2

TOEFL Reading 빈출 주제

〔생물학, 천문학 등〕

어휘와 지문을 교과서처럼
완벽하게 학습하도록 구성!

3

기출 반영 실전 문제
집중 연습을 통해
실전 응용력이 상승하여
고득점 달성!

토플 정복을 위한 확실한 왕도!

입문 및 초급 [40~65점]

TOEFL Basic

한 권으로 토플 시험을 체계적으로 완벽히 이해하는
입문자들의 필독서

기본 및 중급 [60~85점]

TOEFL Intermediate (80+)

한 권으로 시원스쿨 토플 스타 강사진의
과목별 노하우 습득 및 80+ 달성

정규 및 고급 [80~115점]

TOEFL Reading   TOEFL Listening   TOEFL Speaking   TOEFL Writing

토플 기출 족보를 낱낱이 분석해 정리한 최빈출 주제 학습 + 스피킹/라이팅 만점 수강생 다수 배출한 만점 강사의 템플릿 완벽 공개

실전 및 심화 [90~120점]

TOEFL Actual Tests

실제 시험 진행과 동일한 TOEFL 고득점용
최종 마무리 실전 모의고사

어휘 정복

TOEFL Vocabulary

정답과 연관된 토플 기출 단어만을 수록한
진정한 토플 전문 보카 학습서

고득점을 위한 토플 리딩 기본서

SIWONSCHOOL
TOEFL
Reading

시원스쿨어학연구소 · 류형진

시원스쿨 **LAB**

SIWONSCHOOL
TOEFL Reading

초판 1쇄 발행 2023년 1월 2일
개정 2쇄 발행 2023년 9월 15일

지은이 시원스쿨어학연구소, 류형진
펴낸곳 (주)에스제이더블유인터내셔널
펴낸이 양홍걸 이시원

홈페이지 www.siwonschool.com
주소 서울시 영등포구 국회대로74길 12 시원스쿨
교재 구입 문의 02)2014-8151
고객센터 02)6409-0878

ISBN 979-11-6150-730-9 13740
Number 1-110505-18180400-09

머리말

토플 시험 개정 반영,
시원스쿨 토플 TOEFL Reading!

시원스쿨어학연구소가 토플 왕초보를 위한 [시원스쿨 처음토플]과 토플 전용 어휘집인
[시원스쿨 토플 기출 보카]를 출간하고 나서, 독자분들로부터 다음 학습 단계에 대해 많은 문의가 쇄도했
습니다. 이 문의에 대한 응답으로 중급 학습자를 위한 [TOEFL 80+], 시험을 앞둔 실전 학생들을 위한
[TOEFL Actual Tests]를 출간하였습니다. 또한 최신 토플 트렌드를 학습자들에게 제공하고자 [처음토플]
을 [TOEFL Basic]으로, [TOEFL 80+]를 [TOEFL Intermediate]으로 개정하였습니다.

그리고 이제, 시원스쿨 토플 라인업을 완성하는 과목별 토플 정규서가 세상에 나오게 되었습니다. 그동안
시원스쿨어학연구소는 학습자의 학습 편의와 효율성을 위해 한 권에 4과목을 다 아우르는 교재를 출간하여
왔습니다. 하지만 이번 정규라인은 가장 넓은 점수대(80~115점)를 대상으로 하고 있으며, 많은 문제 양을
풀어보며 점수를 올리는 것이 중요하기에, 기존과 달리 과목별 분권으로 나오게 되었습니다.

시원스쿨어학연구소는 과목별 전문성을 최대한 높이기 위해 오프라인 학원에서 인정받은 선생님들과 함께
도서 작업을 하였습니다. 선생님들은 본인들이 과목별 만점을 받은 것은 물론, 다수의 수강생들을 해당 과목
만점으로 이끈 전문가들로, 오프라인 강의에서 소수의 학생들에게만 공개하던 토플 학습 비법들을 이번 도서
에서 전격 공개하였습니다.

「시원스쿨 토플 TOEFL Reading」은

① 확실히 점수를 올려줍니다.

　토플 교과서를 지향하는 본 도서는 TOEFL Reading 시험에 빈출하는 과목별/전공별로 챕터를 구성하였
　습니다. 학습자는 해당 과목(예: 생물학, 천문학 등)의 배경지식 및 기출 토픽을 이해하고 빈출 어휘를 암
　기합니다. 이후 관련 실전 문제를 집중 학습함으로써 확실한 점수 상승이 이루어집니다.

② 학습자의 독해력 및 어휘력을 향상시킵니다.

　TOEFL Reading이 어려운 이유가 지문의 내용을 이해하기 어렵기 때문인데, 내용 이해에 초점을 맞춘
　지문 중심 학습은 독해력 및 어휘력을 향상시킵니다.

③ 토플 시험 기출 족보를 정리하였습니다.

　국내 유명 토플 선생님, 다수의 원어민 연구원들과 토플 고득점 연구원들이 토플 기출 족보를 낱낱이 분석
　해 정리한 도서로, 학습자는 기출 문제 위주로 공부할 수 있습니다.

아무쪼록 이 도서를 통해 영어 실력이 상승하고 토플 목표 점수를 달성하여 성공적인 유학의 길로 나아갈 수
있기를 진심으로 바랍니다.

시원스쿨어학연구소·류형진 드림

목차

- 머리말   3
- 목차   4
- 이 책의 구성과 특징   6
- 토플 시험 소개   8
- TOEFL Reading 정복 학습 플랜   10

Introduction   Question Types   12

Chapter 1   Biology   26

Passage 1: Feeding Strategies in the Ocean   30
Passage 2: Thermoregulation in Amphibians   42
Passage 3: Transgenic Plants   52

Chapter 2   Ecology   62

Passage 1: Direct Species Translocation   66
Passage 2: Evolution of Flowering Plants   78
Passage 3: Coral Reefs   90

Chapter 3   Art   100

Passage 1: Pottery in the Roman Empire   104
Passage 2: The Creation of Cave Paintings   116
Passage 3: The Theater Audience   128

Chapter 4   Geology   138

Passage 1: Soil Quality of Tropical Rainforests   142
Passage 2: The Influence of Glaciers   152
Passage 3: Understanding Earth's Interior   162

Chapter 5 Astronomy 170

Passage 1: Star Death 174
Passage 2: Planets in Our Solar System 186
Passage 3: Structure and Composition of Comets 198

Chapter 6 History 208

Passage 1: The Culture of Britain Under Rome 212
Passage 2: Innovation in Ancient Iran 224
Passage 3: Sumerian City-States 236

Chapter 7 Education 248

Passage 1: Autobiographical Memory 252
Passage 2: Early Childhood Education 262
Passage 3: Reflection in Teaching 274

Chapter 8 Economics 284

Passage 1: The Commercialization of Lumber 288
Passage 2: The Revolution of Cheap Print 298
Passage 3: European Economic Growth in the 17th Century 310

Actual Tests 320

Actual Test 1 322
Actual Test 2 346

• 별책 해설집: 해설, 모범 답안, 어휘 정리

이 책의 구성과 특징

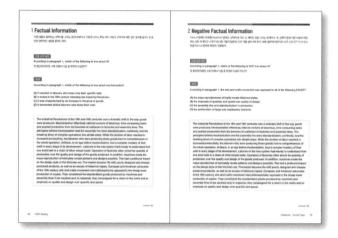

Introduction:
빠르게 기출 문제 유형 파악

10개의 TOEFL Reading 기출 문제 유형에 대한 핵심 설명과 함께 실제 지문에 어떻게 등장하는지 풀어보면서 기출 문제 유형을 빠르게 파악할 수 있다.

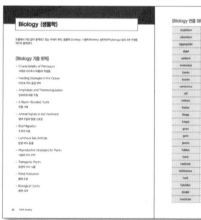

과목별/전공별
빈출 토픽 집중 학습

본문은 8개의 과목별/전공별로 챕터로 구성되어 있다. 학습자는 해당 과목(예: 생물학, 천문학 등)의 배경지식 및 기출 토픽을 이해하고 빈출 어휘를 암기함으로써 TOEFL Reading에서 꼭 필요한 해당 전공의 기본 지식을 습득하게 된다.

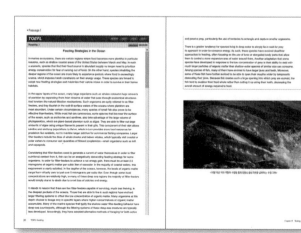

실전 문제 집중 연습

토플 기출 족보를 낱낱이 분석해 정리한 토픽별 기출 반영 실전 문제를 집중적으로 풀어보면서 실전 응용력을 높인다.

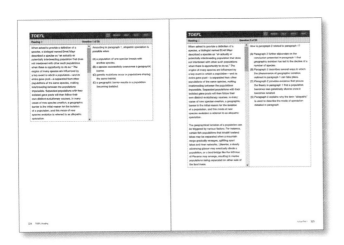

실전 모의고사

최신 개정 출제 경향이 반영된 실전 모의고사 2세트를
풀어보면서 자신의 실력을 점검해 보고 앞에서 학습한
내용을 다시 한번 복습한다.

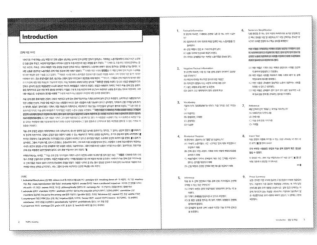

해설집

별책으로 제공하는 해설집을 통해 지문 및 문제 해석과
어휘를 보다 편하게 확인할 수 있다. 특히 해당 지문에
정답 단서 밑줄과 추가적인 정답 해설을 통해 학습자들
의 독학을 최대한 돕고 있다.

토플 시험 소개

▪토플 시험

TOEFL(Test of English as a Foreign Language)은 미국 대학에서 수학할 비영어권 학생을 선별하기 위해 미국 ETS(Educational Testing Service)가 개발한 영어 능력 평가 시험이다. 즉, 미국을 비롯한 영어권 국가 대학에서 수학할 능력의 영어 수준이 되는지를 측정하는 시험인데, 보통 토플 시험이라고 하면 컴퓨터 인터넷 연결로 시험을 보는 iBT(internet-based test) TOEFL을 말한다.

▪시험 영역

영역	지문 및 문제 수	시간	배점
Reading	총 2개 지문 (한 지문에 10문제씩 출제)	약 35분	0~30점
Listening	총 2개 대화 + 강의 3개 (대화 하나에 5문제, 강의 하나에 6문제씩 출제)	약 36분	0~30점
Speaking	총 4문제 (독립형 1번, 통합형 2, 3, 4번)	약 16분	0~30점
Writing	총 2문제 (통합형 1번, 토론형 2번)	약 30분	0~30점
합계	약 2시간, 120점 만점		

▪2023년 7월 26일 이후 시험 변경 내용

1. Reading 또는 Listening에 나오던 더미 문제(점수에 포함되지 않는 연습 문제)가 사라짐
2. Reading 지문 세트가 3개에서 2개로 변경
3. Writing 독립형(Independent) 대신 토론형(Academic Discussion) 출제
4. 전체 시험 시간이 약 3시간에서 2시간으로 단축

▪시험 접수

접수 방법	▹ 시험일로부터 최소 7일 전 ETS 토플 홈페이지에서 접수
접수 비용	▹ 시험 접수 비용: US $220(2023년 7월 기준) ▹ 추가 접수 비용: US $260 　└ 시험일로부터 7일~2일 사이 접수 시 연체료(late fee) US $40 추가 ▹ 날짜 변경 비용: US $60 ▹ 재채점 비용: US $80(Speaking/Writing 각각, Reading/Listening 불가) ▹ 추가 리포팅 비용: US $20(건당) 　└ 시험 접수 시, 무료로 4개까지 성적 리포팅 받을 기관 선택 가능 ▹ 취소 성적 복원 비용: US $20
접수 취소	▹ ETS 토플 홈페이지에서 취소 가능 ▹ 응시료 환불은 시험 접수 후 7일 이내 100%, 응시 4일 전까지는 50%, 응시일로부터 3일 이내는 환불 불가
시험일	▹ 1년에 50회 정도로 보통 주말마다 실시되며, 실시 국가마다 차이가 있음
시험 장소	▹ 다수의 컴퓨터를 비치하고 있는 전국/전세계 교육기관 또는 ETS Test Center에서 시행 ▹ 집에서 Home Edition으로도 응시 가능

▪시험 당일 준비물

공인된 신분증(여권, 주민등록증, 운전면허증, 군인신분증 중 하나)의 원본을 반드시 지참한다. 참고로 필기도구 및 노트는 시험장에서 제공되는 것만 사용할 수 있기에 따로 준비할 필요는 없다.

▪성적 확인

시험 응시일로부터 약 6일 후에 온라인으로 성적이 공개된다. PDF 형식의 성적표는 온라인 성적 공개 2일 후부터 다운로드 가능하다. 성적표 유효기간은 시험 응시일로부터 2년이다.

TOEFL Reading 정복
학습 플랜

- 반드시 실제 시험 문제를 풀듯이 문제를 풀어본다.
- 풀어본 지문은 다시 해석을 꼼꼼하게 해보고 몰랐던 어휘는 완벽하게 암기한다.
- 교재를 끝까지 한 번 보고 나면 2회독에 도전한다. 같은 교재를 여러 번 읽을수록 훨씬 효과가 좋으니 다독하도록 한다.
- 혼자서 학습하기 어렵다면, 시원스쿨 토플 홈페이지(toefl.siwonschool.com)에서 토플 스타 강사진의 강의를 들으면 보다 쉽고 재미있게 공부할 수 있다.

▪ 초고속 10일 완성 학습 플랜

1일	2일	3일	4일	5일
Chapter 1 Biology	Chapter 2 Ecology	Chapter 3 Art	Chapter 4 Geology	Chapter 5 Astronomy

6일	7일	8일	9일	10일
Chapter 6 History	Chapter 7 Education	Chapter 8 Economics	Actual Tests Actual Test 1	Actual Tests Actual Test 2

▪40일 완성 학습 플랜

1일	2일	3일	4일	5일
Introduction Question Types	Chapter 1 Biology 토픽 및 어휘	Chapter 1 Biology Passage 1	Chapter 1 Biology Passage 2	Chapter 1 Biology Passage 3

6일	7일	8일	9일	10일
Chapter 2 Ecology 토픽 및 어휘	Chapter 2 Ecology Passage 1	Chapter 2 Ecology Passage 2	Chapter 2 Ecology Passage 3	Chapter 3 Art 토픽 및 어휘

11일	12일	13일	14일	15일
Chapter 3 Art Passage 1	Chapter 3 Art Passage 2	Chapter 3 Art Passage 3	Chapter 4 Geology 토픽 및 어휘	Chapter 4 Geology Passage 1

16일	17일	18일	19일	20일
Chapter 4 Geology Passage 2	Chapter 4 Geology Passage 3	Chapter 5 Astronomy 토픽 및 어휘	Chapter 5 Astronomy Passage 1	Chapter 5 Astronomy Passage 2

21일	22일	23일	24일	25일
Chapter 5 Astronomy Passage 3	Chapter 6 History 토픽 및 어휘	Chapter 6 History Passage 1	Chapter 6 History Passage 2	Chapter 6 History Passage 3

26일	27일	28일	29일	30일
Chapter 7 Education 토픽 및 어휘	Chapter 7 Education Passage 1	Chapter 7 Education Passage 2	Chapter 7 Education Passage 3	Chapter 8 Economics 토픽 및 어휘

31일	32일	33일	34일	35일
Chapter 8 Economics Passage 1	Chapter 8 Economics Passage 2	Chapter 8 Economics Passage 3	Actual Test 1 Passage 1	Actual Test 1 Passage 2

36일	37일	38일	39일	40일
Actual Test 1 복습	Actual Test 2 Passage 1	Actual Test 2 Passage 2	Actual Test 2 복습	총복습

Introduction
Question Types

1 Factual Information

2 Negative Factual Information

3 Vocabulary

4 Rhetorical Purpose

5 Inference

6 Sentence Simplification

7 Reference

8 Insert Text

9 Prose Summary

10 Fill in a Table

TOEFL Reading Overview

· TOEFL Reading에 나오는 지문은 미국 대학 교재 수준의 학문적(Academic) 글의 발췌문(Passage)으로 길이는 700 단어 내외이다.

· 자주 나오는 전공 지문은 생물학(Biology), 예술(Art), 역사(History), 지질학 (Geology) 등으로, 이러한 전공의 특정 토픽을 설명하는 글들이 출제된다.

· TOEFL Reading 문제는 다음의 10개 유형으로 출제되는데, 미리 문제 유형을 숙지해 두면, 문제의 의도를 파악하는 시간을 현저하게 줄일 수 있다.

문제 유형	출제 빈도 (한 지문 – 10 문제 기준)
1. Factual Information 옳은 정보 찾기 2. Negative Factual Information 틀린 정보 찾기	두 유형 합쳐서 4 문제 정도 출제 (Factual Information 유형이 다수 출제)
3. Vocabulary 어휘	1~3 문제 (평균 2 문제 출제)
4. Rhetorical Purpose 수사적 의도 파악	1 문제 정도 (간혹 안 나옴)
5. Inference 추론	1 문제 정도 (간혹 안 나옴)
6. Sentence Simplification 문장 간략화	1 문제 정도 (간혹 안 나옴)
7. Reference 지시 대상 찾기	1 문제 정도 (거의 안 나옴)
8. Insert Text 문장 삽입	1 문제 정도 (9번 문제로 출제)
9. Prose Summary 지문 요약 10. Fill in a Table 표 채우기	1문제 (10번 문제로 둘 중 하나만 나오는데 거의 Prose Summary만 나옴)

1 Factual Information

지문 내용과 일치하는 선택지를 고르는 문제 유형이다. 지문에 나오는 특정 세부 사항과 선택지에 대한 정보 일치를 묻거나 한 문단의 전반적인 내용을 묻기도 한다.

빈출 질문 패턴

According to paragraph 1, which of the following is true about A?

첫 문단에 따르면, A에 관해서 다음 중 무엇이 사실인가?

예제

According to paragraph 1, which of the following is true about mechanization?

(A) It resulted in laborers who knew only their specific task.
(B) It ended in the 19th century following the Industrial Revolution.
(C) It was characterized by an increase in the price of goods.
(D) It demanded skilled laborers who knew their craft.

The Industrial Revolutions of the 18th and 19th centuries saw a dramatic shift in the way goods were produced. Mechanization effectively relieved workers of laborious, time-consuming tasks and pushed production from the benches of craftsmen to factories and assembly lines. The principles behind mechanization and the assembly line were standardization, continuity, and the breaking down of complex operations into simple steps. While the division of labor resulted in increased productivity, the laborers who were producing these goods had no comprehension of the whole operation. Artisans, in an age before mechanization, had a complex mastery of their craft in every stage of its development. Laborers in the new system had merely to understand their one small task in a chain of other simple tasks. Operators of factories often strove for quantity of production over the quality and design of the goods produced. In addition, machines made the mass reproduction of intricately ornate patterns and designs possible. This had a profound impact on the design style of the Victorian era. The market became rife with poorly designed and cheaply produced products, as well as an excess of historical copies. European and American advocates of the 19th century arts and crafts movement were philosophically opposed to the cheap mass production of copies. They considered the standardized goods produced by machines and assembly lines to be soulless and, in response, they campaigned for a return to the crafts and an emphasis on quality and design over quantity and speed.

Answer: (A)

2 Negative Factual Information

Factual 문제의 부정형(negative) 문제로, 선택지 중 아닌 것, 예외인 것을 고르는 문제이다. 즉, 선택지 중에 지문 내용과 부합하는 것은 세 개이고 나머지 하나만 그렇지 않은데, 이 한 개를 골라내야 한다. 보통 질문에 대문자로 NOT, EXCEPT가 써 있는 만큼 Factual 문제와 확연히 구분된다.

빈출 질문 패턴

According to paragraph 1, which of the following is NOT true about A?

첫 문단에 따르면, A에 관해서 다음 중 무엇이 사실이 아닌가?

예제

According to paragraph 1, the arts and crafts movement was opposed to all of the following EXCEPT

(A) the mass reproductions of highly ornate historical styles
(B) the emphasis of quantity and speed over quality of design
(C) the assembly line and standardization in production
(D) the proliferation of large and unattractive factories

The Industrial Revolutions of the 18th and 19th centuries saw a dramatic shift in the way goods were produced. Mechanization effectively relieved workers of laborious, time-consuming tasks and pushed production from the benches of craftsmen to factories and assembly lines. The principles behind mechanization and the assembly line were standardization, continuity, and the breaking down of complex operations into simple steps. While the division of labor resulted in increased productivity, the laborers who were producing these goods had no comprehension of the whole operation. Artisans, in an age before mechanization, had a complex mastery of their craft in every stage of its development. Laborers in the new system had merely to understand their one small task in a chain of other simple tasks. Operators of factories often strove for quantity of production over the quality and design of the goods produced. In addition, machines made the mass reproduction of intricately ornate patterns and designs possible. This had a profound impact on the design style of the Victorian era. The market became rife with poorly designed and cheaply produced products, as well as an excess of historical copies. European and American advocates of the 19th century arts and crafts movement were philosophically opposed to the cheap mass production of copies. They considered the standardized goods produced by machines and assembly lines to be soulless and, in response, they campaigned for a return to the crafts and an emphasis on quality and design over quantity and speed.

Answer: (D)

3 Vocabulary

지문의 특정 단어나 어구의 의미를 묻는 문제로, 10가지 문제 유형 중 Reference와 함께 가장 쉽게, 빨리 풀 수 있는 문제 유형이다.

빈출 질문 패턴

The word "A" in the passage is closest in meaning to

지문의 어휘 "A"와 의미가 가장 가까운 것은 무엇인가?

예제

The word "profound" in the passage is closest in meaning to

(A) direct
(B) far-reaching
(C) positive
(D) strange

The Industrial Revolutions of the 18th and 19th centuries saw a dramatic shift in the way goods were produced. Mechanization effectively relieved workers of laborious, time-consuming tasks and pushed production from the benches of craftsmen to factories and assembly lines. The principles behind mechanization and the assembly line were standardization, continuity, and the breaking down of complex operations into simple steps. While the division of labor resulted in increased productivity, the laborers who were producing these goods had no comprehension of the whole operation. Artisans, in an age before mechanization, had a complex mastery of their craft in every stage of its development. Laborers in the new system had merely to understand their one small task in a chain of other simple tasks. Operators of factories often strove for quantity of production over the quality and design of the goods produced. In addition, machines made the mass reproduction of intricately ornate patterns and designs possible. This had a profound impact on the design style of the Victorian era. The market became rife with poorly designed and cheaply produced products, as well as an excess of historical copies. European and American advocates of the 19th century arts and crafts movement were philosophically opposed to the cheap mass production of copies. They considered the standardized goods produced by machines and assembly lines to be soulless and, in response, they campaigned for a return to the crafts and an emphasis on quality and design over quantity and speed.

Answer: (B)

4 Rhetorical Purpose

저자의 의도 파악 문제로, 저자가 왜 그 부분을 언급하는지, 또는 전체적인 맥락에서 특정 문단이 어떠한 의도로 사용되었는지 등을 묻는다.

빈출 질문 패턴

Why does the author mention "A"?

왜 저자는 "A"를 언급하는가?

예제

In paragraph 1, why does the author mention "Artisans"?

(A) To argue that laborers in the 18th century worked on time-consuming tasks
(B) To show how the whole operation in production had changed after mechanization
(C) To provide evidence that artists had to master every step of their craft
(D) To provide an example of a problem related to the Industrial Revolution

The Industrial Revolutions of the 18th and 19th centuries saw a dramatic shift in the way goods were produced. Mechanization effectively relieved workers of laborious, time-consuming tasks and pushed production from the benches of craftsmen to factories and assembly lines. The principles behind mechanization and the assembly line were standardization, continuity, and the breaking down of complex operations into simple steps. While the division of labor resulted in increased productivity, the laborers who were producing these goods had no comprehension of the whole operation. Artisans, in an age before mechanization, had a complex mastery of their craft in every stage of its development. Laborers in the new system had merely to understand their one small task in a chain of other simple tasks. Operators of factories often strove for quantity of production over the quality and design of the goods produced. In addition, machines made the mass reproduction of intricately ornate patterns and designs possible. This had a profound impact on the design style of the Victorian era. The market became rife with poorly designed and cheaply produced products, as well as an excess of historical copies. European and American advocates of the 19th century arts and crafts movement were philosophically opposed to the cheap mass production of copies. They considered the standardized goods produced by machines and assembly lines to be soulless and, in response, they campaigned for a return to the crafts and an emphasis on quality and design over quantity and speed.

Answer: (B)

5 Inference

추론 문제로, 지문에 명백하게 드러나지 않지만 지문 속 Fact를 바탕으로 반드시 참인 사실을 파악해야 한다. 질문에 infer(암시하다, 추론하다), imply(암시하다, 시사하다), suggest(암시하다, 시사하다) 등의 동사가 사용되는 특징이 있다.

빈출 질문 패턴

Which of the following can be inferred about A?

A에 대해 다음 중 무엇이 추론될 수 있는가?

예제

Which of the following can be inferred from paragraph 2 about proponents of the arts and crafts movement?

(A) They agreed that machines should be replaced by skilled craftspeople.
(B) They argued that machines could improve upon the crafts.
(C) They were not in agreement as to the usefulness of machines in creating quality goods.
(D) They advocated for the importance of both physical labor and subtle skill in the crafts.

Advocates of the arts and crafts movement maintained that a healthy society depended on having a resource of skilled and talented craftspeople. Aesthetic and beautifully designed goods, they believed, should be accessible to all people – not merely those who could afford them. While mechanization had decreased the price of goods, it had also decreased the quality. In addition, with mass reproduction, original and individual designs had fallen by the wayside. Like any movement, proponents of the arts and crafts ideology expressed various levels of conviction. Some maintained that machines, being the sole cause of the evils of mechanization, should be completely eliminated, and that a return to the crafts was needed in order to heal a society that had become dependent on soulless and mundane labor. Others believed that machines had simply been put to the wrong use. These people acknowledged the benefits of machines that could relieve a craftsman of the ignoble, physically laborious aspects of his work in order to free him up for the more subtle and skilled aspects of the craft.

Answer: (C)

6 Sentence Simplification

지문에 하이라이트 표시된 문장을 보다 짧게 만드는 문제로, 간략화 문제 또는 하이라이트 문제라고도 한다. 정답 문장에는 하이라이트 문장의 핵심 정보가 반드시 들어가야 하며 덜 중요한 정보는 생략된다.

Which of the following best expresses the essential information in the highlighted sentence? Incorrect answer choices change the meaning in important ways or leave out essential information.

다음 문장들 중 어느 것이 지문의 하이라이트 표기된 문장에 담긴 핵심 정보를 가장 잘 표현하는가?
오답 선택지는 중요한 방식으로 의미를 변경하거나 핵심 정보를 배제한다.

Which of the following best expresses the essential information in the highlighted sentence? Incorrect answer choices change the meaning in important ways or leave out essential information.

(A) Some maintained that machines were the cause of all evils and that they had made society unhealthy.
(B) Some advocated for the elimination of machines and a return to the crafts in order to heal society.
(C) Some believed that the crafts could cure a society that was dependent on mundane labor.
(D) Some supported the notion that crafts would eliminate the necessity of soulless and mundane labor.

Advocates of the arts and crafts movement maintained that a healthy society depended on having a resource of skilled and talented craftspeople. Aesthetic and beautifully designed goods, they believed, should be accessible to all people – not merely those who could afford them. While mechanization had decreased the price of goods, it had also decreased the quality. In addition, with mass reproduction, original and individual designs had fallen by the wayside. Like any movement, proponents of the arts and crafts ideology expressed various levels of conviction. Some maintained that machines, being the sole cause of the evils of mechanization, should be completely eliminated, and that a return to the crafts was needed in order to heal a society that had become dependent on soulless and mundane labor. Others believed that machines had simply been put to the wrong use. These people acknowledged the benefits of machines that could relieve a craftsman of the ignoble, physically laborious aspects of his work in order to free him up for the more subtle and skilled aspects of the craft.

Answer: (B)

7 Reference

지문에 제시되는 대명사(this, that, it, its, they, them, some, one, who, which 등) 또는 구문이 무엇을 가리키는지 묻는 문제이다. 가장 쉬운 문제 유형이지만 출제 빈도가 아주 낮다.

빈출 질문 패턴

The word "A" in the passage refers to

해당 지문의 어휘 "A"는 무엇을 가리키는가?

예제

The word "they" in the passage refers to

(A) American designers
(B) architects
(C) proponents of the arts and crafts
(D) machines

In America, however, proponents of the arts and crafts movement did not want to return to a time before machines; rather, they wanted to create a marriage between mechanization and aesthetics. They utilized cost-lowering machinery while at the same time emphasizing the materials of the product. The American designers and architects of the arts and crafts movement focused on the quality of the materials and the simplicity of design. They often intentionally left aspects of the product unfinished in order to highlight the grain of the wood or the texture of the stone. This lent their style a folksy and hardy quality.

Answer: (C)

8 Insert Text

문장 삽입 문제로, 문제에 삽입 문장이 하나 소개되고 이 문장을 지문 곳곳에 있는 네 개의 네모 표기들 중 하나에 넣었을 때 가장 자연스러운 위치를 고르는 문제이다. 항상 각 지문의 9번 문제로 출제된다.

Look at the four squares [▮] that indicate where the following sentence could be added to the passage.
다음 문장이 지문에 추가될 수 있는 곳을 나타내는 네 개의 네모 표기 [▮]를 찾아 보시오.

[삽입 문장 제시]

Where would be the sentence best fit? Click on a square [▮] to add the sentence to the passage.
위 문장은 어느 곳에 가장 적합하겠는가? 네모 표기[▮]를 클릭해 지문에 이 문장을 추가하시오.

예제

Look at the four squares [▮] that indicate where the following sentence could be added to the passage.

Only the wealthy could enjoy the fruits of the European arts and crafts movement.

Where would be the sentence best fit? Click on a square [▮] to add the sentence to the passage.

The arts and crafts movement emerged in both Europe and America, and while they shared a similar philosophical approach, the results were quite different. ▮ Like their American counterpart, the European movement began with the initial impetus to produce artfully made goods that could be accessible to the general public. ▮ But in Europe, proponents of the arts and crafts also wanted to make a complete return to the heroic craft that they felt Industrialization was destroying. ▮ The craftsmen, they asserted, must be revered, respected, and reimbursed accordingly. The sole reliance on hand-made crafts combined with the generous salary people offered to the craftsmen, paradoxically raised the price of the goods they were creating. As a result, products of the European arts and crafts became prohibitively expensive for the common people. ▮

Answer: 4th ▮

9 Prose Summary

지문 요약 문제로 각 지문에서 10번 문제로 출제된다. 문제에는 도입 문장(introductory sentence)과 6개의 선택지가 주어지는데, 도입 문장은 전체 지문을 한 줄로 요약한 문장이다. 도입 문장과 전체 지문 내용을 바탕으로 지문의 핵심 아이디어들을 가장 잘 나타낸 선택지 3개를 고르는 문제로, 하나도 제대로 고르지 못하거나 하나만 맞히면 0점, 두 개를 맞히면 1점, 세 개 모두 맞히면 2점이 주어진다.

빈출 질문 패턴

Directions: An introductory sentence for a brief summary of the passage is provided below. Complete the summary by selecting the THREE answer choices that express the most important ideas in the passage. Some sentences do not belong in the summary because they express ideas that are not presented in the passage or are minor ideas in the passage. **This question is worth 2 points.**

설명: 간략한 지문 요약에 필요한 도입 문장이 아래에 제공되어 있다. 지문에서 가장 중요한 개념들을 나타내는 세 가지 답안 선택지를 골라 요약 내용을 완성하시오. 일부 답안 선택지는 지문에 제시되지 않는 개념을 나타내거나 지문에서 중요하지 않은 개념들이므로 요약 내용에 속하지 않는다. **이 문제는 2 점에 해당된다.**

예제

> **Directions:** An introductory sentence for a brief summary of the passage is provided below. Complete the summary by selecting the THREE answer choices that express the most important ideas in the passage. Some sentences do not belong in the summary because they express ideas that are not presented in the passage or are minor ideas in the passage. **This question is worth 2 points.**
>
> Drag your answer choices to the space where they belong. To remove an answer choice, click on it. To review the passage, click on **VIEW TEXT.**
>
> **This passage discusses the arts and crafts movement that appeared in the 19th century.**
> -
> -
> -

(A) Mechanization allowed craftsmen to focus on the more subtle and skilled aspects of the craft.
(B) The arts and crafts movements in Europe and America brought the same outcome.
(C) The proponents of the arts and crafts emphasized the importance of skilled craftsmen.
(D) The arts and crafts movements occurred only in Europe and America.
(E) Some of the proponents of the arts and crafts admitted the advantages of mechanization.
(F) The price of goods in Europe soared due to the arts and crafts movement.

The Industrial Revolutions of the 18th and 19th centuries saw a dramatic shift in the way goods were produced. Mechanization effectively relieved workers of laborious, time-consuming tasks and pushed production from the benches of craftsmen to factories and assembly lines. The principles behind mechanization and the assembly line were standardization, continuity, and the breaking down of complex operations into simple steps. While the division of labor resulted in increased productivity, the laborers who were producing these goods had no comprehension of the whole operation. Artisans, in an age before mechanization, had a complex mastery of their craft in every stage of its development. Laborers in the new system had merely to understand their one small task in a chain of other simple tasks. Operators of factories often strove for quantity of production over the quality and design of the goods produced. In addition, machines made the mass reproduction of intricately ornate patterns and designs possible. This had a profound impact on the design style of the Victorian era. The market became rife with poorly designed and cheaply produced products, as well as an excess of historical copies. European and American advocates of the 19th century arts and crafts movement were philosophically opposed to the cheap mass production of copies. They considered the standardized goods produced by machines and assembly lines to be soulless and, in response, they campaigned for a return to the crafts and an emphasis on quality and design over quantity and speed.

Advocates of the arts and crafts movement maintained that a healthy society depended on having a resource of skilled and talented craftspeople. Aesthetic and beautifully designed goods, they believed, should be accessible to all people – not merely those who could afford them. While mechanization had decreased the price of goods, it had also decreased the quality. In addition, with mass reproduction, original and individual designs had fallen by the wayside. Like any movement, proponents of the arts and crafts ideology expressed various levels of conviction. Some maintained that machines, being the sole cause of the evils of mechanization, should be completely eliminated, and that a return to the crafts was needed in order to heal a society that had become dependent on soulless and mundane labor. Others believed that machines had simply been put to the wrong use. These people acknowledged the benefits of machines that could relieve a craftsman of the ignoble, physically laborious aspects of his work in order to free him up for the more subtle and skilled aspects of the craft.

The arts and crafts movement emerged in both Europe and America, and while they shared a similar philosophical approach, the results were quite different. Like their American counterpart, the European movement began with the initial impetus to produce artfully made goods that could be accessible to the general public. But in Europe, proponents of the arts and crafts also wanted to make a complete return to the heroic craft that they felt Industrialization was destroying. The craftsmen, they asserted, must be revered, respected, and reimbursed accordingly. The sole reliance on hand-made crafts combined with the generous salary people offered to the craftsmen, paradoxically raised the price of the goods they were creating. As a result, products of the European arts and crafts became prohibitively expensive for the common people.

In America, however, proponents of the arts and crafts movement did not want to return to a time before machines; rather, they wanted to create a marriage between mechanization and aesthetics. They utilized cost-lowering machinery while at the same time emphasizing the materials of the product. The American designers and architects of the arts and crafts movement focused on the quality of the materials and the simplicity of design. They often intentionally left aspects of the product unfinished in order to highlight the grain of the wood or the texture of the stone. This lent their style a folksy and hardy quality.

Answer: (C), (E), (F)

10 Fill in a Table

카테고리에 맞게 구분하는 문제 유형으로 보통 표(Table)와 선택지 7개가 주어지는데, 표 내용에 알맞게 선택지 중 5개를 정답으로 고르는 문제이다. 전체 지문을 보고 풀어야 하는 3점짜리 문제로, 5개 정답 중 3개를 맞히면 1점, 4개는 2점, 5개 전부는 3점이 주어진다.

빈출 질문 패턴

Directions: Select the appropriate phrases from the answer choices and match them to the type to which they relate. TWO of the answer choices will NOT be used. **This question is worth 3 points.**

설명: 선택지에서 적절한 문구를 골라서 연관되는 유형에 연결하시오. 선택지 중 두 개는 사용되지 않는다. 이 문제는 3점에 해당된다.

예제

Directions: Select the appropriate phrases from the answer choices and match them to the type to which they relate. TWO of the answer choices will NOT be used. **This question is worth 3 points.**

Drag your answer choices to the space where they belong. To remove an answer choice, click on it. To review the passage, click on **VIEW TEXT.**

The European Arts and Crafts Movement	The American Arts and Crafts Movement
• •	• • •

(A) The complete return to the noble crafts and the elimination of machinery
(B) The style emphasized the qualities of the material
(C) The preference of quantity and speed over quality and design
(D) A reliance on mundane and repetitive labor
(E) Exposed joints and unfinished surfaces gave the furniture a rustic, folksy style
(F) Goods that were costly to produce and therefore inaccessible to most people
(G) A marriage between mechanization and aesthetics

The Industrial Revolutions of the 18th and 19th centuries saw a dramatic shift in the way goods were produced. Mechanization effectively relieved workers of laborious, time-consuming tasks and pushed production from the benches of craftsmen to factories and assembly lines. The principles behind mechanization and the assembly line were standardization, continuity, and the breaking down of complex operations into simple steps. While the division of labor resulted in increased productivity, the laborers who were producing these goods had no comprehension of the whole operation. Artisans, in an age before mechanization, had a complex mastery of their craft in every stage of its development. Laborers in the new system had merely to understand their one small task in a chain of other simple tasks. Operators of factories often strove for quantity of production over the quality and design of the goods produced. In addition, machines made the mass reproduction of intricately ornate patterns and designs possible. This had a profound impact on the design style of the Victorian era. The market became rife with poorly designed and cheaply produced products, as well as an excess of historical copies. European and American advocates of the 19th century arts and crafts movement were philosophically opposed to the cheap mass production of copies. They considered the standardized goods produced by machines and assembly lines to be soulless and, in response, they campaigned for a return to the crafts and an emphasis on quality and design over quantity and speed.

Advocates of the arts and crafts movement maintained that a healthy society depended on having a resource of skilled and talented craftspeople. Aesthetic and beautifully designed goods, they believed, should be accessible to all people – not merely those who could afford them. While mechanization had decreased the price of goods, it had also decreased the quality. In addition, with mass reproduction, original and individual designs had fallen by the wayside. Like any movement, proponents of the arts and crafts ideology expressed various levels of conviction. Some maintained that machines, being the sole cause of the evils of mechanization, should be completely eliminated, and that a return to the crafts was needed in order to heal a society that had become dependent on soulless and mundane labor. Others believed that machines had simply been put to the wrong use. These people acknowledged the benefits of machines that could relieve a craftsman of the ignoble, physically laborious aspects of his work in order to free him up for the more subtle and skilled aspects of the craft.

The arts and crafts movement emerged in both Europe and America, and while they shared a similar philosophical approach, the results were quite different. Like their American counterpart, the European movement began with the initial impetus to produce artfully made goods that could be accessible to the general public. But in Europe, proponents of the arts and crafts also wanted to make a complete return to the heroic craft that they felt Industrialization was destroying. The craftsmen, they asserted, must be revered, respected, and reimbursed accordingly. The sole reliance on hand-made crafts combined with the generous salary people offered to the craftsmen, paradoxically raised the price of the goods they were creating. As a result, products of the European arts and crafts became prohibitively expensive for the common people.

In America, however, proponents of the arts and crafts movement did not want to return to a time before machines., rather, they wanted to create a marriage between mechanization and aesthetics. They utilized cost-lowering machinery while at the same time emphasizing the materials of the product. The American designers and architects of the arts and crafts movement focused on the quality of the materials and the simplicity of design. They often intentionally left aspects of the product unfinished in order to highlight the grain of the wood or the texture of the stone. This lent their style a folksy and hardy quality.

Answer: European (A), (F) / American (B), (E), (G)

Chapter

01

Biology

Passage 1   Feeding Strategies in the Ocean

Passage 2   Thermoregulation in Amphibians

Passage 3   Transgenic Plants

ESTIMATED NUMBER OF KNOWN
LIVING SPECIES

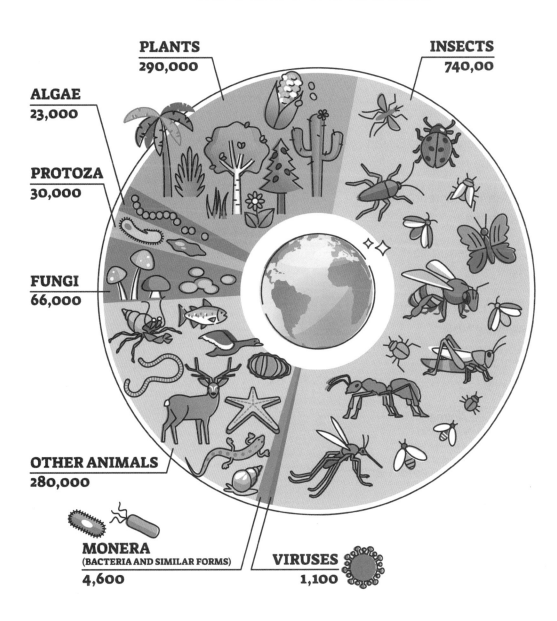

PLANTS
290,000

INSECTS
740,00

ALGAE
23,000

PROTOZA
30,000

FUNGI
66,000

OTHER ANIMALS
280,000

MONERA
(BACTERIA AND SIMILAR FORMS)
4,600

VIRUSES
1,100

Biology (생물학)

토플에서 가장 많이 출제되고 있는 주제로 특히, 동물학(Zoology), 식물학(Botany), 생리학(Physiology) 등의 세부 주제들 위주로 출제된다.

[Biology 기출 토픽]

- Characteristics of Pterosaurs
  프테로사우루스(익룡)의 특징들

- Feeding Strategies in the Ocean
  바닷속 먹이 공급 전략

- Amphibian Thermoregulation
  양서류의 체온 조절

- A Warm-Blooded Turtle
  온혈 거북

- Animal Signals in the Rainforest
  열대 우림의 동물 신호들

- Bird Migration
  조류의 이동

- Luminous Sea Animals
  발광 바다 동물

- Reproductive Strategies for Plants
  식물의 번식 전략

- Transgenic Plants
  유전자 이식 식물

- Wind Pollination
  풍매 수분

- Biological Clocks
  생체 시계

[Biology 빈출 어휘]

amphibian	양서류	luminous	야광의
adaptation	적응	mammal	포유류
aggregation	집단, 집합	mechanism	(작용) 방식, 기제
algae	해조류	metabolic	(신진) 대사의
ambient	주위의	migrate	이주하다
anatomical	해부학적인	navigate	길을 찾다
barren	척박한, 불임의	organism	생물, 유기체
burrow	(서식지로서의) 굴	pest-resistant	해충에 저항력을 지닌
carnivorous	육식성의	photosynthesis	광합성
cell	세포	physiological	생리학적인
embryo	배아, 수정란	population	인구, 개체 수
feather	깃털	predator	포식자
forage	먹이를 찾아다니다	prey	먹이
fungus	균류, 곰팡이류	propagate	(식물이) 번식하다
game	사냥감	reproduce	번식하다
gene	유전자	reptile	파충류
groom	~을 손질하다	substance	물질
habitat	서식지	taxonomy	분류 체계
hatch	부화하다	thermal	열의
herbicide	제초제	thermoregulation	체온 조절
herbivorous	초식성의	tissue	세포 조직
herd	무리, 떼	transgenic	유전자가 이식된
hybridize	잡종 교배하다	vegetation	초목, 식물
inhabit	~에 서식하다, 살다	vertebrate	척추동물
insecticide	살충제	vulnerable	취약한

■ Passage 1

Feeding Strategies in the Ocean

In marine ecosystems, there are certain regions where food becomes more plentiful in particular seasons, such as shallow coastal areas of the United States between March and May. In such a scenario, species that find their food source in abundant supply no longer need to prioritize energy conservation for fear of running out of food. On the other hand, species inhabiting the deeper regions of the ocean are more likely to experience periods where food is exceedingly scarce, which imposes harsh constraints on their energy usage. These species are forced to adopt new feeding strategies and maximize their calorie intake in order to survive in their barren habitats.

In the upper layers of the ocean, many large organisms such as whales consume huge amounts of plankton by separating them from streams of water that pass through anatomical structures that function like natural filtration mechanisms. Such organisms are aptly referred to as filter-feeders, and they flourish in the well-lit surface waters of the oceans where plankton are most abundant. Under certain circumstances, many species of small fish also prove to be effective filter-feeders. While most fish are carnivorous, some species that live near the surface of the ocean, such as anchovies and sardines, also take advantage of the large volume of phytoplankton, which are plant-based plankton such as algae. They are able to filter out large amounts of algae using unique filaments present in their gills. This component of their diet allows sardine and anchovy populations to thrive, which in turn provides more food resources for predators like seabirds, not to mention larger catches for commercial fishing companies. Larger filter-feeders include the likes of whale sharks and baleen whales, which typically visit coastal or polar waters to consume vast quantities of filtered zooplankton—small organisms such as krill and copepods.

Considering that filter-feeders need to generate a current of water themselves in order to filter nutritional content from it, this can be an energetically demanding feeding strategy for some organisms. In order for filter-feeders to achieve a net energy gain, there must be at least 2.5 micrograms of organic matter per cubic liter of seawater. In the majority of coastal waters, this requirement is easily satisfied. In the depths of the oceans, however, the levels of organic matter range from virtually zero to just over 5 micrograms per cubic liter. Even though some local concentrations are relatively high, in many of these deep-sea regions the majority of filter-feeders would simply starve to death due to a net loss of calories and energy.

It stands to reason that there are few filter-feeders capable of surviving, much less thriving, in the deepest pockets of the oceans. Those that are able to live in such regions have evolved larger filtering systems to offset the low concentration of organic matter. Many organisms at this depth choose to forage only in specific layers where higher concentrations of organic matter accumulate. Many of the marine species that typify the shallow-water filter-feeding behavior have deep-sea counterparts, although the filtering systems of these deep-sea creatures are typically less developed. Accordingly, they have adopted alternative methods of foraging for both active and passive prey, particularly the use of tentacles to entangle and capture smaller organisms.

There is a greater tendency for species living in deep water to simply lie in wait for prey to approach in order to conserve energy. As such, these species have evolved stealthier approaches to feeding, often focusing on the use of lures or elongated body parts that allow them to control a more expansive area of water around them. Another adaptation that some species have developed in response to the low concentration of prey is their ability to deal with much larger particles of organic matter than shallow-water species of similar size can consume. Among species of fish, many of them have evolved to have larger jaws and teeth. Moreover, some of these fish have further evolved to be able to open their mouths wider by temporarily dislocating their jaws. Because this creates such a large opening into which prey are sucked, the fish tend to swallow their food whole rather than cutting it up using their teeth, decreasing the overall amount of energy required to feed.

<이빨 대신 여과 역할의 수염을 통해 동물성 플랑크톤을 섭취하는 수염 고래>

In marine ecosystems, there are certain regions where food becomes more plentiful in particular seasons, such as shallow coastal areas of the United States between March and May. In such a scenario, species that find their food source in abundant supply no longer need to prioritize energy conservation for fear of running out of food. On the other hand, species inhabiting the deeper regions of the ocean are more likely to experience periods where food is exceedingly scarce, which imposes harsh constraints on their energy usage. These species are forced to adopt new feeding strategies and maximize their calorie intake in order to survive in their barren habitats.

What can be inferred from paragraph 1 about marine organisms inhabiting coastal waters between March and May?

(A) They expend less energy to find food.
(B) They struggle to source abundant supplies of food.
(C) They increase their calorie intake after May.
(D) They prioritize energy conservation to evade predators.

In the upper layers of the ocean, many large organisms such as whales consume huge amounts of plankton by separating them from streams of water that pass through anatomical structures that function like natural filtration mechanisms. Such organisms are aptly referred to as filter-feeders, and they flourish in the well-lit surface waters of the oceans where plankton are most abundant. Under certain circumstances, many species of small fish also prove to be effective filter-feeders. While most fish are carnivorous, some species that live near the surface of the ocean, such as anchovies and sardines, also take advantage of the large volume of phytoplankton, which are plant-based plankton such as algae. They are able to filter out large amounts of algae using unique filaments present in their gills. This component of their diet allows sardine and anchovy populations to thrive, which in turn provides more food resources for predators like seabirds, not to mention larger catches for commercial fishing companies. Larger filter-feeders include the likes of whale sharks and baleen whales, which typically visit coastal or polar waters to consume vast quantities of filtered zooplankton—small organisms such as krill and copepods.

What is indicated about fish in paragraph 2?

(A) The majority of fish are dependent on phytoplankton.
(B) Most fish species prefer to avoid well-lit ocean layers.
(C) Some typically carnivorous fish consume plant-based food.
(D) Few fish species are effective foragers in near-surface layers.

In the upper layers of the ocean, many large organisms such as whales consume huge amounts of plankton by separating them from streams of water that pass through anatomical structures that function like natural filtration mechanisms. Such organisms are aptly referred to as filter-feeders, and they flourish in the well-lit surface waters of the oceans where plankton are most abundant. Under certain circumstances, many species of small fish also prove to be effective filter-feeders. While most fish are carnivorous, some species that live near the surface of the ocean, such as anchovies and sardines, also take advantage of the large volume of phytoplankton, which are plant-based plankton such as algae. They are able to filter out large amounts of algae using unique filaments present in their gills. This component of their diet allows sardine and anchovy populations to thrive, which in turn provides more food resources for predators like seabirds, not to mention larger catches for commercial fishing companies. Larger filter-feeders include the likes of whale sharks and baleen whales, which typically visit coastal or polar waters to consume vast quantities of filtered zooplankton—small organisms such as krill and copepods.

According to paragraph 2, how do sardines and anchovies feed in the upper layers of the ocean?

(A) They bring food sources from the deeper ocean regions.

(B) They compete with seabirds for organic matter.

(C) They consume organisms discarded by fishing vessels.

(D) They utilize their gills to filter algae from seawater.

Considering that filter-feeders need to generate a current of water themselves in order to filter nutritional content from it, this can be an energetically demanding feeding strategy for some organisms. In order for filter-feeders to achieve a net energy gain, there must be at least 2.5 micrograms of organic matter per cubic liter of seawater. In the majority of coastal waters, this requirement is easily satisfied. In the depths of the oceans, however, the levels of organic matter range from virtually zero to just over 5 micrograms per cubic liter. Even though some local concentrations are relatively high, in many of these deep-sea regions the majority of filter-feeders would simply starve to death due to a net loss of calories and energy.

Which of the sentences below best expresses the essential information in the highlighted sentence in the passage? Incorrect choices change the meaning in important ways or leave out essential information.

(A) In order to generate a sufficiently strong current of water, filter-feeders must conserve energy in between periods of feeding.
(B) Most filter-feeders are able to satisfy their energy requirements by filtering nutritional content from the natural currents of the ocean.
(C) Because filter-feeders create water currents in order to feed, they expend less energy than marine species that do not filter food from seawater.
(D) Large energy demands are placed on organisms that filter seawater to meet their nutritional needs since they need to create their own water currents.

It stands to reason that there are few filter-feeders capable of surviving, much less thriving, in the deepest pockets of the oceans. Those that are able to live in such regions have evolved larger filtering systems to offset the low concentration of organic matter. Many organisms at this depth choose to forage only in specific layers where higher concentrations of organic matter accumulate. Many of the marine species that typify the shallow-water filter-feeding behavior have deep-sea counterparts, although the filtering systems of these deep-sea creatures are typically less developed. Accordingly, they have adopted alternative methods of foraging for both active and passive prey, particularly the use of tentacles to entangle and capture smaller organisms.

According to paragraph 4, filter-feeders in deep ocean regions have adopted all of the following feeding strategies EXCEPT

(A) rising to the surface when local food sources run low
(B) foraging in deep regions where organic matter is most plentiful
(C) utilizing larger filtering systems
(D) immobilizing prey using tentacles

There is a greater tendency for species living in deep water to simply lie in wait for prey to approach in order to conserve energy. As such, these species have evolved stealthier approaches to feeding, often focusing on the use of lures or elongated body parts that allow them to control a more expansive area of water around them. Another adaptation that some species have developed in response to the low concentration of prey is their ability to deal with much larger particles of organic matter than shallow-water species of similar size can consume. Among species of fish, many of them have evolved to have larger jaws and teeth. Moreover, some of these fish have further evolved to be able to open their mouths wider by temporarily dislocating their jaws. Because this creates such a large opening into which prey are sucked, the fish tend to swallow their food whole rather than cutting it up using their teeth, decreasing the overall amount of energy required to feed.

Why does the writer mention that organisms in the ocean depths often rely on "lures" and "elongated body parts"?

(A) To illustrate how organisms in the deepest layers of the oceans are able to trap and consume filter-feeders

(B) To challenge a hypothesis that deep-ocean organisms expend more energy when foraging than shallow-water species do

(C) To identify adaptations some organisms have undergone in order to feed effectively in regions where food is scarce

(D) To provide examples of anatomical features that help deep-ocean creatures to move rapidly through water currents

There is a greater tendency for species living in deep water to simply lie in wait for prey to approach in order to conserve energy. As such, these species have evolved stealthier approaches to feeding, often focusing on the use of lures or elongated body parts that allow them to control a more expansive area of water around them. Another adaptation that some species have developed in response to the low concentration of prey is their ability to deal with much larger particles of organic matter than shallow-water species of similar size can consume. Among species of fish, many of them have evolved to have larger jaws and teeth. Moreover, some of these fish have further evolved to be able to open their mouths wider by temporarily dislocating their jaws. Because this creates such a large opening into which prey are sucked, the fish tend to swallow their food whole rather than cutting it up using their teeth, decreasing the overall amount of energy required to feed.

The phrase "deal with" in the passage is closest in meaning to

(A) trade
(B) process
(C) distribute
(D) attract

There is a greater tendency for species living in deep water to simply lie in wait for prey to approach in order to conserve energy. As such, these species have evolved stealthier approaches to feeding, often focusing on the use of lures or elongated body parts that allow them to control a more expansive area of water around them. Another adaptation that some species have developed in response to the low concentration of prey is their ability to deal with much larger particles of organic matter than shallow-water species of similar size can consume. Among species of fish, many of them have evolved to have larger jaws and teeth. Moreover, some of these fish have further evolved to be able to open their mouths wider by temporarily dislocating their jaws. Because this creates such a large opening into which prey are sucked, the fish tend to swallow their food whole rather than cutting it up using their teeth, decreasing the overall amount of energy required to feed.

According to paragraph 5, why do some fish swallow their prey whole?

(A) They do not want to risk dislocating their jaws.
(B) They lack teeth to bite into their prey.
(C) Intact organic matter provides higher nutritional content.
(D) Swallowing prey involves lower energy expenditure.

■ There is a greater tendency for species living in deep water to simply lie in wait for prey to approach in order to conserve energy. ■ As such, these species have evolved stealthier approaches to feeding, often focusing on the use of lures or elongated body parts that allow them to control a more expansive area of water around them. ■ Another adaptation that some species have developed in response to the low concentration of prey is their ability to deal with much larger particles of organic matter than shallow-water species of similar size can consume. ■ Among species of fish, many of them have evolved to have larger jaws and teeth. Moreover, some of these fish have further evolved to be able to open their mouths wider by temporarily dislocating their jaws. Because this creates such a large opening into which prey are sucked, the fish tend to swallow their food whole rather than cutting it up using their teeth, decreasing the overall amount of energy required to feed.

Look at the four squares [■] that indicate where the following sentence could be added to the passage.

Creatures adopting this passive approach are forced to take advantage of unique strategies in order to meet their nutritional needs.

Where would the sentence best fit? Click on a square [■] to add the sentence to the passage.

Directions: An introductory sentence for a brief summary of the passage is provided below. Complete the summary by selecting the THREE answer choices that express the most important ideas in the passage. Some sentences do not belong in the summary because they express ideas that are not presented in the passage or are minor ideas in the passage. **This question is worth 2 points.**

Drag your answer choices to the space where they belong. To remove an answer choice, click on it. To review the passage, click on **VIEW TEXT.**

Ocean animals have developed various strategies for maximizing energy input from food.

-
-
-

Answer Choices

(A) In deep-ocean layers, the majority of plankton are zooplankton rather than plant-based phytoplankton found near the surface.

(B) The higher concentration of organic matter in shallow or near-surface regions is exploited by organisms capable of filtering food from the water.

(C) Animals in deeper water have evolved strategies that allow them to minimize movement and the need to forage and let prey come to them.

(D) Near the surface of the water, some fish that typically consume meat have adapted to also consume large amounts of plant-based plankton.

(E) Filter-feeders tend to move between shallow and deep regions to avoid being pursued by larger carnivorous predators.

(F) In the depths of the ocean, organisms expend less energy while feeding due to the relatively weak ocean currents.

■ Passage 2

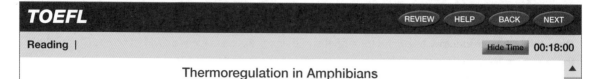

Thermoregulation in Amphibians

Unlike mammals and birds, amphibians have the unique capability to use their own metabolic activity to generate thermal energy. This enables them to regulate their own body temperature regardless of the environmental temperature of their surroundings. Thanks to this physiological adaptation, amphibians are able to inhabit various locations where extreme climate conditions exist.

The range of temperatures within which a species can survive is referred to as its body temperature tolerance range. For example, there is a certain species of newt found in North America that can still freely move around when its body temperature falls below 0°C, while one South American frog can function normally with a body temperature of just over 40°C, higher than that of any other amphibian. Researchers have identified some species of toads and frogs in North America that can live for almost a week with a body temperature just below -5°C and almost half of their internal fluids frozen. The other tissues do not freeze due to the presence of frost-protective substances such as glucose and glycerin. Also, the tolerance boundaries in many species are not fixed, and long-term exposure to specific conditions can change them as a result of acclimatization.

There are some frog species that exhibit remarkable skin structure modifications that function as morphological adaptations, allowing the frogs to remain exposed to the sun despite high temperatures. Most amphibians lack a barrier against solar radiation and evaporation because their skin is completely water-permeable. However, the African savanna frog's skin contains crystals of guanine, which turn the skin into a reflective solar radiation shield, preventing the frog from overheating. Some species of tree frogs mitigate water losses through evaporation by secreting a greasy substance over its entire body that stops it from drying out.

While physiological adaptations are important, the most crucial factor in thermoregulation is behavior. Behavioral thermoregulation includes strategies such as hibernation and estivation, which refers to a reduction in activity during cold and hot periods, respectively; diurnal and annual avoidance behaviors, such as moving to shaded areas during the day to stay cool; thigmothermy, which involves direct heat exchange between the body and environmental objects like soil and rock; and heliothermy, also known as basking, which refers to heat gain through direct sunlight.

Hibernation among amphibians is often used as a means of avoiding frost by burrowing into mud or deep holes. Natterjack toads that inhabit a region north of the Pyrenees Mountains hibernate through the winter by digging into the sandy ground. On the other hand, natterjacks that live in southern Spain remain active during the region's relatively warm winters, and instead enter a state of inactivity during the summer, when the climate is particularly hot and dry. This estivation is achieved by digging into the ground or sheltering in deep, cool fissures in rocks to avoid the extreme climate, which can rapidly dry out and kill the natterjacks.

Amphibians engage in avoidance behavior whenever they are unable to maintain body temperature within their vital range through physiological and morphological adaptations. One common thermoregulatory behavior of avoidance is the nocturnal behavior of amphibians that have low tolerance for high ambient temperatures. In addition, seasonal avoidance behavior is crucial to the survival of many amphibians. Species who live in arid and semiarid regions must take avoidance measures during the long dry, hot summers, while those dwelling in temperate regions must try to avoid the potentially fatal low temperatures in winter.

Frogs and toads can often be seen basking during the day, which helps to raise their body temperature by at least 10°C. For instance, the Andean toad stretches out on exposed, moist ground as soon as the sun rises, and this allows it to reach its target body temperature long before the surrounding air has warmed to that temperature. This approach is beneficial in that it speeds up the digestion of food eaten during the night, which also boosts its growth rate. Similarly, a large number of amphibian species engage in thigmothermy behavior. This serves two functions: water absorption through the skin and heat absorption by conductivity. The Andean toad utilizes thigmothermy during periods of heavy rain. As such, it is able to raise its body temperature to match the temperature of the warm earth rather than let it fall to correspond with the cooler temperature of the air. As is clear from the mechanisms described above, amphibians are adept at coping with extreme ambient temperatures since they have several ways to control their body temperature.

<추운 날씨 속에 활동 가능한 특정 뉴트 종>

The range of temperatures within which a species can survive is referred to as its body temperature tolerance range. For example, there is a certain species of newt found in North America that can still freely move around when its body temperature falls below 0°C, while one South American frog can function normally with a body temperature of just over 40°C, higher than that of any other amphibian. Researchers have identified some species of toads and frogs in North America that can live for almost a week with a body temperature just below -5°C and almost half of their internal fluids frozen. The other tissues do not freeze due to the presence of frost-protective substances such as glucose and glycerin. Also, the tolerance boundaries in many species are not fixed, and long-term exposure to specific conditions can change them as a result of acclimatization.

In paragraph 2, why does the author mention a "South American frog"?

(A) To provide an example of an amphibian that has adapted to relatively high-temperature conditions
(B) To show how extreme temperatures can cause damage to physiological structures
(C) To compare its physiological adaptations with those of the North American newt
(D) To emphasize that the adaptation of amphibians is a process requiring millions of years

There are some frog species that exhibit remarkable skin structure modifications that function as morphological adaptations, allowing the frogs to remain exposed to the sun despite high temperatures. Most amphibians lack a barrier against solar radiation and evaporation because their skin is completely water-permeable. However, the African savanna frog's skin contains crystals of guanine, which turn the skin into a reflective solar radiation shield, preventing the frog from overheating. Some species of tree frogs mitigate water losses through evaporation by secreting a greasy substance over its entire body that stops it from drying out.

According to the passage, the "African savanna frog" has an adaptation that

(A) provides protection to its respiratory system
(B) limits the amount of fluid it can secrete
(C) turns its skin into a barrier to sunlight
(D) converts solar radiation into energy

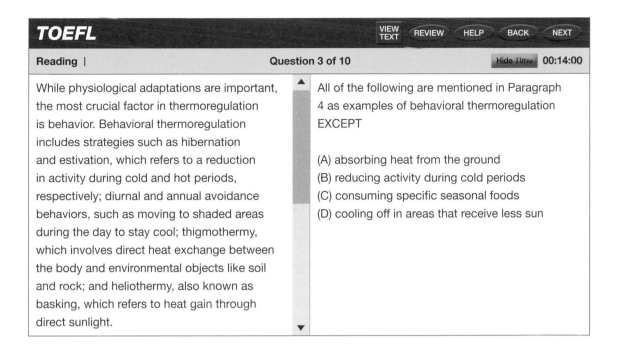

While physiological adaptations are important, the most crucial factor in thermoregulation is behavior. Behavioral thermoregulation includes strategies such as hibernation and estivation, which refers to a reduction in activity during cold and hot periods, respectively; diurnal and annual avoidance behaviors, such as moving to shaded areas during the day to stay cool; thigmothermy, which involves direct heat exchange between the body and environmental objects like soil and rock; and heliothermy, also known as basking, which refers to heat gain through direct sunlight.

All of the following are mentioned in Paragraph 4 as examples of behavioral thermoregulation EXCEPT

(A) absorbing heat from the ground
(B) reducing activity during cold periods
(C) consuming specific seasonal foods
(D) cooling off in areas that receive less sun

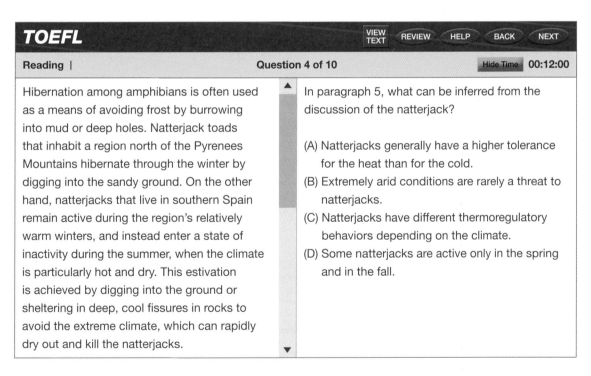

Hibernation among amphibians is often used as a means of avoiding frost by burrowing into mud or deep holes. Natterjack toads that inhabit a region north of the Pyrenees Mountains hibernate through the winter by digging into the sandy ground. On the other hand, natterjacks that live in southern Spain remain active during the region's relatively warm winters, and instead enter a state of inactivity during the summer, when the climate is particularly hot and dry. This estivation is achieved by digging into the ground or sheltering in deep, cool fissures in rocks to avoid the extreme climate, which can rapidly dry out and kill the natterjacks.

In paragraph 5, what can be inferred from the discussion of the natterjack?

(A) Natterjacks generally have a higher tolerance for the heat than for the cold.
(B) Extremely arid conditions are rarely a threat to natterjacks.
(C) Natterjacks have different thermoregulatory behaviors depending on the climate.
(D) Some natterjacks are active only in the spring and in the fall.

Amphibians engage in avoidance behavior whenever they are unable to maintain body temperature within their vital range through physiological and morphological adaptations. One common thermoregulatory behavior of avoidance is the nocturnal behavior of amphibians that have low tolerance for high ambient temperatures. In addition, seasonal avoidance behavior is crucial to the survival of many amphibians. Species who live in arid and semiarid regions must take avoidance measures during the long dry, hot summers, while those dwelling in temperate regions must try to avoid the potentially fatal low temperatures in winter.

According to paragraph 6, why is avoidance behavior important for some amphibians?

(A) Their habitats often experience extreme temperature fluctuations throughout the day.
(B) They lack adequate physiological adaptations for dealing with ambient temperatures.
(C) Their tolerance for extreme ambient temperatures is inhibited by genetic abnormalities.
(D) They are able to avoid potential predators that hunt at certain times of the day.

Frogs and toads can often be seen basking during the day, which helps to raise their body temperature by at least 10°C. For instance, the Andean toad stretches out on exposed, moist ground as soon as the sun rises, and this allows it to reach its target body temperature long before the surrounding air has warmed to that temperature. This approach is beneficial in that it speeds up the digestion of food eaten during the night, which also boosts its growth rate. Similarly, a large number of amphibian species engage in thigmothermy behavior. This serves two functions: water absorption through the skin and heat absorption by conductivity. The Andean toad utilizes thigmothermy during periods of heavy rain. As such, it is able to raise its body temperature to match the temperature of the warm earth rather than let it fall to correspond with the cooler temperature of the air. As is clear from the mechanisms described above, amphibians are adept at coping with extreme ambient temperatures since they have several ways to control their body temperature.

The "Andean toad" is a good example of an amphibian with which of the following behavioral modifications?

(A) Burrowing underground to stay cool
(B) Annual avoidance behavior
(C) Reflecting radiation from the sun
(D) Absorbing heat through direct sunlight

Frogs and toads can often be seen basking during the day, which helps to raise their body temperature by at least 10°C. For instance, the Andean toad stretches out on exposed, moist ground as soon as the sun rises, and this allows it to reach its target body temperature long before the surrounding air has warmed to that temperature. This approach is beneficial in that it speeds up the digestion of food eaten during the night, which also boosts its growth rate. Similarly, a large number of amphibian species engage in thigmothermy behavior. This serves two functions: water absorption through the skin and heat absorption by conductivity. The Andean toad utilizes thigmothermy during periods of heavy rain. As such, it is able to raise its body temperature to match the temperature of the warm earth rather than let it fall to correspond with the cooler temperature of the air. As is clear from the mechanisms described above, amphibians are adept at coping with extreme ambient temperatures since they have several ways to control their body temperature.

The phrase "This approach" in the passage refers to

(A) ensuring body temperature remains low
(B) accelerating the increase of body temperature
(C) maintaining body temperature at 10°C
(D) allowing body temperature to fluctuate regularly

Frogs and toads can often be seen basking during the day, which helps to raise their body temperature by at least 10°C. For instance, the Andean toad stretches out on exposed, moist ground as soon as the sun rises, and this allows it to reach its target body temperature long before the surrounding air has warmed to that temperature. This approach is beneficial in that it speeds up the digestion of food eaten during the night, which also boosts its growth rate. Similarly, a large number of amphibian species engage in thigmothermy behavior. This serves two functions: water absorption through the skin and heat absorption by conductivity. The Andean toad utilizes thigmothermy during periods of heavy rain. As such, it is able to raise its body temperature to match the temperature of the warm earth rather than let it fall to correspond with the cooler temperature of the air. As is clear from the mechanisms described above, amphibians are adept at coping with extreme ambient temperatures since they have several ways to control their body temperature.

Which of the sentences below best expresses the essential information in the highlighted sentence in the passage? Incorrect choices change the meaning in important ways or leave out essential information.

(A) Therefore, despite amphibians having the various mechanisms described above, they only have limited control of their body temperature.

(B) The various methods covered above exemplify how amphibians are capable of withstanding extreme climates by virtue of having control over body temperature.

(C) Thus, without using the mechanisms described above, amphibians would have great difficulty in moving between regions with different ambient temperatures.

(D) As well as the aforementioned mechanisms, amphibians have several other strategies for surviving in habitats that experience temperature extremes.

The range of temperatures within which a species can survive is referred to as its body temperature tolerance range. For example, there is a certain species of newt found in North America that can still freely move around when its body temperature falls below 0°C, while one South American frog can function normally with a body temperature of just over 40°C, higher than that of any other amphibian. ∎ Researchers have identified some species of toads and frogs in North America that can live for almost a week with a body temperature just below -5°C and almost half of their internal fluids frozen. ∎ The other tissues do not freeze due to the presence of frost-protective substances such as glucose and glycerin. ∎ Also, the tolerance boundaries in many species are not fixed, and long-term exposure to specific conditions can change them as a result of acclimatization. ∎

Look at the four squares [∎] that indicate where the following sentence could be added to the passage.

On the other hand, amphibians that inhabit very hot regions can decrease their body temperature through evaporative cooling by secreting mucus from specialized glands.

Where would the sentence best fit? Click on a square [∎] to add the sentence to the passage.

Directions: An introductory sentence for a brief summary of the passage is provided below. Complete the summary by selecting the THREE answer choices that express the most important ideas in the passage. Some sentences do not belong in the summary because they express ideas that are not presented in the passage or are minor ideas in the passage. **This question is worth 2 points.**

Drag your answer choices to the space where they belong. To remove an answer choice, click on it. To review the passage, click on **VIEW TEXT.**

Amphibians take advantage of several thermoregulatory adaptations and behaviors in order to survive in harsh climates.

-
-
-

Answer Choices

(A) Some amphibian species take advantage of several mechanisms by which they can maintain an optimal body temperature by absorbing heat from the sun or ground.

(B) Amphibians that engage in thigmothermy are capable of sharing body heat with other members of their surrounding community.

(C) Some amphibians can function normally in extreme climates as a result of physiological adaptations in their skin and other organs.

(D) Estivation and avoidance behaviors allow amphibians to avoid extremely dry and hot conditions.

(E) Many amphibian species choose to move around and hunt after sunrise in order to maintain an optimal body temperature.

(F) Cold cracks in rocks and other shaded areas can serve as ideal places for amphibians to hibernate during winter months.

Transgenic Plants

Thanks to modern advances in science, it is now possible to insert genes from virtually any source, whether it be human, animal, or even virus, into plants in order to create transgenic plants. Transgenic crops now take up approximately 110 million acres of agricultural land throughout the world, with the vast majority being grown in North America. Corn, canola, soybeans, and cotton are the most widely grown transgenic crops, and they typically contain a pest-resistant gene that produces a protein called Bt toxin, or a gene that confers resistance to an herbicide called glyphosate.

Those who support the cultivation of transgenic crops argue that these crops offer various environmental benefits. For instance, the growth of such crops requires fewer potentially-damaging chemicals, and those that are used pose less threat to the environment than the typical chemicals used in crop production. In fact, studies have shown that the growing of transgenic cotton containing the Bt toxin requires 20 percent less insecticide overall. Additionally, by creating transgenic crops with glyphosate resistance, glyphosate can be applied to kill weeds, instead of using more harmful herbicides.

On the other hand, an increasing number of people believe that more extensive research must be carried out before global crop producers begin cultivating transgenic crops on a large scale. In particular, there has been growing concern regarding the effects that Bt plants might have on nontarget organisms such as birds and insects that feed on the transgenic plants. One specific case that has come under the spotlight is that of the monarch caterpillar. When this species feeds on milkweed plants planted alongside Bt cornfields, it will inadvertently consume corn pollen that has drifted over to the milkweed plants in the wind. Although field studies have thus far failed to show any adverse effects of Bt pollen consumption on monarch caterpillars, laboratory findings indicate that it could potentially kill them. However, it is also true that nontarget species are at serious risk from pesticides that would be used if the Bt plants were replaced with normal crops.

Another potential problem is the accidental transfer of herbicide-resistant genes into weed populations. Crop plants may on occasion be grown in close proximity to wild weedy relatives, and if these weedy relatives were to reproduce with the transgenic crops, then the herbicide-resistant gene would be passed on to the offspring. When this occurs, the herbicide-resistant gene will enter the weed population. The main problem this causes is that the weed populations will no longer be killed when farmers attempt to eradicate them using a substance such as glyphosate. A situation like this is far less likely to occur when the transgenic crop plant has no weedy relative species growing in nearby areas. However, this could still pose a very serious problem in specific cases. For instance, herbicide-resistant genes can quite easily pass from transgenic canola into weed populations because canola is known to hybridize with several mustard weed species.

It is widely acknowledged that large-scale production of transgenic plants will have effects on evolution over a prolonged period of time. One of the most pressing concerns is that insects will eventually develop resistance to the Bt toxin. While this pesticide has been used in farming for several decades, insect populations have failed to acquire widespread resistance to it. However, the Bt toxin is expressed in all structures of transgenic Bt plants during their entire growing period. This means that any insects expressing genes that make them vulnerable to the toxin will inevitably perish, leaving behind only the insects with an established genetic resistance. Mating between these resistant insects has a high likelihood of producing offspring that are also resistant to the Bt toxin, and this will eventually lead to resistance across an entire population. In an effort to inhibit the evolution of insect resistance to Bt toxin, crop producers are planting rows of nontransgenic crops for vulnerable insects to feed on. Measures such as this may result in insect populations retaining a certain level of Bt vulnerability.

One of the biggest arguments against current methods of transgenic crop production is that they incentivize farmers to abandon sustainable farming approaches that enable the continual regeneration of natural resources over time. At least on a superficial level, transgenics make farming a lot easier by removing some of the typical choices farmers would normally be required to make. Growing crops with glyphosate resistance necessitates the use of only that herbicide, while other herbicides and weed-control practices are ignored. Also, farmers who grow Bt crops are unlikely to incorporate pest-management strategies that focus on pesticide application or the use of beneficial insects. It would be far more of a sustainable practice to grow nontransgenic crops, observe crops closely during growing season, and then make a decision regarding pesticide application based on the condition of the crops.

<유전자 이식 식물>

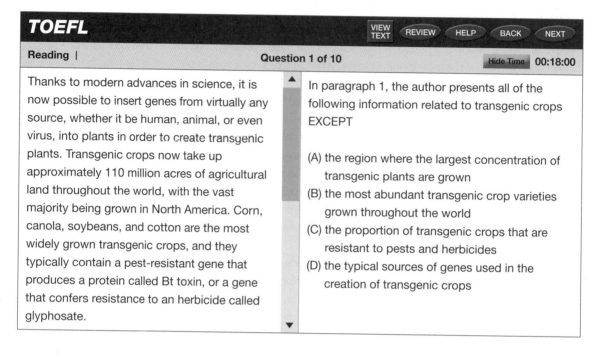

Thanks to modern advances in science, it is now possible to insert genes from virtually any source, whether it be human, animal, or even virus, into plants in order to create transgenic plants. Transgenic crops now take up approximately 110 million acres of agricultural land throughout the world, with the vast majority being grown in North America. Corn, canola, soybeans, and cotton are the most widely grown transgenic crops, and they typically contain a pest-resistant gene that produces a protein called Bt toxin, or a gene that confers resistance to an herbicide called glyphosate.

In paragraph 1, the author presents all of the following information related to transgenic crops EXCEPT

(A) the region where the largest concentration of transgenic plants are grown
(B) the most abundant transgenic crop varieties grown throughout the world
(C) the proportion of transgenic crops that are resistant to pests and herbicides
(D) the typical sources of genes used in the creation of transgenic crops

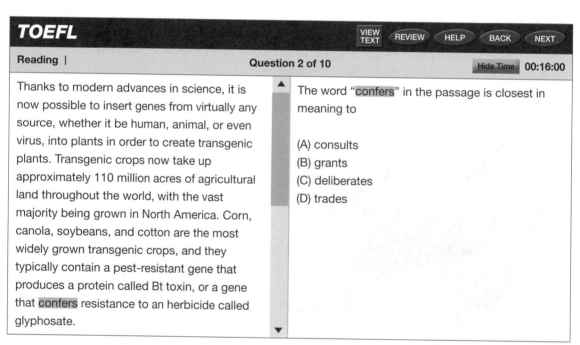

Thanks to modern advances in science, it is now possible to insert genes from virtually any source, whether it be human, animal, or even virus, into plants in order to create transgenic plants. Transgenic crops now take up approximately 110 million acres of agricultural land throughout the world, with the vast majority being grown in North America. Corn, canola, soybeans, and cotton are the most widely grown transgenic crops, and they typically contain a pest-resistant gene that produces a protein called Bt toxin, or a gene that confers resistance to an herbicide called glyphosate.

The word "confers" in the passage is closest in meaning to

(A) consults
(B) grants
(C) deliberates
(D) trades

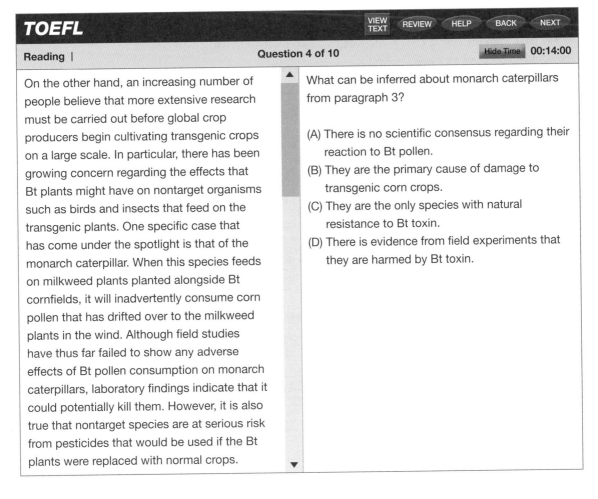

Those who support the cultivation of transgenic crops argue that these crops offer various environmental benefits. For instance, the growth of such crops requires fewer potentially-damaging chemicals, and those that are used pose less threat to the environment than the typical chemicals used in crop production. In fact, studies have shown that the growing of transgenic cotton containing the Bt toxin requires 20 percent less insecticide overall. Additionally, by creating transgenic crops with glyphosate resistance, glyphosate can be applied to kill weeds, instead of using more harmful herbicides.

What purported benefit of transgenic crops does the author describe in paragraph 2?

(A) Less land will be required for agriculture.
(B) A wider variety of crops will become available.
(C) Fewer harmful substances will be applied to crops.
(D) Crops will no longer compete for space with weeds.

On the other hand, an increasing number of people believe that more extensive research must be carried out before global crop producers begin cultivating transgenic crops on a large scale. In particular, there has been growing concern regarding the effects that Bt plants might have on nontarget organisms such as birds and insects that feed on the transgenic plants. One specific case that has come under the spotlight is that of the monarch caterpillar. When this species feeds on milkweed plants planted alongside Bt cornfields, it will inadvertently consume corn pollen that has drifted over to the milkweed plants in the wind. Although field studies have thus far failed to show any adverse effects of Bt pollen consumption on monarch caterpillars, laboratory findings indicate that it could potentially kill them. However, it is also true that nontarget species are at serious risk from pesticides that would be used if the Bt plants were replaced with normal crops.

What can be inferred about monarch caterpillars from paragraph 3?

(A) There is no scientific consensus regarding their reaction to Bt pollen.
(B) They are the primary cause of damage to transgenic corn crops.
(C) They are the only species with natural resistance to Bt toxin.
(D) There is evidence from field experiments that they are harmed by Bt toxin.

Another potential problem is the accidental transfer of herbicide-resistant genes into weed populations. Crop plants may on occasion be grown in close proximity to wild weedy relatives, and if these weedy relatives were to reproduce with the transgenic crops, then the herbicide-resistant gene would be passed on to the offspring. When this occurs, the herbicide-resistant gene will enter the weed population. The main problem this causes is that the weed populations will no longer be killed when farmers attempt to eradicate them using a substance such as glyphosate. A situation like this is far less likely to occur when the transgenic crop plant has no weedy relative species growing in nearby areas. However, this could still pose a very serious problem in specific cases. For instance, herbicide-resistant genes can quite easily pass from transgenic canola into weed populations because canola is known to hybridize with several mustard weed species.

The phrase "passed on" in the passage is closest in meaning to

(A) skipped
(B) overtaken
(C) achieved
(D) transferred

Another potential problem is the accidental transfer of herbicide-resistant genes into weed populations. Crop plants may on occasion be grown in close proximity to wild weedy relatives, and if these weedy relatives were to reproduce with the transgenic crops, then the herbicide-resistant gene would be passed on to the offspring. When this occurs, the herbicide-resistant gene will enter the weed population. The main problem this causes is that the weed populations will no longer be killed when farmers attempt to eradicate them using a substance such as glyphosate. A situation like this is far less likely to occur when the transgenic crop plant has no weedy relative species growing in nearby areas. However, this could still pose a very serious problem in specific cases. For instance, herbicide-resistant genes can quite easily pass from transgenic canola into weed populations because canola is known to hybridize with several mustard weed species.

Why does the author mention "mustard weed species" in paragraph 4?

(A) To support the theory that transgenic crops are more likely to flourish when planted in close proximity to certain weed species.
(B) To provide an example of weeds that could potentially reproduce with transgenic plants and acquire resistance to substances like glyphosate.
(C) To give evidence that transgenic crops have successfully reduced populations of weedy relatives in agricultural regions.
(D) To argue that the creation of transgenic plants through hybridization with weedy relatives is less challenging than creating them in a lab.

It is widely acknowledged that large-scale production of transgenic plants will have effects on evolution over a prolonged period of time. One of the most pressing concerns is that insects will eventually develop resistance to the Bt toxin. While this pesticide has been used in farming for several decades, insect populations have failed to acquire widespread resistance to it. However, the Bt toxin is expressed in all structures of transgenic Bt plants during their entire growing period. This means that any insects expressing genes that make them vulnerable to the toxin will inevitably perish, leaving behind only the insects with an established genetic resistance. Mating between these resistant insects has a high likelihood of producing offspring that are also resistant to the Bt toxin, and this will eventually lead to resistance across an entire population. In an effort to inhibit the evolution of insect resistance to Bt toxin, crop producers are planting rows of nontransgenic crops for vulnerable insects to feed on. Measures such as this may result in insect populations retaining a certain level of Bt vulnerability.

In Paragraph 5, the author claims all of the following about Bt resistance in insect populations EXCEPT

(A) Planting nontransgenic plants in areas adjacent to Bt transgenic crops will accelerate the development of Bt-resistance among insect populations.

(B) An eventual uniform Bt-resistance among insect populations is inevitable if the use of transgenic plants becomes widespread.

(C) While the use of Bt pesticides has not led to Bt resistance in insect populations, there is a higher chance of this occurring through Bt crop planting.

(D) Because Bt plants express the toxin in all structures at all times, they are highly likely to kill off all Bt-susceptible members of insect populations.

One of the biggest arguments against current methods of transgenic crop production is that they incentivize farmers to abandon sustainable farming approaches that enable the continual regeneration of natural resources over time. At least on a superficial level, transgenics make farming a lot easier by removing some of the typical choices farmers would normally be required to make. Growing crops with glyphosate resistance necessitates the use of only that herbicide, while other herbicides and weed-control practices are ignored. Also, farmers who grow Bt crops are unlikely to incorporate pest-management strategies that focus on pesticide application or the use of beneficial insects. It would be far more of a sustainable practice to grow nontransgenic crops, observe crops closely during growing season, and then make a decision regarding pesticide application based on the condition of the crops.

Which of the sentences below best expresses the essential information in the highlighted sentence in the passage? Incorrect choices change the meaning in important ways or leave out essential information.

(A) Many people argue that transgenic crop plants of the future will be far more sustainable than those that are being produced using today's farming approaches.

(B) Farmers who grow transgenic crops are rapidly embracing sustainable farming practices that allow the environment to rejuvenate itself naturally.

(C) One of the biggest disadvantages of transgenic crops is that they require more resources than crops grown using sustainable agriculture strategies.

(D) There is a serious concern that farmers are encouraged to grow transgenic crops instead of helping to renew natural resources through sustainable farming methods.

Another potential problem is the accidental transfer of herbicide-resistant genes into weed populations. Crop plants may on occasion be grown in close proximity to wild weedy relatives, and if these weedy relatives were to reproduce with the transgenic crops, then the herbicide-resistant gene would be passed on to the offspring. ■ When this occurs, the herbicide-resistant gene will enter the weed population. ■ The main problem this causes is that the weed populations will no longer be killed when farmers attempt to eradicate them using a substance such as glyphosate. ■ A situation like this is far less likely to occur when the transgenic crop plant has no weedy relative species growing in nearby areas. ■ However, this could still pose a very serious problem in specific cases. For instance, herbicide-resistant genes can quite easily pass from transgenic canola into weed populations because canola is known to hybridize with several mustard weed species.

Look at the four squares [■] that indicate where the following sentence could be added to the passage.

Considering that most of the crops grown in the United States originated elsewhere, it is particularly rare for it to happen there.

Where would the sentence best fit? Click on a square [■] to add the sentence to the passage.

Directions: An introductory sentence for a brief summary of the passage is provided below. Complete the summary by selecting the THREE answer choices that express the most important ideas in the passage. Some sentences do not belong in the summary because they express ideas that are not presented in the passage or are minor ideas in the passage. **This question is worth 2 points.**

Drag your answer choices to the space where they belong. To remove an answer choice, click on it. To review the passage, click on **VIEW TEXT.**

The development of transgenic plants is a topic that generates many opposing viewpoints, particularly regarding the safety of the practice and its effect on the environment.

-
-
-

Answer Choices

(A) Many of the current problems associated with transgenic plants will likely disappear in the future as more environmentally friendly methods are integrated.

(B) Supporters of transgenic plants maintain that the approach facilitates the use of more environmentally friendly herbicides and cuts down on the use of harmful chemicals.

(C) Over a prolonged period, glyphosate resistance in transgenic plants is likely to diminish through evolution and hybridization with plant relatives.

(D) One potentially negative side effect of transgenic crops is that farmers will favor them over traditional crops that can be grown using sustainable methods.

(E) Transgenic plants may have been the cause of the decline in monarch caterpillar populations throughout North America.

(F) There is grave concern that large-scale production of crops that produce Bt toxin will eventually result in widespread Bt resistance among insect populations.

Chapter

02

Ecology

Passage 1   **Direct Species Translocation**

Passage 2   **Evolution of Flowering Plants**

Passage 3   **Coral Reefs**

LIVING WORLD BIOSPHERE

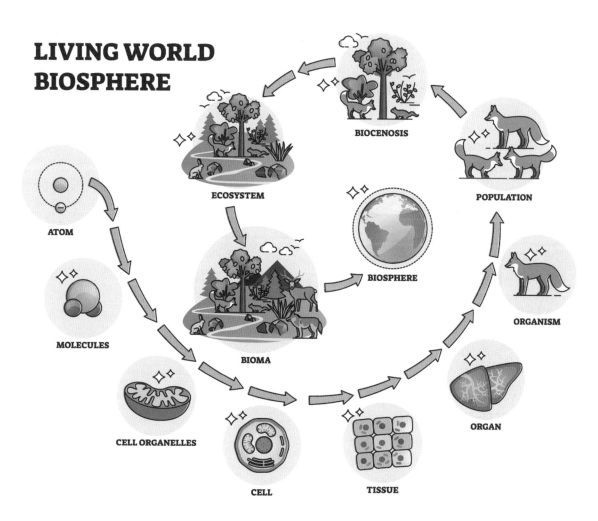

ATOM

MOLECULES

CELL ORGANELLES

CELL

TISSUE

ORGAN

ORGANISM

POPULATION

BIOCENOSIS

ECOSYSTEM

BIOMA

BIOSPHERE

Ecology (생태학)

생물들 사이 그리고 생물과 물리적 환경 간의 상호작용을 과학적으로 연구하는 학문으로 생물학과 토픽 및 어휘면에서 유사하다.

[Ecology 기출 토픽]

- The Long-Term Stability of Ecosystems
  장기간의 생태계 안정화

- Deer Populations of the Puget Sound
  퓨젯 사운드(해협, 작은 만)의 사슴 개체 수

- Mass Extinctions
  집단 멸종

- The Cambrian Explosion
  캄브리아기 폭발(다양한 생명체의 증가)

- Plant Colonization
  식물의 군집화

- Plant Symbiosis
  식물의 공생

- Evolution of Flowering Plants
  꽃식물의 진화

- Coral Reefs
  산호초

- Direct Species Translocation
  종의 강제 이주(야생 동물을 인위적으로 옮겨 정착시킴)

- Succession, Climax, and Ecosystem
  천이(일정한 지역의 식물 군락이 시간의 추이에 따라 변천하여 가는 현상),
  극상(천이에 의한 변화가 장기간 안정을 지속하는 상태) 그리고 생태계

[Ecology 빈출 어휘]

ancestor	조상, 선조	hypothesis	가설
biodiverse	생물이 다양한	immune	면역성이 있는
breeding	번식	invasive	침입하는
catastrophe	재해	isolate	~을 구분하다, 고립시키다
channel	해협	latitude	위도
contaminate	~을 오염시키다	mitigate	~을 완화하다
criteria	기준	olfactory	후각의
degraded	퇴화한	originate	비롯되다, 유래하다
demographic	인구 통계학적인	paleontologist	고생물학자
density	밀도	perish	사라지다, 죽다
deposit	퇴적물	pollen	꽃가루
diagnose	(질병을) 진단하다	protrude	돌출되다
disease	질병	rejuvenation	회복, 활기를 되찾음
dispersal	확산, 분산	relics	유물
dominate	~보다 우세하다	sanitary	위생적인
dwindling	줄어드는	scatter	흩어지다
equator	적도	sediment	침전물
erosion	침식	splintered	분열된
evolve	발전하다, 진화하다	stimulus	자극
facilitate	~을 촉진하다	succession	연속, 계승, 천이
fern	양치 식물	swamp	습지
fossilized	화석화된	symbiosis	공생
genetic	유전의	threshold	한계치
genuine	진정한, 진짜의	trace	~을 추적하다
go extinct	멸종되다	transmission	전염, 전파

Direct Species Translocation

Direct species translocation refers to the moving of several wild animals, or even an entire species, from one location to a different one. When conservationists do this in order to establish a new population in a region where a population of a specific species of animals or plants has gone extinct, it is referred to as reintroduction. Reinforcement, on the other hand, refers to cases where animals are translocated in order to add individuals to an existing population.

Long before conservation became a pressing issue, direct translocation was already being used to move a wide range of plants and animals—typically used as food sources—in order to maintain their populations. As the concept of conservation grew in popularity, so too has the number of translocations that are being carried out, and the technique has come under increased scrutiny due to a lack of evidence concerning its effectiveness, and because of its potential disadvantages. Translocation can occur in various forms, from well-organized and well-funded national or international programs, to the small-scale release of rescued animals by animal enthusiasts with good intentions. Because many populations and habitats are isolated from one another in today's splintered world, translocation can theoretically function as a highly effective conservation approach. It allows conservationists to increase the number or size of existing populations, or improve the demographic balance and genetic diversity of small populations, thereby boosting a population's chances of survival.

Translocation plays an important role in the rejuvenation of species that have substantially diminished, and it is one of the most effective methods for restoring such species back to their former population range. However, potentially serious downsides of reinforcement translocations are the introduction of harmful genes to the existing population and the transmission of disease from one population to another. Furthermore, when predators or competitive species are translocated, it may have an adverse effect on other species and lead to a loss of biodiversity in the region. Another drawback is that this strategy requires a great deal of hard work and resources, so evidence of tangible benefits must be shown in order to justify the costs.

Numerous translocations have been carried out all over the world, but there is barely any significant evidence that they yielded substantial benefits. Admittedly, this is because the majority of translocations have not been overseen by official scientific organizations, and in many cases, have not been legal or for the purpose of conservation. Although a handful of successful translocations have been documented, most of the numerous failures are unlikely to be recorded or reported. This makes it exceedingly difficult to properly appraise the strategy. Moreover, it is difficult to define what a successful transition entails. Should translocation be considered a success if the moved organisms survive for only one month, or for one year? Or must they reproduce over several years in order for the technique to be viewed as successful? Regardless of the definition, what is obvious is that appropriate guidelines must be established to ensure that translocation efforts are warranted, are subject to stringent monitoring and evaluation, and have a high likelihood of succeeding.

One case of direct species translocation that appears to be a genuine success is that of the threatened Seychelles warbler. Once found only on Cousin Island, part of the Seychelles island chain, the species had declined to a population of only 26. This number was increased to over 300 individuals as a result of careful habitat management, but the population was still in danger of extinction from natural catastrophes. A decision was made to mitigate this risk by translocating the warblers to two nearby islands. The translocation to the first island was carried out in 1988, and the translocation to the second one in 1990, and healthy breeding populations were established in both locations. Red howler monkeys in French Guyana serve as another example of a successful translocation project. When a site was to be flooded for hydroelectric power generation, a local population of howler monkeys was translocated to a region where the local howler population had declined due to overhunting. Around 15 of the female monkeys released into the region were monitored by radio tracking. Some early adjustment problems caused the tracked females to scatter at first, but their behavioral patterns became normal fairly quickly.

Sadly, accounts of failures outweigh the evidence of success. Researchers Richard A. Siegel and C. Kenneth Dodd assessed numerous cases of reptile and amphibian translocation and found that very few of them could be considered a success in terms of conservation. Thus, they recommended that such methods should not be deemed as viable species management practices.

<멸종 위기에 처한 세이셸 울새의 강제 이주 작업>

Long before conservation became a pressing issue, direct translocation was already being used to move a wide range of plants and animals—typically used as food sources—in order to maintain their populations. As the concept of conservation grew in popularity, so too has the number of translocations that are being carried out, and the technique has come under increased scrutiny due to a lack of evidence concerning its effectiveness, and because of its potential disadvantages. Translocation can occur in various forms, from well-organized and well-funded national or international programs, to the small-scale release of rescued animals by animal enthusiasts with good intentions. Because many populations and habitats are isolated from one another in today's splintered world, translocation can theoretically function as a highly effective conservation approach. It allows conservationists to increase the number or size of existing populations, or improve the demographic balance and genetic diversity of small populations, thereby boosting a population's chances of survival.

In paragraph 2, all of the following are indicated about species translocation EXCEPT

(A) Increasing interest in conservation led to a rise in the frequency of translocations.
(B) Its potential disadvantages were disproven by several international research studies.
(C) It was primarily utilized to maintain food sources before it was used for conservation.
(D) It is carried out by a wide variety of groups conducting projects of varying scopes.

Translocation plays an important role in the rejuvenation of species that have substantially diminished, and it is one of the most effective methods for restoring such species back to their former population range. However, potentially serious downsides of reinforcement translocations are the introduction of harmful genes to the existing population and the transmission of disease from one population to another. Furthermore, when predators or competitive species are translocated, it may have an adverse effect on other species and lead to a loss of biodiversity in the region. Another drawback is that this strategy requires a great deal of hard work and resources, so evidence of tangible benefits must be shown in order to justify the costs.

The word "substantially" in the passage is closest in meaning to

(A) tentatively
(B) surreptitiously
(C) instantaneously
(D) considerably

Translocation plays an important role in the rejuvenation of species that have substantially diminished, and it is one of the most effective methods for restoring such species back to their former population range. However, potentially serious downsides of reinforcement translocations are the introduction of harmful genes to the existing population and the transmission of disease from one population to another. Furthermore, when predators or competitive species are translocated, it may have an adverse effect on other species and lead to a loss of biodiversity in the region. Another drawback is that this strategy requires a great deal of hard work and resources, so evidence of tangible benefits must be shown in order to justify the costs.

In paragraph 3, all of the following are indicated to be potential drawbacks of species translocation EXCEPT

(A) a loss of biodiversity
(B) the spread of disease
(C) a rise in competition for food
(D) the significant costs involved

Numerous translocations have been carried out all over the world, but there is barely any significant evidence that they yielded substantial benefits. Admittedly, this is because the majority of translocations have not been overseen by official scientific organizations, and in many cases, have not been legal or for the purpose of conservation. Although a handful of successful translocations have been documented, most of the numerous failures are unlikely to be recorded or reported. This makes it exceedingly difficult to properly appraise the strategy. Moreover, it is difficult to define what a successful transition entails. Should translocation be considered a success if the moved organisms survive for only one month, or for one year? Or must they reproduce over several years in order for the technique to be viewed as successful? Regardless of the definition, what is obvious is that appropriate guidelines must be established to ensure that translocation efforts are warranted, are subject to stringent monitoring and evaluation, and have a high likelihood of succeeding.

The word "appraise" in the passage is closest in meaning to

(A) commend
(B) improve
(C) evaluate
(D) apply

Numerous translocations have been carried out all over the world, but there is barely any significant evidence that they yielded substantial benefits. Admittedly, this is because the majority of translocations have not been overseen by official scientific organizations, and in many cases, have not been legal or for the purpose of conservation. Although a handful of successful translocations have been documented, most of the numerous failures are unlikely to be recorded or reported. This makes it exceedingly difficult to properly appraise the strategy. Moreover, it is difficult to define what a successful transition entails. Should translocation be considered a success if the moved organisms survive for only one month, or for one year? Or must they reproduce over several years in order for the technique to be viewed as successful? Regardless of the definition, what is obvious is that appropriate guidelines must be established to ensure that translocation efforts are warranted, are subject to stringent monitoring and evaluation, and have a high likelihood of succeeding.

Which of the following can be inferred from paragraph 4 about translocation efforts?

(A) The techniques used to drive translocation efforts have evolved rapidly.

(B) The available records showing the effectiveness of translocation efforts are not reliable.

(C) Illegal translocations appear to have been more successful than most official translocations.

(D) Researchers worldwide have reached a consensus on the definition of a successful translocation.

One case of direct species translocation that appears to be a genuine success is that of the threatened Seychelles warbler. Once found only on Cousin Island, part of the Seychelles island chain, the species had declined to a population of only 26. This number was increased to over 300 individuals as a result of careful habitat management, but the population was still in danger of extinction from natural catastrophes. A decision was made to mitigate this risk by translocating the warblers to two nearby islands. The translocation to the first island was carried out in 1988, and the translocation to the second one in 1990, and healthy breeding populations were established in both locations. Red howler monkeys in French Guyana serve as another example of a successful translocation project. When a site was to be flooded for hydroelectric power generation, a local population of howler monkeys was translocated to a region where the local howler population had declined due to overhunting. Around 15 of the female monkeys released into the region were monitored by radio tracking. Some early adjustment problems caused the tracked females to scatter at first, but their behavioral patterns became normal fairly quickly.

According to paragraph 5, why did conservationists translocate Seychelles warblers from Cousin Island to two other islands?

(A) They were unsuccessful in earlier efforts to increase the population of warblers on Cousin Island.

(B) They believed the translocation of the warblers would increase biodiversity on all three islands.

(C) They anticipated a decline in the warbler population on Cousin Island due to disease.

(D) They were concerned that the warbler population would perish in a disaster on Cousin Island.

One case of direct species translocation that appears to be a genuine success is that of the threatened Seychelles warbler. Once found only on Cousin Island, part of the Seychelles island chain, the species had declined to a population of only 26. This number was increased to over 300 individuals as a result of careful habitat management, but the population was still in danger of extinction from natural catastrophes. A decision was made to mitigate this risk by translocating the warblers to two nearby islands. The translocation to the first island was carried out in 1988, and the translocation to the second one in 1990, and healthy breeding populations were established in both locations. Red howler monkeys in French Guyana serve as another example of a successful translocation project. When a site was to be flooded for hydroelectric power generation, a local population of howler monkeys was translocated to a region where the local howler population had declined due to overhunting. Around 15 of the female monkeys released into the region were monitored by radio tracking. Some early adjustment problems caused the tracked females to scatter at first, but their behavioral patterns became normal fairly quickly.

According to paragraph 5, why were the howler monkeys in French Guyana translocated?

(A) Several potential predators were introduced to their original habitat.
(B) Climate conditions were having an adverse effect on their population density.
(C) An imbalance of genders meant that females struggled to find mates.
(D) Their original habitat was going to be altered by human activity.

Sadly, accounts of failures outweigh the evidence of success. Researchers Richard A. Siegel and C. Kenneth Dodd assessed numerous cases of reptile and amphibian translocation and found that very few of them could be considered a success in terms of conservation. Thus, they recommended that such methods should not be deemed as viable species management practices.

In paragraph 6, the author mentions the work of Richard A. Siegel and C. Kenneth Dodd in order to

(A) provide details of the criteria that are used to determine the potential effectiveness of translocation

(B) support the claim that repeated failures make it difficult to justify species translocation efforts

(C) show how the translocation of reptiles and amphibians is more difficult than that of other animals

(D) emphasize that translocation techniques are improving as researchers become more knowledgeable

One case of direct species translocation that appears to be a genuine success is that of the threatened Seychelles warbler. Once found only on Cousin Island, part of the Seychelles island chain, the species had declined to a population of only 26. This number was increased to over 300 individuals as a result of careful habitat management, but the population was still in danger of extinction from natural catastrophes. ■ A decision was made to mitigate this risk by translocating the warblers to two nearby islands. ■ The translocation to the first island was carried out in 1988, and the translocation to the second one in 1990, and healthy breeding populations were established in both locations. ■ Red howler monkeys in French Guyana serve as another example of a successful translocation project. ■ When a site was to be flooded for hydroelectric power generation, a local population of howler monkeys was translocated to a region where the local howler population had declined due to overhunting. Around 15 of the female monkeys released into the region were monitored by radio tracking. Some early adjustment problems caused the tracked females to scatter at first, but their behavioral patterns became normal fairly quickly.

Look at the four squares [■] that indicate where the following sentence could be added to the passage.

This is certainly not the only case of positive results coming from a large-scale translocation.

Where would the sentence best fit? Click on a square [■] to add the sentence to the passage.

Directions: An introductory sentence for a brief summary of the passage is provided below. Complete the summary by selecting the THREE answer choices that express the most important ideas in the passage. Some sentences do not belong in the summary because they express ideas that are not presented in the passage or are minor ideas in the passage. **This question is worth 2 points.**

Drag your answer choices to the space where they belong. To remove an answer choice, click on it. To review the passage, click on **VIEW TEXT.**

Translocation is a technique employed in the reintroduction or reinforcement of species.

-
-
-

Answer Choices

(A) While translocation can be extremely useful as a conservation tool, it can also have several adverse effects on species and habitats.

(B) Data indicates that the vast majority of successful translocation efforts have been carried out on a small scale by wildlife enthusiasts.

(C) It is critical that translocation projects be properly evaluated to ensure that the chance of success is high enough to justify the cost.

(D) The translocation of red howler monkeys was deemed a success despite initial concerns over the behavior patterns of the females.

(E) Species translocation can be used to increase dwindling populations of a specific species or to repopulate a region where a species is no longer present.

(F) Illegal translocations have been blamed for the negative portrayal of direct species translocation by the worldwide media.

■ Passage 2

Evolution of Flowering Plants

When considering the evolutionary pathways of flowering plants, or angiosperms, several questions remain largely unanswered. Scientists have uncovered fossilized stems, leaves, pollen, and fruits, and less commonly, flowers, and these provide useful evidence of the earliest angiosperms. There has also been extensive scientific research carried out on the morphology (structure) and genetics of modern plants in order to identify which of the present-day species are closely related to the ancient ancestors of angiosperms. Despite over two centuries of intensive research, scientists have still not reached a consensus on which specific type of plant was the ancestor of angiosperms, nor have they determined where and when angiosperms began evolving. In fact, even the renowned Charles Darwin used the term "an abominable mystery" when referring to the origin of angiosperms.

In attempting to figure out what type of plant was the ancestor to the angiosperms, the majority of botanists now agree that angiosperms are monophyletic in origin, which means they evolved from a common ancestor. According to some paleontologists, the common ancestor is likely to have been a variety of cycad, which is a type of seed plant found in tropical regions. Others, however, believe that flowering plants evolved from seed-bearing ferns. Another hypothesis, based on studies of morphological features of some primitive living plants, is that the ancestor may have been a relative of modern pine trees. In short, the true ancestry of flowering plants is a matter that remains unresolved.

For many decades, there has been a great focus on figuring out the approximate time and place of the first appearance of angiosperms. Based on fossil evidence, early angiosperms, some of which appear similar to modern magnolias, existed more than 100 million years ago in the Early Cretaceous geologic period. During this period, angiosperms began growing in increasing numbers, accounting for around one percent of all plant life. During the Late Cretaceous, which lasted from around 100 million to 65 million years ago, angiosperms grew in abundance and made up more than 50 percent of plant life. It was during this period that many of the modern plant families began to appear. In the following geologic period, the Early Tertiary, angiosperms continued to flourish and spread, eventually comprising at least 90 percent of Earth's total plant life. But where exactly did these successful plants originate?

Biogeographers have analyzed the geographic distribution and fossil leaf structure of the earliest flowering plants from the Cretaceous, concluding that they likely evolved in the tropical regions and then migrated toward the Earth's poles. It was not until the Late Cretaceous that flowering plants became prevalent in the high latitudes. In eastern South America and western Africa, paleontologists have recovered fossilized parts of flowering plants from deposits dating back to the Early Cretaceous. Two supercontinents existed at that time, and Africa and South America comprised part of the supercontinent known as Gondwanaland. These early angiosperm fossils were unearthed in regions that would have been close to the equator during the Early Cretaceous, and this backs up the theory of poleward migration from tropical regions.

Some botanists disagree with the notion of an African-South American origin for the evolution and dispersal of flowering plants, highlighting the fact that several of the earliest types of flowering plants are still present in South Pacific countries such as Australia, Fiji, New Guinea, and throughout the Malay Archipelago. Recent studies on plant genetics have indicated that the living plant that bears the closest resemblance to the ancient ancestor of all angiosperms is Amborella. This relatively rare tropical shrub, which has red fruit and small yellow-white flowers, grows only on the South Pacific islands of New Caledonia. The large number of primitive living angiosperms in the South Pacific region has led several leading botanists to conclude that this is where angiosperms first evolved, and relics of this early evolution can be seen in these modern species. DNA from hundreds of species of flowering plants has been compared with the DNA of Amborella, and the findings indicate that the first flowering plant emerged and began evolving into several distinct species approximately 135 million years ago.

However, fossils that have recently been unearthed further compound our understanding of the origin of flowering plants. Chinese paleontologists have found well-preserved fossils of a flowering plant, including seeds and flowers, in deposits dating back to the Jurassic geologic period at a site near modern Beijing. This makes the new fossil plant found at the site the oldest known angiosperm, with an estimated age of 130 million years old. The primitive morphology of the flowers, not to mention the age of the fossils, has led the discoverers to speculate that the earliest angiosperms may have evolved in northern Asia.

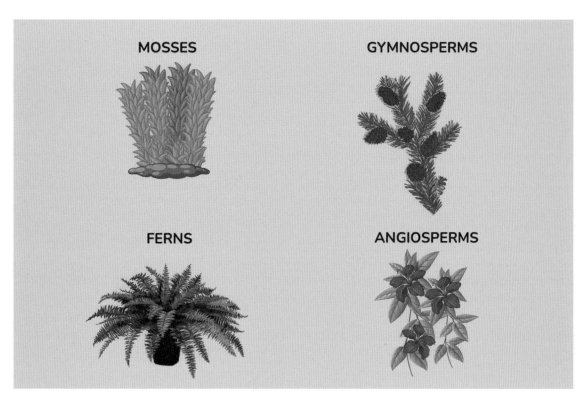

<이끼식물, 양치식물, 겉씨식물, 속씨식물로 구분되는 식물군>

When considering the evolutionary pathways of flowering plants, or angiosperms, several questions remain largely unanswered. Scientists have uncovered fossilized stems, leaves, pollen, and fruits, and less commonly, flowers, and these provide useful evidence of the earliest angiosperms. There has also been extensive scientific research carried out on the morphology (structure) and genetics of modern plants in order to identify which of the present-day species are closely related to the ancient ancestors of angiosperms. Despite over two centuries of intensive research, scientists have still not reached a consensus on which specific type of plant was the ancestor of angiosperms, nor have they determined where and when angiosperms began evolving. In fact, even the renowned Charles Darwin used the term "an abominable mystery" when referring to the origin of angiosperms.

The word "intensive" in the passage is closest in meaning to

(A) optimistic
(B) diverse
(C) thorough
(D) alarming

When considering the evolutionary pathways of flowering plants, or angiosperms, several questions remain largely unanswered. Scientists have uncovered fossilized stems, leaves, pollen, and fruits, and less commonly, flowers, and these provide useful evidence of the earliest angiosperms. There has also been extensive scientific research carried out on the morphology (structure) and genetics of modern plants in order to identify which of the present-day species are closely related to the ancient ancestors of angiosperms. Despite over two centuries of intensive research, scientists have still not reached a consensus on which specific type of plant was the ancestor of angiosperms, nor have they determined where and when angiosperms began evolving. In fact, even the renowned Charles Darwin used the term "an abominable mystery" when referring to the origin of angiosperms.

According to paragraph 1, all of the following types of evidence have been crucial to studying the history of angiosperms EXCEPT

(A) research on angiosperm adaptations to climate change
(B) genetic analyses of modern angiosperms
(C) knowledge of the structure of modern angiosperms
(D) fossils of angiosperm stems and leaves

In attempting to figure out what type of plant was the ancestor to the angiosperms, the majority of botanists now agree that angiosperms are monophyletic in origin, which means they evolved from a common ancestor. According to some paleontologists, the common ancestor is likely to have been a variety of cycad, which is a type of seed plant found in tropical regions. Others, however, believe that flowering plants evolved from seed-bearing ferns. Another hypothesis, based on studies of morphological features of some primitive living plants, is that the ancestor may have been a relative of modern pine trees. In short, the true ancestry of flowering plants is a matter that remains unresolved.

The word "matter" in the passage is closest in meaning to

(A) substance
(B) trait
(C) consequence
(D) issue

For many decades, there has been a great focus on figuring out the approximate time and place of the first appearance of angiosperms. Based on fossil evidence, early angiosperms, some of which appear similar to modern magnolias, existed more than 100 million years ago in the Early Cretaceous geologic period. During this period, angiosperms began growing in increasing numbers, accounting for around one percent of all plant life. During the Late Cretaceous, which lasted from around 100 million to 65 million years ago, angiosperms grew in abundance and made up more than 50 percent of plant life. It was during this period that many of the modern plant families began to appear. In the following geologic period, the Early Tertiary, angiosperms continued to flourish and spread, eventually comprising at least 90 percent of Earth's total plant life. But where exactly did these successful plants originate?

In paragraph 3, which of the following is indicated about angiosperms during the Early Cretaceous?

(A) They rarely left behind any fossilized remains.
(B) They represented approximately 1 percent of plant life.
(C) Their numbers significantly declined during this period.
(D) They bore no resemblance to plants living today.

Biogeographers have analyzed the geographic distribution and fossil leaf structure of the earliest flowering plants from the Cretaceous, concluding that they likely evolved in the tropical regions and then migrated toward the Earth's poles. It was not until the Late Cretaceous that flowering plants became prevalent in the high latitudes. In eastern South America and western Africa, paleontologists have recovered fossilized parts of flowering plants from deposits dating back to the Early Cretaceous. Two supercontinents existed at that time, and Africa and South America comprised part of the supercontinent known as Gondwanaland. These early angiosperm fossils were unearthed in regions that would have been close to the equator during the Early Cretaceous, and this backs up the theory of poleward migration from tropical regions.

Why does the author mention "Gondwanaland" in paragraph 4?

(A) To provide evidence that flowering plants adapted in similar ways all over the world
(B) To refute the idea that flowering plants moved toward the poles during the Cretaceous
(C) To provide support for the theory that flowering plants originated in the tropics
(D) To explain how geographical barriers impeded the migration of some species

Some botanists disagree with the notion of an African-South American origin for the evolution and dispersal of flowering plants, highlighting the fact that several of the earliest types of flowering plants are still present in South Pacific countries such as Australia, Fiji, New Guinea, and throughout the Malay Archipelago. Recent studies on plant genetics have indicated that the living plant that bears the closest resemblance to the ancient ancestor of all angiosperms is Amborella. This relatively rare tropical shrub, which has red fruit and small yellow-white flowers, grows only on the South Pacific islands of New Caledonia. The large number of primitive living angiosperms in the South Pacific region has led several leading botanists to conclude that this is where angiosperms first evolved, and relics of this early evolution can be seen in these modern species. DNA from hundreds of species of flowering plants has been compared with the DNA of Amborella, and the findings indicate that the first flowering plant emerged and began evolving into several distinct species approximately 135 million years ago.

In paragraph 5, what can be inferred about primitive living angiosperms in the South Pacific?

(A) They have only been studied on the group of islands known as New Caledonia.
(B) They prove that angiosperms evolved in several sites simultaneously around the world.
(C) They have numerous similarities with angiosperm plants found in South America and Africa.
(D) They more closely resemble the earliest angiosperms than other living angiosperms do.

However, fossils that have recently been unearthed further compound our understanding of the origin of flowering plants. Chinese paleontologists have found well-preserved fossils of a flowering plant, including seeds and flowers, in deposits dating back to the Jurassic geologic period at a site near modern Beijing. This makes the new fossil plant found at the site the oldest known angiosperm, with an estimated age of 130 million years old. The primitive morphology of the flowers, not to mention the age of the fossils, has led the discoverers to speculate that the earliest angiosperms may have evolved in northern Asia.

According to paragraph 6, which of the following is true of angiosperm fossils discovered in China?

(A) They are almost identical to angiosperm fossils discovered in the South Pacific.
(B) They have made it more difficult to ascertain the true origin of angiosperms.
(C) They include fossilized flowers that dated back to the Late Cretaceous.
(D) They indicate that flowering plants did not originate in northern Asia.

Some botanists disagree with the notion of an African-South American origin for the evolution and dispersal of flowering plants, highlighting the fact that several of the earliest types of flowering plants are still present in South Pacific countries such as Australia, Fiji, New Guinea, and throughout the Malay Archipelago. Recent studies on plant genetics have indicated that the living plant that bears the closest resemblance to the ancient ancestor of all angiosperms is Amborella. This relatively rare tropical shrub, which has red fruit and small yellow-white flowers, grows only on the South Pacific islands of New Caledonia. The large number of primitive living angiosperms in the South Pacific region has led several leading botanists to conclude that this is where angiosperms first evolved, and relics of this early evolution can be seen in these modern species. DNA from hundreds of species of flowering plants has been compared with the DNA of Amborella, and the findings indicate that the first flowering plant emerged and began evolving into several distinct species approximately 135 million years ago.

Which of the sentences below best expresses the essential information in the highlighted sentence in the passage? Incorrect choices change the meaning in important ways or leave out essential information.

(A) Angiosperms in Australia, Fiji, New Caledonia, New Guinea, and the Malay Archipelago have more primitive features than angiosperms in Africa and South America do.

(B) Botanists struggle to reach a consensus on whether the most primitive forms of living plants are located in parts of Africa and South America or in the South Pacific.

(C) Some botanists believe that the very primitive forms of angiosperms that live in the South Pacific cast doubt on the theory that angiosperm evolution originated in Africa and South America.

(D) Some botanists who support the idea of Africa and South America forming the center for the evolution of flowering plants cite primitive angiosperms in the South Pacific as evidence.

When considering the evolutionary pathways of flowering plants, or angiosperms, several questions remain largely unanswered. Scientists have uncovered fossilized stems, leaves, pollen, and fruits, and less commonly, flowers, and these provide useful evidence of the earliest angiosperms. ■ There has also been extensive scientific research carried out on the morphology (structure) and genetics of modern plants in order to identify which of the present-day species are closely related to the ancient ancestors of angiosperms. ■ Despite over two centuries of intensive research, scientists have still not reached a consensus on which specific type of plant was the ancestor of angiosperms, nor have they determined where and when angiosperms began evolving. ■ In fact, even the renowned Charles Darwin used the term "an abominable mystery" when referring to the origin of angiosperms. ■

Look at the four squares [■] that indicate where the following sentence could be added to the passage.

With that said, the precise origin and time of angiosperm evolution remain unclear.

Where would the sentence best fit? Click on a square [■] to add the sentence to the passage.

Directions: An introductory sentence for a brief summary of the passage is provided below. Complete the summary by selecting the THREE answer choices that express the most important ideas in the passage. Some sentences do not belong in the summary because they express ideas that are not presented in the passage or are minor ideas in the passage. **This question is worth 2 points.**

Drag your answer choices to the space where they belong. To remove an answer choice, click on it. To review the passage, click on **VIEW TEXT.**

Despite decades of research, there are still unanswered questions regarding the history of flowering plants.

-
-
-

Answer Choices

(A) The fact that angiosperm fossils are very rarely discovered makes it very difficult to study the evolution of flowering plants.

(B) Based on fossil evidence, some botanists have concluded that angiosperms first evolved in the tropics and then gradually migrated toward the poles.

(C) Recent studies on fossils found in South America, the South Pacific, and Asia suggest that the first flowering plants emerged more recently than previously estimated.

(D) Although the original ancestor of flowering plants is not certain, they had appeared by the Early Cretaceous and eventually made up the vast majority of Earth's plant life.

(E) Analyses of Early Cretaceous fossil deposits show that the ancestor to all flowering plants was a plant bearing a strong similarity to the modern magnolia.

(F) Research on living angiosperms in the South Pacific and the discovery of fossils in China have resulted in new theories about the origin of angiosperm evolution.

Passage 3

Coral Reefs

Coral reefs are important habitats that are found in the intertropical zone of the ocean, where the temperature of the water rarely drops below 21°C, and underwater visibility is not impeded by significant amounts of sediment. In order for them to develop and thrive, reefs generally require a sturdy base with access to sunlight, roughly 30 to 40 meters below the surface, because they do not grow well in very deep, dark water. The vast majority of their physical structure is made up of coral skeletons, which are carnivorous organisms that feed on zooplankton. In addition to corals, massive accumulations of algae are used as building blocks in the construction of the reefs. Reefs can vary greatly in size, and while most of them are relatively small, some atolls such as Kwajalein in the South Pacific Marshall Islands are as large as 120 kilometers in length and 24 kilometers in breadth. The complex of reefs named the Great Barrier Reef, which creates a 2,000-kilometer-long natural breakwater off the northeast coast of Australia, is the most massive coral structure on Earth by a wide margin.

Scientists have been fascinated with coral reefs for centuries, and Charles Darwin is regarded as having made some of the most pertinent observations of them during his expedition on The Beagle during the 1830s. He identified three distinct types of reef: atolls, barrier reefs, and fringing reefs. Darwin also concluded that they were related to one another in a logical and gradational sequence. Fringing reefs are formed off the coasts of islands or continents. The surface of a fringing reef creates a rough platform that runs parallel to the shore of the land mass, not far below the surface of the water, with its outer edge sloping down into the deeper water. Occasionally, a channel or lagoon is created between the land and a fringing reef, and when this becomes deep and wide and the reef is sufficiently far from the shore and protrudes above the water's surface, the structure is referred to as a barrier reef. A reef that is shaped like a horseshoe or a ring, with a lagoon in the center, is typically known as an atoll.

Darwin theorized that upward growth of coral from a sinking platform could trigger the succession from one coral reef type to another, with an initial fringing reef progressing through the barrier reef stage, and the eventual subsidence of the central portion of the barrier reef leaving behind a reef-enclosed lagoon or atoll. In the 1950s, more than 100 years after Darwin had put forward this theory, research scientists drilled deep boreholes in the Pacific atolls. The drills bored through more than a thousand meters of coral before eventually reaching the hard rock that makes up the ocean floor. The researchers concluded that the coral had been growing upward as the Earth's crust subsided at a rate of 50 meters per million years over tens of millions of years. These findings essentially supported Darwin's theory of reef succession.

Coral reefs are vital habitats for thousands of species, and species diversity is at its highest in the coral reefs that have formed in the warm waters of the Indian Ocean and the western Pacific. In fact, the reefs are often considered the aquatic equivalent of the tropical rainforest in terms of their richness of species and biological productivity. They also play an important role in protecting coastal areas, providing recreational opportunities such as snorkeling, and producing useful substances, some of which are used in medicinal drugs. They are at increasing risk from a variety of threats, most notably from dredging and the adverse effects of increased siltation resulting from the accelerated erosion of coastlines.

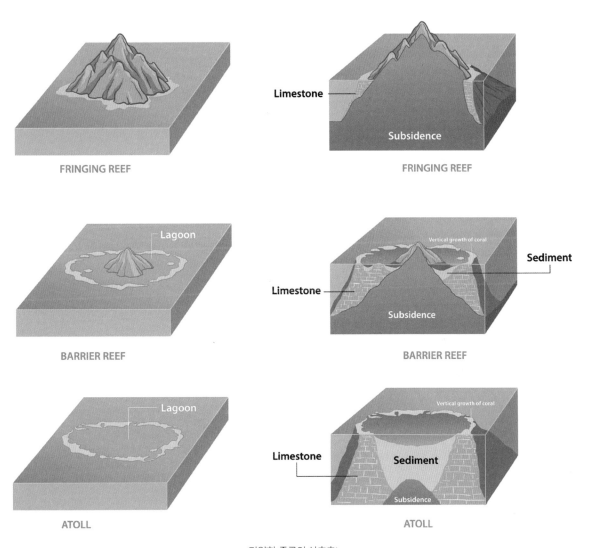

<다양한 종류의 산호초>

Coral reefs are important habitats that are found in the intertropical zone of the ocean, where the temperature of the water rarely drops below 21°C, and underwater visibility is not impeded by significant amounts of sediment. In order for them to develop and thrive, reefs generally require a sturdy base with access to sunlight, roughly 30 to 40 meters below the surface, because they do not grow well in very deep, dark water. The vast majority of their physical structure is made up of coral skeletons, which are carnivorous organisms that feed on zooplankton. In addition to corals, massive accumulations of algae are used as building blocks in the construction of the reefs. Reefs can vary greatly in size, and while most of them are relatively small, some atolls such as Kwajalein in the South Pacific Marshall Islands are as large as 120 kilometers in length and 24 kilometers in breadth. The complex of reefs named the Great Barrier Reef, which creates a 2000-kilometer-long natural breakwater off the northeast coast of Australia, is the most massive coral structure on Earth by a wide margin.

According to paragraph 1, all of the following are needed for the growth of coral reef EXCEPT

(A) a solid foundation to grow on
(B) exposure to sunlight
(C) water temperatures of approximately 21 °C
(D) a sufficiently high level of sediment

Coral reefs are important habitats that are found in the intertropical zone of the ocean, where the temperature of the water rarely drops below 21°C, and underwater visibility is not impeded by significant amounts of sediment. In order for them to develop and thrive, reefs generally require a sturdy base with access to sunlight, roughly 30 to 40 meters below the surface, because they do not grow well in very deep, dark water. The vast majority of their physical structure is made up of coral skeletons, which are carnivorous organisms that feed on zooplankton. In addition to corals, massive accumulations of algae are used as building blocks in the construction of the reefs. Reefs can vary greatly in size, and while most of them are relatively small, some atolls such as Kwajalein in the South Pacific Marshall Islands are as large as 120 kilometers in length and 24 kilometers in breadth. The complex of reefs named the Great Barrier Reef, which creates a 2000-kilometer-long natural breakwater off the northeast coast of Australia, is the most massive coral structure on Earth by a wide margin.

The word "complex" in the passage is closest in meaning to

(A) region
(B) pillar
(C) system
(D) dilemma

Scientists have been fascinated with coral reefs for centuries, and Charles Darwin is regarded as having made some of the most pertinent observations of them during his expedition on The Beagle during the 1830s. He identified three distinct types of reef: atolls, barrier reefs, and fringing reefs. Darwin also concluded that they were related to one another in a logical and gradational sequence. Fringing reefs are formed off the coasts of islands or continents. The surface of a fringing reef creates a rough platform that runs parallel to the shore of the land mass, not far below the surface of the water, with its outer edge sloping down into the deeper water. Occasionally a channel or lagoon is created between the land and a fringing reef, and when this becomes deep and wide and the reef is sufficiently far from the shore and protrudes above the water's surface, the structure is referred to as a barrier reef. A reef that is shaped like a horseshoe or a ring, with a lagoon in the center, is typically known as an atoll.

The word "pertinent" in the passage is closest in meaning to

(A) relevant
(B) controversial
(C) bold
(D) accurate

Scientists have been fascinated with coral reefs for centuries, and Charles Darwin is regarded as having made some of the most pertinent observations of them during his expedition on The Beagle during the 1830s. He identified three distinct types of reef: atolls, barrier reefs, and fringing reefs. Darwin also concluded that they were related to one another in a logical and gradational sequence. Fringing reefs are formed off the coasts of islands or continents. The surface of a fringing reef creates a rough platform that runs parallel to the shore of the land mass, not far below the surface of the water, with its outer edge sloping down into the deeper water. Occasionally a channel or lagoon is created between the land and a fringing reef, and when this becomes deep and wide and the reef is sufficiently far from the shore and protrudes above the water's surface, the structure is referred to as a barrier reef. A reef that is shaped like a horseshoe or a ring, with a lagoon in the center, is typically known as an atoll.

According to paragraph 2, which of the following is NOT a characteristic of a barrier reef?

(A) It is typically found in deep ocean water.
(B) It circles around a central lagoon.
(C) It is separated from coastal land by a wide channel.
(D) It is situated far from the shore of the nearest land mass.

Darwin theorized that upward growth of coral from a sinking platform could trigger the succession from one coral reef type to another, with an initial fringing reef progressing through the barrier reef stage, and the eventual subsidence of the central portion of the barrier reef leaving behind a reef-enclosed lagoon or atoll. In the 1950s, more than 100 years after Darwin had put forward this theory, research scientists drilled deep boreholes in the Pacific atolls. The drills bored through more than a thousand meters of coral before eventually reaching the hard rock that makes up the ocean floor. The researchers concluded that the coral had been growing upward as the Earth's crust subsided at a rate of 50 meters per million years over tens of millions of years. These findings essentially supported Darwin's theory of reef succession.

Which of the sentences below best expresses the essential information in the highlighted sentence in the passage? Incorrect choices change the meaning in important ways or leave out essential information.

(A) According to Darwin's theory, the vast majority of coral reefs began as atolls and then gradually turned into barrier reefs or fringing reefs.
(B) Darwin recognized that the succession of coral reefs was dependent on a wide variety of environmental factors such as the direction of coral growth.
(C) Darwin believed that as a coral reef grew upward, it would progress from a fringing reef to a barrier reef, and it would eventually become an atoll as the middle section subsided to form a lagoon.
(D) Darwin's theory helped explain how coral reefs contributed to the disappearance of several islands which are believed to have sunk below the surface of the ocean.

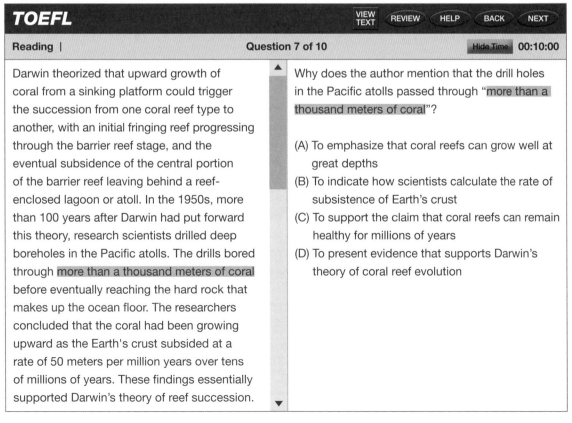

Darwin theorized that upward growth of coral from a sinking platform could trigger the succession from one coral reef type to another, with an initial fringing reef progressing through the barrier reef stage, and the eventual subsidence of the central portion of the barrier reef leaving behind a reef-enclosed lagoon or atoll. In the 1950s, more than 100 years after Darwin had put forward this theory, research scientists drilled deep boreholes in the Pacific atolls. The drills bored through more than a thousand meters of coral before eventually reaching the hard rock that makes up the ocean floor. The researchers concluded that the coral had been growing upward as the Earth's crust subsided at a rate of 50 meters per million years over tens of millions of years. These findings essentially supported Darwin's theory of reef succession.

Which of the following can be inferred from paragraph 3 about the Pacific atolls?

(A) They could transform into fringing reefs over millions of years.
(B) They were originally discovered by Darwin during his voyage on the Beagle.
(C) They are located where the ocean floor is at its softest.
(D) They originated as fringing reefs along the coasts of islands.

Darwin theorized that upward growth of coral from a sinking platform could trigger the succession from one coral reef type to another, with an initial fringing reef progressing through the barrier reef stage, and the eventual subsidence of the central portion of the barrier reef leaving behind a reef-enclosed lagoon or atoll. In the 1950s, more than 100 years after Darwin had put forward this theory, research scientists drilled deep boreholes in the Pacific atolls. The drills bored through more than a thousand meters of coral before eventually reaching the hard rock that makes up the ocean floor. The researchers concluded that the coral had been growing upward as the Earth's crust subsided at a rate of 50 meters per million years over tens of millions of years. These findings essentially supported Darwin's theory of reef succession.

Why does the author mention that the drill holes in the Pacific atolls passed through "more than a thousand meters of coral"?

(A) To emphasize that coral reefs can grow well at great depths
(B) To indicate how scientists calculate the rate of subsistence of Earth's crust
(C) To support the claim that coral reefs can remain healthy for millions of years
(D) To present evidence that supports Darwin's theory of coral reef evolution

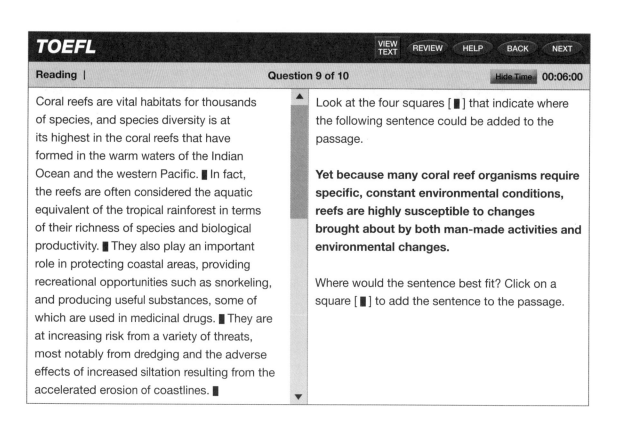

Coral reefs are vital habitats for thousands of species, and species diversity is at its highest in the coral reefs that have formed in the warm waters of the Indian Ocean and the western Pacific. In fact, the reefs are often considered the aquatic equivalent of the tropical rainforest in terms of their richness of species and biological productivity. They also play an important role in protecting coastal areas, providing recreational opportunities such as snorkeling, and producing useful substances, some of which are used in medicinal drugs. They are at increasing risk from a variety of threats, most notably from dredging and the adverse effects of increased siltation resulting from the accelerated erosion of coastlines.

According to paragraph 4, why have coral reefs been compared to tropical rainforests?

(A) They are both found in abundance near the Indian and western Pacific Oceans.
(B) They are both known for their rich biodiversity.
(C) They both play a crucial role in protecting coastlines.
(D) They are both negatively impacted by land erosion.

Coral reefs are vital habitats for thousands of species, and species diversity is at its highest in the coral reefs that have formed in the warm waters of the Indian Ocean and the western Pacific. ■ In fact, the reefs are often considered the aquatic equivalent of the tropical rainforest in terms of their richness of species and biological productivity. ■ They also play an important role in protecting coastal areas, providing recreational opportunities such as snorkeling, and producing useful substances, some of which are used in medicinal drugs. ■ They are at increasing risk from a variety of threats, most notably from dredging and the adverse effects of increased siltation resulting from the accelerated erosion of coastlines. ■

Look at the four squares [■] that indicate where the following sentence could be added to the passage.

Yet because many coral reef organisms require specific, constant environmental conditions, reefs are highly susceptible to changes brought about by both man-made activities and environmental changes.

Where would the sentence best fit? Click on a square [■] to add the sentence to the passage.

Directions: An introductory sentence for a brief summary of the passage is provided below. Complete the summary by selecting the THREE answer choices that express the most important ideas in the passage. Some sentences do not belong in the summary because they express ideas that are not presented in the passage or are minor ideas in the passage. **This question is worth 2 points.**

Drag your answer choices to the space where they belong. To remove an answer choice, click on it. To review the passage, click on **VIEW TEXT.**

Coral reefs are critical tropical environments that serve as habitats for a rich variety of ocean life.

-
-
-

Answer Choices

(A) Fringing reefs are located near the shore of continents and islands, facilitating the movement of species between the land mass and the sea.

(B) Coral reefs are structures comprising numerous living creatures and can grow only in specific ocean conditions.

(C) While coral reefs bring multiple benefits to nature and humans, they are currently under threat from human activity and natural degradation.

(D) Coral reefs are categorized as fringing reefs, barrier reefs, or atolls, all of which are steps in a sequence of progressive development.

(E) Although atolls are home to numerous species of marine life, barrier reefs are by far the most biodiverse of all reef habitats.

(F) Scientists believe coral reefs are as important as mangrove swamps as habitats for numerous plant and animal species.

Chapter

03

Art

Passage 1	Pottery in the Roman Empire
Passage 2	The Creation of Cave Paintings
Passage 3	The Theater Audience

Art (예술)

토플에서 예술은 역사 등과 결부되어 특정 예술, 작품, 기법의 기원 등 예술사가 주로 출제되며, 고대 공예품에서부터 현대 영화까지 다양한 시기의 세부 토픽들이 등장한다.

[Art 기출 토픽]

- Architecture
  건축

- Paleolithic Cave Paintings
  구석기 동굴 벽화

- Chinese Pottery
  중국의 도자기

- Ancient Egyptian Sculpture
  고대 이집트 조각

- Pottery in the Roman Empire
  로마 제국의 도자기

- Crafts in the Ancient Near East
  고대 근동의 공예

- Chartres Cathedral
  샤르트르 대성당

- Early Writing Systems
  초기 표기 체계

- The Birth of Photography
  사진술의 탄생

- The Origins of Theater
  연극의 기원

- Early Cinema
  초기 영화

- Transition to Sound in Film
  유성 영화로 변천

[Art 빈출 어휘]

artisan	장인	gloss	광택, 윤
abstract	추상적인	grandeur	장엄함
adorn	~을 장식하다	imbue	(감정, 사상 등)을 불어넣다
aesthetic	심미적인	in bulk	대량으로
appreciate	~을 감상하다	lackluster	생기 없는
archaeological	고고학적인	magnificent	장엄한
carving	조각(술)	marvel	경이, 경이로워하다
cavern	동굴	mason	석공
chamber	공간, 방	molding	주형물
chasm	깊은 틈	motif	모티프, 주제
coarse	저급한, 조잡한	Paleolithic era	구석기 시대
collapse	무너지다	prevalence	보편적임, 만연함
communal	공동의	prominence	두드러짐
conjure	~을 떠올리게 하다	rarified	세련된
contribute to	~에 도움이 되다	reproduction	재현, 복제
counterpart	(대응 관계) 대상	scope	범위, 규모
deform	~을 변형시키다	signify	~을 의미하다
descendant	후손	staples	주요 산물
dispose of	~을 처분하다	statuette	작은 조각품
dumpsite	쓰레기 매립지	sturdy	견고한, 튼튼한
evocative	연상시키는	thrive	번성하다, 발전하다
excess	여분의, 초과한	ubiquitous	어디에나 있는
feature	~을 특징으로 하다	universal	보편적인
fragile	깨지기 쉬운	urn	단지, 항아리
geometrical	기하학적인	utilitarian	실용적인, 공리적인

Pottery in the Roman Empire

Expertly crafted pottery was ubiquitous in the Ancient Roman Empire. Light yet sturdy, Roman pottery was primarily manufactured for utilitarian purposes. While the Ancient Greeks adorned pots and urns with elaborate paintings that depicted anything from personal biographies to epic adventures, the pottery of the Ancient Romans served basic functions, such as cooking, storage, or transportation. This is not to say the pottery lacked aesthetic qualities—its exceptional craftmanship alone is enough to marvel at—but instead the pieces, and the quantity in which they were produced, signify the advanced industrial and economic workings of the Roman Empire.

Roman pottery is often classified into two groups. The first is fine wares, which were skillfully crafted serving vessels and tableware. Used for official dinner occasions, fine wares were both decorative and practical. The most prominent example of fine wares was *terra sigillata*, a red-gloss ware that was made in the regions of northern Italy and France. These pieces were well-fired and adequately hard with a naturally glossy surface slip. *Terra sigillata* pieces were produced on an industrial scale—the largest kilns could fire tens of thousands of pieces at a time—and exported throughout the empire. Red-gloss potsherds, or shards of pottery, have been recovered all the way from India to Scotland. Many bore the signatures of their crafters or manufacturers, with pieces from the same artist or factory appearing in distant locations. Made to be aesthetically appealing, *terra sigillata* pieces were like the artistic work of Grecian pieces, though they were not painted. Instead, crafters adorned the pieces with reliefs—moldings or carvings that stood out from the surface of the pottery.

Coarse wares represented the other sphere of Ancient Roman pottery. Unlike fine wares, coarse wares were manufactured purely for function. These common vessels were made and sold locally and used chiefly for cooking, storage, and transportation. They were staples of Roman households, regardless of rank or class. Though they were not made for display, they were still finely crafted. They were sturdy yet light, and smooth in the hand. Their glossy, sealed surfaces made them ideal for the storage of liquids such as olive oil, fish sauce, and wine. Crafters followed standardized sizes that made the pottery conducive to stacking and efficient, long-term storage. Amphorae were a common piece of coarse ware. These cone-shaped storage vessels allowed them to fit securely into storerooms and the holds of merchant ships. Their valuable contents were protected during marine transport, so the large-scale production of amphorae served a crucial role in the trade of the Roman Empire.

As is common in archaeology, only a sparse sample of the total amount of pottery created and used in Ancient Rome will ever be recovered. However, one exceptional dumpsite exists that hints at the massive scale of pottery production in Ancient Rome. Monte Testaccio is an artificial hill around 50 meters high that is located on the left bank of the Tiber River in Rome, a site near one of the ancient river ports. It is composed entirely of discarded and broken amphorae, most of which are dated from the second and third centuries A.D. Archeologists estimate that more than 50 million amphorae have contributed to the building of Monte Testaccio. Given what we know of the capacity of the containers, it is likely that more than six billion liters of olive oil had been imported into the city from overseas. Monte Testaccio attests to the massive scope and complexity of Ancient Rome's imports, and conjures the image of a society not so different from modern ones. It produced and shipped goods across the expanse of its empire via high-quality, optimized containers that could simply be discarded upon delivery, if necessary.

Monte Testaccio and other sites throughout the empire indicate that Roman pottery was transported in bulk over vast distances, yet they also show how every level of Ancient Roman society had access to fine products. Roman pottery, from the humblest pieces to the finest wares, serves as a standard of everyday life in the empire.

Glossary	X

slip: a mixture of clay and water used to decorate pottery
kiln: a furnace or oven for baking, burning, or drying, especially one for firing pottery

▼

<테라 시길라타라고 알려진 광택이 나는 붉은 표면을 가진 고대 로마 도자기>

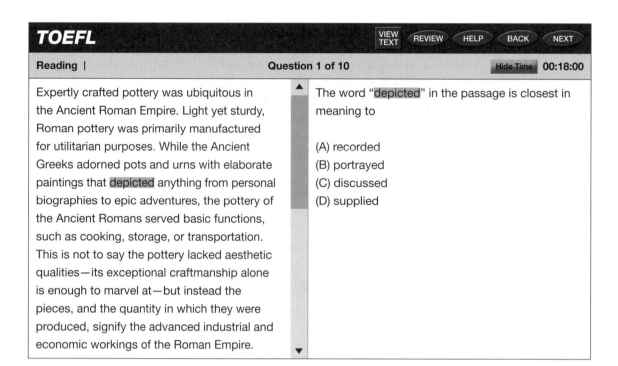

Expertly crafted pottery was ubiquitous in the Ancient Roman Empire. Light yet sturdy, Roman pottery was primarily manufactured for utilitarian purposes. While the Ancient Greeks adorned pots and urns with elaborate paintings that depicted anything from personal biographies to epic adventures, the pottery of the Ancient Romans served basic functions, such as cooking, storage, or transportation. This is not to say the pottery lacked aesthetic qualities—its exceptional craftmanship alone is enough to marvel at—but instead the pieces, and the quantity in which they were produced, signify the advanced industrial and economic workings of the Roman Empire.

The word "depicted" in the passage is closest in meaning to

(A) recorded
(B) portrayed
(C) discussed
(D) supplied

Expertly crafted pottery was ubiquitous in the Ancient Roman Empire. Light yet sturdy, Roman pottery was primarily manufactured for utilitarian purposes. While the Ancient Greeks adorned pots and urns with elaborate paintings that depicted anything from personal biographies to epic adventures, the pottery of the Ancient Romans served basic functions, such as cooking, storage, or transportation. This is not to say the pottery lacked aesthetic qualities—its exceptional craftmanship alone is enough to marvel at—but instead the pieces, and the quantity in which they were produced, signify the advanced industrial and economic workings of the Roman Empire.

The author's description of Roman pottery in paragraph 1 mentions all of the following EXCEPT

(A) It was well made.
(B) It was widely distributed.
(C) It was useful.
(D) It was made for display.

Roman pottery is often classified into two groups. The first is fine wares, which were skillfully crafted serving vessels and tableware. Used for official dinner occasions, fine wares were both decorative and practical. The most prominent example of fine wares was *terra sigillata*, a red-gloss ware that was made in the regions of northern Italy and France. These pieces were well-fired and adequately hard with a naturally glossy surface slip. *Terra sigillata* pieces were produced on an industrial scale—the largest kilns could fire tens of thousands of pieces at a time—and exported throughout the empire. Red-gloss potsherds, or shards of pottery, have been recovered all the way from India to Scotland. Many bore the signatures of their crafters or manufacturers, with pieces from the same artist or factory appearing in distant locations. Made to be aesthetically appealing, *terra sigillata* pieces were like the artistic work of Grecian pieces, though they were not painted. Instead, crafters adorned the pieces with reliefs—moldings or carvings that stood out from the surface of the pottery.

Which of the following can be inferred from paragraph 2 about *terra sigillata*?

(A) Pieces fired together in the same kiln were identical.

(B) The style varied depending on where it was made.

(C) It was mainly used by the elites of Roman society.

(D) It was more fragile than coarse ware pottery.

Roman pottery is often classified into two groups. The first is fine wares, which were skillfully crafted serving vessels and tableware. Used for official dinner occasions, fine wares were both decorative and practical. The most prominent example of fine wares was *terra sigillata*, a red-gloss ware that was made in the regions of northern Italy and France. These pieces were well-fired and adequately hard with a naturally glossy surface slip. *Terra sigillata* pieces were produced on an industrial scale—the largest kilns could fire tens of thousands of pieces at a time—and exported throughout the empire. Red-gloss potsherds, or shards of pottery, have been recovered all the way from India to Scotland. Many bore the signatures of their crafters or manufacturers, with pieces from the same artist or factory appearing in distant locations. Made to be aesthetically appealing, *terra sigillata* pieces were like the artistic work of Grecian pieces, though they were not painted. Instead, crafters adorned the pieces with reliefs—moldings or carvings that stood out from the surface of the pottery.

According to paragraph 2, *terra sigillata* differed from Grecian pottery because

(A) it was decorated with reliefs instead of paint.
(B) it was popular for its striking designs.
(C) it was produced in large numbers.
(D) it has been found across the Mediterranean region.

Coarse wares represented the other sphere of Ancient Roman pottery. Unlike fine wares, coarse wares were manufactured purely for function. These common vessels were made and sold locally and used chiefly for cooking, storage, and transportation. They were staples of Roman households, regardless of rank or class. Though they were not made for display, they were still finely crafted. They were sturdy yet light, and smooth in the hand. Their glossy, sealed surfaces made them ideal for the storage of liquids such as olive oil, fish sauce, and wine. Crafters followed standardized sizes that made the pottery conducive to stacking and efficient, long-term storage. Amphorae were a common piece of coarse ware. These cone-shaped storage vessels allowed them to fit securely into storerooms and the holds of merchant ships. Their valuable contents were protected during marine transport, so the large-scale production of amphorae served a crucial role in the trade of the Roman Empire.

According to paragraph 3, crafters followed standardized sizes so that

(A) various products could be transported via ship.
(B) larger quantities of goods could be imported to Rome.
(C) pieces remained consistently sturdy no matter their size.
(D) coarse ware pottery could store goods efficiently.

Coarse wares represented the other sphere of Ancient Roman pottery. Unlike fine wares, coarse wares were manufactured purely for function. These common vessels were made and sold locally and used chiefly for cooking, storage, and transportation. They were staples of Roman households, regardless of rank or class. Though they were not made for display, they were still finely crafted. They were sturdy yet light, and smooth in the hand. Their glossy, sealed surfaces made them ideal for the storage of liquids such as olive oil, fish sauce, and wine. Crafters followed standardized sizes that made the pottery conducive to stacking and efficient, long-term storage. Amphorae were a common piece of coarse ware. These cone-shaped storage vessels allowed them to fit securely into storerooms and the holds of merchant ships. Their valuable contents were protected during marine transport, so the large-scale production of amphorae served a crucial role in the trade of the Roman Empire.

Why does the author mention "merchant ships"?

(A) To indicate amphorae were frequently transported by ship
(B) To suggest that amphorae were a popular trade good
(C) To contrast the shape of amphorae with that of other pottery vessels
(D) To argue that the majority of goods were imported into Rome

As is common in archaeology, only a sparse sample of the total amount of pottery created and used in Ancient Rome will ever be recovered. However, one exceptional dumpsite exists that hints at the massive scale of pottery production in Ancient Rome. Monte Testaccio is an artificial hill around 50 meters high that is located on the left bank of the Tiber River in Rome, a site near one of the ancient river ports. It is composed entirely of discarded and broken amphorae, most of which are dated from the second and third centuries A.D. Archeologists estimate that more than 50 million amphorae have contributed to the building of Monte Testaccio. Given what we know of the capacity of the containers, it is likely that more than six billion liters of olive oil had been imported into the city from overseas. Monte Testaccio attests to the massive scope and complexity of Ancient Rome's imports, and conjures the image of a society not so different from modern ones. It produced and shipped goods across the expanse of its empire via high-quality, optimized containers that could simply be discarded upon delivery, if necessary.

The word "entirely" in the passage is closest in meaning to

(A) traditionally
(B) steadily
(C) apparently
(D) completely

Monte Testaccio and other sites throughout the empire indicate that Roman pottery was transported in bulk over vast distances, yet they also show how every level of Ancient Roman society had access to fine products. Roman pottery, from the humblest pieces to the finest wares, serves as a standard of everyday life in the empire.

Which of the sentences below best expresses the essential information in the highlighted sentence in the passage? Incorrect answer choices change the meaning in important ways or leave out essential information.

(A) The massive amount of pottery that arrived in Monte Testaccio suggests that nearly every person in Rome owned pottery.

(B) The recovery of pottery at various locations shows that fine pottery was moved in large amounts across the empire and possessed by all Romans.

(C) As Roman citizens got higher-quality pottery, they discarded their old pieces at places such as Monte Testaccio, and this implies a surplus of goods in the empire.

(D) Every territory in the Ancient Roman Empire had a communal site like Mount Testaccio where the people could dispose of their excess pottery.

As is common in archaeology, only a sparse sample of the total amount of pottery created and used in Ancient Rome will ever be recovered. ▌ However, one exceptional dumpsite exists that hints at the massive scale of pottery production in Ancient Rome. ▌ Monte Testaccio is an artificial hill around 50 meters high that is located on the left bank of the Tiber River in Rome, a site near one of the ancient river ports. ▌ It is composed entirely of discarded and broken amphorae, most of which are dated from the second and third centuries A.D. ▌ Archeologists estimate that more than 50 million amphorae have contributed to the building of Monte Testaccio. Given what we know of the capacity of the containers, it is likely that more than six billion liters of olive oil had been imported into the city from overseas. Monte Testaccio attests to the massive scope and complexity of Ancient Rome's imports, and conjures the image of a society not so different from modern ones. It produced and shipped goods across the expanse of its empire via high-quality, optimized containers that could simply be discarded upon delivery, if necessary.

Look at the four squares [▌] that indicate where the following sentence could be added to the passage.

Considering this, it is difficult to estimate how much was produced.

Where would the sentence best fit? Click on a square [▌] to add the sentence to the passage.

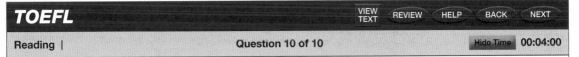
Directions: An introductory sentence for a brief summary of the passage is provided below. Complete the summary by selecting the THREE answer choices that express the most important ideas in the passage. Some sentences do not belong in the summary because they express ideas that are not presented in the passage or are minor ideas in the passage. **This question is worth 2 points.**

Drag your answer choices to the space where they belong. To remove an answer choice, click on it. To review the passage, click on **VIEW TEXT.**

The exceptional pottery of Ancient Rome showcases several of the Empire's strengths.

-
-
-

Answer Choices

(A) *Terra sigillata* pieces were used mainly for the transportation of liquids such as olive oil.

(B) The collection of amphorae at Monte Testaccio details the magnitude of Ancient Rome's importing and trade industries.

(C) The universal presence of pottery around the Roman Empire shows that all people had access to quality goods.

(D) Popular crafters and manufacturers distributed their wares throughout the empire, from India to Scotland.

(E) Fine ware and coarse ware pieces were expertly crafted and manufactured in great amounts.

(F) The Ancient Romans modeled their pottery on the artistic works of the Ancient Greeks.

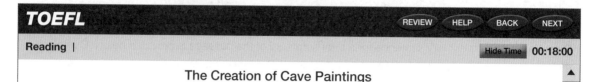

The Creation of Cave Paintings

Cave paintings dating from the end of the Paleolithic era represent the earliest works of human art. Discovered mainly in caverns and chasms around Spain and France, the paintings depict bulls, aurochs, horses, and other animals from the time in surprising detail. Lascaux and Chauvet in France are some of the most well-known of these sites. If these paintings do represent the first human attempts at art, how do we explain the motivation behind their creation? What purpose did they serve? In his classic work *Poetics*, Aristotle claims that people "naturally take delight in works of imitation." If a sunset is a temporary glimpse of beauty, recreating it via art makes at least a suggestion of its grandeur readily available. If we, the descendants, can enjoy art in such a simple, direct manner, then it is quite possible that our ancestors enjoyed it in much the same way.

By this reasoning, the caves at Lascaux could have existed as a sort of prehistoric gallery, where early people could journey to take in the beautiful masterpieces of accomplished artists. Access to such leisurely activities would have required some reprieve from the incessant demands of survival. If there was an abundance of food in Paleolithic Europe, this might have been a plausible scenario. However, there are numerous issues with this assumption. For one thing, the abundance of archaeological sites that have been discovered, including cave painting locations of unknown ages, offers a strikingly narrow range of artistic subjects. Each site has the same recurring images or motifs of animals. Rarely are there depictions of human figures, and when there are, they lack the attention to detail given to the animals. If the Paleolithic artists worked to recreate beauty, then their scope was extremely limited. Why did they ignore flowers and trees, the stars and the sky?

The notion that early people were exploring art as a way of recreating beauty is further challenged by the prevalence of abstract images with no apparent counterparts in reality. These marks—usually simple geometrical patterns composed of lines and dots—appear by themselves or alongside the typical depictions of animals. Cave art in the Lot region of France, namely the grotto of Pech Merle, show both animal paintings and abstract markings. Namely, paintings of stout-bellied horses adorn the walls. However, the outlines of the animals are covered by dark spots that deform the otherwise realistic drawing of the horses. It is unknown what function the spots serve, other than to detract from the naturalistic reproduction. In addition, if the images are made to be viewed and appreciated, then their location is problematic. While the caves of Lascaux would have been accessible to Paleolithic gallery-goers, other sites would test even experienced cavers. Drawings in narrow nooks and shallow chambers would have required impressive contortions by the artists and seem, if anything, to dissuade the approach of would-be viewers.

Furthermore, the overall assumption that Paleolithic painters could enjoy art for art's sake hinges on the relative calm of daily life, that food was plentiful and basic survival was not a constant demand. During this time, Europe was still experiencing an ice age, and it has been estimated that a human at that time would have needed to take in about 2,000 calories a day to survive. Extracting this amount of sustenance from an icy, harsh terrain would have taken top priority. The emphasis on animal paintings and the harsh lifestyle of Paleolithic people has led some archaeologists to believe that cave paintings must have served a practical purpose and somehow aided in their main means of survival: hunting.

A new theory emerged in the early 20th century that centered on how cave paintings could assist in survival. French archaeologist Henri Breuil proposed the idea of "sympathetic magic." He argued that the artists worked in such detail to capture the spirit of the animal being depicted. The more realistic and evocative the image, the better it would trap the prey. Under this idea, the artist's precise paintings had the magical capacity to imbue the hunter's task with luck and good fortune.

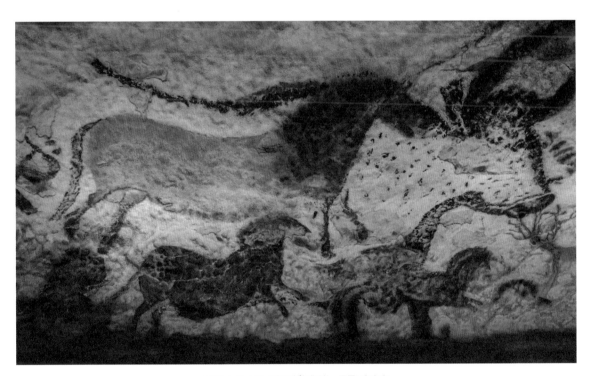

<프랑스 라스코 동굴 벽화에 있는 동물 이미지>

Cave paintings dating from the end of the Paleolithic era represent the earliest works of human art. Discovered mainly in caverns and chasms around Spain and France, the paintings depict bulls, aurochs, horses, and other animals from the time in surprising detail. Lascaux and Chauvet in France are some of the most well-known of these sites. If these paintings do represent the first human attempts at art, how do we explain the motivation behind their creation? What purpose did they serve? In his classic work *Poetics*, Aristotle claims that people "naturally take delight in works of imitation." If a sunset is a temporary glimpse of beauty, recreating it via art makes at least a suggestion of its grandeur readily available. If we, the descendants, can enjoy art in such a simple, direct manner, then it is quite possible that our ancestors enjoyed it in much the same way.

According to paragraph 1, what is significant about cave paintings?

(A) They represent the earliest artwork of humanity.
(B) They appear in areas that are difficult to reach.
(C) They were the only means of delight for early ancestors.
(D) They accurately portray common plants and animals.

Cave paintings dating from the end of the Paleolithic era represent the earliest works of human art. Discovered mainly in caverns and chasms around Spain and France, the paintings depict bulls, aurochs, horses, and other animals from the time in surprising detail. Lascaux and Chauvet in France are some of the most well-known of these sites. If these paintings do represent the first human attempts at art, how do we explain the motivation behind their creation? What purpose did they serve? In his classic work *Poetics*, Aristotle claims that people "naturally take delight in works of imitation." If a sunset is a temporary glimpse of beauty, recreating it via art makes at least a suggestion of its grandeur readily available. If we, the descendants, can enjoy art in such a simple, direct manner, then it is quite possible that our ancestors enjoyed it in much the same way.

In paragraph 1, why does the writer mention Aristotle?

(A) To demonstrate how the Ancient Greeks viewed Paleolithic art
(B) To share a theory about the creation of art that might apply to cave paintings
(C) To suggest that Paleolithic artists had different reasons for creating art
(D) To highlight a connection between Paleolithic art and Ancient Greek art

By this reasoning, the caves at Lascaux could have existed as a sort of prehistoric gallery, where early people could journey to take in the beautiful masterpieces of accomplished artists. Access to such leisurely activities would have required some reprieve from the incessant demands of survival. If there was an abundance of food in Paleolithic Europe, this might have been a plausible scenario. However, there are numerous issues with this assumption. For one thing, the abundance of archaeological sites that have been discovered, including cave painting locations of unknown ages, offer a strikingly narrow range of artistic subjects. Each site has the same recurring images or motifs of animals. Rarely are there depictions of human figures, and when there are, they lack the attention to detail given to the animals. If the Paleolithic artists worked to recreate beauty, then their scope was extremely limited. Why did they ignore flowers and trees, the stars and the sky?

In paragraph 2, the author suggests that the cave art in Europe could have only been made for pleasure if

(A) enough natural light was available in the caves.
(B) artists in the Paleolithic era possessed outstanding artistic skills.
(C) the basic needs of survival were easily met.
(D) enough people were interested in visiting the galleries.

By this reasoning, the caves at Lascaux could have existed as a sort of prehistoric gallery, where early people could journey to take in the beautiful masterpieces of accomplished artists. Access to such leisurely activities would have required some reprieve from the incessant demands of survival. If there was an abundance of food in Paleolithic Europe, this might have been a plausible scenario. However, there are numerous issues with this assumption. For one thing, the abundance of archaeological sites that have been discovered, including cave painting locations of unknown ages, offer a strikingly narrow range of artistic subjects. Each site has the same recurring images or motifs of animals. Rarely are there depictions of human figures, and when there are, they lack the attention to detail given to the animals. If the Paleolithic artists worked to recreate beauty, then their scope was extremely limited. Why did they ignore flowers and trees, the stars and the sky?

The word "scope" in the passage is closest in meaning to

(A) shape
(B) extent
(C) talent
(D) sight

The notion that early people were exploring art as a way of recreating beauty is further challenged by the prevalence of abstract images with no apparent counterparts in reality. These marks—usually simple geometrical patterns composed of lines and dots—appear by themselves or alongside the typical depictions of animals. Cave art in the Lot region of France, namely the grotto of Pech Merle, show both animal paintings and abstract markings. Namely, paintings of stout-bellied horses adorn the walls. However, the outlines of the animals are covered by dark spots that deform the otherwise realistic drawing of the horses. It is unknown what function the spots serve, other than to detract from the naturalistic reproduction. In addition, if the images are made to be viewed and appreciated, then their location is problematic. While the caves of Lascaux would have been accessible to Paleolithic gallery-goers, other sites would test even experienced cavers. Drawings in narrow nooks and shallow chambers would have required impressive contortions by the artists and seem, if anything, to dissuade the approach of would-be viewers.

In paragraph 3, what is NOT mentioned about the abstract figures that appear in cave art?

(A) They are located on animal paintings.
(B) Their purpose is unknown.
(C) They can be found in Pech Merle.
(D) They are intricately designed.

The notion that early people were exploring art as a way of recreating beauty is further challenged by the prevalence of abstract images with no apparent counterparts in reality. These marks—usually simple geometrical patterns composed of lines and dots—appear by themselves or alongside the typical depictions of animals. Cave art in the Lot region of France, namely the grotto of Pech Merle, show both animal paintings and abstract markings. Namely, paintings of stout-bellied horses adorn the walls. However, the outlines of the animals are covered by dark spots that deform the otherwise realistic drawing of the horses. It is unknown what function the spots serve, other than to detract from the naturalistic reproduction. In addition, if the images are made to be viewed and appreciated, then their location is problematic. While the caves of Lascaux would have been accessible to Paleolithic gallery-goers, other sites would test even experienced cavers. Drawings in narrow nooks and shallow chambers would have required impressive contortions by the artists and seem, if anything, to dissuade the approach of would-be viewers.

In paragraph 3, what can be inferred about the cave paintings at Lascaux?

(A) They were mostly done on the ceiling of the cave.
(B) The artists who made them were extremely nimble.
(C) They were painted in easily accessible areas.
(D) Caving gear is required to approach them.

Furthermore, the overall assumption that Paleolithic painters could enjoy art for art's sake hinges on the relative calm of daily life, that food was plentiful and basic survival was not a constant demand. During this time, Europe was still experiencing an ice age, and it has been estimated that a human at that time would have needed to take in about 2,000 calories a day to survive. Extracting this amount of sustenance from an icy, harsh terrain would have taken top priority. The emphasis on animal paintings and the harsh lifestyle of Paleolithic people has led some archaeologists to believe that cave paintings must have served a practical purpose and somehow aided in their main means of survival: hunting.

Which of the sentences below best expresses the essential information in the highlighted sentence in the passage? Incorrect answer choices change the meaning in important ways or leave out essential information.

(A) Hunters used cave art in a useful manner by recording detailed images of animals, which made hunting easier and the people safer in general.

(B) Paleolithic people who had difficulty surviving had to focus on hunting, while those who did not were able to spend their time painting cave art of animals.

(C) By hunting, Paleolithic artists were able to closely observe animals for their paintings, which overall helped people to survive.

(D) The number of animal paintings and the difficulty of survival at the time suggest that cave paintings were meant to support hunting in some way.

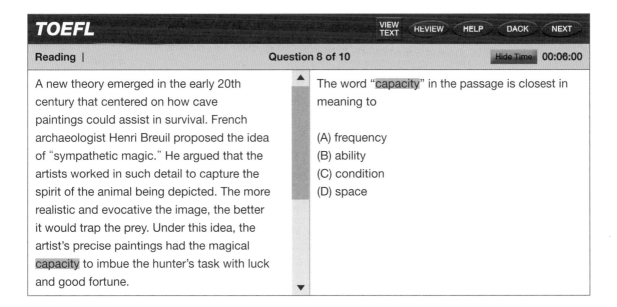

A new theory emerged in the early 20th century that centered on how cave paintings could assist in survival. French archaeologist Henri Breuil proposed the idea of "sympathetic magic." He argued that the artists worked in such detail to capture the spirit of the animal being depicted. The more realistic and evocative the image, the better it would trap the prey. Under this idea, the artist's precise paintings had the magical capacity to imbue the hunter's task with luck and good fortune.

The word "capacity" in the passage is closest in meaning to

(A) frequency
(B) ability
(C) condition
(D) space

By this reasoning, the caves at Lascaux could have existed as a sort of prehistoric gallery, where early people could journey to take in the beautiful masterpieces of accomplished artists. Access to such leisurely activities would have required some reprieve from the incessant demands of survival. If there was an abundance of food in Paleolithic Europe, this might have been a plausible scenario. However, there are numerous issues with this assumption. For one thing, the abundance of archaeological sites that have been discovered, including cave painting locations of unknown ages, offer a strikingly narrow range of artistic subjects. ▪ Each site has the same recurring images or motifs of animals. ▪ Rarely are there depictions of human figures, and when there are, they lack the attention to detail given to the animals. ▪ If the Paleolithic artists worked to recreate beauty, then their scope was extremely limited. ▪ Why did they ignore flowers and trees, the stars and the sky?

Look at the four squares [▪] that indicate where the following sentence could be added to the passage.

There are no self-portraits, or paintings of communities.

Where would the sentence best fit? Click on a square [▪] to add the sentence to the passage.

Directions: An introductory sentence for a brief summary of the passage is provided below. Complete the summary by selecting the THREE answer choices that express the most important ideas in the passage. Some sentences do not belong in the summary because they express ideas that are not presented in the passage or are minor ideas in the passage. **This question is worth 2 points.**

Drag your answer choices to the space where they belong. To remove an answer choice, click on it. To review the passage, click on **VIEW TEXT.**

> **Paleolithic cave paintings were most likely not created just for enjoyment because of several reasons.**
>
> •
> •
> •

Answer Choices

(A) People living during the Paleolithic era most likely did not have leisure time, and most paintings were located in difficult-to-reach areas.

(B) The idea of art as a form of entertainment did not gain prominence until Classical Greece.

(C) Artists did not paint humans because it was believed that doing so would trap the soul of the person in the painting.

(D) The importance of hunting in the Paleolithic era and the art's focus on animals suggest that cave paintings were made to benefit hunters.

(E) The paintings only represented a small portion of the natural world, and some paintings were abstract.

(F) The realistic depiction of animals in cave art served to warn people about the danger of the creatures.

■ Passage 3

The Theater Audience

No amount of rehearsal or preparation can give an actor control over how a live audience will impact their performance. An actor who has been brilliant in rehearsal can collapse in front of a real audience, their energy dissipating in the hesitancy of stage fright. Other performers who have been dull and lackluster in rehearsal can be electrified by the live audience. This transformation was seen in Lee J. Cobb's lead performance in the original production of Arthur Miller's *Death of a Salesman*. The director and Miller himself feared that Cobb had decided to play the role as if with one foot in the grave, so dreary was he in rehearsal. But then, on opening night, Cobb lit up and left the audience stunned and silent for minutes after the final curtain fell. An audience can affect a performance in any other number of ways. It can turn the serious role comical or make the painted clown the production's sober voice of reason.

Radical departures from rehearsed performances, to be sure, are not anticipated on opening night, and they surely are not the goal. Well-trained and disciplined actors aim to perfect their performance in dress rehearsal and transplant it into opening night, fully intact and unaltered. This is, after all, the purpose of all those rehearsals. Once, actors thought to save their emotion and passion for an explosive expression on opening night, but this practice is now shunned, and such recklessness is an obvious sign of an amateur. Those who rely on guts and sudden inspiration will surely leave their fellow players stranded on stage. Likewise, purposefully playing to a crowd, or altering a planned performance in response to the audience's laughter or applause, is scorned in any serious theater.

While it should not be forced, the actor's performance will regardless be influenced by the audience, and this will undoubtedly cause a shift between rehearsal and performance—and indeed, this is a main ingredient in the exotic dish that is live theater. The actor, however, acutely aware of the audience, will subtly adjust to the reactions of the crowd automatically—the performance evolves under observation. This creates a distinction between performances, even in shows that have run countless times. The changes can be small but significant. The actor waits a second longer to deliver a line, allowing laughter time to settle, or there is a subtle tilt of the head to emphasize a line or hint at a concealed character trait.

A great actor also impresses themselves on the audience through their presence, a powerful but difficult-to-define quality in the world of theater. Presence can lift both the character and the actor to new heights before the audience. With presence, the actor commands both the stage and the audience and thrives under the spectators' view. The actor presents, and the audience responds. Both parties interact in different but equal manners. It is a unique communication, a give and take, that employs speech and action from the actor and applause, laughter, and even silence from the audience as its unique code.

The absence of reaction can be just as inspirational. An unmoving, silent audience, invisible to the actor thanks to the intensity of the stage lights, can be just as impressive, or oppressive, to those on stage. Everything becomes a sign, a signal. Having a hundred people sit still, not sniffling, not rummaging through their pockets, but paying full, unimpeded attention to the world on the stage is the grand ambition of the stage actor. The audience's chuckles and gasps carry the same weight for the actor—the communication is transmitted, and the actor responds. The experienced actor knows how to respond to these cues and seize the moment, to turn a chuckle into an uproar of laughter, to turn a sigh into a soul-expressing gale. Likewise, they can turn the tide and grab the focus of a restless audience or wake up a drowsy crowd. Reading the audience in such a way is difficult if not impossible to learn through training and must be felt; it is instinctual. It is a matter of timing, not unlike any other social grace. And, as with most aspects of the stage, experience is the best teacher.

<무대에서 연기하는 배우들>

No amount of rehearsal or preparation can give an actor control over how a live audience will impact their performance. An actor who has been brilliant in rehearsal can collapse in front of a real audience, their energy dissipating in the hesitancy of stage fright. Other performers who have been dull and lackluster in rehearsal can be electrified by the live audience. This transformation was seen in Lee J. Cobb's lead performance in the original production of Arthur Miller's *Death of a Salesman*. The director and Miller himself feared that Cobb had decided to play the role as if with one foot in the grave, so dreary was he in rehearsal. But then, on opening night, Cobb lit up and left the audience stunned and silent for minutes after the final curtain fell. An audience can affect a performance in any other number of ways. It can turn the serious role comical or make the painted clown the production's sober voice of reason.

The word "impact" in the passage is closest in meaning to

(A) create
(B) damage
(C) criticize
(D) affect

No amount of rehearsal or preparation can give an actor control over how a live audience will impact their performance. An actor who has been brilliant in rehearsal can collapse in front of a real audience, their energy dissipating in the hesitancy of stage fright. Other performers who have been dull and lackluster in rehearsal can be electrified by the live audience. This transformation was seen in Lee J. Cobb's lead performance in the original production of Arthur Miller's *Death of a Salesman*. The director and Miller himself feared that Cobb had decided to play the role as if with one foot in the grave, so dreary was he in rehearsal. But then, on opening night, Cobb lit up and left the audience stunned and silent for minutes after the final curtain fell. An audience can affect a performance in any other number of ways. It can turn the serious role comical or make the painted clown the production's sober voice of reason.

Which of the following can be inferred about the lead actor's performance in the opening night of *Death of a Salesman*?

(A) It became the standard way for portraying that character in the play.
(B) It surprised the people who had observed the actor in rehearsal.
(C) It would have been improved had there been more rehearsals with live audiences.
(D) It showed that an experienced actor can turn a comedic role into a serious one.

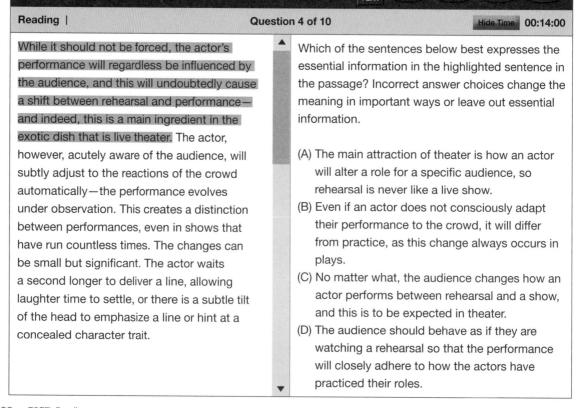

Radical departures from rehearsed performances, to be sure, are not anticipated on opening night, and they surely are not the goal. Well-trained and disciplined actors aim to perfect their performance in dress rehearsal and transplant it into opening night, fully intact and unaltered. This is, after all, the purpose of all those rehearsals. Once, actors thought to save their emotion and passion for an explosive expression on opening night, but this practice is now shunned, and such recklessness is an obvious sign of an amateur. Those who rely on guts and sudden inspiration will surely leave their fellow players stranded on stage. Likewise, purposefully playing to a crowd, or altering a planned performance in response to the audience's laughter or applause, is scorned in any serious theater.

According to paragraph 2, an actor who deliberately alters their performance for opening night will most likely

(A) express more emotion in their role.
(B) capture the attention of a live audience.
(C) irritate everyone else in the production.
(D) discover a new way to play a role.

While it should not be forced, the actor's performance will regardless be influenced by the audience, and this will undoubtedly cause a shift between rehearsal and performance— and indeed, this is a main ingredient in the exotic dish that is live theater. The actor, however, acutely aware of the audience, will subtly adjust to the reactions of the crowd automatically—the performance evolves under observation. This creates a distinction between performances, even in shows that have run countless times. The changes can be small but significant. The actor waits a second longer to deliver a line, allowing laughter time to settle, or there is a subtle tilt of the head to emphasize a line or hint at a concealed character trait.

Which of the sentences below best expresses the essential information in the highlighted sentence in the passage? Incorrect answer choices change the meaning in important ways or leave out essential information.

(A) The main attraction of theater is how an actor will alter a role for a specific audience, so rehearsal is never like a live show.
(B) Even if an actor does not consciously adapt their performance to the crowd, it will differ from practice, as this change always occurs in plays.
(C) No matter what, the audience changes how an actor performs between rehearsal and a show, and this is to be expected in theater.
(D) The audience should behave as if they are watching a rehearsal so that the performance will closely adhere to how the actors have practiced their roles.

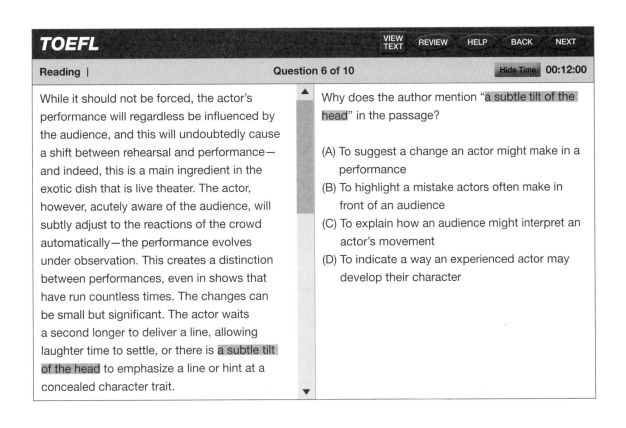

While it should not be forced, the actor's performance will regardless be influenced by the audience, and this will undoubtedly cause a shift between rehearsal and performance— and indeed, this is a main ingredient in the exotic dish that is live theater. The actor, however, acutely aware of the audience, will subtly adjust to the reactions of the crowd automatically—the performance evolves under observation. This creates a distinction between performances, even in shows that have run countless times. The changes can be small but significant. The actor waits a second longer to deliver a line, allowing laughter time to settle, or there is a subtle tilt of the head to emphasize a line or hint at a concealed character trait.

The word "automatically" in the passage is closest in meaning to

(A) naturally
(B) mechanically
(C) rigidly
(D) frequently

While it should not be forced, the actor's performance will regardless be influenced by the audience, and this will undoubtedly cause a shift between rehearsal and performance— and indeed, this is a main ingredient in the exotic dish that is live theater. The actor, however, acutely aware of the audience, will subtly adjust to the reactions of the crowd automatically—the performance evolves under observation. This creates a distinction between performances, even in shows that have run countless times. The changes can be small but significant. The actor waits a second longer to deliver a line, allowing laughter time to settle, or there is a subtle tilt of the head to emphasize a line or hint at a concealed character trait.

Why does the author mention "a subtle tilt of the head" in the passage?

(A) To suggest a change an actor might make in a performance
(B) To highlight a mistake actors often make in front of an audience
(C) To explain how an audience might interpret an actor's movement
(D) To indicate a way an experienced actor may develop their character

The absence of reaction can be just as inspirational. An unmoving, silent audience, invisible to the actor thanks to the intensity of the stage lights, can be just as impressive, or oppressive, to those on stage. Everything becomes a sign, a signal. Having a hundred people sit still, not sniffling, not rummaging through their pockets, but paying full, unimpeded attention to the world on the stage is the grand ambition of the stage actor. The audience's chuckles and gasps carry the same weight for the actor—the communication is transmitted, and the actor responds. The experienced actor knows how to respond to these cues and seize the moment, to turn a chuckle into an uproar of laughter, to turn a sigh into a soul-expressing gale. Likewise, they can turn the tide and grab the focus of a restless audience or wake up a drowsy crowd. Reading the audience in such a way is difficult if not impossible to learn through training and must be felt; it is instinctual. It is a matter of timing, not unlike any other social grace. And, as with most aspects of the stage, experience is the best teacher.

According to paragraph 5, what does a silent audience indicate?

(A) The audience is confused by the actor's performance.
(B) The audience does not want to distract the actor.
(C) The actor has the full attention of the audience.
(D) The actor has failed to trigger a response in the audience.

The absence of reaction can be just as inspirational. An unmoving, silent audience, invisible to the actor thanks to the intensity of the stage lights, can be just as impressive, or oppressive, to those on stage. Everything becomes a sign, a signal. Having a hundred people sit still, not sniffling, not rummaging through their pockets, but paying full, unimpeded attention to the world on the stage is the grand ambition of the stage actor. The audience's chuckles and gasps carry the same weight for the actor—the communication is transmitted, and the actor responds. The experienced actor knows how to respond to these cues and seize the moment, to turn a chuckle into an uproar of laughter, to turn a sigh into a soul-expressing gale. Likewise, they can turn the tide and grab the focus of a restless audience or wake up a drowsy crowd. Reading the audience in such a way is difficult if not impossible to learn through training and must be felt; it is instinctual. It is a matter of timing, not unlike any other social grace. And, as with most aspects of the stage, experience is the best teacher.

In paragraph 5, what is NOT mentioned about an actor's ability to read an audience?

(A) It can change the audience's mood.
(B) It is taught by experienced teachers.
(C) It depends on the actor's instincts.
(D) It can enhance the audience's responses.

A great actor also impresses themselves on the audience through their presence, a powerful but difficult-to-define quality in the world of theater. Presence can lift both the character and the actor to new heights before the audience. With presence, the actor commands both the stage and the audience and thrives under the spectators' view. ■ The actor presents, and the audience responds. ■ Both parties interact in different but equal manners. ■ It is a unique communication, a give and take, that employs speech and action from the actor and applause, laughter, and even silence from the audience as its unique code. ■

Look at the four squares [■] that indicate where the following sentence could be added to the passage.

In this way, performance is not a one-sided relationship with only the stage informing the house.

Where would the sentence best fit? Click on a square [■] to add the sentence to the passage.

Directions: An introductory sentence for a brief summary of the passage is provided below. Complete the summary by selecting the THREE answer choices that express the most important ideas in the passage. Some sentences do not belong in the summary because they express ideas that are not presented in the passage or are minor ideas in the passage. **This question is worth 2 points.**

Drag your answer choices to the space where they belong. To remove an answer choice, click on it. To review the passage, click on **VIEW TEXT.**

A unique relationship exists between the actors and the audience during a live theater performance.

-
-
-

Answer Choices

(A) A skilled performer will change their performance for the audience, even if it makes a serious role comical.

(B) Skilled actors know how to make subtle changes in response to an audience and demonstrate presence on stage.

(C) Amateur actors easily learn how to change their delivery of a line to draw out more laughter from the audience.

(D) The audience communicates to the actors through a variety of ways, including sight, laughter, applause, and even silence.

(E) A disrespectful audience will disrupt the performance and cause an actor to express more anger on stage.

(F) While the performance should match the rehearsal, it cannot completely prepare actors for a performance before a live audience.

Chapter

04

Geology

Passage 1   **Soil Quality of Tropical Rainforests**

Passage 2   **The Influence of Glaciers**

Passage 3   **Understanding Earth's Interior**

GEOLOGIC TIMELINE

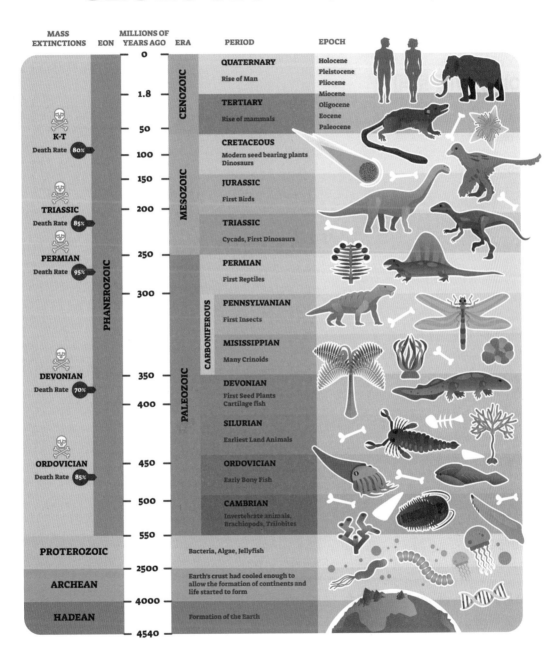

MASS EXTINCTIONS	EON	MILLIONS OF YEARS AGO	ERA	PERIOD	EPOCH
		0	CENOZOIC	**QUATERNARY** Rise of Man	Holocene Pleistocene Pliocene
		1.8		**TERTIARY** Rise of mammals	Miocene Oligocene Eocene Paleocene
K-T Death Rate 80%		50			
		100	MESOZOIC	**CRETACEOUS** Modern seed bearing plants Dinosaurs	
		150		**JURASSIC** First Birds	
TRIASSIC Death Rate 85%		200		**TRIASSIC** Cycads, First Dinosaurs	
PERMIAN Death Rate 95%	PHANEROZOIC	250	PALEOZOIC	**PERMIAN** First Reptiles	
		300		**PENNSYLVANIAN** First Insects	
				MISISSIPPIAN Many Crinoids	
DEVONIAN Death Rate 70%		350		**DEVONIAN** First Seed Plants Cartilage fish	
		400		**SILURIAN** Earliest Land Animals	
ORDOVICIAN Death Rate 85%		450		**ORDOVICIAN** Early Bony Fish	
		500		**CAMBRIAN** Invertebrate animals, Brachiopods, Trilobites	
		550			
	PROTEROZOIC			Bacteria, Algae, Jellyfish	
	ARCHEAN	2500		Earth's crust had cooled enough to allow the formation of continents and life started to form	
	HADEAN	4000		Formation of the Earth	
		4540			

Note: CARBONIFEROUS spans the PENNSYLVANIAN and MISISSIPPIAN periods.

Geology (지질학)

지구의 구성 물질, 형성 과정, 화석 등 광범위한 토픽이 출제되고 있으며, 특별히 사막, 빙하, 화산 등 다양한 지형의 형성 과정이 자주 나온다.

[Geology 기출 토픽]

- Geothermal Energy
  지열 에너지

- Rainforest Soils
  열대 우림 토양

- Desert Formation
  사막 형성

- Groundwater
  지하수

- Lake Water
  호수

- Soil Formation
  토양 형성

- Glacier Formation
  빙하 형성

- Earth's Age
  지구의 나이

- Earth's Core
  지구의 중심(핵)

- The Formation of Volcanic Islands
  화산섬의 형성

- The Geologic History of the Mediterranean
  지중해의 지질학적 역사

- Fossil
  화석

[Geology 빈출 어휘]

alteration	변화		glacier	빙하
aquifer	대수층		gravel	자갈
classify	~을 분류하다		humus	부엽토
composition	구성 요소		hydrologic	물의
compounds	화합물		ice sheet	대륙 빙하
concentric	동심원의		inhabitant	서식 동물
conductive	전도성의		intensity	강도
consistency	농도		magnetic field	자기장
decaying	부패하는		medium	매개물
decompose	~을 분해하다		melting point	용해점, 녹는 점
disparity	차이		microbes	미생물
disperse	~을 분산시키다		nitrogen	질소
displace	~을 옮겨 놓다		obliterate	~을 없애다
drift	이동		penetrate	~을 관통하다
electrical conductor	전기 전도체		phosphorus	인(화학 원소)
electron	전자		precipitation	강수(량)
elucidate	~을 설명하다		radius	반지름
encompassing	둘러싸고 있는		retreat	후퇴하다
evaporation	증발		seismic	지진의
exert	(힘)을 가하다		shrink	수축하다, 수축되다
facilitator	촉진제		sustain	~을 지속하다
far-reaching	광범위한		temperate	온난한, 온화한
fracture	~을 갈라지게 하다		trajectory	궤적
disparity	차이		transformation	탈바꿈, 변모
fungal	균류의		transmission	전송, 전달, 전파

Soil Quality of Tropical Rainforests

One would assume that a rainforest, with its dense vegetation and diverse inhabitants, would be supported from the ground up by nutrient-rich soil. After all, healthy plant life requires healthy soil in most cases. However, though various soils make up rainforests, they all lack nutrients. The constant rainfall in rainforests washes the nutrients of the soil out through a process known as leaching. As a result of leaching, the soils in tropical rainforests have very low mineral contents, a stark difference from grassland soils. In addition, tropical rainforest soils contain clays that are resistant to binding mineral ions, save for aluminum, which is the most prevalent mineral in most tropical soils. This element is not in demand by plants; in fact, it can be toxic to them in high amounts. The presence of aluminum also reduces that of phosphorus, an element critical to plants.

Compared to grasslands and temperate rainforest soils, tropical rainforest soils also contain less humus, or organic materials. The perpetual humidity and high temperatures of the tropics promote the development of microbes that decompose humus-forming compounds in the soil. These compounds would typically improve the clays in the soil, helping to loosen them, hold water, and draw mineral nutrients. Without such aid, the clay within tropical rainforest soils becomes even less conducive to supporting plant life: as the clays harden, plant roots cannot penetrate them, and the lack of water in them threatens plants during dry spells. This imbalance of minerals is easily observable in the color of the clay. Lacking the dark hues of organic material, the soil instead adopts a rusty-red color from its high iron-oxide content, or yellow from aluminum. The soil also becomes as hard as rock when it dries. For this reason, it has historically been successfully used in ancient construction and roads.

Yet rainforests support some of the most abundant ecosystems on Earth—how do they do so with nutrient-depleted soil? Instead of depending on soil, rainforests recycle vital nutrients and minerals through their biomass. Unlike grasslands, which have most of their biomass underground, the biomass of a tropical rainforests exists above ground, in the trees and canopy. The forest's waste rarely even reaches the surface before it is completely broken down by efficient bacterial and fungal decomposers. Shallow plants below the canopy feed on the mineral contents of the decaying biomass and store it in their tissue. Then the minerals are transported and shared through a complex mycorrhizal network, wherein fungi assist roots in absorbing, transmitting, and dispersing nutrients. They also help the plants to absorb nutrients they are unable to, such as much-needed phosphorus. Fungi, bacteria, and other decomposers act as the facilitators in the continuous recycling of nutrients and minerals that sustains tropical rainforests.

Rainforests have also evolved to combat the loss of nutrients through leaching by developing closed nutrient systems. In such a system, minerals are transmitted between organisms without leaking much of them into the surrounding soil. By keeping minerals within the closed system, rainforests can promote plant growth and prevent the total loss of minerals. This is a clear adaptation that rainforests undergo in response to leaching. Nutrient systems in rainforests where the soil is rich are open and more akin to those found in grasslands. However, in areas with the poorest soils, the systems are closed and thus guarded against leaching.

Nitrogen is also vitally important to rainforest plants, and while it is abundant in the atmosphere, plants require it to be bound in molecules to absorb it. Here, rainforest plant life is once again assisted by special bacteria that capture nitrogen and transfer it to plants. The legume family of plants, which many rainforest species belong to, is known to coexist with nitrogen-fixing bacteria, which they harbor within their roots. Other species of plants, such as cycads, have adapted to grow their roots above ground to attract these special bacteria. Above ground, the roots are exposed to sunlight, which the bacteria need to grow. By supporting the growth of nitrogen-fixing bacteria, the plants can obtain nitrogen and thrive.

Glossary	X
biomass: the mass of living biological organisms in a given area or ecosystem at a given time mycorrhizal network: underground fungal systems that connect individual plants together and transfer water, nutrients, and minerals	

<브라질의 열대 우림>

One would assume that a rainforest, with its dense vegetation and diverse inhabitants, would be supported from the ground up by nutrient-rich soil. After all, healthy plant life requires healthy soil in most cases. However, though various soils make up rainforests, they all lack nutrients. The constant rainfall in rainforests washes the nutrients of the soil out through a process known as leaching. As a result of leaching, the soils in tropical rainforests have very low mineral contents, a stark difference from grassland soils. In addition, tropical rainforest soils contain clays that are resistant to binding mineral ions, save for aluminum, which is the most prevalent mineral in most tropical soils. This element is not in demand by plants; in fact, it can be toxic to them in high amounts. The presence of aluminum also reduces that of phosphorus, an element critical to plants.

Which of the following can be inferred about grasslands in paragraph 1?

(A) They consist of a wide variety of soil types.
(B) They have soil that receives nutrients from streams.
(C) They support sparse plant life compared to rainforests.
(D) They do not experience as much rainfall as rainforests.

One would assume that a rainforest, with its dense vegetation and diverse inhabitants, would be supported from the ground up by nutrient-rich soil. After all, healthy plant life requires healthy soil in most cases. However, though various soils make up rainforests, they all lack nutrients. The constant rainfall in rainforests washes the nutrients of the soil out through a process known as leaching. As a result of leaching, the soils in tropical rainforests have very low mineral contents, a stark difference from grassland soils. In addition, tropical rainforest soils contain clays that are resistant to binding mineral ions, save for aluminum, which is the most prevalent mineral in most tropical soils. This element is not in demand by plants; in fact, it can be toxic to them in high amounts. The presence of aluminum also reduces that of phosphorus, an element critical to plants.

According to paragraph 1, why do tropical rainforest soils have relatively low mineral content? Select TWO answers.

(A) The density of plant life in rainforests drains all minerals from the soil.

(B) The clay in rainforest soil does not bind mineral ions effectively.

(C) The streams that flow through rainforests do not replenish the soil with minerals.

(D) The heavy rainfall washes the minerals out of the rainforest soil.

Compared to grasslands and temperate rainforest soils, tropical rainforest soils also contain less humus, or organic materials. The perpetual humidity and high temperatures of the tropics promote the development of microbes that decompose humus-forming compounds in the soil. These compounds would typically improve the clays in the soil, helping to loosen them, hold water, and draw mineral nutrients. Without such aid, the clay within tropical rainforest soils becomes even less conducive to supporting plant life: as the clays harden, plant roots cannot penetrate them, and the lack of water in them threatens plants during dry spells. This imbalance of minerals is easily observable in the color of the clay. Lacking the dark hues of organic material, the soil instead adopts a rusty-red color from its high iron-oxide content, or yellow from aluminum. The soil also becomes as hard as rock when it dries. For this reason, it has historically been successfully used in ancient construction and roads.

The word "draw" in the passage is closest in meaning to

(A) attract
(B) enclose
(C) illustrate
(D) approach

Compared to grasslands and temperate rainforest soils, tropical rainforest soils also contain less humus, or organic materials. The perpetual humidity and high temperatures of the tropics promote the development of microbes that decompose humus-forming compounds in the soil. These compounds would typically improve the clays in the soil, helping to loosen them, hold water, and draw mineral nutrients. Without such aid, the clay within tropical rainforest soils becomes even less conducive to supporting plant life: as the clays harden, plant roots cannot penetrate them, and the lack of water in them threatens plants during dry spells. This imbalance of minerals is easily observable in the color of the clay. Lacking the dark hues of organic material, the soil instead adopts a rusty-red color from its high iron-oxide content, or yellow from aluminum. The soil also becomes as hard as rock when it dries. For this reason, it has historically been successfully used in ancient construction and roads.

In paragraph 2, why does the author mention "ancient construction and roads"?

(A) To provide an example of a material's uses
(B) To demonstrate the durability of a material
(C) To contrast the qualities of two materials
(D) To explain how a material was used in the past

Yet rainforests support some of the most abundant ecosystems on Earth—how do they do so with nutrient-depleted soil? Instead of depending on soil, rainforests recycle vital nutrients and minerals through their biomass. Unlike grasslands, which have most of their biomass underground, the biomass of a tropical rainforests exists above ground, in the trees and canopy. The forest's waste rarely even reaches the surface before it is completely broken down by efficient bacterial and fungal decomposers. Shallow plants below the canopy feed on the mineral contents of the decaying biomass and store it in their tissue. Then the minerals are transported and shared through a complex mycorrhizal network, wherein fungi assist roots in absorbing, transmitting, and dispersing nutrients. They also help the plants to absorb nutrients they are unable to, such as much-needed phosphorus. Fungi, bacteria, and other decomposers act as the facilitators in the continuous recycling of nutrients and minerals that sustains tropical rainforests.

According to paragraph 3, rainforest plants gather nutrients through

(A) the organic material stored below ground
(B) the assistance of bacteria within the soil
(C) the absorption of fungal organisms
(D) the constant reuse of the forest's biomass

Rainforests have also evolved to combat the loss of nutrients through leaching by developing closed nutrient systems. In such a system, minerals are transmitted between organisms without leaking much of them into the surrounding soil. By keeping minerals within the closed system, rainforests can promote plant growth and prevent the total loss of minerals. This is a clear adaptation that rainforests undergo in response to leaching. Nutrient systems in rainforests where the soil is rich are open and more akin to those found in grasslands. However, in areas with the poorest soils, the systems are closed and thus guarded against leaching.

All of the following benefits of a closed nutrient system are mentioned in paragraph 4 EXCEPT

(A) the prevention of mineral loss
(B) the enrichment of poor soil types
(C) the sharing of nutrients between organisms
(D) the support of healthy plant growth

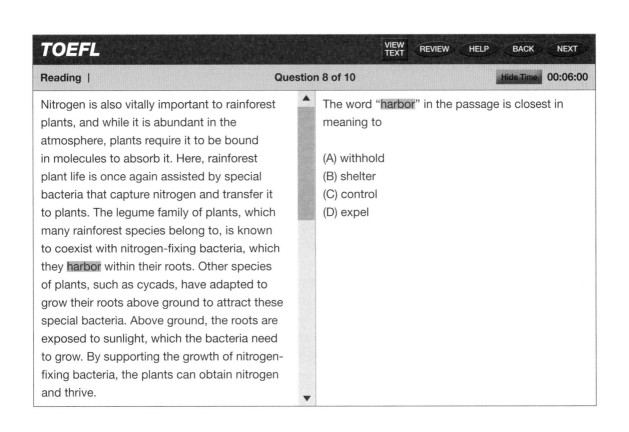

Nitrogen is also vitally important to rainforest plants, and while it is abundant in the atmosphere, plants require it to be bound in molecules to absorb it. Here, rainforest plant life is once again assisted by special bacteria that capture nitrogen and transfer it to plants. The legume family of plants, which many rainforest species belong to, is known to coexist with nitrogen-fixing bacteria, which they harbor within their roots. Other species of plants, such as cycads, have adapted to grow their roots above ground to attract these special bacteria. Above ground, the roots are exposed to sunlight, which the bacteria need to grow. By supporting the growth of nitrogen-fixing bacteria, the plants can obtain nitrogen and thrive.

Which of the sentences below best expresses the essential information in the highlighted sentence in the passage? Incorrect answer choices change the meaning in important ways or leave out essential information.

(A) Plants are required to combine nitrogen with other elements to maintain the health of the atmosphere.

(B) Even though there is plenty of nitrogen available in the air, plants cannot access it unless it is part of a compound.

(C) Rainforests are rich in nitrogen, and plants use it to create a vast array of unique chemical compounds.

(D) Nitrogen is only present in the atmosphere in molecules, and plants can only use it if it is isolated from other elements.

Nitrogen is also vitally important to rainforest plants, and while it is abundant in the atmosphere, plants require it to be bound in molecules to absorb it. Here, rainforest plant life is once again assisted by special bacteria that capture nitrogen and transfer it to plants. The legume family of plants, which many rainforest species belong to, is known to coexist with nitrogen-fixing bacteria, which they harbor within their roots. Other species of plants, such as cycads, have adapted to grow their roots above ground to attract these special bacteria. Above ground, the roots are exposed to sunlight, which the bacteria need to grow. By supporting the growth of nitrogen-fixing bacteria, the plants can obtain nitrogen and thrive.

The word "harbor" in the passage is closest in meaning to

(A) withhold
(B) shelter
(C) control
(D) expel

Yet rainforests support some of the most abundant ecosystems on Earth—how do they do so with nutrient-depleted soil? Instead of depending on soil, rainforests recycle vital nutrients and minerals through their biomass. Unlike grasslands, which have most of their biomass underground, the biomass of a tropical rainforests exists above ground, in the trees and canopy. ■ The forest's waste rarely even reaches the surface before it is completely broken down by efficient bacterial and fungal decomposers. Shallow plants below the canopy feed on the mineral contents of the decaying biomass and store it in their tissue. ■ Then the minerals are transported and shared through a complex mycorrhizal network, wherein fungi assist roots in absorbing, transmitting, and dispersing nutrients. ■ They also help the plants to absorb nutrients they are unable to, such as much-needed phosphorus. ■ Fungi, bacteria, and other decomposers act as the facilitators in the continuous recycling of nutrients and minerals that sustains tropical rainforests.

Look at the four squares [■] that indicate where the following sentence could be added to the passage.

Thus, the thick topsoil of a tropical rainforest is composed mostly of decaying material—fallen branches, leaves, and dead animals.

Where would the sentence best fit? Click on a square [■] to add the sentence to the passage.

Directions: An introductory sentence for a brief summary of the passage is provided below. Complete the summary by selecting the THREE answer choices that express the most important ideas in the passage. Some sentences do not belong in the summary because they express ideas that are not presented in the passage or are minor ideas in the passage. **This question is worth 2 points.**

Drag your answer choices to the space where they belong. To remove an answer choice, click on it. To review the passage, click on **VIEW TEXT.**

Rainforests have adapted to the low nutrient content of their soils in several ways.

-
-
-

Answer Choices

(A) A system of fungal connections collects and transfers nutrients from decayed biomass throughout the rainforest.

(B) Humus, organic material gathered in soil, makes clays more suitable for sustaining plant life.

(C) Plant species in rainforests have adapted to form beneficial relationships with bacteria capable of collecting specific nutrients.

(D) Rainforests have developed closed nutrient systems to prevent nutrient loss in the soil.

(E) Nutrients are continuously transferred from streams and rivers to rainforest soils through the water cycle.

(F) Most nutrients in rainforest soils are lost due to heavy rainfall through a process known as leaching.

The Influence of Glaciers

Glaciers are huge masses of slow-moving ice that accumulate in areas where more snow falls than melts. Glaciers are often referred to as "rivers of ice," since, though slow, they are in constant motion. There are two types of glaciers—alpine glaciers and ice sheets. Alpine glaciers form on mountainsides and carve down through valleys; ice sheets form on flat land with large central domes that spread outward. However, both types form in much the same manner. All snow falls as hexagonal crystals and, upon reaching the ground, becomes compacted into smaller, denser grains, due to the escape of air between the crystals. As more air is forced out, the grains of snow compact further and become denser. The grains melt and refreeze and eventually become firn, a crystallized intermediate stage of snow between flakes and ice. Firn appears light and powdery, like packed sugar, but is as hard as ice. With more time, pressure, and freezing cycles, even more air is pushed out until the firn granules lock together into larger crystals of pure, blue, glacial ice. The frozen aggregate officially becomes a glacier once it thickens to about 30 meters, upon which the total weight of the snow, ice, and firn will cause the crystals at the lowest levels to attain plasticity, or a liquid-like consistency. With this slick base, the glacier begins to flow outward or downward from its central mass.

A glacier is in constant development via an input-output system wherein snow adds to the glacier and meltwater subtracts. Precipitation and temperature are the two main climatic factors that influence this balance. Glaciers can only grow if enough snow falls to regain the mass loss through melting, evaporation, and, for coastal glaciers, calving—the breaking off of large chunks of a glacier into the sea or lakes. Warmer seasons and reduced snowfall can cause a glacier to shrink and retreat, which can have dramatic effects on local ecosystems, economies, and even global geology. Glaciers can be further classified by their temperature, with temperate glaciers existing at a constant melting point, resulting in a mix of ice and flowing water. They are faster-moving than polar glaciers, or those that are always below the freezing point.

Like oceans and rivers, glaciers are a part of the Earth's hydrologic cycle. Only the ocean contains more water than glaciers, which hold about two percent of the planet's water in their ice; however, this figure is misleading since glaciers contain over 80 percent of the fresh water on Earth. Antarctica itself holds a huge amount of the world's fresh water, so much so that, if it were to hypothetically melt, global sea levels would rise by a cataclysmic sixty meters. Islands would be submerged, and coastal nations would be greatly reduced. Conversely, if the planet were to experience another ice age, the sea level would drop as water froze. Sea levels were nearly 120 meters lower during the last ice age compared to what they are now.

Although glaciers move slowly—about 25 centimeters per day, on average—they are incredibly powerful and shape the land they flow across. Like bulldozers, they obliterate every land feature in their path, clearing entire forests and moving mountains. As they erode the ground below them, they push soil, rock, and clay across great distances. The rocks and dirt displaced by glaciers are called glacial erratics. They are easily identifiable as they rarely match the landscape upon which they have settled. Once glaciers retreat, perhaps hundreds of thousands of years later, they leave behind entirely new mountain ranges, deep lakes, and vast canyons. Glaciers shape the Earth, gradually but powerfully.

Throughout the far-reaching ages of the Earth, glaciers are rare. However, during our time, glaciers cover nearly 10 percent of the Earth's land surface. Antarctica and Greenland are covered by massive ice sheets, and alpine glaciers exist on every continent except for Australia. During the most recent ice age in the Pleistocene epoch, a third of the planet was concealed below thousands of meters of ice. As they grow and shift, glaciers will continue to influence the face of the Earth.

<남극대륙을 뒤덮고 있는 대륙 빙하>

Glaciers are huge masses of slow-moving ice that accumulate in areas where more snow falls than melts. Glaciers are often referred to as "rivers of ice," since, though slow, they are in constant motion. There are two types of glaciers—alpine glaciers and ice sheets. Alpine glaciers form on mountainsides and carve down through valleys; ice sheets form on flat land with large central domes that spread outward. However, both types form in much the same manner. All snow falls as hexagonal crystals and, upon reaching the ground, becomes compacted into smaller, denser grains, due to the escape of air between the crystals. As more air is forced out, the grains of snow compact further and become denser. The grains melt and refreeze and eventually become firn, a crystallized intermediate stage of snow between flakes and ice. Firn appears light and powdery, like packed sugar, but is as hard as ice. With more time, pressure, and freezing cycles, even more air is pushed out until the firn granules lock together into larger crystals of pure, blue, glacial ice. The frozen aggregate officially becomes a glacier once it thickens to about 30 meters, upon which the total weight of the snow, ice, and firn will cause the crystals at the lowest levels to attain plasticity, or a liquid-like consistency. With this slick base, the glacier begins to flow outward or downward from its central mass.

According to paragraph 1, which of the following is NOT a part of the glacial formation process?

(A) Snow crystals fall and become compacted into smaller grains.
(B) Ice thickens until the lowest levels become similar to fluid.
(C) Hexagonal crystals of snow interlock to become glacial ice.
(D) Air departs from between snow crystals, changing snow to firn.

Glaciers are huge masses of slow-moving ice that accumulate in areas where more snow falls than melts. Glaciers are often referred to as "rivers of ice," since, though slow, they are in constant motion. There are two types of glaciers—alpine glaciers and ice sheets. Alpine glaciers form on mountainsides and carve down through valleys; ice sheets form on flat land with large central domes that spread outward. However, both types form in much the same manner. All snow falls as hexagonal crystals and, upon reaching the ground, becomes compacted into smaller, denser grains, due to the escape of air between the crystals. As more air is forced out, the grains of snow compact further and become denser. The grains melt and refreeze and eventually become firn, a crystallized intermediate stage of snow between flakes and ice. Firn appears light and powdery, like packed sugar, but is as hard as ice. With more time, pressure, and freezing cycles, even more air is pushed out until the firn granules lock together into larger crystals of pure, blue, glacial ice. The frozen aggregate officially becomes a glacier once it thickens to about 30 meters, upon which the total weight of the snow, ice, and firn will cause the crystals at the lowest levels to attain plasticity, or a liquid-like consistency. With this slick base, the glacier begins to flow outward or downward from its central mass.

The word "attain" in the passage is closest in meaning to

(A) maintain
(B) achieve
(C) replace
(D) transform

A glacier is in constant development via an input-output system wherein snow adds to the glacier and meltwater subtracts. Precipitation and temperature are the two main climatic factors that influence this balance. Glaciers can only grow if enough snow falls to regain the mass loss through melting, evaporation, and, for coastal glaciers, calving—the breaking off of large chunks of a glacier into the sea or lakes. Warmer seasons and reduced snowfall can cause a glacier to shrink and retreat, which can have dramatic effects on local ecosystems, economies, and even global geology. Glaciers can be further classified by their temperature, with temperate glaciers existing at a constant melting point, resulting in a mix of ice and flowing water. They are faster-moving than polar glaciers, or those that are always below the freezing point.

Paragraph 2 suggests that enough snowfall influences a glacier by

(A) offsetting losses of ice due to melting, evaporation, and calving.
(B) making the ground near a glacier slick.
(C) adding extra weight that leads to calving.
(D) preventing the ice from reaching its melting point.

A glacier is in constant development via an input-output system wherein snow adds to the glacier and meltwater subtracts. Precipitation and temperature are the two main climatic factors that influence this balance. Glaciers can only grow if enough snow falls to regain the mass loss through melting, evaporation, and, for coastal glaciers, calving—the breaking off of large chunks of a glacier into the sea or lakes. Warmer seasons and reduced snowfall can cause a glacier to shrink and retreat, which can have dramatic effects on local ecosystems, economies, and even global geology. Glaciers can be further classified by their temperature, with temperate glaciers existing at a constant melting point, resulting in a mix of ice and flowing water. They are faster-moving than polar glaciers, or those that are always below the freezing point.

According to paragraph 2, which of the following is true about fast-moving glaciers?

(A) Polar glaciers do not have enough land to move across quickly.
(B) Fast-moving glaciers experience a higher frequency of calving.
(C) Warmer climates will have glaciers that move at quicker rates.
(D) Smaller glaciers move faster than larger ones.

Like oceans and rivers, glaciers are a part of the Earth's hydrologic cycle. Only the ocean contains more water than glaciers, which hold about two percent of the planet's water in their ice; however, this figure is misleading since glaciers contain over 80 percent of the fresh water on Earth. Antarctica itself holds a huge amount of the world's fresh water, so much so that, if it were to hypothetically melt, global sea levels would rise by a cataclysmic sixty meters. Islands would be submerged, and coastal nations would be greatly reduced. Conversely, if the planet were to experience another ice age, the sea level would drop as water froze. Sea levels were nearly 120 meters lower during the last ice age compared to what they are now.

Which of the sentences below best expresses the essential information in the highlighted sentence in the passage? Incorrect answer choices change the meaning in important ways or leave out essential information.

(A) Glaciers' holding only two percent of the Earth's water is deceiving since they hold a vast majority of the planet's fresh water.
(B) While 80 percent of the Earth's water is found in the ocean, two percent of it can be found in glaciers as fresh water.
(C) Oceans are home to the majority of Earth's water, and 80 percent of the water in glaciers can be used as a source of fresh water.
(D) Two percent of the ocean's water is held in glaciers, but 80 percent of it makes up Earth's fresh water.

Like oceans and rivers, glaciers are a part of the Earth's hydrologic cycle. Only the ocean contains more water than glaciers, which hold about two percent of the planet's water in their ice; however, this figure is misleading since glaciers contain over 80 percent of the fresh water on Earth. Antarctica itself holds a huge amount of the world's fresh water, so much so that, if it were to hypothetically melt, global sea levels would rise by a cataclysmic sixty meters. Islands would be submerged, and coastal nations would be greatly reduced. Conversely, if the planet were to experience another ice age, the sea level would drop as water froze. Sea levels were nearly 120 meters lower during the last ice age compared to what they are now.

In paragraph 3, why does the author mention what would happen if Antarctica's glaciers melted?

(A) To illustrate how much water is contained within glaciers
(B) To emphasize how long the glaciers have existed
(C) To contrast the effects of an ice age with those of global warming
(D) To suggest that more water is in glaciers than in the sea

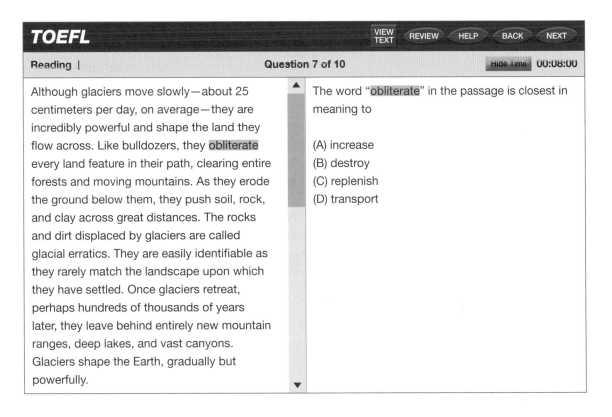

Although glaciers move slowly—about 25 centimeters per day, on average—they are incredibly powerful and shape the land they flow across. Like bulldozers, they obliterate every land feature in their path, clearing entire forests and moving mountains. As they erode the ground below them, they push soil, rock, and clay across great distances. The rocks and dirt displaced by glaciers are called glacial erratics. They are easily identifiable as they rarely match the landscape upon which they have settled. Once glaciers retreat, perhaps hundreds of thousands of years later, they leave behind entirely new mountain ranges, deep lakes, and vast canyons. Glaciers shape the Earth, gradually but powerfully.

The word "obliterate" in the passage is closest in meaning to

(A) increase
(B) destroy
(C) replenish
(D) transport

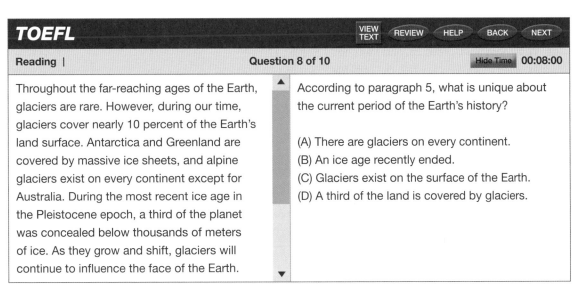

Throughout the far-reaching ages of the Earth, glaciers are rare. However, during our time, glaciers cover nearly 10 percent of the Earth's land surface. Antarctica and Greenland are covered by massive ice sheets, and alpine glaciers exist on every continent except for Australia. During the most recent ice age in the Pleistocene epoch, a third of the planet was concealed below thousands of meters of ice. As they grow and shift, glaciers will continue to influence the face of the Earth.

According to paragraph 5, what is unique about the current period of the Earth's history?

(A) There are glaciers on every continent.
(B) An ice age recently ended.
(C) Glaciers exist on the surface of the Earth.
(D) A third of the land is covered by glaciers.

Glaciers are huge masses of slow-moving ice that accumulate in areas where more snow falls than melts. Glaciers are often referred to as "rivers of ice," since, though slow, they are in constant motion. There are two types of glaciers—alpine glaciers and ice sheets. Alpine glaciers form on mountainsides and carve down through valleys; ice sheets form on flat land with large central domes that spread outward. ▮ However, both types form in much the same manner. ▮ All snow falls as hexagonal crystals and, upon reaching the ground, becomes compacted into smaller, denser grains, due to the escape of air between the crystals. ▮ As more air is forced out, the grains of snow compact further and become denser. ▮ The grains melt and refreeze and eventually become firn, a crystallized intermediate stage of snow between flakes and ice. Firn appears light and powdery, like packed sugar, but is as hard as ice. With more time, pressure, and freezing cycles, even more air is pushed out until the firn granules lock together into larger crystals of pure, blue, glacial ice. The frozen aggregate officially becomes a glacier once it thickens to about 30 meters, upon which the total weight of the snow, ice, and firn will cause the crystals at the lowest levels to attain plasticity, or a liquid-like consistency. With this slick base, the glacier begins to flow outward or downward from its central mass.

Look at the four squares [▮] that indicate where the following sentence could be added to the passage.

The process hinges on the transformation of snow into glacial ice.

Where would the sentence best fit? Click on a square [▮] to add the sentence to the passage.

Directions: An introductory sentence for a brief summary of the passage is provided below. Complete the summary by selecting the THREE answer choices that express the most important ideas in the passage. Some sentences do not belong in the summary because they express ideas that are not presented in the passage or are minor ideas in the passage. **This question is worth 2 points.**

Drag your answer choices to the space where they belong. To remove an answer choice, click on it. To review the passage, click on **VIEW TEXT.**

Glaciers influence the planet in several ways.

-
-
-

Answer Choices

(A) They raise sea levels when they melt.

(B) They move quicker the colder they become.

(C) They reduce the temperatures of a climate.

(D) They hold a vast amount of fresh water.

(E) They form when snow evaporates and becomes firn.

(F) They shape the landscape as they flow and retreat.

■ Passage 3

Understanding Earth's Interior

Geologists use earthquakes and the planet-spanning seismic waves they create to analyze the depths of the Earth. There are several types of seismic waves, but primary waves (P-waves) and secondary waves (S-waves) are the most elucidating toward these studies. Both types travel deep within the Earth, providing vital data to scientists grounded on the surface. Sudden changes in the trajectory and velocity of the waves at different depths have revealed the division of the Earth's interior into the central core, the thick mantle on top of it, and the encompassing crust. Marked transitions in the characteristics of seismic waves are called discontinuities.

The Gutenberg discontinuity, located at a depth of about 2,900 kilometers, is about halfway to the center of the Earth and indicates the outer limit of the Earth's core. Both S-waves and P-waves behave strangely at this limit: S-waves cannot continue, while P-waves slow and bend. The reason for these odd behaviors is due to the outer core being liquid. Since S-waves are unable to travel through fluids, the outer layer absorbs them. This is why S-waves originating from one side of the planet do not appear at seismograph stations on the opposite side. In addition, while P-waves can pass through fluid, they are rapidly slowed and refracted in a liquid medium. In this way, P-waves traveling through the Earth's molten outer core have their velocity reduced and are redirected downward. Therefore, the behavior of both types of waves point to the core having a liquid outer shell.

The core is composed of concentric shells with an outer liquid layer and an inner solid core. The radius of the entire core is 3,500 kilometers, while the inner, solid core's radius is 1,220 kilometers. The composition of the inner and outer core is the same, but the extreme pressure being exerted on the inner core forces it to only exist in a solid state. Subsequent alterations to the velocity and trajectory of P-waves reveal that the core's consistency changes between the outer and inner layers, and additional evidence lends further support to its solidity.

Data regarding the Earth's density suggest an inner solid core. The overall density of Earth is 5.5 grams per cubic centimeter; however, the average density of rocks on the surface and in the crust is less than 3.0 grams per cubic centimeter. The disparity between the two numbers indicates that the material deeper in the planet must have a higher density that would raise the average. Considering the immense pressure at the core, iron mixed with nickel would be dense enough to make up the difference in density. It is probable, however, that some lighter elements are also mixed in, as laboratory experiments suggest that an iron-nickel alloy under extreme pressure would be too dense. Silicon, sulfur, carbon, or oxygen could all be likely candidates that help lighten the heavy core.

Looking outwards can also help scientists understand what is inside the Earth. The theory that the core comprises iron and nickel is supported by the study of meteorites. Most meteorites that have been recovered are made up of an iron-nickel alloy. It is suspected that the meteorites that inhabit the solar system are the remaining debris from the core of a shattered planet. If the core of this ancient planet was composed of iron and nickel, then the core of the Earth could be similar.

A basic understanding of magnets also lends support to the idea of Earth's solid metallic core. Earth's magnetic field is obvious to anyone who has ever used a compass, as the planet itself acts like a massive bar magnet with a north and south pole. The presence and flow of a magnetic field require strong electrical conductors, and since the silicate rocks in the crust and mantle are not very conductive, they could not support a magnetic field on their own. However, iron and nickel are highly conductive. The circulation of extreme heat in the core and the force generated by the Earth's rotation could create the necessary flow of electrons around the inner core that would support the magnetic field. If there were no metallic core, the magnetic field could not exist.

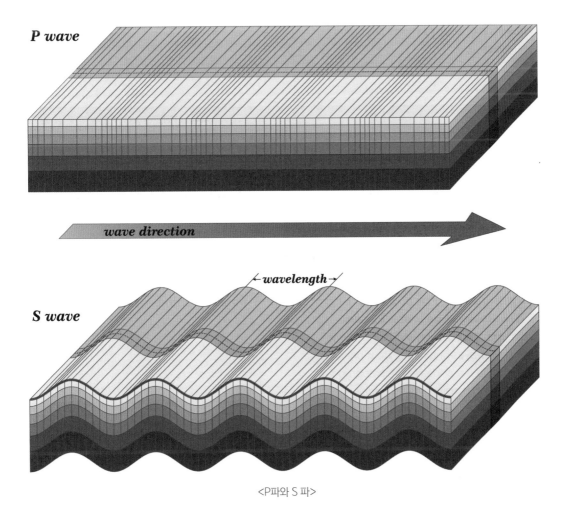

<P파와 S 파>

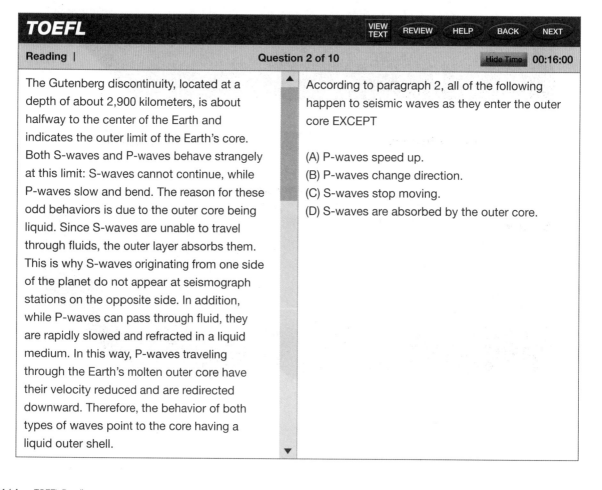

Geologists use earthquakes and the planet-spanning seismic waves they create to analyze the depths of the Earth. There are several types of seismic waves, but primary waves (P-waves) and secondary waves (S-waves) are the most elucidating toward these studies. Both types travel deep within the Earth, providing vital data to scientists grounded on the surface. Sudden changes in the trajectory and velocity of the waves at different depths have revealed the division of the Earth's interior into the central core, the thick mantle on top of it, and the encompassing crust. Marked transitions in the characteristics of seismic waves are called discontinuities.

According to paragraph 1, which of the following findings supports the idea that the Earth's interior is divided into three sections?

(A) Earth's mantle is too weak to support the crust.
(B) Discontinuities appear at specific depths inside the Earth.
(C) All seismic waves register on the opposite side of the Earth.
(D) P-waves become S-waves as they pass through the layers.

The Gutenberg discontinuity, located at a depth of about 2,900 kilometers, is about halfway to the center of the Earth and indicates the outer limit of the Earth's core. Both S-waves and P-waves behave strangely at this limit: S-waves cannot continue, while P-waves slow and bend. The reason for these odd behaviors is due to the outer core being liquid. Since S-waves are unable to travel through fluids, the outer layer absorbs them. This is why S-waves originating from one side of the planet do not appear at seismograph stations on the opposite side. In addition, while P-waves can pass through fluid, they are rapidly slowed and refracted in a liquid medium. In this way, P-waves traveling through the Earth's molten outer core have their velocity reduced and are redirected downward. Therefore, the behavior of both types of waves point to the core having a liquid outer shell.

According to paragraph 2, all of the following happen to seismic waves as they enter the outer core EXCEPT

(A) P-waves speed up.
(B) P-waves change direction.
(C) S-waves stop moving.
(D) S-waves are absorbed by the outer core.

Data regarding the Earth's density suggest an inner solid core. The overall density of Earth is 5.5 grams per cubic centimeter; however, the average density of rocks on the surface and in the crust is less than 3.0 grams per cubic centimeter. The disparity between the two numbers indicates that the material deeper in the planet must have a higher density that would raise the average. Considering the immense pressure at the core, iron mixed with nickel would be dense enough to make up the difference in density. It is probable, however, that some lighter elements are also mixed in, as laboratory experiments suggest that an iron-nickel alloy under extreme pressure would be too dense. Silicon, sulfur, carbon, or oxygen could all be likely candidates that help lighten the heavy core.

The word "disparity" in the passage is closest in meaning to

(A) accumulation
(B) confusion
(C) error
(D) difference

Data regarding the Earth's density suggest an inner solid core. The overall density of Earth is 5.5 grams per cubic centimeter; however, the average density of rocks on the surface and in the crust is less than 3.0 grams per cubic centimeter. The disparity between the two numbers indicates that the material deeper in the planet must have a higher density that would raise the average. Considering the immense pressure at the core, iron mixed with nickel would be dense enough to make up the difference in density. It is probable, however, that some lighter elements are also mixed in, as laboratory experiments suggest that an iron-nickel alloy under extreme pressure would be too dense. Silicon, sulfur, carbon, or oxygen could all be likely candidates that help lighten the heavy core.

According to paragraph 4, why does the Earth's core likely contain elements such as silicon, sulfur, carbon, or oxygen?

(A) Other elements are needed in order for iron and nickel to combine.
(B) Samples from the core contain traces of silicon, sulfur, carbon, and oxygen.
(C) Rocks on the surface also contain dense mixes of various elements.
(D) Iron and nickel alone would be too dense under so much pressure.

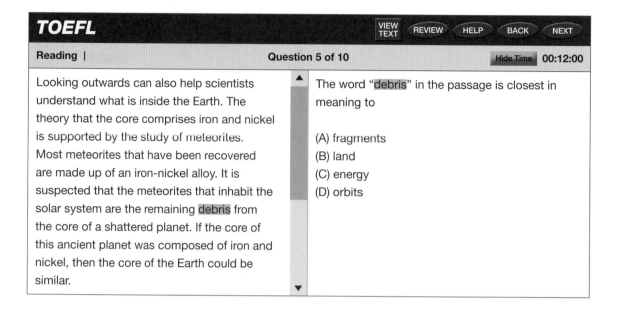

Looking outwards can also help scientists understand what is inside the Earth. The theory that the core comprises iron and nickel is supported by the study of meteorites. Most meteorites that have been recovered are made up of an iron-nickel alloy. It is suspected that the meteorites that inhabit the solar system are the remaining debris from the core of a shattered planet. If the core of this ancient planet was composed of iron and nickel, then the core of the Earth could be similar.

The word "debris" in the passage is closest in meaning to

(A) fragments
(B) land
(C) energy
(D) orbits

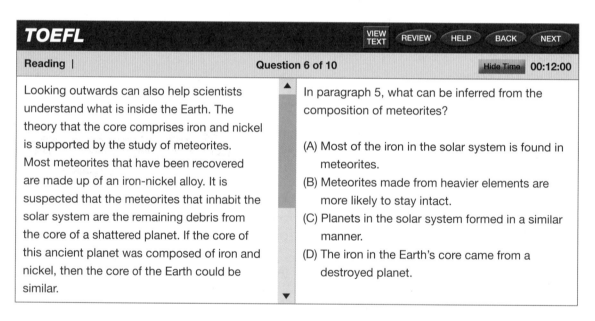

Looking outwards can also help scientists understand what is inside the Earth. The theory that the core comprises iron and nickel is supported by the study of meteorites. Most meteorites that have been recovered are made up of an iron-nickel alloy. It is suspected that the meteorites that inhabit the solar system are the remaining debris from the core of a shattered planet. If the core of this ancient planet was composed of iron and nickel, then the core of the Earth could be similar.

In paragraph 5, what can be inferred from the composition of meteorites?

(A) Most of the iron in the solar system is found in meteorites.
(B) Meteorites made from heavier elements are more likely to stay intact.
(C) Planets in the solar system formed in a similar manner.
(D) The iron in the Earth's core came from a destroyed planet.

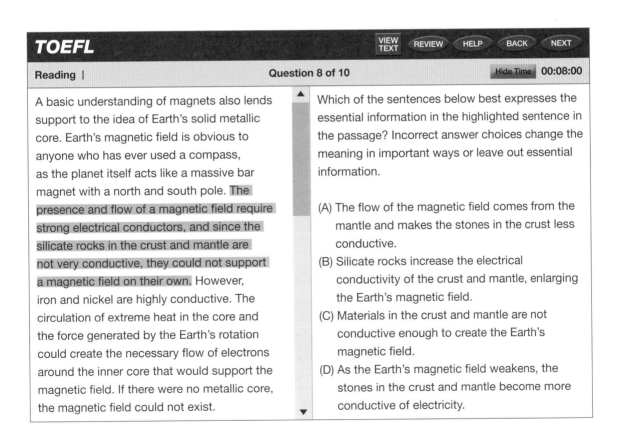

A basic understanding of magnets also lends support to the idea of Earth's solid metallic core. Earth's magnetic field is obvious to anyone who has ever used a compass, as the planet itself acts like a massive bar magnet with a north and south pole. The presence and flow of a magnetic field require strong electrical conductors, and since the silicate rocks in the crust and mantle are not very conductive, they could not support a magnetic field on their own. However, iron and nickel are highly conductive. The circulation of extreme heat in the core and the force generated by the Earth's rotation could create the necessary flow of electrons around the inner core that would support the magnetic field. If there were no metallic core, the magnetic field could not exist.

In paragraph 6, the author discusses the Earth's magnetic field to

(A) present a mystery concerning Earth's core that remains unsolved.
(B) explain why so many iron-based meteorites fall toward Earth.
(C) provide another reason why the Earth must have an iron-nickel core.
(D) highlight an opposing theory about the composition of the Earth's core.

A basic understanding of magnets also lends support to the idea of Earth's solid metallic core. Earth's magnetic field is obvious to anyone who has ever used a compass, as the planet itself acts like a massive bar magnet with a north and south pole. The presence and flow of a magnetic field require strong electrical conductors, and since the silicate rocks in the crust and mantle are not very conductive, they could not support a magnetic field on their own. However, iron and nickel are highly conductive. The circulation of extreme heat in the core and the force generated by the Earth's rotation could create the necessary flow of electrons around the inner core that would support the magnetic field. If there were no metallic core, the magnetic field could not exist.

Which of the sentences below best expresses the essential information in the highlighted sentence in the passage? Incorrect answer choices change the meaning in important ways or leave out essential information.

(A) The flow of the magnetic field comes from the mantle and makes the stones in the crust less conductive.
(B) Silicate rocks increase the electrical conductivity of the crust and mantle, enlarging the Earth's magnetic field.
(C) Materials in the crust and mantle are not conductive enough to create the Earth's magnetic field.
(D) As the Earth's magnetic field weakens, the stones in the crust and mantle become more conductive of electricity.

The core is composed of concentric shells with an outer liquid layer and an inner solid core. ■ The radius of the entire core is 3,500 kilometers, while the inner, solid core's radius is 1,220 kilometers. ■ The composition of the inner and outer core is the same, but the extreme pressure being exerted on the inner core forces it to only exist in a solid state. ■ Subsequent alterations to the velocity and trajectory of P-waves reveal that the core's consistency changes between the outer and inner layers, and additional evidence lends further support to its solidity. ■

Look at the four squares [■] that indicate where the following sentence could be added to the passage.

It is slightly smaller than the Moon with its radius of 1,700 kilometers.

Where would the sentence best fit? Click on a square [■] to add the sentence to the passage.

Directions: An introductory sentence for a brief summary of the passage is provided below. Complete the summary by selecting the THREE answer choices that express the most important ideas in the passage. Some sentences do not belong in the summary because they express ideas that are not presented in the passage or are minor ideas in the passage. **This question is worth 2 points.**

Drag your answer choices to the space where they belong. To remove an answer choice, click on it. To review the passage, click on **VIEW TEXT.**

A variety of techniques have been used to understand the interior of the Earth.

-
-
-

Answer Choices

(A) Abrupt changes in the transmission of seismic waves within the planet at different depths reveal that the Earth's interior is divided into three main layers.

(B) The outer liquid core is composed of iron, while the solid inner core is nickel combined with lighter elements, such as sulfur and oxygen.

(C) Seismic waves that travel through the Earth's interior show that the Earth's core is mainly composed of metals.

(D) The Earth's overall density and the composition of meteorites from around the solar system suggest that the Earth's inner core is metallic and solid.

(E) The intensity of the pressure in the Earth's inner core means that it exists in a liquid state.

(F) The existence of the Earth's magnetic field requires the Earth to have a metallic inner core that can conduct electricity.

Chapter

05

Astronomy

Passage 1   **Star Death**

Passage 2   **Planets in Our Solar System**

Passage 3   **Structure and Composition of Comets**

Astronomy (천문학)

우주를 구성하는 천체에서 일어나는 각종 자연 현상을 화학, 지질학 및 물리학 등의 과학적 지식을 바탕으로 연구하는 학문이다.

[Astronomy 기출 토픽]

- Star Death
  별의 죽음

- Planets in Our Solar System
  우리 태양계에 속한 행성들

- The Surface of Mars
  화성의 표면

- Structure and Composition of Comets
  혜성의 구조 및 구성 요소

- Surface Fluids on Venus and Earth
  금성과 지구의 표면 유체

- Age of the Universe
  우주의 나이

- The Two Moons of Mars
  화성의 두 달

- The Climate of Venus
  금성의 기후

- Callisto and Ganymede
  칼리스토와 가니메데

- The Allende Meteorite
  알렌데 운석

[Astronomy 빈출 어휘]

asteroid	소행성	mass	질량
astronomer	천문학자	Mercury	수성
atmosphere	대기	meteorite	운석
bulge	볼록한 부분	molecule	분자
by-product	부산물	momentum	운동량, 기세, 힘
celestial	천체의, 하늘의	Neptune	해왕성
collision	충돌	neutron	중성자
comet	혜성	nuclei	핵(nucleus의 복수)
condense	응축되다	orbit	궤도(를 돌다)
contract	수축하다	phenomenon	현상
crust	(딱딱한) 표면	planet	행성
debris	잔해, 쓰레기	proton	양성자
diameter	지름	proximity	가까움, 근접
dim	밝기가 낮은	radiation	방사선, (열 등의) 복사
emit	~을 방출하다	Saturn	토성
evaporate	증발하다	shrinking	수축
expel	~을 배출하다	solar	태양의
friction	마찰	sphere	구, 구체
galaxy	은하	star	별, 항성
gravitational	중력의	terrestrial	지구의, 육생의
halo	광륜, 후광	tilt	기울어짐, 경사
Jupiter	목성	universe	우주, 세계
luminosity	광도, 광채	Uranus	천왕성
magnetic	자성의	velocity	속도
Mars	화성	Venus	금성

Star Death

Until around the mid-1900s, there was a consensus among scientists that shrinking is a necessary process for generating energy in stars. They believed that, as stars contract, their heat increases, and they give off a greater amount of light. However, this could not be the primary mechanism by which stars shine. If it were, they would struggle to burn brightly for even a million years, let alone the billions of years we know that they typically shine for. What we do now know is that nuclear fusion provides stars with their power. Energy is released as a by-product each time fusion takes place within a star, and this energy that is expelled into space is what we refer to as starlight. The process of fusion starts when two hydrogen nuclei collide at high speed, giving rise to a particle called a deuteron, which is a combination of a neutron and a proton. Deuterons readily combine with extra protons to form helium molecules, which can fuse together into heavier elements such as carbon. In the case of most stars, significant quantities of heavy elements are accumulated through the continual fusing of molecules.

It is important to point out the differences between two different stellar groups: the relatively young Population I and the much older Population II. It is also possible to distinguish between these groups based on their locations. Take for example our galaxy, the Milky Way, which is shaped like a central bulge surrounded by a flat disk. Population I stars are typically located within the galactic disk, whereas Population II stars are generally found in the galaxy's central bulge and its surrounding halo.

Most Population II stars have existed since the early stages of the universe and were formed when the cosmos was largely comprised of hydrogen and helium gases. At first, such stars contained virtually no heavy elements. Once their fusible material has run out, they cease to shine and then die, spreading material out into space in the form of dust. A lot of this dust is subsequently combined with newly formed Population I stars. Population I stars are composed primarily of hydrogen and helium gases, but they also include heavy elements, which make up roughly 1 or 2 percent of their total mass. These heavier elements are formed by the fusing of lighter elements that the stars have accumulated. It follows, then, that Population I stars contain materials that were at some point released by stars from previous generations. Perhaps the best-known example of a Population I star is our Sun.

So, what will happen when the Sun eventually expires? Several billion years from now, the Sun will burn even brighter than it does now. More and more of its nuclear fuel will be exhausted, until barely any of its original hydrogen remains. Eventually, there will no longer be any nuclear reactions or activity in the Sun's center.

The Sun will effectively separate into two distinct regions, an inner zone and an outer zone, once it commences its "post-nuclear" phase. While the inner zone will be completely devoid of hydrogen fuel, the outer zone will retain a small amount. Very rapid changes will start to occur, and these changes will effectively rip the Sun apart. Without any nuclear reactions taking place within, the inner zone will begin to collapse under its own weight, contracting into a hot, dense, and dim core. The outer zone, which will resemble a ball of gas that is held together loosely, will undergo an extremely different type of transformation. When the inner zone contracts, it will trigger a shock wave that will send ripples through the expiring star, forcing the material within the stellar exterior farther and farther outward. This in turn causes the outer envelope to rapidly expand until it is hundreds of times larger than its original size. As it grows, its temperature will drop by thousands of degrees. In the end, the Sun will become a red giant star. It will be cool and bright, and so large that it will take up the entire space where Earth used to orbit. And it will shine so brilliantly that it would theoretically be possible to see it with the naked eye from thousands of light-years away. This is the state it will remain in for millions of years, during which time the material of its outer envelope will gradually be expelled into space. Eventually, there will be no remnants of the Sun's gaseous exterior whatsoever, and all that will be left will be a hot, white core. The Sun will then be classified as a white dwarf star, until its core shrinks, the last of its energy is emitted, and it finally dies.

<태양계가 속한 우리 은하>

Until around the mid-1900s, there was a consensus among scientists that shrinking is a necessary process for generating energy in stars. They believed that, as stars contract, their heat increases and they give off a greater amount of light. However, this could not be the primary mechanism by which stars shine. If it were, they would struggle to burn brightly for even a million years, let alone the billions of years we know that they typically shine for. What we do now know is that nuclear fusion provides stars with their power. Energy is released as a by-product each time fusion takes place within a star, and this energy that is expelled into space is what we refer to as starlight. The process of fusion starts when two hydrogen nuclei collide at high speed, giving rise to a particle called a deuteron, which is a combination of a neutron and a proton. Deuterons readily combine with extra protons to form helium molecules, which can fuse together into heavier elements such as carbon. In the case of most stars, significant quantities of heavy elements are accumulated through the continual fusing of molecules.

The word "form" in the passage is closest in meaning to

(A) guide
(B) repel
(C) separate
(D) create

Until around the mid-1900s, there was a consensus among scientists that shrinking is a necessary process for generating energy in stars. They believed that, as stars contract, their heat increases and they give off a greater amount of light. However, this could not be the primary mechanism by which stars shine. If it were, they would struggle to burn brightly for even a million years, let alone the billions of years we know that they typically shine for. What we do now know is that nuclear fusion provides stars with their power. Energy is released as a by-product each time fusion takes place within a star, and this energy that is expelled into space is what we refer to as starlight. The process of fusion starts when two hydrogen nuclei collide at high speed, giving rise to a particle called a deuteron, which is a combination of a neutron and a proton. Deuterons readily combine with extra protons to form helium molecules, which can fuse together into heavier elements such as carbon. In the case of most stars, significant quantities of heavy elements are accumulated through the continual fusing of molecules.

According to paragraph 1, the energy that comes from stars and that is seen as light is the result of

(A) the fusing together of various particles
(B) heavy elements discarding their atoms
(C) helium atoms merging with protons
(D) hydrogen molecules splitting apart

Until around the mid-1900s, there was a consensus among scientists that shrinking is a necessary process for generating energy in stars. They believed that, as stars contract, their heat increases and they give off a greater amount of light. However, this could not be the primary mechanism by which stars shine. If it were, they would struggle to burn brightly for even a million years, let alone the billions of years we know that they typically shine for. What we do now know is that nuclear fusion provides stars with their power. Energy is released as a by-product each time fusion takes place within a star, and this energy that is expelled into space is what we refer to as starlight. The process of fusion starts when two hydrogen nuclei collide at high speed, giving rise to a particle called a deuteron, which is a combination of a neutron and a proton. Deuterons readily combine with extra protons to form helium molecules, which can fuse together into heavier elements such as carbon. In the case of most stars, significant quantities of heavy elements are accumulated through the continual fusing of molecules.

In paragraph 1, why does the author point out that stars are billions of years old?

(A) To explain that starlight is produced by a continual process rather than a one-time event
(B) To suggest that stars contract at a much slower rate than was previously estimated
(C) To illustrate that fusion in a star decelerates as increasing amounts of heavy elements accumulate
(D) To argue that the primary mechanism by which stars generate energy cannot be their shrinking

It is important to point out the differences between two different stellar groups: the relatively young Population I and the much older Population II. It is also possible to distinguish between these groups based on their locations. Take for example our galaxy, the Milky Way, which is shaped like a central bulge surrounded by a flat disk. Population I stars are typically located within the galactic disk, whereas Population II stars are generally found in the galaxy's central bulge and its surrounding halo.

Most Population II stars have existed since the early stages of the universe and were formed when the cosmos was largely comprised of hydrogen and helium gases. At first, such stars contained virtually no heavy elements. Once their fusible material has run out, they cease to shine and then die, spreading material out into space in the form of dust. A lot of this dust is subsequently combined with newly formed Population I stars. Population I stars are composed primarily of hydrogen and helium gases, but they also include heavy elements, which make up roughly 1 or 2 percent of their total mass. These heavier elements are formed by the fusing of lighter elements that the stars have accumulated. It follows, then, that Population I stars contain materials that were at some point released by stars from previous generations. Perhaps the best known example of a Population I star is our Sun.

According to paragraphs 2 and 3, all of the following are true of Population I stars EXCEPT

(A) They are partly comprised of materials that were once components of Population II stars.
(B) Their lifespan is generally much shorter than that of Population II stars.
(C) They contain elements that were created through the fusion of lighter elements.
(D) They are mostly composed of hydrogen and helium gases.

So, what will happen when the Sun eventually expires? Several billion years from now, the Sun will burn even brighter than it does now. More and more of its nuclear fuel will be exhausted, until barely any of its original hydrogen remains. Eventually, there will no longer be any nuclear reactions or activity in the Sun's center.

The word "exhausted" in the passage is closest in meaning to

(A) depleted

(B) allocated

(C) retracted

(D) distributed

The Sun will effectively separate into two distinct regions, an inner zone and an outer zone, once it commences its "post-nuclear" phase. While the inner zone will be completely devoid of hydrogen fuel, the outer zone will retain a small amount. Very rapid changes will start to occur, and these changes will effectively rip the Sun apart. Without any nuclear reactions taking place within, the inner zone will begin to collapse under its own weight, contracting into a hot, dense, and dim core. The outer zone, which will resemble a ball of gas that is held together loosely, will undergo an extremely different type of transformation. When the inner zone contracts, it will trigger a shock wave that will send ripples through the expiring star, forcing the material within the stellar exterior farther and farther outward. This in turn causes the outer envelope to rapidly expand until it is hundreds of times larger than its original size. As it grows, its temperature will drop by thousands of degrees. In the end, the Sun will become a red giant star. It will be cool and bright, and so large that it will take up the entire space where Earth used to orbit. And it will shine so brilliantly that it would theoretically be possible to see it with the naked eye from thousands of light-years away. This is the state it will remain in for millions of years, during which time the material of its outer envelope will gradually be expelled into space. Eventually, there will be no remnants of the Sun's gaseous exterior whatsoever, and all that will be left will be a hot, white core. The Sun will then be classified as a white dwarf star, until its core shrinks, the last of its energy is emitted, and it finally dies.

According to paragraph 5, when the Sun enters its "post-nuclear" phase, the outer zone will differ from the inner zone in that the outer zone will

(A) change size by a far less significant extent
(B) still contain some trace amounts of hydrogen
(C) cease to generate any energy whatsoever
(D) become hotter and denser over time

The Sun will effectively separate into two distinct regions, an inner zone and an outer zone, once it commences its "post-nuclear" phase. While the inner zone will be completely devoid of hydrogen fuel, the outer zone will retain a small amount. Very rapid changes will start to occur, and these changes will effectively rip the Sun apart. Without any nuclear reactions taking place within, the inner zone will begin to collapse under its own weight, contracting into a hot, dense, and dim core. The outer zone, which will resemble a ball of gas that is held together loosely, will undergo an extremely different type of transformation. When the inner zone contracts, it will trigger a shock wave that will send ripples through the expiring star, forcing the material within the stellar exterior farther and farther outward. This in turn causes the outer envelope to rapidly expand until it is hundreds of times larger than its original size. As it grows, its temperature will drop by thousands of degrees. In the end, the Sun will become a red giant star. It will be cool and bright, and so large that it will take up the entire space where Earth used to orbit. And it will shine so brilliantly that it would theoretically be possible to see it with the naked eye from thousands of light-years away. This is the state it will remain in for millions of years, during which time the material of its outer envelope will gradually be expelled into space. Eventually, there will be no remnants of the Sun's gaseous exterior whatsoever, and all that will be left will be a hot, white core. The Sun will then be classified as a white dwarf star, until its core shrinks, the last of its energy is emitted, and it finally dies.

According to paragraph 5, which of the following will be true about the inner core of the dying Sun?

(A) It will shrink as a result of the increasing weight of the outer envelope.

(B) It will absorb vast amounts of material from the stellar exterior.

(C) It will continue to expand until it is hundreds of times its original size.

(D) It will contract and cause an energy wave to pass through the rest of the star.

The Sun will effectively separate into two distinct regions, an inner zone and an outer zone, once it commences its "post-nuclear" phase. While the inner zone will be completely devoid of hydrogen fuel, the outer zone will retain a small amount. Very rapid changes will start to occur, and these changes will effectively rip the Sun apart. Without any nuclear reactions taking place within, the inner zone will begin to collapse under its own weight, contracting into a hot, dense, and dim core. The outer zone, which will resemble a ball of gas that is held together loosely, will undergo an extremely different type of transformation. When the inner zone contracts, it will trigger a shock wave that will send ripples through the expiring star, forcing the material within the stellar exterior farther and farther outward. This in turn causes the outer envelope to rapidly expand until it is hundreds of times larger than its original size. As it grows, its temperature will drop by thousands of degrees. In the end, the Sun will become a red giant star. It will be cool and bright, and so large that it will take up the entire space where Earth used to orbit. And it will shine so brilliantly that it would theoretically be possible to see it with the naked eye from thousands of light-years away. This is the state it will remain in for millions of years, during which time the material of its outer envelope will gradually be expelled into space. Eventually, there will be no remnants of the Sun's gaseous exterior whatsoever, and all that will be left will be a hot, white core. The Sun will then be classified as a white dwarf star, until its core shrinks, the last of its energy is emitted, and it finally dies.

Paragraph 5 supports which of the following statements about the death of the Sun?

(A) The Sun's outer envelope will expand rapidly as a result of falling temperatures in the outer zone.
(B) While the outer region of the Sun expands, all its material will be released into space.
(C) Nuclear fusion will continue in the remaining core for a limited period after the Sun releases the material of its outer envelope into space.
(D) The Sun will stay in the red giant stage for millions of years before it becomes a white dwarf star.

Until around the mid-1900s, there was a consensus among scientists that shrinking is a necessary process for generating energy in stars. ■ They believed that, as stars contract, their heat increases and they give off a greater amount of light. ■ However, this could not be the primary mechanism by which stars shine. ■ If it were, they would struggle to burn brightly for even a million years, let alone the billions of years we know that they typically shine for. ■ What we do now know is that nuclear fusion provides stars with their power. Energy is released as a by-product each time fusion takes place within a star, and this energy that is expelled into space is what we refer to as starlight. The process of fusion starts when two hydrogen nuclei collide at high speed, giving rise to a particle called a deuteron, which is a combination of a neutron and a proton. Deuterons readily combine with extra protons to form helium molecules, which can fuse together into heavier elements such as carbon. In the case of most stars, significant quantities of heavy elements are accumulated through the continual fusing of molecules.

Look at the four squares [■] that indicate where the following sentence could be added to the passage.

Clearly, it was necessary to identify a more plausible mechanism to explain how stars generate energy.

Where would the sentence best fit? Click on a square [■] to add the sentence to the passage.

Directions: An introductory sentence for a brief summary of the passage is provided below. Complete the summary by selecting the THREE answer choices that express the most important ideas in the passage. Some sentences do not belong in the summary because they express ideas that are not presented in the passage or are minor ideas in the passage. **This question is worth 2 points.**

Drag your answer choices to the space where they belong. To remove an answer choice, click on it. To review the passage, click on **VIEW TEXT.**

While scientists once believed that stars generate energy by contracting, they now know that it occurs as a by-product of nuclear fusion.

-
-
-

Answer Choices

(A) The outer envelope of the Sun and other similar stars release their energy into space, and the inner cores will become white dwarfs before they emit the last of their last energy.

(B) Formed from hydrogen and helium gases, Population II stars are the oldest stars and they shine until they exhaust their fusible material.

(C) The Sun and other similar stars will separate into inner cores and outer envelopes prior to the cessation of all nuclear reactions in the cores.

(D) The Sun is a good example of a Population I star because it creates its energy through nuclear fusion rather than through contraction.

(E) Population I stars such as the Sun are fairly young stars that are mostly composed of hydrogen and helium gases, but also contain heavier elements.

(F) In the Milky Way, Population II stars are found in the galactic disk while Population I stars are found in and around the central bulge.

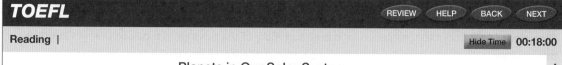

Planets in Our Solar System

The Sun is the central body of a massive rotating solar system comprising nine planets, their various moons and satellites, and countless smaller objects such as meteoroids, comets, and asteroids. Approximately 99.85 percent of our solar system's total mass is contained within the Sun, while the remaining 0.15 percent is collectively made up of the planets. In order of their distance from the Sun, the planets are arranged as follows: Mercury, Venus, Earth, Mars, Jupiter, Saturn, Uranus, and Neptune. The Sun's gravitational force exerts control over the movement of all planets, all of which travel in the same direction and maintain an elliptical orbit around the Sun.

The planets in our solar system can be categorized as either terrestrial or Jovian. Mercury, Venus, Earth, and Mars are terrestrial planets, or Earth-like planets, while Jupiter, Saturn, Uranus and Neptune are Jovian planets, or Jupiter-like planets. One of the clearest differences between the terrestrial and the Jovian planets is their size. Earth is the largest terrestrial planet, yet its diameter is only a quarter of the size of the diameter of the smallest Jovian planet, Neptune, and its mass is only one seventeenth as great. As such, the Jovian planets are commonly referred to as giants. Also, based on the planets' locations relative to one another, the four terrestrial planets are known as the inner planets, while the four Jovian planets are known as the outer planets.

The terrestrial and Jovian planets also significantly differ in terms of their density and composition. Terrestrial planets, on average, are roughly 5 times denser than water, whereas the Jovian planets tend to be around 1.5 times denser than water. In fact, Saturn is only 0.7 times denser than water, which means that the planet of Saturn would theoretically float in water. These large differences in density are attributed to variations in the composition of the planets. The materials that comprise planets in both categories can be separated into three groups— gases, rocks, and ices—depending on their melting points. The terrestrial planets are primarily made up of dense rocks and metallic material, plus relatively small amounts of gases. On the other hand, the Jovian planets are largely composed of the hydrogen and helium gases, and they also contain minor amounts of ices in the form of frozen water, ammonia, and methane, but no rocky material.

The atmospheres of the Jovian planets are very thick and contain varying amounts of hydrogen, helium, methane, and ammonia. The atmospheres of the terrestrial planets are fairly insubstantial by comparison. The key factors that govern a planet's ability to retain an atmosphere are its temperature and mass. Basically, gas molecules are likely to "evaporate" from a planet's atmosphere if they reach a speed referred to as the escape velocity. In the case of Earth, the escape velocity is 11 kilometers per second. The Jovian planets have much higher escape velocities, generally between 21 and 60 kilometers per second, than the terrestrial planets, due to their greater masses and higher surface gravities. Therefore, it is far more unlikely that gases will attain the required velocity that would allow them to escape into space from the atmosphere. Also, the speed of gas molecules is greatly influenced by temperature, and the low temperatures of the Jovian planets prevent even the lightest gases from reaching the escape velocity. On the other hand, Earth's moon, which is a relatively warm body with low surface gravity, is not capable of retaining even the heaviest gases, so it lacks an atmosphere. The larger terrestrial planets of Venus, Earth, and Mars are capable of retaining some heavy gases like carbon dioxide, but their atmospheres still only comprise a very tiny percentage of their overall mass.

Because our solar system is organized so optimally, most astronomers believe that all of its planets were created at roughly the same time and from the same material as the Sun. According to a generally accepted hypothesis, all of the planets condensed from a primordial cloud of dust and gas that had a composition comparable to the composition of Jupiter. However, unlike Jupiter, the terrestrial planets today are essentially devoid of ices and light gases. One explanation could be that the terrestrial planets were at one point much larger, with a greater abundance of these materials, but eventually lost them due to their close proximity to the Sun and their relatively high temperatures.

<태양계 행성들: 지구형 행성과 목성형 행성>

The Sun is the central body of a massive rotating solar system comprising nine planets, their various moons and satellites, and countless smaller objects such as meteoroids, comets, and asteroids. Approximately 99.85 percent of our solar system's total mass is contained within the Sun, while the remaining 0.15 percent is collectively made up of the planets. In order of their distance from the Sun, the planets are arranged as follows: Mercury, Venus, Earth, Mars, Jupiter, Saturn, Uranus, and Neptune. The Sun's gravitational force exerts control over the movement of all planets, all of which travel in the same direction and maintain an elliptical orbit around the Sun.

The planets in our solar system can be categorized as either terrestrial or Jovian. Mercury, Venus, Earth, and Mars are terrestrial planets, or Earth-like planets, while Jupiter, Saturn, Uranus and Neptune are Jovian planets, or Jupiter-like planets. One of the clearest differences between the terrestrial and the Jovian planets is their size. Earth is the largest terrestrial planet, yet its diameter is only a quarter of the size of the diameter of the smallest Jovian planet, Neptune, and its mass is only one seventeenth as great. As such, the Jovian planets are commonly referred to as giants. Also, based on the planets' locations relative to one another, the four terrestrial planets are known as the inner planets, while the four Jovian planets are known as the outer planets.

According to the passage, each of the following statements comparing terrestrial planets with Jovian planets is true EXCEPT

(A) Terrestrial planets are located nearer to the Sun than Jovian planets are.
(B) The diameters of terrestrial planets are smaller than those of Jovian planets.
(C) Terrestrial planets and Jovian planets travel in different directions around the Sun.
(D) The masses of Jovian planets are greater than those of terrestrial planets.

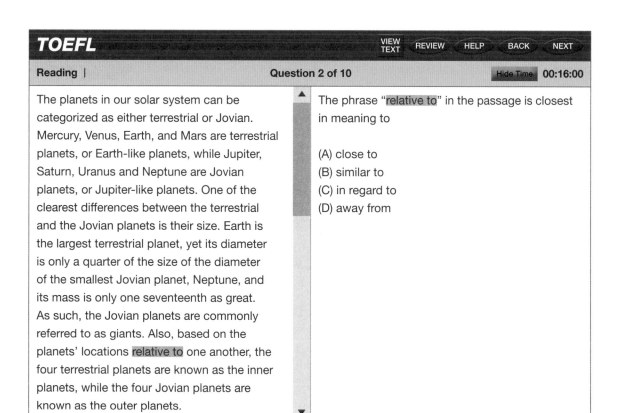

The planets in our solar system can be categorized as either terrestrial or Jovian. Mercury, Venus, Earth, and Mars are terrestrial planets, or Earth-like planets, while Jupiter, Saturn, Uranus and Neptune are Jovian planets, or Jupiter-like planets. One of the clearest differences between the terrestrial and the Jovian planets is their size. Earth is the largest terrestrial planet, yet its diameter is only a quarter of the size of the diameter of the smallest Jovian planet, Neptune, and its mass is only one seventeenth as great. As such, the Jovian planets are commonly referred to as giants. Also, based on the planets' locations relative to one another, the four terrestrial planets are known as the inner planets, while the four Jovian planets are known as the outer planets.

The phrase "relative to" in the passage is closest in meaning to

(A) close to
(B) similar to
(C) in regard to
(D) away from

The terrestrial and Jovian planets also significantly differ in terms of their density and composition. Terrestrial planets, on average, are roughly 5 times denser than water, whereas the Jovian planets tend to be around 1.5 times denser than water. In fact, Saturn is only 0.7 times denser than water, which means that the planet of Saturn would theoretically float in water. These large differences in density are attributed to variations in the composition of the planets. The materials that comprise planets in both categories can be separated into three groups—gases, rocks, and ices—depending on their melting points. The terrestrial planets are primarily made up of dense rocks and metallic material, plus relatively small amounts of gases. On the other hand, the Jovian planets are largely composed of the hydrogen and helium gases, and they also contain minor amounts of ices in the form of frozen water, ammonia, and methane, but no rocky material.

Paragraph 3 mentions which of the following as a reason why terrestrial planets are dense?

(A) They are composed mainly of rocky and metallic materials.
(B) They are made up of three groups of substances.
(C) They contain a greater amount of ice than Jovian planets do.
(D) They barely contain any water.

The terrestrial and Jovian planets also significantly differ in terms of their density and composition. Terrestrial planets, on average, are roughly 5 times denser than water, whereas the Jovian planets tend to be around 1.5 times denser than water. In fact, Saturn is only 0.7 times denser than water, which means that the planet of Saturn would theoretically float in water. These large differences in density are attributed to variations in the composition of the planets. The materials that comprise planets in both categories can be separated into three groups—gases, rocks, and ices—depending on their melting points. The terrestrial planets are primarily made up of dense rocks and metallic material, plus relatively small amounts of gases. On the other hand, the Jovian planets are largely composed of the hydrogen and helium gases, and they also contain minor amounts of ices in the form of frozen water, ammonia, and methane, but no rocky material.

Paragraph 3 supports each of the following statements about Saturn EXCEPT

(A) It is not as dense as any of the terrestrial planets.
(B) It is primarily composed of gases.
(C) It contains ices such as frozen methane.
(D) It contains small amounts of rocky material.

The atmospheres of the Jovian planets are very thick and contain varying amounts of hydrogen, helium, methane, and ammonia. The atmospheres of the terrestrial planets are fairly insubstantial by comparison. The key factors that govern a planet's ability to retain an atmosphere are its temperature and mass. Basically, gas molecules are likely to "evaporate" from a planet's atmosphere if they reach a speed referred to as the escape velocity. In the case of Earth, the escape velocity is 11 kilometers per second. The Jovian planets have much higher escape velocities, generally between 21 and 60 kilometers per second, than the terrestrial planets, due to their greater masses and higher surface gravities. Therefore, it is far more unlikely that gases will attain the required velocity that would allow them to escape into space from the atmosphere. Also, the speed of gas molecules is greatly influenced by temperature, and the low temperatures of the Jovian planets prevent even the lightest gases from reaching the escape velocity. On the other hand, Earth's moon, which is a relatively warm body with low surface gravity, is not capable of retaining even the heaviest gases, so it lacks an atmosphere. The larger terrestrial planets of Venus, Earth, and Mars are capable of retaining some heavy gases like carbon dioxide, but their atmospheres still only comprise a very tiny percentage of their overall mass.

According to paragraph 4, which of the following statements is true of both Jovian and terrestrial planets?

(A) The thinner the atmosphere, the greater the planet's mass.
(B) The lower the surface gravity, the lower the escape velocity.
(C) The lower the number of the gases in the atmosphere, the lower the temperature.
(D) The greater extent that the atmosphere contributes to the total mass, the higher the temperature.

The atmospheres of the Jovian planets are very thick and contain varying amounts of hydrogen, helium, methane, and ammonia. The atmospheres of the terrestrial planets are fairly insubstantial by comparison. The key factors that govern a planet's ability to retain an atmosphere are its temperature and mass. Basically, gas molecules are likely to "evaporate" from a planet's atmosphere if they reach a speed referred to as the escape velocity. In the case of Earth, the escape velocity is 11 kilometers per second. The Jovian planets have much higher escape velocities, generally between 21 and 60 kilometers per second, than the terrestrial planets, due to their greater masses and higher surface gravities. Therefore, it is far more unlikely that gases will attain the required velocity that would allow them to escape into space from the atmosphere. Also, the speed of gas molecules is greatly influenced by temperature, and the low temperatures of the Jovian planets prevent even the lightest gases from reaching the escape velocity. On the other hand, Earth's moon, which is a relatively warm body with low surface gravity, is not capable of retaining even the heaviest gases, so it lacks an atmosphere. The larger terrestrial planets of Venus, Earth, and Mars are capable of retaining some heavy gases like carbon dioxide, but their atmospheres still only comprise a very tiny percentage of their overall mass.

According to paragraph 4, what is a major reason that Jovian planets have much thicker atmospheres than terrestrial planets do?

(A) Jovian planets have lower gravitational force on their surfaces.
(B) Jovian planets' gas molecules are capable of traveling at greater speeds.
(C) Jovian planets have much lower escape velocities.
(D) Jovian planets have lower surface temperatures.

The atmospheres of the Jovian planets are very thick and contain varying amounts of hydrogen, helium, methane, and ammonia. The atmospheres of the terrestrial planets are fairly insubstantial by comparison. The key factors that govern a planet's ability to retain an atmosphere are its temperature and mass. Basically, gas molecules are likely to "evaporate" from a planet's atmosphere if they reach a speed referred to as the escape velocity. In the case of Earth, the escape velocity is 11 kilometers per second. The Jovian planets have much higher escape velocities, generally between 21 and 60 kilometers per second, than the terrestrial planets, due to their greater masses and higher surface gravities. Therefore, it is far more unlikely that gases will attain the required velocity that would allow them to escape into space from the atmosphere. Also, the speed of gas molecules is greatly influenced by temperature, and the low temperatures of the Jovian planets prevent even the lightest gases from reaching the escape velocity. On the other hand, Earth's moon, which is a relatively warm body with low surface gravity, is not capable of retaining even the heaviest gases, so it lacks an atmosphere. The larger terrestrial planets of Venus, Earth, and Mars are capable of retaining some heavy gases like carbon dioxide, but their atmospheres still only comprise a very tiny percentage of their overall mass.

Paragraph 4 supports which of the following statements about the ability of planets to retain gases?

(A) Planets are less likely to retain light gases than heavy gases.
(B) Planets of greater mass are less able to retain gases than those of relatively low mass.
(C) Jovian planets have extreme difficulty in retaining the lightest gases.
(D) Only terrestrial planets have the capability to retain carbon dioxide.

Because our solar system is organized so optimally, most astronomers believe that all of its planets were created at roughly the same time and from the same material as the Sun. According to a generally accepted hypothesis, all of the planets condensed from a primordial cloud of dust and gas that had a composition comparable to the composition of Jupiter. However, unlike Jupiter, the terrestrial planets today are essentially devoid of ices and light gases. One explanation could be that the terrestrial planets were at one point much larger, with a greater abundance of these materials, but eventually lost them due to their close proximity to the Sun and their relatively high temperatures.

In calling the cloud of gas and dust from which the Sun and all the planets are thought to have condensed "primordial," the author means that the cloud was

(A) larger than any other body
(B) similar in structure to the Sun
(C) composed of a diverse range of materials
(D) present at the inception of our solar system

The terrestrial and Jovian planets also significantly differ in terms of their density and composition. Terrestrial planets, on average, are roughly 5 times denser than water, whereas the Jovian planets tend to be around 1.5 times denser than water. In fact, Saturn is only 0.7 times denser than water, which means that the planet of Saturn would theoretically float in water. These large differences in density are attributed to variations in the composition of the planets. ■ The materials that comprise planets in both categories can be separated into three groups—gases, rocks, and ices—depending on their melting points. ■ The terrestrial planets are primarily made up of dense rocks and metallic material, plus relatively small amounts of gases. ■ On the other hand, the Jovian planets are largely composed of the hydrogen and helium gases, and they also contain minor amounts of ices in the form of frozen water, ammonia, and methane, but no rocky material. ■

Look at the four squares [■] that indicate where the following sentence could be added to the passage.

This accounts for their relatively low densities.

Where would the sentence best fit? Click on a square [■] to add the sentence to the passage.

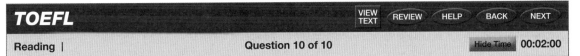

Directions: From the seven answer choices below, select the two phrases that correctly characterize the terrestrial planets and the three phrases that correctly characterize the Jovian planets. Drag each phrase you select into the appropriate column of the table. Two of the phrases will NOT be used. **This question is worth 3 points.**

Drag your answer choices to the space where they belong. To remove an answer choice, click on it. To review the passage, click on **VIEW TEXT.**

Jovian

-
-
-

Terrestrial

-
-

Answer Choices

(A) Possess relatively high escape velocities

(B) Possess densities that are typically lower than that of water

(C) Contain relatively large amounts of helium gases

(D) Are characterized by relatively high temperatures

(E) Have a relatively similar composition to the cloud from which they formed

(F) Are grouped together in the same category with Earth's moon

(G) Are of relatively small size

■ Passage 3

Structure and Composition of Comets

When comets are far from the Sun, they are relatively small objects measuring only a few kilometers in diameter. They are mainly composed of water ice, methane ice, and ammonia ice, as well as embedded dust particles, and they generally appear as a dirty ice ball. Whenever a comet moves closer to the Sun, radiation causes the icy matter to vaporize, which in turn releases much of the embedded dust. This creates a massive halo that envelops the ice ball. This halo is called a coma, and it can stretch out tens of thousands of kilometers from the icy core of a comet. The coma is often visible to people on Earth due to sunlight reflecting off the dust particles. Moreover, the vapor molecules are broken down into their constituent elements by the Sun's ultraviolet radiation, and these components become excited through the absorption of radiation from the Sun. When the excited atoms and ions return to a state of lower energy, they emit light and contribute to the luminosity of the coma.

As the comet draws even nearer to the Sun, its most recognizable and remarkable feature—the tail—begins to form. Comets technically have two separate tails, the dust tail and the ion tail. The dust tail is the product of the Sun's light reflecting off the coma's dust particles. When a photon reflects off a dust particle, it exerts a slight change on the dust particle's momentum, pushing it away from the coma. As the comet continues its orbit, an arcing trail of dust is left behind it. This visible dust tail can stretch for tens or hundreds of millions of kilometers out from the coma of the comet. Most dust tails are characterized by their gently curved shape and faintly yellow color.

The ion tail is formed by a slightly different mechanism. As the comet approaches the Sun, ultraviolet radiation in solar wind ionizes and excites the atoms in the coma. The high-velocity charged particles of the solar wind interact with the electrically charged excited ions in the coma, forcing them away from the head of the comet. When these excited ions return to lower-energy states, they emit photons and create a luminous, bluish-colored tail that stretches out from the comet in the opposite direction from the Sun. Since both types of tails result from radiation streaming out from the Sun, they both generally stretch out from the coma in the direction away from the Sun, and a comet may have several tails of each type.

As a comet travels through the inner solar system, it leaves a trail of debris behind it. Occasionally, this matter may get strewn across Earth's orbital path around the Sun. When Earth reaches this section of its orbit, it travels through the debris left behind by the dust trail. This may result in numerous particles entering Earth's atmosphere at high velocity. The resulting friction in the air can give rise to sudden streaks of light as the particles burn up in the atmosphere.

Each time a comet passes by the Sun, it loses more matter, and once all of the matter has been depleted, the comet will no longer be visible. What that essentially means is that comets that travel close to the Sun have finite lifetimes. Considering the average sizes of comets and the normal rates at which they lose matter, astronomers have come to the conclusion that comets that orbit close enough to the Sun to be seen from Earth have much shorter lifespans than the age of our solar system. So, where do new comets emerge from to take the place of those that burn out and disappear from view?

One proposal put forward by the Dutch astronomer Jan Oort is that a giant cloud of matter that remains from the creation of the solar system surrounds the Sun and extends out to about 50,000 astronomical units. Within this cloud are large chunks of matter, some of which are the cores of comets. When a star passes by the cloud, its gravitational influence can be significant enough that it affects the orbit of one of these chunks, sending it in the direction of the inner solar system and bringing it into closer proximity to the Sun.

<지구 근처에서 날아가는 혜성>

When comets are far from the Sun, they are relatively small objects measuring only a few kilometers in diameter. They are mainly composed of water ice, methane ice, and ammonia ice, as well as embedded dust particles, and they generally appear as a dirty ice ball. Whenever a comet moves closer to the Sun, radiation causes the icy matter to vaporize, which in turn releases much of the embedded dust. This creates a massive halo that envelops the ice ball. This halo is called a coma, and it can stretch out tens of thousands of kilometers from the icy core of a comet. The coma is often visible to people on Earth due to sunlight reflecting off the dust particles. Moreover, the vapor molecules are broken down into their constituent elements by the Sun's ultraviolet radiation, and these components become excited through the absorption of radiation from the Sun. When the excited atoms and ions return to a state of lower energy, they emit light and contribute to the luminosity of the coma.

Select the TWO answer choices from paragraph 1 that describe changes that occur as a comet approaches the Sun. To receive credit, you must select TWO answers.

(A) The halo of the comet will reduce in size.
(B) The comet's icy matter will begin to vaporize.
(C) A coma will begin to form from dust particles and vapor.
(D) A core is formed through condensation of water, methane, and ammonia.

When comets are far from the Sun, they are relatively small objects measuring only a few kilometers in diameter. They are mainly composed of water ice, methane ice, and ammonia ice, as well as embedded dust particles, and they generally appear as a dirty ice ball. Whenever a comet moves closer to the Sun, radiation causes the icy matter to vaporize, which in turn releases much of the embedded dust. This creates a massive halo that envelops the ice ball. This halo is called a coma, and it can stretch out tens of thousands of kilometers from the icy core of a comet. The coma is often visible to people on Earth due to sunlight reflecting off the dust particles. Moreover, the vapor molecules are broken down into their constituent elements by the Sun's ultraviolet radiation, and these components become excited through the absorption of radiation from the Sun. When the excited atoms and ions return to a state of lower energy, they emit light and contribute to the luminosity of the coma.

The word "envelops" in the passage is closest in meaning to

(A) sends
(B) surrounds
(C) scatters
(D) seals

As the comet draws even nearer to the Sun, its most recognizable and remarkable feature—the tail—begins to form. Comets technically have two separate tails, the dust tail and the ion tail. The dust tail is the product of the Sun's light reflecting off the coma's dust particles. When a photon reflects off a dust particle, it exerts a slight change on the dust particle's momentum, pushing it away from the coma. As the comet continues its orbit, an arcing trail of dust is left behind it. This visible dust tail can stretch for tens or hundreds of millions of kilometers out from the coma of the comet. Most dust tails are characterized by their gently curved shape and faintly yellow color.

The ion tail is formed by a slightly different mechanism. As the comet approaches the Sun, ultraviolet radiation in solar wind ionizes and excites the atoms in the coma. The high-velocity charged particles of the solar wind interact with the electrically charged excited ions in the coma, forcing them away from the head of the comet. When these excited ions return to lower-energy states, they emit photons and create a luminous, bluish-colored tail that stretches out from the comet in the opposite direction from the Sun. Since both types of tails result from radiation streaming out from the Sun, they both generally stretch out from the coma in the direction away from the Sun, and a comet may have several tails of each type.

According to paragraphs 2 and 3, all of the following statements about comet tails are true EXCEPT

(A) Ion tails are yellowish in color and have a curved shape.
(B) Photons are involved in the formation of both ion tails and dust tails.
(C) Dust tails extend large distances behind comets.
(D) The creation of ion tails requires ultraviolet radiation.

The ion tail is formed by a slightly different mechanism. As the comet approaches the Sun, ultraviolet radiation in solar wind ionizes and excites the atoms in the coma. The high-velocity charged particles of the solar wind interact with the electrically charged excited ions in the coma, forcing them away from the head of the comet. When these excited ions return to lower-energy states, they emit photons and create a luminous, bluish-colored tail that stretches out from the comet in the opposite direction from the Sun. Since both types of tails result from radiation streaming out from the Sun, they both generally stretch out from the coma in the direction away from the Sun, and a comet may have several tails of each type.

According to paragraph 3, the tails of a comet

(A) are stretched toward the Sun.

(B) become more curved as the comet gets closer to the Sun.

(C) can be separated from the comet's core by powerful solar winds.

(D) move in the same direction as the radiation that creates them.

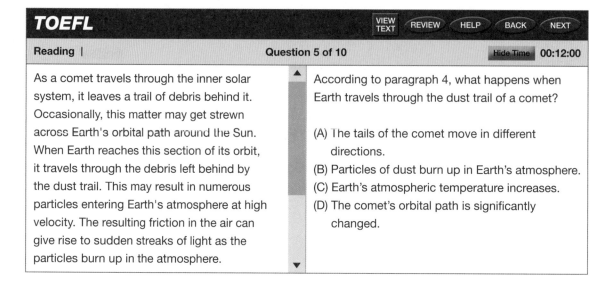

As a comet travels through the inner solar system, it leaves a trail of debris behind it. Occasionally, this matter may get strewn across Earth's orbital path around the Sun. When Earth reaches this section of its orbit, it travels through the debris left behind by the dust trail. This may result in numerous particles entering Earth's atmosphere at high velocity. The resulting friction in the air can give rise to sudden streaks of light as the particles burn up in the atmosphere.

According to paragraph 4, what happens when Earth travels through the dust trail of a comet?

(A) The tails of the comet move in different directions.
(B) Particles of dust burn up in Earth's atmosphere.
(C) Earth's atmospheric temperature increases.
(D) The comet's orbital path is significantly changed.

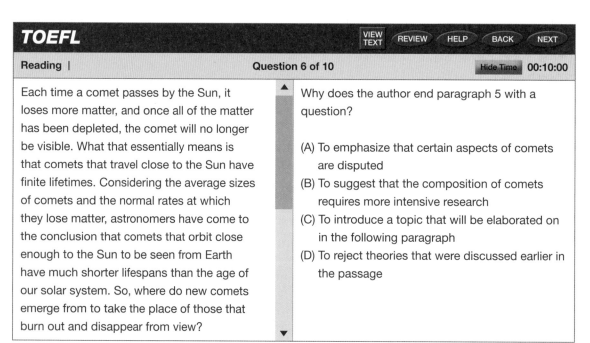

Each time a comet passes by the Sun, it loses more matter, and once all of the matter has been depleted, the comet will no longer be visible. What that essentially means is that comets that travel close to the Sun have finite lifetimes. Considering the average sizes of comets and the normal rates at which they lose matter, astronomers have come to the conclusion that comets that orbit close enough to the Sun to be seen from Earth have much shorter lifespans than the age of our solar system. So, where do new comets emerge from to take the place of those that burn out and disappear from view?

Why does the author end paragraph 5 with a question?

(A) To emphasize that certain aspects of comets are disputed
(B) To suggest that the composition of comets requires more intensive research
(C) To introduce a topic that will be elaborated on in the following paragraph
(D) To reject theories that were discussed earlier in the passage

One proposal put forward by the Dutch astronomer Jan Oort is that a giant cloud of matter that remains from the creation of the solar system surrounds the Sun and extends out to about 50,000 astronomical units. Within this cloud are large chunks of matter, some of which are the cores of comets. When a star passes by the cloud, its gravitational influence can be significant enough that it affects the orbit of one of these chunks, sending it in the direction of the inner solar system and bringing it into closer proximity to the Sun.

According to paragraph 6, how did astronomer Jan Oort contribute to our understanding of comets?

(A) He showed that old comets do not really disappear; they just move beyond the limits of the solar system.

(B) He proposed a method for comparing comets that orbit other stars with those found in our own solar system.

(C) He proved that a comet's lifetime is dependent on its distance from the Sun during the formation of the solar system.

(D) He theorized that comets are created when chunks of old debris are pushed from the outer to the inner solar system.

Each time a comet passes by the Sun, it loses more matter, and once all of the matter has been depleted, the comet will no longer be visible. What that essentially means is that comets that travel close to the Sun have finite lifetimes. Considering the average sizes of comets and the normal rates at which they lose matter, astronomers have come to the conclusion that comets that orbit close enough to the Sun to be seen from Earth have much shorter lifespans than the age of our solar system. So, where do new comets emerge from to take the place of those that burn out and disappear from view?

Which of the sentences below best expresses the essential information in the highlighted sentence in the passage? Incorrect choices change the meaning in important ways or leave out essential information.

(A) Each time a comet comes in close contact with the Sun, it becomes increasingly hard to detect with the naked eye.

(B) When comets pass by the Sun, the amount of matter they lose depends on the distance between the comets and the Sun.

(C) Comets lose more and more matter every time they pass by the Sun and eventually become impossible to see once all matter has been lost.

(D) A comet will no longer be visible once all of its matter has been depleted during its orbit around the Sun.

As a comet travels through the inner solar system, it leaves a trail of debris behind it. Occasionally, this matter may get strewn across Earth's orbital path around the Sun. ■ When Earth reaches this section of its orbit, it travels through the debris left behind by the dust trail. ■ This may result in numerous particles entering Earth's atmosphere at high velocity. ■ The resulting friction in the air can give rise to sudden streaks of light as the particles burn up in the atmosphere. ■

Look at the four squares [■] that indicate where the following sentence could be added to the passage.

These speeding particles collide with other particles present in Earth's atmosphere.

Where would the sentence best fit? Click on a square [■] to add the sentence to the passage.

Directions: An introductory sentence for a brief summary of the passage is provided below. Complete the summary by selecting the THREE answer choices that express the most important ideas in the passage. Some sentences do not belong in the summary because they express ideas that are not presented in the passage or are minor ideas in the passage. **This question is worth 2 points.**

Drag your answer choices to the space where they belong. To remove an answer choice, click on it. To review the passage, click on **VIEW TEXT.**

> **Astronomers have acquired much information about the composition of comets and the ways comets change as they move through the solar system.**
>
> -
> -
> -

Answer Choices

(A) Comets may form several types of tail depending on their primary components.

(B) Comets lose matter each time they pass by the Sun and eventually burn out.

(C) Comets are composed of ices and dust which create a halo known as a coma.

(D) The coma of most comets is significantly larger than the tail.

(E) A comet forms a coma as well as multiple tails as it gets nearer the Sun.

(F) The solar system contains debris from old comets that expired long ago.

Chapter

06

History

Passage 1   The Culture of Britain Under Rome

Passage 2   Innovation in Ancient Iran

Passage 3   Sumerian City-States

History

History (역사)

고대 이집트, 메소포타미아, 중국, 그리스, 로마를 비롯하여 중남미의 테오티우아칸 등 고대 역사 위주로 출제되고 있다.

[History 기출 토픽]

- The Nile and Ancient Egypt
  나일강과 고대 이집트

- Memphis: United Egypt's First Capital
  멤피스: 통일 이집트의 첫 번째 수도

- Sumer and the First Cities of the Ancient East
  수메르와 고대 중동의 최초 도시들

- Innovation in Ancient Iran
  고대 이란에서의 혁신

- Early Athens
  고대 아테네

- The Empire of Alexander the Great
  알렉산더 대왕의 제국

- The Roman Empire
  로마 제국

- The Culture of Britain Under Rome
  로마 통치 하의 영국 문화

- Colonizing the Americas via the Northwest Coast
  북서해안을 통한 아메리카 대륙 정착

- The Rise of Teotihuacán
  테오티우아칸의 번영

- The Use of Bronze and Jade in China
  중국에서 청동과 옥의 사용

- Siam 1851–1910
  시암(옛 타이 왕국) 1851년~1910년

[History 빈출 어휘]

adherence	준수, 고수	incise	~을 새기다
attest	증명하다	intact	온전한
authority	권위	intricate	복잡한
canal	수로, 운하	irrigation	관개
catastrophic	대재앙의	isolated	고립된
cluster	무리	lavish	호화로운
collective	집단의, 공동의	nomadism	유목 생활
conducive to	~에 도움이 되는	opulent	호화로운
consolidate	~을 통합하다	pagan	이교도의
constitute	~을 구성하다	pastoral	전원적인
culminate	끝나다, 절정에 이르다	plateau	고원 지대
deity	신	predominant	지배적인
desolate	황폐한	realm	영역
diplomat	외교관	reclaim	~을 개간하다
distinctive	독특한	scarcity	부족
divine	신의, 신성한	secular	세속적인
esteem	존중, 존경	settlement	정착지
ethnic	민족의	shaft	수직 갱도
fecund	비옥한	subsequent	그 이후의
fertile	비옥한	subterranean	지하의
flourish	번영하다	throne	왕좌
forge	(금속)을 단조하다	tract	넓은 지대, 지역
garner	~을 얻다	treasure	~을 귀하게 여기다
gradient	경사도	upsurge	급증
graze	방목하다	worship	예배, 숭배

■ Passage 1

The Culture of Britain Under Rome

A wave of social, political, and cultural influences accompanied the Roman invasion of Britain between A.D. 43 and 87. Roman goods and ideas flowed along the streets and were as evident as the soldiers, administrators, and troops that occupied the British settlements. The most obvious among these new cultural influences were the influx of Roman goods, the arrival of skilled artisans from within the Empire, and the construction of massive civil architecture.

The objects the Romans carried into Britain were by no means of artistic value; in fact, they were widely utilitarian only. However, the impact they had on the British was no less significant. The imported tools, cooking ware, and clothing quickly became treasured by the British people and came with the added mark of social status. Possession of terra sigillata, the red-gloss pottery of the Empire, granted the owner a cultured air, even if they were ignorant to the tales and mythology decorating the wares, and introduced them to the rarified style and artistic concepts of the Greco-Roman civilization. While most items were mass-produced and domestically used, a few more aesthetic pieces were also common, such as statuettes. Most probably arrived in Britain for use in religious ceremonies or were gifted to regional leaders during cultural exchanges. The diplomatic and religious value of the statuettes lent them a desirable quality that saw their fashion and acquisition spread quickly across Britain.

Some of the British welcomed the style and culture of the Romans with open arms and fully adopted it. Fishbourne Villa, built later in the first century, was likely designed and constructed at the behest of the regional king Cogidubnus and showcased his many Roman inclinations. It featured both imported marble and the colorful mosaics popular in Rome at the time, while Greco-Roman sculptures and other artwork decorated Fishbourne's lavish halls. So alike was the design of Fishbourne to Roman aesthetics that a visiting diplomat would have surely felt as though they were in the heart of the empire, rather than some provincial backwater of Roman conquest. While the king lacked the social esteem of being a true Roman, he no doubt garnered a certain amount of respect by so aptly espousing the cultural symbols and identity of the empire.

With such sterling examples to live up to, Roman style flourished, and demand rose for similar designs. Since the native British were yet to master artisan work such as stone carving, an influx of craft workers from the mainland was necessary. An early product of their work was the magnificent temple at Bath, which was built relatively quickly after the conquest. It bore similarities with the designs of northeast Gaul, indicating further that its builders likely came from that region. In order to construct these facilities, Roman administrators used their personal network to connect British workers with skilled architects and masons from within the empire. Eventually, the skills were passed on to the native workers, allowing for the rise of a more independent style using these new artisanal skills. This encouraged a wider upsurge in artistic work, including mosaic, decorative wall painting, ceramics, and metalworking throughout Britain, all of which eventually led to the creation of a distinctive Romano-British style.

Roman influences did not all casually seep into British culture. Some, like architecture, arrived intently with the conquering empire. Before the Romans, settlements in Britain were isolated. People rarely traveled, and, aside from war or infrequent religious festivals, did not gather together in large groups. It was a loosely connected society of small communities, composed of clusters of humble huts and dwellings. Most buildings were hardly taller than the adults who inhabited them, and their construction from organic material—peat and wood—and rounded shapes merged them with the natural landscape. But the effect of Roman architecture was the opposite. Massive and opulent, it sought to intimidate the conquered people as they witnessed the might of the Roman empire through its monolithic structures. Their straight lines and hard angles contrasted sharply with the curves of British structures and attested to Roman engineering and adherence to principle and authority.

<로마 건축 양식에 영향받은 영국 바스>

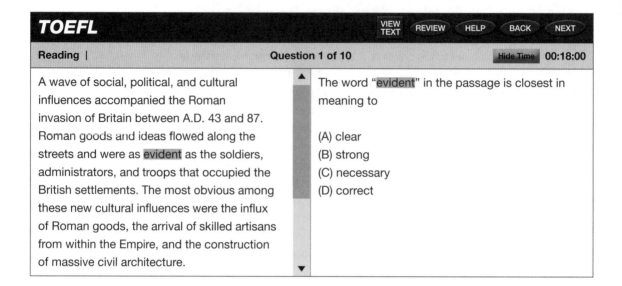

A wave of social, political, and cultural influences accompanied the Roman invasion of Britain between A.D. 43 and 87. Roman goods and ideas flowed along the streets and were as evident as the soldiers, administrators, and troops that occupied the British settlements. The most obvious among these new cultural influences were the influx of Roman goods, the arrival of skilled artisans from within the Empire, and the construction of massive civil architecture.

The word "evident" in the passage is closest in meaning to

(A) clear
(B) strong
(C) necessary
(D) correct

The objects the Romans carried into Britain were by no means of artistic value; in fact, they were widely utilitarian only. However, the impact they had on the British was no less significant. The imported tools, cooking ware, and clothing quickly became treasured by the British people and came with the added mark of social status. Possession of terra sigillata, the red-gloss pottery of the Empire, granted the owner a cultured air, even if they were ignorant to the tales and mythology decorating the wares, and introduced them to the rarified style and artistic concepts of the Greco-Roman civilization. While most items were mass-produced and domestically used, a few more aesthetic pieces were also common, such as statuettes. Most probably arrived in Britain for use in religious ceremonies or were gifted to regional leaders during cultural exchanges. The diplomatic and religious value of the statuettes lent them a desirable quality that saw their fashion and acquisition spread quickly across Britain.

According to paragraph 2, a possible benefit of attaining a Roman-made object was

(A) a higher quality of product.
(B) an increase in social standing.
(C) an introduction to Roman mythology.
(D) participation in religious ceremonies.

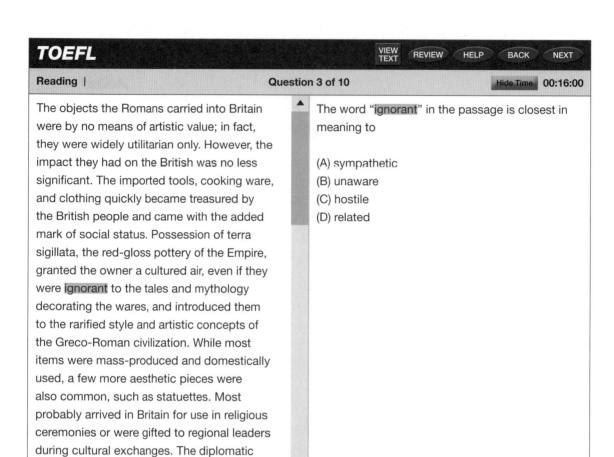

The objects the Romans carried into Britain were by no means of artistic value; in fact, they were widely utilitarian only. However, the impact they had on the British was no less significant. The imported tools, cooking ware, and clothing quickly became treasured by the British people and came with the added mark of social status. Possession of terra sigillata, the red-gloss pottery of the Empire, granted the owner a cultured air, even if they were ignorant to the tales and mythology decorating the wares, and introduced them to the rarified style and artistic concepts of the Greco-Roman civilization. While most items were mass-produced and domestically used, a few more aesthetic pieces were also common, such as statuettes. Most probably arrived in Britain for use in religious ceremonies or were gifted to regional leaders during cultural exchanges. The diplomatic and religious value of the statuettes lent them a desirable quality that saw their fashion and acquisition spread quickly across Britain.

The word "ignorant" in the passage is closest in meaning to

(A) sympathetic
(B) unaware
(C) hostile
(D) related

Some of the British welcomed the style and culture of the Romans with open arms and fully adopted it. Fishbourne Villa, built later in the first century, was likely designed and constructed at the behest of the regional king Cogidubnus and showcased his many Roman inclinations. It featured both imported marble and the colorful mosaics popular in Rome at the time, while Greco-Roman sculptures and other artwork decorated Fishbourne's lavish halls. So alike was the design of Fishbourne to Roman aesthetics that a visiting diplomat would have surely felt as though they were in the heart of the empire, rather than some provincial backwater of Roman conquest. While the king lacked the social esteem of being a true Roman, he no doubt garnered a certain amount of respect by so aptly espousing the cultural symbols and identity of the empire.

What can be inferred about Cogidubnus?

(A) He was quickly replaced by a Roman administrator.
(B) He had visited Rome before the conquest.
(C) He was familiar with the current fashions of the empire.
(D) He aided the Romans during the conquest.

Some of the British welcomed the style and culture of the Romans with open arms and fully adopted it. Fishbourne Villa, built later in the first century, was likely designed and constructed at the behest of the regional king Cogidubnus and showcased his many Roman inclinations. It featured both imported marble and the colorful mosaics popular in Rome at the time, while Greco-Roman sculptures and other artwork decorated Fishbourne's lavish halls. So alike was the design of Fishbourne to Roman aesthetics that a visiting diplomat would have surely felt as though they were in the heart of the empire, rather than some provincial backwater of Roman conquest. While the king lacked the social esteem of being a true Roman, he no doubt garnered a certain amount of respect by so aptly espousing the cultural symbols and identity of the empire.

Which of the sentences below best expresses the essential information in the highlighted sentence in the passage? Incorrect answer choices change the meaning in important ways or leave out essential information.

(A) Fishbourne was closely modeled after a Roman villa even though it was located in the British countryside.

(B) A Roman who went to Fishbourne Villa would think its design was more similar to Rome's than Britain's.

(C) Lost Romans often ended up at Fishbourne because it resembled their homes back in Rome.

(D) Diplomats often met at Fishbourne because it was more suitable for their needs than most British structures.

With such sterling examples to live up to, Roman style flourished and demand rose for similar designs. Since the native British were yet to master artisan work such as stone carving, an influx of craft workers from the mainland was necessary. An early product of their work was the magnificent temple at Bath, which was built relatively quickly after the conquest. It bore similarities with the designs of northeast Gaul, indicating further that its builders likely came from that region. In order to construct these facilities, Roman administrators used their personal network to connect British workers with skilled architects and masons from within the empire. Eventually, the skills were passed on to the native workers, allowing for the rise of a more independent style using these new artisanal skills. This encouraged a wider upsurge in artistic work, including mosaic, decorative wall painting, ceramics, and metalworking throughout Britain, all of which eventually led to the creation of a distinctive Romano-British style.

According to paragraph 4, one factor that aided the quick development of Roman-styled construction in Britain was

(A) the wide availability of stone and marble in the country.

(B) the skilled workers from the empire who had previously moved to Britain.

(C) the expert stone carving skills of the native Britons.

(D) the personal contacts of Roman administrators with craftsmen.

Roman influences did not all casually seep into British culture. Some, like architecture, arrived intently with the conquering empire. Before the Romans, settlements in Britain were isolated. People rarely traveled, and, aside from war or infrequent religious festivals, did not gather together in large groups. It was a loosely connected society of small communities, composed of clusters of humble huts and dwellings. Most buildings were hardly taller than the adults who inhabited them, and their construction from organic material—peat and wood— and rounded shapes merged them with the natural landscape. But the effect of Roman architecture was the opposite. Massive and opulent, it sought to intimidate the conquered people as they witnessed the might of the Roman empire through its monolithic structures. Their straight lines and hard angles contrasted sharply with the curves of British structures and attested to Roman engineering and adherence to principle and authority.

Why does the author mention that Britons rarely traveled?

(A) To show how the Roman conquest provided access to transportation

(B) To suggest that Britons had little contact with other cultures

(C) To explain why British architecture was not built to be large

(D) To argue that domestic life was a higher priority to Britons

Roman influences did not all casually seep into British culture. Some, like architecture, arrived intently with the conquering empire. Before the Romans, settlements in Britain were isolated. People rarely traveled, and, aside from war or infrequent religious festivals, did not gather together in large groups. It was a loosely connected society of small communities, composed of clusters of humble huts and dwellings. Most buildings were hardly taller than the adults who inhabited them, and their construction from organic material—peat and wood— and rounded shapes merged them with the natural landscape. But the effect of Roman architecture was the opposite. Massive and opulent, it sought to intimidate the conquered people as they witnessed the might of the Roman empire through its monolithic structures. Their straight lines and hard angles contrasted sharply with the curves of British structures and attested to Roman engineering and adherence to principle and authority.

According to paragraph 5, pre-Roman buildings differed from those built by the Romans in all the following ways EXCEPT

(A) their geometric shapes
(B) their effect on people
(C) their placement in clusters
(D) their scale

With such sterling examples to live up to, Roman style flourished and demand rose for similar designs. ■ Since the native British were yet to master artisan work such as stone carving, an influx of craft workers from the mainland was necessary. ■ An early product of their work was the magnificent temple at Bath, which was built relatively quickly after the conquest. ■ It bore similarities with the designs of northeast Gaul, indicating further that its builders likely came from that region. ■ In order to construct these facilities, Roman administrators used their personal network to connect British workers with skilled architects and masons from within the empire. Eventually, the skills were passed on to the native workers, allowing for the rise of a more independent style using these new artisanal skills. This encouraged a wider upsurge in artistic work, including mosaic, decorative wall painting, ceramics, and metalworking throughout Britain, all of which eventually led to the creation of a distinctive Romano-British style.

Look at the four squares [■] that indicate where the following sentence could be added to the passage.

These artisans came mainly from Gaul and Germany.

Where would the sentence best fit? Click on a square [■] to add the sentence to the passage.

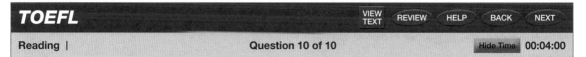

Directions: An introductory sentence for a brief summary of the passage is provided below. Complete the summary by selecting the THREE answer choices that express the most important ideas in the passage. Some sentences do not belong in the summary because they express ideas that are not presented in the passage or are minor ideas in the passage. **This question is worth 2 points.**

Drag your answer choices to the space where they belong. To remove an answer choice, click on it. To review the passage, click on **VIEW TEXT.**

The Roman Empire's conquest of Britain affected several cultural changes.

-
-
-

Answer Choices

(A) New education opportunities were available to Britons as they traveled to Gaul to learn advanced trade skills.

(B) A range of new objects came into Britain, from everyday goods such a pottery to decorative items used for special events.

(C) Roman designs for buildings and interiors required advanced skills, so workers were brought in from the empire's other provinces.

(D) British villages were replaced by luxurious villas as Roman administrators moved into the countryside.

(E) Pagan ceremonies held by the British were modified to accommodate the various deities of the Romans.

(F) The modest buildings of Britain were dwarfed by the massive size and straight lines of Roman structures.

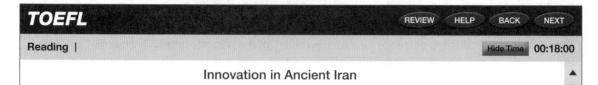

Innovation in Ancient Iran

The history of Iran has been defined in part by its geographical limitations. While the fertile valleys and plains in regions that receive adequate rainfall could support livestock, the total amount of vegetation was insufficient. If the animals grazed in one spot for too long, they quickly consumed all the available food. These conditions gave rise to the practice of pastoral nomadism, wherein shepherds would tend their livestock—namely sheep and goats—by herding them across vast stretches of countryside. Pastoral nomadism shaped the economy of early Iran and several other facets of its society. The movement of herds generally followed a vertical pattern, with shepherds descending to the lowlands for the winter season and returning to the highlands again in the summer. The goods produced by the nomadic livestock were valuable and diverse. They included copious material for the crafting of carpets, clothing, and shelters, as well as dairy and meat. Pockets of social identities formed as nomads converged into tribes capable of controlling great tracts of land for their roaming herds.

The tribes of pastoral nomads constituted an influential social and political force in Iran from ancient times to the 20th century. Most of all, the skills inherent and crucial in their livelihood— hunting predators, navigating open country, disciplining initiates, and protecting territory—were perfectly suited for military purposes. Most rulers and soldiers emerged from the tribes, which also worked closely with the dynasties that led the country. In fact, the political realm of Iran was deeply involved with handling the tribes. This meant cultivating support and goodwill with the friendly ones and trying to enforce rule over or totally remove the more hostile among them, either through combat, intimidation, or other means. Even by the start of the 20th century, Iran's tribes still held considerable sway over the political system, with tribal people comprising at least a quarter of the population. However, the nomadic way of life began to diminish in the 1930s with the arrival of mechanized warfare, which allowed the government to push back against the power of the tribes and force them to settle. The campaign was a success, and the tribes have minimal presence in modern Iran's society and economy, with less than 5 percent of the population representative of the traditional nomadic pastoral lifestyle.

Iran's scarcity of water required additional innovations. With arid conditions across the plateau, Iran lacked the copious water supplies of its neighbors, such as Mesopotamia with its life-sustaining rivers. Early farmers solved this problem with one of the most remarkable agricultural innovations of the ancient world, one that made it possible to create farmland beyond the scant oases that dotted the flatlands. This innovation was the development of qanats, vast subterranean canals that allowed for the irrigation of groundwater via the natural gradient of the plateau basin. The system started with a well dug in the foothills of the mountains, where it would accumulate the water from melting snow. From there, additional wells and shafts were constructed that connected to underground canals running to different areas ready for cultivation in various villages. Some special attention was required, as the natural slopes encouraged erosion and the interiors of wells and shafts required routine repairs to keep them intact.

Qanats were a marvel of ancient ingenuity in multiple ways. While aboveground systems would be vulnerable to evaporation, the qanats were underground and thus avoided the problem. No mechanical systems were necessary as gravity facilitated all the movement of the water. By dividing the length of the canal by wells and shafts, each track was kept short and manageable, and repairs of individual sections were easily managed. Development of the qanats occurred over multiple centuries, culminating in a massive network. It has been estimated that the system in its entirety—including the wells, shafts, and canals—is more than 300,000 kilometers long. However, this resourcefulness did not result in great returns; agriculture in Iran was still a dire prospect, and the peasant farmers only received a fraction of the agricultural goods after taxation.

<여전히 유목 생활 전통을 따르는 이란의 일부 부족민들>

The history of Iran has been defined in part by its geographical limitations. While the fertile valleys and plains in regions that receive adequate rainfall could support livestock, the total amount of vegetation was insufficient. If the animals grazed in one spot for too long, they quickly consumed all the available food. These conditions gave rise to the practice of pastoral nomadism, wherein shepherds would tend their livestock—namely sheep and goats—by herding them across vast stretches of countryside. Pastoral nomadism shaped the economy of early Iran and several other facets of its society. The movement of herds generally followed a vertical pattern, with shepherds descending to the lowlands for the winter season and returning to the highlands again in the summer. The goods produced by the nomadic livestock were valuable and diverse. They included copious material for the crafting of carpets, clothing, and shelters, as well as dairy and meat. Pockets of social identities formed as nomads converged into tribes capable of controlling great tracts of land for their roaming herds.

According to paragraph 1, pastoral nomads needed to herd their livestock from one area to the next because of

(A) territorial disputes with other nomads.
(B) the lack of vegetation available for grazing.
(C) seasonal climate changes in different regions.
(D) the difficulties of raising livestock at high altitudes.

The history of Iran has been defined in part by its geographical limitations. While the fertile valleys and plains in regions that receive adequate rainfall could support livestock, the total amount of vegetation was insufficient. If the animals grazed in one spot for too long, they quickly consumed all the available food. These conditions gave rise to the practice of pastoral nomadism, wherein shepherds would tend their livestock—namely sheep and goats—by herding them across vast stretches of countryside. Pastoral nomadism shaped the economy of early Iran and several other facets of its society. The movement of herds generally followed a vertical pattern, with shepherds descending to the lowlands for the winter season and returning to the highlands again in the summer. The goods produced by the nomadic livestock were valuable and diverse. They included copious material for the crafting of carpets, clothing, and shelters, as well as dairy and meat. Pockets of social identities formed as nomads converged into tribes capable of controlling great tracts of land for their roaming herds.

The word "converged" in the passage is closest in meaning to

(A) competed
(B) migrated
(C) assembled
(D) rotated

The tribes of pastoral nomads constituted an influential social and political force in Iran from ancient times to the 20th century. Most of all, the skills inherent and crucial in their livelihood—hunting predators, navigating open country, disciplining initiates, and protecting territory—were perfectly suited for military purposes. Most rulers and soldiers emerged from the tribes, which also worked closely with the dynasties that led the country. In fact, the political realm of Iran was deeply involved with handling the tribes. This meant cultivating support and goodwill with the friendly ones and trying to enforce rule over or totally remove the more hostile among them, either through combat, intimidation, or other means. Even by the start of the 20th century, Iran's tribes still held considerable sway over the political system, with tribal people comprising at least a quarter of the population. However, the nomadic way of life began to diminish in the 1930s with the arrival of mechanized warfare, which allowed the government to push back against the power of the tribes and force them to settle. The campaign was a success, and the tribes have minimal presence in modern Iran's society and economy, with less than 5 percent of the population representative of the traditional nomadic pastoral lifestyle.

What can be inferred from paragraph 2 about how Iranian rulers used the nomadic tribes?

(A) The rulers consulted with tribal leaders before making major administrative decisions.
(B) The rulers recruited friendly tribes to fight against tribes that did not support them.
(C) The rulers depended on the trade created by the tribes' economic activities.
(D) The rulers inspired conflicts between the tribes to weaken their collective power.

The tribes of pastoral nomads constituted an influential social and political force in Iran from ancient times to the 20th century. Most of all, the skills inherent and crucial in their livelihood—hunting predators, navigating open country, disciplining initiates, and protecting territory—were perfectly suited for military purposes. Most rulers and soldiers emerged from the tribes, which also worked closely with the dynasties that led the country. In fact, the political realm of Iran was deeply involved with handling the tribes. This meant cultivating support and goodwill with the friendly ones and trying to enforce rule over or totally remove the more hostile among them, either through combat, intimidation, or other means. Even by the start of the 20th century, Iran's tribes still held considerable sway over the political system, with tribal people comprising at least a quarter of the population. However, the nomadic way of life began to diminish in the 1930s with the arrival of mechanized warfare, which allowed the government to push back against the power of the tribes and force them to settle. The campaign was a success, and the tribes have minimal presence in modern Iran's society and economy, with less than 5 percent of the population representative of the traditional nomadic pastoral lifestyle.

According to paragraph 2, nomadic pastoralists played a significant role in Iranian history for all of the following reasons EXCEPT

(A) Many Iranian rulers came from the tribes.
(B) Their skills were of value to Iranian rulers.
(C) They helped introduce mechanized labor.
(D) They composed a large part of the population.

Iran's scarcity of water required additional innovations. With arid conditions across the plateau, Iran lacked the copious water supplies of its neighbors, such as Mesopotamia with its life-sustaining rivers. Early farmers solved this problem with one of the most remarkable agricultural innovations of the ancient world, one that made it possible to create farmland beyond the scant oases that dotted the flatlands. This innovation was the development of qanats, vast subterranean canals that allowed for the irrigation of groundwater via the natural gradient of the plateau basin. The system started with a well dug in the foothills of the mountains, where it would accumulate the water from melting snow. From there, additional wells and shafts were constructed that connected to underground canals running to different areas ready for cultivation in various villages. Some special attention was required, as the natural slopes encouraged erosion and the interiors of wells and shafts required routine repairs to keep them intact.

In paragraph 3, why does the author compare Iran's geography with that of Mesopotamia?

(A) To demonstrate the influence of Mesopotamia's rivers throughout the region

(B) To explain why neighboring regions did not adopt the qanat system

(C) To emphasize how the entire Middle East depended on irrigation

(D) To show the motivation behind the development of qanats in Iran

Iran's scarcity of water required additional innovations. With arid conditions across the plateau, Iran lacked the copious water supplies of its neighbors, such as Mesopotamia with its life-sustaining rivers. Early farmers solved this problem with one of the most remarkable agricultural innovations of the ancient world, one that made it possible to create farmland beyond the scant oases that dotted the flatlands. This innovation was the development of qanats, vast subterranean canals that allowed for the irrigation of groundwater via the natural gradient of the plateau basin. The system started with a well dug in the foothills of the mountains, where it would accumulate the water from melting snow. From there, additional wells and shafts were constructed that connected to underground canals running to different areas ready for cultivation in various villages. Some special attention was required, as the natural slopes encouraged erosion and the interiors of wells and shafts required routine repairs to keep them intact.

Which of the sentences below best expresses the essential information in the highlighted sentence in the passage? Incorrect answer choices change the meaning in important ways or leave out essential information.

(A) Qanats needed extra care to continue functioning.

(B) Erosion caused multiple structural problems for qanats.

(C) Being built on a slope prevented the interiors of qanats from degrading.

(D) Fixing qanats was difficult due to the steepness of the openings.

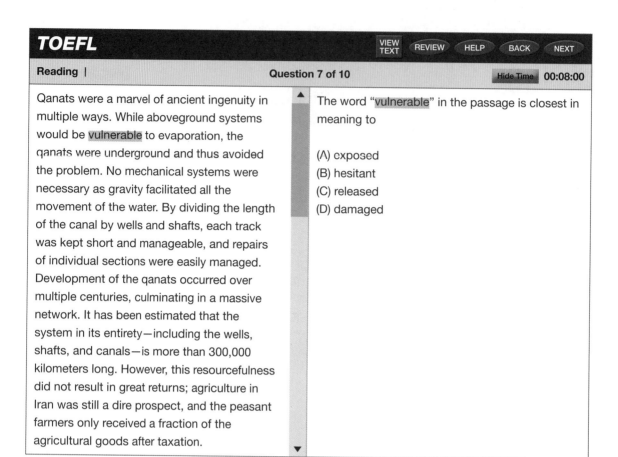

Qanats were a marvel of ancient ingenuity in multiple ways. While aboveground systems would be vulnerable to evaporation, the qanats were underground and thus avoided the problem. No mechanical systems were necessary as gravity facilitated all the movement of the water. By dividing the length of the canal by wells and shafts, each track was kept short and manageable, and repairs of individual sections were easily managed. Development of the qanats occurred over multiple centuries, culminating in a massive network. It has been estimated that the system in its entirety—including the wells, shafts, and canals—is more than 300,000 kilometers long. However, this resourcefulness did not result in great returns; agriculture in Iran was still a dire prospect, and the peasant farmers only received a fraction of the agricultural goods after taxation.

The word "vulnerable" in the passage is closest in meaning to

(A) exposed
(B) hesitant
(C) released
(D) damaged

Qanats were a marvel of ancient ingenuity in multiple ways. While aboveground systems would be vulnerable to evaporation, the qanats were underground and thus avoided the problem. No mechanical systems were necessary as gravity facilitated all the movement of the water. By dividing the length of the canal by wells and shafts, each track was kept short and manageable, and repairs of individual sections were easily managed. Development of the qanats occurred over multiple centuries, culminating in a massive network. It has been estimated that the system in its entirety—including the wells, shafts, and canals—is more than 300,000 kilometers long. However, this resourcefulness did not result in great returns; agriculture in Iran was still a dire prospect, and the peasant farmers only received a fraction of the agricultural goods after taxation.

According to paragraph 4, why were the qanats built with numerous wells and shafts?

(A) To collect more water from melting snow
(B) To promote a quicker flow of water
(C) To allow various communities to draw water from them
(D) To make separate sections easier to maintain

Qanats were a marvel of ancient ingenuity in multiple ways. While aboveground systems would be vulnerable to evaporation, the qanats were underground and thus avoided the problem. No mechanical systems were necessary as gravity facilitated all the movement of the water. By dividing the length of the canal by wells and shafts, each track was kept short and manageable, and repairs of individual sections were easily managed. ∎ Development of the qanats occurred over multiple centuries, culminating in a massive network. ∎ It has been estimated that the system in its entirety—including the wells, shafts, and canals—is more than 300,000 kilometers long. ∎ However, this resourcefulness did not result in great returns; agriculture in Iran was still a dire prospect, and the peasant farmers only received a fraction of the agricultural goods after taxation. ∎

Look at the four squares [∎] that indicate where the following sentence could be added to the passage.

As this is the same distance as that between the Earth and the Moon, one can easily see how much time and money went into the construction of the qanats.

Where would the sentence best fit? Click on a square [∎] to add the sentence to the passage.

Directions: An introductory sentence for a brief summary of the passage is provided below. Complete the summary by selecting the THREE answer choices that express the most important ideas in the passage. Some sentences do not belong in the summary because they express ideas that are not presented in the passage or are minor ideas in the passage. **This question is worth 2 points.**

Drag your answer choices to the space where they belong. To remove an answer choice, click on it. To review the passage, click on **VIEW TEXT.**

The arid climate and sparse landscape of Iran affected its social and economic development.

-
-
-

Answer Choices

(A) To successfully raise livestock for food and materials, pastoral nomads herded animals across the countryside.

(B) The nomadic tribes of Iran successfully integrated into Iranian cities and towns in the 1900s.

(C) The natural slope of the Iranian landscape made the construction of irrigation canals possible.

(D) Nomadic tribal communities held great social and economic influence for centuries, into the 20th century.

(E) Qanats created an intricate irrigation system and made possible the expansion of Iranian farming.

(F) Throughout its history, the government of Iran relied on the nomadic tribes to defend it from invaders.

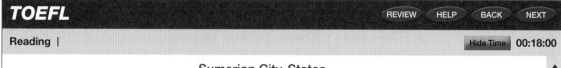

Sumerian City-States

Sumer was the earliest known civilization of Mesopotamia, the fertile region between the Tigris and Euphrates Rivers in the Middle East, and one of the first in the world. It emerged on the southern tip of the Mesopotamian plain, which was, at first, an unlikely location to foster civilization. The plains were largely desolate with few natural resources such as timber, stone, and metal. Rainfall was also sparse, but annual floods descended as melted snow washed across the plain. In addition, due to the slight natural gradient, the riverbeds of the plain shifted frequently. However, these difficulties proved conducive to civilization as they demanded the development of irrigation, a massive undertaking that required social organization and cooperation. Once a system was introduced and nutrient-rich silt flowed across the farmlands, crops flourished. The irrigated land produced nearly five times more than the normal land. The resulting crop surpluses led to the establishment of an elite class, needed to manage and distribute resources, and a subsequent social class order.

With the beginnings of social order in place, urban settlements naturally followed. However, it is unclear what the exact factors were that led to the establishment of the first city-states. One possibility is religion. The earliest city-state, Eridu, founded around 4500 B.C.E., rose around an impressive mud-brick temple. Similarly, Uruk, founded about a thousand years later, housed a temple at its city center. The elites likely used religion to consolidate their power and backed it with divine justification. Furthermore, the cities had patron gods. Uruk, for example, had two: Anu, the god of the sky and chief deity of the pantheon, and Inanna, the goddess of love and war. The catastrophic flood, the same that appears in later religious texts, likely had its earliest version with the Sumerian gods, who, in their own legend, destroyed the human race merely for being too noisy.

The central presence of temples and intricacy of the mythology suggested that religious figures most likely led the cities. However, it is now believed that this was not the case, and the cities likely had secular leaders even from their earliest days. Under secular leadership, various occupations arose, generating diversity in city life. Professionals included administrators, craftspeople, and merchants. Given the land's limited natural resources, a robust trade system developed as most raw materials had to be imported. Increasing sophistication in administration and trade led to the invention of a writing system around 3300 B.C.E. Initial versions of the writing were based on logograms, symbols that represented entire words. These logograms were incised on clay tablets using a stylus with a wedge-shaped head. The Romans later called this system of writing cuneiform as the shape of the stylus was a cuneus.

The earliest records depict over 2,000 logograms, but the system was simplified as it began to use symbols to express a syllable rather than an entire word. For example, the original symbol for the word "master"—"en"—resembled a throne, though over time it was simplified, with the symbol itself referring to the syllable instead. Any word that included the sound "en" would use that sign, and the rest of the syllables would be expressed via other signs. Around one thousand years after its first appearance, cuneiform had been reduced to about 600 symbols, while the variety of words able to be expressed grew. Texts concerning economic matters were predominant, though works of literature, theology, history, and law also appeared, including the epic of Gilgamesh.

Sumerian city-states also benefitted from other innovations. The wheel likely appeared in the fourth millennium B.C.E., originally for use in pottery. The first sign of wheels being applied to transportation was seen on a tablet from around 3000 B.C.E., which depicted a box-like cart being pulled on four wheels. The discovery of bronze, which occurred around the same time, also marked major progress for Sumer. Sumerians had been using copper since 3500 B.C.E. but did not smelt it with tin to create significantly stronger bronze until about 500 years later. Bronze did not completely replace copper and stone tools, but it could be forged with sharp edges, making it the superior material for saws, scythes, and all manner of weapons. The discovery of bronze initiated the Bronze Age, which lasted from 3000 to 1000 B.C.E.

<고대 수메르 신과 쐐기 문자>

Sumer was the earliest known civilization of Mesopotamia, the fertile region between the Tigris and Euphrates Rivers in the Middle East, and one of the first in the world. It emerged on the southern tip of the Mesopotamian plain, which was, at first, an unlikely location to foster civilization. The plains were largely desolate with few natural resources such as timber, stone, and metal. Rainfall was also sparse, but annual floods descended as melted snow washed across the plain. In addition, due to the slight natural gradient, the riverbeds of the plain shifted frequently. However, these difficulties proved conducive to civilization as they demanded the development of irrigation, a massive undertaking that required social organization and cooperation. Once a system was introduced and nutrient-rich silt flowed across the farmlands, crops flourished. The irrigated land produced nearly five times more than the normal land. The resulting crop surpluses led to the establishment of an elite class, needed to manage and distribute resources, and a subsequent social class order.

The word "it" in the passage refers to

(A) Sumer
(B) civilization
(C) Mesopotamia
(D) the Middle East

Sumer was the earliest known civilization of Mesopotamia, the fertile region between the Tigris and Euphrates Rivers in the Middle East, and one of the first in the world. It emerged on the southern tip of the Mesopotamian plain, which was, at first, an unlikely location to foster civilization. The plains were largely desolate with few natural resources such as timber, stone, and metal. Rainfall was also sparse, but annual floods descended as melted snow washed across the plain. In addition, due to the slight natural gradient, the riverbeds of the plain shifted frequently. However, these difficulties proved conducive to civilization as they demanded the development of irrigation, a massive undertaking that required social organization and cooperation. Once a system was introduced and nutrient-rich silt flowed across the farmlands, crops flourished. The irrigated land produced nearly five times more than the normal land. The resulting crop surpluses led to the establishment of an elite class, needed to manage and distribute resources, and a subsequent social class order.

All of the following are mentioned in paragraph 1 as disadvantages of the Mesopotamian plain EXCEPT

(A) Natural resources like wood and ore were not present.
(B) The riverbeds did not contain sufficient silt.
(C) Flooding occurred yearly due to melting snow.
(D) Rain was infrequent for most of the year.

With the beginnings of social order in place, urban settlements naturally followed. However, it is unclear what the exact factors were that led to the establishment of the first city-states. One possibility is religion. The earliest city-state, Eridu, founded around 4500 B.C.E., rose around an impressive mud-brick temple. Similarly, Uruk, founded about a thousand years later, housed a temple at its city center. The elites likely used religion to consolidate their power and backed it with divine justification. Furthermore, the cities had patron gods. Uruk, for example, had two: Anu, the god of the sky and chief deity of the pantheon, and Inanna, the goddess of love and war. The catastrophic flood, the same that appears in later religious texts, likely had its earliest version with the Sumerian gods, who, in their own legend, destroyed the human race merely for being too noisy.

According to paragraph 2, Eridu and Uruk were both urban settlements that

(A) depended on irrigation for their crops.
(B) flourished while other Sumerian city-states struggled.
(C) were built around large religious structures.
(D) supported a ruling class of elites.

The central presence of temples and intricacy of the mythology suggested that religious figures most likely led the cities. However, it is now believed that this was not the case, and the cities likely had secular leaders even from their earliest days. Under secular leadership, various occupations arose, generating diversity in city life. Professionals included administrators, craftspeople, and merchants. Given the land's limited natural resources, a robust trade system developed as most raw materials had to be imported. Increasing sophistication in administration and trade led to the invention of a writing system around 3300 B.C.E. Initial versions of the writing were based on logograms, symbols that represented entire words. These logograms were incised on clay tablets using a stylus with a wedge-shaped head. The Romans later called this system of writing cuneiform as the shape of the stylus was a cuneus.

What can be inferred from paragraph 3 about the city-states?

(A) Their functions were more economic than religious.
(B) They developed economies based around their religious practices.
(C) They did not support a large variety of trade skills.
(D) Their writing system was based on those encountered during trade.

The central presence of temples and intricacy of the mythology suggested that religious figures most likely led the cities. However, it is now believed that this was not the case, and the cities likely had secular leaders even from their earliest days. Under secular leadership, various occupations arose, generating diversity in city life. Professionals included administrators, craftspeople, and merchants. Given the land's limited natural resources, a robust trade system developed as most raw materials had to be imported. Increasing sophistication in administration and trade led to the invention of a writing system around 3300 B.C.E. Initial versions of the writing were based on logograms, symbols that represented entire words. These logograms were incised on clay tablets using a stylus with a wedge-shaped head. The Romans later called this system of writing cuneiform as the shape of the stylus was a cuneus.

The word "incised" in the passage is closest in meaning to

(A) discovered
(B) placed
(C) displayed
(D) engraved

The earliest records depict over 2,000 logograms, but the system was simplified as it began to use symbols to express a syllable rather than an entire word. For example, the original symbol for the word "master"—"en"—resembled a throne, though over time it was simplified, with the symbol itself referring to the syllable instead. Any word that included the sound "en" would use that sign, and the rest of the syllables would be expressed via other signs. Around one thousand years after its first appearance, cuneiform had been reduced to about 600 symbols, while the variety of words able to be expressed grew. Texts concerning economic matters were predominant, though works of literature, theology, history, and law also appeared, including the epic of Gilgamesh.

In paragraph 4, why does the author mention that the number of symbols used in cuneiform decreased from 2,000 to 600?

(A) To suggest that the range of available words fluctuated depending on the time period
(B) To show how cuneiform began to be used for more specific purposes
(C) To demonstrate how cuneiform became more efficient by expressing syllables
(D) To provide statistics regarding how cuneiform began to decline in use

The earliest records depict over 2,000 logograms, but the system was simplified as it began to use symbols to express a syllable rather than an entire word. For example, the original symbol for the word "master"—"en"— resembled a throne, though over time it was simplified, with the symbol itself referring to the syllable instead. Any word that included the sound "en" would use that sign, and the rest of the syllables would be expressed via other signs. Around one thousand years after its first appearance, cuneiform had been reduced to about 600 symbols, while the variety of words able to be expressed grew. Texts concerning economic matters were predominant, though works of literature, theology, history, and law also appeared, including the epic of Gilgamesh.

The word "predominant" in the passage is closest in meaning to

(A) complicated
(B) lengthy
(C) primary
(D) uncommon

Sumerian city-states also benefitted from other innovations. The wheel likely appeared in the fourth millennium B.C.E., originally for use in pottery. The first sign of wheels being applied to transportation was seen on a tablet from around 3000 B.C.E., which depicted a box-like cart being pulled on four wheels. The discovery of bronze, which occurred around the same time, also marked major progress for Sumer. Sumerians had been using copper since 3500 B.C.E. but did not smelt it with tin to create significantly stronger bronze until about 500 years later. Bronze did not completely replace copper and stone tools, but it could be forged with sharp edges, making it the superior material for saws, scythes, and all manner of weapons. The discovery of bronze initiated the Bronze Age, which lasted from 3000 to 1000 B.C.E.

According to paragraph 5, the Sumerians first used the wheel to

(A) make pottery.
(B) transport trade goods.
(C) develop roads between cities.
(D) craft box-like carts.

With the beginnings of social order in place, urban settlements naturally followed. However, it is unclear what the exact factors were that led to the establishment of the first city-states. One possibility is religion. The earliest city-state, Eridu, founded around 4500 B.C.E., rose around an impressive mud-brick temple. Similarly, Uruk, founded about a thousand years later, housed a temple at its city center. ■ The elites likely used religion to consolidate their power and backed it with divine justification. ■ Furthermore, the cities had patron gods. ■ Uruk, for example, had two: Anu, the god of the sky and chief deity of the pantheon, and Inanna, the goddess of love and war. ■ The catastrophic flood, the same that appears in later religious texts, likely had its earliest version with the Sumerian gods, who, in their own legend, destroyed the human race merely for being too noisy.

Look at the four squares [■] that indicate where the following sentence could be added to the passage.

All powerful, the gods controlled the meek lives of their worshippers.

Where would the sentence best fit? Click on a square [■] to add the sentence to the passage.

Directions: An introductory sentence for a brief summary of the passage is provided below. Complete the summary by selecting the THREE answer choices that express the most important ideas in the passage. Some sentences do not belong in the summary because they express ideas that are not presented in the passage or are minor ideas in the passage. **This question is worth 2 points.**

Drag your answer choices to the space where they belong. To remove an answer choice, click on it. To review the passage, click on **VIEW TEXT.**

The necessity of irrigation led to the rise of the Sumerian civilization in southern Mesopotamia around 4500 B.C.E.

-
-
-

Answer Choices

(A) The elite class of Mesopotamia gathered the scarce resources of the plain and used them to make the first city-states.

(B) The first city-states honored their patron gods and featured large temples and sites of worship.

(C) Writing was developed in the form of logographs but evolved into a more efficient system based on syllables.

(D) The city-states were ruled by priests who oversaw the economic and political activities of the people.

(E) Technological innovations such as the wheel and the crafting of bronze goods helped the city-states develop.

(F) The city-state of Eridu depended economically on its irrigated crops, while Uruk was known for its pottery and metalwork.

Chapter

07

Education

Passage 1　　Autobiographical Memory

Passage 2　　Early Childhood Education

Passage 3　　Reflection in Teaching

VISUAL
PERCEPTION

IMAGINATION

FINE MOTOR
SKILLS

SPEECH

FINE MOTOR
SKILLS

MEMORY

COLOR &
SHAPE

LOGICAL
THINKING

FINE MONOR
SKILLS

ARTICULATION

VISUAL
PERCEPTION

CONCENTRATION
OF ATTENTION

HEARING

MEMORY

CONCENTRATION
OF ATTENTION

GAMES

CREATIVITY

EDUCATION

PURPOSEFULNESS

BRAIN

Education (교육학)

토플에서는 주로 영유아 발달에 초점을 맞추어 나오고 있으며, 심리학 및 생리학 내용과도 연계되어 출제된다.

[Education 기출 토픽]

- Early Childhood Education
  유아 교육

- Autobiographical Memory
  자서전적 기억

- Reflection in Teaching
  교직에서의 성찰

- Types of Social Groups
  사회 집단의 유형

- Children and Advertising
  아이들과 광고

- Auditory Perception in Infancy
  영아기의 청각적 지각

- Methods of Studying Infant Perception
  영아 지각 연구의 방법들

- Infantile Amnesia
  영아기 기억 상실

- Role of Play in Development
  성장 발달에서 놀이의 역할

[Education 빈출 어휘]

adolescent	청소년		inherited	선천적인
adopt	~을 택하다		inhibition	억제
amnesia	기억 상실		innate	타고난
cognitive	인지의		instill	(생각 등)을 불어넣다
cohesive	응집력 있는		instinctively	본능적으로
conscious	자각하는, 의식적인		interrelated	상호 연관된
continuity	연속성, 지속성		intervention	개입, 중재
correlation	상호 관계		investigation	연구, 조사
discipline	수련(법), 훈육		juvenile	청소년의
discourage	~을 단념하게 하다		kindergarten	유치원
elaboration	정밀화, 정교화		maturation	성숙
embrace	~을 수용하다		nurture	~을 양육하다
empathy	공감, 감정이입		obstacle	장애(물)
engaged	몰입한, 관여한		parental	부모의
entity	실체, 존재		practitioner	실천하는 사람
externally	외면적으로		principle	원리, 원칙
extracurricular	과외의		puberty	사춘기
findings	연구 결과들		recall	~을 회상하다
foster	~을 발전시키다		recount	~을 말하다
fundamental	근본적인		refine	~을 개선하다
grasp	~을 이해하다		reflection	성찰, 반성
imitate	~을 모방하다		reproach	~을 혼내다
implement	~을 이행하다		toddler	유아
infant	영아		verbal	언어의, 말로 하는
influence	~에 영향을 미치다		yield	(결과 등)을 낳다

Autobiographical Memory

If you were asked to recount the earliest memory you have of your life, approximately what age would you have been? The vast majority of people find it impossible to recall memories of things that occurred before they turned three years old, and this phenomenon is referred to as infantile amnesia. Psychologists have spent decades trying to understand why infantile amnesia occurs, despite plenty of evidence that infants and young children have otherwise impressive memory capabilities. Some have suggested that the phenomenon might be better understood if we learn more about the general mechanisms of autobiographical memory, which refers to the memory of events that have occurred in one's own life. Most children are able to give fairly lengthy and cohesive descriptions of past events once they reach three or four years old. So, what factors influence this crucial point in development?

Some possible answers can be found in theories put forward by the renowned Swiss psychologist Jean Piaget. For instance, Piaget asserted that children under two process and recount events in a qualitatively different manner than older children do. This would also mean that the verbal abilities that emerge in two-year-olds enable the coding and expression of events in a significantly different form than the action-based coding form of infants. In fact, verbal abilities of one-year-olds are connected to their memories of events when they attempt to recall them one year later. When researchers asked one-year-olds to imitate an action sequence one year after they first saw it, there was a correlation between their success on the memory task and the children's verbal skills in the past, when they first saw the event. However, even children with poor verbal ability were able to remember the event to some degree, indicating that while memories may be helped by verbal skills, they are not dependent on them.

Another theory is that children must have a fair understanding of the self as a psychological entity before they are able to talk about past events in their lives. Typically, when children are aged between one and two, they develop an understanding of the self, and this undergoes rapid elaboration over the next few years. According to this hypothesis, the emergence of autobiographical memory is dependent on the realization that the physical self has continuity in time.

A third theory is that children need to learn about the general structure of narrative storytelling before they are equipped to tell their own "life story." In other words, they need to experience social interactions, particularly the act of being read stories by parents and being talked to by parents about past events, in order to acquire the necessary knowledge about narratives. When parents discuss things that they did with their children today, or last week, or a year ago, the children begin to understand how to convey stories about past events. This also reminds children about the function of memory and those memories are valued as part of the cultural experience. Interestingly, researchers have found that Korean children are less likely to remember very early memories than Caucasian American children are. Furthermore, other researchers have concluded that Korean parent-child pairs talk about past life experiences three times less often than Caucasian American parent-child pairs do. This indicates that the development of autobiographical memories is influenced by the types of social experiences children have.

One final theory is that, before they can discuss their own past memories, children must first develop an understanding of mental states, such as thoughts, feelings, beliefs, and desires, in themselves and in those around them. Studies have suggested that improvements in memory seem to occur once children become able to answer questions like "What does it mean to believe something?" or "What does it mean to remember something?"

It may be the case that all of the aforementioned factors are interrelated and influence one another. For instance, discussing past events with parents may foster the understanding of the concept of the self while simultaneously helping the child to grasp what it means to "remember." Regardless, it can be said with assurance that the ability to talk about one's past represents a higher level of memory complexity than simply recognizing or recalling a person or event.

<잠자리에 들기 전에 침대에서 책을 읽는 엄마와 딸>

If you were asked to recount the earliest memory you have of your life, approximately what age would you have been? The vast majority of people find it impossible to recall memories of things that occurred before they turned three years old, and this phenomenon is referred to as infantile amnesia. Psychologists have spent decades trying to understand why infantile amnesia occurs, despite plenty of evidence that infants and young children have otherwise impressive memory capabilities. Some have suggested that the phenomenon might be better understood if we learn more about the general mechanisms of autobiographical memory, which refers to the memory of events that have occurred in one's own life. Most children are able to give fairly lengthy and cohesive descriptions of past events once they reach three or four years old. So, what factors influence this crucial point in development?

According to paragraph 1, what indicates that a child has developed autobiographical memory?

(A) The child is able to recall events that occurred before the age of three.

(B) The child is able to form new memories about current events.

(C) The child is aware that some thoughts they have are in fact memories.

(D) The child is able to describe past events coherently and at sufficient length.

Some possible answers can be found in theories put forward by the renowned Swiss psychologist Jean Piaget. For instance, Piaget asserted that children under two process and recount events in a qualitatively different manner than older children do. This would also mean that the verbal abilities that emerge in two-year-olds enable the coding and expression of events in a significantly different form than the action-based coding form of infants. In fact, verbal abilities of one-year-olds are connected to their memories of events when they attempt to recall them one year later. When researchers asked one-year-olds to imitate an action sequence one year after they first saw it, there was a correlation between their success on the memory task and the children's verbal skills in the past, when they first saw the event. However, even children with poor verbal ability were able to remember the event to some degree, indicating that while memories may be helped by verbal skills, they are not dependent on them.

In paragraph 2, why does the author include the information that children with poor verbal skills have shown evidence of remembering past events?

(A) To argue that one-year-olds should be given ample opportunities for verbal interaction
(B) To challenge the notion that one-year-olds are incapable of recognizing others
(C) To provide evidence that memories do not depend only upon verbal skills
(D) To suggest that Piaget's correlation between memory and verbal ability was flawed

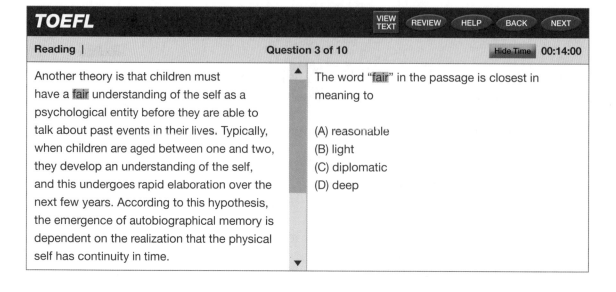

Another theory is that children must have a fair understanding of the self as a psychological entity before they are able to talk about past events in their lives. Typically, when children are aged between one and two, they develop an understanding of the self, and this undergoes rapid elaboration over the next few years. According to this hypothesis, the emergence of autobiographical memory is dependent on the realization that the physical self has continuity in time.

The word "fair" in the passage is closest in meaning to

(A) reasonable
(B) light
(C) diplomatic
(D) deep

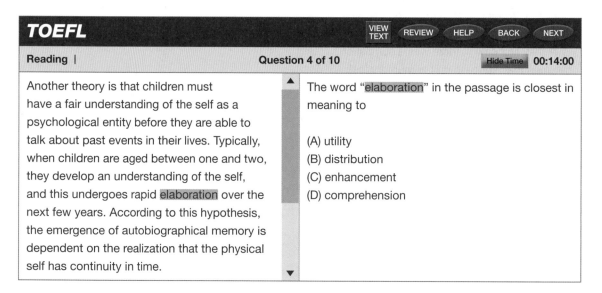

Another theory is that children must have a fair understanding of the self as a psychological entity before they are able to talk about past events in their lives. Typically, when children are aged between one and two, they develop an understanding of the self, and this undergoes rapid elaboration over the next few years. According to this hypothesis, the emergence of autobiographical memory is dependent on the realization that the physical self has continuity in time.

The word "elaboration" in the passage is closest in meaning to

(A) utility
(B) distribution
(C) enhancement
(D) comprehension

Another theory is that children must have a fair understanding of the self as a psychological entity before they are able to talk about past events in their lives. Typically, when children are aged between one and two, they develop an understanding of the self, and this undergoes rapid elaboration over the next few years. According to this hypothesis, the emergence of autobiographical memory is dependent on the realization that the physical self has continuity in time.

According to paragraph 3, what is the relationship between the development of an understanding of the self and the development of autobiographical memory?

(A) Children can quickly gain an understanding of the self by discussing prior events in their lives.

(B) Autobiographical memory helps children to better understand their own strengths and weaknesses.

(C) The development of autobiographical memory is a prerequisite for an understanding of the self.

(D) An understanding that the self remains constant over time facilitates the development of autobiographical memory.

A third theory is that children need to learn about the general structure of narrative storytelling before they are equipped to tell their own "life story." In other words, they need to experience social interactions, particularly the act of being read stories by parents and being talked to by parents about past events, in order to acquire the necessary knowledge about narratives. When parents discuss things that they did with their children today, or last week, or a year ago, the children begin to understand how to convey stories about past events. This also reminds children about the function of memory and those memories are valued as part of the cultural experience. Interestingly, researchers have found that Korean children are less likely to remember very early memories than Caucasian American children are. Furthermore, other researchers have concluded that Korean parent-child pairs talk about past life experiences three times less often than Caucasian American parent-child pairs do. This indicates that the development of autobiographical memories is influenced by the types of social experiences children have.

All of the following are mentioned in paragraph 4 as ways in which parents help their children understand the structure of storytelling EXCEPT

(A) asking children to create their own stories
(B) reading stories to their children
(C) showing children that memories are important
(D) discussing past events with their children

Another theory is that children must have a fair understanding of the self as a psychological entity before they are able to talk about past events in their lives. Typically, when children are aged between one and two, they develop an understanding of the self, and this undergoes rapid elaboration over the next few years. According to this hypothesis, the emergence of autobiographical memory is dependent on the realization that the physical self has continuity in time.

A third theory is that children need to learn about the general structure of narrative storytelling before they are equipped to tell their own "life story." In other words, they need to experience social interactions, particularly the act of being read stories by parents and being talked to by parents about past events, in order to acquire the necessary knowledge about narratives. When parents discuss things that they did with their children today, or last week, or a year ago, the children begin to understand how to convey stories about past events. This also reminds children about the function of memory and those memories are valued as part of the cultural experience. Interestingly, researchers have found that Korean children are less likely to remember very early memories than Caucasian American children are. Furthermore, other researchers have concluded that Korean parent-child pairs talk about past life experiences three times less often than Caucasian American parent-child pairs do. This indicates that the development of autobiographical memories is influenced by the types of social experiences children have.

One final theory is that, before they can discuss their own past memories, children must first develop an understanding of mental

The organization of the passage can best be described as

(A) the definition of a psychological condition followed by its evolution over the years
(B) the description of a learning technique followed by its benefits and drawbacks
(C) an explanation of a phenomenon followed by multiple theories about its development
(D) an outline of memory-processing followed by the significance of memories in various cultures

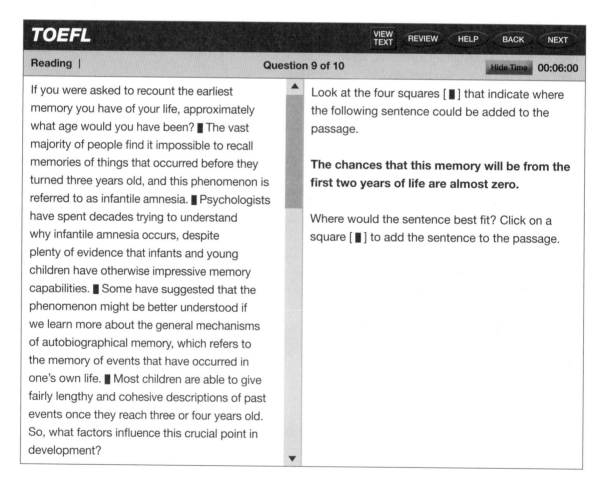

It may be the case that all of the aforementioned factors are interrelated and influence one another. For instance, discussing past events with parents may foster the understanding of the concept of the self while simultaneously helping the child to grasp what it means to "remember." Regardless, it can be said with assurance that the ability to talk about one's past represents a higher level of memory complexity than simply recognizing or recalling a person or event.

The passage supports which of the following statements about the development of autobiographical memory?

(A) An understanding of what it means to remember things is the most crucial factor in the development of autobiographical memory.
(B) Jean Piaget was the first psychologist to fully comprehend the development of autobiographical memory.
(C) Research on the development of autobiographical memory may help psychologists prevent infant amnesia.
(D) The development of autobiographical memory likely results from a combination of different factors.

If you were asked to recount the earliest memory you have of your life, approximately what age would you have been? ■ The vast majority of people find it impossible to recall memories of things that occurred before they turned three years old, and this phenomenon is referred to as infantile amnesia. ■ Psychologists have spent decades trying to understand why infantile amnesia occurs, despite plenty of evidence that infants and young children have otherwise impressive memory capabilities. ■ Some have suggested that the phenomenon might be better understood if we learn more about the general mechanisms of autobiographical memory, which refers to the memory of events that have occurred in one's own life. ■ Most children are able to give fairly lengthy and cohesive descriptions of past events once they reach three or four years old. So, what factors influence this crucial point in development?

Look at the four squares [■] that indicate where the following sentence could be added to the passage.

The chances that this memory will be from the first two years of life are almost zero.

Where would the sentence best fit? Click on a square [■] to add the sentence to the passage.

Directions: An introductory sentence for a brief summary of the passage is provided below. Complete the summary by selecting the THREE answer choices that express the most important ideas in the passage. Some sentences do not belong in the summary because they express ideas that are not presented in the passage or are minor ideas in the passage. **This question is worth 2 points.**

Drag your answer choices to the space where they belong. To remove an answer choice, click on it. To review the passage, click on **VIEW TEXT.**

The capability to create autobiographical memories—coherent narratives about events from one's past—may be affected by several social and intellectual developments.

-
-
-

Answer Choices

(A) The development of autobiographical memory allows children to appreciate meaningful moments that helped shape their development.

(B) Verbal skills and comprehension of narrative structures are believed to play vital roles in the construction of autobiographical memories.

(C) While children are capable of performing simple memory tasks early in life, they do not develop the capacity for autobiographical memory until at least the age of three.

(D) Studies indicate that children who have an understanding of their own mental states and those of others find it easier to formulate and discuss their personal memories.

(E) Children who have acquired a concept of the self and of various mental states are generally able to talk about their own past memories.

(F) Children's earliest autobiographical memories are typically focused around social interactions with their parents.

■ Passage 2

Early Childhood Education

Throughout the world, different cultures hold different opinions when it comes to the purpose of early childhood education. As such, preschools, educational facilities typically designed for children aged five and under, vary considerably from one country to the next. For example, when comparing preschools in the United States, Japan, and China, researchers noted significant differences in the ways that parents in each of the countries view the function of preschools. Whereas parents in Japan view them primarily as a way of giving children the opportunity to be members of a group, Chinese parents see preschools as a crucial first step in their children's academic journey. Meanwhile, in the United States, parents tend to believe the primary purpose of preschools is to instill values of independence and self-reliance in their children, although introducing children to group experiences and academic learning is also a valued aspect.

While many preschool programs are geared primarily toward social and emotional factors, some are designed to promote cognitive development and to make preschoolers better prepared for the more formal learning environments they will experience from kindergarten onwards. In the United States, one of the most well-known programs that aim to promote future academic success is Head Start. The program was established when the United States declared the War on Poverty in the 1960s, and it has now served over 12 million children. The program places a large focus on parental involvement and was created with the "whole child" in mind. As such, it seeks to enhance children's social and emotional development, social responsibility, physical health, and self-assuredness.

It is a matter of personal perspective whether or not Head Start has been a successful program. If success is measured in terms of providing long-term increases in IQ (intelligence quotient) scores, then the program would be seen as a disappointment. While those who graduate from Head Start programs often display immediate IQ increases, these gains tend to fade steadily over time. On the other hand, Head Start does appear to succeed in terms of preparing preschoolers for school. Head Start graduates tend to achieve future school grades that are well above average. Also, researchers have found that Head Start graduates ultimately show higher academic performance at the end of high school, even if the increase in achievement is modest.

Similarly, results from other types of preschool readiness programs show that those who graduate from them are less likely to fail classes and need to repeat grades, and they are more likely to complete school. This indicates that preschool readiness programs are a good long-term investment. Based on cost-benefit analysis research findings, by the time graduates of readiness programs reach the age of 27, taxpayers will have saved seven dollars for every dollar spent on the readiness programs.

Recently, a comprehensive study of early intervention programs indicated that, as a whole, preschool programs have the potential to be highly beneficial, and that governments would be wise to channel funding into such programs in order to reduce potential future costs. For example, compared with children who did not enroll in early intervention programs, the graduates from these programs displayed improved health-related behaviors, increased economic self-sufficiency, better educational outcomes, gains in emotional or cognitive development, and reduced levels of criminal activity. Moreover, some researchers have pointed out that numerous affordable programs have recorded the same positive outcomes as the more expensive ones such as Head Start. In general, the findings of the study were extremely promising, suggesting that early intervention has the potential to yield significant long-term benefits.

However, there are some individuals who oppose programs that seek to enhance academic skills during the preschool years. In fact, the renowned developmental psychologist David Elkind argues that the society within the United States has a tendency to push young learners so relentlessly that they begin to buckle under the stress and pressure. Elkind believes that academic success is primarily influenced by a child's rate of maturation and their inherited abilities—factors that are beyond parental control. It follows, then, that children of a particular age cannot be expected to achieve academic excellence without considering their current level of cognitive development. Ultimately, it is crucial that children receive an appropriate education that takes into account both the unique characteristics of a given child and the general development stages of most children.

<미국 미취학 아동의 헤드 스타트 프로그램>

Throughout the world, different cultures hold different opinions when it comes to the purpose of early childhood education. As such, preschools, educational facilities typically designed for children aged five and under, vary considerably from one country to the next. For example, when comparing preschools in the United States, Japan, and China, researchers noted significant differences in the ways that parents in each of the countries view the function of preschools. Whereas parents in Japan view them primarily as a way of giving children the opportunity to be members of a group, Chinese parents see preschools as a crucial first step in their children's academic journey. Meanwhile, in the United States, parents tend to believe the primary purpose of preschools is to instill values of independence and self-reliance in their children, although introducing children to group experiences and academic learning is also a valued aspect.

According to paragraph 1, what is true regarding parents from the United States, Japan, and China?

(A) They believe preschools are less important than later education programs.

(B) They are dissatisfied with the current education systems in their respective countries.

(C) They have higher expectations of their children than parents in other countries do.

(D) They have differing perspectives on the goals of early education.

While many preschool programs are geared primarily toward social and emotional factors, some are designed to promote cognitive development and to make preschoolers better prepared for the more formal learning environments they will experience from kindergarten onwards. In the United States, one of the most well-known programs that aims to promote future academic success is Head Start. The program was established when the United States declared the War on Poverty in the 1960s, and it has now served over 12 million children. The program places a large focus on parental involvement and was created with the "whole child" in mind. As such, it seeks to enhance children's social and emotional development, social responsibility, physical health, and self-assuredness.

It can be inferred from paragraph 2 that the Head Start program was created to assist children who

(A) were born in the 1950s
(B) had struggled with typical kindergarten material
(C) came from families that were struggling financially
(D) lacked social skills and verbal abilities

It is a matter of personal perspective whether or not Head Start has been a successful program. If success is measured in terms of providing long-term increases in IQ (intelligence quotient) scores, then the program would be seen as a disappointment. While those who graduate from Head Start programs often display immediate IQ increases, these gains tend to fade steadily over time. On the other hand, Head Start does appear to succeed in terms of preparing preschoolers for school. Head Start graduates tend to achieve future school grades that are well above average. Also, researchers have found that Head Start graduates ultimately show higher academic performance at the end of high school, even if the increase in achievement is modest.

In paragraph 3, the author mentions "long-term increases in IQ" to

(A) provide one factor in which Head Start has performed underwhelmingly.
(B) oppose an argument that Head Start is less effective than preschool readiness programs.
(C) indicate that a high IQ is the most reliable indicator of success in most preschool readiness programs.
(D) emphasize the benefits of participating in preschool readiness programs.

Similarly, results from other types of preschool readiness programs show that those who graduate from them are less likely to fail classes and need to repeat grades, and they are more likely to complete school. This indicates that preschool readiness programs are a good long-term investment. Based on cost-benefit analysis research findings, by the time graduates of readiness programs reach the age of 27, taxpayers will have saved seven dollars for every dollar spent on the readiness programs.

According to paragraph 4, a cost-benefit analysis of preschool readiness programs revealed that

(A) readiness programs result in higher taxes for taxpayers in the United States.

(B) participants in readiness programs made more money than their peers by the age of 27.

(C) taxpayers save money in the long term as a result of readiness programs.

(D) the amount of dollars allocated for readiness programs should be increased.

Recently, a comprehensive study of early intervention programs indicated that, as a whole, preschool programs have the potential to be highly beneficial, and that governments would be wise to channel funding into such programs in order to reduce potential future costs. For example, compared with children who did not enroll in early intervention programs, the graduates from these programs displayed improved health-related behaviors, increased economic self-sufficiency, better educational outcomes, gains in emotional or cognitive development, and reduced levels of criminal activity. Moreover, some researchers have pointed out that numerous affordable programs have recorded the same positive outcomes as the more expensive ones such as Head Start. In general, the findings of the study were extremely promising, suggesting that early intervention has the potential to yield significant long-term benefits.

The word "comprehensive" in the passage is closest in meaning to

(A) understandable
(B) thorough
(C) respectable
(D) knowledgeable

Recently, a comprehensive study of early intervention programs indicated that, as a whole, preschool programs have the potential to be highly beneficial, and that governments would be wise to channel funding into such programs in order to reduce potential future costs. For example, compared with children who did not enroll in early intervention programs, the graduates from these programs displayed improved health-related behaviors, increased economic self-sufficiency, better educational outcomes, gains in emotional or cognitive development, and reduced levels of criminal activity. Moreover, some researchers have pointed out that numerous affordable programs have recorded the same positive outcomes as the more expensive ones such as Head Start. In general, the findings of the study were extremely promising, suggesting that early intervention has the potential to yield significant long-term benefits.

According to paragraph 5, which of the following is true about the benefits of early intervention programs?

(A) Even relatively cheap programs can provide several benefits.
(B) Only the benefits of the most expensive programs are worthy of investment.
(C) The programs produce good short-term benefits but few long-term benefits.
(D) The Head Start program provides more benefits than any other program.

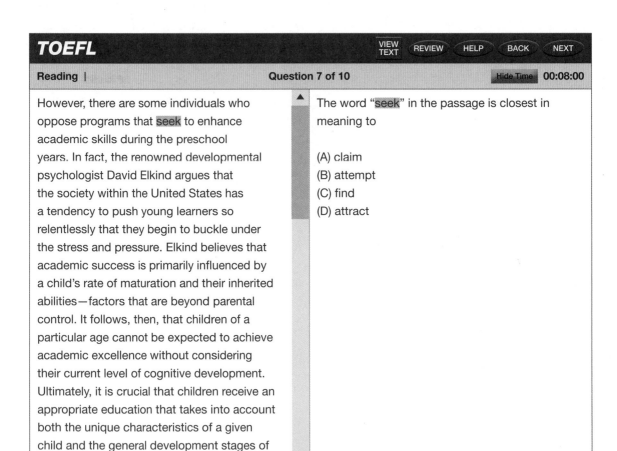

However, there are some individuals who oppose programs that seek to enhance academic skills during the preschool years. In fact, the renowned developmental psychologist David Elkind argues that the society within the United States has a tendency to push young learners so relentlessly that they begin to buckle under the stress and pressure. Elkind believes that academic success is primarily influenced by a child's rate of maturation and their inherited abilities—factors that are beyond parental control. It follows, then, that children of a particular age cannot be expected to achieve academic excellence without considering their current level of cognitive development. Ultimately, it is crucial that children receive an appropriate education that takes into account both the unique characteristics of a given child and the general development stages of most children.

The word "seek" in the passage is closest in meaning to

(A) claim
(B) attempt
(C) find
(D) attract

However, there are some individuals who oppose programs that seek to enhance academic skills during the preschool years. In fact, the renowned developmental psychologist David Elkind argues that the society within the United States has a tendency to push young learners so relentlessly that they begin to buckle under the stress and pressure. Elkind believes that academic success is primarily influenced by a child's rate of maturation and their inherited abilities—factors that are beyond parental control. It follows, then, that children of a particular age cannot be expected to achieve academic excellence without considering their current level of cognitive development. Ultimately, it is crucial that children receive an appropriate education that takes into account both the unique characteristics of a given child and the general development stages of most children.

The passage mentions "developmental psychologist David Elkind" in order to

(A) provide an example of an expert who has launched an effective preschool program.
(B) introduce an opposing viewpoint on the value of early childhood education programs.
(C) help explain why early childhood education programs are only effective in certain countries.
(D) disprove a theory that academic success is dependent on factors outside the control of parents.

However, there are some individuals who oppose programs that seek to enhance academic skills during the preschool years. ■ In fact, the renowned developmental psychologist David Elkind argues that the society within the United States has a tendency to push young learners so relentlessly that they begin to buckle under the stress and pressure. ■ Elkind believes that academic success is primarily influenced by a child's rate of maturation and their inherited abilities—factors that are beyond parental control. ■ It follows, then, that children of a particular age cannot be expected to achieve academic excellence without considering their current level of cognitive development. ■ Ultimately, it is crucial that children receive an appropriate education that takes into account both the unique characteristics of a given child and the general development stages of most children.

Look at the four squares [■] that indicate where the following sentence could be added to the passage.

In Elkind's view, not only does this lead to emotional distress, but it also fails to foster the desired cognitive gains.

Where would the sentence best fit? Click on a square [■] to add the sentence to the passage.

Directions: An introductory sentence for a brief summary of the passage is provided below. Complete the summary by selecting the THREE answer choices that express the most important ideas in the passage. Some sentences do not belong in the summary because they express ideas that are not presented in the passage or are minor ideas in the passage. **This question is worth 2 points.**

Drag your answer choices to the space where they belong. To remove an answer choice, click on it. To review the passage, click on **VIEW TEXT.**

Preschool programs provide opportunities for young children to develop socially, emotionally, and cognitively.

-
-
-

Answer Choices

(A) Head Start and other preschool programs have been shown to help prepare children for school and may also have long-term benefits in helping children develop various life skills.

(B) As well as stressing academic development, preschools should be fun learning environments, since children benefit more from programs they find enjoyable.

(C) The main purpose of preschool programs differs by country, with some focusing on providing group experience, and others promoting self-reliance and preparation for later education.

(D) Research shows that preschool programs are most effective when they focus on only one developmental factor rather than trying to serve the "whole child."

(E) David Elkind has opposed publicly funded preschool programs, arguing that the parents cannot influence their children's emotional development.

(F) Opponents of preschool programs claim that they put undue pressure on children and are ineffective in cases where children are not developmentally ready for academic work.

Reflection in Teaching

It is believed by many that teachers can greatly benefit from reflection, that is, the practice of thinking deeply about and evaluating the events and interactions that occur within their own classrooms. In 1987, education researchers T. Wildman and J. Niles outlined a method for developing the practice of reflection in experienced teachers. They argued that reflective practice could help teachers to feel more engaged in their teaching roles, from an intellectual perspective, and help them to deal with the scarcity of scientific facts in the discipline of teaching.

Of particular interest to Wildman and Niles were the conditions that could potentially be required for reflection to flourish. They felt this topic had not been adequately covered in scientific literature and warranted further investigation. As part of their experimental strategy, they assembled a group of forty teachers in Virginia and worked with them over several years. Wildman and Niles harbored concerns that many participants would be keen to embrace these radical teaching concepts only to find that the act of reflection is difficult to apply in practice to a complex task such as teaching. As such, they guided the teachers through a program in which they first learned how to talk about teaching events, then how to reflect on specific issues in a group, and eventually, how to reflect on these issues by oneself.

Wildman and Niles concluded that successful reflection on teaching depended on an individual having a strong ability to evaluate classroom interactions objectively. At first, many of the teachers involved in their program were described as being utilitarian and possibly incapable of systematic reflection. This was because teachers rarely have the time or opportunities to assess their own teaching experiences, or those of others, from an impartial viewpoint. Wildman and Niles noted a tendency among the teachers to consider only events that took place in the classroom, rather than evaluate the potential contributing factors in a deep and balanced manner.

Encouraging this group of teachers to change the manner in which they thought about classroom events became a fundamental aim of the program. This process was fairly time-consuming, requiring not only a great deal of patience but also highly effective trainers. According to the researchers, training the teachers to consider classroom events objectively took as much as 30 hours, and a similar length of time was required to practice and refine reflection skills.

During their research, Wildman and Niles determined that three factors facilitate reflective practice in a teaching environment. First, support from administrators in the education system enables teachers to comprehend the requirements of reflective practice and its beneficial connection to teaching. Second, teachers require adequate time and space. The teachers who participated in the program complained that they found it difficult to allocate time to develop their own reflection ability because they constantly had to deal with the urgent demands of others. Third, a collaborative environment should be created and supported by other teachers.

The teachers involved with the program noted that support and encouragement helped them cope with aspects of their professional life that they were dissatisfied with. In their final report, Wildman and Niles concluded: "Perhaps the most important thing we learned is the idea of the teacher-as-reflective-practitioner will not happen simply because it is a good or even compelling idea."

The research carried out by Wildman and Niles highlights how critical it is to understand the difficulties of implementing reflective practice in teaching. Other researchers have also noted the cultural inhibitions of teachers with regard to reflective practice. In their 1987 paper, Zeichner and Liston discussed the problems that can arise when teachers attempt to take on two roles: one role being that of the typical teacher educating their students, and the other that of a more reflective decision maker. In addition to cultural issues, there is also the matter of motivation. Hard work is necessary in order to become a reflective practitioner and many individuals struggle to motivate themselves due to the seemingly few immediate benefits and the lack of clearly outlined goals. Some outspoken critics have questioned why a teacher would want to become reflective at all. It seems that the primary reason that some teachers work toward adopting reflective practice is that teacher educators believe it to be beneficial. Indeed, there are many unexplored matters concerning the motivation to reflect, particularly when comparing those who are externally motivated to reflect with those who reflect instinctively and naturally.

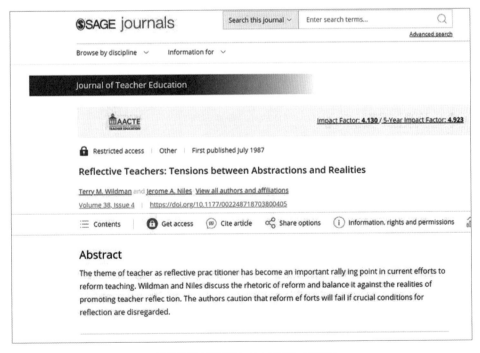

<와일드먼과 나일즈의 논문, '성찰하는 교사들'>

It is believed by many that teachers can greatly benefit from reflection, that is, the practice of thinking deeply about and evaluating the events and interactions that occur within their own classrooms. In 1987, education researchers T. Wildman and J. Niles outlined a method for developing the practice of reflection in experienced teachers. They argued that reflective practice could help teachers to feel more engaged in their teaching roles, from an intellectual perspective, and help them to deal with the scarcity of scientific facts in the discipline of teaching.

According to paragraph 1, it was believed that the act of reflection could benefit teachers by helping them to

(A) establish a more discipline-oriented method of teaching.

(B) understand the core principles of classroom-based learning.

(C) use scientific facts to improve teaching approaches.

(D) enhance their intellectual connection to teaching.

Of particular interest to Wildman and Niles were the conditions that could potentially be required for reflection to flourish. They felt this topic had not been adequately covered in scientific literature and warranted further investigation. As part of their experimental strategy, they assembled a group of forty teachers in Virginia and worked with them over several years. Wildman and Niles harbored concerns that many participants would be keen to embrace these radical teaching concepts only to find that the act of reflection is difficult to apply in practice to a complex task such as teaching. As such, they guided the teachers through a program in which they first learned how to talk about teaching events, then how to reflect on specific issues in a group, and eventually, how to reflect on these issues by oneself.

The word "warranted" in the passage is closest in meaning to

(A) approved
(B) justified
(C) identified
(D) deliberated

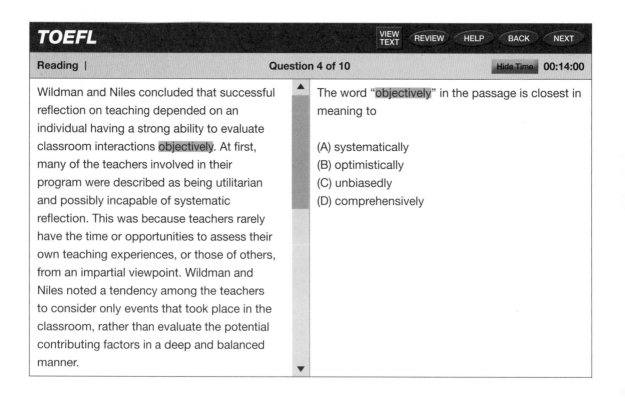

Of particular interest to Wildman and Niles were the conditions that could potentially be required for reflection to flourish. They felt this topic had not been adequately covered in scientific literature and warranted further investigation. As part of their experimental strategy, they assembled a group of forty teachers in Virginia and worked with them over several years. Wildman and Niles harbored concerns that many participants would be keen to embrace these radical teaching concepts only to find that the act of reflection is difficult to apply in practice to a complex task such as teaching. As such, they guided the teachers through a program in which they first learned how to talk about teaching events, then how to reflect on specific issues in a group, and eventually, how to reflect on these issues by oneself.

All of the following are mentioned about the experimental strategy described in paragraph 2 EXCEPT

(A) It required teachers to write down their reflections about teaching.
(B) It was adopted by a group of experienced teachers for a number of years.
(C) It involved having teachers discuss events that took place in their classrooms.
(D) It was designed to ultimately help teachers reflect without help from others.

Wildman and Niles concluded that successful reflection on teaching depended on an individual having a strong ability to evaluate classroom interactions objectively. At first, many of the teachers involved in their program were described as being utilitarian and possibly incapable of systematic reflection. This was because teachers rarely have the time or opportunities to assess their own teaching experiences, or those of others, from an impartial viewpoint. Wildman and Niles noted a tendency among the teachers to consider only events that took place in the classroom, rather than evaluate the potential contributing factors in a deep and balanced manner.

The word "objectively" in the passage is closest in meaning to

(A) systematically
(B) optimistically
(C) unbiasedly
(D) comprehensively

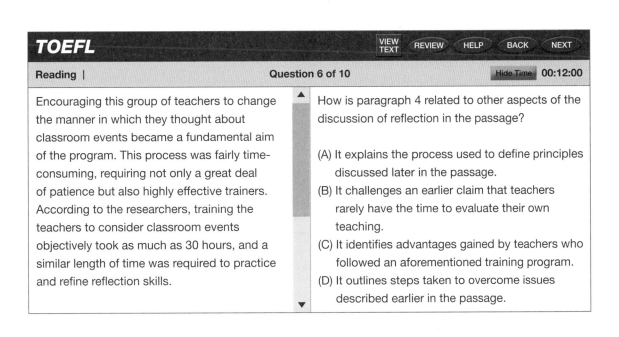

Wildman and Niles concluded that successful reflection on teaching depended on an individual having a strong ability to evaluate classroom interactions objectively. At first, many of the teachers involved in their program were described as being utilitarian and possibly incapable of systematic reflection. This was because teachers rarely have the time or opportunities to assess their own teaching experiences, or those of others, from an impartial viewpoint. Wildman and Niles noted a tendency among the teachers to consider only events that took place in the classroom, rather than evaluate the potential contributing factors in a deep and balanced manner.

According to paragraph 3, what did the teachers working with Wildman and Niles often fail to do when they attempted to reflect?

(A) Accurately calculate the amount of time required for the act of reflection
(B) Consider the potential causes of events that transpired in their classrooms
(C) Compare and contrast various methods used to reflect on events
(D) Establish achievable long-term goals prior to engaging in reflection

Encouraging this group of teachers to change the manner in which they thought about classroom events became a fundamental aim of the program. This process was fairly time-consuming, requiring not only a great deal of patience but also highly effective trainers. According to the researchers, training the teachers to consider classroom events objectively took as much as 30 hours, and a similar length of time was required to practice and refine reflection skills.

How is paragraph 4 related to other aspects of the discussion of reflection in the passage?

(A) It explains the process used to define principles discussed later in the passage.
(B) It challenges an earlier claim that teachers rarely have the time to evaluate their own teaching.
(C) It identifies advantages gained by teachers who followed an aforementioned training program.
(D) It outlines steps taken to overcome issues described earlier in the passage.

The research carried out by Wildman and Niles highlights how critical it is to understand the difficulties of implementing reflective practice in teaching. Other researchers have also noted the cultural inhibitions of teachers with regard to reflective practice. In their 1987 paper, Zeichner and Liston discussed the problems that can arise when teachers attempt to take on two roles: one role being that of the typical teacher educating their students, and the other that of a more reflective decision maker. In addition to cultural issues, there is also the matter of motivation. Hard work is necessary in order to become a reflective practitioner and many individuals struggle to motivate themselves due to the seemingly few immediate benefits and the lack of clearly outlined goals. Some outspoken critics have questioned why a teacher would want to become reflective at all. It seems that the primary reason that some teachers work toward adopting reflective practice is that teacher educators believe it to be beneficial. Indeed, there are many unexplored matters concerning the motivation to reflect, particularly when comparing those who are externally motivated to reflect with those who reflect instinctively and naturally.

According to paragraph 6, teachers may be reluctant to practice reflection because

(A) it is difficult to keep track of events that occur each day.

(B) it is typically discouraged by those involved in teacher education.

(C) the rewards of reflection may not be immediately apparent.

(D) they feel it uses up valuable time that could be spent with students.

The research carried out by Wildman and Niles highlights how critical it is to understand the difficulties of implementing reflective practice in teaching. Other researchers have also noted the cultural inhibitions of teachers with regard to reflective practice. In their 1987 paper, Zeichner and Liston discussed the problems that can arise when teachers attempt to take on two roles: one role being that of the typical teacher educating their students, and the other that of a more reflective decision maker. In addition to cultural issues, there is also the matter of motivation. Hard work is necessary in order to become a reflective practitioner and many individuals struggle to motivate themselves due to the seemingly few immediate benefits and the lack of clearly outlined goals. Some outspoken critics have questioned why a teacher would want to become reflective at all. It seems that the primary reason that some teachers work toward adopting reflective practice is that teacher educators believe it to be beneficial. Indeed, there are many unexplored matters concerning the motivation to reflect, particularly when comparing those who are externally motivated to reflect with those who reflect instinctively and naturally.

Which of the sentences below best expresses the essential information in the highlighted sentence in the passage? Incorrect choices change the meaning in important ways or leave out essential information.

(A) More research certainly must be carried out on what motivates people to reflect, especially the differences between people who are encouraged to reflect and people who do it naturally.

(B) Most teachers need to explore different strategies to help them reflect independently rather than require the support of others.

(C) Many of the unknown factors related to the practice of being reflective are likely to be better understood by studying people who are reflective without external motivation.

(D) There has been very little research conducted on the ways we can motivate teachers to incorporate reflection into their standard teaching approach.

Encouraging this group of teachers to change the manner in which they thought about classroom events became a fundamental aim of the program. ▮ This process was fairly time-consuming, requiring not only a great deal of patience but also highly effective trainers. ▮ According to the researchers, training the teachers to consider classroom events objectively took as much as 30 hours, and a similar length of time was required to practice and refine reflection skills.

▮ During their research, Wildman and Niles determined that three factors facilitate reflective practice in a teaching environment. ▮ First, support from administrators in the education system enables teachers to comprehend the requirements of reflective practice and its beneficial connection to teaching. Second, teachers require adequate time and space. The teachers who participated in the program complained that they found it difficult to allocate time to develop their own reflection ability because they constantly had to deal with the urgent demands of others. Third, a collaborative environment should be created and supported by other teachers. The teachers involved with the program noted that support and encouragement helped them cope with aspects of their professional life that they were dissatisfied with. In their final report, Wildman and Niles concluded: "Perhaps the most important thing we learned is the idea of the teacher-as-reflective-practitioner will not happen simply because it is a good or even compelling idea."

Look at the four squares [▮] that indicate where the following sentence could be added to the passage.

However, changing teachers' attitudes toward reflection will not be successful unless there is support for reflection in the teaching environment.

Where would the sentence best fit? Click on a square [▮] to add the sentence to the passage.

Directions: An introductory sentence for a brief summary of the passage is provided below. Complete the summary by selecting the THREE answer choices that express the most important ideas in the passage. Some sentences do not belong in the summary because they express ideas that are not presented in the passage or are minor ideas in the passage. **This question is worth 2 points.**

Drag your answer choices to the space where they belong. To remove an answer choice, click on it. To review the passage, click on **VIEW TEXT.**

Wildman and Niles conducted an extensive research study on reflection in teaching.

-
-
-

Answer Choices

(A) Wildman and Niles concluded that teachers can successfully practice reflection if they have sufficient resources as well as the cooperation and encouragement of others.

(B) By working with Virginia teachers, Wildman and Niles were able to prove conclusively that reflection benefits both teachers and students in various ways.

(C) Wildman and Niles described three strategies that teachers could use to help themselves handle issues that occur as a result of reflection.

(D) A teacher's ability to overcome the difficulties involved in reflection depends on his or her initial motivation to reflect.

(E) Research indicates that there are several obstacles to implementing reflection in schools and insufficient understanding of why teachers might want to reflect.

(F) Wildman and Niles found that significant amounts of training and practice are required to understand classroom events and develop the skills required for reflection.

Chapter

08

Economics

Passage 1   The Commercialization of Lumber

Passage 2   The Revolution of Cheap Print

Passage 3   European Economic Growth in the
             17th Century

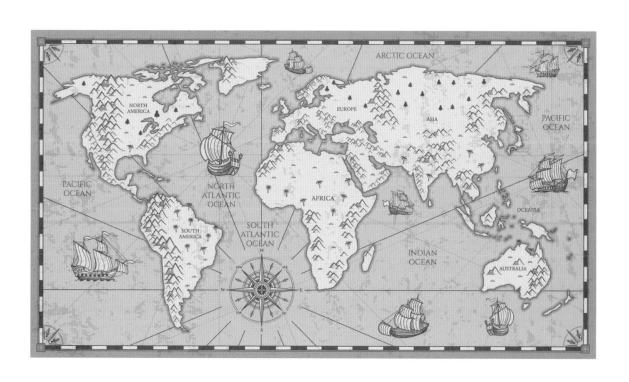

Economics (경제학)

토플에서 경제학은 엄밀히 말해 역사 속 경제, 특정 물품의 역사 또는 특정 시기의 특정 지역 경제를 배경으로 한 지문이 주로 출제된다.

[Economics 기출 토픽]

- Background for the Industrial Revolution
  산업 혁명의 배경

- Industrialization in the Netherlands and Scandinavia
  네덜란드와 스칸디나비아에서의 산업화

- The Commercialization of Lumber
  목재의 상업화

- The Revolution of Cheap Print
  저가 인쇄의 혁명

- European Economic Growth in the 17th Century
  17세기 유럽의 경제 성장

- Trade and the Ancient Middle East
  무역과 고대 중동

- Europe's Early Sea Trade with Asia
  유럽의 초기 아시아 해상 무역

- Megalopolis: The Urbanized Northeastern Seaboard of the United States
  메갈로폴리스: 도시화된 미동북부 해안 지방

- Trade and Early State Formation
  무역과 초기 국가의 형성

- The Commercial Revolution in Medieval Europe
  중세 유럽의 상업 혁명

[Economics 빈출 어휘]

advent	출현, 도래	industrialist	기업가, 실업가
affluent	부유한	infusion	투입
bolster	~을 강화하다	ingenuity	독창성
boom	호황을 누리다	instrumental	중요한
boost	~을 증대하다	intensively	집중적으로
capital	자본금, 자금	intermittent	간헐적인
carrier	운송회사, 운반자	meager	변변치 않은
circulate	~을 유포하다	mill	공장
coincide	동시에 일어나다	peasant	소작농
commercialization	상업화	prosperous	번영하는, 번창하는
commodity	상품	remoteness	멀리 떨어져 있음
comprehensive	포괄적인, 종합적인	revolution	혁명
consecutive	연속적인	rural	시골의
criticize	~을 비판하다	scrap	폐품
deliberately	의도적으로, 고의로	sophistication	세련됨
dependence on	~에 대한 의존(도)	sphere	분야, 영역
drastic	급격한	spur	~에 박차를 가하다
drive	원동력	subsidize	~에게 보조금을 주다
economic gains	경제적 이득	supplement	~을 보충하다
equivalent	상당하는 것	surplus	잉여, 과잉
exacerbate	~을 악화시키다	take advantage of	~을 활용하다
facilitate	~을 용이하게 하다	take place	일어나다, 발생하다
feasible	실현 가능한	trigger	~을 촉발시키다
herald	~을 예고하다	unprecedented	전례 없는
incentive	자극(제), 동기	watershed	분수령

■ Passage 1

The Commercialization of Lumber

In America during the 1800s, almost everything that was built was manufactured from wood. One of the most valuable types of wood for building purposes was pine. It is soft enough to be easily fashioned using simple hand tools, but also relatively durable and strong. It also floats well on water, which made it easy to transport to distant markets throughout the country. States such as Michigan, Wisconsin, and Minnesota, which are situated around the Great Lakes, all boasted expansive pine forests and large rivers, facilitating the transportation of logs into the Great Lakes and onwards toward international shipping hubs.

By the mid-19th century, timber shortages in the East and the settlement of the American West both had an impact on the pine forests around the Great Lakes. Over the next three decades, the lumbering industry boomed in Michigan, Wisconsin, and Minnesota. Newly established lumbering corporations purchased huge tracts of pineland and began cutting down the trees at a rapid pace. Timber was regarded as a valuable commodity by both the colonists and the later industrialists, but the latter group took a far more comprehensive and aggressive approach to removing trees. As a result, the period between 1860 and 1890 represented a drastic change in the way lumber had been traded in the past. Farmers seeking extra ways to make money were no longer the main source for firewood or other wood products. As early as the 1870s, both farmers and city folk had begun purchasing lumber products from large manufacturing companies based in the Great Lakes states instead of cutting down trees themselves or buying wood from local sources.

Technological developments played a large role in the commercialization of lumbering. The thick saw blades that had originally been used were very inefficient, wasting as much as a third of each log, which would be left behind as sawdust or scrap. However, in the 1870s, the British-invented band saw, with its thinner blade, soon became the preferred cutting tool in the lumber factories throughout the Great Lakes states. Around the same time, the advent of steam-powered mills facilitated lumber production by allowing for the more continuous and efficient cutting of logs. In fact, steam power brought automation to a wide range of tasks, one of which was the transportation of waste products. Steam-powered mills also provided heat to log ponds, keeping them unfrozen all year round so that lumber production could continue without delays.

Lumber companies had to come up with methods to neutralize the effects of the seasons in order for industrial lumber production to succeed. Tree cutting typically took place during the winter, as logs could be easily dragged on sleds across snow and ice to the banks of rivers. As soon as the rivers and lakes had thawed, workers would load the logs onto rafts and transport them to mills, where they would be chopped into lumber during the summer. If the seasons behaved unpredictably, such as an unseasonably warm winter or a delayed spring thaw, lumber production was adversely affected. Loggers devised several techniques for transporting logs out of the forests when the climate conditions were not ideal. In the 1870s, logging teams in the Great Lakes states started to sprinkle water on sleigh roads, promoting the formation of an artificial ice layer to facilitate transportation. The reduced friction provided by the ice allowed workers to transport larger and heavier loads.

However, there was no such quick fix to counter the greater issue of uncharacteristically warm winters, during which the sleigh roads would quickly turn to mud. After a series of consecutive snowless winters, lumber companies began focusing on ways in which they could reduce their dependence on Mother Nature and the seasons. The first thing they thought of was railroad expansion. Initially, common carriers were reluctant to lay the proposed track due to the remoteness of the pine forests, but rising lumber prices in the late 1870s and the intermittent warm, dry winters left loggers little choice but to turn to iron rails. By 1887, Michigan was home to a network of 89 logging railroads, and logging had transformed into a year-round activity rather than merely a winter one.

Even after the logs arrived at a river, the remaining leg of the journey downstream to a mill was often challenging. It was common to have logjams—accumulations of logs that prevented logs from floating along the river—that could stretch as far as 15 kilometers, and this problem was exacerbated as increased pressure was placed on the northern Midwest pinelands. Log and chain barriers called booms had to be constructed to help keep the logs moving steadily and control their direction.

<베어진 나무(timber)가 운반을 위해 잘려져 통나무(log)가 된 후 공장에서 가공되어 목재(lumber)가 됨>

By the mid-19th century, timber shortages in the East and the settlement of the American West both had an impact on the pine forests around the Great Lakes. Over the next three decades, the lumbering industry boomed in Michigan, Wisconsin, and Minnesota. Newly established lumbering corporations purchased huge tracts of pineland and began cutting down the trees at a rapid pace. Timber was regarded as a valuable commodity by both the colonists and the later industrialists, but the latter group took a far more comprehensive and aggressive approach to removing trees. As a result, the period between 1860 and 1890 represented a drastic change in the way lumber had been traded in the past. Farmers seeking extra ways to make money were no longer the main source for firewood or other wood products. As early as the 1870s, both farmers and city folk had begun purchasing lumber products from large manufacturing companies based in the Great Lakes states instead of cutting down trees themselves or buying wood from local sources.

What can be inferred from paragraph 2 about timber in America before the year 1860?

(A) Timber was less readily available prior to 1860 and hence more expensive.
(B) Timber was mainly manufactured by large companies based in the East.
(C) Farmers who wished to supplement their income were the primary source of lumber.
(D) Farmers of the American West became rich by selling timber to newly arrived settlers.

Technological developments played a large role in the commercialization of lumbering. The thick saw blades that had originally been used were very inefficient, wasting as much as a third of each log, which would be left behind as sawdust or scrap. However, in the 1870s, the British-invented band saw, with its thinner blade, soon became the preferred cutting tool in the lumber factories throughout the Great Lakes states. Around the same time, the advent of steam-powered mills facilitated lumber production by allowing for the more continuous and efficient cutting of logs. In fact, steam power brought automation to a wide range of tasks, one of which was the transportation of waste products. Steam-powered mills also provided heat to log ponds, keeping them unfrozen all year round so that lumber production could continue without delays.

Why does the author mention "the British-invented band saw"?

(A) To exemplify the influence of new technology on the lumber industry
(B) To illustrate how steam power resulted in several technological advancements
(C) To explain how thicker saw blades helped to reduce waste from logs
(D) To show how American lumber companies worked closely with British lumber companies

Technological developments played a large role in the commercialization of lumbering. The thick saw blades that had originally been used were very inefficient, wasting as much as a third of each log, which would be left behind as sawdust or scrap. However, in the 1870s, the British-invented band saw, with its thinner blade, soon became the preferred cutting tool in the lumber factories throughout the Great Lakes states. Around the same time, the advent of steam-powered mills facilitated lumber production by allowing for the more continuous and efficient cutting of logs. In fact, steam power brought automation to a wide range of tasks, one of which was the transportation of waste products. Steam-powered mills also provided heat to log ponds, keeping them unfrozen all year round so that lumber production could continue without delays.

The phrase "allowing for" in the passage is closest in meaning to

(A) approving
(B) encouraging
(C) preparing
(D) enabling

Lumber companies had to come up with methods to neutralize the effects of the seasons in order for industrial lumber production to succeed. Tree cutting typically took place during the winter, as logs could be easily dragged on sleds across snow and ice to the banks of rivers. As soon as the rivers and lakes had thawed, workers would load the logs onto rafts and transport them to mills, where they would be chopped into lumber during the summer. If the seasons behaved unpredictably, such as an unseasonably warm winter or a delayed spring thaw, lumber production was adversely affected. Loggers devised several techniques for transporting logs out of the forests when the climate conditions were not ideal. In the 1870s, logging teams in the Great Lakes states started to sprinkle water on sleigh roads, promoting the formation of an artificial ice layer to facilitate transportation. The reduced friction provided by the ice allowed workers to transport larger and heavier loads.

The word "facilitate" in the passage is closest in meaning to

(A) ease
(B) produce
(C) evaluate
(D) shorten

Lumber companies had to come up with methods to neutralize the effects of the seasons in order for industrial lumber production to succeed. Tree cutting typically took place during the winter, as logs could be easily dragged on sleds across snow and ice to the banks of rivers. As soon as the rivers and lakes had thawed, workers would load the logs onto rafts and transport them to mills, where they would be chopped into lumber during the summer. If the seasons behaved unpredictably, such as an unseasonably warm winter or a delayed spring thaw, lumber production was adversely affected. Loggers devised several techniques for transporting logs out of the forests when the climate conditions were not ideal. In the 1870s, logging teams in the Great Lakes states started to sprinkle water on sleigh roads, promoting the formation of an artificial ice layer to facilitate transportation. The reduced friction provided by the ice allowed workers to transport larger and heavier loads.

According to paragraph 4, how could a warm winter negatively impact lumber production?

(A) Rivers would not flow quickly enough to power lumber mills.
(B) Transportation of logs to rivers and lakes would become too difficult.
(C) Some tree species would yield lumber of unsatisfactory quality.
(D) Logs were more likely to become jammed on water transportation routes.

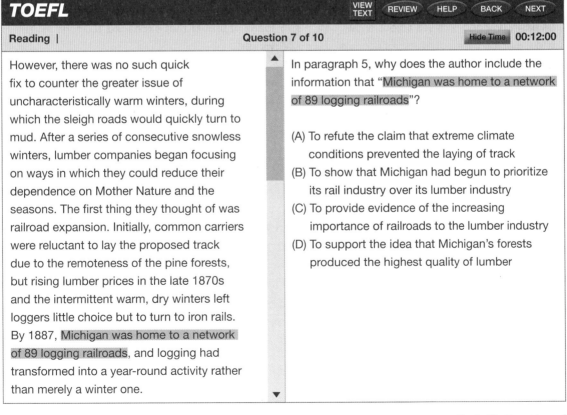

However, there was no such quick fix to counter the greater issue of uncharacteristically warm winters, during which the sleigh roads would quickly turn to mud. After a series of consecutive snowless winters, lumber companies began focusing on ways in which they could reduce their dependence on Mother Nature and the seasons. The first thing they thought of was railroad expansion. Initially, common carriers were reluctant to lay the proposed track due to the remoteness of the pine forests, but rising lumber prices in the late 1870s and the intermittent warm, dry winters left loggers little choice but to turn to iron rails. By 1887, Michigan was home to a network of 89 logging railroads, and logging had transformed into a year-round activity rather than merely a winter one.

The word "remoteness" in the passage is closest in meaning to

(A) density
(B) stagnation
(C) isolation
(D) scarcity

However, there was no such quick fix to counter the greater issue of uncharacteristically warm winters, during which the sleigh roads would quickly turn to mud. After a series of consecutive snowless winters, lumber companies began focusing on ways in which they could reduce their dependence on Mother Nature and the seasons. The first thing they thought of was railroad expansion. Initially, common carriers were reluctant to lay the proposed track due to the remoteness of the pine forests, but rising lumber prices in the late 1870s and the intermittent warm, dry winters left loggers little choice but to turn to iron rails. By 1887, Michigan was home to a network of 89 logging railroads, and logging had transformed into a year-round activity rather than merely a winter one.

In paragraph 5, why does the author include the information that "Michigan was home to a network of 89 logging railroads"?

(A) To refute the claim that extreme climate conditions prevented the laying of track
(B) To show that Michigan had begun to prioritize its rail industry over its lumber industry
(C) To provide evidence of the increasing importance of railroads to the lumber industry
(D) To support the idea that Michigan's forests produced the highest quality of lumber

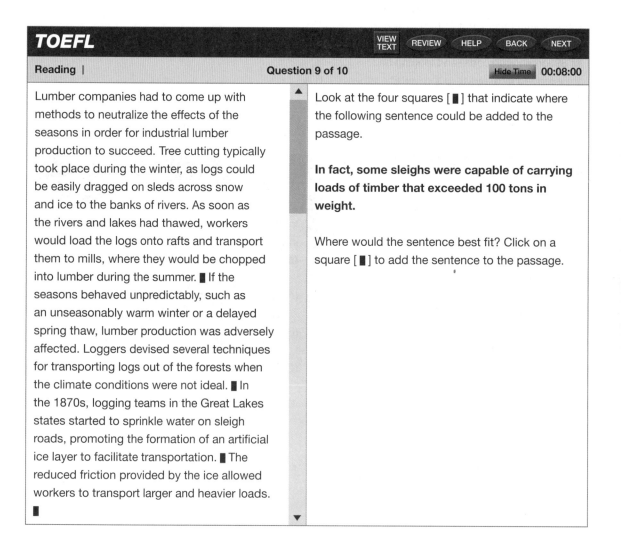

Even after the logs arrived at a river, the remaining leg of the journey downstream to a mill was often challenging. It was common to have logjams—accumulations of logs that prevented logs from floating along the river—that could stretch as far as 15 kilometers, and this problem was exacerbated as increased pressure was placed on the northern Midwest pinelands. Log and chain barriers called booms had to be constructed to help keep the logs moving steadily and control the direction of them.

According to paragraph 6, the construction of booms benefited the logging industry by

(A) helping logs to travel downstream more quickly and easily.

(B) reducing the expense of logging around the Great Lakes states.

(C) shortening the length of the downstream journey from logging sites to mills.

(D) increasing the number of logs that could be stored in lakes.

Lumber companies had to come up with methods to neutralize the effects of the seasons in order for industrial lumber production to succeed. Tree cutting typically took place during the winter, as logs could be easily dragged on sleds across snow and ice to the banks of rivers. As soon as the rivers and lakes had thawed, workers would load the logs onto rafts and transport them to mills, where they would be chopped into lumber during the summer. ∎ If the seasons behaved unpredictably, such as an unseasonably warm winter or a delayed spring thaw, lumber production was adversely affected. Loggers devised several techniques for transporting logs out of the forests when the climate conditions were not ideal. ∎ In the 1870s, logging teams in the Great Lakes states started to sprinkle water on sleigh roads, promoting the formation of an artificial ice layer to facilitate transportation. ∎ The reduced friction provided by the ice allowed workers to transport larger and heavier loads.

∎

Look at the four squares [∎] that indicate where the following sentence could be added to the passage.

In fact, some sleighs were capable of carrying loads of timber that exceeded 100 tons in weight.

Where would the sentence best fit? Click on a square [∎] to add the sentence to the passage.

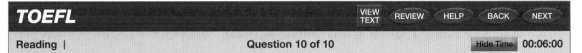
Directions: An introductory sentence for a brief summary of the passage is provided below. Complete the summary by selecting the THREE answer choices that express the most important ideas in the passage. Some sentences do not belong in the summary because they express ideas that are not presented in the passage or are minor ideas in the passage. **This question is worth 2 points.**

Drag your answer choices to the space where they belong. To remove an answer choice, click on it. To review the passage, click on **VIEW TEXT.**

Increasing demands for timber in nineteenth-century America transformed lumbering in the Great Lakes region.

-
-
-

Answer Choices

(A) By innovating new technology such as band saws, American lumber companies profited by exporting lumbering equipment to Britain and other countries.

(B) The development of steam power and other technological advances led to increased productivity, efficiency, and commercialization of the lumbering industry.

(C) During the 1800s, lumbering became a large-scale industry involving manufacturing companies rather than a local enterprise created by local farmers.

(D) After 1860, farmers began collaborating with lumber companies to efficiently transport and manufacture logs into wood products.

(E) New techniques for transporting logs to mills were introduced, and these helped transform lumbering from a seasonal activity to a year-round activity.

(F) Unpredictable seasonal weather in the Great Lakes states made it virtually impossible to lay tracks for logging railroads.

The Revolution of Cheap Print

Significant changes in the economics of the printed word occurred in both the United States and Europe during the first half of the nineteenth century, although the changes generally began earlier and had a wider impact in the US. During the 1830s and 1840s, the advent of the era of cheap print was heralded by drastic price reductions for books and newspapers in America. Whereas daily newspapers had normally cost six cents per issue, some began to sell for only a penny or two. Likewise, books that had once cost two dollars started selling for 25 cents, even though the same books cost the equivalent of seven dollars in Britain. The drops in the price of print were so steep and happened so rapidly that they were described as an information-price revolution. Several similar instances of sharp price declines have occurred between then and the modern day, profoundly affecting our culture and the spread of information.

In the mid-nineteenth century, two American cultural innovations related to the printed word were named to acknowledge their low price. The "dime novel" and the "penny press" were considered cheap in both senses of the word; they may have been pleasingly low in price, but they were also criticized for being low in sophistication. However, low price did not necessarily mean low taste, and publishers increasingly printed highly regarded works in cheap formats to reach as many customers as possible. The information-price revolution also had a profound impact on religion and politics, as groups within both spheres understood that, for the first time in history, the publishing of printed works was the most effective tool of mass persuasion.

The availability of cheap printed works was not entirely unprecedented. In England and France during the 1600s and 1700s, it was fairly common for people among the lower classes to circulate cheap collections of stories, ballads, and plays. The vast majority of the poor were unable to read, so those who could read would read the works aloud to large groups. In this way, cheap print captivated a listening audience more so than it did a reading audience. The rise of cheap print in the 1800s in America and Europe took place on a much greater scale, and it coincided with substantial increases in literacy to create a sort of cultural watershed. Historically, even in the homes of literate people, books and other published works were fairly uncommon and special items, often only consisting of religious texts that were read repeatedly. But with the sharp rise of cheap print, reading habits became more varied, and people began to enjoy reading newspapers, magazines, and cheap books and then sharing them with others. While people still indulged in intensive reading of religious texts, reading quickly also became popular as an enjoyable and relaxing form of recreation.

When attempting to provide an explanation for the rise of cheap print, most sources tend to emphasize the importance of technological developments. Without a doubt, technological change was instrumental in the development of cheap print. However, print prices had already begun to fall in America before technological advances occurred. In other words, new technology arrived while the price drops were already underway, so while it helped to accelerate the trend, it did not trigger it. In fact, it was the steady expansion of print that triggered a drive to innovate new technology. To consider technology as the main cause of cheap print would be rather ignorant, as politics, culture, and markets played critical roles in shaping the conditions that made it feasible to invest in new technology for print purposes.

Whereas European governments taxed print publications such as newspapers, the United States did not, and even subsidized them through the postal system. The rising popularity of cheap printed works in the United States also highlighted clear trends in American consumer markets in the 19th century. Nathan Rosenberg, an economic historian, cited the cases of cutlery, guns, boots, and clothing, saying, "Americans readily accepted products which had been deliberately designed for low cost, mass production methods," even though demand for unique, bespoke goods persisted among consumers in countries like Britain. So, it is not surprising that books followed this pattern. Furthermore, much of the new manufacturing technology that was introduced to facilitate the mass production of books was not the product of American ingenuity. In fact, most of the major developments in printing before 1850 had not traveled east across the Atlantic toward Britain, but in the opposite direction. But the mass production of books advanced more rapidly in the United States, where the market was much larger than Britain's and more concerned about price than quality, probably because a relatively small percentage of book purchasers were sophisticated readers.

<미국의 저가 신문(페니 프레스)>

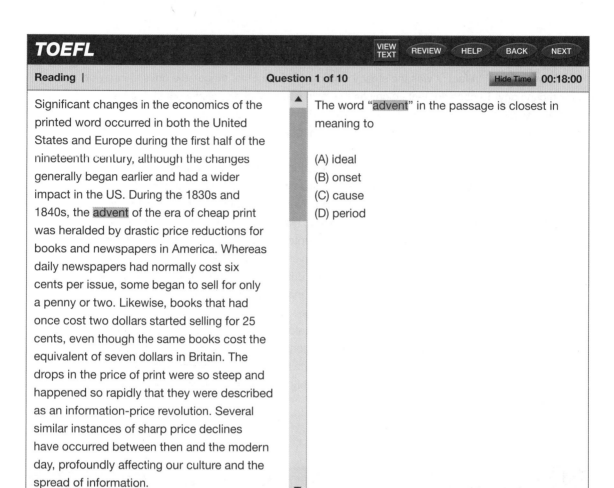

Significant changes in the economics of the printed word occurred in both the United States and Europe during the first half of the nineteenth century, although the changes generally began earlier and had a wider impact in the US. During the 1830s and 1840s, the advent of the era of cheap print was heralded by drastic price reductions for books and newspapers in America. Whereas daily newspapers had normally cost six cents per issue, some began to sell for only a penny or two. Likewise, books that had once cost two dollars started selling for 25 cents, even though the same books cost the equivalent of seven dollars in Britain. The drops in the price of print were so steep and happened so rapidly that they were described as an information-price revolution. Several similar instances of sharp price declines have occurred between then and the modern day, profoundly affecting our culture and the spread of information.

The word "advent" in the passage is closest in meaning to

(A) ideal
(B) onset
(C) cause
(D) period

In the mid-nineteenth century, two American cultural innovations related to the printed word were named to acknowledge their low price. The "dime novel" and the "penny press" were considered cheap in both senses of the word; they may have been pleasingly low in price, but they were also criticized for being low in sophistication. However, low price did not necessarily mean low taste, and publishers increasingly printed highly regarded works in cheap formats to reach as many customers as possible. The information-price revolution also had a profound impact on religion and politics, as groups within both spheres understood that, for the first time in history, the publishing of printed works was the most effective tool of mass persuasion.

Which of the following claims is made about the low-price publications mentioned in paragraph 2?

(A) Book publishers stopped printing well-known literary works and focused on cheap stories.

(B) Consumers were impressed with the high quality of writing in dime novels.

(C) Inexpensive novels became largely popular with the upper class.

(D) The criticism that all cheap novels are unsophisticated is not always accurate.

The availability of cheap printed works was not entirely unprecedented. In England and France during the 1600s and 1700s, it was fairly common for people among the lower classes to circulate cheap collections of stories, ballads, and plays. The vast majority of the poor were unable to read, so those who could read would read the works aloud to large groups. In this way, cheap print captivated a listening audience more so than it did a reading audience. The rise of cheap print in the 1800s in America and Europe took place on a much greater scale, and it coincided with substantial increases in literacy to create a sort of cultural watershed. Historically, even in the homes of literate people, books and other published works were fairly uncommon and special items, often only consisting of religious texts that were read repeatedly. But with the sharp rise of cheap print, reading habits became more varied, and people began to enjoy reading newspapers, magazines, and cheap books and then sharing them with others. While people still indulged in intensive reading of religious texts, reading quickly also became popular as an enjoyable and relaxing form of recreation.

The word "unprecedented" in the passage is closest in meaning to

(A) consistent
(B) exceptional
(C) acceptable
(D) documented

The availability of cheap printed works was not entirely unprecedented. In England and France during the 1600s and 1700s, it was fairly common for people among the lower classes to circulate cheap collections of stories, ballads, and plays. The vast majority of the poor were unable to read, so those who could read would read the works aloud to large groups. In this way, cheap print captivated a listening audience more so than it did a reading audience. The rise of cheap print in the 1800s in America and Europe took place on a much greater scale, and it coincided with substantial increases in literacy to create a sort of cultural watershed. Historically, even in the homes of literate people, books and other published works were fairly uncommon and special items, often only consisting of religious texts that were read repeatedly. But with the sharp rise of cheap print, reading habits became more varied, and people began to enjoy reading newspapers, magazines, and cheap books and then sharing them with others. While people still indulged in intensive reading of religious texts, reading quickly also became popular as an enjoyable and relaxing form of recreation.

According to paragraph 3, reading changed in all of the following ways after the rise of cheap print EXCEPT

(A) Reading for enjoyment became more common.
(B) Readers began to share books with acquaintances.
(C) People began to read a more diverse range of publications.
(D) People began to study religious texts more intensively.

When attempting to provide an explanation for the rise of cheap print, most sources tend to emphasize the importance of technological developments. Without a doubt, technological change was instrumental in the development of cheap print. However, print prices had already begun to fall in America before technological advances occurred. In other words, new technology arrived while the price drops were already underway, so while it helped to accelerate the trend, it did not trigger it. In fact, it was the steady expansion of print that triggered a drive to innovate new technology. To consider technology as the main cause of cheap print would be rather ignorant, as politics, culture, and markets played critical roles in shaping the conditions that made it feasible to invest in new technology for print purposes.

In paragraph 4, the author expresses which of the following points of view on the relationship between technology and the development of cheap print?

(A) The introduction of new technology enabled the early development of cheap print.
(B) The print revolution could not have happened without significant technological developments.
(C) The growth of cheap print provided an incentive to begin developing new technology.
(D) Cultural and political groups were opposed to using new technology to produce cheap print.

Whereas European governments taxed print publications such as newspapers, the United States did not, and even subsidized them through the postal system. The rising popularity of cheap printed works in the United States also highlighted clear trends in American consumer markets in the 19th century. Nathan Rosenberg, an economic historian, cited the cases of cutlery, guns, boots, and clothing, saying, "Americans readily accepted products which had been deliberately designed for low cost, mass production methods," even though demand for unique, bespoke goods persisted among consumers in countries like Britain. So, it is not surprising that books followed this pattern. Furthermore, much of the new manufacturing technology that was introduced to facilitate the mass production of books was not the product of American ingenuity. In fact, most of the major developments in printing before 1850 had not traveled east across the Atlantic toward Britain, but in the opposite direction. But the mass production of books advanced more rapidly in the United States, where the market was much larger than Britain's and more concerned about price than quality, probably because a relatively small percentage of book purchasers were sophisticated readers.

Why does the author refer to Nathan Rosenberg's remarks on "the cases of cutlery, guns, boots and clothing"?

(A) To support the idea that books fit a trend observed in nineteenth-century American consumer markets

(B) To highlight how manufacturing techniques used for books were also used to produce other goods

(C) To show the similarities between consumer trends in Britain and in the United States

(D) To explain why bespoke products were less popular in America than they were in other countries

Whereas European governments taxed print publications such as newspapers, the United States did not, and even subsidized them through the postal system. The rising popularity of cheap printed works in the United States also highlighted clear trends in American consumer markets in the 19th century. Nathan Rosenberg, an economic historian, cited the cases of cutlery, guns, boots, and clothing, saying, "Americans readily accepted products which had been deliberately designed for low cost, mass production methods," even though demand for unique, bespoke goods persisted among consumers in countries like Britain. So, it is not surprising that books followed this pattern. Furthermore, much of the new manufacturing technology that was introduced to facilitate the mass production of books was not the product of American ingenuity. In fact, most of the major developments in printing before 1850 had not traveled east across the Atlantic toward Britain, but in the opposite direction. But the mass production of books advanced more rapidly in the United States, where the market was much larger than Britain's and more concerned about price than quality, probably because a relatively small percentage of book purchasers were sophisticated readers.

The word "persisted" in the passage is closest in meaning to

(A) argued
(B) elevated
(C) continued
(D) preserved

Whereas European governments taxed print publications such as newspapers, the United States did not, and even subsidized them through the postal system. The rising popularity of cheap printed works in the United States also highlighted clear trends in American consumer markets in the 19th century. Nathan Rosenberg, an economic historian, cited the cases of cutlery, guns, boots, and clothing, saying, "Americans readily accepted products which had been deliberately designed for low cost, mass production methods," even though demand for unique, bespoke goods persisted among consumers in countries like Britain. So, it is not surprising that books followed this pattern. Furthermore, much of the new manufacturing technology that was introduced to facilitate the mass production of books was not the product of American ingenuity. In fact, most of the major developments in printing before 1850 had not traveled east across the Atlantic toward Britain, but in the opposite direction. But the mass production of books advanced more rapidly in the United States, where the market was much larger than Britain's and more concerned about price than quality, probably because a relatively small percentage of book purchasers were sophisticated readers.

Which of the following is suggested in Paragraph 5 about books in Britain?

(A) Britain developed the most innovative technology for book printing prior to 1850.
(B) Government subsidies allowed European publishers to produce more books.
(C) British and American book markets were in direct competition in the nineteenth century.
(D) Mass-produced books were less popular in Britain than they were in the United States.

The availability of cheap printed works was not entirely unprecedented. In England and France during the 1600s and 1700s, it was fairly common for people among the lower classes to circulate cheap collections of stories, ballads, and plays. The vast majority of the poor were unable to read, so those who could read would read the works aloud to large groups. In this way, cheap print captivated a listening audience more so than it did a reading audience. The rise of cheap print in the 1800s in America and Europe took place on a much greater scale, and it coincided with substantial increases in literacy to create a sort of cultural watershed. ■ Historically, even in the homes of literate people, books and other published works were fairly uncommon and special items, often only consisting of religious texts that were read repeatedly. ■ But with the sharp rise of cheap print, reading habits became more varied, and people began to enjoy reading newspapers, magazines, and cheap books and then sharing them with others. ■ While people still indulged in intensive reading of religious texts, reading quickly also became popular as an enjoyable and relaxing form of recreation. ■

Look at the four squares [■] that indicate where the following sentence could be added to the passage.

Although people did not read a broad range of materials, they tended to read the limited number of books at their disposal intensively and on a regular basis.

Where would the sentence best fit? Click on a square [■] to add the sentence to the passage.

Directions: An introductory sentence for a brief summary of the passage is provided below. Complete the summary by selecting the THREE answer choices that express the most important ideas in the passage. Some sentences do not belong in the summary because they express ideas that are not presented in the passage or are minor ideas in the passage. **This question is worth 2 points.**

Drag your answer choices to the space where they belong. To remove an answer choice, click on it. To review the passage, click on **VIEW TEXT.**

Cheap print experienced early success in the United States.

-
-
-

Answer Choices

(A) As early as the 1830s, America began experiencing an information-price revolution which saw published works selling far cheaper than they were in Britain.

(B) Very few readers in seventeenth- and eighteenth-century England and France were interested in reading printed materials that were non-religious.

(C) As was the case with a wide variety of products, American consumers were more willing to embrace mass-produced books than European consumers were.

(D) Cheap print was opposed by some governments who feared that religious texts would disappear and be replaced by unsophisticated print materials.

(E) Most advances in printing technology originated in Europe and American publishers were reluctant to embrace these new approaches.

(F) The rapid rise of cheap print gave American readers greater access to different kinds of publications, changing the way people read and their primary reasons for reading.

■ Passage 3

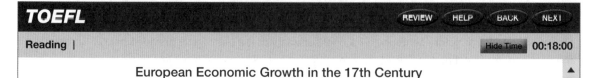

European Economic Growth in the 17th Century

In the late 16th century and early 17th century, economic growth in Europe continued and allowed most European countries to make significant economic gains after the less prosperous medieval period. Several factors played a crucial role in this growth, including the expansion of trade networks and increased agricultural productivity.

It is virtually impossible for populations to grow if the rural economy is unable to produce enough extra food to feed everyone. During the sixteenth century, farmers converted vast tracts of forests and low-lying wetlands into land that was suitable for crop cultivation. One notable example of this is the Dutch land reclamation in the Netherlands in the 16th and 17th centuries. This extensive expansion of farmland resulted in the Dutch reclaiming more than 36,000 acres of land between 1590 and 1615.

What may have appeared as small, unremarkable villages actually played a considerable role in European economic development. These rural settlements were typically situated in regions where agricultural production was relatively advanced, ensuring not only the livelihoods of the village dwellers but also a surplus of agricultural products for sale and trade. Moreover, the farmers in these small villages had fairly easy access to city merchants, markets, and trade routes. As agricultural production increased in the countryside, companies began establishing industrial facilities in rural areas, which played a pivotal role in the expansion of industry. In particular, textile manufacturers took advantage of cheap and plentiful rural labor and employed countless peasants to produce goods in their own village homes. Throughout Germany, destruction brought about by the Thirty Years' War (1618-1648) pushed textile production even further into the countryside. Entire families of poor villagers spun or wove cloth and linens in their humble shacks in an effort to supplement their typical meager family income, despite being poorly paid for their work.

The expansion of trading networks also helped to boost Europe's economy during this period. Ships set sail from England and the Netherlands to pick up rye from the Baltic states, and they stopped off in Spain and Portugal during the return trip to trade various goods. The growth of populations, and subsequently workforces, in places like England, Belgium, northern Italy, and parts of Spain led to the expansion of small-scale manufacturing of textiles and production of metal in those regions. At that time, manufacturing industries required very little capital and quickly turned a profit. The only business ventures that required a significant initial financial investment were mining and iron smelting.

The expansion of trade was helped by the development of banking and other financial services. By the middle of the sixteenth century, money lenders and merchants had begun accepting bills of exchange rather than insisting upon the use of gold or silver. Bills of exchange first saw use in medieval Italy. These were written guarantees that an individual would pay a specified amount of money by a certain date, so they were similar to providing a person with credit in today's world. Around the middle of the century, a financier from Antwerp made the bold claim that, "One can no more trade without bills of exchange than sail without water." The use of bills of exchange meant that merchants no longer had to risk carrying desirable gold and silver on long, dangerous journeys. A merchant from London who wished to buy olives from a merchant in Madrid could go to an exchanger and pay the exchanger the equivalent sum in pounds, the British currency. The exchanger would then send a bill of exchange to a colleague in Madrid, giving him approval to pay the Madrid merchant in reals, the Spanish currency at the time, after the goods had been handed over to the London merchant.

As Spanish ships returned to Europe carrying gold and silver mined from the Americas, this infusion of capital further spurred the expansion of international trade. The increase of capital boosted the production of goods and led to increased trade, and even credit across the European continent. Furthermore, bankers and affluent merchants offered investments and loans to states, increasing the credit supply, and an English innovation called a joint-stock partnership became more common. Joint-stock companies differed from typical short-term financial arrangements between investors and businesses, as they would provide long-term permanent funding of capital by selling shares to wealthy merchants and other investors and using the money generated through shares to bolster the company.

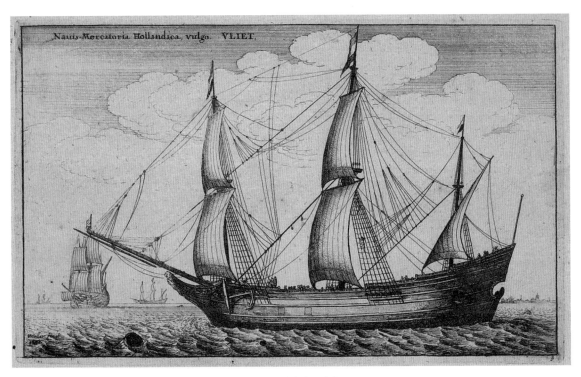

<17세기 네덜란드 상선>

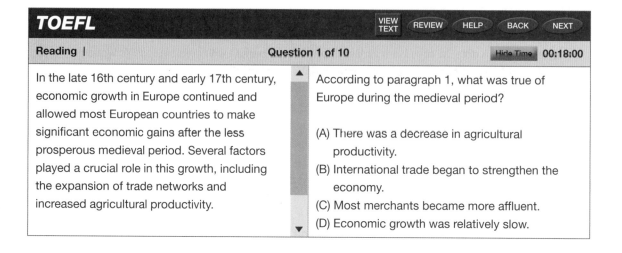

In the late 16th century and early 17th century, economic growth in Europe continued and allowed most European countries to make significant economic gains after the less prosperous medieval period. Several factors played a crucial role in this growth, including the expansion of trade networks and increased agricultural productivity.

According to paragraph 1, what was true of Europe during the medieval period?

(A) There was a decrease in agricultural productivity.
(B) International trade began to strengthen the economy.
(C) Most merchants became more affluent.
(D) Economic growth was relatively slow.

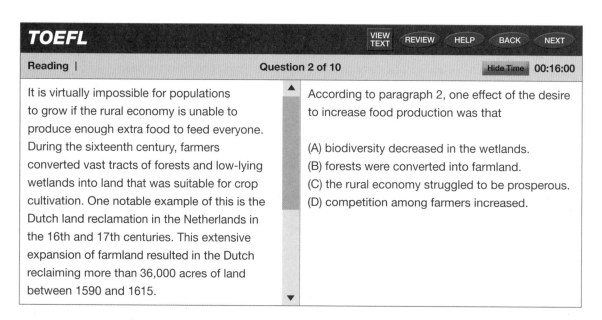

It is virtually impossible for populations to grow if the rural economy is unable to produce enough extra food to feed everyone. During the sixteenth century, farmers converted vast tracts of forests and low-lying wetlands into land that was suitable for crop cultivation. One notable example of this is the Dutch land reclamation in the Netherlands in the 16th and 17th centuries. This extensive expansion of farmland resulted in the Dutch reclaiming more than 36,000 acres of land between 1590 and 1615.

According to paragraph 2, one effect of the desire to increase food production was that

(A) biodiversity decreased in the wetlands.
(B) forests were converted into farmland.
(C) the rural economy struggled to be prosperous.
(D) competition among farmers increased.

What may have appeared as small, unremarkable villages actually played a considerable role in European economic development. These rural settlements were typically situated in regions where agricultural production was relatively advanced, ensuring not only the livelihoods of the village dwellers but also a surplus of agricultural products for sale and trade. Moreover, the farmers in these small villages had fairly easy access to city merchants, markets, and trade routes. As agricultural production increased in the countryside, companies began establishing industrial facilities in rural areas, which played a pivotal role in the expansion of industry. In particular, textile manufacturers took advantage of cheap and plentiful rural labor and employed countless peasants to produce goods in their own village homes. Throughout Germany, destruction brought about by the Thirty Years' War (1618-1648) pushed textile production even further into the countryside. Entire families of poor villagers spun or wove cloth and linens in their humble shacks in an effort to supplement their typical meager family income, despite being poorly paid for their work.

The word "meager" in the passage is closest in meaning to

(A) gradual
(B) intermittent
(C) ordinary
(D) inadequate

What may have appeared as small, unremarkable villages actually played a considerable role in European economic development. These rural settlements were typically situated in regions where agricultural production was relatively advanced, ensuring not only the livelihoods of the village dwellers but also a surplus of agricultural products for sale and trade. Moreover, the farmers in these small villages had fairly easy access to city merchants, markets, and trade routes. As agricultural production increased in the countryside, companies began establishing industrial facilities in rural areas, which played a pivotal role in the expansion of industry. In particular, textile manufacturers took advantage of cheap and plentiful rural labor and employed countless peasants to produce goods in their own village homes. Throughout Germany, destruction brought about by the Thirty Years' War (1618-1648) pushed textile production even further into the countryside. Entire families of poor villagers spun or wove cloth and linens in their humble shacks in an effort to supplement their typical meager family income, despite being poorly paid for their work.

Why does the author mention the "Thirty Years' War" in paragraph 3?

(A) To show the negative consequences of poor trade relationships
(B) To describe one of several factors that led to increased rural industry
(C) To contrast the differences between two European conflicts
(D) To argue that international trade had been stronger prior to the war

The expansion of trading networks also helped to boost Europe's economy during this period. Ships set sail from England and the Netherlands to pick up rye from the Baltic states, and they stopped off in Spain and Portugal during the return trip to trade various goods. The growth of populations, and subsequently workforces, in places like England, Belgium, northern Italy, and parts of Spain led to the expansion of small-scale manufacturing of textiles and production of metal in those regions. At that time, manufacturing industries required very little capital and quickly turned a profit. The only business ventures that required a significant initial financial investment were mining and iron smelting.

In paragraph 4, the author suggests that the textile industry grew as a result of

(A) improved conditions in rural settlements.
(B) the discovery of new types of raw materials for use by industry.
(C) an increase in the number of available workers.
(D) profits accumulated through mining and smelting.

The expansion of trade was helped by the development of banking and other financial services. By the middle of the sixteenth century, money lenders and merchants had begun accepting bills of exchange rather than insisting upon the use of gold or silver. Bills of exchange first saw use in medieval Italy. These were written guarantees that an individual would pay a specified amount of money by a certain date, so they were similar to providing a person with credit in today's world. Around the middle of the century, a financier from Antwerp made the bold claim that, "One can no more trade without bills of exchange than sail without water." The use of bills of exchange meant that merchants no longer had to risk carrying desirable gold and silver on long, dangerous journeys. A merchant from London who wished to buy olives from a merchant in Madrid could go to an exchanger and pay the exchanger the equivalent sum in pounds, the British currency. The exchanger would then send a bill of exchange to a colleague in Madrid, giving him approval to pay the Madrid merchant in reals, the Spanish currency at the time, after the goods had been handed over to the London merchant.

What can be inferred from paragraph 5 about merchants undertaking business trips in Europe?

(A) They generally chose to travel in groups.
(B) They rarely accepted bills of exchange.
(C) They preferred to meet buyers at a neutral location.
(D) They risked being robbed of their valuables.

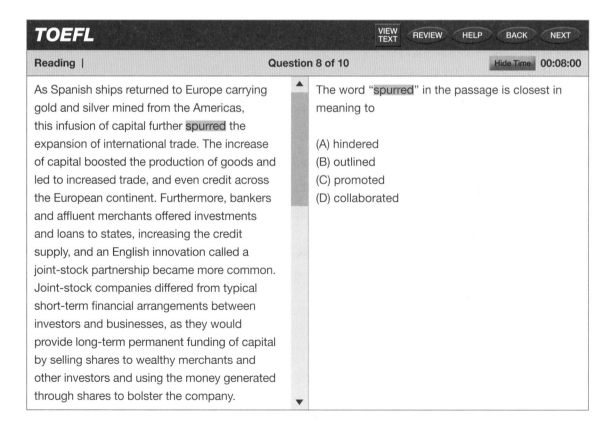

As Spanish ships returned to Europe carrying gold and silver mined from the Americas, this infusion of capital further spurred the expansion of international trade. The increase of capital boosted the production of goods and led to increased trade, and even credit across the European continent. Furthermore, bankers and affluent merchants offered investments and loans to states, increasing the credit supply, and an English innovation called a joint-stock partnership became more common. Joint-stock companies differed from typical short-term financial arrangements between investors and businesses, as they would provide long-term permanent funding of capital by selling shares to wealthy merchants and other investors and using the money generated through shares to bolster the company.

In paragraph 6, all of the following are indicated about joint-stock companies EXCEPT

(A) They were originally conceived in England.
(B) They provided financial backing for businesses.
(C) They typically entered into short-term financial arrangements.
(D) They were involved in the selling of shares in businesses.

As Spanish ships returned to Europe carrying gold and silver mined from the Americas, this infusion of capital further spurred the expansion of international trade. The increase of capital boosted the production of goods and led to increased trade, and even credit across the European continent. Furthermore, bankers and affluent merchants offered investments and loans to states, increasing the credit supply, and an English innovation called a joint-stock partnership became more common. Joint-stock companies differed from typical short-term financial arrangements between investors and businesses, as they would provide long-term permanent funding of capital by selling shares to wealthy merchants and other investors and using the money generated through shares to bolster the company.

The word "spurred" in the passage is closest in meaning to

(A) hindered
(B) outlined
(C) promoted
(D) collaborated

The expansion of trade was helped by the development of banking and other financial services. By the middle of the sixteenth century, money lenders and merchants had begun accepting bills of exchange rather than insisting upon the use of gold or silver. ▪ Bills of exchange first saw use in medieval Italy. These were written guarantees that an individual would pay a specified amount of money by a certain date, so they were similar to providing a person with credit in today's world. ▪ Around the middle of the century, a financier from Antwerp made the bold claim that, "One can no more trade without bills of exchange than sail without water." The use of bills of exchange meant that merchants no longer had to risk carrying desirable gold and silver on long, dangerous journeys. ▪ A merchant from London who wished to buy olives from a merchant in Madrid could go to an exchanger and pay the exchanger the equivalent sum in pounds, the British currency. ▪ The exchanger would then send a bill of exchange to a colleague in Madrid, giving him approval to pay the Madrid merchant in reals, the Spanish currency at the time, after the goods had been handed over to the London merchant.

Look at the four squares [▪] that indicate where the following sentence could be added to the passage.

They could also avoid having to identify and assess the value of the various currencies used at each trading destination.

Where would the sentence best fit? Click on a square [▪] to add the sentence to the passage.

Directions: An introductory sentence for a brief summary of the passage is provided below. Complete the summary by selecting the THREE answer choices that express the most important ideas in the passage. Some sentences do not belong in the summary because they express ideas that are not presented in the passage or are minor ideas in the passage. **This question is worth 2 points.**

Drag your answer choices to the space where they belong. To remove an answer choice, click on it. To review the passage, click on **VIEW TEXT.**

> **In late 16th-and early 17th-century Europe, increased agricultural production and the expansion of trade helped drive economic growth.**
>
> •
> •
> •

Answer Choices

(A) Most countryside settlements established arrangements with urban markets that allowed them to sell any handicrafts they produced.

(B) The expansion of trade was facilitated by improvements to financial services and a huge influx of capital thanks to gold and silver brought back from the Americas.

(C) The rise of rural industry and its large workforce resulted in a boom in textile manufacturing, much of it taking place within the homes of village residents.

(D) Increased capital was required for the production of more sophisticated goods, which were increasingly desirable to European consumers.

(E) Converting land into farmland allowed farmers to produce more food to bolster the rural economies and accumulate surpluses of products for trading.

(F) Bills of exchange gradually fell out of favor with international traders as banks began to provide loans for merchants.

Actual Tests

01 **Actual Test 1**

02 **Actual Test 2**

Actual Test 1

Geographic Isolation of Species

When asked to provide a definition of a species, a biologist named Ernst Mayr described a species as "an actually or potentially interbreeding population that does not interbreed with other such populations when there is opportunity to do so." The origins of many species are influenced by a key event in which a population—and its entire gene pool—is separated from other populations of the same species, making interbreeding between the populations impossible. Separated populations with their isolated gene pools will then follow their own distinct evolutionary courses. In many cases of new species creation, a geographic barrier is the initial reason for the isolation of a population, and this mode of new species evolution is referred to as allopatric speciation.

The geographical isolation of a population can be triggered by various factors. For instance, certain fish populations that inhabit lowland lakes may be separated when a mountain range gradually emerges, splitting apart lakes and river networks. Likewise, a slowly advancing glacier may eventually divide a population, or a land bridge like the Isthmus of Panama may emerge, resulting in marine populations being separated on either side of the land mass.

How substantial and massive does a geographic barrier need to be in order to keep populations separated? That depends on a given species' ability to traverse such barriers. Mountains and rivers pose no obstacle to birds, or even adaptable mammals like coyotes. In the case of plants, wind-blown pollen is also unhindered by such barriers, and plant seeds can still be carried back and forth on insects and other animals. Small rodents, on the other hand, will find no way to pass a wide river or a deep canyon. One good example of this is the separation of the white-tailed antelope squirrel and the closely related Harris' antelope squirrel by the Grand Canyon in the southwestern United States. The Harris' antelope squirrel is present in a limited range in deserts south of the Grand Canyon, while the smaller white-tailed antelope squirrel inhabits deserts north of the canyon and west of the Colorado River in southern California.

Although geographic isolation gives rise to opportunities for new species to develop, allopatric speciation can only occur when the gene pool is changed significantly enough to establish reproductive barriers between the parent population and the isolated population. The chances of allopatric speciation occurring increase when a population is both small and isolated, as there is a higher chance of its gene pool changing substantially. For instance, in under two million years, tiny populations of foreign animal and plant species originating from the South American mainland managed to colonize the Galapagos Islands, creating all the unique species that now live on the islands.

Oceanic islands that are close enough to allow occasional population movement to occur, but far enough apart to ensure most populations evolve in isolation, serve as valuable outdoor laboratories where the process of evolution is on full view. Nowhere is this more apparent than the Galapagos Islands. The islands emerged as a result of underwater volcanic eruptions, and they were gradually populated by organisms who had strayed from their habitats, often carried by wind and oceanic currents from far away continents and islands. Also, some species most likely reached the island chain by being transported by other organisms, such as seeds entangled in the feathers of sea birds.

The vast majority of species on the Galapagos Islands today are found nowhere else and are the descendants of organisms that were blown or floated across the sea from the South American mainland. For example, the island chain is home to the Galapagos finches: thirteen species of closely related birds. While these birds share a lot of similarities, their feeding habits differ, as do their beak types, which are specially adapted to better suit their feeding habits. Much evidence has been gathered that indicates all thirteen finch species descended from one single small population of birds that colonized one of the islands. Once the founder population had become isolated on the island after traveling from the mainland, its gene pool must have undergone significant changes, essentially creating a new species. Later, some organisms belonging to this new species were likely carried to a neighboring island by a storm. This second founder population, now isolated on its island, would then have evolved into a second new species, which could later recolonize the island from which its founding population emigrated. Recent studies show that each island of the Galapagos now has multiple species of finches, with some islands having as many as ten distinct species.

When asked to provide a definition of a species, a biologist named Ernst Mayr described a species as "an actually or potentially interbreeding population that does not interbreed with other such populations when there is opportunity to do so." The origins of many species are influenced by a key event in which a population—and its entire gene pool—is separated from other populations of the same species, making interbreeding between the populations impossible. Separated populations with their isolated gene pools will then follow their own distinct evolutionary courses. In many cases of new species creation, a geographic barrier is the initial reason for the isolation of a population, and this mode of new species evolution is referred to as allopatric speciation.

According to paragraph 1, allopatric speciation is possible when

(A) a population of one species breeds with another species.

(B) a species successfully overcomes a geographic barrier.

(C) genetic mutations occur in populations sharing the same habitat.

(D) a geographic barrier results in a population becoming isolated.

When asked to provide a definition of a species, a biologist named Ernst Mayr described a species as "an actually or potentially interbreeding population that does not interbreed with other such populations when there is opportunity to do so." The origins of many species are influenced by a key event in which a population—and its entire gene pool—is separated from other populations of the same species, making interbreeding between the populations impossible. Separated populations with their isolated gene pools will then follow their own distinct evolutionary courses. In many cases of new species creation, a geographic barrier is the initial reason for the isolation of a population, and this mode of new species evolution is referred to as allopatric speciation.

The geographical isolation of a population can be triggered by various factors. For instance, certain fish populations that inhabit lowland lakes may be separated when a mountain range gradually emerges, splitting apart lakes and river networks. Likewise, a slowly advancing glacier may eventually divide a population, or a land bridge like the Isthmus of Panama may emerge, resulting in marine populations being separated on either side of the land mass.

How is paragraph 2 related to paragraph 1?

(A) Paragraph 2 further elaborates on the conclusion presented in paragraph 1 that geographic isolation has led to the decline of a number of species.

(B) Paragraph 2 describes several ways in which the phenomenon of geographic isolation outlined in paragraph 1 can take place.

(C) Paragraph 2 provides evidence that proves the theory in paragraph 1 that a population becomes less genetically diverse once it becomes isolated.

(D) Paragraph 2 explains why the term "allopatric" is used to describe the mode of speciation detailed in paragraph

How substantial and massive does a geographic barrier need to be in order to keep populations separated? That depends on a given species' ability to traverse such barriers. Mountains and rivers pose no obstacle to birds, or even adaptable mammals like coyotes. In the case of plants, wind-blown pollen is also unhindered by such barriers, and plant seeds can still be carried back and forth on insects and other animals. Small rodents, on the other hand, will find no way to pass a wide river or a deep canyon. One good example of this is the separation of the white-tailed antelope squirrel and the closely related Harris' antelope squirrel by the Grand Canyon in the southwestern United States. The Harris' antelope squirrel is present in a limited range in deserts south of the Grand Canyon, while the smaller white-tailed antelope squirrel inhabits deserts north of the canyon and west of the Colorado River in southern California.

In paragraph 3, the author provides examples using various organisms to explain which of the following points?

(A) Populations of plants are less likely to be separated by geographic barriers than populations of animals.

(B) Populations of large organisms are more likely to be kept isolated by geographic barriers than populations of small organisms.

(C) The capability that organisms have to move across geographic barriers directly relates to the effectiveness of the barriers.

(D) Only those members of a species that have undergone evolutionary adaptations are able to cross geographic barriers.

How substantial and massive does a geographic barrier need to be in order to keep populations separated? That depends on a given species' ability to traverse such barriers. Mountains and rivers pose no obstacle to birds, or even adaptable mammals like coyotes. In the case of plants, wind-blown pollen is also unhindered by such barriers, and plant seeds can still be carried back and forth on insects and other animals. Small rodents, on the other hand, will find no way to pass a wide river or a deep canyon. One good example of this is the separation of the white-tailed antelope squirrel and the closely related Harris' antelope squirrel by the Grand Canyon in the southwestern United States. The Harris' antelope squirrel is present in a limited range in deserts south of the Grand Canyon, while the smaller white-tailed antelope squirrel inhabits deserts north of the canyon and west of the Colorado River in southern California.

According to paragraph 3, white-tailed antelope squirrels and Harris' antelope squirrels have which of the following in common?

(A) They are the two smallest rodents native to California.
(B) They are unable to cross the Grand Canyon.
(C) They are found across the continental United States.
(D) They struggle to survive in desert conditions.

Although geographic isolation gives rise to opportunities for new species to develop, allopatric speciation can only occur when the gene pool is changed significantly enough to establish reproductive barriers between the parent population and the isolated population. The chances of allopatric speciation occurring increase when a population is both small and isolated, as there is a higher chance of its gene pool changing substantially. For instance, in under two million years, tiny populations of foreign animal and plant species originating from the South American mainland managed to colonize the Galapagos Islands, creating all the unique species that now live on the islands.

Which of the sentences below best expresses the essential information in the highlighted sentence in the passage? Incorrect choices change the meaning in important ways or leave out essential information.

(A) Geographic isolation can result in the development of new species only if the gene pool of the isolated population was altered to such an extent that it prevents reproduction with the parent population.

(B) Genetic changes in geographically isolated populations often change the reproductive behavior of organisms and this can result in the gene pool of a species shrinking.

(C) Geographical isolation permits separated populations to evolve independently of each other and reproduce with populations that inhabit remote habitats.

(D) Geographic isolation often leads to the formation of reproductive barriers between a parent population and the populations that descend from it.

Although geographic isolation gives rise to opportunities for new species to develop, allopatric speciation can only occur when the gene pool is changed significantly enough to establish reproductive barriers between the parent population and the isolated population. The chances of allopatric speciation occurring increase when a population is both small and isolated, as there is a higher chance of its gene pool changing substantially. For instance, in under two million years, tiny populations of foreign animal and plant species originating from the South American mainland managed to colonize the Galapagos Islands, creating all the unique species that now live on the islands.

The word "managed" in the passage is closest in meaning to

(A) were controlled
(B) were able
(C) were likely
(D) were available

Oceanic islands that are close enough to allow occasional population movement to occur, but far enough apart to ensure most populations evolve in isolation, serve as valuable outdoor laboratories where the process of evolution is on full view. Nowhere is this more apparent than the Galapagos Islands. The islands emerged as a result of underwater volcanic eruptions, and they were gradually populated by organisms who had strayed from their habitats, often carried by wind and oceanic currents from far away continents and islands. Also, some species most likely reached the island chain by being transported by other organisms, such as seeds entangled in the feathers of sea birds.

Paragraph 5 indicates that the Galapagos Islands are a good example of one of Earth's "valuable outdoor laboratories" primarily because of

(A) the richness of the volcanic soil that the islands are primarily composed of
(B) the long period of time it took organisms to colonize the islands
(C) the distance between the individual islands and from the mainland
(D) the optimal climate required for several species to flourish

The vast majority of species on the Galapagos Islands today are found nowhere else and are the descendants of organisms that were blown or floated across the sea from the South American mainland. For example, the island chain is home to the Galapagos finches: thirteen species of closely related birds. While these birds share a lot of similarities, their feeding habits differ, as do their beak types, which are specially adapted to better suit their feeding habits. Much evidence has been gathered that indicates all thirteen finch species descended from one single small population of birds that colonized one of the islands. Once the founder population had become isolated on the island after traveling from the mainland, its gene pool must have undergone significant changes, essentially creating a new species. Later, some organisms belonging to this new species were likely carried to a neighboring island by a storm. This second founder population, now isolated on its island, would then have evolved into a second new species, which could later recolonize the island from which its founding population emigrated. Recent studies show that each island of the Galapagos now has multiple species of finches, with some islands having as many as ten distinct species.

According to paragraph 6, what is true about the thirteen species of Galapagos finches?

(A) All thirteen species are now present on most of the islands in the Galapagos chain.
(B) All thirteen species exist in small numbers and are in danger of extinction.
(C) All thirteen species evolved on the mainland before traveling to the island chain.
(D) All thirteen species have descended from the same population of ancestral birds.

The vast majority of species on the Galapagos Islands today are found nowhere else and are the descendants of organisms that were blown or floated across the sea from the South American mainland. For example, the island chain is home to the Galapagos finches: thirteen species of closely related birds. While these birds share a lot of similarities, their feeding habits differ, as do their beak types, which are specially adapted to better suit their feeding habits. Much evidence has been gathered that indicates all thirteen finch species descended from one single small population of birds that colonized one of the islands. Once the founder population had become isolated on the island after traveling from the mainland, its gene pool must have undergone significant changes, essentially creating a new species. ■ Later, some organisms belonging to this new species were likely carried to a neighboring island by a storm. ■ This second founder population, now isolated on its island, would then have evolved into a second new species, which could later recolonize the island from which its founding population emigrated. ■ Recent studies show that each island of the Galapagos now has multiple species of finches, with some islands having as many as ten distinct species. ■

Look at the four squares [■] that indicate where the following sentence could be added to the passage.

This process of speciation and colonization would have continued with a third and a fourth species and beyond, slowly dispersing across all the islands in the chain.

Where would the sentence best fit? Click on a square [■] to add the sentence to the passage.

Directions: An introductory sentence for a brief summary of the passage is provided below. Complete the summary by selecting the THREE answer choices that express the most important ideas in the passage. Some sentences do not belong in the summary because they express ideas that are not presented in the passage or are minor ideas in the passage. **This question is worth 2 points.**

Drag your answer choices to the space where they belong. To remove an answer choice, click on it. To review the passage, click on **VIEW TEXT.**

The geographic isolation of a population can result in the rise of a new species.

-
-
-

Answer Choices

(A) Studies show that the first organisms to colonize the Galapagos Islands were finches, which gradually evolved into thirteen distinct species.

(B) Speciation is more likely to occur when an isolated population is small because significant genetic changes are more common in a small population than in a large one.

(C) Isolation can occur when a geographic barrier separates a population or when some organisms inadvertently travel across a geographic barrier by wind or sea and create a new population.

(D) Due to the geographic isolation of the Galapagos Islands, many species that inhabit them have not undergone many evolutionary changes.

(E) Bird populations are less easily isolated by geographic barriers than fish and mammal populations due to their ability to fly.

(F) The Galapagos Islands are ideal for speciation because they can isolate populations while also allowing occasional dispersions of organisms between islands.

Symbiotic Relationship

When there is an interaction between two or more species in which one of the species lives in or on the other species, this is an example of a symbiotic relationship. Symbiotic interactions can be broadly categorized as parasitism, commensalism, and mutualism. In the structure of a biological community—that is, all the populations of organisms interacting with one another in a given ecosystem—parasitism and mutualism are particularly important forms of symbiotic relationships.

Generally speaking, parasitism describes a predator-prey relationship in which one organism, the host, makes certain sacrifices to provide food or resources to its symbiotic partner, the parasite. In most cases, parasitic organisms are smaller than their host organisms. One common example of a parasite is the tapeworm, which lives inside the intestines of larger organisms and leeches nutrients from its host. Parasites that are well-adapted to seeking out and feeding on hosts are favored by natural selection, as are the defensive abilities of hosts. For instance, some plants produce chemicals that are toxic to fungal and bacterial parasites, and others that are toxic to predatory animals. And, in most vertebrates, the body's immune system provides multiple means of defense against internal parasites.

Sometimes we are able to observe the effects of natural selection in host-parasite relationships. For instance, during the 1940s in Australia, hundreds of millions of European rabbits overran rural areas. The rabbits ruined large swathes of Australian farmland and posed a serious risk to the sheep and cattle industries. In 1950, the Australian government intentionally introduced the myxoma virus, a parasite that is fatal to rabbits, in an effort to drastically reduce the rabbit population. The virus was spread rapidly by mosquitoes, decimating the rabbit population. However, the virus was less effective in killing the offspring of surviving rabbits, and it proved less and less useful over the years. It became apparent that the parasitic-resistant genotypes, or the genetic composition of organisms, were being favored in the population of rabbits. As such, the most fatal strains of the virus died out along with the host rabbits, as natural selection favored strains that could infect hosts but not kill them. Thus, this host-parasite relationship was stabilized through natural selection.

Commensalism differs from parasitism in that one member of a relationship benefits without the other one being affected. Absolute commensalism is relatively rare in nature, as it is unlikely that the non-benefitting member will be completely unaffected. Commensal interactions often involve the obtaining of food by one species after it has been inadvertently exposed by another. For example, grazing cattle expose insects in grass that many species of birds swoop down to feed on. It is difficult to conceive how this could have a detrimental effect on the cattle, but there remains a possibility that the relationship may help or hinder them in some way that has yet to be determined.

Lastly, there is a form of symbiosis called mutualism, which confers benefits upon both members in the relationship. This mutualistic association is exemplified in the interactions between flowering plants and their pollinators, and in legume plants and their nitrogen-fixing bacteria. In the first case, pollinators such as birds and insects obtain food from flowering plants while helping the plant to disperse pollen and seeds much more efficiently than they would by wind alone. In the second case, the bacteria are provided with carbohydrates and other organic compounds by the plants, while the plants take advantage of nitrogen that the bacteria gradually add to the soil. Mutualism is also evident in the case of the bull's horn acacia tree, which is found throughout Central and South America. Ants belonging to the genus Pseudomyrmex commonly use the trees as nesting sites. They inhabit the trees' large, hollow thorns and feed on sugar secreted by the trees. The trees also have yellow structures at the tip of their leaflets, and these protein-rich features seem to serve no purpose to the trees, other than to attract the ants. The host trees receive benefits in that the ants attack almost any other species that come close to the trees. Other insects and large herbivores risk being stung by the ants, so they tend to leave the trees alone. The ants have even been observed clipping the surrounding vegetation in order to provide more space for the trees to grow. When the ants are taken away, the trees typically perish because they are no longer protected from herbivores and will be forced to compete with surrounding plants for space and resources.

When there is an interaction between two or more species in which one of the species lives in or on the other species, this is an example of a symbiotic relationship. Symbiotic interactions can be broadly categorized as parasitism, commensalism, and mutualism. In the structure of a biological community—that is, all the populations of organisms interacting with one another in a given ecosystem— parasitism and mutualism are particularly important forms of symbiotic relationships.

Which of the following statements about commensalism can be inferred from paragraph 1?

(A) It plays a relatively minor role in the organization of biological communities.

(B) It is integral to a biological community's ability to flourish.

(C) It excludes interactions between more than two species.

(D) It has the potential to severely disrupt the structure of biological populations.

Generally speaking, parasitism describes a predator-prey relationship in which one organism, the host, makes certain sacrifices to provide food or resources to its symbiotic partner, the parasite. In most cases, parasitic organisms are smaller than their host organisms. One common example of a parasite is the tapeworm, which lives inside the intestines of larger organisms and leeches nutrients from its host. Parasites that are well-adapted to seeking out and feeding on hosts are favored by natural selection, as are the defensive abilities of hosts. For instance, some plants produce chemicals that are toxic to fungal and bacterial parasites, and others that are toxic to predatory animals. And, in most vertebrates, the body's immune system provides multiple means of defense against internal parasites.

The word "favored" in the passage is closest in meaning to

(A) connected
(B) affordable
(C) reluctant
(D) preferred

Sometimes, we are able to observe the effects of natural selection in host-parasite relationships. For instance, during the 1940s in Australia, hundreds of millions of European rabbits overran rural areas. The rabbits ruined large swathes of Australian farmland and posed a serious risk to the sheep and cattle industries. In 1950, the Australian government intentionally introduced the myxoma virus, a parasite that is fatal to rabbits, in an effort to drastically reduce the rabbit population. The virus was spread rapidly by mosquitoes, decimating the rabbit population. However, the virus was less effective in killing the offspring of surviving rabbits, and it proved less and less useful over the years. It became apparent that the parasitic-resistant genotypes, or the genetic composition of organisms, were being favored in the population of rabbits. As such, the most fatal strains of the virus died out along with the host rabbits, as natural selection favored strains that could infect hosts but not kill them. Thus, this host-parasite relationship was stabilized through natural selection.

Which of the following can be concluded from the discussion in paragraph 3 about the Australian rabbit population?

(A) Human interference in host-parasite relationships can negatively impact the environment.

(B) The benefits of introducing foreign species into a biological community greatly outweigh the risks.

(C) Human intervention may cause changes to occur in the host, the parasite, and their relationship.

(D) Species that survive a parasitic attack are likely to reproduce in record numbers.

Sometimes, we are able to observe the effects of natural selection in host-parasite relationships. For instance, during the 1940s in Australia, hundreds of millions of European rabbits overran rural areas. The rabbits ruined large swathes of Australian farmland and posed a serious risk to the sheep and cattle industries. In 1950, the Australian government intentionally introduced the myxoma virus, a parasite that is fatal to rabbits, in an effort to drastically reduce the rabbit population. The virus was spread rapidly by mosquitoes, decimating the rabbit population. However, the virus was less effective in killing the offspring of surviving rabbits, and it proved less and less useful over the years. It became apparent that the parasitic-resistant genotypes, or the genetic composition of organisms, were being favored in the population of rabbits. As such, the most fatal strains of the virus died out along with the host rabbits, as natural selection favored strains that could infect hosts but not kill them. Thus, this host-parasite relationship was stabilized through natural selection.

According to paragraph 3, all of the following characterize the way natural selection stabilized the Australian rabbit population EXCEPT

(A) The most deadly virus strains vanished along with their hosts.

(B) The surviving rabbits showed increased immunity to the virus.

(C) Rabbits with specific genotypes were more likely to resist the virus.

(D) The decline of the mosquito population reduced the effectiveness of the virus.

Commensalism differs from parasitism in that one member of a relationship benefits without the other one being affected. Absolute commensalism is relatively rare in nature, as it is unlikely that the non-benefitting member will be completely unaffected. Commensal interactions often involve the obtaining of food by one species after it has been inadvertently exposed by another. For example, grazing cattle expose insects in grass that many species of birds swoop down to feed on. It is difficult to conceive how this could have a detrimental effect on the cattle, but there remains a possibility that the relationship may help or hinder them in some way that has yet to be determined.

The word "inadvertently" in the passage is closest in meaning to

(A) inversely
(B) unintentionally
(C) significantly
(D) intermittently

Lastly, there is a form of symbiosis called mutualism, which confers benefits upon both members in the relationship. This mutualistic association is exemplified in the interactions between flowering plants and their pollinators, and in legume plants and their nitrogen-fixing bacteria. In the first case, pollinators such as birds and insects obtain food from flowering plants while helping the plant to disperse pollen and seeds much more efficiently than they would by wind alone. In the second case, the bacteria are provided with carbohydrates and other organic compounds by the plants, while the plants take advantage of nitrogen that the bacteria gradually add to the soil. Mutualism is also evident in the case of the bull's horn acacia tree, which is found throughout Central and South America. Ants belonging to the genus Pseudomyrmex commonly use the trees as nesting sites. They inhabit the trees' large, hollow thorns and feed on sugar secreted by the trees. The trees also have yellow structures at the tip of their leaflets, and these protein-rich features seem to serve no purpose to the trees, other than to attract the ants. The host trees receive benefits in that the ants attack almost any other species that come close to the trees. Other insects and large herbivores risk being stung by the ants, so they tend to leave the trees alone. The ants have even been observed clipping the surrounding vegetation in order to provide more space for the trees to grow. When the ants are taken away, the trees typically perish because they are no longer protected from herbivores and will be forced to compete with surrounding plants for space and resources.

According to paragraph 5, the relationship between legumes and bacteria benefits the soil by

(A) absorbing carbohydrates from the soil
(B) enriching the soil with nitrogen
(C) removing toxins from the atmosphere
(D) accelerating the decomposition of organic matter

Lastly, there is a form of symbiosis called mutualism, which confers benefits upon both members in the relationship. This mutualistic association is exemplified in the interactions between flowering plants and their pollinators, and in legume plants and their nitrogen-fixing bacteria. In the first case, pollinators such as birds and insects obtain food from flowering plants while helping the plant to disperse pollen and seeds much more efficiently than they would by wind alone. In the second case, the bacteria are provided with carbohydrates and other organic compounds by the plants, while the plants take advantage of nitrogen that the bacteria gradually add to the soil. Mutualism is also evident in the case of the bull's horn acacia tree, which is found throughout Central and South America. Ants belonging to the genus Pseudomyrmex commonly use the trees as nesting sites. They inhabit the trees' large, hollow thorns and feed on sugar secreted by the trees. The trees also have yellow structures at the tip of their leaflets, and these protein-rich features seem to serve no purpose to the trees, other than to attract the ants. The host trees receive benefits in that the ants attack almost any other species that come close to the trees. Other insects and large herbivores risk being stung by the ants, so they tend to leave the trees alone. The ants have even been observed clipping the surrounding vegetation in order to provide more space for the trees to grow. When the ants are taken away, the trees typically perish because they are no longer protected from herbivores and will be forced to compete with surrounding plants for space and resources.

Which of the sentences below best expresses the essential information in the highlighted sentence in the passage? Incorrect choices change the meaning in important ways or leave out essential information.

(A) Animals and insects seek out flowering plants in an effort to find food that comprises a large part of their daily diet.
(B) In some cases, birds and insects are drawn to flowering plants by following pollen and seeds that are carried by the wind.
(C) The wind enables the flowering plants to distribute their seeds and pollen among birds and insects that consume them.
(D) Birds and insects acquire food from the flowering plants and also provide a better means of pollen and seed dispersal than the wind.

Lastly, there is a form of symbiosis called mutualism, which confers benefits upon both members in the relationship. This mutualistic association is exemplified in the interactions between flowering plants and their pollinators, and in legume plants and their nitrogen-fixing bacteria. In the first case, pollinators such as birds and insects obtain food from flowering plants while helping the plant to disperse pollen and seeds much more efficiently than they would by wind alone. In the second case, the bacteria are provided with carbohydrates and other organic compounds by the plants, while the plants take advantage of nitrogen that the bacteria gradually add to the soil. Mutualism is also evident in the case of the bull's horn acacia tree, which is found throughout Central and South America. Ants belonging to the genus Pseudomyrmex commonly use the trees as nesting sites. They inhabit the trees' large, hollow thorns and feed on sugar secreted by the trees. The trees also have yellow structures at the tip of their leaflets, and these protein-rich features seem to serve no purpose to the trees, other than to attract the ants. The host trees receive benefits in that the ants attack almost any other species that come close to the trees. Other insects and large herbivores risk being stung by the ants, so they tend to leave the trees alone. The ants have even been observed clipping the surrounding vegetation in order to provide more space for the trees to grow. When the ants are taken away, the trees typically perish because they are no longer protected from herbivores and will be forced to compete with surrounding plants for space and resources.

According to paragraph 5, which of the following is NOT true of the relationship between the bull's horn acacia tree and the Pseudomyrmex ants?

(A) The ants assist the acacia tree in producing its own chemical defenses.
(B) The acacia trees serve as a valuable source of nutrition for the ants.
(C) The ants defend the host trees against potential predators.
(D) The ants help the trees by reducing competition from surrounding vegetation.

Sometimes, we are able to observe the effects of natural selection in host-parasite relationships. For instance, during the 1940s in Australia, hundreds of millions of European rabbits overran rural areas. ■ The rabbits ruined large swathes of Australian farmland and posed a serious risk to the sheep and cattle industries. ■ In 1950, the Australian government intentionally introduced the myxoma virus, a parasite that is fatal to rabbits, in an effort to drastically reduce the rabbit population. ■ The virus was spread rapidly by mosquitoes, decimating the rabbit population. ■ However, the virus was less effective in killing the offspring of surviving rabbits, and it proved less and less useful over the years. It became apparent that the parasitic-resistant genotypes, or the genetic composition of organisms, were being favored in the population of rabbits. As such, the most fatal strains of the virus died out along with the host rabbits, as natural selection favored strains that could infect hosts but not kill them. Thus, this host-parasite relationship was stabilized through natural selection.

Look at the four squares [■] that indicate where the following sentence could be added to the passage.

This huge number originated from only twelve pairs of imported rabbits that were introduced a century earlier and reproduced at a rapid rate.

Where would the sentence best fit? Click on a square [■] to add the sentence to the passage.

Directions: An introductory sentence for a brief summary of the passage is provided below. Complete the summary by selecting the THREE answer choices that express the most important ideas in the passage. Some sentences do not belong in the summary because they express ideas that are not presented in the passage or are minor ideas in the passage. **This question is worth 2 points.**

Drag your answer choices to the space where they belong. To remove an answer choice, click on it. To review the passage, click on **VIEW TEXT.**

Symbiotic relationships involve the interaction of two or more organisms and beneficial outcomes for one or both of the organisms involved.

-
-
-

Answer Choices

(A) The structure of biological communities is dependent on the types of relationships that exist among the species within the communities.

(B) Commensal relationships ordinarily allow one member of the relationship to benefit at no perceived cost to the other member.

(C) Mutualism is unique among symbiotic relationships in that it confers benefits on both members involved in the relationship.

(D) Parasitic relationships typically include a parasite and a host and result in the parasite receiving benefits at the expense of the host.

(E) The introduction of parasites initially helped to control Australian rabbit populations until the host-parasite relationship was stabilized through natural selection.

(F) Mutualism more commonly occurs between two members of the same species than between two members of different species.

Actual Test 2

Surface Fluids on Venus and Earth

When a substance, typically a liquid or a gas, consists of particles that can move past one another, we refer to it as a fluid. Whatever type of container a fluid is placed inside, the fluid will conform to its shape. When fluids move across the surface of a planet, the geologic processes that occur can significantly alter the planet's surface. Most of these processes are driven by solar power and the gravitational forces of the planet itself. As fluids flow over the surface, particles are shifted around, and the fluids bring about chemical reactions that can modify particles or produce new materials. Typically, only a very low amount of the planetary mass flows as surface fluids on a solid planet with a hydrosphere and an atmosphere. However, the movements of these fluids can still drastically transform a planet.

Let us consider Venus and Earth, two terrestrial planets that have atmospheres. While Venus and Earth are often referred to as twin planets, they are far from identical. At their birth, the two planets likely had comparable levels of carbon dioxide and oxygen, and they are roughly the same size and composed of similar substances. However, due to their being located at different distances from the Sun, the twins evolved to have significant differences from one another. Venus harbors a massive amount of internal heat and is highly geologically active due to volcanoes, rifting, and folding. However, there is no evidence of any sort of a hydrologic system (water circulation and distribution); there are no glaciers, rivers, or bodies of water whatsoever. Probes sent into space indicate that Venus may once have had as much water as Earth, but that water could not be sustained in liquid form. The increased amount of heat that Venus receives from the Sun caused the water released from the interior to evaporate and rise to the upper atmosphere, where its molecules were broken apart by the Sun's ultraviolet rays. Most of the released hydrogen drifted out into space, leaving Venus with a carbon dioxide-rich atmosphere and no water, very unlike Earth. The carbon dioxide in the atmosphere creates an intense greenhouse effect, causing surface temperatures to soar to such extreme highs that they can melt lead and prohibit the formation of carbonate minerals. Over countless years, volcanoes have continually erupted, filling the atmosphere with more and more carbon dioxide. On Earth, carbon dioxide is removed from the atmosphere by liquid water and is then combined with calcium produced by rock weathering, eventually forming carbonate sedimentary rocks. Lacking such liquid water, Venus is unable to remove carbon from the atmosphere, so its level of atmospheric carbon dioxide remains extremely high.

Earth is similar to Venus in that it is massive enough for its gravitational field to retain an atmosphere and for it to be geologically active. However, it differs significantly from Venus in that its ideal distance from the Sun results in desirable temperatures that allow water to be present as a liquid, a solid, and a gas. This increases the mobility of water and allows it to move freely across the planet in a continuous hydrologic cycle. Ocean water is heated by the Sun and enters the atmosphere, where it forms into rain and falls to create river systems that crisscross the continents, before eventually being deposited back into Earth's vast oceans. As a result of this continuous cycle, there have been numerous changes made to Earth's surface, which has been eroded into intricate networks of river valleys, making it stand out from other planet surfaces that are characterized by impact craters.

Almost every part of Earth has been shaped by the flow of water. In a similar fashion, wind has eroded rocks over the millennia and carried fine particles across large distances, creating expansive sand seas dominated by dunes, or sheets of fine-grained soil deposits called loess. These fluid movements are largely driven by gravitational forces and the Sun's heat. Geologic changes can also take place when rocks on the planet's surface react with water or atmospheric gases to give rise to new chemical compounds with unique properties. One notable example of this process was the formation of carbonate rocks as a result of the removal of most of Earth's carbon dioxide from its atmosphere. However, if Earth were situated farther from the Sun, its oceans would completely freeze, and if it were any closer to the Sun, all of its water would evaporate. Thanks to the presence of liquid water, Earth was capable of developing and sustaining life by using its self-replicating molecules of carbon, hydrogen, and oxygen, resulting in altered land masses that are covered with lush vegetation. As such, with its oxygen- and nitrogen-rich atmosphere and moderate temperatures, Earth is an ideal planet where all manner of living things can grow and flourish.

When a substance, typically a liquid or a gas, consists of particles that can move past one another, we refer to it as a fluid. Whatever type of container a fluid is placed inside, the fluid will conform to its shape. When fluids move across the surface of a planet, the geologic processes that occur can significantly alter the planet's surface. Most of these processes are driven by solar power and the gravitational forces of the planet itself. As fluids flow over the surface, particles are shifted around, and the fluids bring about chemical reactions that can modify particles or produce new materials. Typically, only a very low amount of the planetary mass flows as surface fluids on a solid planet with a hydrosphere and an atmosphere. However, the movements of these fluids can still drastically transform a planet.

According to paragraph 1, what influences geological processes on Earth and Venus?

(A) Water level and pH
(B) Seasonal climate and rainfall
(C) Orbit speed and diameter
(D) Gravity and the Sun

When a substance, typically a liquid or a gas, consists of particles that can move past one another, we refer to it as a fluid. Whatever type of container a fluid is placed inside, the fluid will conform to its shape. When fluids move across the surface of a planet, the geologic processes that occur can significantly alter the planet's surface. Most of these processes are driven by solar power and the gravitational forces of the planet itself. As fluids flow over the surface, particles are shifted around, and the fluids bring about chemical reactions that can modify particles or produce new materials. Typically, only a very low amount of the planetary mass flows as surface fluids on a solid planet with a hydrosphere and an atmosphere. However, the movements of these fluids can still drastically transform a planet.

The word "drastically" in the passage is closest in meaning to

(A) disastrously
(B) permanently
(C) significantly
(D) continuously

Let us consider Venus and Earth, two terrestrial planets that have atmospheres. While Venus and Earth are often referred to as twin planets, they are far from identical. At their birth, the two planets likely had comparable levels of carbon dioxide and oxygen, and they are roughly the same size and composed of similar substances. However, due to their being located at different distances from the Sun, the twins evolved to have significant differences from one another. Venus harbors a massive amount of internal heat and is highly geologically active due to volcanoes, rifting, and folding. However, there is no evidence of any sort of a hydrologic system (water circulation and distribution); there are no glaciers, rivers, or bodies of water whatsoever. Probes sent into space indicate that Venus may once have had as much water as Earth, but that water could not be sustained in liquid form. The increased amount of heat that Venus receives from the Sun caused the water released from the interior to evaporate and rise to the upper atmosphere, where its molecules were broken apart by the Sun's ultraviolet rays. Most of the released hydrogen drifted out into space, leaving Venus with a carbon dioxide-rich atmosphere and no water, very unlike Earth. The carbon dioxide in the atmosphere creates an intense greenhouse effect, causing surface temperatures to soar to such extreme highs that they can melt lead and prohibit the formation of carbonate minerals. Over countless years, volcanoes have continually erupted, filling the atmosphere with more and more carbon dioxide. On Earth, carbon dioxide is removed from the atmosphere by liquid water and is then combined with calcium produced by rock weathering, eventually forming carbonate sedimentary rocks. Lacking such liquid water, Venus is unable to remove carbon from the atmosphere, so its level of atmospheric carbon dioxide remains extremely high.

The word "prohibit" in the passage is closest in meaning to

(A) promote
(B) decrease
(C) eradicate
(D) prevent

Let us consider Venus and Earth, two terrestrial planets that have atmospheres. While Venus and Earth are often referred to as twin planets, they are far from identical. At their birth, the two planets likely had comparable levels of carbon dioxide and oxygen, and they are roughly the same size and composed of similar substances. However, due to their being located at different distances from the Sun, the twins evolved to have significant differences from one another. Venus harbors a massive amount of internal heat and is highly geologically active due to volcanoes, rifting, and folding. However, there is no evidence of any sort of a hydrologic system (water circulation and distribution); there are no glaciers, rivers, or bodies of water whatsoever. Probes sent into space indicate that Venus may once have had as much water as Earth, but that water could not be sustained in liquid form. The increased amount of heat that Venus receives from the Sun caused the water released from the interior to evaporate and rise to the upper atmosphere, where its molecules were broken apart by the Sun's ultraviolet rays. Most of the released hydrogen drifted out into space, leaving Venus with a carbon dioxide-rich atmosphere and no water, very unlike Earth. The carbon dioxide in the atmosphere creates an intense greenhouse effect, causing surface temperatures to soar to such extreme highs that they can melt lead and prohibit the formation of carbonate minerals. Over countless years, volcanoes have continually erupted, filling the atmosphere with more and more carbon dioxide. On Earth, carbon dioxide is removed from the atmosphere by liquid water and is then combined with calcium produced by rock weathering, eventually forming carbonate sedimentary rocks. Lacking such liquid water, Venus is unable to remove carbon from the atmosphere, so its level of atmospheric carbon dioxide remains extremely high.

According to paragraph 2, what is one way in which Earth and Venus differ?

(A) Only Earth has a hydrologic system.
(B) Earth has less water in its atmosphere than Venus.
(C) Venus is less geologically active than Earth.
(D) Earth has greater amounts of carbon dioxide than Venus.

Let us consider Venus and Earth, two terrestrial planets that have atmospheres. While Venus and Earth are often referred to as twin planets, they are far from identical. At their birth, the two planets likely had comparable levels of carbon dioxide and oxygen, and they are roughly the same size and composed of similar substances. However, due to their being located at different distances from the Sun, the twins evolved to have significant differences from one another. Venus harbors a massive amount of internal heat and is highly geologically active due to volcanoes, rifting, and folding. However, there is no evidence of any sort of a hydrologic system (water circulation and distribution); there are no glaciers, rivers, or bodies of water whatsoever. Probes sent into space indicate that Venus may once have had as much water as Earth, but that water could not be sustained in liquid form. The increased amount of heat that Venus receives from the Sun caused the water released from the interior to evaporate and rise to the upper atmosphere, where its molecules were broken apart by the Sun's ultraviolet rays. Most of the released hydrogen drifted out into space, leaving Venus with a carbon dioxide-rich atmosphere and no water, very unlike Earth. The carbon dioxide in the atmosphere creates an intense greenhouse effect, causing surface temperatures to soar to such extreme highs that they can melt lead and prohibit the formation of carbonate minerals. Over countless years, volcanoes have continually erupted, filling the atmosphere with more and more carbon dioxide. On Earth, carbon dioxide is removed from the atmosphere by liquid water and is then combined with calcium produced by rock weathering, eventually forming carbonate sedimentary rocks. Lacking such liquid water, Venus is unable to remove carbon from the atmosphere, so its level of atmospheric carbon dioxide remains extremely high.

According to paragraph 2, all of the following played a role in keeping carbon dioxide levels high in the atmosphere of Venus EXCEPT

(A) the escape of hydrogen into space
(B) the formation of carbonate materials
(C) the evaporation of water released from the planet
(D) the splitting of water molecules by solar rays

Earth is similar to Venus in that it is massive enough for its gravitational field to retain an atmosphere and for it to be geologically active. However, it differs significantly from Venus in that its ideal distance from the Sun results in desirable temperatures that allow water to be present as a liquid, a solid, and a gas. This increases the mobility of water and allows it to move freely across the planet in a continuous hydrologic cycle. Ocean water is heated by the Sun and enters the atmosphere, where it forms into rain and falls to create river systems that crisscross the continents, before eventually being deposited back into Earth's vast oceans. As a result of this continuous cycle, there have been numerous changes made to Earth's surface, which has been eroded into intricate networks of river valleys, making it stand out from other planet surfaces that are characterized by impact craters.

According to paragraph 3, why is water able to move so freely on Earth?

(A) Earth's temperature allows water to exist in solid, liquid, and gas forms.
(B) Earth's gravitational field is strong enough to affect ocean tides.
(C) Earth's mountainous regions accelerate the flow of rivers.
(D) Earth has active winds that create currents in seas and oceans.

Earth is similar to Venus in that it is massive enough for its gravitational field to retain an atmosphere and for it to be geologically active. However, it differs significantly from Venus in that its ideal distance from the Sun results in desirable temperatures that allow water to be present as a liquid, a solid, and a gas. This increases the mobility of water and allows it to move freely across the planet in a continuous hydrologic cycle. Ocean water is heated by the Sun and enters the atmosphere, where it forms into rain and falls to create river systems that crisscross the continents, before eventually being deposited back into Earth's vast oceans. As a result of this continuous cycle, there have been numerous changes made to Earth's surface, which has been eroded into intricate networks of river valleys, making it stand out from other planet surfaces that are characterized by impact craters.

According to paragraph 3, Earth's surface differs from that of many other planets in which of the following ways?

(A) It has been eroded by the flow of water.
(B) It is characterized by impact craters.
(C) It contains a thicker layer of rock.
(D) It experiences more frequent temperature changes.

Almost every part of Earth has been shaped by the flow of water. In a similar fashion, wind has eroded rocks over the millennia and carried fine particles across large distances, creating expansive sand seas dominated by dunes, or sheets of fine-grained soil deposits called loess. These fluid movements are largely driven by gravitational forces and the Sun's heat. Geologic changes can also take place when rocks on the planet's surface react with water or atmospheric gases to give rise to new chemical compounds with unique properties. One notable example of this process was the formation of carbonate rocks as a result of the removal of most of Earth's carbon dioxide from its atmosphere. However, if Earth were situated farther from the Sun, its oceans would completely freeze, and if it were any closer to the Sun, all of its water would evaporate. Thanks to the presence of liquid water, Earth was capable of developing and sustaining life by using its self-replicating molecules of carbon, hydrogen, and oxygen, resulting in altered land masses that are covered with lush vegetation. As such, with its oxygen- and nitrogen-rich atmosphere and moderate temperatures, Earth is an ideal planet where all manner of living things can grow and flourish.

Why does the author point out that on Earth "rocks on the planet's surface react with water or atmospheric gases to give rise to new chemical compounds"?

(A) To explain why certain regions of Earth have remained untouched by flowing water

(B) To provide an example of one of the various ways by which the surface of a planet is altered

(C) To illustrate how chemical compounds play a crucial role in facilitating the flow of water

(D) To give evidence that Earth has undergone more extensive geological change than Venus has

Let us consider Venus and Earth, two terrestrial planets that have atmospheres. While Venus and Earth are often referred to as twin planets, they are far from identical. At their birth, the two planets likely had comparable levels of carbon dioxide and oxygen, and they are roughly the same size and composed of similar substances. However, due to their being located at different distances from the Sun, the twins evolved to have significant differences from one another. Venus harbors a massive amount of internal heat and is highly geologically active due to volcanoes, rifting, and folding. ■ However, there is no evidence of any sort of a hydrologic system (water circulation and distribution); there are no glaciers, rivers, or bodies of water whatsoever. ■ Probes sent into space indicate that Venus may once have had as much water as Earth, but that water could not be sustained in liquid form. ■ The increased amount of heat that Venus receives from the Sun caused the water released from the interior to evaporate and rise to the upper atmosphere, where its molecules were broken apart by the Sun's ultraviolet rays. ■ Most of the released hydrogen drifted out into space, leaving Venus with a carbon dioxide-rich atmosphere and no water, very unlike Earth. The carbon dioxide in the atmosphere creates an intense greenhouse effect, causing surface temperatures to soar to such extreme highs that they can melt lead and prohibit the formation of carbonate minerals. Over countless years, volcanoes have continually erupted, filling the atmosphere with more and more carbon dioxide. On Earth, carbon dioxide is removed from the atmosphere by liquid water and is then combined with calcium produced by rock weathering, eventually forming carbonate sedimentary rocks. Lacking such liquid water, Venus is unable to remove carbon from the atmosphere, so its level of atmospheric carbon dioxide remains extremely high.

Look at the four squares [■] that indicate where the following sentence could be added to the passage.

Venus may actually have been quite different in the past.

Where would the sentence best fit? Click on a square [■] to add the sentence to the passage.

Directions: An introductory sentence for a brief summary of the passage is provided below. Complete the summary by selecting the THREE answer choices that express the most important ideas in the passage. Some sentences do not belong in the summary because they express ideas that are not presented in the passage or are minor ideas in the passage. **This question is worth 2 points.**

Drag your answer choices to the space where they belong. To remove an answer choice, click on it. To review the passage, click on **VIEW TEXT.**

Over time, the movement of surface fluids has greatly changed Venus and Earth.

-
-
-

Answer Choices

(A) While Earth and Venus are of comparable size, the greater volcanic activity of Venus has significantly increased carbon dioxide levels in its atmosphere.

(B) Earth's atmosphere has far higher levels of oxygen and nitrogen than does the atmosphere of Venus.

(C) Chemical reactions involving fluids remove carbon dioxide from Earth's atmosphere by forming carbonate rocks, while wind moves fine particles from one place to another.

(D) Because all water evaporated from Venus, the carbon dioxide-rich atmosphere caused the planet to increase in temperature.

(E) On Earth, a continual hydrologic cycle controls atmospheric carbon and has created a surface landscape characterized by river valleys.

(F) The evaporation of liquid water from Earth's surface is prevented due to extensive vegetation coverage on most continents.

Auditory Perception in Infancy

The reason that infants are born with fairly good auditory perception is that they receive a surprising amount of hearing practice prior to their birth. Indeed, during the first two years of life, an infant is more sensitive to certain extremely high and low frequencies than adults are. Conversely, infants are initially less sensitive to middle-range frequencies when compared with adults. Over time, though, their auditory perception within the middle range will become much more sensitive.

Although there is no definitive explanation for the improvement in sensitivity to sounds in infants, many researchers believe it is connected to the maturation of the nervous system. There is even less of a consensus when it comes to explaining why, after infancy, a child's ability to hear extremely high and low frequencies gradually diminishes. One theory is that increased exposure to loud noise may reduce a child's capability to perceive sound at these extreme frequencies.

In order to hear effectively, infants need several other abilities in addition to the ability to detect sound. For example, sound localization enables infants to accurately determine the direction from which a sound is coming. Infants are at a disadvantage compared with adults when it comes to this ability, as effective sound localization relies on the slight discrepancy in the times at which the two ears individually hear a sound. Because the distance between an infant's ears is shorter than that between an adult's, sounds arrive at both ears more quickly than they do in the case of an adult. However, even with this potential limitation, the sound localization abilities of infants are relatively strong even at birth, and they typically reach adult levels of effectiveness by the time an infant is one year old. It is interesting to note that their improvement is not linear. Sound localization ability actually worsens over the first two months after birth before it begins to improve, and there is no clear explanation why that occurs.

Young infants are also capable of recognizing subtle distinctions between various sounds, and this is crucial to their future understanding of language. For example, in one well-known study, a group of infants aged between four weeks and four months sucked on nipples that played a recording of an adult saying "ba" whenever it was sucked. To begin with, the infants sucked vigorously due to their keen interest in the recorded voice. After a while, however, they lost interest in the sound and their sucking became less enthusiastic. The experimenters then changed the sound to "pa," and the infants' enthusiasm was immediately renewed, causing them to suck harder once more. The findings clearly indicated that infants as young as four weeks old could make the distinction between two similar sounds.

Another interesting aspect of auditory perception in infants is their ability to identify certain characteristics that differentiate between various spoken languages. Research has shown that even two-day-olds have a preference for the language spoken by those around them over unfamiliar languages. Their ability to distinguish between languages develops rapidly over the first few months of life. By the age of five months, they can recognize the differences between spoken passages in English and Spanish, even when the speakers employ the same speaking speed, intonation, and number of syllables.

Knowing that infants are capable of discriminating very slight differences in speech, such as the difference between two consonants, it is not surprising that they can also identify different people based on their voices. At an early age, infants display clear preferences for specific voices. This was shown to great effect in an experiment in which newborns were allowed to suck a nipple that activated a recording of an adult reading a story. When the voice belonged to a stranger, the infants sucked with significantly less enthusiasm and for a shorter amount of time than they did when the recording was of the voice of their mother.

Researchers have long been curious about how such preferences might arise. Proponents of this theory often provide supporting evidence that indicates that newborns do not show a preference for their fathers' voices over other male voices. Moreover, newborns prefer hearing songs that had been sung to them while in the womb to songs sung to them only after birth. Therefore, it is apparent that the listening preferences of infants are influenced by prenatal exposure to their mothers' voices, even though sounds are muffled due to the liquid environment of the womb.

The reason that infants are born with fairly good auditory perception is that they receive a surprising amount of hearing practice prior to their birth. Indeed, during the first two years of life, an infant is more sensitive to certain extremely high and low frequencies than adults are. Conversely, infants are initially less sensitive to middle-range frequencies when compared with adults. Over time, though, their auditory perception within the middle range will become much more sensitive

The word "fairly" in the passage is closest in meaning to

(A) equally
(B) clearly
(C) reasonably
(D) occasionally

The reason that infants are born with fairly good auditory perception is that they receive a surprising amount of hearing practice prior to their birth. Indeed, during the first two years of life, an infant is more sensitive to certain extremely high and low frequencies than adults are. Conversely, infants are initially less sensitive to middle-range frequencies when compared with adults. Over time, though, their auditory perception within the middle range will become much more sensitive.

According to paragraph 1, which of the following statements is NOT accurate regarding the auditory capability of infants?

(A) An infant's sensitivity to middle-range frequencies becomes more enhanced as the child ages.
(B) Infants up to age two are more capable of hearing extreme frequencies than adults are.
(C) Infants have more sensitivity to high and low frequencies than they do to middle frequencies.
(D) Infants are unfamiliar with any type of auditory stimuli prior to their birth.

Although there is no definitive explanation for the improvement in sensitivity to sounds in infants, many researchers believe it is connected to the maturation of the nervous system. There is even less of a consensus when it comes to explaining why, after infancy, a child's ability to hear extremely high and low frequencies gradually diminishes. One theory is that increased exposure to loud noise may reduce a child's capability to perceive sound at these extreme frequencies.

Which of the following best describes the organization of paragraph 2?

(A) Two theories about auditory perception followed by descriptions of experiments that have proven those theories.
(B) A history of auditory perception research followed by a comparison of two recent studies on the topic.
(C) A brief discussion of two developments in auditory perception together with potential explanations of them.
(D) Two methods used to test the auditory perception capacity of children aged two and under.

In order to hear effectively, infants need several other abilities in addition to the ability to detect sound. For example, sound localization enables infants to accurately determine the direction from which a sound is coming. Infants are at a disadvantage compared with adults when it comes to this ability, as effective sound localization relies on the slight discrepancy in the times at which the two ears individually hear a sound. Because the distance between an infant's ears is shorter than that between an adult's, sounds arrive at both ears more quickly than they do in the case of an adult. However, even with this potential limitation, the sound localization abilities of infants are relatively strong even at birth, and they typically reach adult levels of effectiveness by the time an infant is one year old. It is interesting to note that their improvement is not linear. Sound localization ability actually worsens over the first two months after birth before it begins to improve, and there is no clear explanation why that occurs.

According to paragraph 3, which of the following statements does NOT accurately characterize infants' sound localization capabilities?

(A) By the age of one year, the sound localization capabilities of infants are basically equal to those of adults.

(B) The reason that sound localization capabilities of infants do not improve steadily is unknown.

(C) The sound localization capabilities of infants are potentially less accurate than those of adults due to the relatively short distance between their ears.

(D) The ability to localize sound accurately declines steadily after two months of age but then increases after the age of one.

Young infants are also capable of recognizing subtle distinctions between various sounds, and this is crucial to their future understanding of language. For example, in one well-known study, a group of infants aged between four weeks and four months sucked on nipples that played a recording of an adult saying "ba" whenever it was sucked. To begin with, the infants sucked vigorously due to their keen interest in the recorded voice. After a while, however, they lost interest in the sound and their sucking became less enthusiastic. The experimenters then changed the sound to "pa," and the infants' enthusiasm was immediately renewed, causing them to suck harder once more. The findings clearly indicated that infants as young as four weeks old could make the distinction between two similar sounds.

Which of the following statements describes a finding from the well-known study on infants' auditory perception that is discussed in paragraph 4?

(A) Infants tend to lose interest when the sound they have been hearing is changed.
(B) Some consonant sounds are easier for infants to recognize than others.
(C) Even very young infants are capable of detecting small differences in sound.
(D) Infants show more interest in spoken sounds than sounds made by objects.

Another interesting aspect of auditory perception in infants is their ability to identify certain characteristics that differentiate between various spoken languages. Research has shown that even two-day-olds have a preference for the language spoken by those around them over unfamiliar languages. Their ability to distinguish between languages develops rapidly over the first few months of life. By the age of five months, they can recognize the differences between spoken passages in English and Spanish, even when the speakers employ the same speaking speed, intonation, and number of syllables.

The word "employ" in the passage is closest in meaning to

(A) recruit
(B) utilize
(C) strive
(D) learn

Another interesting aspect of auditory perception in infants is their ability to identify certain characteristics that differentiate between various spoken languages. Research has shown that even two-day-olds have a preference for the language spoken by those around them over unfamiliar languages. Their ability to distinguish between languages develops rapidly over the first few months of life. By the age of five months, they can recognize the differences between spoken passages in English and Spanish, even when the speakers employ the same speaking speed, intonation, and number of syllables.

What is the main point of paragraph 5?

(A) Children are able to easily recognize only similar sounding words in various languages.
(B) Intonation and speaking speed are two characteristics children use to determine which language they are hearing.
(C) Many children are capable of learning both English and Spanish at a very young age.
(D) Even when only a few months old, infants can distinguish between the sounds of different languages.

Knowing that infants are capable of discriminating very slight differences in speech, such as the difference between two consonants, it is not surprising that they can also identify different people based on their voices. At an early age, infants display clear preferences for specific voices. This was shown to great effect in an experiment in which newborns were allowed to suck a nipple that activated a recording of an adult reading a story. When the voice belonged to a stranger, the infants sucked with significantly less enthusiasm and for a shorter amount of time than they did when the recording was of the voice of their mother.

Paragraph 6 answers which of the following questions about the auditory abilities of infants?

(A) Can newborns recognize differences in stories read by their mothers?
(B) Can infants distinguish when the readers of story recordings are switched?
(C) Do newborns gain more benefit from listening to stories spoken by people they are unfamiliar with?
(D) What type of voice has the most soothing effect on young children?

Researchers have long been curious about how such preferences might arise. ■ Proponents of this theory often provide supporting evidence that indicates that newborns do not show a preference for their fathers' voices over other male voices. ■ Moreover, newborns prefer hearing songs that had been sung to them while in the womb to songs sung to them only after birth. ■ Therefore, it is apparent that the listening preferences of infants are influenced by prenatal exposure to their mothers' voices, even though sounds are muffled due to the liquid environment of the womb. ■

Look at the four squares [■] that indicate where the following sentence could be added to the passage.

One theory is that the most crucial factor is prenatal exposure to the mother's voice.

Where would the sentence best fit? Click on a square [■] to add the sentence to the passage.

Directions: An introductory sentence for a brief summary of the passage is provided below. Complete the summary by selecting the THREE answer choices that express the most important ideas in the passage. Some sentences do not belong in the summary because they express ideas that are not presented in the passage or are minor ideas in the passage. **This question is worth 2 points.**

Drag your answer choices to the space where they belong. To remove an answer choice, click on it. To review the passage, click on **VIEW TEXT.**

Studies have shown that auditory perception in infants is quite sophisticated.

-
-
-

Answer Choices

(A) The preference of newborns for their mother's voice and for songs heard during pregnancy indicates that prenatal exposure to sounds affects auditory development in the womb.

(B) In one well-known study, infants enthusiastically sucked on a nipple upon hearing a recording of a person saying "ba" but became less energetic when the sound changed to "pa."

(C) Because the liquid environment of the womb limits exposure to a father's voice, newborns typically show a preference for their mother's voice.

(D) During the first two years of life, infants respond to sounds at middle-range frequencies more accurately than sounds at extreme frequencies.

(E) Infants' capabilities to hear very high and low frequencies surpass those of even adults, and their ability to determine the source of sounds is also extraordinarily good.

(F) From an early age, the auditory perception of infants allows them to make auditory discriminations not only between two similar sounds, but also between different languages and different voices.

시원스쿨 토플 전문강사
류형진 선생님

시원스쿨
TOEFL Reading
온라인 강의

빈출 토픽별 학습으로 문제풀이 원리 터득

시원스쿨 TOEFL Reading 강의 POINT 3

토플 시험에 자주 나오는
과학, 역사, 예술 등
빈출 토픽별 학습

빈출 주제에 대한
배경지식을 넓히고
관련 어휘 습득

오답 및 정답을 분석,
친절한 해설을 통해
토플 문제 풀이의 원리 터득

시원스쿨LAB(lab.siwonschool.com)에서 유료강의를 수강하실 수 있습니다.

고득점을 위한 **토플** 리딩 기본서

SIWONSCHOOL
TOEFL

Reading

정답 및 해설

시원스쿨 **LAB**

고득점을 위한 **토플** 리딩 **기본서**

SIWONSCHOOL
TOEFL
Reading

정답 및 해설

시원스쿨 **LAB**

Introduction

[전체 지문 보기]

18세기와 19세기에는 산업 혁명으로 인해 상품이 생산되는 방식에 있어 급격한 변화가 일어났다. 기계회는 노동자들에게서 고되고 시간 소모적인 일을 없애 주었고, 수공예 작업자들의 의자에서 공장 및 조립 라인으로 생산 과정을 옮겨 주었다. [2(C)]기계화 및 조립 라인 이면에 존재하는 원칙은 표준화, 지속성, 그리고 복잡한 작업 공정을 단순한 단계로 바꾸는 세분화였다. 노동력의 분배가 생산성 증가라는 결과를 낳기는 했지만, 이러한 상품을 생산하던 노동자들은 전체 작업 공정에 대한 이해가 없었다. [4(B)]기계화 이전 시대의 장인들은 각 개발 단계에 있어 자신의 수공예품에 대한 복잡한 장인 기술을 갖고 있었다. [1(A)]새로운 시스템 하의 노동자들은 일련의 다른 단순한 작업들 속에서 그저 각자의 작은 일 한 가지만 이해해야 했다. 공장 운영자들은 종종, 생산되는 상품의 질과 디자인보다 생산량을 위해 애썼다. [2(A)]게다가, 기계들로 인해 복잡하게 화려한 패턴과 디자인에 대한 대량 재생산이 가능하게 되었다. 이는 빅토리아 시대의 디자인 양식에 [3(B)]아주 큰 영향을 미쳤다. 당시의 시장은 형편없이 디자인되고 값싸게 생산된 제품들뿐만 아니라 과도한 역사적 복제품들로 가득하게 되었다. 유럽과 아메리카 지역의 19세기 미술 공예 운동 옹호자들은 철학적으로 값싼 대량 복제 생산을 반대했다. 이들은 기계 및 조립 라인에 의해 생산되어 표준화된 상품을 혼이 없는 것으로 여겼으며, 그에 대한 대응으로, 수공예로의 회귀를 비롯해 [2(B)]수량과 속도가 아닌 품질과 디자인에 대한 강조를 캠페인했다.

미술 공예 운동 옹호자들은 건강한 사회가 숙련되고 능력 있는 공예 작업자라는 자원의 보유에 달려 있다고 주장했다. 심미적이고 아름답게 디자인된 상품을 단순히 그것을 얻을 여유가 있는 사람들이 아니라 모든 사람들이 이용 가능해야 한다고 생각했다. 기계화가 상품 가격을 낮춰 주기는 했지만, 품질도 떨어뜨렸다. 더욱이, 대량 재생산이 이뤄지면서, 독창적이고 개성 있는 디자인들이 살아남지 못하게 되었다. [5(C)]다른 모든 운동과 마찬가지로, 미술 공예 이데올로기 지지자들은 다양한 수준의 신념을 표현했다. [6(B)]어떤 이들은 기계라는 악폐의 유일한 원인인 기계들이 완전히 사라져야 한다고 주장하기도 했고, 혼이 담겨 있지 않고 일상적인 노동에 의존하게 된 사회를 치유하기 위해 수공예로의 회귀가 필요하다고 주장하기도 했다. 또 다른 이들은 기계가 그저 잘못 이용되었다고 생각하기도 했다. 이 사람들은 수공예가 지닌 더 미묘하면서 숙련된 기술을 요하는 측면들에 대해 자유로워지게 하기 위해 수공예 작업자에게서 그 일의 열등하고 신체적으로 힘든 측면들을 없애 줄 수 있는 기계의 이점들을 인정했다.

미술 공예 운동은 유럽과 아메리카에서 모두 나타났으며, 유사한 철학적 접근 방식을 공유하기는 했지만, 그 결과는 상당히 달랐다. ■ 아메리카의 경우와 마찬가지로, 유럽의 운동은 일반 대중이 이용할 수 있는 예술적으로 제작된 상품을 생산하자는 초기의 원동력과 함께 시작되었다. ■ 하지만 유럽에서, 미술 공예 운동 지지자들은 또한 산업화가 파괴하고 있다고 생각했던 대담한 수공예로 완전히 회귀하기를 원했다. ■ 수공예 작업자들은, 그들이 주장하기를, 반드시 존경받고, 존중되어야 하며, 그에 따라 비용 보상을 받아야 한다. 사람들이 수공예 작업자들에게 제공하는 넉넉한 봉급과 결합된 수작업 공예품에 대한 유일한 의존은, 역설적이게도 그들이 만들어내던 상품의 가격을 인상시켰다. 결과적으로, 유럽 미술 공예 운동 제품들은 일반인들에게 엄두도 못 내 만큼 비싼 것이 되었다. [8]■

아메리카에서는, 하지만, [7(C)]미술 공예 운동 지지자들이 기계가 나오기 이전의 시대로 회귀하기를 원치 않은 대신, [7(C)]이들은 기계화와 미학 사이에서 조화를 만들어내고 싶어했다. 이들은 비용을 낮추는 기계를 활용함과 동시에 제품의 재료를 강조했다. 아메리카 미술 공예 운동 디자이너들과 건축자들은 재료의 질과 디자인의 단순함에 초점을 맞췄다. 이들은 나무의 결 또는 돌의 질감을 강조하기 위해 흔히 의도적으로 제품의 여러 측면을 미완성 상태로 남겨두었다. 이는 그들의 양식에 서민적이고 강인한 특성을 더해 주었다.

[어휘]

1. Industrial Revolution 산업 혁명 relieve A of B A에게서 B를 없애 주다 principle 원칙 breaking down of ~의 세분화, ~의 구분 mastery 숙달, 통달 mass reproduction 대량 재생산 intricately 복잡하게 ornate 화려한 have a profound impact on ~에 아주 큰 영향을 미치다 rife with ~로 가득한 excess 과도함, 지나침 philosophically 철학적으로 campaign for ~에 찬성하는 운동을 벌이다, 캠페인하다
2. advocate 옹호자 maintain 주장하다 aesthetic 심미적인 fall by the wayside 살아남지 못하다, 도중에 실패하다 conviction 신념 mundane 일상적인 be put to the wrong use 잘못 이용되다 ignoble 열등한, 조악한 laborious 힘든 aspect 측면, 양상 subtle 미묘한
3. counterpart (대응 관계에 있는) 상대, 대상 impetus 원동력, 자극(제) heroic 대담한 assert 주장하다 revere ~을 존경하다, ~을 숭배하다 reimburse ~에게 비용을 보상해주다 paradoxically 역설적이게 prohibitively 엄두도 내지 못할 만큼
4. proponent 지지자 marriage 조화 grain (나무, 돌 등의) 결 lend A B A에게 B를 주다, 부여하다

1. Factual Information
첫 문단에 따르면, 기계화와 관련해 다음 중 어느 것이 사실인가?
(A) 결과적으로 오직 각자의 특정 임무만 아는 노동자들을 만들어냈다.
(B) 산업 혁명이 있은 후 19세기에 끝이 났다.
(C) 상품 가격의 인상으로 특징지어졌다.
(D) 각자의 공예품을 아는 숙련된 노동자들을 필요로 했다.

2. Negative Factual Information
첫 문단에 따르면, 다음 중 미술 공예 운동이 반대하지 않았던 것은 무엇인가?
(A) 대단히 화려한 역사적인 양식의 대량 재생산
(B) 디자인의 품질이 아닌 수량과 속도에 대한 강조
(C) 생산 과정의 조립 라인 및 표준화
(D) 규모가 크고 매력적이지 못한 공장의 확산

3. Vocabulary
지문의 단어 "profound"와 의미가 가장 가까운 것은 무엇인가?
(A) 직접적인
(B) 광범위한, 지대한
(C) 긍정적인
(D) 이상한

4. Rhetorical Purpose
첫 문단에서, 글쓴이는 왜 "장인"을 언급하는가?
(A) 18세기 노동자들이 시간 소모적인 일에 대해 작업했다고 주장하기 위해
(B) 전체 생산 작업 과정이 기계화 후에 어떻게 변화되었음을 보여주기 위해
(C) 예술가들이 각자의 공예품에 대한 모든 단계를 숙달해야 했다는 증거를 제공하기 위해
(D) 산업 혁명과 관련된 문제에 대한 예시를 제공하기 위해

5. Inference
다음 중 두 번째 문단에서 미술 공예 운동 지지자들과 관련해 유추할 수 있는 것은 무엇인가?
(A) 기계가 숙련된 공예 작업자들로 대체되어야 한다는 데 동의했다.
(B) 기계가 공예품을 향상시킬 수 있다고 주장했다.
(C) 질 좋은 상품을 만드는 데 있어 기계의 유용함과 관련해 동의하지 않았다.
(D) 공예품에 필요한 신체 노동과 미묘한 기술 모두의 중요성을 옹호했다.

6. Sentence Simplification
다음 문장들 중 어느 것이 지문의 하이라이트 표기된 문장에 담긴 핵심 정보를 가장 잘 표현하는가? 오답 선택지는 중요한 방식으로 의미를 변경하거나 핵심 정보를 배제한다.

어떤 이들은 기계화라는 악폐의 유일한 원인인 기계들이 완전히 사라져야 한다고 주장하기도 했고, 혼이 담겨 있지 않고 일상적인 노동에 의존하게 된 사회를 치유하기 위해 수공예로의 회귀가 필요하다고 주장하기도 했다.

(A) 어떤 이들은 기계가 모든 악폐의 원인이며 사회를 건강하지 못하게 만들었다고 주장했다.
(B) 어떤 이들은 사회를 치유하기 위해 기계의 폐기 및 공예 작업으로의 회귀를 옹호했다.
(C) 어떤 이들은 공예품이 일상적인 노동에 의존하는 사회를 치유할 수 있다고 생각했다.
(D) 어떤 이들은 공예품이 혼이 담겨 있지 않은 일상적인 노동의 필요성을 없애 줄 것이라는 생각을 지지했다.

7. Reference
해당 단락의 단어 "they"는 무엇을 가리키는가?
(A) 아메리카의 디자이너들
(B) 건축가들
(C) 미술 공예 운동 지지자들
(D) 기계들

8. Insert Text
다음 문장이 지문에 추가될 수 있는 곳을 나타내는 네 개의 네모 표기 [■]를 찾아 보시오.

오직 부유한 사람들만 유럽의 미술 공예 운동이 맺은 결실을 즐길 수 있었다.

위 문장은 어느 곳에 가장 적합하겠는가? 네모 표기 [■]를 클릭해 지문에 이 문장을 추가하시오.

4th ■

9. Prose Summary
설명: 간략한 지문 요약에 필요한 도입 문장이 아래에 제공되어 있다. 지문에서 가장 중요한 개념들을 나타내는 세 가지 답안 선택지를 골라 요약 내용을 완성하시오. 일부 답안 선택지는 지문에 제시되지 않는 개념을 나타내거나 지문에서 중요하지 않은 개념들이므로 요약 내용에 속하지 않는다. 이 문제는 2점에 해당된다.

> 이 지문은 19세기에 나타났던 미술 공예 운동을 이야기하고 있다.
> - (C) 미술 공예 운동 지지자들이 숙련된 공예 작업자들의 중요성을 강조했다.
> - (E) 일부 미술 공예 운동 지지자들은 기계화의 장점을 인정했다.
> - (F) 유럽의 상품 가격이 미술 공예 운동으로 인해 치솟았다.

(A) 기계화로 인해 공예 작업자들이 공예품의 더 미묘하고 숙련된 기술을 요하는 측면에 초점을 맞출 수 있게 되었다.
(B) 유럽과 아메리카의 미술 공예 운동이 동일한 결과를 가져왔다.
(C) 미술 공예 운동 지지자들이 숙련된 공예 작업자들의 중요성을 강조했다.
(D) 미술 공예 운동이 오직 유럽과 아메리카에서만 일어났다.
(E) 일부 미술 공예 운동 지지자들은 기계화의 장점을 인정했다.
(F) 유럽의 상품 가격이 미술 공예 운동으로 인해 치솟았다.

10. Fill in a Table

설명: 선택지에서 적절한 문구를 골라서 연관되는 유형에 연결하시오. 선택지 중 두 개는 사용되지 않는다. 이 문제는 3점에 해당된다.

유럽의 미술 공예 운동	아메리카의 미술 공예 운동
- (A) 고귀한 공예 작업으로이 완전한 회귀 및 기계의 폐기 - (F) 생산하는 데 많은 비용이 들어서 대부분의 사람들이 이용 불가능한 상품	- (B) 재료의 특성을 강조한 양식 - (E) 노출된 접합부 및 미완성 상태의 표면으로 인해 가구에 나타난 투박하고 서민적인 양식 - (G) 기계화와 미학 사이의 조화

(A) 고귀한 공예 작업으로의 완전한 회귀 및 기계의 폐기
(B) 재료의 특성을 강조한 스타일
(C) 품질과 디자인이 아닌 수량과 속도에 대한 선호
(D) 일상적이고 반복적인 노동에 대한 의존
(E) 노출된 접합부 및 미완성 상태의 표면으로 인해 가구에 나타난 투박하고 서민적인 양식
(F) 생산하는 데 많은 비용이 들어서 대부분의 사람들이 이용 불가능한 상품
(G) 기계화와 미학 사이의 조화

Passage 1

Answers

1. A	2. C	3. D	4. D	5. A	6. C	7. B	8. D	9. B	10. BCD

바닷속 먹이 공급 전략

해양 생태계에는, ^{1(A)}3월에서 5월 사이에 해당되는 미국의 얕은 연안 지역들처럼 먹이가 특정 계절 중에 더 풍부해지는 특정 지역들이 존재한다. 이러한 시나리오에서, 풍부한 먹이 공급원을 찾은 종들은 먹이가 바닥나는 것에 대한 두려움으로 인한 에너지 보존을 더 이상 우선시할 필요가 없어진다. 반면에, 바다의 더 깊은 지역에서 서식하는 종들은 먹이가 극도로 부족한 기간을 겪을 가능성이 더 높아지며, 이는 그들의 에너지 사용에 있어 가혹한 제약을 가하게 된다. 이러한 종들은 어쩔 수 없이 새로운 먹이 공급 전략을 택해 척박한 서식지에서 생존하기 위해 칼로리 섭취량을 극대화해야 한다.

바다의 상층부에서는, 고래 같은 많은 대형 생물체들이 자연 여과 장치처럼 기능하는 해부학적 구조를 통해 지나가는 물의 흐름으로부터 플랑크톤을 분리하는 방식으로 엄청난 양의 플랑크톤을 먹어치운다. 이러한 생물체들은 여과 섭식 동물이라고 적절히 일컬어지고 있으며, 이들은 바다에서 플랑크톤이 가장 풍부하고 빛이 잘 드는 표층수에서 잘 자란다. 특정 환경 하에서는, 많은 작은 물고기 종들도 효과적인 여과 섭식 동물인 것으로 드러나고 있다. ^{2(C)}대부분의 물고기가 육식성이긴 하지만, 바다의 표면 근처에 사는 멸치나 정어리 같은 일부 종들은 해조류 같은 식물 기반의 플랑크톤인 식물성 플랑크톤 또한 다량 섭취한다. ^{3(D)}이들은 아가미에 있는 독특한 섬유 조직을 활용해 많은 양의 해조류를 걸러 낼 수 있다. 이들의 식단을 구성하는 이러한 요소는 정어리 및 멸치 개체수가 번성할 수 있게 해주며, 이는 결과적으로 상업용 어업 회사들이 더 많은 어획량을 얻는 것은 말할 것도 없고 바닷새 같은 포식자들에게도 더 많은 먹이 자원을 제공한다. 더 큰 여과 섭식 동물에는 고래 상어나 수염 고래 같은 것들이 포함되며, 이들은 일반적으로 엄청난 양의 여과된 동물성 플랑크톤(크릴 새우나 요각류 같은 작은 생물)을 먹기 위해 연안 해역이나 한대 해역을 찾는다.

^{4(D)}여과 섭식 동물이 영양 성분을 물에서 걸러 내기 위해 직접 물살을 만들어내야 한다는 점을 감안하면, 이는 일부 생물체들에게 있어 에너지 부담이 큰 먹이 공급 전략일 수 있다. 여과 섭식 동물이 순 에너지 이득을 얻으려면, 반드시 바닷물 1큐빅리터당 최소 2.5마이크로그램의 유기 물질이 있어야 한다. 대부분의 연안 해역에서, 이러한 요건은 쉽게 충족된다. 하지만, 깊은 바다에서는, 유기 물질의 수준이 사실상 1큐빅리터당 0에서 5마이크로그램을 간신히 넘는 범위에 이른다. 일부 지역의 밀도가 상대적으로 높기는 하지만, 이러한 심해 지역의 많은 곳에서 대부분의 여과 섭식 동물은 칼로리 및 에너지 순손실로 인해 그야말로 굶어 죽게 될 것이다.

바다의 가장 깊은 지역에서 번성하는 것은 고사하고 생존할 수 있는 여과 섭식 동물이 거의 없다는 사실은 누가 봐도 당연하다. 그러한 지역에서 살 수 있는 것들은 ^{5(C)}유기 물질의 낮은 밀도를 상쇄할 수 있는 더 큰 여과 시스템을 발달시켜왔다. ^{5(B)}이 정도 깊이에 사는 많은 생물들은 유기 물질이 더 많이 집중되어 축적되는 특정 층에서만 먹이를 찾아 다니기를 택한다. 전형적으로 얕은 물에서 여과 섭식 행위를 보이는 많은 해양 종들과 마찬가지로 심해에도 그러한 행위를 보이는 종들이 있기는 하지만, 이 심해 생물들의 여과 시스템은 일반적으로 덜 발달되어 있다. 따라서, 이들은 활동적인 먹이와 수동적인 먹이를 모두 잡으러 다니기 위해 대체 방법을 택해왔는데, ^{5(D)}특히 크기가 더 작은 생물들을 걸러지게 해서 붙잡는 데 사용하는 촉수가 그 방법이다.

■ ^{6(C)}심해에 사는 종들은 에너지를 아끼기 위해 먹이가 다가오기를 기다리면서 그저 가만히 있는 경향이 더 크다. ^{9(B)}■ 이에 따라, 이 종들은 더 은밀한 먹이 공급 방법을 발달시켜왔으며, 흔히 주변의 더 넓은 수중 공간을 통제할 수 있게 해주는 유인 장치나 길쭉한 신체 부위의 활용에 초점을 맞춘다. ■ 낮은 먹이 밀도에 대한 대응으로 일부 종들이 발달시켜온 또 다른 적응 방식은 얕은 물에 사는 유사한 크기의 종들이 먹을 수 있는 것보다 훨씬 더 큰 유기 물질 입자를 ^{7(B)}처리하는 능력이다. ■ 물고기 종들 사이에서, 많은 종들이 더 큰 아래턱과 이빨을 지니도록 진화해왔다. 더욱이, 이 물고기들 중 일부는 일시적으로 아래턱을 탈구시켜 입을 더 크게 벌릴 수 있도록 진화해왔다. 이런 방법이 먹이가 빨려 들어 가는

구멍을 아주 넓게 만들어 주기 때문에, [8(D)]해당 물고기는 이빨을 이용해 먹이를 잘게 자르는 대신 통째로 삼키는 경향이 있는데, 이는 먹이를 먹는 데 필요한 총 에너지량을 줄여준다.

[어휘]

1. shallow 얕은 prioritize ~을 우선시하다 inhabit ~에 서식하다, 살다 exceedingly 극도로 scarce 부족한 impose constraints on ~에 제약을 가하다 maximize ~을 극대화하다 barren 척박한

2. consume ~을 소비하다, 먹다 anatomical 해부학적인 filtration mechanism 여과 장치 be referred to as ~라고 일컬어지다 aptly 적절히 filter-feeder 여과 섭식 동물(물 속의 유기 물질이나 미생물 등을 여과해 섭취하는 동물) flourish 번성하나, 질 자라디 carnivorous 육식성의 anchovy 멸치 sardine 정어리 take advantage of ~을 이용하다 phytoplankton 식물성 플랑크톤 algae 해조류 filament 섬유, 가는 실 gill 아가미 catch 잡은 양 zooplankton 동물성 플랑크톤

3. nutritional content 영양 성분 net 순 ~ range from A to B A에서 B의 범위에 이르다 concentration 밀도, 농도

4. It stands to reason that ~인 것이 누가 봐도 당연하다 pocket 지역 offset ~을 상쇄하다 forage 먹이를 찾아다니다 typify ~의 전형이다, ~을 대표하다 counterpart 대응 관계에 있는 사물이나 사람 tentacle 촉수 entangle ~을 걸려들게 하다

5. lure 유인 장치 elongated 길쭉한 adaptation 적응 (방식) particle 입자 jaw 아래턱 dislocate ~을 탈구시키다 swallow A whole A를 통째로 삼키다

---

1. 첫 번째 문단에서 3월에서 5월 사이에 연안 해역에 서식하는 해양 생물과 관련해 유추할 수 있는 것은 무엇인가?
(A) 먹이를 찾는 데 에너지를 덜 쏟는다.
(B) 풍부한 먹이 공급량을 얻기 위해 애쓴다.
(C) 5월이 지나면 칼로리 섭취량을 늘린다.
(D) 포식자들을 피하기 위해 에너지 보존을 우선시한다.

해설 얕은 연안 지역에서 먹이가 풍부하다고 언급되어 있고, 그렇지 않은 깊은 지역에서는 먹이를 찾는 데 에너지를 더 쏟아야 된다고 나오므로, 연안 지역 해양 생물들은 먹이를 찾는 데 에너지를 덜 쏟는 것을 유추할 수 있다. 따라서, (A)가 정답이다.

어휘 expend (에너지, 시간 등) ~을 쏟다, 들이다 source ~을 얻다, 공급받다 evade ~을 피하다

2. 두 번째 문단에서 물고기와 관련해 알 수 있는 것은 무엇인가?
(A) 대부분의 물고기가 식물성 플랑크톤에 의존한다.
(B) 대부분의 물고기 종들이 빛이 잘 드는 해수 층을 피하는 것을 선호한다.
(C) 일부 육식성 물고기는 식물 기반의 먹이도 먹는다.
(D) 수면과 가까운 층에서 효과적인 먹이 사냥꾼인 물고기 종은 거의 없다.

해설 대부분의 물고기가 육식성이지만 바다표면에 사는 일부 물고기들은 식물성 플랑크톤을 섭취하기도 한다는 점을 확인할 수 있으므로 (C)가 정답이다.

3. 두 번째 문단에 따르면, 정어리와 멸치는 바다의 상층부에서 어떻게 먹이를 얻는가?
(A) 바다의 더 깊은 지역에서 먹이 공급원을 가져온다.
(B) 유기 물질을 얻기 위해 바닷새들과 경쟁한다.
(C) 어업용 선박이 버린 생물들을 먹는다.

(D) 아가미를 활용해 바닷물에서 해조류를 걸러 낸다.

해설 멸치와 정어리들은 아가미에 있는 독특한 섬유 조직을 활용해 많은 양의 해조류를 걸러 낼 수 있다는 점을 토대로 (D)가 정답이라는 점을 유추할 수 있다.

어휘 discard ~을 버리다, 폐기하다

4. 다음 문장들 중 어느 것이 지문의 하이라이트 표기된 문장에 담긴 핵심 정보를 가장 잘 표현하는가? 오답 선택지는 중요한 방식으로 의미를 변경하거나 핵심 정보를 배제한다.

여과 섭식 동물이 영양 성분을 물에서 걸러 내기 위해 직접 물살을 만들어내야 한다는 점을 감안하면, 이는 일부 생물체들에게 있어 에너지 부담이 큰 먹이 공급 전략일 수 있다.

(A) 충분히 강력한 물살을 만들어 내기 위해, 여과 섭식 동물은 반드시 먹이 공급 사이의 기간에 에너지를 아껴야 한다.
(B) 대부분의 여과 섭식 동물은 자연적인 바다 물살에서 영양 성분을 걸러 냄으로써 에너지 필요 조건을 충족할 수 있다.
(C) 여과 섭식 동물이 먹이를 공급받기 위해 물살을 만들어 내기 때문에, 바닷물에서 먹이를 걸러 내지 않는 해양 종들보다 에너지를 덜 쏟는다.
(D) 그들 스스로 물살을 만들어 내야 하기 때문에, 필요한 영양분을 충족하기 위해 바닷물을 걸러 내는 생물체들에게 많은 에너지가 요구된다.

해설 명확한 인과관계가 드러나는 보기가 정답임을 유추할 수 있다. 직접 물살을 만들어내야 한다는 점을 감안한다는 정보가 (D)에서 'since they need to create their own water currents'로 등장하고, 많은 에너지가 요구되어야 한다는 점이 앞에 'Large energy demands are placed on'이라는 표현으로 제시된다. (A)는 'conserve energy' 라는 점이 틀렸고, (B)는

직접 물살을 만들어낸다는 점을 고려한다는 내용이 누락되어 있으며, (C)는 'expend less energy than'이라는 해당 사항이 없는 정보가 제시되어 오답이다.

5. 네 번째 문단에 따르면, 다음 중 심해 지역에 사는 여과 섭식 동물이 택한 먹이 공급 전략이 아닌 것은 무엇인가?
(A) 지역 내 먹이 공급원이 모자라게 될 때 수면 쪽으로 올라가는 것
(B) 유기 물질이 가장 풍부한 심해 지역에서 먹이를 찾아다니는 것
(C) 더 큰 여과 시스템을 활용하는 것
(D) 촉수를 이용해 먹이가 움직이지 못하게 하는 것

해설 (C)는 문단 초반부에 낮은 밀도를 상쇄할 수 있는 더 큰 여과 시스템을 발달시켜왔다는 부분에서 확인할 수 있고, (D)는 마지막인 촉수 언급을 하는 부분에서 확인할 수 있다. (B)는 유기 물질이 더 많이 집중되어 축적되는 특정 층에서만 먹이를 찾아다닌다는 중간 부분에서 확인할 수 있다. (A)의 수면 쪽으로 올라간다는 점은 지문에 언급되지 않는다.

어휘 run low 모자라게 되다, 부족해지다 utilize ~을 활용하다
immobilize ~을 움직이지 못하게 하다

6. 글쓴이는 왜 바다 깊은 곳의 생물들이 흔히 "유인 장치"와 "길쭉한 신체 부위"에 의존한다고 언급하는가?
(A) 바닷속 가장 깊은 층에 사는 생물들이 어떻게 여과 섭식 동물을 잡아 먹을 수 있는지 설명하기 위해
(B) 먹이를 찾아다닐 때 얕은 물에 사는 종들보다 심해 생물들이 더 많은 에너지를 쏟는다는 가설에 이의를 제기하기 위해
(C) 일부 생물들이 먹이가 부족한 지역에서 효과적으로 먹이를 먹기 위해 거쳐온 적응 방식을 확인하기 위해
(D) 심해 생물들이 물살을 헤치고 빠르게 이동하는 것을 도와주는 해부학적 특징들의 예시를 제공하기 위해

해설 다섯 번째 문단의 첫 문장부터 심해에 사는 종은 에너지를 아끼기 위해 먹이가 다가오기를 기다린다는 점을 언급해주고 있고, 이어지는 문장에서 더 넓은 수중 공간을 통제하기 위한 유인 장치 또는 길쭉한 신체부위 활용을 언급하기 때문에 (C)가 답이라는 점을 유추할 수 있다.

어휘 hypothesis 가설 feature 특징

7. 지문의 표현 "deal with"와 의미가 가장 가까운 것은 무엇인가?
(A) ~을 거래하다, 교환하다
(B) ~을 처리하다
(C) ~을 분배하다
(D) ~을 끌어들이다

해설 deal with(처리하다)와 process(처리하다)는 동의어로 정답

은 (B)이다.

8. 다섯 번째 문단에 따르면, 일부 물고기는 왜 먹이를 통째로 삼키는가?
(A) 아래턱을 탈구시키는 위험을 감수하고 싶어하지 않는다.
(B) 먹이를 덥석 물 수 있는 이빨이 부족하다.
(C) 온전한 유기 물질이 더 높은 영양 성분을 제공한다.
(D) 먹이를 삼키는 것이 더 적은 에너지 소비를 수반한다.

해설 다섯 번째 문단 마지막 부분을 보면 먹이를 먹는 데 필요한 총 에너지량을 줄여준다는 점을 명시하고 있으므로 (D)가 정답이다.

어휘 risk -ing ~하는 위험을 감수하다 intact 온전한
expenditure 소비

9. 다음 문장이 지문에 추가될 수 있는 곳을 나타내는 네 개의 네모 표기 [▮]를 찾아 보시오.

이 수동적인 접근 방식을 택한 생물체는 필요한 영양분을 충족하기 위해 어쩔 수 없이 독특한 전략을 이용해야 한다.

위 문장은 어느 곳에 가장 적합하겠는가? 네모 표기[▮]를 클릭해 지문에 이 문장을 추가하시오.

(A) 1번
(B) 2번
(C) 3번
(D) 4번

해설 1번 네모 뒤 문장에서 심해에 사는 종들이 가만히 있는 경향이 크다는 점을 명시하고 있다. 이를 일컫는 'this passive approach'라는 표현이 그 뒤에 나오는 것이 합리적이다. 이뿐만 아니라 주어진 문장에 등장하는 'unique strategies'라는 개념을 2번 네모에 넣었을 때, 이후 내용에서 등장하는 은밀한 먹이 공급 방법과 유인 장치 활용 등이 논리적으로 이어질 수 있다.

10. 설명: 간략한 지문 요약에 필요한 도입 문장이 아래에 제공되어 있다. 지문에서 가장 중요한 개념들을 나타내는 세 가지 답안 선택지를 골라 요약 내용을 완성하시오. 일부 답안 선택지는 지문에 제시되지 않는 개념을 나타내거나 지문에서 중요하지 않은 개념들이므로 요약 내용에 속하지 않는다. **이 문제는 2점에 해당된다.**

해양 동물들은 먹이를 통해 얻는 에너지를 극대화하기 위해 다양한 전략을 발전시켜왔다.

(A) 심해 층에서는, 대부분의 플랑크톤이 수면 가까이에서 발견되는 식물 기반의 식물성 플랑크톤이 아니라 동물성 플랑크톤이다.

(B) 얕은 지역 또는 수면과 가까운 지역의 밀도가 더 높은 유기 물질은 물에서 먹이를 걸러 낼 수 있는 생물들에 의해 이용되고 있다.

(C) 더 깊은 물 속에 사는 동물들은 움직임과 먹이를 찾아다닐 필요성을 최소화하고 먹이가 그들에게 오게 하는 전략들을 발전시켜왔다.

(D) 수면 가까운 곳에서는, 일반적으로 고기를 먹는 일부 물고기가 많은 양의 식물 기반 플랑크톤도 먹을 수 있도록 적응해왔다.

(E) 여과 섭식 동물은 더 큰 육식성 포식자들에게 쫓기는 것을 피하기 위해 얕은 지역과 깊은 지역 사이를 이동하는 경향

이 있다.

(F) 바다 깊은 곳에서는, 생물들이 상대적으로 약한 바다 물살로 인해 먹이를 먹는 동안 에너지를 덜 쏟는다.

해설 (B)의 경우 두 번째 문단에서 '바다의 상층부에서는, 고래 같은 많은 대형 생물체들이 자연 여과 장치처럼 기능하는 해부학적 구조'를 활용하며 이를 여과 섭식 동물이라고 일컫는다는 점을 토대로 정답임을 유추할 수 있다. 다섯 번째 문단을 통해 (C) 내용이 정답임을 확인할 수 있다. (D)는 두 번째 문단 중반부에서 멸치와 정어리 예를 통해 설명하고 있다.

어휘 exploit ~을 이용하다 adapt 적응하다 tend to do ~하는 경향이 있다

Passage 2

Answers

1. A	2. C	3. C	4. C	5. B	6. D	7. B	8. B	9. C	10. ACD

양서류의 체온 조절

포유류나 조류와 달리, 양서류는 자체 대사 활동을 이용해 열에너지를 생성하는 특별한 능력을 지니고 있다. 이로 인해 양서류는 주변의 환경 온도와 상관없이 체온을 조절할 수 있게 된다. 이러한 생리학적 적응 방식 덕분에, 양서류는 극한의 기후 조건이 존재하는 다양한 곳에서 서식할 수 있다.

한 가지 종이 생존할 수 있는 기온 범위를 체온 내성 범위라고 일컫는다. 예를 들어, 북미 지역에서 발견되는 특정 뉴트 종은 체온이 섭씨 0도 아래로 떨어지는 상황에서도 여전히 자유롭게 돌아다닐 수 있으며, 반면에 [1(A)]한 남아메리카 개구리는 다른 어떤 양서류보다 높은 수준인 섭씨 40도를 약간 웃도는 체온에서도 정상적으로 활동할 수 있다. ■ 연구가들은 북미 지역에서 체온이 섭씨 영하 5도 바로 밑으로 떨어져 내부 체액의 거의 절반이 얼어붙은 상태에서도 거의 일주일 동안 살 수 있는 일부 두꺼비 및 개구리 종을 발견했다. ■ 나머지 신체 조직은 포도당 및 글리세린 같은 동결 방지 물질의 존재로 인해 얼지 않는다. [9(C)] ■ 또한, 많은 종에게 있어 내성 한계는 고정된 것이 아니며, 특정 환경에 대한 장기적인 노출은 기후순응에 따른 결과로서 그 한계를 변경시킬 수 있다. ■

높은 기온에도 불구하고 계속 태양에 노출된 상태로 유지할 수 있게 해주는 형태학적 적응 방식의 역할을 하는 놀랄 만한 피부 조직 변형 능력을 발휘하는 일부 개구리 종도 존재한다. 대부분의 양서류는 피부에 완전히 물이 스며들 수 있기 때문에 태양 복사열과 증발 건조를 막아주는 방어막이 부족하다. 하지만, [2(C)]아프리카 사바나 개구리의 피부는 구아닌 결정체들을 포함하고 있는데, 이는 피부를 태양 복사열을 반사하는 방패로 탈바꿈시켜, 개구리가 과열되지 않도록 방지해 준다. 일부 청개구리 종은 말라붙는 것을 막아주는 미끌미끌한 물질을 몸 전체에 걸쳐 분비함으로써 증발 건조로 인한 수분 손실을 완화시킨다.

생리학적 적응 방식이 중요하기는 하지만, 체온 조절에 있어 가장 결정적인 요소는 행동이다. 행동적 체온 조절은 [3(B)]각각 추운 기간과 더운 기간 중의 활동 감소를 가리키는 동면이 하면과, [3(D)]몸을 시원하게 유지하기 위해 낮 시간 중에 그늘진 공간으로 이동하는 것과 같이 낮 동안 또는 해마다 나타나는 회피 행동, [3(A)]흙과 암석 같은 환경적 물체와 신체 사이의 직접적인 열 교환을 수반하는 '밀착 접촉', 태양 직사광을 통한 발열로서 햇빛 쪼이기로도 알려진 '일광욕'과 같은 전략들을 포함한다.

양서류 사이에서 나타나는 동면은 진흙이나 깊은 구멍 속으로 굴을 파고 들어가 동결을 피하는 수단으로서 흔히 이용된다. [4(C)]피레네 산맥의 북쪽에 위치한 지역에 서식하는 내터잭 두꺼비는 모래로 된 땅을 파서 겨울 내내 동면한다. 반면에, 남부 스페인에 사는 내터잭 두꺼비는 그 지역의 비교적 따뜻한 겨울 동안 활동적인 상태를 유지하다가, 대신 기후가 특히 덥고 건조한 여름 중에 활동 중단 상태에 접어든다. 이 하면은 내터잭 두꺼비를 말라붙게 해서 죽일 수도 있는 극한 기후를 피하기 위해 땅 속으로 파고 들어가거나 암석의 깊고 시원한 갈라진 틈새에 자리를 마련

함으로써 이뤄진다.

5(B)양서류는 생명 유지의 필수적인 범위 내에서 체온을 유지할 수 없을 때마다 생리학적 적응 반식과 형태학적 적응 방식을 통해 회피 행동을 한다. 한 가지 흔한 체온 조절용 회피 행동은 주위의 높은 온도에 대한 낮은 내성을 가진 양서류의 야간 행동이다. 더욱이, 계절별 회피 행동은 많은 양서류의 생존에 있어 중대하다. 건조 및 반건조 지역에 사는 종들이 길고 건조한 더운 여름 기간 중에 반드시 회피 조치를 취해야 하는 반면, 온화한 지역에 사는 종들은 반드시 겨울 중에 잠재적으로 치명적일 수 있는 낮은 온도를 피하도록 해야 한다.

개구리와 두꺼비가 흔히 낮 시간 중에 햇빛을 쬐는 모습을 볼 수 있는데, 이는 최소 섭씨 10도 정도 체온을 끌어올리는 데 도움을 준다. 예를 들어, 6(D)안데스 두꺼비는 해가 뜨자마자 노출된 촉촉한 땅바닥에 온 몸을 쭉 편 상태로 있는데, 이는 주변의 공기가 데워져서 해당 온도가 되기 훨씬 전에 목표 체온 온도에 이를 수 있게 해준다. 7(B)이러한 방식은 야간에 먹은 음식의 소화 속도를 높이고 성장률도 촉진한다는 점에서 유익하다. 마찬가지로, 아주 많은 양서류 종들이 '밀착 접촉' 행동을 한다. 이는 피부를 통한 수분 흡수와 전도에 의한 열 흡수라는 두 가지 기능을 수행한다. 안데스 두꺼비는 폭우가 내리는 기간 중에 '밀착 접촉' 행동을 활용한다. 따라서, 공기의 더 차가운 온도와 일치하도록 체온을 떨어지게 하는 것이 아니라 따뜻한 지면 온도와 같아지도록 끌어올릴 수 있다. 8(B)지금까지 설명한 방식에서 명확하게 알 수 있듯이, 양서류는 체온을 조절하는 여러 가지 방법이 있기 때문에 극한의 주위 온도에 대처하는 데 능숙하다.

[어휘]
1. thermoregulation 체온 조절 amphibians 양서류 mammals 포유류 metabolic (신진) 대사의 thermal 열의 physiological 생리학적인 adaptation 적응 (방식) inhabit ~에 서식하다, 살다
2. be referred to as ~라고 일컬어지다 tolerance 내성, 저항력 newt 뉴트(도롱뇽의 일종) toad 두꺼비 tissue (신체의) 조직 frost-protective 동결 방지의 substance 물질 glucose 포도당 acclimatization 기후순응
3. exhibit ~을 발휘하다, 드러내다 morphological 형태학적인 radiation 복사열 evaporation 증발 permeable 투과성의 guanine 구아닌(핵산 구성 성분인 퓨린 염기의 일종, 생체 내에서 대사 및 DNA 등의 형성에 관여) secrete ~을 분비하다 greasy 미끈미끈한
4. hibernation 동면(↔ estivation 하면) diurnal 주행성의, 낮 동안의(↔ nocturnal 야행성의) thigmothermy 밀착 접촉 heliothermy 일광욕 bask 햇빛을 조이다
5. burrow 굴을 파고 들어가다 shelter 피할 곳을 마련하다 fissure 갈라진 틈
6. ambient 주위의 arid 건조한 semiarid 반건조의 take measures 조치를 취하다 fatal 치명적인
7. digestion 소화 absorption 흡수 conductivity 전도(성) utilize ~을 활용하다 correspond with ~와 일치하다 mechanism (작용) 방식, 구조, 기제 be adept at ~에 능숙하다 cope with ~에 대처하다

---

1. 두 번째 문단에서, 글쓴이는 왜 "남아메리카 개구리"를 언급하는가?
   (A) 상대적으로 높은 기온 조건에 적응한 양서류의 예시를 제공하기 위해
   (B) 극한의 기온이 어떻게 생리학적 구조에 피해를 초래할 수 있는지 보여주기 위해
   (C) 그 개구리의 생리학적 적응 방식을 북아메리카 뉴트의 것과 비교하기 위해
   (D) 양서류의 적응이 수백만 년을 필요로 하는 과정임을 강조하기 위해

해설 두 번째 문단의 시작부터 체온 내성 범위를 설명하고 있고, 남아메리카 개구리는 타 양서류보다 높은 수준의 체온에서도 살아남을 수 있다는 점을 언급하기 때문에 (A)가 정답이다. (B)의 '피해', (D)의 '수백만 년'은 오답 근거가 되고, (C)의 뉴트는 비교가 아닌 체온 내성 범위의 정도를 설명하기 위한 또 다른 예시로 오답이다.

어휘 adapt to ~에 적응하다 emphasize ~을 강조하다

2. 지문에 따르면, "아프리카 사바나 개구리"는 어떤 적응 방식을 지니고 있는가?
   (A) 호흡기 계통에 보호를 제공하는 방식
   (B) 분비할 수 있는 체액의 양을 제한하는 방식
   (C) 피부를 햇빛에 대한 방어막으로 바꾸는 방식
   (D) 태양 복사열을 에너지로 전환하는 방식

해설 '피부를 태양 복사열을 반사하는 방패로 탈바꿈시켜, 개구리가 과열되지 않도록 방지해 준다'는 점을 토대로 (C)가 정답임을 확인할 수 있다.

어휘 respiratory 호흡기의

3. 다음 중 네 번째 문단에서 행동적 체온 조절의 예시로 언급되지 않은 것은 무엇인가?
   (A) 지면으로부터 열을 흡수하는 것
   (B) 추운 기간 중에 활동을 줄이는 것
   (C) 특정한 계절 먹이를 소비하는 것
   (D) 햇빛을 덜 받는 곳에서 몸을 식히는 것

해설 특정 계절 먹이는 언급된 적이 없으므로 (C)가 정답이다. (A)는

밀착 접촉, (B)는 추운 기간과 더운 기간 중의 활동 감소, (D)는 낮 동안 그늘진 공간으로 이동하는 회피 행동을 통해 각각 언급된다.

4. 다섯 번째 문단에서, 내터잭에 관한 이야기를 통해 유추할 수 있는 것은 무엇인가?

(A) 내터잭은 일반적으로 추위보다 열에 대한 내성이 더 뛰어나다.

(B) 극도로 건조한 환경 조건은 내터잭에게 좀처럼 위협이 되지 못한다.

(C) 내터잭은 기후에 따라 다른 체온 조절 행동을 한다.

(D) 일부 내터잭은 오직 봄과 가을에만 활동적이다.

해설 극한 기후를 피하기 위해 내터잭은 굴을 파고 들어간다는 점을 문단 전반에 걸쳐 설명하고 있기 때문에 (C)를 정답으로 유추할 수 있다. (A)의 경우, 하면(여름 잠)을 하는 내터잭이 있는 점을 미뤄보아 오답임을 알 수 있다. (B)는 위협이 되지 못한다는 점에서 소거할 수 있으며, (D)는 '오직'이라는 부분에서 소거가 가능하다.

5. 여섯 번째 문단에 따르면, 회피 행동이 왜 일부 양서류에게 중요한가?

(A) 서식지가 낮 시간 동안 극심한 기온 변동을 자주 겪는다.

(B) 주변의 기온에 대처하는 데 있어 적절한 생리학적 적응 방식이 부족하다.

(C) 유전적 이상으로 인해 극한의 주변 기온에 대한 내성이 억제된다.

(D) 하루 중 특정 시간대에 사냥하는 잠재 포식자들을 피할 수 있다.

해설 추론의 성격을 지니는 문항으로, 여섯 번째 문단의 첫 문장에서 '필수 범위 내에서 체온을 유지할 수 없을 때마다 회피 행동을 한다'는 점을 명시하고 있다. 그리고 그 조건에는 '생리학적 적응 방식과 형태학적 적응 방식을 통해'라고 언급했기 때문에 (B)가 정답이다.

어휘 fluctuation 변동, 오르내림 inhibit ~을 억제하다 genetic 유전의 abnormality 이상, 비정상

6. "안데스 두꺼비"는 다음 중 어느 행동 변경 능력을 지닌 양서류의 좋은 예시인가?

(A) 몸을 시원하게 유지하기 위해 지하로 굴을 파는 것

(B) 해마다 나타나는 회피 행동

(C) 태양의 복사열을 반사시키는 것

(D) 직사광선을 통해 열을 흡수하는 것

해설 안데스 두꺼비가 활용하는 '밀착 행동'과 관련하여, 해가 뜨자마자 가려지지 않은 촉촉한 땅바닥에 온 몸을 편 상태로 유지하며 주변의 공기가 데워져 해당 온도가 되기 훨씬 전에 목표 체온에 이를 수 있다는 점을 언급한 것으로 보아 직사광선을 통해

열을 흡수한다는 점을 확인할 수 있으므로 (D)가 정답이다.

7. 지문의 표현 "이러한 방식"이 가리키는 것은 무엇인가?

(A) 체온을 낮은 상태로 확실히 유지하는 것

(B) 체온의 증가를 가속화하는 것

(C) 체온을 섭씨 10도로 유지하는 것

(D) 체온이 주기적으로 변동되도록 하는 것

해설 해당 온도가 되기 훨씬 전에 목표 체온 온도에 이를 수 있다는 점을 토대로 (B)가 정답이다.

8. 다음 문장들 중 어느 것이 지문의 하이라이트 표기된 문장에 담긴 핵심 정보를 가장 잘 표현하는가? 오답 선택지는 중요한 방식으로 의미를 변경하거나 핵심 정보를 배제한다.

지금까지 설명한 방식에서 명확하게 알 수 있듯이, 양서류는 체온을 조절하는 여러 가지 방법이 있기 때문에 극한의 주위 온도에 대처하는 데 능숙하다.

(A) 따라서, 양서류가 앞서 설명한 다양한 방식을 갖고 있음에도 불구하고, 자신의 체온에 대해 오직 제한적인 통제력만 지니고 있다.

(B) 앞서 다룬 다양한 방법들은 양서류가 체온에 대한 통제력을 지닌 덕분에 어떻게 극한의 기후를 견딜 수 있는지에 대한 예시가 된다.

(C) 따라서, 앞서 설명한 방법들을 활용하지 않으면, 양서류는 주변 기온이 서로 다른 지역들 사이를 이동하는 데 있어 큰 어려움을 겪을 것이다.

(D) 앞서 언급한 방법들 외에도, 양서류는 극한의 기온을 겪는 서식지에서 생존하는 여러 다른 전략을 갖고 있다.

해설 '지금까지 설명한 방식', '체온을 조절하는 여러 가지 방법' 그리고 '대처에 능숙'의 키워드가 들어가는 지 확인하는 것이 중요하다. 그런 점에서 (B)는 '앞서 다룬 다양한 방법', '통제력을 지닌 덕분'이라는 내용을 모두 충족시키고 있기에 정답이다. (A)는 '불구하고', (C)는 '활용하지 않으면', 그리고 (D)는 '방법들 외에도 ~ 다른 전략'에서 소거가 가능하다.

어휘 exemplify ~의 예시가 되다 withstand ~을 견디다 by virtue of ~ 덕분에 aforementioned 앞서 언급한

9. 다음 문장이 지문에 추가될 수 있는 곳을 나타내는 네 개의 네모 표기 [■]를 찾아 보시오.

반면에, 아주 더운 지역에 서식하는 양서류는 특수 샘에서 점액을 분비함으로써 증발 냉각 작용을 통해 체온을 떨어뜨릴 수 있다.

위 문장은 어느 곳에 가장 적합하겠는가? 네모 표기[■]를 클릭해 지문에 이 문장을 추가하시오.

(A) 1번

(B) 2번

(C) 3번

(D) 4번

해설 문단의 흐름을 보면 '낮은 온도 – 더운 온도 – 추운 온도 – 낮은 온도'의 순서로 설명을 전개한다. 추운 온도에서 동결 방지 물질에 대한 언급을 했기 때문에 세 번째 네모에 문장을 삽입하여 '반면 더운 지역에 서식하는 양서류는 증발 냉각 작용을 활용한다'는 내용을 넣어 매끄럽게 흐름을 이어갈 수 있다. 또한 세 번째 네모에 문장을 넣어야 다음 문장에서 'Also'로 새로운 정보를 제공하는 것과 어울린다.

어휘 evaporative cooling 증발 냉각 작용 mucus 점액 gland 샘, 선(신체 내부에서 물질을 분비)

10. **설명:** 간략한 지문 요약에 필요한 도입 문장이 아래에 제공되어 있다. 지문에서 가장 중요한 개념들을 나타내는 세 가지 답안 선택지를 골라 요약 내용을 완성하시오. 일부 답안 선택지는 지문에 제시되지 않는 개념을 나타내거나 지문에서 중요하지 않은 개념들이므로 요약 내용에 속하지 않는다. **이 문제는 2점에 해당된다.**

양서류는 가혹한 기후에서 생존하기 위해 여러 가지 체온 조절 적응 방식과 행동을 이용한다.

(A) 일부 양서류 종은 태양 또는 지면으로부터 열을 흡수해 최적의 세온을 유지할 수 있는 여러 가지 방법을 이용한다.

(B) 밀착 접촉을 하는 양서류는 주변 공동체의 다른 구성원들과 체열을 공유할 수 있다.

(C) 일부 양서류는 피부 및 다른 신체 기관의 생리학적 적응 방식에 따른 결과로 극한의 기후에서도 정상적으로 활동할 수 있다.

(D) 하면 및 회피 행동은 양서류가 극도로 건조하고 더운 환경 조건을 피할 수 있게 해준다.

(E) 많은 양서류 종이 최적의 체온을 유지하기 위해 일몰 후에 돌아다니며 사냥하는 것을 택한다.

(F) 암석의 시원한 틈과 다른 그늘진 곳들이 양서류가 겨울철에 동면하기에 이상적인 장소의 역할을 할 수 있다.

해설 (A)는 다양한 양서류의 전략 중 밀착 행동이라는 핵심 키워드 내용을 포함하고 있으므로 정답이다. (C)는 네 번째 문단의 핵심 주제로, (D)는 회피 행동이라는 핵심 키워드 내용을 포함하고 있으므로 정답이다. (B)는 체열 공유라는 잘못된 정보를 담고 있고, (E)는 많은 양서류 종을 주어로 언급한 오답이다. (F)는 겨울철에 동면하기에 좋은 장소라는 잘못된 정보를 담고 있어 소거한다.

어휘 take advantage of ~을 이용하다 organ 신체 기관, 장기 optimal 최적의

Passage 3

Answers

1. C	2. B	3. C	4. A	5. D	6. B	7. A	8. D	9. D	10. BDF

유전자 이식 식물

현대적인 과학 발전 덕분에, 유전자 이식 식물을 만들어 내기 위해 이제는 사람이나 동물, 심지어 바이러스든 상관없이 거의 모든 공급원에서 얻은 유전자를 식물에 주입하는 것이 가능하다. 유전자 이식 농작물은 현재 전 세계에 걸쳐 약 1억 1천만 에이커 규모의 농지를 차지하고 있으며, 1(A)그 대부분이 북미 지역에서 재배되고 있다. 1(B)옥수수와 카놀라, 대두, 그리고 면화가 가장 널리 재배되고 있는 유전자 이식 농작물이며, 1(D)이 작물들은 일반적으로 Bt 독소라는 단백질을 만들어 내는 해충에 강한 유전자, 즉 글리포세이트라고 불리는 제초제에 대한 저항력을 2(B)제공해주는 유전자를 지니고 있다.

유전자 이식 농작물의 재배를 지지하는 사람들은 이 농작물이 다양한 환경적 이점을 제공해준다고 주장한다. 3(C)예를 들어, 이러한 농작물의 재배는 잠재적으로 해로운 화학 약품을 더 적게 필요로 하며, 사용되고 있는 것들조차 농작물 생산에 사용되는 일반 화학 약품보다 환경에 더 적은 위협을 가하고 있다. 실제로, 연구에 따르면 Bt 독소를 함유한 유전자 이식 면화의 재배는 전체적으로 20퍼센트나 더 적은 살충제를 필요로 하는 것으로 나타났다. 더욱이, 글리포세이트에 저항력이 있는 유전자 이식 농작물을 만들어 냄으로써, 더 유해한 제초제를 사용하는 대신, 글리포세이트가 잡초를 죽이는 데 적용될 수 있다.

반면, 전 세계의 농작물 생산업체들이 대규모로 유전자 이식 농작물 재배를 시작하기 전에 반드시 더욱 폭넓은 연구가 실행되어야 한다고 생각

하는 사람들이 점점 더 늘고 있다. 특히, 유전자 이식 식물을 먹고 사는 새들이나 곤충들 같은 비표적 생물들에게 Bt 식물이 미칠 수도 있는 영향과 관련한 우려가 계속 커지고 있다. 많은 주목을 받게 된 한 구체적인 사례가 바로 제왕나비 애벌레다. 이 종이 Bt 옥수수 밭에 나란히 심어진 박주가리 식물을 먹을 때, 바람에 날려 박주가리가 있는 쪽으로 떠내려온 옥수수 꽃가루를 무심코 먹게 된다. [4(A)]비록 현장 연구에서는 지금까지 Bt 꽃가루 섭취가 제왕나비 애벌레에 미치는 부정적인 영향을 아무것도 증명하지 못했지만, 실험실 연구 결과에 따르면 애벌레들을 잠재적으로 죽일 수도 있는 것으로 나타났다. 하지만, 비표적 종들이 Bt 식물이 일반 농작물로 대체되는 경우 사용될 살충제로 인한 심각한 위험에 처할 수도 있다는 점 또한 사실이다.

[6(B)]또 다른 삼재적 문제점은 잡초 개체군에 우연히 옮겨지는 제초제 저항 유전자이다. 농작물은 때때로 야생 잡초 유사종들과 아주 가까운 곳에서 재배될 수 있는데, 이 잡초 유사종들이 유전자 이식 농작물과 함께 번식하게 된다면, 제초제 저항 유전자가 그 자손에게 [5(D)]**전해질 것이다.** ■ 이러한 일이 발생할 경우, 제초제 저항 유전자가 잡초 개체군에 유입될 것이다. ■ 이것이 초래하는 주된 문제점은, 농부들이 글리포세이트와 같은 물질을 이용해 잡초 개체군을 박멸하려 할 때 더 이상 죽지 않게 된다는 점이다. ■ 이러한 상황은 유전자 이식 농작물과 가까운 구역에 야생 잡초 유사종들이 자라지 않는 경우에 나타날 가능성이 훨씬 더 적다. [9(D)]■ 하지만, 이는 특정한 경우에 있어 여전히 매우 심각한 문제를 일으킬 수 있다. [6(B)]예를 들어, 카놀라는 여러 종의 겨자 풀과 잡종 교배하는 것으로 알려져 있어 제초제 저항 유전자가 상당히 쉽게 유전자 이식 카놀라에서 잡초 개체군으로 이동할 수 있다.

유전자 이식 식물의 대규모 생산이 장기간에 걸쳐 진화에 영향을 미칠 것이라는 사실은 널리 알려져 있다. 가장 긴급한 우려 사항들 중 하나는 [7(B)]곤충들이 결국 Bt 독소에 대한 저항성을 발달시킬 것이라는 점이다. [7(C)]이 살충제가 수십 년 동안 농업 분야에서 활용되어 오기는 했지만, 곤충 개체군은 그에 대한 폭넓은 저항성을 획득하지는 못했다. 하지만, Bt 독소는 유전자 이식 Bt 식물들의 전체 성장 기간 중에 모든 조직 기관에서 발현된다. [7(D)]이는 해당 독소에 취약하게 만드는 유전자를 발현하는 곤충이면 필연적으로 죽게 되며, 확실한 유전적 저항성을 가진 곤충들만이 살아남는다는 것을 의미한다. 저항력이 있는 이 곤충들 사이에 일어나는 짝짓기는 마찬가지로 Bt 독소에 저항력이 있는 자손을 낳을 가능성이 높으며, 이는 결국 전체 개체군에 걸친 저항성으로 이어질 것이다. [7(A)]Bt 독소에 대한 곤충 저항성의 발전을 억제하기 위한 노력의 일환으로, 농작물 생산업자들은 취약한 곤충들이 먹을 수 있도록 유전자가 이식되지 않은 작물을 여러 줄 심고 있다. 이러한 조치는 곤충 개체군이 일정 수준의 Bt 취약성을 유지하는 결과를 낳을 수 있다.

[8(D)]현재의 유전자 이식 농작물 생산 방법들에 반대하는 가장 강력한 주장 중 하나는 농부들에게 오랜 시간에 걸쳐 천연 자원이 거듭 재생될 수 있게 해주는 지속 가능한 농업 접근법을 포기하도록 조장한다는 점이다. 적어도 피상적인 수준에서 볼 때, 유전자 이식은 농부들이 일반적으로 선택해야 할 몇몇 전형적인 사항들을 제거함으로써 농업을 훨씬 더 쉽게 만들어준다. 글리포세이트 저항성이 있는 농작물의 재배는 오직 그 제초제의 사용만을 필요로 하는 반면, 다른 제초제나 잡초 방제 관행들은 무시된다. 또한, Bt 농작물을 재배하는 농부들은 살충제 살포 또는 이로운 곤충을 활용하는 것에 초점을 맞추는 해충 관리 전략들을 포함할 가능성이 낮아진다. 유전자가 이식되지 않은 농작물을 재배하면서 재배 기간 중에 농작물을 면밀히 관찰한 다음, 해당 농작물의 상태를 바탕으로 살충제 살포와 관련된 결정을 내리는 것이 훨씬 더 지속 가능한 관행이 될 수 있을 것이다.

[어휘]

1. transgenic 유전자가 이식된 gene 유전자 take up ~을 차지하다 pest-resistant 해충에 저항력을 지닌 Bt toxin Bt 독소 confer ~을 주다, 수여하다 herbicide 제초제 glyphosate 글리포세이트(제초제의 하나)

2. pose (위협, 문제 등) ~을 가하다, 일으키다 insecticide 살충제(= pesticide)

3. carry out ~을 실행하다 on a large scale 대규모로 nontarget 대상이 아닌, 목표 (대상) 밖의 organism 생물체 feed on ~을 먹고 살다 come under the spotlight 많은 주목을 받게 되다, 집중 조명을 받게 되다 milkweed 박주가리(여러해살이 덩굴풀로서, 줄기나 잎을 꺾으면 흰 즙이 나옴) inadvertently 무심코, 우연히 pollen 꽃가루, 화분 thus far 지금까지 adverse 부정적인, 불리한 species (동식물의) 종

4. population 개체군, 개체 수 in close proximity to ~와 아주 가까운 곳에 relative 유사 종 reproduce 번식하다 pass A on to B A를 B에게 전하다 eradicate ~을 박멸하다 substance 물질 hybridize 잡종 교배하다

5. evolution 진화, 발전 pressing 긴급한 express (형질 등)을 발현하다 vulnerable to ~에 취약한 inevitably 필연적으로, 불가피하게 perish 죽다 offspring 자손 inhibit ~을 억제하다 retain ~을 유지하다

6. incentivize ~을 조장하다, ~에게 장려하다 abandon ~을 포기하다 sustainable 지속 가능한 continual 거듭되는, 지속되는 superficial 피상적인 necessitate ~을 필요하게 만들다 practice 관행, 관례 incorporate ~을 포함하다, 통합하다

1. 첫 번째 문단에서, 다음 중 글쓴이가 유전자 이식 농작물과 관련해 제공하는 정보가 아닌 것은 무엇인가?

(A) 가장 밀도 높게 유전자 이식 식물이 재배되는 지역

(B) 전 세계에 걸쳐 가장 풍부하게 재배되는 유선자 이식 농작물 종류

(C) 해충 및 제초제에 저항력이 있는 유전자 이식 농작물의 비율

(D) 유전자 이식 농작물을 만드는 데 사용되는 일반적인 유전자 공급원

해설 대부분이 북미 지역에서 재배되고 있다는 정보가 등장하고, 가장 널리 재배되는 유전자 이식 농작물은 옥수수, 카놀라, 대두, 그리고 면화라는 점이 언급되었다. 글리포세이트라고 불리는 저항력을 제공하는 유전자를 지닌다는 점 역시 등장한다. 그러나 비율에 대한 언급은 없으므로 (C)가 정답이다.

어휘 concentration 밀도, 농도　abundant 풍부한

2. 지문의 단어 "confers"와 의미가 가장 가까운 것은 무엇인가?

(A) ~와 상의하다, ~을 참고하다

(B) ~을 주다, 수여하다

(C) ~을 숙고하다

(D) ~을 거래하다

어휘 confer(~을 주다, 수여하다)와 grant(~을 주다, 수여하다)는 동의어로 정답은 (B)이다.

3. 두 번째 문단에서 글쓴이는 유전자 이식 농작물과 관련해 알려진 어떤 이점을 설명하는가?

(A) 농업용 부지가 더 적게 필요할 것이다.

(B) 더 다양한 농작물이 이용 가능하게 될 것이다.

(C) 농작물에 쓰이는 유해 물질이 더 적어질 것이다.

(D) 농작물이 더 이상 잡초와 공간 경쟁을 하지 않을 것이다.

해설 글쓴이는 예시를 들어주며, 이러한 농작물의 재배는 잠재적으로 해로운 화학 약품을 더 적게 필요로 한다는 점을 명시해주고 있으므로 (C)가 정답이다.

어휘 purported ~라고 알려진

4. 세 번째 문단에서 제왕나비 애벌레와 관련해 유추할 수 있는 것은 무엇인가?

(A) Bt 꽃가루에 대한 반응과 관련해 과학적인 의견 일치가 없다.

(B) 유전자 이식 옥수수 작물에 대한 피해의 주요 원인이다.

(C) Bt 독소에 대한 자연적 저항성을 지닌 유일한 종이다.

(D) Bt 독소에 의해 피해를 입는다는 현장 실험의 증거가 있다.

해설 '비록 현장 연구에서는 지금까지 Bt 꽃가루 섭취가 제왕나비 애벌레에 미치는 부정적인 영향을 아무것도 증명하지 못했지만'이라는 부분을 통해 (A)가 정답임을 알 수 있다. (B)의 '주요 원

인', (C)의 '유일한', (D)의 '현장 실험의 증거가 있다'는 부분을 통해 오답을 소거할 수 있다.

어휘 consensus 의견 일치, 합의

5. 지문의 표현 "passed on"과 의미가 가장 가까운 것은 무엇인가?

(A) 건너뛴

(B) 추월된

(C) 달성된

(D) 옮겨진

어휘 passed on(전해진, 옮겨진)과 transferred(전해진, 옮겨진)는 동의어로 정답은 (D)이다.

6. 글쓴이는 왜 네 번째 문단에서 "겨자 풀"을 언급하는가?

(A) 유전자 이식 농작물이 특정 잡초 종과 가까운 곳에 심어질 때 잘 자랄 가능성이 더 크다는 이론을 뒷받침하기 위해

(B) 잠재적으로 유전자 이식 식물과 번식할 가능성이 있으면서 글리포세이트 같은 물질에 대한 저항성을 얻을 수 있는 잡초의 예시를 제공하기 위해

(C) 유전자 이식 농작물이 농업 지역 내에서 성공적으로 유사 잡초 개체군을 줄여주었다는 증거를 제공하기 위해

(D) 잡초 유사종과의 잡종 교배를 통해 유전자 이식 식물을 만드는 것이 실험실에서 만드는 것보다 덜 어렵다는 점을 주장하기 위해

해설 네 번째 문단의 시작에서 또 다른 잠재적 문제점인 제초제 저항 유전자가 우연히 잡초 개체군에 우연히 옮겨질 수 있음을 언급한다. 그리고 구체적인 예시인 카놀라가 여러 종의 겨자 풀과 잡종 교배를 하고, 제초제 저항 유전자가 쉽게 이동할 수 있다는 점을 언급하고 있으므로 (B)가 정답이다.

어휘 hybridization 잡종 교배

7. 다섯 번째 문단에서, 다음 중 곤충 개체군 내의 Bt 저항성과 관련해 글쓴이가 주장하지 않는 것은 무엇인가?

(A) Bt 유전자 이식 농작물과 인접한 지역에 유전자를 이식하지 않은 식물을 심는 것은 곤충 개체군 내에서의 Bt 저항성의 발달을 가속화할 것이다.

(B) 유전자 이식 식물의 활용이 광범위해질 경우 곤충 개체군들 사이에서 결과적으로 균일한 Bt 저항성이 불가피하다.

(C) Bt 살충제의 사용이 곤충 개체군 내의 Bt 저항성으로 이어져 오지 않았던 반면, Bt 농작물을 심는 과정을 통해 이러한 일이 발생할 확률은 더 높다.

(D) Bt 식물들은 언제나 모든 조직 기관에서 해당 독소를 발현하기 때문에, 곤충 개체군 내에 Bt에 취약한 모든 구성원들을 몰살시킬 가능성이 크다.

해설 식물을 심는 것은 Bt 저항성의 발달을 억제하고 일정 수준의 취약성을 유지하게 하는 결과를 만들고자 한 것이기 때문에 (A)

의 경우 글쓴이의 주장과 다르다. (B)는 곤충들이 결국 Bt 독소에 대한 저항성을 발달시킬 것이라는 점이 언급된 부분을 보아 글쓴이의 주장이라 할 수 있다. (C)는 살충제가 수 십년 동안 농업 분야에서 사용되었으나 폭넓은 저항성을 획득하지 못한 반면, 유전자 이식 Bt 식물들의 성장 기간 중에 모든 조직 기관에 발현되었다는 정보를 보아 역시 글쓴이의 주장으로 볼 수 있다. 그리고 확실한 유전적 저항성을 가진 곤충들만이 살아남는다는 본문 내용을 통해 (D) 역시 글쓴이의 주장임을 알 수 있다.

어휘 adjacent to ~와 인접한 accelerate ~을 가속화하다 eventual 결과적으로 나타나는 inevitable 불가피한

8. 다음 문장들 중 어느 것이 지문의 하이라이트 표기된 문장에 담긴 핵심 정보를 가장 잘 표현하는가? 오답 선택지는 중요한 방식으로 의미를 변경하거나 핵심 정보를 배제한다.

현재의 유전자 이식 농작물 생산 방법들에 반대하는 가장 강력한 주장 중 하나는 농부들에게 오랜 시간에 걸쳐 천연 자원이 거듭 재생될 수 있게 해주는 지속 가능한 농업 접근법을 포기하도록 조장한다는 점이다.

(A) 많은 사람들은 미래의 유전자 이식 농작물이 오늘날의 농업 접근법을 활용해 생산되는 것들보다 훨씬 더 지속 가능할 것이라고 주장하고 있다.

(B) 유전자 이식 농작물을 재배하는 농부들은 환경이 자연의 힘으로 스스로 되살아날 수 있도록 하는 지속 가능한 농업 관행을 빠르게 받아들이고 있다.

(C) 유전자 이식 농작물의 가장 큰 단점들 중의 하나는 지속 가능한 농업 전략을 활용해 재배되는 농작물보다 더 많은 자원을 필요로 한다는 점이다.

(D) 농부들이 지속 가능한 농법을 통해 천연 자원을 회복시키는 데 도움을 주는 대신 유전자 이식 농작물을 재배하도록 장려되고 있어 심각한 우려를 낳고 있다.

해설 제시된 문장의 키워드인 '유전자 이식 농작물', '포기', 그리고 '천연 자원이 재생될 수 있도록 하는 지속 가능한 농업 접근법' 있는지 확인한다. (A)의 경우, 지속 가능성 자체의 비교만 언급할 뿐 천원 자원에 대한 언급이 없다. (B)의 경우, 관행을 빠르게 받아들이고 있다는 점에서 정반대의 입장을 취하는 오답이다. (C)는 '더 많은 자원을 필요로 한다'는 점이 오답의 근거가 된다. (D)의 경우, '지속 가능한 농업을 통해 천연 자원을 회복시키는 방식 대신 유전자 이식 농작물 재배'에 관한 키워드를 모두 담고 있기에 정답이다.

어휘 embrace ~을 받아들이다, 포용하다 rejuvenate ~을 되살리다, 회복시키다(= renew)

9. 다음 문장이 지문에 추가될 수 있는 곳을 나타내는 네 개의 네모 표기 [▪]를 찾아 보시오.

미국에서 재배되는 대부분의 농작물이 다른 곳에서 비롯되었

다는 점을 감안하면, 그것이 그곳에서 발생되는 일은 특히 드물다.

위 문장은 어느 곳에 가장 적합하겠는가? 네모 표기[▪]를 클릭해 지문에 이 문장을 추가하시오.

(A) 1번
(B) 2번
(C) 3번
(D) 4번

해설 주어진 문장에서 농작물이 비롯된 장소를 언급하기 때문에 앞의 문장에서 '유전자 이식 농작물과 가까운 구역'이라는 부분을 통해 답의 근거를 찾을 수 있다. 주어진 문장에서 드물다는 점을 언급했을 때, 뒤에 문장에서 '특정한 경우에서 여전히 심각한 문제를 일으킬 수 있다'는 점을 강조해줄 수 있기 때문에 (D)가 정답이다.

10. **설명:** 간략한 지문 요약에 필요한 도입 문장이 아래에 제공되어 있다. 지문에서 가장 중요한 개념들을 나타내는 세 가지 답안 선택지를 골라 요약 내용을 완성하시오. 일부 답안 선택지는 지문에 제시되지 않는 개념을 나타내거나 지문에서 중요하지 않은 개념들이므로 요약 내용에 속하지 않는다. **이 문제는 2점에 해당된다.**

유전자 이식 식물의 개발은 특히 그 실행의 안전성 및 환경에 미치는 영향과 관련하여 반대하는 견해를 많이 낳는 주제이다.

(A) 유전자 이식 식물과 연관된 현재의 문제들 중 많은 것들이 미래에는 더욱 환경 친화적인 방법들이 통합됨에 따라 사라질 가능성이 있을 것이다.

(B) 유전자 이식 식물을 지지하는 사람들은 그 방법이 더 환경 친화적인 제초제의 사용을 촉진하고 유해 화학 약품의 사용을 줄여준다고 주장한다.

(C) 장기간에 걸쳐, 유전자 이식 식물 내의 글리포세이트 저항성은 진화 과정 및 유사 식물 종과의 잡종 교배를 통해 약화될 가능성이 있다.

(D) 유전자 이식 농작물이 지닌 한 가지 잠재적으로 부정적인 부작용 한 가지는 농부들이 지속 가능한 방법을 이용해 재배할 수 있는 전통적인 농작물보다 유전자 이식 농작물을 선호하게 될 것이라는 점이다.

(E) 유전자 이식 식물은 북미 지역 전체에 걸쳐 제왕나비 애벌레 개체수의 감소 원인이었을 수도 있다.

(F) Bt 독소를 만들어 내는 대규모 농작물 생산이 결국 곤충 개체군 내에 널리 퍼지는 Bt 저항성을 초래할 것이라는 심각한 우려가 있다.

해설 (B)는 다양한 환경적 이점을 제시하는 두 번째 문단에서 확인할 수 있다. (F)는 다섯 번째 문단에서 대규모 농작물 생산이 진화에 영향을 미칠 것이며, 그 중에서도 곤충이 가지는 저항성에 대한 내용을 다루기 때문에 정답이다. (D)는 마지막 문단의 첫

문장에서 언급하고 있는 내용이다. (E)는 지나치게 세부적인 예시를 언급하고 있고, (C)는 저항성이 약화될 가능성이 있다는 점을 보아 오답임을 알 수 있다. (A)는 문제들이 사라질 가능성이 있다는 점이 글이 방향성과 맞지 않기에 오답이나.

어휘 opposing 반대하는 associate with ~와 연관된

integrate ~을 통합하다 facilitate ~을 촉진하다 cut down on ~를 줄이다, 감소시키다 diminish 약화되다, 줄어들다 side effect 부작용 favor A over B B보다 A를 선호하다 decline in ~의 감소 grave concern 심각한 우려

Chapter 2 Ecology

Passage 1

Answers

1. B	2. D	3. C	4. C	5. B	6. D	7. D	8. B	9. C	10. ACE

종의 강제 이주

종의 강제 이주는 여러 야생 동물들, 또는 심지어 하나의 종 전체를 한 곳에서 다른 곳으로 이동하는 것을 가리킨다. 환경 보호 운동가들이 특정 동물 종 또는 식물 종 개체군이 멸종된 지역에 새로운 개체군을 확립하기 위해 이렇게 하는 경우에, 이것을 '재도입'이라고 일컫는다. 반면에, '강화'는 기존의 개체군에 개별 구성원들을 추가하기 위해 동물들이 이주되는 경우를 일컫는다.

[1(C)]보존이 긴급한 사안이 되기 오래 전부터, 강제 이주는 개체수를 유지하기 위해 아주 다양한, 일반적으로 식품 공급원으로 쓰이는, 식물과 동물을 옮기는 데 이미 활용되고 있었다. [1(A)]보존이라는 개념이 인기를 얻게 되면서, 이주가 실시되는 횟수도 늘어나게 되었는데, 그 효과성과 관련된 증거 부족으로 인해, 그리고 잠재적인 불이익 때문에 그 방법이 점점 더 많은 정밀 조사를 받게 되었다. [1(D)]이주는 아주 체계적이고 재정 지원이 잘 되는 국가적인 또는 국제적인 프로그램에서부터, 선의를 가진 동물 애호가들에 의해 구조된 동물들의 소규모 방생에 이르기까지 다양한 유형으로 나타날 수 있다. 오늘날과 같이 분열된 세계에서는 많은 개체군과 서식지들이 서로 떨어져 있기 때문에, 이주는 이론적으로 대단히 효과적인 보존 방식으로 기능할 수 있다. 이는 환경 보호 운동가들이 기존 개체군의 수나 규모를 늘리거나, 작은 개체군 내의 인구(개체수) 통계학적 균형과 유전적 다양성을 개선할 수 있게 함으로써, 개체군의 생존 가능성을 높여준다.

이주는 [2(D)]상당히 감소된 종의 회복에 있어 중요한 역할을 하며, 그러한 종을 과거의 개체 수 범위로 다시 되돌릴 수 있는 가장 효과적인 방법들 중 하나이다. [3(B)]하지만, 강화 이주가 지닌 잠재적으로 심각한 단점은 기존의 개체군에 유해한 유전자의 유입 및 한 개체군에서 다른 개체군으로의 질병 전염이다. 게다가, 포식자 또는 경쟁 종이 이주되는 경우, [3(A)]다른 종에 부정적인 영향을 미치게 되어 해당 지역 내의 생물 다양성 상실이라는 결과로 이어질 수 있다. 또 다른 결점은, [3(D)]이 전략이 아주 많은 노력과 자원을 필요로 하기 때문에, 그 비용을 정당화하기 위해 실체적인 이득의 증거가 반드시 나타나야 한다는 점이다.

[5(B)]전 세계 각지에서 수많은 이주가 실시되어 왔지만, 실제적인 이득을 가져왔다는 뚜렷한 증거는 거의 존재하지 않는다. 물론, 이는 대부분의 이주가 공식 과학 기관에 의해 감독되지 않았고, 많은 경우에 있어, 합법적이지 않았거나 보존을 목적으로 하지 않았기 때문이다. 비록 소수의 성공적인 이주가 기록되어 있기는 하지만, 다수의 실패 사례 대부분이 기록되거나 보고되었을 가능성이 낮다. 이로 인해 이 전략을 제대로 [4(C)]평가하는 것이 극도로 어려워진다. 더욱이, 성공적인 이주가 수반하는 것이 무엇인지 정의하기 어렵다. 옮겨진 생물체들이 고작 한달, 또는 일년 밖에 생존하지 못하는 경우에 이주가 성공한 것으로 여겨져야 하는가? 또는 그 방법이 성공적이라고 여겨질 수 있도록 생물체들이 반드시 수년 동안에 걸쳐 번식해야 하는가? 그 정의와 상관없이, 분명한 것은 이주 활동이 보장되고, 엄중한 관찰 및 평가 대상이 되고, 성공할 가능성을 높이기 위해 적절한 가이드라인이 확립되어야 한다는 점이다.

종의 강제 이주가 진정한 성공작으로 보여지는 한 가지 사례가 바로 멸종 위기에 처한 세이셸 울새에 대한 것이다. 한때 세이셸 군도의 일부인 커즌 섬에서만 발견되었던, 이 종은 오직 26마리의 개체수로 줄어들었다. 이 숫자는 신중한 서식지 관리에 따른 결과로 300마리 넘게 증가되었지만, [6(D)]그 개체군은 여전히 자연 재해로 인해 멸종 위기에 처해 있었다. ■ 그 울새들을 근처의 섬 두 곳으로 이주함으로써 이러한 위험을 완화시키려는 결정이 내려졌다. ■ 첫 번째 섬으로의 이주가 1988년에, 두 번째 섬으로의 이주가 1990년에 실시되었으며, 두 곳 모두에서 건강한 번식 개체군이 확립되었다. [9(C)]■ 프랑스령 가이아나의 붉은 고함 원숭이도 성공적인 이주 프로젝트의 또 다른 예시에 해당된다. ■ [7(D)]수력 발전을 위해 한 장소가 침수될 예정이었을 때, 현지의 한 고함 원숭이 개체군이 지나친 사냥으로 인해 고함 원숭이 개체군이 줄어버린 지역으로 이주되었다. 해당 지역에 방생된 약 15마리의 암컷 원숭이들은 전파 추적 방식으로 관찰되었다. 초기의 몇몇 적응 문제로 인해 추적되던 암컷들이 처음에는 뿔뿔이 흩어지는 일이 초래되었지만, 그들의 행동 패턴은 상당히 빨리 정상으로 돌아왔다.

[8(B)]안타깝게도, 실패 이야기가 성공의 증거보다 더 많다. 연구가 리차드 A. 시겔과 C 케네스 도드는 파충류 및 양서류 이주에 내한 수많은 사례를 평가해 보존이라는 측면에 있어 극소수만이 성공작으로 여겨질 수 있다는 사실을 밝혀냈다. [8(B)]이에 따라, 이들은 그러한 방법이 실행 가능한 종 관리 관행으로 여겨지지 말아야 한다고 권고했디.

[어휘]

1. translocation 이주(위치를 옮기는 일) population 개체군, 개체수 go extinct 멸종되다 be referred to as ~라고 일컬어지다 reintroduction 재도입 reinforcement 강화

2. pressing 긴급한 grow in popularity 인기를 얻다 carry out ~을 실시하다 come under scrutiny 정밀 조사를 받다 isolate ~을 구분하다, 고립시키다 splintered 분열된 theoretically 이론적으로 function as ~로서 기능하다 demographic 인구(개체수) 통계학적인 genetic 유전의

3. play an important role in ~에 있어 중요한 역할을 하다 rejuvenation 회복, 활기를 되찾음 substantially 상당히 diminish 줄어들다, 약해지다 restore ~을 회복시키다 downside 단점, 문제점 gene 유전자 transmission 전염, 전파 disease 질병 adverse 부정적인 biodiversity 생물 다양성 drawback 결점 tangible 실체적인, 실재하는 justify ~을 정당화하다

4. yield (결과, 산물 등) ~을 내다, 가져오다 oversee ~을 감독하다 a handful of 소수의 properly 제대로, 적절히 appraise ~을 평가하다 entail ~을 수반하다 warrant ~을 보장하다, 정당화하다(= justify) be subject to ~의 대상이 되다 stringent 엄중한

5. genuine 진정한, 진짜의 extinction 멸종 catastrophe 재해 mitigate ~을 완화하다 breeding 번식 hydroelectric power generation 수력 발전 adjustment 적응 scatter 흩어지다

6. outweigh ~보다 더 많다, 더 중요하다 assess ~을 평가하다 in terms of ~의 측면에서, ~와 관련해서 be deemed as ~로 여겨지다 viable 실행 가능한 practice 관행, 관례

1. 두 번째 문단에서, 다음 중 종의 이주와 관련해 언급되지 않은 것은 무엇인가?

(A) 보존에 대한 관심의 증가가 이주 빈도의 증가로 이어졌다.

(B) 그것의 잠재적 불이익이 여러 국제적인 연구 조사에 의해 틀렸음이 입증되었다.

(C) 보존을 위해 이용되기 전에 식품 공급원을 유지하는 데 주로 활용되었다.

(D) 여러 가지 범위의 프로젝트를 수행하는 아주 다양한 그룹에 의해 실시된다.

해설 (A)는 문단의 두 번째 문장에서 인기와 실시 횟수를 통해 확인할 수 있고, (C)는 문단의 첫 문장에서 등장한다. (D)의 경우, 국제적인 프로그램부터 동물 애호가 등 다양한 프로젝트로 실시되었다는 점이 명시되어 있으므로 정답은 (B)이다. (B)의 경우 효과성과 관련된 증거 부족으로 인해 정밀 조사가 진행되었다는 점으로만 정보가 제공되었다.

어휘 disprove ~가 틀렸음을 입증하다 utilize ~을 활용하다 of varying scopes 여러 가지 범위의

2. 지문의 단어 "substantially"와 의미가 가장 가까운 것은 무엇인가?

(A) 잠정적으로

(B) 몰래, 은밀하게

(C) 즉각적으로

(D) 상당히

해설 substantially(상당히)와 considerably(상당히)는 동의어로 정답은 (D)이다.

3. 세 번째 문단에서, 다음 중 종의 이주가 지니는 잠재적 결점으로 언급되지 않은 것은 무엇인가?

(A) 생물 다양성 상실

(B) 질병 확산

(C) 먹이 경쟁 증가

(D) 상당한 비용 수반

해설 (A)의 경우 포식자나 경쟁 종이 이주되는 경우 부정적인 영향을 미치게 되며 생물 다양성 상실이라는 결과로 이어진다는 점을 언급하고 있다. (B)의 경우 질병 전염이 잠재적으로 심각한 단점임을 언급하고 있다. (D)의 경우 많은 노력과 자원을 필요로 한다고 문단의 마지막 문장에서 언급하고 있다. (C)의 먹이 경쟁 증가는 언급되지 않은 정보이다.

4. 지문의 단어 "appraise"와 의미가 가장 가까운 것은 무엇인가?

(A) ~을 칭찬하다, 추천하다

(B) ~을 향상시키다

(C) ~을 평가하다

(D) ~을 적용하다, 신청하다

해설 appraise(평가하다)와 evaluate(평가하다)는 동의어로 정답은 (C)이다.

5. 다음 중 어느 것이 네 번째 문단에서 이주 활동과 관련해 유추할 수 있는 것인가?

(A) 이주 활동을 추진하는 데 이용되는 방법이 빠르게 발전해

왔다.

(B) 이주 활동의 효과성을 보여주는 데 이용 가능한 기록이 신뢰할 만하지 못하다.

(C) 불법적인 이주 활동이 대부분의 공식적인 이주 활동보다 더 성공적이었던 것으로 보인다.

(D) 전 세계의 연구가들이 성공적인 이주의 정의에 대해 의견 일치에 이르렀다.

해설 네 번째 문단 전체가 이주의 이득을 뒷받침하는 증거가 없다는 점을 명확하게 설명하고 있다. 그리고 그 이유로 공식적 기관의 감독 부재, 합법적이지 않았거나 보존 목적이 아니었던 점, 다수의 실패 사례가 보고되지 않는 점, 정의를 내리기 어려운 점 등을 제시하고 있다. 그러므로 (B)가 정답이다.

어휘 evolve 발전하다, 진화하다 reliable 신뢰할 만한
consensus 의견 일치

6. 다섯 번째 문단에 따르면, 환경 보호 운동가들이 왜 세이셸 울새를 커즌 섬에서 다른 두 곳의 섬으로 이주시켰는가?

(A) 커즌 섬의 울새 개체군을 늘리려 했던 이전의 활동이 성공적이지 못했다.

(B) 울새의 이주가 세 곳의 섬에서 모두 생물 다양성을 늘려줄 것이라고 생각했다.

(C) 질병으로 인해 커즌 섬 울새 개체군의 감소를 예상했다.

(D) 울새 개체군이 커즌 섬의 재해 속에 사라질까 우려했다.

해설 자연 재해로 인해 멸종 위기에 처해 있었고, 이주를 통해 위험을 완화시키려는 결정이 내려졌다는 부분으로 보아 정답을 (D)로 유추할 수 있다.

어휘 perish 사라지다, 죽다 disaster 재해, 재난

7. 다섯 번째 문단에 따르면, 프랑스령 가이아나의 고함 원숭이들은 왜 이주되었는가?

(A) 여러 잠재 포식자들이 그들의 기존 서식지에 유입되었다.

(B) 기후 조건이 그들의 개체군 밀도에 부정적인 영향을 미치고 있었다.

(C) 성비 불균형은 암컷들이 짝을 찾는 데 힘겨워 했음을 의미했다.

(D) 그들의 기존 서식지가 인간 활동에 의해 바뀔 예정이었다.

해설 수력 발전을 위해 인해 한 장소가 침수될 예정이라는 점이 언급되어 있어 인간 활동(human activity)에 의한 변화로 판단하고 (D)를 답으로 선택해야 한다.

어휘 density 밀도 alter ~을 변경하다, 바꾸다

8. 여섯 번째 문단에서, 글쓴이는 무엇을 하기 위해 리차드 A. 시겔과 C. 케네스 도드를 언급하는가?

(A) 이주의 잠재적 효과성을 결정하는 데 이용되는 기준의 상

세 정보를 제공하기 위해

(B) 반복된 실패는 종의 이주 활동을 정당화하기 어렵게 만든다는 주장을 뒷받침하기 위해

(C) 파충류 및 양서류 이주가 다른 동물들의 이주보다 얼마나 더 어려운지 보여주기 위해

(D) 연구가들이 더 많은 지식을 얻게 됨에 따라 이주 방법이 개선되고 있음을 강조하기 위해

해설 글쓴이의 의도를 묻는 문제는 첫번째 문장에서 먼저 방향성을 잡아야 하나. 실패 이야기기 더욱 많은 전을 언급하면서, 마지막 문장에서 종의 이주 활동을 관리 관행으로 여기지 말아야 한다는 점을 제시하는 것을 토대로 (B)가 정답임을 알 수 있다.

어휘 criteria 기준

9. 다음 문장이 지문에 추가될 수 있는 곳을 나타내는 네 개의 [■]를 찾아 보시오.

이는 분명 대규모 이주에서 생겨난 긍정적인 결과들의 유일한 사례가 아니다.

위 문장은 어느 곳에 가장 적합하겠는가? 네모 표기[■]를 클릭해 지문에 이 문장을 추가하시오.

(A) 1번
(B) 2번
(C) 3번
(D) 4번

해설 '이것은 긍정적인 결과들의 유일한 사례가 아니다'라는 점을 언급하는 것으로 보아 이 문장 앞에 긍정적인 사례 한 개가 등장하고, 이후 문장에서 새로운 예시가 등장해야한다는 점을 고려해 볼 때 (C)가 정답이다.

어휘 large-scale 대규모의

10. **설명:** 간략한 지문 요약에 필요한 도입 문장이 아래에 제공되어 있다. 지문에서 가장 중요한 개념들을 나타내는 세 가지 답안 선택지를 골라 요약 내용을 완성하시오. 일부 답안 선택지는 지문에 제시되지 않는 개념을 나타내거나 지문에서 중요하지 않은 개념들이므로 요약 내용에 속하지 않는다. **이 문제는 2점에 해당된다.**

이주는 종의 재도입 또는 강화 과정에서 활용되는 방법이다.

(A) 이주가 보존 수단으로서 대단히 유용할 수는 있지만, 종과 서식지에 여러 부정적인 영향을 미칠 수도 있다.

(B) 데이터에 따르면 대부분의 성공적인 이주 활동은 야생 동물 애호가들에 의해 소규모로 실시되어 왔다.

(C) 성공 가능성이 비용을 정당화할 만큼 충분히 높다는 것을 보증하기 위해 이주 프로젝트들이 제대로 평가되는 것이 대단히 중요하다.

(D) 붉은 고함 원숭이의 이주는 암컷들의 행동 패턴에 대한 초

기의 우려에도 불구하고 성공작으로 여겨졌다.

(E) 종의 이주는 특정 종의 줄어드는 개체군을 늘리거나 한 가
지 종이 더 이상 존재하지 않는 지역에 다시 서식하게 만
드는 데 이용될 수 있다.

(F) 불법적인 이주는 종의 강제 이주에 대한 부정적인 묘사로
인해 전 세계의 언론으로부터 비난받아왔다.

해설 (A)는 세 번째 문단에서 다루고 있는 내용을 요약하고 있는 문
장이라는 점을 알 수 있다. (C)는 네 번째 문단의 핵심 키워드를

담고 있는 보기로 정답임을 알 수 있다. (E)의 경우, 다섯 번째
문단의 사례들을 통해 정답임을 추론할 수 있다.

어휘 employ ~을 활용하다 the vast majority of 대부분의, 대
다수의 dwindling 줄어드는 repopulate ~에 다시 살게 하
다 be blamed for ~로 비난 받다

Passage 2

1. C	2. A	3. D	4. B	5. C	6. D	7. B	8. C	9. B	10. BDF

꽃식물의 진화

꽃식물, 즉 속씨식물의 진화 경로를 고려할 때, 여러 가지 의문점이 대체로 풀리지 않은 채로 남아 있다. 2(D)과학자들은 화석화된 줄기와 잎, 꽃
가루, 열매, 그리고 덜 흔하긴 하지만, 꽃도 발견했으며, 이것들은 가장 오래된 속씨식물에 대한 유용한 증거를 제공해 준다. ■ 또한, 현대의 종들
중 어느 것이 속씨식물의 고대 조상들과 밀접하게 관련되어 있는지를 확인하기 위해 2(B,C)현대 식물의 형태학(구조)과 유전학에 대한 광범위한
과학적 연구도 실시되어 왔다. 9(B)■ 두 세기가 넘는 1(C)집중적인 연구에도 불구하고, 과학자들은 어느 특정 식물 유형이 속씨식물의 조상이었는
지에 대한 의견 일치에 여전히 도달하지 못했을 뿐만 아니라, 언제 그리고 어디에서 속씨식물이 진화하기 시작했는지도 밝혀 내지 못했다. ■ 실
제로, 그 유명한 찰스 다윈조차 속씨식물의 기원을 가리켜 "지독한 미스터리"라는 말을 사용했다. ■

어떤 종류의 식물이 속씨식물의 조상이었는지를 파악하기 위해 시도하는 과정에서, 현재 대부분의 식물학자들은 속씨식물이 그 기원에 있어 단
일 계통에 해당된다는 점에 동의하고 있으며, 이는 공통 조상으로부터 진화했음을 의미한다. 일부 고생물학자들에 따르면, 이 공통 조상은 다양
한 소철, 즉 열대 지방에서 발견되는 일종의 종자 식물이었을 가능성이 있다. 하지만, 다른 이들은 꽃식물이 씨앗을 품는 양치식물로부터 진화했
을 것이라고 생각하고 있다. 살아 있는 일부 원시 식물의 형태적 특징에 대한 연구를 기반으로 하는 또 다른 가설은 그 조상이 현대 소나무의 동
족이었을 수도 있다는 것이다. 간단히 말해서, 꽃식물의 진정한 조상은 여전히 미해결 상태로 남아 있는 3(D)문제이다.

수십 년 동안, 속씨식물이 처음 나타난 대략적인 시기와 장소를 파악하는 데 크게 초점이 맞춰져 있었다. 화석 증거를 바탕으로, 초기 속씨식물
중 현대의 목련과 유사하게 보이는 일부가 1억년도 더 이전인 초기 백악기 지질 시대에 존재했다. 4(B)이 시대에, 속씨식물이 점점 더 그 숫자를
늘려가며 자라기 시작했고, 모든 식물의 약 1퍼센트를 차지했다. 약 1억년 전에서 6,500만년 전까지 지속되었던 후기 백악기에는, 속씨식물이
풍부하게 자라면서 전체 식물의 50퍼센트 넘게 구성했다. 현대의 식물 집단들 중 많은 것들이 나타나기 시작한 때가 바로 이 시기였다. 그 뒤를
잇는 지질 시대인 제삼기 초기에는, 속씨식물이 지속적으로 번성하고 확산되어, 마침내 지구의 전체 식물 중 최소 90퍼센트를 차지하기에 이르
렀다. 하지만 정확히 어디에서 이 성공적인 식물이 비롯된 것일까?

생물 지리학자들은 백악기에 나온 가장 오래된 꽃식물의 지리적 분포와 화석 잎 구조를 분석해, 5(C)그 식물이 열대 지방에서 진화한 뒤에 지구의
극지방으로 이동했을 가능성이 있다는 결론을 내렸다. 꽃식물이 고위도 지방에서 널리 퍼지게 된 것은 후기 백악기나 되어서였다. 남미 동부 지
역과 아프리카 서부 지역에서는, 고생물학자들이 초기 백악기까지 시대가 거슬러 올라가는 퇴적물에서 화석화된 꽃식물의 일부를 복구해냈다.
당시에는 두 개의 초대륙이 존재했으며, 아프리카와 남미 지역이 곤드와나 대륙이라고 알려진 초대륙의 일부를 구성하고 있었다. 5(C)이 초기의
속씨식물 화석들은 초기 백악기 중에 적도와 가까웠을 법한 지역에서 발굴되었으며, 이는 열대 지방에서 극지방으로 향하는 이동 이론을 뒷받침
해준다.

8(C)일부 식물학자들은 가장 오래된 꽃식물 유형이 호주와 피지, 뉴기니 같은 남태평양 국가에, 그리고 말레이 제도 전역에 여전히 존재하고 있다
는 사실을 강조하면서, 꽃식물의 진화 및 확산에 대한 아프리카-남미 기원설에 동의하지 않고 있다. 식물 유전학에 대한 최근 연구에 따르면 모

든 속씨식물의 고대 조상과 가장 밀접하게 닮은 모습을 지닌 살아 있는 식물이 암보렐라인 것으로 나타났다. 비교적 흔치 않은 이 열대 관목은, 붉은색 과일과 작은 백황색 꽃을 지니고 있으며, 오직 뉴칼레도니아의 남태평양 섬에서만 자란다. [6(D)]남태평양 지역에 아주 많이 살아 있는 원시 속씨식물로 인해 여러 손꼽히는 식물학자들이 이곳이 바로 속씨식물이 처음 진화한 곳이어서 이 초기 진화의 유물이 현대의 이 종에서 볼 수 있는 것이라는 결론을 짓기에 이르렀다. 수백 가지 꽃식물 종에서 얻은 DNA가 암보렐라 DNA와 비교되었으며, 그 결과물에 따르면 첫 꽃식물은 약 1억 3,500만년 전에 나타나 뚜렷이 다른 여러 종으로 진화하기 시작했음을 나타내고 있다.

[7(B)]하지만, 최근 발굴된 화석들은 꽃식물의 기원에 대한 우리의 이해를 더욱 복잡하게 만들고 있다. 중국의 고생물학자들이 현재의 베이징 근처에 있는 한 장소에서 쥐라기 지질 시대로 거슬러 올라가는 퇴적물 속에서 씨앗과 꽃을 포함해 잘 보존된 꽃식물 화석을 발견해냈다. 이로 인해 그 현장에서 화석으로 찾은 새 식물이 대략 1억 3,000만년이나 된, 지금까지 알려진 가장 오래된 속씨식물이 되었다. 이 화석의 연대는 말할 것도 없고, 그 꽃에 대한 원시 형태론으로 인해 발견자들이 가장 오래된 속씨식물이 아시아 북부 지역에서 진화했을 수도 있다고 추측하게 되었다.

[어휘]

1. evolutionary pathway 진화 경로 angiosperms 속씨식물 fossilized 화석화된 pollen 꽃가루 morphology 형태학, 형태론 ancestor 조상, 선조 intensive 집중적인 consensus 의견 일치 abominable 지독한, 끔찍한

2. monophyletic 단일 계통의, 단일 종족의 paleontologist 고생물학자 cycad 소철 fern 양치식물 hypothesis 가설 primitive 원시적인 relative 동족 unresolved 미해결된

3. Cretaceous 백악기의 account for (비율 등) ~을 차지하다 make up ~을 구성하다(= comprise) Tertiary 제삼기 originate 비롯되다, 유래하다

4. biogeographer 생물 지리학자 migrate 이동하다, 이주하다 prevalent 널리 퍼진, 일반적인 latitude 위도 deposit 퇴적물 supercontinent 초대륙 unearth ~을 발굴하다 equator 적도 poleward 극지방으로 향하는

5. dispersal 확산, 분산 genetics 유전학 bear resemblance to ~와 닮다 evolve 진화하다, 발전하다 relics 유물 emerge 나타나다 distinct 뚜렷이 다른

6. compound ~을 복잡하게 만들다 estimated 대략의, 추정되는 speculate ~라고 추측하다

---

1. 지문의 단어 "intensive"와 의미가 가장 가까운 것은 무엇인가?
(A) 낙관적인
(B) 다양한
(C) 철저한
(D) 놀라운

해설 intensive(집중적인, 철두철미한)와 thorough(철저한)는 유의어로 정답은 (C)이다.

2. 첫 번째 문단에 따르면, 다음 중 어느 종류의 증거가 속씨식물의 역사를 연구하는 데 있어 중대하지 않았던 것인가?
(A) 속씨식물의 기후 변화 적응에 대한 연구
(B) 현대 속씨식물에 대한 유전학적 분석
(C) 현대 속씨식물의 구조에 대한 지식
(D) 속씨식물의 줄기 화석 및 잎 화석

해설 현대 식물의 형태학과 유전학에 대한 광범위한 과학적 연구가 실시되었다는 점으로 미뤄보아 (B)와 (C)를 소거할 수 있다. 문단의 두 번째 문장에서 화석화된 줄기, 잎 등을 언급하며 이들이 유용한 증거라는 점을 언급하기 때문에 (D) 역시 소거할 수 있다. 따라서 정답은 (A)이다.

어휘 adaptation 적응

3. 지문의 단어 "matter"와 의미가 가장 가까운 것은 무엇인가?
(A) 물질
(B) 특색
(C) 결과
(D) 문제

해설 matter(문제)와 issue(문제)는 동의어로 정답은 (D)이다.

4. 세 번째 문단에서, 다음 중 초기 백악기 중의 속씨식물과 관련해 언급된 것은 무엇인가?
(A) 어떤 화석화된 유해도 좀처럼 남기지 않았다.
(B) 식물의 대략 1퍼센트에 해당했다.
(C) 이 시기에 숫자가 상당히 감소했다.
(D) 오늘날 살고 있는 식물과 닮지 않았다.

해설 세 번째 문단의 세 번째 문장을 보면 초기 백악기 시대에 속씨식물이 점점 숫자를 늘려갔고, 모든 식물의 약 1퍼센트를 차지했다고 언급하기 때문에 정답은 (B)이다.

어휘 leave behind ~을 남겨 놓다 remains 유해, 유적 represent ~을 대표하다, 해당하다

5. 글쓴이는 왜 네 번째 문단에서 "곤드와나 대륙"을 언급하는가?

(A) 꽃식물이 전 세계에서 유사한 방법으로 적응했다는 증거를 제공하기 위해

(B) 꽃식물이 백악기 중에 극지방으로 이동했다는 견해를 반박하기 위해

(C) 꽃식물이 열대 지방에서 비롯되었다는 이론을 뒷받침하기 위해

(D) 지리적인 장벽이 어떻게 일부 종의 이동을 지연시켰는지 설명하기 위해

해설 글쓴이가 특정 키워드를 언급하는 문제를 다루는 경우, 반드시 문단의 첫 문장을 읽고 키워드가 포함된 문장으로 넘어가는 것이 중요하다. 첫 문장에서 열대 지방에서 진화한 뒤 극지방으로 이동했을 가능성에 대해 언급한 후, 곤드와나 대륙을 말해주며 마무리 문장까지 같은 방향성을 보여주고 있기 때문에 (C)가 정답이다.

어휘 adapt 적응하다 refute ~에 반박하다 impede ~을 지연시키다

6. 다섯 번째 문단에서, 남태평양의 살아 있는 원시 속씨식물과 관련해 유추할 수 있는 것은 무엇인가?

(A) 오직 뉴칼레도니아라고 알려진 군도에서만 연구되었다.

(B) 속씨식물이 전 세계의 여러 장소에서 동시에 진화했음을 증명한다.

(C) 남미 및 아프리카 지역에서 발견되는 속씨식물과 많은 유사성을 지니고 있다.

(D) 다른 살아 있는 속씨식물들보다 가장 오래된 속씨식물과 더 밀접하게 닮았다.

해설 남태평양의 많은 원시 속씨식물로 인해 초기 진화의 유물이 현대의 종에서 볼 수 있을 것이라는 내용을 통해 (D)를 정답으로 유추할 수 있다.

어휘 simultaneously 동시에 similarity 유사성 resemble ~을 닮다

7. 여섯 번째 문단에 따르면, 다음 중 어느 것이 중국에서 발견된 속씨식물 화석에 대해 사실인가?

(A) 남태평양에서 발견된 속씨식물 화석과 거의 동일하다.

(B) 속씨식물의 진정한 기원을 알아내기 더욱 어렵게 만들었다.

(C) 후기 백악기로 거슬러 올라가는 화석화된 꽃을 포함한다.

(D) 꽃식물이 북부 아시아에서 유래하지 않았음을 나타낸다.

해설 문단의 첫 번째 문장에서 최근 발굴된 화석들이 기원에 대한 이해를 복잡하게 한다고 정보를 제시하고 있고, 이어 중국에서 발견된 속씨 식물 화석을 언급하고 있기 때문에 정답은 (B)이다.

어휘 identical to ~와 동일한, 똑같은 ascertain ~을 알아내다, 확인하다 date back to (시기 등이) ~로 거슬러 올라가다 originate 유래하다, 비롯되다

8. 다음 문장들 중 어느 것이 지문의 하이라이트 표기된 문장에 담긴 핵심 정보를 가장 잘 표현하는가? 오답 선택지는 중요한 방식으로 의미를 변경하거ㅏ 핵심 정보를 배제한다.

일부 식물학자들은 가장 오래된 꽃식물 유형이 호주와 피지, 뉴기니 같은 남태평양 국가에, 그리고 말레이 제도 전역에 여전히 존재하고 있다는 사실을 강조하면서, 꽃식물의 진화 및 확산에 대한 아프리카-남미 기원설에 동의하지 않고 있다.

(A) 호주와, 피지, 뉴칼레도니아, 뉴기니, 그리고 말레이 제도의 속씨식물은 아프리카와 남미에 있는 속씨식물보다 더 많은 원시적인 특징을 지니고 있다.

(B) 식물학자들은 가장 원시적인 형태의 살아 있는 식물들이 아프리카와 남미의 일부 지역 또는 남태평양에 위치해 있는지에 대해 의견 일치에 도달하는 데 어려움을 겪는다.

(C) 일부 식물학자들은 남태평양에 서식하는 매우 원시적인 형태의 속씨식물이 아프리카와 남미 지역에서 속씨식물의 진화가 유래했다는 이론에 의구심을 갖게 한다고 생각한다.

(D) 아프리카와 남미 지역이 꽃식물 진화의 중심지를 구성한다는 견해를 지지하는 일부 식물학자들은 남태평양의 원시 속씨식물을 증거로 든다.

해설 가장 먼저 초점을 두어야하는 점은 일부 식물학자들이 하나의 주장 또는 개념에 동의하지 않는 점이며, 이를 명확하게 제시하고 있는 보기는 (C)밖에 없다.

어휘 feature 특징 A cast doubt on B A로 인해 B에 대해 의구심을 갖다 cite A as evidence A를 증거로 들다

9. 다음 문장이 지문에 추가될 수 있는 곳을 나타내는 네 개의 네모 표기 [■]를 찾아 보시오.

그러한 의미에서, 속씨식물 진화의 정확한 기원 및 시기는 여전히 불확실한 상태이다.

위 문장은 어느 곳에 가장 적합하겠는가? 네모 표기[■]를 클릭해 지문에 이 문장을 추가하시오.

(A) 1번

(B) 2번

(C) 3번

(D) 4번

해설 주어진 문장을 보면, '그러한 의미에서'라는 표현을 담고 있다. 그 말은 기원 및 시기가 불확실하다는 정보와 관련 있는 내용이 앞에 등장해야 한다는 것을 의미한다. 2번 박스 앞 문장을 보면, '현대 식물의 형태학과 유전학에 대한 광범위한 과학적 연구가 실시되었다'는 내용이 등장한다. 그리고 주어진 문장에 등장하는 '정확한 기원과 시기는 불확실하다'는 정보는 이후 의견 일치에 도달하지 못했다는 내용과 같은 흐름을 지니기 때문에 정답은 (B)이다.

어휘 with that said 그러한 의미에서, 말이 나온 김에

10. 설명: 간략한 지문 요약에 필요한 도입 문장이 아래에 제공되어 있다. 지문에서 가장 중요한 개념들을 나타내는 세 가지 답안 선택지를 골라 요약 내용을 완성하시오. 일부 답안 선택지는 지문에 제시되지 않는 개념을 나타내거나 지문에서 중요하지 않은 개념들이므로 요약 내용에 속하지 않는다. **이 문제는 2점에 해당된다.**

수십 년에 걸친 연구에도 불구하고, 꽃식물의 역사와 관련해 여전히 답을 찾지 못한 의문점들이 존재한다.

(A) 속씨식물 화석이 매우 드물게 발견된다는 사실은 꽃식물의 진화를 연구하기 매우 어렵게 만든다.

(B) 화석 증거를 바탕으로, 일부 식물학자들은 속씨식물이 열대 지방에서 처음 진화한 다음, 점차 극지방으로 이동했다는 결론을 내렸다.

(C) 남미와 남태평양, 그리고 아시아에서 발견된 화석에 대한 최근의 연구에 따르면 최초의 꽃식물이 이전에 추정한 것

보다 더 최근에 나타났음을 보여준다.

(D) 비록 꽃식물의 최초 조상이 확실하진 않지만, 초기 백악기 무렵에 나타났으며 결국 지구 식물의 대부분을 구성하게 되었다.

(E) 초기 백악기 화석 침전물에 대한 분석에 따르면 모든 꽃식물의 조상은 현대의 목련과 큰 유사성을 지닌 식물이었다.

(F) 남태평양의 살아 있는 속씨식물에 대한 연구 및 중국의 화석 발견은 속씨식물 진화의 기원에 관한 새로운 이론들을 낳게 되었다.

해설 (B)의 내용은 두 번째 문단에서 언급하고 있는 '열대 지방'의 키워드로 답을 유추할 수 있다. (D)의 내용은 세 번째 문단에서 '초기 백악기'의 키워드를 통해 확인할 수 있다. (F)의 내용은 여섯 번째 문단의 중국에서 발견된 화석으로 인해 더욱 기원을 유추하기가 어려웠다는 정보에서 답을 확신할 수 있다.

어휘 than previously estimated 이전에 추정한 것보다 the vast majority of 대부분의, 대다수의

Passage 3

Answers

1. D	2. C	3. A	4. B	5. C	6. D	7. D	8. B	9. C	10. BCD

산호초

[1(C)]산호초는 수온이 섭씨 21도 이하로 좀처럼 내려가지 않으면서, [1(D)]수중의 가시성이 상당한 양의 침전물에 의해 방해받지 않는 바다 열대 지역에서 발견되는 중요한 서식지다. 산호초가 발달하고 번성하기 위해서는, 일반적으로 [1(A,B)]수면에서 약 30~40미터 아래에 햇빛을 받을 수 있는 견고한 기반을 필요로 하는데, 아주 깊고 어두운 물 속에서는 잘 자라지 않기 때문이다. 대부분의 물리적 구조는 산호 골격으로 구성되는데, 이는 동물성 플랑크톤을 먹고 사는 육식 생물체이다. 산호 외에, 거대하게 축적된 해조류도 암초 형성의 구성 요소로 쓰인다. 암초는 그 크기가 대단히 다양할 수 있으며, 대부분이 비교적 작긴 하지만, 남태평양 마샬 제도의 콰잘레인 같은 일부 환초는 길이가 120킬로미터에 폭이 24킬로미터나 될 정도로 크다. 그레이트 배리어 리프라고 불리는 암초 [2(C)]집합체는 호주 북동부 해안 앞바다에서 2,000킬로미터 길이의 자연 방파제를 형성하는데, 압도적인 차이로 지구상에서 가장 거대한 산호 구조물이다.

과학자들은 수 세기 동안 산호초에 매료되어 왔으며, 찰스 다윈은 1830년대에 있었던 '비글 호' 탐험 중에 몇몇 가장 [3(A)]적절한 관찰을 했던 사람으로 여겨지고 있다. 그는 뚜렷이 다른 세 가지 유형의 암초, 즉 환초와 보초, 그리고 거초를 발견했다. 다윈은 또한 이들이 논리적이고 단계적인 순서로 서로 관련되어 있다는 결론도 내렸다. 거초는 섬 또는 대륙 앞바다에 형성된다. 거초의 표면은 수면 아래의 깊지 않은 곳에서 바깥쪽 가장자리가 더 깊은 물 속으로 내리막을 이루면서 육지의 해안과 평행으로 이어지는 울퉁불퉁한 지대를 만든다. [4(A,C)]때때로, 해협이나 석호가 육지와 거초 사이에 형성되는데, 이것(해협이나 석호)이 깊고 넓어지며 [4(D)]거초가 해안으로부터 충분히 멀리 떨어진 곳에 위치해 수면 위로 돌출되는 경우에, 그 구조물을 보초라고 일컫는다. [4(B)]말발굽 또는 고리 같은 모양을 하고 있으면서 중앙에 석호가 있는 암초는 일반적으로 환초라고 알려져 있다.

[5(C), 6(D)]다윈은 가라앉는 지대로부터 위쪽을 향해 자라는 산호가 한 가지 산호 유형에서 다른 유형으로 이어지는 천이 작용을 촉발시켜, 최초의 거초가 보초 단계를 거치면서 발달되어 최종적으로는 보초의 중앙 부분이 침하되면서 암초로 둘러싸인 석호 또는 환초를 남길 수 있다는 이론을 제시했다. 다윈이 이러한 이론을 제시한지 100년도 더 지난 1950년대에, 연구 과학자들은 태평양의 여러 환초에서 시추공을 깊게 파고 들어갔

다. 천공기가 산호를 1천 미터 넘게 뚫고 들어간 후에나 마침내 해저를 구성하는 단단한 암석에 도달하게 되었다. 이 연구가들은 지구이 지가이 수칩 만년 동안에 걸쳐 수백만 년에 50미터의 비율보 심하하는 동안 산호가 위쪽을 향해 자라나고 있었다는 결론을 내렸다. [6(D), 7(D)]이 결과물은 다윈의 암초 천이 이론을 근본적으로 뒷받침하는 것이었다.

산호초는 수천 가지 종의 필수 서식지이며, 종의 다양성은 인도양 및 서태평양의 따뜻한 물 속에서 형성된 산호초에서 최고 수준에 이른다. ■ [8(B)] 실제로, 그 산호초는 종의 풍부함 및 생물학적 생산성이라는 측면에 있어 수중의 열대 우림과 같은 것으로 흔히 여겨지고 있다. ■ 또한, 해변 지역 보호, 스노클링 같은 여가 활동 기회 제공, 그리고 일부가 의약품에 쓰이기도 하는 유용한 물질 생산에 있어서도 중요한 역할을 한다. [9(C)]■산호초는 다양한 위협 요소들로 인해 점점 더 많은 위험에 처하고 있으며, 가장 주목할 만한 것으로는 해안 지대 침식 가속화에 따라 증가하고 있는 매몰의 부작용 및 준설 공사가 있다. ■

[어휘]
1. intertropical 열대 지방의 impede ~을 방해하다, 저해하다 sediment 침전물 the vast majority of 대부분의, 대다수의 be made up of ~로 구성되다 coral skeleton 산호 골격 carnivorous 육식의 organism 생물체 zooplankton 동물성 플랑크톤 accumulation 축적, 쌓임 algae 해조류 atoll 환초(중앙에 호수가 있는 고리 모양의 산호초) complex 집합체 breakwater 방파제 by a wide margin 압도적인 차이로
2. pertinent 적절한, 관련 있는 barrier reef 보초(해안에서 약간 떨어진 곳에 있는 산호초) fringing reef 거초(섬 또는 육지 주변에 발달하는 산호초) gradational 단계적인, 점진적인 platform (높은) 지대 run parallel to ~와 평행으로 이어지다 slope down 내리막을 이루다 channel 해협 lagoon 초호(환초로 둘러싸여 바다 안의 호수처럼 된 해면), 석호(바다에서 분리되어 생긴 호수) protrude 돌출되다
3. theorize that ~라는 이론을 제시하다 trigger ~을 촉발시키다 succession 천이(일정한 지역의 식물 군락이 시간의 추이에 따라 변천하여 가는 현상), 연쇄, 연속 subsidence 침하, 침강 put forward ~을 제시하다 borehole 시추공(지질 조사 또는 지하 탐사 등을 위해 뚫는 구멍) bore through ~을 뚫고 들어가다 subside 침하하다
4. species (동식물의) 종 equivalent 동등한 것, 상당하는 것 in terms of ~의 측면에 있어 play an important role in ~에 있어 중요한 역할을 하다 substance 물질 dredging 준설 공사(바닥에 쌓인 모래나 암석 등을 파내는 일) siltation 매몰 accelerated 가속화된 erosion 침식

1. 첫 번째 문단에 따르면, 다음 중 어느 것이 산호초 성장에 필요치 않은가?
(A) 자라나기 위한 단단한 토대
(B) 햇빛에 대한 노출
(C) 섭씨 약 21도의 수온
(D) 충분히 높은 수준의 침전물

해설 섭씨 21도 이하로 내려가지 않는다는 조건에서 (C)를 확인할 수 있다. 두 번째 문장에서 햇빛을 받을 수 있는 견고한 기반을 언급하므로 (A)와 (B)의 내용을 확인할 수 있다.

2. 지문의 단어 "complex"와 의미가 가장 가까운 것은 무엇인가?
(A) 지역
(B) 기둥
(C) 체계, 조직(체)
(D) 딜레마, 진퇴양난

어휘 complex(조직, 집합체)와 system(체계, 조직)은 유의어로 정답은 (C)이다.

3. 지문의 단어 "pertinent"와 의미가 가장 가까운 것은 무엇인가?

(A) 적절한, 관련 있는
(B) 논란이 많은
(C) 대담한
(D) 정확한

해설 pertinent(적절한, 관련 있는)와 relevant(적절한, 관련 있는)는 동의어로 정답은 (A)이다.

4. 두 번째 문단에 따르면, 다음 중 어느 것이 보초의 특징에 해당되지 않는가?
(A) 일반적으로 깊은 바닷물 속에서 발견된다.
(B) 중앙의 석호를 둘러싸고 있다.
(C) 넓은 해협에 의해 해안 지대와 분리되어 있다.
(D) 가장 가까운 육지의 해안으로부터 멀리 떨어진 곳에 위치해 있다.

해설 중앙에 석호가 있는 암초는 일반적으로 환초의 특징으로 마지막 문장에서 언급하기 때문에 (B)를 답으로 확인할 수 있다. (A), (C), (D)는 문단의 후반부에서 정보를 제시하고 있다.

5. 다음 문장들 중 어느 것이 지문의 하이라이트 표기된 문장에 담긴 핵심 정보를 가장 잘 표현하는가? 오답 선택지는 중요한 방식으로 의미를 변경하거나 핵심 정보를 배제한다.

다윈은 가라앉는 지대로부터 위쪽을 향해 자라는 산호가 한 가지 산호 유형에서 다른 유형으로 이어지는 천이 작용을 촉발시켜, 최초의 거초가 보초 단계를 거치면서 발달되어 최종적으로는 보초의 중앙 부분이 침하되면서 암초로 둘러싸인 석호 또는 환초를 남길 수 있다는 이론을 제시했다.

(A) 다윈의 이론에 따르면, 대부분의 산호초가 환초에서 시작된 다음, 점차적으로 보초 또는 거초로 변모했다.
(B) 다윈은 산호초의 천이가 암초 성장의 방향 같은 아주 다양한 환경적 요소에 따라 달라진다는 점을 알게 되었다.
(C) 다윈은 산호초가 위쪽을 향해 자라면서 거초가 보초로 발달했다가 중앙 부분이 침하해 석호를 형성하면서 마침내 환초가 된다고 생각했다.
(D) 다윈의 이론은 산호초가 어떻게 해수면 아래로 가라앉은 것으로 여겨지는 여러 섬의 소멸에 대한 원인이 되었는지 설명하는 데 도움을 주었다.

해설 '다윈이 - 이론을 제시했다'는 부분이 (C)의 '다윈은 - 생각했다'로 구조가 일치한다. 두 번째로 초점을 맞출 부분은 '위쪽을 향해 자라나는 구조가 천이 작용을 촉발시킨다'는 점인데, 이 과정에 대한 내용은 (B)와 (D)에서 찾아볼 수 없다. 그리고 '거초가 보초 단계를 거치고, 중앙 부분이 최종적으로 침하되며 환초를 남긴다'라는 정보를 담고 있는 선택지는 (C)뿐이다. (A)는 그 과정을 반대로 언급하고 있기 때문에 소거한다.

어휘 dependent on ~에 따라 다른, ~에 달려 있는 contribute to ~의 원인이 되다

6. 세 번째 문단에서 태평양의 환초와 관련해 유추할 수 있는 것은 무엇인가?
(A) 수백만 년 동안에 걸쳐 거초로 변형될 수 있었다.
(B) 비글 호 항해 중에 다윈에 의해 처음 발견되었다.
(C) 해저에서 가장 부드러운 곳에 위치해 있다.
(D) 섬의 해안을 따라 위치한 거초에서 비롯되었다.

해설 다윈의 이론을 언급하는 첫 문장에서 '최초의 거초가 보초 단계를 거치며 최종적으로 환초가 된다'는 과정을 언급했고, 이후 내용에서 다윈의 암초 천이 이론을 뒷받침하는 결과를 만들어냈다고 언급했기 때문에 정답을 (D)로 유추할 수 있다.

7. 글쓴이는 왜 태평양 환초의 시추공이 "산호를 1천 미터 넘게" 뚫고 지나갔다는 사실을 언급하는가?
(A) 산호초가 아주 깊은 곳에서 잘 자랄 수 있다는 점을 강조하기 위해
(B) 과학자들이 어떻게 지각의 침하 속도를 계산하는지 나타내기 위해
(C) 산호초가 수백만 년 동안 건강하게 유지될 수 있다는 주장을 뒷받침하기 위해
(D) 다윈의 산호초 진화 이론을 뒷받침하는 증거를 제시하기 위해

해설 글쓴이의 의도를 파악할 땐 문단의 첫 문장을 올바르게 이해하는 것이 중요하다. 다윈의 산호초 진화 이론을 언급한 뒤로, 이를 뒷받침하는 실험으로 시추공에 관한 내용이 제시되고 있기 때문에 정답은 (D)이다.

8. 네 번째 문단에 따르면, 왜 산호초가 열대 우림과 비교되었는가?
(A) 둘 모두 인도양 및 서태평양 근처에서 풍부하게 발견되고 있다.
(B) 둘 모두 풍부한 생물 다양성으로 알려져 있다.
(C) 둘 모두 해안 지대를 보호하는 데 있어 중대한 역할을 한다.
(D) 둘 모두 토양 침식에 의해 부정적으로 영향을 받는다.

해설 네 번째 문단의 두 번째 문장을 보면 종의 풍부함과 생물학적 생산성이라는 공통점을 가지고 있어 수중의 열대 우림과 같다고 표현하기 때문에 정답은 (B)이다.

어휘 impact ~에 영향을 미치다

9. 다음 문장이 지문에 추가될 수 있는 곳을 나타내는 네 개의 네모 표기 [■]를 찾아 보시오.

하지만 많은 산호초 생물체들이 특정하고 지속적인 환경 조건을 필요로 하기 때문에, 암초는 사람이 만든 활동 및 환경 변화 둘 모두에 의해 초래되는 변화에 대단히 취약하다.

위 문장은 어느 곳에 가장 적합하겠는가? 네모 표기[■]를 클릭해 지문에 이 문장을 추가하시오.

(A) 1번
(B) 2번
(C) 3번
(D) 4번

해설 역접을 뜻하는 Yet으로 문장이 시작되기 때문에 주어진 문장에서 제시된 '사람이 만든 활동과 환경 변화에 의해 초래되는 변화'를 언급하는 문장 뒤에 오는 것이 바람직하다고 판단할 수 있다. 그리고 주어진 문장 뒤에는 지속적인 취약성에 대한 이야기가 나와야하는 만큼 정답은 3번째 네모가 적절하다.

어휘 susceptible to ~에 취약한, ~의 영향을 받기 쉬운 bring about ~을 초래하다

10. **설명:** 간략한 지문 요약에 필요한 도입 문장이 아래에 제공되어 있다. 지문에서 가장 중요한 개념들을 나타내는 세 가지 답안 선택지를 골라 요약 내용을 완성하시오. 일부 답안 선택지는 지문에 제시되지 않는 개념을 나타내거나 지문에서 중요하지 않은 개념들이므로 요약 내용에 속하지 않는다. **이 문제는 2점에 해당된다.**

산호초는 아주 다양한 해양 생물의 서식지 역할을 하는 대단

히 중요한 열대 환경이다.

(A) 거초는 대륙과 섬의 해안 근처에 위치해 있으면서, 육지와 바다 사이에서 일어나는 종의 이동을 촉진한다.

(B) 산호초는 많은 살아 있는 생물로 구성된 구조물이며, 오직 특정한 해양 환경에서만 성장할 수 있다.

(C) 산호초가 자연과 인간에게 다양한 혜택을 제공해 주기는 하지만, 현재 인간 활동 및 자연 악화로 인한 위협에 처해 있다.

(D) 산호초는 거초와 보초, 또는 환초로 분류되며, 이 모두는 점진적 발달 과정의 순서상 단계들이다.

(E) 비록 환초가 수많은 해양 생물 종의 서식지이기는 하지만, 보초가 모든 암초 서식지들 중에서 단연코 가장 생물 다양

성이 뛰어나다.

(F) 과학자들은 산호초가 수많은 동식물 종의 서식지로서 맹그로브 습지만큼 중요하다고 생각하고 있다.

해설 첫 번째 문단에서 산호초의 정의와 조건을 설명해주는 정보가 핵심이기 때문에 (B)를 정답으로 선택할 수 있다. 네 번째 문단을 보면 자연과 인간에 대한 혜택과 취약성을 언급하기 때문에 (C)도 정답이다. (D)의 경우 다윈의 가설에서부터 시작되는 세 번째 문단의 천이 이론을 통해 답이라는 점을 유추할 수 있다.

어휘 facilitate ~을 촉진하다 comprise ~으로 구성되다 degradation 악화, 저하 be categorized as ~로 분류되다 by far 단연코 biodiverse 생물이 다양한 mangrove 맹그로브(열대와 아열대의 하구 등에서 자라는 식물 집단) swamp 습지

Chapter 3 Art

Passage 1

Answers

1. B	2. D	3. C	4. A	5. D	6. A	7. D	8. B	9. A	10. BCE

로마 제국의 도자기

²⁽ᴬ⁾훌륭하게 제작된 도자기는 ²⁽ᴮ⁾고대 로마 제국 어디에나 존재했다. 가벼우면서 견고한 로마 도자기는 ²⁽ᶜ⁾주로 실용적인 목적으로 제조되었다. 고대 그리스인들이 개인 전기에서부터 모험 서사시에 이르는 어떤 것이든 ¹⁽ᴮ⁾묘사한 정교한 그림으로 그릇과 단지들을 꾸몄던 반면, ²⁽ᴰ⁾고대 로마의 도자기는 요리와 저장, 또는 운송 같은 기본적인 기능을 했다. 이는 그 도자기의 미적 특징이 부족했다는 말이 아니라 ²⁽ᴬ⁾(그 훌륭한 솜씨 자체는 충분히 경이롭다), 대신 도자기 제품들과 그것들이 제작된 수량이 로마 제국의 선진적인 산업 및 경제 운용 방식을 나타내는 것이다.

로마의 도자기는 흔히 두 가지 종류로 분류된다. 그 첫 번째는 고급 자기로서, 그릇과 식기로 사용하기 위해 솜씨 있게 빚어낸 제품이다. ³⁽ᶜ⁾공식적인 저녁 만찬 행사용으로 쓰였던, 고급 자기는 장식용이면서 실용적이었다. 고급 자기의 가장 중요한 예시가 '테라 시길라타'였는데, 이탈리아 북부와 프랑스 같은 지역에서 만들어졌던 붉은 광택이 도는 자기였다. 이 제품은 잘 구운 다음, 자연스럽게 광택이 나는 표면 슬립을 추가했으며 충분히 단단했다. '테라 시길라타' 제품은 하나의 산업 규모로 생산되었고(가장 큰 가마들은 한 번에 수만 개의 제품을 구울 수 있었다), 로마 제국 전역으로 수출되었다. 붉은 광택이 도는 그릇 파편, 즉 도자기 파편들이 인도에서 스코틀랜드에 이르는 곳곳에서 발견되었다. 그것들을 만든 공예가나 제조사의 서명이 표기된 조각들이 많았으며, 멀리 떨어진 여러 곳에서 동일한 예술가 또는 공장을 통해 나온 제품도 발견되었다. ⁴⁽ᴬ⁾미적으로 매력적이도록 만들어진, '테라 시길라타' 제품은 마치 예술 작품 같은 고대 그리스 도자기 제품과 비슷했지만, 색을 입히진 않았다. 대신, 공예가들은 양각으로, 즉 도자기 표면에서 두드러졌던 주형물이나 조각물로 장식했다.

저급 자기는 고대 로마 도자기의 다른 한 영역을 대표하는 것이었다. 고급 자기와 달리, 저급 자기는 순전히 기능용으로 제작되었다. 이 흔한 그릇들은 현지에서 제작되어 판매되었으며, 주로 요리와 저장, 운송용으로 쓰였다. 이 자기는 신분과 계층에 상관없이 로마 시대 가정의 주요 물품이었다. 진열용으로 만들어진 것은 아니었지만, 그럼에도 불구하고 훌륭하게 제작되었다. 견고하면서 가벼웠고, 손으로 만져보면 부드러웠다. 광택이 있고 보호막 처리가 된 표면으로 인해 올리브 오일이나 생선 소스, 그리고 와인 같은 액체 저장용으로 이상적이었다. ⁵⁽ᴰ⁾공예가들이 규격화된 사이즈를 따랐기 때문에 도자기를 차곡차곡 쌓고 효율적이고 장기적으로 보관하는 데 도움이 되었다. 암포라가 일반적인 저급 자기 제품이었다. ⁶⁽ᴬ⁾이 원뿔 모양의 저장용 그릇은 저장고 및 상선 화물실에 안전하게 들어맞을 수 있었다. 귀중한 내용물이 해상 운송 중에 보호되었기 때문에, 대규모 암포라 생산은 로마 제국의 무역에 있어 중대한 역할을 했다.

고고학에서 흔히 그렇듯이, 고대 로마에서 만들어지고 사용되었던 전체 도자기 수량의 극히 드문 샘플만 앞으로 발견될 것이다. ⁹⁽ᴬ⁾■ 하지만, 고대 로마 시대에 대규모 도자기 생산이 이뤄졌음을 암시하는 특별한 쓰레기 매립지가 한 곳 존재한다. ■ 몬테 테스타치오는 약 50미터 높이의 인공 언덕으로서, 로마의 티베르 강 왼쪽 둑에 고대의 강 항구들 중의 하나와 가까운 곳에 위치해 있다. ■ 이곳은 ⁷⁽ᴰ⁾전적으로 버려지고 깨진 암포라로 구성되어 있으며, 그 대부분은 서기 2~3세기로 거슬러 올라가는 것들이다. ■ 고고학자들은 5천만 개가 넘는 암포라가 몬테 테스타치오 축조에 들어간 것으로 추정하고 있다. 우리가 알고 있는 그 용기들의 용량을 감안할 때, 60억 리터가 넘는 올리브 오일이 해외에서 이 도시로 수입되었을 가능성이 있다. 몬테 테스타치오는 고대 로마 시대의 엄청난 수입품 규모와 복잡성을 증명하는 것이며, 오늘날과 크게 다르지 않은 사회의 이미지를 떠올리게 한다. 고대 로마는, 필요할 경우에, 운송 즉시 간단하게 처리될 수 있는 고품질의 최적화된 용기들을 통해 그 제국의 전체 지역에 걸쳐 상품을 생산하고 수송했다.

⁸⁽ᴮ⁾몬테 테스타치오를 비롯해 로마 제국 전역에 위치한 다른 부지들을 보면 로마의 도자기가 아주 먼 거리에 걸쳐 대량으로 운송되었다는 사실을 나타낼 뿐만 아니라, 어떻게 고대 로마 사회의 모든 계층이 훌륭한 제품을 이용했는지도 나타난다. 변변치 못한 제품에서부터 고급 자기에 이르기까지, 로마의 도자기는 그 제국의 일상 생활을 엿볼 수 있는 기준의 역할을 한다.

용어 설명 슬립: 점토와 물을 섞은 혼합물로서, 도자기를 장식하는 데 사용

가마: 굽고 태우기니 긴조를 위한 화로나 화덕으로서, 특히 도자기를 굽는 데 쓰이는 것

[어휘]

1. ubiquitous 어디에나 있는 utilitarian 실용적인 adorn ~을 장식하다 urn 단지, 항아리 aesthetic 미적인 marvel at ~을 경이로워하다 signify ~을 의미하다 working 운용, 작용

2. be classified into ~로 분류되다 ware 자기, 도기 fire (도자기 등) ~을 굽다 gloss 광택, 윤 potsherd 그릇 조각 shard 조각, 파편 Grecian 고대 그리스의 relief 양각(으로 만든 것) molding 주형물

3. coarse 저급한, 조잡한 sphere 영역, 범주 staples 주요 산물, 중요 상품 standardized 규격화된, 표준화된 conducive to ~에 좋은, 도움이 되는 amphora 암포라(고대 로마 시대에 쓰던 항아리, amphorae는 복수형) serve a crucial role in ~에 있어 중대한 역할을 하다

4. sparse 드문 dumpsite 쓰레기 매립지 hint at ~을 암시하다 be composed of ~로 구성되다 discard ~을 처리하다, 버리다 contribute to ~에 도움이 되다 attest to ~을 증명하다 scope 범위, 규모 conjure ~을 떠올리게 하다 expanse (넓은) 지역, 공간 optimized 최적화된

5. in bulk 대량으로 have access to ~을 이용하다, ~에 접근하다 humble 변변치 못한

1. 지문의 단어 "depicted"와 의미가 가장 가까운 것은 무엇인가?

(A) 기록했다

(B) 묘사했다

(C) 논의했다

(D) 공급했다

해설 depicted(묘사했다)와 portrayed(묘사했다)는 동의어로 정답은 (B)이다.

2. 다음 중 첫 번째 문단에서 글쓴이가 묘사하는 로마의 도자기와 관련해 언급되지 않은 것은 무엇인가?

(A) 잘 만들어졌다.

(B) 널리 유통되었다.

(C) 유용했다.

(D) 진열용으로 만들어졌다.

해설 (D)를 제외한 나머지 보기의 내용은 첫 문단에 고르게 설명되어 있다. '진열용'과 관련된 내용은 언급된 적이 없다.

3. 다음 중 어느 것이 '테라 시길라타'와 관련해 두 번째 문단에서 유추할 수 있는 내용인가?

(A) 같은 가마에서 함께 구운 제품들은 동일했다.

(B) 만들어진 곳에 따라 그 양식이 다양했다.

(C) 로마 사회의 엘리트 계층이 주로 사용했다.

(D) 저급 도자기보다 더 취약했다.

해설 특정 키워드를 언급하는 경우 문단의 초반부에서 그 힌트를 얻어야 한다. 고급 자기와 관련해 '공식적인 저녁 만찬 행사 및 장식품'이라는 표현이 쓰여 있고, 그 예시로 '테라 시길라타'를 언급하고 있어 상위계층이 즐겨 사용한 자기라는 점을 유추할 수 있다. 따라서 (C)가 정답이다.

어휘 identical 동일한 depending on ~에 따라 다른, ~에 달려 있는 fragile 취약한, 깨지기 쉬운

4. 두 번째 문단에 따르면, '테라 시길라타'가 고대 그리스의 도자기와 달랐던 이유는 무엇인가?

(A) 페인트 대신 양각으로 장식되었다.

(B) 매력적인 디자인으로 인해 인기가 있었다.

(C) 대량으로 생산되었다.

(D) 지중해 지역 전체에 걸쳐 발견되었다.

해설 문단의 마지막 부분을 보면 그리스 도자기 제품과 비슷했지만, 색을 입히지 않고 양각을 활용하였다는 점이 언급되므로 정답은 (A)이다.

5. 세 번째 문단에 따르면, 공예가들이 규격화된 사이즈를 따름으로써 어떤 결과가 나타났는가?

(A) 다양한 제품이 배를 통해 운송될 수 있었다.

(B) 더 많은 양의 상품이 로마로 수입될 수 있었다.

(C) 사이즈와 상관없이 제품이 한결같이 견고한 상태를 유지했다.

(D) 저급 도자기가 상품을 효율적으로 저장할 수 있었다.

해설 세 번째 문단 중간에 보면 규격화된 사이즈를 따름으로써 효율적이고 장기적인 보관에 도움이 되었다는 정보를 확인할 수 있으므로 정답은 (D)이다.

어휘 consistently 한결같이, 지속적으로 sturdy 견고한, 튼튼한

6. 글쓴이는 왜 "상선"을 언급하는가?

(A) 암포라가 자주 배로 운송되었다는 점을 나타내기 위해

(B) 암포라가 인기 있는 교역품이었음을 주장하기 위해

(C) 암포라의 형태를 다른 도자기 그릇의 형태와 대비시키기 위해

(D) 대부분의 상품이 로마로 수입되었음을 주장하기 위해

해설 해당 문장과 다음 문장을 보면 원뿔 모양의 저장용 그릇이 안전하게 들어맞을 수 있었고, 내용물이 보호될 수 있다는 점을 언급하고 있으므로 (A)를 정답으로 유추할 수 있다.

어휘   trade good 교역품   the majority of 대부분의, 대다수의

7. 지문의 단어 "entirely"와 의미가 가장 가까운 것은 무엇인가?
     (A) 전통적으로
     (B) 변함없이
     (C) 분명히
     (D) 전적으로

해설   entirely(완전히, 전적으로)와 completely(완전히, 전적으로)는 동의어로 정답은 (D)이다.

8. 다음 문장들 중 어느 것이 지문의 하이라이트 표기된 문장에 담긴 핵심 정보를 가장 잘 표현하는가? 오답 선택지는 중요한 방식으로 의미를 변경하거나 핵심 정보를 배제한다.

몬테 테스타치오를 비롯해 로마 제국 전역에 위치한 다른 부지들을 보면 로마의 도자기가 아주 먼 거리에 걸쳐 대량으로 운송되었다는 사실을 나타낼 뿐만 아니라, 어떻게 고대 로마 사회의 모든 계층이 훌륭한 제품을 이용했는지도 나타난다.

     (A) 몬테 테스타치오에 도착한 대량의 도자기는 거의 모든 로마 사람이 도자기를 소유했음을 나타낸다.
     (B) 다양한 곳에서 발견된 도자기를 보면 고급 도자기가 로마 제국 전역에서 대량으로 운송되어 모든 로마인들이 소유했음을 나타낸다.
     (C) 로마 시민들이 품질이 더 뛰어난 도자기를 얻게 되면서, 몬테 테스타치오 같은 곳에 기존의 제품을 버렸으며, 이는 로마 제국의 상품 과잉을 암시하는 것이다.
     (D) 고대 로마 제국의 모든 영토에는 몬테 테스타치오처럼 사람들이 여분의 도자기를 처리할 수 있었던 공동 부지가 있었다.

해설   주어진 문장은 큰 정보를 두 개 담고 있는데, 하나는 몬테 테스타치오 및 다양한 부지가 도자기의 대량 운송을 나타낸다는 점이다. 이 내용을 담고 있는 보기는 (B)뿐이다. 그리고 두 번째 정보는 로마 사회의 모든 계층이 훌륭한 제품을 이용했다는 것인데 이도 (B)에서만 확인할 수 있다.

어휘   possess ~을 소유하다   surplus 과잉, 잉여   territory 영토, 영역   communal 공동의   dispose of ~을 처리하다, 처분하다   excess 여분의, 초과한

9. 다음 문장이 지문에 추가될 수 있는 곳을 나타내는 네 개의 [■]를 찾아 보시오.

이것을 감안하면, 얼마나 많이 생산되었는지 추정하기 어렵다.

     위 문장은 어느 곳에 가장 적합하겠는가? 네모 표기[■]를 클릭해 지문에 이 문장을 추가하시오.
     (A) 1번

     (B) 2번
     (C) 3번
     (D) 4번

해설   '이것을 감안하면'이라는 표현을 통해 앞에 수량에 대한 이야기가 반드시 등장해야 한다. 그렇기 때문에 극히 드문 양의 샘플만 발견될 것이라고 말하는 문장 뒤에 위치한 1번 박스가 정답 후보에 해당된다. 그리고 얼마나 생산되었는지 추정하기 힘들다는 말 뒤에 역접을 나타내는 However와 함께 대규모 도자기 생산을 암시하는 매립지 이야기가 이어지는 것이 자연스러우므로 정답은 (A) 이다.

10. 설명: 간략한 지문 요약에 필요한 도입 문장이 아래에 제공되어 있다. 지문에서 가장 중요한 개념들을 나타내는 세 가지 답안 선택지를 골라 요약 내용을 완성하시오. 일부 답안 선택지는 지문에 제시되지 않는 개념을 나타내거나 지문에서 중요하지 않은 개념들이므로 요약 내용에 속하지 않는다. **이 문제는 2점에 해당된다.**

고대 로마의 훌륭한 도자기는 그 제국이 지닌 여러 가지 장점을 보여준다.

     (A) '테라 시길라타' 제품은 올리브 오일 같은 액체 운송에 주로 사용되었다.
     (B) 몬테 테스타치오의 암포라 더미는 고대 로마의 수출 및 무역 산업의 규모를 자세히 나타낸다.
     (C) 로마 제국 전역에 걸쳐 보편적으로 존재했던 도자기는 모든 사람들이 질 좋은 제품을 이용했음을 보여준다.
     (D) 인기 있는 공예가와 제조업체들이 인도에서 스코틀랜드에 이르기까지 그 제국 전역에서 도기를 유통시켰다.
     (E) 고급 자기 제품과 저급 자기 제품이 전문적으로 만들어지고 대량으로 제조되었다.
     (F) 고대 로마인들은 고대 그리스인들의 예술 작품을 본받아 도자기를 만들었다.

해설   네 번째 문단과 다섯 번째 문단의 정보를 통해 몬테 테스타치오와 암포라 더미가 고대 로마 수출 및 무역 규모를 보여준다는 점을 알 수 있으므로 (B)가 정답이다. 다섯 번째 문단은 (C)의 정보도 포함하고 있으므로 정답이다. 첫 번째, 두 번째, 그리고 세 번째 문단을 통해 고급 자기와 저급 자기가 모두 대량으로 만들어졌다는 점을 토대로 (E)도 정답으로 유추할 수 있다.

어휘   magnitude 규모   universal 보편적인   in great amounts 대량으로   model A on B A에 대해 B를 본받다, B를 A의 모델로 삼다

Passage 2

1. A	2. B	3. C	4. B	5. D	6. C	7. D	8. B	9. C	10. ADE

동굴 벽화의 창조

^{1(A)}구석기 시대 말기에 시작된 동굴 벽화는 최초의 인간 예술 작품을 상징하는 그림이다. 주로 스페인과 프랑스 곳곳의 큰 동굴과 깊게 갈라진 지면 틈에서 발견된 동굴 벽화는 당시의 황소와 오록스, 말을 비롯한 여러 동물을 놀라울 정도로 자세히 묘사하고 있다. 프랑스의 라스코와 쇼베는 이러한 곳으로 가장 잘 알려져 있는 몇몇 장소에 해당된다. ^{2(B)}만일 이 벽화들이 정말로 초기 인류가 시도한 예술을 상징하는 것이라면, 어떻게 그 창조 이면에 숨어 있는 동기를 설명할 것인가? 그 벽화들은 어떤 목적을 지니고 있는가? 고전 작품 <시학>을 통해, 아리스토텔레스는 사람들이 "모방된 작품에서 자연적으로 즐거움을 얻는다"라고 주장했다. 일몰이 일시적으로 언뜻 보이는 아름다움이라면, 예술을 통한 재창조가 적어도 그 장엄함에 대한 연상이 즉시 가능하도록 만들어준다. 만약 후손들인 우리가 그렇게 간단하면서도 직접적인 방식으로 예술을 즐길 수 있다면, ^{2(B)}우리의 조상들도 거의 비슷한 방법으로 즐겼을 가능성이 꽤 높다.

이렇게 추론해 보자면, 라스코의 동굴들은 초기 인류가 뛰어난 화가들의 아름다운 걸작을 보러 가기 위한 여행을 떠날 수 있었던 일종의 선사 시대 미술관으로서 존재했을 수도 있다. ^{3(C)}이렇게 여유 있는 활동을 누릴 수 있는 기회는 끊임없는 생존 요구에 대한 일시적 모면을 필요로 했을 것이다. 구석기 시대의 유럽에 식량이 풍부하게 존재했다면, 이는 그럴듯한 시나리오였을지도 모른다. 하지만, 이러한 가정에는 수많은 문제들이 존재한다. 우선 한 가지는, 시대를 알 수 없는 동굴 벽화 장소들을 포함해 그동안 발견된 많은 고고학적 유적지들은 놀라울 정도로 좁은 범위의 예술 주제를 제공하고 있다. ■ 각 유적지에는 동일하게 반복되는 동물 이미지나 모티프가 있다. ■ 인간의 모습에 대한 묘사는 좀처럼 나타나 있지 않으며, 존재한다 하더라도, 동물에게 기울였던 것과 같은 세부 요소에 대한 주의력이 부족하다. ^{9(C)}■ 구석기 시대의 미술가들이 아름다움을 재창조하기 위해 작업한 것이라면, 그 ^{4(B)}범위는 대단히 한정적이었다. ■ 이들은 왜 꽃과 나무들, 별들과 하늘을 무시했던 것일까?

초기 인류가 아름다움의 재창조 수단으로서 예술을 탐구했다는 개념은 현실에 분명한 대상이 존재하지 않는 추상적인 이미지들의 보편화로 인해 추가적으로 이의가 제기되고 있다. ^{5(A)}이러한 표시들은(^{5(D)}일반적으로 선과 점으로 구성된 단순한 기하학적 무늬들) 독자적으로 나타나 있거나 전형적인 동물 묘사와 함께 나타나 있다. ^{5(C)}프랑스의 로트 지역, 즉 페슈 메를의 작은 동굴에 그려진 벽화를 보면 동물 그림과 추상적인 무늬가 모두 나타나 있다. 다시 말해서 배가 불룩한 말 그림들이 그곳의 벽들을 장식하고 있다. 하지만, 이 동물 그림들의 윤곽선은 그와 달리 현실적인 말 그림을 기형적으로 보이게 만드는 어두운 점들로 덮여 있다. 이 점들이 자연주의적 재현 작업의 가치를 떨어뜨린다는 것 외에는 ^{5(B)}어떤 기능을 하는지 알려져 있지 않다. 게다가, 이 이미지들이 관람 및 감상용으로 만들어진 것이라면, 그 위치에도 문제가 있다. ^{6(C)}라스코의 동굴들이 구석기 시대 미술관 관람객들이 접근하기 쉬웠을 수 있었던 반면, 다른 곳들은 심지어 경험 많은 동굴 탐험가들조차 시험에 들게 할 수 있다. 좁은 구석 자리와 얕은 공간에 있는 그림들을 보면 그것을 그린 미술가들은 인상적일 정도로 뒤틀린 자세가 필요했을 것이며, 오히려, 관람을 바라는 사람들의 접근을 가로막는 것처럼 보인다.

게다가, 구석기 시대 미술가들이 예술을 위한 예술을 즐겼을 수 있다는 전반적인 가정은, 식량이 풍족하고 기본적인 생존이 지속적인 요구 사항이 아닌 경우, 즉 비교적 차분한 일상 생활을 전제로 한다. 이 시기에, 유럽은 여전히 빙하 시대를 겪고 있었으며, 당시의 사람은 생존을 위해 하루에 약 2,000칼로리를 섭취해야 했을 것으로 추정되어 왔다. 얼어붙어 있는 가혹한 땅에서 이 정도 양의 자양물을 얻는 것은 최우선 과제였을 것이다. ^{7(D)}동물 그림 및 구석기 시대 사람들의 가혹한 생활 방식에 대한 강조로 인해 일부 고고학자들은 동굴 벽화가 분명 실용적인 목적으로 만들어졌고 당시 사람들의 주요 생존 수단인 '사냥'에 어떻게든 도움이 되었을 것이라고 믿게 되었다.

어떻게 동굴 벽화가 생존에 도움이 될 수 있었는지에 초점을 맞춘 새로운 이론 하나가 20세기 초에 등장했다. 프랑스의 고고학자 앙리 브뢰이유는 '공감 주술'이라는 개념을 제시했다. 그는 묘사되는 동물의 혼을 담아 두기 위해 당시 미술가들이 그렇게 세부적으로 작업했다고 주장했다. 더 현실적이고 더 잘 연상되는 이미지일수록, 그것이 먹이를 더 잘 잡을 수 있다는 것이다. 이러한 개념에 따르면, 미술가의 정확한 그림은 사냥꾼의 활동에 행운과 길운이 깃들게 해줄 주술적 ^{8(B)}능력을 지니고 있었다.

[어휘]
1. date from (기원 등) ~부터 시작되다   Paleolithic era 구석기 시대   represent ~을 상징하다, 대표하다   cavern 동굴   chasm 깊은 틈   aurochs

오록스(옛날의 몸집이 큰 야생 소) glimpse 얼핏 봄, 언뜻 봄 suggestion 연상 (작용) grandeur 장엄함 descendant 후손 ancestor 선조, 조상

2. take in 보러 가다, 받아들이다 accomplished 뛰어난 (실력을 지닌) access to ~에 대한 접근, 이용 reprieve 일시적 모면 incessant 끊임없는 plausible 그럴듯한 assumption 가정, 추정 archaeological 고고학적인 recurring 반복적인 motif 모티프, 주제 attention 주의(력), 주목, 관심 scope 시야, 범위

3. challenge ~에 이의를 제기하다 prevalence 보편적임, 만연함 abstract 추상적인 counterpart (대응 관계에 있는) 대상 geometrical 기하학적인 composed of ~로 구성된 grotto 작은 동굴 stout-bellied 배가 불룩한 adorn ~을 장식하다 deform ~을 기형으로 만들다, 변형시키다 detract from ~의 가치를 떨어뜨리다 reproduction 재현, 복제 appreciate ~을 감상하다 nook 구석(진 곳) chamber 공간, 방 contortion 뒤틀림, 일그러짐 if anything 오히려 dissuade ~하지 못하게 하다, ~을 단념하게 만들다 would-be ~가 되려고 하는

4. for A's sake A를 위한 hinge on (전적으로) ~에 달려 있다, …에 따라 결정되다 extract ~을 얻어내다, 추출하다 sustenance 자양물 A lead B to do A로 인해 B가 ~하게 되다, ~하기에 이르다

5. emerge 나타나다, 떠오르다 centered on ~에 초점을 맞춘 evocative 연상시키는, 환기시키는 imbue A with B A에 B가 깃들다, A에 B가 가득하다

---

1. 첫 번째 문단에 따르면, 동굴 벽화와 관련해 무엇이 중요한가?
(A) 인류 최초의 예술 작품을 상징한다.
(B) 도달하기 어려운 지역에서 나타난다.
(C) 초기 선조들이 누린 유일한 즐거움의 수단이었다.
(D) 일반적인 동식물들을 정교하게 묘사하고 있다.

해설 문단의 가장 첫 부분에서 동굴 벽화는 최초의 인간 예술 작품을 상징하는 그림이라는 점을 언급한다. 그리고 이후 문단의 중반에서도 어떻게 동기를 설명할 것인가라는 질문을 던지기 때문에 정답은 (A)이다. (C)의 경우, '유일한'이라는 표현이 소거의 대상이 되고, (B)와 (D)는 동굴 벽화에 대한 기본적인 정보에 불과하므로 중요한 정보로 볼 수 없다.

2. 첫 번째 문단에서, 글쓴이는 왜 아리스토텔레스를 언급하는가?
(A) 고대 그리스인들이 어떻게 구석기 시대 예술을 바라봤는지 입증하기 위해
(B) 동굴 벽화에 적용될 만한 예술 창조와 관련된 이론을 공유하기 위해
(C) 구석기 시대 예술가들이 예술 창조에 대해 다른 이유를 지니고 있었음을 주장하기 위해
(D) 구석기 시대 예술과 고대 그리스 예술 사이의 연관성을 강조하기 위해

해설 창조 이면에 숨어 있는 동기를 질문하는 문장 뒤에 아리스토텔레스를 언급했기 때문에 예술 창조와 관련된 이론을 제시하기 위해서라고 판단할 수 있다. 그리고 문단의 마지막에서도 아리스토텔레스가 언급한 '모방된 작품에서 얻는 즐거움'을 긍정적으로 바라보고 있기 때문에 정답은 (B)이다.

3. 두 번째 문단에서, 글쓴이는 어떤 경우에 유럽의 동굴 벽화가 오직 즐거움을 위해 만들어졌을 수도 있다고 주장하는가?
(A) 충분한 자연광이 동굴 내에서 이용 가능한 경우에
(B) 구석기 시대의 예술가들이 뛰어난 예술적 능력을 지니고 있었을 경우에
(C) 생존에 대한 기본적인 요구가 손쉽게 충족된 경우에

(D) 충분한 사람들이 그 미술관을 방문하는 데 관심이 있었을 경우에

해설 두 번째 문장에 제시된 '여유로운 활동을 누리는 기회는 생존 요구에 대한 일시적인 모면이 없다면 불가능했을 것'이라는 내용을 토대로 기본적인 요구가 충족이 되었을 경우라는 전제 조건을 유추할 수 있다. 그리고 세 번째 문장에서도 식량이 풍부했다면 그럴듯한 시나리오였을지도 모른다는 점을 말하는 것을 토대로 정답이 (C)라는 점을 확인할 수 있다.

4. 지문의 단어 "scope"와 의미가 가장 가까운 것은 무엇인가?
(A) 형태
(B) 범위, 정도
(C) 재능
(D) 시야, 견해

해설 scope(범위, 정도)와 extent(범위, 정도)는 동의어로 정답은 (B)이다.

5. 세 번째 문단에서, 동굴 벽화에 나타나 있는 추상적인 형체와 관련해 언급되지 않은 것은 무엇인가?
(A) 동물 그림에 위치해 있다.
(B) 그 목적은 알려져 있지 않다.
(C) 페슈 메를에서 찾아볼 수 있다.
(D) 복잡하게 고안되어 있다.

해설 중간 부분의 '기능과 관련된 의문점'을 통해 (B)가 소거된다. 그리고 두 번째 문장에서 동물 그림을 언급하고 있기 때문에 (A)를 소거하고, 세 번째 문장의 내용을 통해 (C)를 소거하여 정답은 (D)로 판단한다. 복잡함은 언급되지 않았으며 오히려 '단순한 기하학적 무늬들(simple geometrical patterns)'이라고 나와 있다.

어휘 intricately 복잡하게

6. 세 번째 문단에서, 라스코 동굴 벽화와 관련해 유추할 수 있는

것은 무엇인가?

(A) 대부분 동굴 천장 부분에 완성되었다.

(B) 그것들을 만든 미술가들이 대단히 민첩했다.

(C) 쉽게 접근할 수 있는 곳에 그려졌다.

(D) 접근하는 데 동굴 탐험용 장비가 필요하다.

해설 세 번째 문단 후반부에 '라스코 동굴들이 구석기 시대 미술관 관람객들이 접근하기 쉬웠을 것으로 보이는 반면'이라는 내용을 토대로 정답이 (C)임을 확인할 수 있다.

어휘 nimble 민첩한, 재빠른

7. 다음 문장들 중 어느 것이 지문의 하이라이트 표기된 문장에 담긴 핵심 정보를 가장 잘 표현하는가? 오답 선택지는 중요한 방식으로 의미를 변경하거나 핵심 정보를 배제한다.

동물 그림 및 구석기 시대 사람들의 가혹한 생활 방식에 대한 강조로 인해 일부 고고학자들은 동굴 벽화가 분명 실용적인 목적으로 만들어졌고 당시 사람들의 주요 생존 수단인 '사냥'에 어떻게든 도움이 되었을 것이라고 믿게 되었다.

(A) 사냥꾼들은 동물들의 상세 이미지를 기록함으로써 유용한 방식으로 동굴 벽화를 이용했으며, 이는 일반적으로 사냥은 더 쉽게, 그리고 사람들은 더 안전하게 만들어주었다.

(B) 생존에 어려움을 겪었던 구석기 시대 사람들은 사냥에 초점을 맞춰야 했던 반면, 그렇지 않았던 사람들은 동물을 동굴 벽화로 그리면서 시간을 보낼 수 있었다.

(C) 사냥을 통해, 구석기 시대 미술가들은 그림에 필요한 동물을 가까이에서 관찰할 수 있었으며, 이는 전반적으로 사람들이 생존하는 데 도움이 되었다.

(D) 동물 그림의 숫자 및 당시 생존의 어려움은 동굴 그림들이 어떤 식으로든 사냥에 도움이 될 것이었음을 나타낸다.

해설 동물 그림 및 가혹한 생활 방식에 대한 강조가 실용적인 목적을 지녔을 것이라는 핵심 정보를 포함하는 선택지를 찾는 것이 매우 중요하다. 그런 의미에서 이러한 그림이 생존 수단인 사냥에 도움이 되었을 것이라는 점을 토대로 정답이 (D)임을 확인할 수 있다.

어휘 in general 일반적으로, 전반적으로 observe ~을 관찰하다 overall 전반적으로 be meant to do ~할 것으로 여겨지다, ~하기로 되어 있다, ~하지 않으면 안 되다

8. 지문의 단어 "capacity"와 의미가 가장 가까운 것은 무엇인가?

(A) 빈도

(B) 능력

(C) 상태, 조건

(D) 공간, 장소

해설 capacity(능력)와 ability(능력)는 동의어로 정답은 (B)이다.

9. 다음 문장이 지문에 추가될 수 있는 곳을 나타내는 네 개의 네모 표기 [▮]를 찾아 보시오.

자화상 또는 지역 공동세를 그린 그림은 존재하지 않는다.

위 문장은 어느 곳에 가장 적합하겠는가? 네모 표기 [▮]를 클릭해 지문에 이 문장을 추가하시오.

(A) 1번

(B) 2번

(C) 3번

(D) 4번

해설 주어진 문장에 자화상이 언급되므로 인간의 모습에 대한 묘사는 좀처럼 나타나 있지 않다는 점을 언급하는 문장이 주어진 문장 주변에 있어야 한다. 2번 박스에 적합하지 않은 이유는 앞 문장에 드러난 '동물 이미지나 모티프'라는 키워드와 관련된 '동물에게 기울였던 것과 같은 세부 요소에 대한 주의력'이 제시되기 때문에 두 문장은 이어져 있다. 따라서 3번 박스에 넣는 것이 더욱 알맞다.

10. **설명:** 간략한 지문 요약에 필요한 도입 문장이 아래에 제공되어 있다. 지문에서 가장 중요한 개념들을 나타내는 세 가지 답안 선택지를 골라 요약 내용을 완성하시오. 일부 답안 선택지는 지문에 제시되지 않는 개념을 나타내거나 지문에서 중요하지 않은 개념들이므로 요약 내용에 속하지 않는다. **이 문제는 2점에 해당된다.**

구석기 시대 동굴 벽화는 여러 가지 이유로 인해 단순히 즐거움만을 위해 만들어지지 않았을 가능성이 매우 크다.

(A) 구석기 시대에 살았던 사람들은 여가 시간이 없었을 가능성이 매우 크며, 대부분의 그림들은 도달하기 어려운 곳에 위치해 있었다.

(B) 오락의 한 형태로서 예술에 대한 개념은 고대 그리스 시대가 되어서야 두드러지게 되었다.

(C) 미술가들은 사람을 그리지 않았는데, 그렇게 하는 것이 그림 속에 그 사람의 혼을 담게 될 것이라고 믿었기 때문이었다.

(D) 구석기 시대의 사냥이 지니는 중요성 및 동물에 초점을 맞춘 예술은 동굴 벽화가 사냥꾼에게 유익하도록 만들어졌다는 것을 나타낸다.

(E) 그 그림들은 오직 자연 세계의 작은 일부분만 표현했으며, 일부 그림들은 추상적이었다.

(F) 동굴 벽화의 현실적인 동물 묘사는 그 생물체들의 위험성과 관련해 사람들에게 주의를 주는 역할을 했다.

해설 (A)의 앞부분은 여러가지 근거를 제시하는 두 번째 문단의 내용을 통해, 뒷부분은 세 번째 문단 후반부를 통해 정답임을 확인할 수 있다. (D)의 경우, 네 번째 문단과 그 문단에 있는 강조된 문장을 토대로 답임을 확인할 수 있다. (E)의 경우, 그림의 대상 범위가 좁고, 추상적임을 나타내는 두 번째 문단과 세 번째 문단을 통해 답임을 유추할 수 있다.

어휘   prominence 두드러짐, 중요성, 명성 benefit ~에게 유익하
다, 이롭다 depiction 묘사 serve to do ~하는 역할을 하다

Passage 3

Answers

1. D	2. B	3. C	4. B	5. A	6. A	7. C	8. B	9. D	10. BDF

연극 관객

리허설이나 준비 과정은 현장 관객이 공연에 어떻게 [1](D)영향을 미칠지에 대해 조금도 배우에게 통제권을 제공해 주지 못한다. 리허설 중에 훌륭한 모습을 보였던 배우도 무대 공포증에 따른 망설임으로 에너지가 허비되어 실제 관객들 앞에서는 무너질 수 있다. 리허설 중에 활기도 없고 생기 없는 모습을 보였던 다른 연기자들은 현장 관객들로 인해 짜릿함을 얻을 수도 있다. 이러한 변화는 아서 밀러의 <세일즈맨의 죽음> 초연 당시 리 J. 콥이 주인공으로서 펼친 연기에서 나타났다. [2](B)연출가와 밀러 자신은 콥이 마치 다 죽어가는 사람인 것처럼 그 역할을 연기하겠다고 결정하면서 리허설 중에 아주 음울한 모습을 보인 것을 우려했다. 하지만 그 뒤로, 개막일 밤에, 콥은 번뜩였고, 막이 내린 후에도 몇 분 동안이나 관객들을 놀라움과 침묵 상태로 빠트렸다. 관객은 여러 가지 다른 모든 방식으로 공연에 영향을 미칠 수 있다. 심각한 역할을 코믹하게 바꿔버릴 수도 있고, 분장한 광대를 해당 공연 작품에서 엄숙한 이성의 목소리로 만들 수도 있다.

리허설을 마친 공연에서 완전히 벗어나는 상황은 틀림없이 개막일 밤에 기대되는 일이 아니며, 당연히 그것이 목표도 아니다. 잘 훈련되고 통솔된 배우는 드레스 리허설 중에 자신의 연기를 완벽하게 가다듬어 개막일 밤 공연에 전적으로 온전하고 바뀌지 않은 상태로 이식하는 것을 목표로 한다. 이것이 결국 그 모든 리허설의 목적이다. [3](C)한때, 배우들은 개막일 밤 공연에서의 폭발적인 감정 표현을 위해 감정과 열정을 아껴야 한다고 생각했지만, 이러한 관행은 현재 기피되고 있으며, 그러한 무모함은 아마추어임을 나타내는 명백한 표시이다. 배짱과 순간적인 영감에 의존하는 배우들은 분명 무대에서 동료 배우들을 오도가도 못하게 만들 것이다. 마찬가지로, 목적을 갖고 사람들 앞에서 연기하거나 관객의 웃음 또는 박수에 반응해 계획된 연기를 변경하는 것은 모든 진지한 연극에서 괄시를 받는다.

[4](B)강요되어야 하는 일은 아니지만, 배우의 연기는 그럼에도 불구하고 관객에 의해 영향을 받게 되는데, 이는 의심의 여지없이 리허설과 공연 사이에서 변화를 초래하며, 실제로, 이는 라이브 공연 극장이라는 이국적인 요리의 주된 재료와 같다. [6](A)하지만, 관객을 정확히 인식하는 배우는 [5](A)자동적으로 사람들의 반응에 따라 미묘하게 적응한다. 즉, 연기는 관찰을 통해 변화한다. 이는 공연들 사이에서, 심지어 셀 수 없이 많이 상연된 공연에서조차 차이를 만들어낸다. 그 변화는 작으면서 중요할 수 있다. 웃음이 가라앉을 시간을 주기 위해 배우가 잠깐 더 기다렸다가 대사를 전달하기도 하고, [6](A)미묘한 머리 기울임을 통해 대사를 강조하거나 인물의 숨겨진 특성을 암시하기도 한다.

뛰어난 배우는 또한 자신의 존재감을 통해 관객들에게 깊은 인상을 남기는데, 이는 연극의 세계에서 강력하면서도 정의하기 어려운 특성이다. 존재감은 등장 인물과 해당 배우를 모두 관객 앞에서 새로운 수준으로 끌어올릴 수 있다. 존재감을 통해, 배우는 무대와 관객을 모두 장악하며, 관객들의 관람에 영향을 받아 발전하게 된다. ■ 배우가 표현하고, 관객은 반응한다. ■ 양측은 서로 다르면서도 동일한 방식으로 교감한다. ■ 이는 배우의 말과 행동, 관객의 박수와 웃음, 심지어 침묵을 특별한 코드로 활용하여 서로 주고받는 독특한 의사소통이다. [9](D)■

반응 부재도 그에 못지않게 영감을 줄 수 있다. 무대 조명의 강렬함으로 인해 배우에게 보이진 않지만 움직임 없이 침묵하고 있는 관객은 무대 위의 배우들에게 있어 그만큼 인상적이거나 억압적일 수 있다. 모든 것이 표시이자 신호가 된다. [7](A)100명의 사람들이 훌쩍이지도 않고 주머니를 뒤적거리지도 않는 채로 가만히 앉아 있지만, 무대 위의 세상에 아무런 방해도 없이 온전하게 주의를 기울이게 만드는 일은 연극 배우의 원대한 야망이다. 관객의 낄낄거리는 웃음과 헐떡이는 숨소리는 배우에게 동일한 무게감으로 전달되는데, 즉 의사소통이 이뤄지고 배우는 반응한다. [8](D)경험 많은 배우는 이러한 신호에 반응해 낄낄대는 웃음을 시끌벅적한 큰 웃음소리로 바꾸거나 한숨을 혼이 담긴 감정 폭발로 바꾸기 위해 그 순간을 포착하는 방법을 알고 있다. [8](A)마찬가지로, 이 배우들은 분위기를 전환시켜 들썩이는 관객의 중심을 잡아주거나 졸린 사람들을 깨울 수도 있다. 이렇게 관객들의 생각을 읽는 일은 훈련을 통해 터득하는 것이 불가능하지는 않다 하더라도 어려운 일이며, 반드시 스스로 느껴야 하는, [8](C)즉 본능적인 부분이다. 이는 타이밍의 문제이며, 다른 모든 사교적 능력도 크게 다르지 않다. 그리고, 무대와 관련된 대부분의 측면들이 그러하듯, [8](B)경험이 최고의 선생님이다.

[어휘]

1. theater 연극, 극장 impact ~에 영향을 미치다 collapse 무너지다, 실패하다 dissipate 허비되다, 소멸되다 dull 활기 없는, 따분한 lackluster 생기 없는 electrify ~을 짜릿하게 만들다, 흥분하게 만들다 transformation 변화 production 제작(물), 작품 as if 마치 ~인 것처럼 with one foot in the grave 다 죽어가는 듯한, 오래 못 살 것 같은 dreary 음울한 light up (기쁨 등으로 인해) 밝아지다, 빛이 나다 sober 엄숙한, 진지한

2. radical departure from ~로부터 완전히 벗어남, ~에서의 완전한 이탈 disciplined 통제된, 규율에 따르는 transplant ~을 이식하다 intact 온전한, 원래대로인 practice 관행, 관례 shun ~을 피하다 recklessness 무모함 rely on ~에 의존하다 guts 배짱 stranded 오도가도 못하게 된, 꼼짝 못하게 된 scorn ~을 괄시하다, 경멸하다

3. regardless 그럼에도 불구하고, 여하튼 subtly 미묘하게 adjust to ~에 적응하다 evolve 발전하다, 진화하다 observation 관찰 distinction 차이 settle 안정되다 tilt 기울임 conceal ~을 숨기다 trait 특징

4. impress oneself on ~에게 깊은 인상을 남기다 quality 특성 command ~을 장악하다 thrive 발전하다, 번성하다

5. invisible to ~에게 보이지 않는 oppressive 억압적인 sniffle 훌쩍거리다 rummage 뒤적거리다 unimpeded 방해 받지 않는 chuckle 킬킬거리는 웃음 gasp 헐떡거림 transmit ~을 전하다, 전달하다 uproar 시끌벅적함, 떠들썩함 sigh 한숨 soul-expressing 혼이 담긴 gale 감정 폭발 turn the tide 분위기를 전환하다, 전세를 뒤엎다 restless 들썩이는, 가만히 있지 못하는 instinctual 본능적인 social grace 사교적 능력 aspect 측면, 양상

1. 지문의 단어 "impact"와 의미가 가장 가까운 것은 무엇인가?
(A) ~을 만들어내다
(B) ~을 손상시키다, ~에 피해를 입히다
(C) ~을 비난하다, 비판하다
(D) ~에 영향을 미치다

해설 impact(영향을 미치다)와 affect(영향을 미치다)는 동의어로 정답은 (D)이다.

2. 다음 중 어느 것이 <세일즈맨의 죽음> 개막일 밤에 있었던 주인공의 연기와 관련해 유추할 수 있는 내용인가?
(A) 그 연극의 해당 인물을 묘사하는 일반적인 방식이 되었다.
(B) 리허설에서 그 배우를 관찰했던 사람들을 놀라게 했다.
(C) 현장 관객들이 있는 리허설을 더 많이 했다면 향상되었을 것이다.
(D) 경험 많은 배우가 코믹한 역할을 진지한 것으로 바꿀 수 있다는 점을 보여주었다.

어휘 첫 번째 문단의 중간 부분에 등장하는 내용으로 음울한 모습을 보였던 리허설과 달리 개막일 밤에 몇 분 동안이나 관객들을 놀라움과 침묵의 상태로 빠트렸다는 점을 미뤄보아 정답은 (B)임을 확인할 수 있다.

어휘 portray ~을 묘사하다 observe ~을 관찰하다

3. 두 번째 문단에 따르면, 개막일 밤에 의도적으로 연기를 변경하는 배우는 무엇을 할 가능성이 가장 큰가?
(A) 맡은 역할 속에서 감정을 더 많이 표현하는 일
(B) 현장 관객들의 이목을 사로잡는 일
(C) 작품 속 다른 모든 사람을 거슬리게 하는 일
(D) 역할을 연기하는 새로운 방법을 발견하는 일

해설 문단 전체가 의도적으로 리허설을 벗어나는 행위 자체가 문제가 된다는 점을 명확하게 언급하기 때문에 정답은 (C)이다.

어휘 deliberately 의도적으로, 고의로 irritate ~을 거슬리게 하다, 짜증나게 하다

4. 다음 문장들 중 어느 것이 지문의 하이라이트 표기된 문장에 담긴 핵심 정보를 가장 잘 표현하는가? 오답 선택지는 중요한 방식으로 의미를 변경하거나 핵심 정보를 배제한다.

강요되어야 하는 일은 아니지만, 배우의 연기는 그럼에도 불구하고 관객에 의해 영향을 받게 되는데, 이는 의심의 여지 없이 리허설과 공연 사이에서 변화를 초래하며, 실제로, 이는 라이브 공연 극장이라는 이국적인 요리의 주된 재료와 같다.

(A) 연극 공연의 주된 매력은 배우가 특정 관객을 대상으로 역할을 변화시키는 방식이므로, 리허설은 절대로 현장 공연과 같지 않다.
(B) 설사 배우가 의식적으로 관객에게 연기를 맞추지 않는다 하더라도, 이러한 변화는 연극 속에서 항상 발생되므로 연습과 달라질 것이다.
(C) 무엇이 됐든, 관객들은 배우가 리허설과 공연 사이에서 연기하는 방식을 변화시키며, 이는 연극 공연 속에서 예상되는 일이다.
(D) 관객들이 마치 리허설을 보고 있는 것처럼 행동해야 배우들이 각자의 역할을 연습한 방식이 공연에서 면밀하게 지켜질 것이다.

해설 주어진 문장의 핵심인 '배우의 연기가 관객의 영향을 반드시 받게 되어 리허설과 실제 공연에서 변화가 있다'는 내용이 제대로 반영된 (B)가 정답이다. 관객은 연기의 변화에 영향을 주는 것이고 연기의 변화 주체는 배우이기에, 변화의 주체를 관객으로 설명한 (C)는 오답이다. (A)는 핵심 내용이 누락되어 있고, (D)는 언급되지 않은 내용이 들어가 있다.

어휘 consciously 의식적으로 adapt A to B A를 B에 맞추다, 적응시키다 no matter what 무엇이 됐든 adhere to ~을 준수하다, 지키다

5. 지문 단어 "automatically"와 의미가 가장 가까운 것은 무엇인가?

    (A) 자연적으로

    (B) 기계적으로

    (C) 엄격하게

    (D) 자주, 빈번히

해설 automatically(자동적으로, 무의식적으로)와 naturally(자연적으로)는 유의어로 정답은 (A)이다.

6. 글쓴이는 왜 지문에서 "미묘한 머리 기울임"을 언급하는가?

    (A) 배우가 공연 중에 만들어 낼 수도 있는 변화를 말하기 위해

    (B) 배우들이 관객들 앞에서 흔히 저지르는 실수를 강조하기 위해

    (C) 관객들이 배우의 움직임을 어떻게 해석할 수 있는지 설명하기 위해

    (D) 경험 많은 배우가 자신이 맡은 인물을 발전시킬 수 있는 방식을 나타내기 위해

해설 문단의 중간을 보면, 관객을 정확히 인식하는 배우가 사람들의 반응에 따라 미묘하게 적응하고 차이를 만들어낸다는 점을 언급하고 있다. 이러한 내용의 구체적인 예시 중 하나가 미묘한 머리 기울임이기 때문에 정답은 (A)이다.

어휘 highlight ~을 강조하다, 집중 조명하다 interpret ~을 해석하다

7. 다섯 번째 문단에 따르면, 침묵을 지키는 관객들은 무엇을 나타내는가?

    (A) 관객들이 배우의 연기에 혼란스러워하는 것이다.

    (B) 관객들이 배우에게 지장을 주고 싶어하지 않는다.

    (C) 배우가 관객들로부터 온전한 주목을 받고 있다.

    (D) 배우가 관객들의 반응을 촉발하지 못했다.

해설 문단의 초반부를 보면, 침묵은 '인상적이거나 억압적'일 수 있는데, '무대 위의 세상에 아무런 방해도 없이 온전하게 주의를 기울이게 만드는 일'은 연극 배우의 야망이라는 점을 토대로 침묵은 관객들의 주목을 의미한다는 점을 유추할 수 있다. 그러므로 정답은 (C)이다.

어휘 distract ~에게 지장을 주다, ~을 방해하다 fail to do ~하지 못하다 trigger ~을 촉발하다

8. 다섯 번째 문단에서, 관객들의 마음을 읽는 배우의 능력과 관련해 언급되지 않은 것은 무엇인가?

    (A) 관객들의 기분을 변화시킬 수 있다.

    (B) 경험 많은 선생님을 통해 배우는 것이다.

    (C) 배우의 본능에 따라 좌우된다.

    (D) 관객들의 반응을 향상시킬 수 있다.

해설 (B)의 '경험 많은 선생님'은 해당 문단 마지막 문장에 등장하는 키워드를 활용한 함정이며, '경험이 최고의 선생님이다'라고 말하는 마지막 부분과 다른 의미를 지닌 (B)가 정답이다.

어휘 depend on ~에 좌우되다, ~에 달려 있다 instinct 본능 enhance ~을 향상시키다, 강화하다

9. 다음 문장이 지문에 추가될 수 있는 곳을 나타내는 네 개의 네모 표기 [■]를 찾아 보시오.

    이렇게 하면, 공연은 오직 무대에서 객석에 전달하기만 하는 일방적인 관계가 되지 않는다.

    위 문장은 어느 곳에 가장 적합하겠는가? 네모 표기[■]를 클릭해 지문에 이 문장을 추가하시오.

    (A) 1번

    (B) 2번

    (C) 3번

    (D) 4번

해설 문단의 흐름을 보면 존재감에 대한 정의와 관련해 언급한 다음, 배우의 표현과 관객의 반응을 통한 교감이 특별한 의사소통임을 설명하고 있다. 다시 말해 공연이라는 것은 일방적인 방식이 아니라는 점을 토대로 주어진 문장이 문단의 총 정리를 해주고 있다는 점을 파악할 수 있다. 그러므로 4번째 박스에 넣는 것이 알맞다.

어휘 one-sided relationship 일방적인 관계 house 객석

10. **설명:** 간략한 지문 요약에 필요한 도입 문장이 아래에 제공되어 있다. 지문에서 가장 중요한 개념들을 나타내는 세 가지 답안 선택지를 골라 요약 내용을 완성하시오. 일부 답안 선택지는 지문에 제시되지 않는 개념을 나타내거나 지문에서 중요하지 않은 개념들이므로 요약 내용에 속하지 않는다. **이 문제는 2점에 해당된다.**

현장 연극 공연 중에 배우들과 관객들 사이에 특별한 관계가 존재한다.

    (A) 숙련된 연기자는 심각한 역할을 코믹하게 만든다 하더라도 관객들을 위해 자신의 연기를 변화시킨다.

    (B) 숙련된 배우는 관객의 반응에 따라 미묘한 변화를 만들어내고 무대 위에서 존재감을 보여주는 방법을 알고 있다.

    (C) 아마추어 배우는 관객들에게서 더 많은 웃음을 이끌어내기 위해 대사 전달을 변경하는 방법을 쉽게 배운다.

    (D) 관객들은 눈에 보이는 것, 웃음, 박수, 그리고 심지어 침묵까지 포함한 다양한 방법을 통해 배우들과 의사소통한다.

    (E) 무례한 관객들은 공연에 지장을 주며, 배우에게 무대에서 분노를 더 많이 표출하도록 초래한다.

    (F) 공연이 리허설과 일치해야 하기는 하지만, 배우들에게 현장 관객들 앞에서 펼쳐지는 공연에 대해 완전히 대비하게

해주지는 못한다.

해설   세 번째 문단에서 (B)에 관련된 내용을 정확히 기술하고 있다. (D)는 네 번째 문단과 다섯 번째 분단에서 파악할 수 있는 내용으로 궁극적으로 관객과 배우가 상호 소통한다는 점을 명확하게 설명해주고 있다. (F)의 경우, 두 번째 문단과 세 번째 문단에서 리허설의 의의와 실제 공연에서 발생하는 일의 설명을 포괄하고 있는 선택지로 볼 수 있다.

어휘   demonstrate ~을 보여주다, 입증하다 draw out A from B B에게서 A를 이끌어내다 disrespectful 무례한 cause A to do A에게 ~하도록 초래하다, ~하게 만들다

Passage 1

열대 우림의 토양 특성

혹자는 울창한 초목과 다양한 서식 동물이 존재하는 우림이 처음부터 영양분이 풍부한 토양에 의해 지탱될 것으로 생각할 수도 있다. 어쨌든, 대부분의 경우에 있어 건강한 식물은 건강한 토양을 필요로 한다. 하지만, 다양한 토양이 우림을 구성한다 하더라도, 모든 토양은 영양분이 부족하다. ¹⁽ᴰ⁾, ²⁽ᴰ⁾우림 지역에 지속적으로 내리는 비는 침출이라고 알려진 과정을 통해 토양의 영양분을 쓸려 보낸다. 침출에 따른 결과로, 열대 우림의 토양은 무기물 함량이 매우 낮아져, 초원의 토양과 극명한 차이를 보이게 된다. ²⁽ᴮ⁾게다가, 열대 우림의 토양은 알루미늄을 제외한, 무기물 이온을 결합시키는 데 저항력이 있는 점토를 함유하는데, 알루미늄은 대부분의 열대 지역 토양에서 가장 보편적인 무기물이다. 이 성분은 식물이 필요로 하는 것이 아니며, 실제로는, 그 양이 많으면 유독할 수 있다. 알루미늄의 존재는 식물에게 대단히 중요한 원소인 인의 존재를 감소시키기도 한다.

초원 및 온대 우림의 토양에 비해, 열대 우림의 토양은 부엽토, 즉 유기물도 더 적게 함유하고 있다. 열대 지역의 끊임없이 지속되는 습기와 높은 온도는 토양 속에서 부엽토를 형성하는 화합물을 분해하는 미생물의 성장을 촉진시킨다. 이 화합물은 일반적으로 토양 속의 점토를 개선시켜, 그것이 풀어지게 만들고, 물을 함유하면서 무기질 영양분을 ³⁽ᴬ⁾끌어들이는 데 도움을 준다. 이러한 도움이 없다면, 열대 우림의 토양 속에 들어 있는 점토는 식물을 지탱하는 데 훨씬 덜 도움이 되는데, 점토가 굳으면서, 식물 뿌리가 그 속을 관통하지 못하게 되고, 토양 속 수분 부족이 건조기 중에 식물을 위협하게 되기 때문이다. 이 무기질 불균형 문제는 점토의 색을 통해 쉽게 관찰할 수 있다. 유기물의 어두운 색조가 부족한 경우, 그 토양은 대신 높은 산화철 함유량으로 인한 적갈색이나 알루미늄으로 인한 황색을 띠게 된다. ⁴⁽ᴮ⁾그 토양은 또한 건조해지면 암석처럼 단단하게 변하기도 한다. 이런 이유로 인해, 역사적으로 고대의 건설 공사와 도로 공사에 성공적으로 이용된 바 있다.

그럼에도 불구하고 우림은 지구상에서 몇몇 가장 풍부한 생태계를 지탱하는데, 어떻게 영양분이 고갈된 토양으로 그럴 수 있는 것일까? ⁵⁽ᴰ⁾토양에 의존하는 대신, 우림은 생물량을 통해 필수 영양분과 무기질을 재활용한다. 대부분의 생물량이 지하에 있는 초원과 달리, 열대 우림의 생물량은 지상에, 즉 나무를 비롯해 숲의 우거진 윗부분에 존재한다. ⁹⁽ᴬ⁾■ 그곳의 삼림 폐기물은 심지어 효율적인 박테리아 분해자 및 균류 분해자에 의해 완전히 분해되기 전에는 좀처럼 지표면에 이르지도 못한다. 숲의 우거진 윗부분보다 밑에 있는 얕은 식물들은 부패하는 생물량에 함유된 무기물을 먹고 살며, 세포 조직 속에 저장한다. ■ 그런 다음, 그 무기물은 복잡한 균근 조직망을 통해 운반되고 공유되며, 그 과정에서 뿌리가 영양분을 흡수하고 전달하며 분산시키는 데 있어 균류가 도움을 준다. ■ 또한, 균류는 식물들이 크게 필요로 하는 인 같이 식물이 흡수할 수 없는 영양분을 흡수하도록 돕기도 한다. ■ ⁵⁽ᴰ⁾균류와 박테리아, 그리고 다른 분해자들은 열대 우림을 지속시키는 영양분과 무기물의 지속적인 재활용에 있어 촉진제의 역할을 한다.

우림은 또한 폐쇄적인 영양분 체계를 발전시켜 침출을 통한 영양분 손실을 방지하도록 진화하기도 했다. ⁶⁽ᶜ⁾이러한 시스템 하에서, 무기물은 생물체들 사이에서 주변의 토양으로 많이 누출되지 않은 채로 전달된다. ⁶⁽ᴰ⁾이 폐쇄적인 체계 내에서 무기물을 유지함으로써, 우림은 식물 성장을 촉진하고 ⁶⁽ᴬ⁾전체적인 무기물 손실을 예방할 수 있다. 이는 우림이 침출에 대응하기 위해 거치게 되는 명백한 적응 방식이다. 토양이 비옥한 우림의 영양분 체계는 개방적이며, 초원에서 볼 수 있는 것과 더 유사하다. 하지만, 토양의 수준이 최악인 곳에서는, 그 체계가 폐쇄적이므로 침출에 대비해 방어적이다.

⁷⁽ᴮ⁾질소 또한 우림 지역 식물에게 극도로 중요하며, 대기 중에 많이 있기는 하지만, 식물이 흡수하기 위해서는 분자 상태로 결합되어 있어야 한다. 여기서, 우림 지역 식물은 질소를 포착해 식물에게 전해주는 특별한 박테리아의 도움을 다시 한번 받는다. 많은 우림 식물 종이 속하는 콩과 식물은 뿌리에 ⁸⁽ᴮ⁾잠복하면서 질소를 마련해주는 박테리아와 공존하는 것으로 알려져 있다. 소철 같은 다른 식물 종은 이 특별한 박테리아를

끌어들이기 위해 지상으로 뿌리가 자라도록 적응해왔다. 지상에서, 이 뿌리는 햇빛에 노출되는데, 이는 그 박테리아가 자라는 데 필요한 것이다. 질소를 마련해주는 박테리아의 성장을 도움으로써, 이 식물은 질소를 얻어 무성해질 수 있게 된다.

용어 설명 생물량: 특정 시기에 특정 지역이니 생태계에 살고 있는 생물체의 양
균근 조직망: 개별 식물들을 서로 연결하고, 물과 영양분, 그리고 무기질을 운반하는 지하 균류 체계

[어휘]
1. inhabitant 서식 동물 from the ground up 처음부터, 완전히 nutrient-rich 영양분이 풍부한 make up ~을 구성하다 leaching 침출(너무 많은 물이 토양의 중요한 영양분을 쓸려 보내 손실시키는 것) resistant to ~에 저항력이 있는 save for ~을 제외하고 phosphorus 인
2. humus 부엽토(풀이나 낙엽, 가지 등이 미생물에 의해 분해되어 생긴 흙) microbes 미생물 decompose ~을 분해하다 compounds 화합물 conducive to ~에 도움이 되는 penetrate ~을 관통하다 dry spell 건조기 hue 색조 iron-oxide 산화철
3. nutrient-depleted 영양분이 고갈된 biomass 생물량 canopy 숲의 우거진 윗부분 break down ~을 분해하다 fungal 균류의 decaying 부패하는 tissue 세포 조직 mycorrhizal network 균근 조직망 disperse ~을 분산시키다 facilitator 촉진제 sustain ~을 지속하다, 지탱하다
4. combat ~을 방지하다 adaptation 적응 akin to ~와 유사한 guarded 방어적인
5. nitrogen 질소 molecule 분자 legume family 콩과 harbor 잠복하다, 살다

1. 다음 중 어느 것이 첫 번째 문단에서 초원과 관련해 유추할 수 있는 내용인가?
(A) 아주 다양한 토양 종류로 구성되어 있다.
(B) 시냇물에서 영양분을 얻는 토양이 있다.
(C) 우림에 비해 드물게 자라는 식물을 지탱한다.
(D) 우림만큼 많은 강우량을 경험하지 않는다.

해설 초원의 토양과 극명한 차이를 보여주는 우림 지역의 토양은 지속적으로 내리는 비로 인한 침출과 영양분의 차이라는 것을 토대로 정답이 (D)임을 유추할 수 있다.

2. 첫 번째 문단에 따르면, 열대 우림 지역의 토양은 왜 상대적으로 무기물 함유량이 적은가? 두 개의 답변을 고르시오.
(A) 우림의 식물 밀도는 토양으로부터 모든 무기물을 고갈시킨다.
(B) 우림 지역 토양의 점토는 무기물 이온을 효과적으로 결합하지 못한다.
(C) 우림 지역 내에서 흐르는 시냇물은 토양을 무기물로 보충해주지 못한다.
(D) 폭우가 우림 지역 토양에서 무기물을 쓸려 보낸다.

해설 (B)의 경우 문단의 중간 이후 부분에서 등장하는 '무기물 이온을 결합시키는 데 저항력이 있는 점토를 함유한다'는 내용을 근거로 삼을 수 있다. (D)의 경우 문단 상단 부분에 '침출의 결과로 영양분이 쓸려 보내지면서 무기물 함량이 낮아진다'라는 내용을 통해 확인할 수 있다.

어휘 density 밀도 drain ~을 고갈시키다, 빠져 나가게 하다 replenish A with B A를 B로 보충하다, 다시 채우다

3. 지문의 단어 "draw"와 의미가 가장 가까운 것은 무엇인가?
(A) ~을 끌어들이다

(B) ~을 에워싸다
(C) ~을 설명하다, 분명히 보여주다
(D) ~에 접근하다

해설 draw(끌어들이다)와 attract(끌어들이다)는 동의어로 정답은 (A)이다.

4. 두 번째 문단에서, 글쓴이는 왜 "고대의 건설 공사와 도로 공사"를 언급하는가?
(A) 한 가지 재료의 여러 용도에 대한 예시를 제공하기 위해
(B) 한 가지 재료의 내구성을 입증하기 위해
(C) 두 가지 재료의 특성을 대조하기 위해
(D) 한 가지 재료가 과거에 어떻게 쓰였는지 설명하기 위해

해설 무기질 불균형을 시작으로, 토양이 건조해지면 암석처럼 변한다는 내용을 기반으로 건설과 도로에 쓰일 정도로 내구성이 강하다는 점을 확인할 수 있다. 그러므로 정답은 (B)이다.

어휘 demonstrate ~을 입증하다 durability 내구성 contrast ~을 대조하다

5. 세 번째 문단에 따르면, 우림 지역의 식물은 무엇을 통해 영양분을 모으는가?
(A) 지하에 저장되어 있는 유기물
(B) 토양 내에 있는 박테리아의 도움
(C) 균류 생물체의 흡수
(D) 삼림 생물량의 지속적인 재활용

해설 해당 문단의 두 번째 문장에서 '우림은 생물량을 통해 필수 영양분과 무기질을 재활용한다'라는 정답 근거를 확인할 수 있고, 문단의 마지막 문장도 동일한 정보를 제공하므로 정답은 (D)이다.

6. 다음 중 폐쇄적인 영양분 체계의 이점으로 네 번째 문단에서 언급되지 않은 것은 무엇인가?

(A) 무기물 손실의 방지

(B) 좋지 못한 토양 종류의 비옥화

(C) 생물체들 사이에서의 영양분 공유

(D) 건강한 식물 성장을 지탱

해설 문단 전체에서 '주변의 토양으로 누출되지 않는 무기물', '식물 성장을 촉진하고 전체적인 무기물 손실을 예방', 그리고 '영양분 체계가 개방적이다'라는 내용을 확인할 수 있으나, 좋지 않은 토양 종류의 비옥화는 언급된 적이 없다. 정답은 (B)이다.

7. 다음 문장들 중 어느 것이 지문의 하이라이트 표기된 문장에 담긴 핵심 정보를 가장 잘 표현하는가? 오답 선택지는 중요한 방식으로 의미를 변경하거나 핵심 정보를 배제한다.

질소 또한 우림 지역 식물에게 극도로 중요하며, 대기 중에 많이 있기는 하지만, 식물이 흡수하기 위해서는 분자 상태로 결합되어 있어야 한다.

(A) 식물들은 대기의 건강을 유지하기 위해 질소를 다른 원소들과 결합해야 한다.

(B) 공기 중에 이용 가능한 질소가 많기는 하지만, 식물들은 그것이 화합물의 일부가 아니라면 이용할 수 없다.

(C) 우림 지역에 질소가 풍부하며, 식물들은 아주 다양한 특별한 화학 혼합물을 만들기 위해 그것을 이용한다.

(D) 질소는 대기 중에 오직 분자의 형태로만 존재하며, 식물들은 오직 그것이 다른 원소들과 분리되어 있는 경우에만 이용할 수 있다.

해설 질소가 대기 중에 많이 있지만 '흡수를 위해 분자 상태로 결합되어 있어야 한다'는 내용이(to be bound in molecules) 화합물의 일부로 표현된(part of a compound) (B)가 정답이다.

어휘 access ~을 이용하다   a vast array of 아주 다양한
isolate ~을 분리하다

8. 지문의 단어 "harbor"와 의미가 가장 가까운 것은 무엇인가?

(A) 억제하다, 보류하다

(B) 숨다, 피하다

(C) 통제하다, 조절하다

(D) 쫓아내다

해설 harbor(잠복하다, 살다)와 shelter(숨다, 피하다)는 유의어로 정답은 (B)이다.

9. 다음 문장이 지문에 추가될 수 있는 곳을 나타내는 네 개의 [■]를 찾아 보시오.

따라서, 열대 우림의 두터운 표토는 대부분 떨어진 나뭇가지

와 낙엽, 죽은 동물 같이 부패하는 물체로 구성된다.

위 문장은 어느 곳에 가장 적합하겠는가? 네모 표기[■]를 클릭해 지문에 이 문장을 추가하시오.

(A) 1번

(B) 2번

(C) 3번

(D) 4번

해설 해당 문단의 세 번째 문장을 보면, '생물량이 지하에 있는 초원과 달리 열대 우림의 생물량은 지상에, 숲의 우거신 윗부분에 존재한다'는 내용이 있는데, 이는 주어진 문장과 자연스럽게 이어지는 내용이다. 1번 박스 뒤에는 주어진 문장의 '부패하는 물체'와 상응하는 '삼림 폐기물'이라는 키워드가 있다. 그러므로 정답은 (A)이다.

10. **설명:** 간략한 지문 요약에 필요한 도입 문장이 아래에 제공되어 있다. 지문에서 가장 중요한 개념들을 나타내는 세 가지 답안 선택지를 골라 요약 내용을 완성하시오. 일부 답안 선택지는 지문에 제시되지 않는 개념을 나타내거나 지문에서 중요하지 않은 개념들이므로 요약 내용에 속하지 않는다. **이 문제는 2점에 해당된다.**

우림은 여러 가지 방식으로 토양의 낮은 영양분 함유량에 적응해왔다.

(A) 균류의 연결 체계가 우림 전역에서 부패한 생물량으로부터 영양분을 모으고 전달해준다.

(B) 토양 속에 모인 유기물인 부엽토는 식물을 지탱하는 데 있어 점토를 더욱 적합하게 만들어준다.

(C) 우림의 식물 종은 특정 영양분을 모을 수 있는 박테리아와 유익한 관계를 형성하도록 적응해왔다.

(D) 우림은 토양 내의 영양분 손실을 방지하기 위해 폐쇄적인 영양분 체계를 발전시켜왔다.

(E) 영양분은 물 순환을 통해 지속적으로 시내와 강에서 우림 지역의 토양으로 운반된다.

(F) 우림 지역 토양의 영양분 대부분은 폭우로 인해 침출이라고 알려진 과정을 거치면서 손실된다.

해설 두 번째 문단과 세 번째 문단의 내용을 토대로 우림이 부패한 생물량으로부터 영양분을 모은다는 점과, 박테리아와의 관계 형성에 대한 이야기를 언급하고 있으므로 (A)와 (C)를 빠르게 답으로 선택한다. 그리고 (D)의 경우, 네 번째 문단의 내용을 토대로 우림은 토양 내 영양분 손실 방지를 위해 폐쇄적인 영양분 체계를 발전시켰다는 것을 알 수 있다.

어휘 water cycle 물 순환

Passage 2

빙하의 영향

빙하는 눈이 녹는 양보다 내리는 양이 더 많은 곳에서 축적되어 서서히 움직이는 엄청난 크기의 얼음 덩어리이다. 빙하는 비록 느리기는 하지만 지속적으로 움직이는 상태이기 때문에 "얼음의 강"이라고 일컫는다. 빙하에는 고산 빙하와 대륙 빙하, 두 가지 종류가 있다. 고산 빙하는 산등성이에서 형성되어 골짜기들을 따라 자리잡게 되며, 대륙 빙하는 평지에서 중심부를 이루는 큰 반구 모양의 얼음이 바깥쪽으로 확산되면서 형성된다. ■ 하지만, 두 가지 종류 모두 거의 유사한 방식으로 형성된다. ⁹⁽ᴮ⁾ ■ ¹⁽ᴬ⁾모든 눈은 6각형의 결정체로 내리며, 지면에 닿는 즉시, 결정체들 사이에서 발생되는 공기 배출로 인해 더 작고 더 밀도 높은 알갱이로 압축된 상태가 된다. ■ ¹⁽ᴰ⁾더 많은 공기가 배출됨에 따라, 눈 알갱이는 더욱 압축되어 더 밀도 높은 상태로 변한다. ■ 그 알갱이들이 녹았다가 다시 얼면서 결국 만년설이 되는데, 이는 눈송이와 얼음 사이에 해당되는 눈의 결정화 중간 단계이다. 만년설은 마치 단단히 다져진 설탕처럼 가볍고 가루 같은 상태이지만, 얼음처럼 단단하다. 더 많은 시간과 압력, 그리고 결빙 과정이 이어지면, 훨씬 더 많은 공기가 빠져나오면서 만년설 과립자들이 하나로 고착되어 더 큰 순수한 푸른 빛의 빙하 결정체를 이루게 된다. ¹⁽ᴮ⁾그 얼어붙은 집합체가 약 30미터의 두께로 두꺼워지면 정식으로 빙하가 되며, 그 눈과 얼음, 그리고 만년설의 전체 무게로 인해 가장 아래쪽의 결정체들은 가소성, 즉 액체 같은 밀도에 ²⁽ᴮ⁾이르게 된다. 맨 아래 부분이 이렇게 미끌미끌한 빙하는 중심부의 덩어리에서 바깥쪽으로 또는 아래쪽으로 흘러가기 시작한다.

빙하는 눈이 추가되고 해빙수가 빠져나가는 일종의 입출력 시스템을 통해 지속적인 발전 상태를 유지한다. 강수량 및 기온이 이러한 균형에 영향을 미치는 두 가지 주된 기후적 요소이다. ³⁽ᴬ⁾빙하는 용해와 증발, 그리고 해안 빙하의 경우에 있어, 빙하 분리(빙하에서 큰 덩어리들이 떨어져 나와 바다나 호수로 흘러 들어가는 것)를 통해 질량 손실을 되돌릴 정도로 충분한 눈이 내리는 경우에만 커질 수 있다. 더 따뜻한 계절 및 강설량 감소로 인해 빙하가 수축되거나 후퇴할 수 있으며, 이는 지역 생태계와 경제, 그리고 심지어 전 세계의 지질에 급격한 영향을 미칠 수 있다. ⁴⁽ᶜ⁾빙하는 그 온도에 따라 추가적으로 분류될 수 있으며, 일정한 용해점에서 존재하면서 얼음과 흐르는 물이 공존하는 결과를 낳는 온빙하가 있다. 이 빙하는 극빙하, 또는 항상 영하의 수준에 머물러 있는 빙하보다 더 빠르게 움직인다.

바다나 강과 마찬가지로, 빙하도 지구 물 순환의 일부분이다. ⁵⁽ᴬ⁾오직 바다만 빙하보다 더 많은 물을 포함하고 있고, 빙하는 그 얼음 속에 지구의 물 중 약 2퍼센트를 보유하고 있지만, 이 수치가 오해의 소지가 있는 이유는 빙하가 지구상의 담수를 80퍼센트 넘게 포함하고 있기 때문이다. ⁶⁽ᴬ⁾남극 대륙 자체만해도 전 세계의 담수 중에서 엄청난 양을 보유하고 있고, 그 양이 하도 많아서, 가설적으로 그것이 녹는다면, 전 세계의 해수면 높이는 격변 수준에 해당되는 60미터나 높아질 것이다. 섬들은 물 속에 잠기게 될 것이며, 해안 국가들은 크게 줄어들 것이다. 반대로, 지구가 또 다른 빙하 시대를 겪게 된다면, 물이 얼면서 해수면 높이는 낮아질 것이다. 마지막 빙하 시대의 해수면 높이는 현재 수준에 비해 거의 120미터나 더 낮았다.

빙하가 서서히 움직이기는 하지만(평균적으로 하루에 약 25센티미터), 믿을 수 없을 정도로 강력하며, 곳곳으로 흘러 다니면서 육지의 형태에 영향을 미친다. 마치 불도저처럼, 숲 전체를 없애고 산을 이동시키면서, 길을 가로막는 모든 육지의 특징을 ⁷⁽ᴮ⁾없애버린다. 아래에 놓여 있는 땅을 침식시키면서, 토양과 암석, 그리고 점토를 아주 먼 거리까지 밀어 보내기도 한다. 빙하에 의해 옮겨지는 암석과 흙은 빙하 표석이라고 부른다. 표석은 자리잡은 곳의 풍경과 좀처럼 어울리지 않기 때문에 쉽게 알아볼 수 있다. 빙하가 후퇴하고 나면, 아마 수십만 년 후에는, 완전히 새로운 산맥과 깊은 호수, 그리고 어마어마한 협곡을 남겨놓게 될 것이다. 빙하는 서서히, 하지만 강력하게 지구의 형태에 영향을 미친다.

지구의 광범위한 시대들을 통틀어 볼 때, 빙하는 드문 존재이다. ⁸⁽ᶜ⁾하지만, 현대에는, 빙하가 지구 육지 표면의 거의 10퍼센트를 덮고 있다. 남극 대륙과 그린란드는 거대한 대륙 빙하로 덮여 있으며, 고산 빙하는 호주를 제외한 모든 대륙에 존재한다. 최신세(홍적세)에 있었던 가장 최근의 빙하 시대 중에, 지구의 3분의 1이 얼음 속 수천 미터 아래에 숨겨졌다. 규모가 커지고 변화하면서, 빙하는 지속적으로 지구의 표면에 영향을 미칠 것이다.

[어휘]
1. accumulate 축적되다 be referred to as ~라고 일컬어지다 alpine glaciers 고산 빙하 ice sheet 대륙 빙하 carve down through ~을 따

라 자리잡다 **hexagonal** 6각형의 **be forced out** 강제 배출되다 **firm** 만년설 **granule** 과립자 **aggregate** 집합(체) **plasticity** 가소성(외부적 요인에 의해 변화된 물체가 그 요인이 없어져도 원래의 형태로 돌아오지 않는 성질) **consistency** 농도, 밀도 **slick** 미끄러운

2. **subtract** 빠지다 **precipitation** 강수(량) **regain** ~을 되돌리다 **evaporation** 증발 **calving** 빙하 분리 **shrink** 수축되다 **retreat** 후퇴하다 **classify** ~을 분류하다 **temperate** 온난한, 온화한 **melting point** 용해점, 녹는 점 **below the freezing point** 영하의, 빙점 이하의

3. **hydrologic cycle** 물 순환 **Antarctica** 남극 대륙 **so much so that** (앞서 언급된 것에 대해) 하도 그래서 ~하다 **hypothetically** 가설적으로 **cataclysmic** 격변하는 (수준의) **submerge** ~을 물 속에 가라앉히다

4. **obliterate** ~을 흔적도 없이 없애다 **erode** ~을 침식시키다 **displace** ~을 옮겨 놓다 **erratic** 표석(빙하에 의해 운반되었다가 빙하가 녹은 후에 그대로 남은 암석)

5. **far-reaching** 광범위한 **Pleistocene** 최신세, 홍적세(지질 시대 중 신생대 제4기의 전반에 해당되는 세) **epoch** 시대, 세

---

1. 첫 번째 문단에 따르면, 다음 중 어느 것이 빙하 형성 과정의 일부에 해당되지 않는가?
(A) 눈 결정체들이 내려와 더 작은 알갱이로 압축된 상태가 된다.
(B) 가장 낮은 부분이 액체와 유사한 상태가 될 때까지 얼음이 두터워진다.
(C) 6각형의 눈 결정체들이 서로 맞물려 빙하가 된다.
(D) 공기가 눈 결정체들 사이에서 이탈해, 눈을 만년설로 바꾼다.

해설 해당 문단의 중간에 보면, '결정체들 사이에서 발생하는 공기 배출로 인해 더 작고 밀도 높은 알갱이가 된다는 점'을 기반으로 (A)를 소거한다. (D)는 공기 배출 과정을 통해 만년설이 된다는 점이 언급되어 있으므로 소거한다. (B)의 경우 문단의 하단 부분에서 '액체와 같은 밀도'에 이른다는 점을 토대로 소거한다. 그러므로 정답은 (C)이다.

어휘 **interlock** 서로 맞물리다 **depart from** ~에서 이탈하다

2. 지문의 단어 "attain"과 의미가 가장 가까운 것은 무엇인가?
(A) ~을 유지하다
(B) ~을 이루다, 달성하다
(C) ~을 대체하다
(D) ~을 변형시키다

해설 attain(이르다, 이루다, 달하다)과 achieve(달성하다)는 유의어로 정답은 (B)이다.

3. 두 번째 문단은 충분한 강설량이 무엇에 의해 빙하에 영향을 미친다고 주장하는가?
(A) 용해, 증발 그리고 분리로 인한 얼음의 손실을 상쇄함으로써
(B) 빙하 근처의 땅을 매끈하게 만듦으로써
(C) 빙하 분리로 이어지는 별도의 무게를 추가함으로써
(D) 얼음이 용해점에 도달하지 못하게 막음으로써

해설 지문의 regain the mass loss가 offsetting losses of ice로 패러프레이징된 (A)가 정답이다.

어휘 **offset** ~을 상쇄하다

4. 두 번째 문단에 따르면, 다음 중 어느 것이 빠르게 움직이는 빙하와 관련해 사실인가?
(A) 극빙하는 빠르게 곳곳으로 옮겨 다닐 육지가 충분하지 않다.
(B) 빠르게 움직이는 빙하는 빙하 분리를 겪는 빈도가 더 높다.
(C) 기후가 더 따뜻하면 더 빠른 속도로 움직이는 빙하가 나타난다.
(D) 더 작은 빙하는 더 큰 것들보다 더 빠르게 움직인다.

해설 해당 문단의 중간 부분에 따뜻한 계절이 영향을 미칠 수 있다는 점을 언급한 뒤, 마지막 두 문장에서 온빙하가 극빙하보다 더욱 빠르게 움직인다는 점을 설명하기 때문에 정답은 (C)이다.

5. 다음 문장들 중 어느 것이 지문의 하이라이트 표기된 문장에 담긴 핵심 정보를 가장 잘 표현하는가? 오답 선택지는 중요한 방식으로 의미를 변경하거나 핵심 정보를 배제한다.

오직 바다만 빙하보다 더 많은 물을 포함하고 있고, 빙하는 그 얼음 속에 지구의 물 중 약 2퍼센트를 보유하고 있지만, 이 수치가 오해의 소지가 있는 이유는 빙하가 지구상의 담수를 80퍼센트 넘게 포함하고 있기 때문이다.

(A) 빙하가 지구의 물 중 오직 2퍼센트만 포함하고 있다는 것은 빙하에 지구의 담수 대부분이 들어 있기 때문에 잘못 생각할 수 있는 부분이다.
(B) 지구의 물 중 80퍼센트가 바다에 존재하는 반면, 2퍼센트는 빙하 속에서 담수로 존재할 수 있다.
(C) 바다는 지구의 물 대부분의 근거지로, 빙하에 담긴 물의 80퍼센트는 담수 공급원으로서 이용될 수 있다.
(D) 바다의 물 중 2퍼센트가 빙하 속에 담겨 있지만, 그 80퍼센트가 지구의 담수를 구성한다.

해설 제시된 문장에서 '오해의 소지가 있는' (misleading)이라는 키워드에만 집중해도 정답은 (A) 밖에 없다는 사실을 확인할 수 있다. 그리고 세부사항을 보면, 현재 지구상의 담수 대부분을 차지하고 있다는 말이 80%와 동일한 맥락이기에 정답임을 확신할 수 있다. 참고로, (A)의 holding은 명사가 아닌 hold의 동명사이다.

어휘 **deceiving** 잘못 생각하게 만드는, 속이는 **a vast majority of** 대부분의, 대다수의 **make up** ~을 구성하다

6. 세 번째 문단에서, 글쓴이는 왜 남극 대륙의 빙하가 녹을 경우에 일어날 수 있는 일을 언급하는가?

(A) 빙하 속에 얼마나 많은 물이 담겨 있는지 설명하기 위해

(B) 그 빙하가 얼마나 오래 존재해왔는지 강조하기 위해

(C) 빙하 시대의 영향을 지구 온난화의 영향과 대조해 보기 위해

(D) 바다보다 빙하 속에 더 많은 물이 있다고 주장하기 위해

해설 해당 문단의 내용을 보면, 엄청난 양의 담수를 보유하고 있고, 그 양이 많아 전 세계의 해수면 높이가 높아질 것이라는 점을 언급하고 있으므로 (A)가 정답이다.

어휘 emphasize ~을 강조하다 contrast A with B A를 B와 대조하다, 대비시키다

7. 지문의 단어 "obliterate"와 의미가 가장 가까운 것은 무엇인가?

(A) ~을 증가시키다

(B) ~을 파괴하다

(C) ~을 보충하다

(D) ~을 옮기다

해설 obliterate(없애다, 제거하다)와 destroy(파괴하다)는 유의어로 정답은 (B)이다.

8. 다섯 번째 문단에 따르면, 지구 역사 중에서 현재의 시대와 관련해 무엇이 특별한가?

(A) 모든 대륙에 빙하가 있다.

(B) 빙하 시대가 최근에 끝났다.

(C) 빙하가 지구의 지표면에 존재한다.

(D) 육지의 3분의 1이 빙하로 덮여 있다.

해설 기존 시대를 통틀어 볼 때 드문 존재인 빙하가 현재에는 육지 표면의 10퍼센트를 덮고 있다는 내용을 기반으로 정답을 (C)로 판단할 수 있다.

9. 다음 문장이 지문에 추가될 수 있는 곳을 나타내는 네 개의 네모 표기 [■]를 찾아 보시오.

그 과정은 눈이 빙하로 탈바꿈되는 일에 달려 있다.

위 문장은 어느 곳에 가장 적합하겠는가? 네모 표기[■]를 클릭해 지문에 이 문장을 추가하시오.

(A) 1번

(B) 2번

(C) 3번

(D) 4번

해설 1번 박스의 앞뒤 내용을 보면, 대륙 빙하의 형성 과정을 설명하다가, 두 가지 종류 모두가 유사한 방식으로 형성된다는 문장이 있다. 그리고 그 이후 내용에 눈이 압축되고, 녹았다 얼면서 변

하는 과정을 설명하기 때문에 2번째 박스에 넣어야 올바르다

어휘 hinge on ~에 달려 있다 transformation 탈바꿈, 변모

10. **설명:** 간략한 지문 요약에 필요한 도입 문장이 아래에 제공되어 있다. 지문에서 가장 중요한 개념들을 나타내는 세 가지 답안 선택지를 골라 요약 내용을 완성하시오. 일부 답안 선택지는 지문에 제시되지 않는 개념을 나타내거나 지문에서 중요하지 않은 개념들이므로 요약 내용에 속하지 않는다. **이 문제는 2점에 해당된다.**

빙하는 여러 면에서 지구에 영향을 미친다.

(A) 빙하가 녹으면 해수면을 상승시킨다.

(B) 빙하는 더 차가워질수록 더 빠르게 움직인다.

(C) 빙하는 기후의 온도를 낮춘다.

(D) 빙하는 담수의 아주 많은 양을 담고 있다.

(E) 빙하는 눈이 증발해 만년설이 될 때 형성된다.

(F) 빙하가 흘러 다니고 후퇴할 때 풍경이 형성된다.

해설 세 번째 문단에서 빙하가 상당량의 담수를 담고 있고, 녹았을 때의 상황을 확인할 수 있기에 (A)와 (D)를 정답으로 선택한다. 그리고 네 번째 문단에서 (F)의 정보를 찾을 수 있다. 지문 요약 문제를 풀 때, 항상 모든 문단의 핵심 정보를 파악해둔 상태가 되는 것이 좋다.

Passage 3

지구의 내부 이해하기

지질학자들은 지진 및 지진이 지구에 걸쳐 만들어내는 지진파를 이용해 지구의 깊은 곳을 분석한다. 지진파에는 여러 종류가 있지만, 가장 먼저 기록되는 파(P파)와 두 번째로 기록되는 파(S파)가 이러한 연구를 가장 잘 설명해준다. 두 종류 모두 지구 내부로 깊숙이 이동해, 지표면에 기반을 두고 있는 과학자들에게 필수적인 데이터를 제공해준다. [1(B)]깊이가 다른 지점에서 나타나는 지진파의 갑작스러운 궤적 및 속도 변화를 통해 지구의 내부가 중심 핵과 그 위에 존재하는 두꺼운 맨틀, 그리고 겉부분을 둘러싸고 있는 지각으로 구분된다는 사실이 밝혀졌다. 지진파가 지닌 특징의 뚜렷한 변화를 불연속면이라 일컫는다.

약 2,900킬로미터 깊이에 위치한 구텐베르크 불연속면은 지구 중심부에 이르는 거리의 약 절반 지점에 해당되며, 지구 핵의 외측 경계를 나타낸다. S파와 P파 모두 이 경계에서 이상하게 반응하는데, [2(C)]S파는 지속되지 못하고, [2(B)]P파는 느려지면서 휘어진다. 이러한 이상 반응에 대한 이유는 외핵이 액체로 되어 있기 때문이다. [2(D)]S파가 액체를 통과해 이동할 수 없기 때문에, 외층이 S파를 흡수한다. 이것이 바로 지구의 한쪽에서 비롯된 S파가 반대편에 위치한 지진계 관측 기관에 나타나지 않는 이유이다. [2(A)]게다가, P파는 액체를 통과해 지날 수는 있지만, 액체 매개물 속에서는 급격히 느려지면서 굴절된다. 이러한 방식으로, 지구의 녹아 있는 외핵을 통과해 이동하는 [2(B)]P파는 속도가 감소되고 아래쪽으로 방향이 바뀌게 된다. 따라서, 이 두 가지 지진파가 모두 보이는 반응은 핵이 액체로 된 외형 구조를 지니고 있음을 나타내는 것이다.

핵은 바깥쪽의 액체로 된 층과 내부의 고체로 된 중심부가 있는 동심원 외형 구조로 구성되어 있다. ■ 전체 핵의 반지름은 3,500킬로미터이지만, 내부의 고체로 된 핵의 반지름은 1,220킬로미터이다. [9(B)]■ 내핵과 외핵의 구성 요소가 동일하지만, 내핵은 그것에 가해지는 극도의 압력으로 인해 어쩔 수 없이 고체 상태로만 존재한다. ■ 그 이후에 P파에 나타나는 속도 및 궤적의 변화는 핵의 농도가 외층과 내층 사이에서 변화한다는 것을 나타내며, 추가적인 증거가 그 고체성에 한층 더 신빙성을 더해 주고 있다. ■

지구의 밀도와 관련된 데이터를 보면 내부에 고체 핵이 존재한다는 것을 알 수 있다. 지구의 전반적인 밀도는 1입방 센티미터당 5.5그램이지만, 지표면과 지각에 위치한 암석들의 평균 밀도는 1입방 센티미터당 3.0그램이 채 되지 않는다. 이 두 수치들 사이의 [3(D)]차이는 지구의 더 깊은 곳에 있는 물질이 평균 수치를 높일 만큼 밀도가 더 높은 것이 틀림없다는 사실을 나타낸다. [4(D)]핵에 가해지는 엄청난 압력을 감안할 때, 니켈이 섞인 철은 밀도의 차이를 보완해줄 정도로 충분히 밀도가 높을 것이다. 하지만, 연구소 실험을 통해 극한의 압력을 받는 철–니켈 합금은 밀도가 너무 높을 것으로 나타남에 따라, 몇몇 더 가벼운 원소들도 섞여 있을 가능성이 있다. 규소와 황, 탄소, 또는 산소가 모두 무거운 핵을 가볍게 하는 데 도움이 되는 후보자일 가능성이 있다.

외부로 눈을 돌려보는 것도 지구 내부에 무엇이 있는지 이해하는 데 있어 과학자들에게 도움을 줄 수 있다. 핵이 철과 니켈로 구성되어 있다는 이론은 운석 연구에 의해 뒷받침되고 있다. [6(C)]그 동안 되찾아낸 대부분의 운석은 철–니켈 합금으로 구성되어 있다. 태양계에 존재하는 운석들이 산산조각난 행성의 핵에서 비롯되어 남은 [5(A)]잔해라는 의혹이 있다. 이 고대 행성의 핵이 철과 니켈로 구성되어 있었다면, 지구의 핵도 유사할 수 있다.

[7(C)]자석에 대한 기본적인 이해 또한 지구의 핵이 금속성 고체라는 아이디어에 신빙성을 더해주고 있다. 지구의 자기장은 나침반을 한 번이라도 이용해본 사람이라면 누구나 명확히 알 수 있는데, 지구 자체가 마치 북극과 남극이 있는 하나의 거대한 자석과 같은 역할을 하기 때문이다. [8(C)]자기장의 존재 및 흐름은 강력한 전기 전도체를 필요로 하며, 지각과 맨틀 내의 규소암은 전도성이 아주 뛰어나진 않기 때문에, 스스로 자기장을 지탱할 수 없을 것이다. [7(C)]하지만, 철과 니켈은 대단히 전도성이 뛰어나다. 핵 내부에 나타나는 극도의 열 순환과 지구의 자전에 의해 발생되는 힘은 내핵 주변에서 자기장을 지탱하는 데 필요할 만한 전자의 흐름을 만들어낼 수 있을 것이다. 금속성 핵이 없다면, 자기장은 존재할 수 없을 것이다.

[어휘]
1. planet-spanning 지구 전체에 걸친 seismic waves 지진파(지진에 의해 발생되는 진동의 움직임) elucidating 설명해주는 grounded on ~에 기반을 둔 trajectory 궤적 velocity 속도 encompassing 둘러싸고 있는 transition 변화 discontinuity 불연속면

2. **behave** 반응하다 **originate from** ~에서 비롯되다 **seismograph** 지진계 **refracted** 굴절된 **medium** 매개물 **molten** 녹아 있는 **point to** ~을 나타내다, 가리키다

3. **be composed of** ~로 구성되다 **concentric** 동심원의, 중심이 같은 **radius** 반지름 **composition** 구성 요소 **exert** (힘)을 가하다 **subsequent** 그 이후의 **alteration** 변화 **consistency** 농도 **lend support to** ~에 신빙성을 더하다

4. **density** 밀도 **disparity** 차이 **make up** ~을 보완하다, 보충하다

5. **comprise** ~로 구성되다(= be made up of) **meteorite** 운석 **inhabit** ~에 존재하다 **debris** 잔해, 쓰레기, 파편

6. **magnetic field** 자기장 **electrical conductor** 전기 전도체 **conductive** 전도성의 **electron** 전자

1. 첫 번째 문단에 따르면, 다음 중 어느 결과물이 지구의 내부가 세 부분으로 나뉜다는 생각을 뒷받침하는가?
(A) 지구의 맨틀은 지각을 지탱하기엔 너무 약하다.
(B) 지구 내부의 특정 깊이에서 불연속면이 나타난다.
(C) 모든 지진파가 지구 반대편에서 기록된다.
(D) P파는 여러 층을 통과해 지나면서 S파가 된다.

해설 첫 번째 문단의 마지막 부분을 통해 불연속면이 나타난다는 점을 토대로 정답이 (B)임을 유추할 수 있다.

2. 두 번째 문단에 따르면, 다음 중 지진파가 외핵으로 들어가면서 발생되지 않는 일은 무엇인가?
(A) P파의 속도가 높아진다.
(B) P파가 방향을 바꾼다.
(C) S파가 움직임을 멈춘다.
(D) S파가 외핵에 의해 흡수된다.

어휘 두 번째 문단의 초반부를 보면, 이미 P파는 느려지면서 휘어진다는 점을 설명하고 있다. 이후 내용에서 액체로 되어 있는 외핵을 통해 이동하는 P파의 속도가 감소된다는 점을 다시 언급하므로 정답은 (A)이다.

3. 지문의 단어 "disparity"와 의미가 가장 가까운 것은 무엇인가?
(A) 축적
(B) 혼란, 혼동
(C) 오류, 실수
(D) 차이

해설 disparity(차이)와 difference(차이)는 동의어로 정답은 (D)이다.

4. 네 번째 문단에 따르면, 지구의 핵은 왜 규소와 황, 탄소, 또는 산소 같은 원소를 포함하고 있을 가능성이 있는가?
(A) 철과 니켈이 결합하기 위해 다른 원소가 필요하다.
(B) 핵에서 얻은 샘플에 극미량의 규소와 황, 탄소, 그리고 산소가 들어 있다.
(C) 지표면의 암석에도 밀도 높게 혼합된 다양한 원소가 들어 있다.
(D) 철과 니켈 자체가 아주 큰 압력 하에서는 밀도가 너무 높

을 수 있다.

해설 해당 문단의 중간 지점을 보면, 핵에 가해지는 압력을 감안하면, 니켈이 섞인 철은 충분히 밀도가 높고, 실제 실험을 통해 철-니켈 합금은 밀도가 너무 높을 것으로 나타나기 때문에 가벼운 원소들도 섞여 있을 가능성이 있다고 언급되어 있으므로 정답은 (D)이다.

어휘 **combine** 결합하다 **trace** 극미량, 흔적, 자취

5. 지문의 단어 "debris"와 의미가 가장 가까운 것은 무엇인가?
(A) 잔해
(B) 육지, 땅
(C) 에너지
(D) 궤도

해설 debris(잔해, 파편)와 fragments(파편, 잔해)는 동의어로 정답은 (A)이다.

6. 다섯 번째 문단에서, 운석 구성 요소와 관련해 유추할 수 있는 것은 무엇인가?
(A) 태양계에 있는 철 대부분은 운석에서 발견된다.
(B) 더 무거운 원소로 만들어진 운석은 온전한 상태로 유지될 가능성이 더 크다.
(C) 태양계 내의 행성은 유사한 방식으로 형성되었다.
(D) 지구의 핵 속에 들어 있는 철은 파괴된 행성에서 비롯되었다.

해설 문단 후반부에 태양계에 존재하는 운석들의 성분과 지구 핵의 구성 요소 사이에 나타나는 유사성을 언급하고 있으므로 (C)가 정답이다.

어휘 **intact** 온전한, 원래대로인

7. 여섯 번째 문단에서, 글쓴이는 무엇을 하기 위해 지구의 자기장을 이야기하는가?
(A) 미해결 상태로 남아 있는 지구의 핵과 관련된 미스터리를 제시하기 위해
(B) 철을 기반으로 하는 운석이 왜 그렇게 많이 지구에 떨어지는지 설명하기 위해
(C) 지구에 철과 니켈로 된 핵이 있는 것이 틀림없는 또 다른 이유를 제공하기 위해

해설 (D) 지구의 핵 구성 요소와 관련된 반대 이론을 강조하기 위해 문단 초반부에 마치 자석 같은 지구의 자기장을 언급해 지구의 핵이 금속성 고체임을 증명하는 내용이 제시되어 있다. 그 성분이 앞서 설명한 철과 니켈이므로 이러한 정보를 담고 있는 (C)가 정답이다.

8. 다음 문장들 중 어느 것이 지문의 하이라이트 표기된 문장에 담긴 핵심 정보를 가장 잘 표현하는가? 오답 선택지는 중요한 방식으로 의미를 변경하거나 핵심 정보를 배제한다.

자기장의 존재 및 흐름은 강력한 전기 전도체를 필요로 하며, 지각과 맨틀 내의 규소암은 전도성이 아주 뛰어나진 않기 때문에, 스스로 자기장을 지탱할 수 없을 것이다.

(A) 자기장의 흐름은 맨틀에서 비롯되며, 지각 내에 있는 암석들의 전도성을 약화시킨다.
(B) 규소암은 지각과 맨틀의 전기 전도성을 높여, 지구의 자기장을 확대시킨다.
(C) 지각과 맨틀 내의 물체들은 지구의 자기장을 만들어낼 정도로 충분히 전도성이 좋지 못하다.
(D) 지구의 자기장이 약해지면, 지각과 맨틀 내의 암석들은 전기 전도성이 더 높아진다.

해설 주어진 문장에 '맨틀 내의 규소암은 전도성이 좋지 않다'는 내용을 담고 있어야 하기 때문에 (C)의 '지각과 맨틀 내의 물체'라는 단어로 규소암을 포함하고, '충분히 전도성이 좋지 못하다'는 내용을 통해 주어진 문장과 핵심 내용이 일치한다는 점을 확인할 수 있다. 그리고 '스스로 자기장을 지탱할 수 없을 것이다'라는 정보도 (C)에 들어가 있으므로 정답은 (C)이다.

9. 다음 문장이 지문에 추가될 수 있는 곳을 나타내는 네 개의 네모 표기 [▪]를 찾아 보시오.

그것은 반지름이 1,700킬로미터인 달보다 약간 더 작다.

위 문장은 어느 곳에 가장 적합하겠는가? 네모 표기 [▪]를 클릭해 지문에 이 문장을 추가하시오.

(A) 1번
(B) 2번
(C) 3번
(D) 4번

해설 지구 핵의 반지름 수치를 제시하는 문장 뒤에 위치한 두 번째 박스에 들어가 그 크기를 비교하는 흐름이 되어야 자연스러우므로 정답은 (B)이다.

10. **설명:** 간략한 지문 요약에 필요한 도입 문장이 아래에 제공되어 있다. 지문에서 가장 중요한 개념들을 나타내는 세 가지 답안 선택지를 골라 요약 내용을 완성하시오. 일부 답안 선택지는 지

문에 제시되지 않는 개념을 나타내거나 지문에서 중요하지 않은 개념들이므로 요약 내용에 속하지 않는다. **이 문제는 2점에 해당된다.**

지구의 내부를 이해하기 위해 다양한 기술이 활용되었다.

(A) 지구 내부의 다른 깊이에서 갑작스럽게 나타나는 지진파의 전송 변화는 지구의 내부가 세 가지 주된 층으로 나뉘어 있다는 사실을 나타낸다.
(B) 외부의 액체 핵은 철로 구성되어 있는 반면, 내부의 고체 핵은 황이나 산소 같이 더 가벼운 원소와 결합한 니켈로 되어 있다.
(C) 지구의 내부를 통과해 이동하는 지진파는 지구의 핵이 주로 금속으로 구성되어 있다는 것을 나타낸다.
(D) 지구의 전반적인 밀도 및 태양계 곳곳에서 날아온 운석의 구성 요소는 지구의 내핵이 금속성이며 고체라는 것을 나타낸다.
(E) 지구 내핵 속의 압력 강도는 내핵이 액체 상태로 존재하고 있다는 것을 뜻한다.
(F) 지구 자기장의 존재로 인해 지구는 전기를 전도할 수 있는 금속성 내핵을 지니고 있어야 한다.

해설 (A)의 세 가지 지구 내부 층은 첫 번째 문단에서, (D)의 운석 내용은 다섯 번째 문단에서 확인된다. (F)의 자기장 내용은 마지막 문단에서 찾을 수 있다.

어휘 abrupt 갑작스러운 transmission 전송, 전달, 전파 intensity 강도 conduct ~을 전도하다

Passage 1

Answers

1. D	2. A	3. D	4. B	5. A	6. B	7. D	8. D	9. D	10. ABE

별의 죽음

1900년대 중반 무렵까지는, 과학자들 사이에서 수축이 별 내부에서 에너지를 생성하는 데 필수적인 과정이라는 의견 일치가 존재했다. ■ [3(D)]이들은 별이 수축함에 따라 온도가 상승하고 더 많은 양의 빛을 발산한다고 생각했다. ■ 하지만, 이는 별이 빛을 내는 주요 작용 방식이 될 수 없다. ■ 만일 그렇다면, 일반적으로 별이 빛을 내는 기간이라고 우리가 알고 있는 수십 억 년은 고사하고 1백만 년 동안 밝게 타는 것조차 힘겨울 것이다. [9(D)]현재 우리가 알고 있는 것은 핵융합이 별에게 그 힘을 제공해 준다는 점이다. [2(A)]핵융합이 별 내부에서 발생될 때마다 부산물로서 에너지가 방출되며, 우주로 배출되는 이 에너지가 바로 우리가 별빛이라고 일컫는 것이다. 그 융합 과정은 두 개의 수소 핵이 높은 속도로 충돌하면서 하나의 중성자와 하나의 양성자로 구성된 조합인 중양자라고 부르는 입자를 만들어내면서 시작된다. 중양자는 즉시 추가 양성자와 결합해 헬륨 분자들을 [1(D)]형성하는데, 이 분자들은 탄소 같이 더 무거운 원소로 융합할 수 있다. 대부분 별들의 경우에, 상당한 양의 무거운 원소들이 거듭되는 분자 융합을 통해 축적된다.

두 가지 서로 다른 별 집단, 즉 상대적으로 젊은 종족 I과 훨씬 더 늙은 종족 II 사이의 차이점을 짚고 넘어가는 것이 중요하다. 또한, 위치를 바탕으로 이 집단들을 구별하는 것도 가능하다. 불룩한 중심부가 평평한 원반으로 둘러싸인 모양을 하고 있는 우리 은하, 즉 은하수를 예로 들어 보자. 종족 I에 속하는 별들은 일반적으로 은하 원반부 내에 위치해 있는 반면, 종족 II에 속하는 별들은 보통 은하 중심부의 불룩한 부분과 그 주변 광륜에서 발견된다.

종족 II에 속하는 대부분의 별들은 우주의 초기 단계에서부터 존재해 왔으며, 우주가 대체로 수소 가스 및 헬륨 가스로 구성되어 있었을 때 형성되었다. 처음에, 그 별들은 사실상 어떤 무거운 원소도 포함하고 있지 않았다. 일단 그 별들의 가용성 물질이 다 떨어지고 나면, 그들은 빛을 잃고 죽게 되어, 먼지의 형태로 물질을 우주에 퍼트리게 된다. [4(A)]이 먼지의 상당 부분이 그 후에 새롭게 형성된 종족 I 별들과 결합한다. [4(D)]종족 I 별들은 주로 수소 가스와 헬륨 가스로 구성되지만, [4(C)]무거운 원소들도 포함하고 있고, 이 원소들은 별들의 전체 질량에서 대략 1~2퍼센트를 차지한다. 더 무거운 이 원소들은 별들이 축적해온 더 가벼운 원소들과의 융합을 통해 형성된다. 그러면 결과적으로 종족 I에 속하는 별들은 이전 세대의 별들에 의해 어느 시점에 방출된 물질을 포함하게 된다. 아마 종족 I에 속하는 별들의 가장 잘 알려진 예는 우리의 태양일 것이다.

그럼, 태양이 마침내 그 수명을 다하게 되면 어떤 일이 벌어질까? 지금으로부터 수십 억 년 뒤에는, 태양이 지금보다 훨씬 더 밝게 탈 것이다. 점점 더 많은 핵 연료가 [5(A)]고갈되어, 애초의 수소가 거의 조금도 남아 있지 않은 상태가 될 것이다. 결국, 태양의 중심부에서는 더 이상 어떤 핵 반응이나 활동도 나타나지 않을 것이다.

일단 태양이 "핵 활동 이후의" 단계를 시작하게 되면, 사실상 내부 영역과 외부 영역으로 구성된 두 가지 뚜렷이 구별되는 지역으로 분리될 것이다. [6(B)]내부 영역은 수소 연료가 전혀 없는 상태가 되는 반면, 외부 영역은 소량을 유지하게 된다. 대단히 빠른 변화들이 나타나기 시작해, 이 변화들이 사실상 태양을 산산조각 낼 것이다. 안에서 어떠한 핵 반응도 일어나지 않는 채로, 내부 영역은 자체 무게로 인해 붕괴되어, 뜨겁고 밀도가 높으면서 밝기가 낮은 중심핵으로 수축되기 시작할 것이다. 외부 영역은, 가스가 엉성하게 뭉쳐 있는 공 모양을 닮게 될 것이며, 매우 다른 종류의 변형 과정을 거치게 된다. [7(D)]내부 영역이 수축하면, 소멸하는 별을 통과해 잔물결을 보내는 충격파를 촉발시켜, 별 외부에 속하는 물질을 바깥쪽으로 더욱 더 멀리 떠밀어 보내게 된다. 이는 결과적으로 외피 부분이 애초의 크기보다 수백 배 더 커질 때까지 빠르게 팽창하도록 초래한다. 크기가 커지면서, 온도는 수천 도의 차이로 떨어지게 된다. [8(C)]결국, 태양은 적색 거성이 되는 것이다. 차갑게 식고 밝으며, 너무 커져서 지구가 공전하던 전체 영역을 차지하게 된다. 그리고 너무 밝게 빛나게 되어 이론적으로는 수천 광년 떨어진 곳에서도 육안으로 보는 것이 가능할 것이다. 이것이 바로 태양이 수백 만 년 동안 유지될 상태이며, 그 기간 중에 외피 부분의 물질은 점차 우주 속으로 배출될 것이다. [8(D)]마침내,

기체로 되어 있는 태양의 외부 형태 중 어떤 것도 남아있지 않게 되며, 오직 뜨거운 백색 중심핵만 남아 있게 된다. 그 후에 태양은 중심핵이 수축해 마지막 에너지를 방출하고 마침내 죽게 될 때까지 백색 왜성으로 분류될 것이다.

[어휘]

1. shrinking 수축 contract 수축하다 let alone ~은 고사하고 by-product 부산물 expel ~을 배출하다 refer A to as B A를 B라고 일컫다 nuclei 핵(nucleus의 복수) collide 충돌하다 give rise to ~을 만들어내다, 일으키다 deuteron 중양자 neutron 중성자 proton 양성자 molecule 분자 element 원소, 요소 accumulate ~을 축적하다, 축적되다

2. distinguish 구별하다 bulge 불룩한 부분 galactic disk 은하 원반부 halo 광륜, 후광

3. be comprised of ~로 구성되다(= be composed of) virtually 거의, 사실상 fusible 가용성의 cease to do ~하기를 중단하다, 멈추다 subsequently 그 후에, 그 뒤에 make up ~을 차지하다 mass 질량

4. exhaust ~을 다 써버리다, 고갈시키다

5. effectively 사실상 devoid of ~가 결여된, 전혀 없는 rip A apart A를 산산조각 내다, 갈가리 찢다 dim 밝기가 낮은 resemble ~을 닮다 be held together 뭉쳐 있다 trigger ~을 촉발시키다 shock wave 충격파 ripple 잔물결 in turn 결과적으로, 결국 envelope 외피 red giant star 적색 거성 take up ~을 차지하다 orbit 공전하다 remnant 남은 부분, 나머지 gaseous 기체로 되어 있는 whatsoever ~하는 그 어떤 것이든 be classified as ~로 분류되다 white dwarf star 백색 왜성 emit ~을 방출하다

1. 지문의 단어 "form"과 의미가 가장 가까운 것은 무엇인가?
(A) ~을 이끌다
(B) ~을 쫓아 버리다
(C) ~을 분리하다
(D) ~을 만들다

해설 form(형성하다)과 create(만들다)은 유의어로 정답은 (D)이다.

2. 첫 번째 문단에 따르면, 별에서 비롯되어 빛으로 보이는 에너지는 무엇에 따른 결과인가?
(A) 다양한 입자들이 함께 이루는 융합
(B) 원자를 버리는 무거운 원소들
(C) 양성자들과 결합되는 헬륨 원자들
(D) 분열을 일으키는 수소 분자들

해설 해당 문단의 중간을 보면, 핵융합이 별 내부에서 발생될 때마다 부산물로 에너지가 방출되며, 이 에너지가 별빛이라고 일컫는다고 정보를 제공하고 있다. 정답은 (A)이다.

3. 첫 번째 문단에서, 글쓴이는 왜 별들이 수십 억 년이나 되었다는 점을 지적하는가?
(A) 별빛이 일회성 사건이 아니라 거듭되는 과정에 의해 생성된다는 점을 설명하기 위해
(B) 별들이 이전에 추정되었던 것보다 훨씬 더 느린 속도로 수축한다는 것을 주장하기 위해
(C) 점점 더 많은 양의 무거운 원소들이 축적됨에 따라 별의 융합 과정 속도가 둔화된다는 점을 설명하기 위해
(D) 별들이 에너지를 만들어내는 주된 작용 방식이 수축 과정일 수 없다는 점을 주장하기 위해

해설 첫 번째 문단의 두 번째 문장을 보면, 수축함에 따라 더 많은 빛을 발산한다고 생각했는데, 이는 빛을 내는 주요 방식이 될 수

없었으며 일반적으로 별이 빛을 내는 기간이 힘겨울 것이다는 언급을 통해 (D)가 정답이다.

어휘 estimate ~을 추정하다 decelerate 속도가 둔화되다

4. 두 번째 문단과 세 번째 문단에 따르면, 다음 중 종족 I에 속하는 별들과 관련해 사실이 아닌 것은 무엇인가?
(A) 한때 종족 II에 속하는 별들의 구성 요소였던 물질들로 일부분 구성되어 있다.
(B) 수명이 일반적으로 종족 II에 속하는 별들보다 훨씬 더 짧다.
(C) 더 가벼운 원소들의 융합을 통해 만들어진 원소들을 포함한다.
(D) 대부분 수소 가스와 헬륨 가스로 구성되어 있다.

해설 세 번째 문단의 중간을 보면, 종족 I에 속하는 별들은 주로 수소 가스와 헬륨 가스로 구성되어 있다는 점을 토대로 (D)를 소거한다. 그리고 바로 이어지는 문장에서 (C)의 내용을 확인할 수 있다. (A) 역시, 앞에서 종족 II에 속하는 별들의 가용성 물질이 다 떨어지면, 먼지의 형태로 물질을 우주에 퍼뜨리며 이 먼지 상당 부분이 새롭게 형성된 종족 I 별과 결합함을 명시하고 있다. (B)는 언급된 적이 없다.

5. 지문의 단어 "exhausted"와 의미가 가장 가까운 것은 무엇인가?
(A) 고갈된
(B) 할당된
(C) 철회된
(D) 분배된

해설 exhausted(고갈된)와 depleted(고갈된)는 동의어로 정답은 (A)이다.

6. 다섯 번째 문단에 따르면, 태양이 "핵 활동 이후의" 단계에 접어들 때, 외부 영역이 무엇을 하게 된다는 점에서 내부 영역과 달라질 것인가?

(A) 훨씬 덜 현저한 정도로 크기가 변화될 것이다.

(B) 여전히 극소량의 수소를 포함할 것이다.

(C) 그 어떤 것이든 에너지 생성을 멈출 것이다.

(D) 시간이 흐를수록 더 뜨거워지고 밀도가 높아질 것이다.

해설 다섯 번째 문단의 두 번째 문장을 보면 내부 영역은 수소 연료가 전혀 없는 상태가 되는 반면, 외부 영역은 소량을 유지하게 되므로 정답은 (B)이다.

어휘 trace amount 극소량

7. 다섯 번째 문단에 따르면, 다음 중 어느 것이 죽어가는 태양의 내부 중심핵과 관련해 사실일 것인가?

(A) 외피 부분의 무게 증가에 따른 영향으로 수축될 것이다.

(B) 별 외부로부터 엄청난 양의 물질을 흡수할 것이다.

(C) 애초의 크기보다 수백 배 커질 때까지 계속 팽창할 것이다.

(D) 수축하면서 별의 나머지 부분을 통과하는 에너지파를 초래할 것이다.

해설 해당 문단의 중간을 보면, 내부 영역이 수축하면, 소멸하는 별을 통과해 잔물결을 보내는 충격파를 촉발시켜, 별 외부에 속하는 물질을 바깥쪽으로 더욱 멀리 떠밀어 보내게 된다는 점을 통해 정답이 (D)임을 확인할 수 있다.

8. 다섯 번째 문단은 태양의 죽음과 관련해 다음 중 어느 내용을 뒷받침하는가?

(A) 외부 영역의 온도 하락에 따른 결과로 태양의 외피 부분이 빠르게 팽창할 것이다.

(B) 태양의 외부 영역이 팽창하는 동안, 그곳의 모든 물질이 우주로 방출될 것이다.

(C) 태양이 외피 부분의 물질을 우주로 방출한 후 남아 있는 중심핵에서 핵융합이 한시적으로 지속될 것이다.

(D) 태양은 수백 만 년 동안 적색 거성 단계에 머물러 있다가 백색 왜성이 될 것이다.

해설 다섯 번째 문단 중간 이하 내용에서 결국 태양은 적색 거성이 된다는 점이 언급되어 있다. 그리고 문단의 마지막 부분을 보면, 중심핵이 수축해 마지막 에너지를 방출하고 백색 왜성이 된다는 점이 명시되어 있으므로 정답은 (D)이다.

9. 다음 문장이 지문에 추가될 수 있는 곳을 나타내는 네 개의 네모 표기 [■]를 찾아 보시오.

분명히, 별들이 어떻게 에너지를 생성하는지를 설명하기 위해 더욱 그럴 듯한 작용 방식을 발견하는 것이 필수적이었다.

위 문장은 어느 곳에 가장 적합하겠는가? 네모 표기[■]를 클릭해 지문에 이 문장을 추가하시오.

(A) 1번

(B) 2번

(C) 3번

(D) 4번

해설 1번 박스 앞 문장에서, 과거에는 의견 일치가 존재했다는 점을 언급하고 이러한 내용이 1번 박스 뒤 문장에서 자연스럽게 연결된다. 또한 역접으로 2번 박스 앞뒤 문장이 연결되고 가정을 통해 3번 박스 앞뒤 문장도 내용이 자연스럽게 연결된다. 주어진 문장이 4번 박스에 들어가야, "현재 우리가 알고 있는 것은 핵융합이 별에게 그 힘을 제공해 준다"는 뒤 문장과 흐름이 이어진다. 그러므로 정답은 (D)이다.

어휘 plausible 타당한, 그럴 듯한

10. **설명:** 간략한 지문 요약에 필요한 도입 문장이 아래에 제공되어 있다. 지문에서 가장 중요한 개념들을 나타내는 세 가지 답안 선택지를 골라 요약 내용을 완성하시오. 일부 답안 선택지는 지문에 제시되지 않는 개념을 나타내거나 지문에서 중요하지 않은 개념들이므로 요약 내용에 속하지 않는다. 이 문제는 2점에 해당된다.

과학자들은 한때 별들이 수축 과정에 의해 에너지를 생성한다고 생각했지만, 지금은 그것이 핵융합의 부산물로서 일어난다는 것을 알고 있다.

(A) 태양과 다른 유사한 별들의 외피는 우주로 에너지를 방출하며, 내부 중심핵은 마지막 에너지를 방출하기 전 백색 왜성이 된다.

(B) 수소 가스와 헬륨 가스로부터 형성된, 종족 II 별들은 가장 오래된 별들이며, 그들은 가용성 물질을 다 써버릴 때까지 빛난다.

(C) 태양과 다른 유사한 별들은 중심핵에서 이루어지는 모든 핵 반응의 중단에 앞서 내부 중심핵과 외피 부분으로 분리될 것이다.

(D) 태양은 수축보다는 핵융합을 통해서 에너지를 만들어 내기 때문에 종족 I에 속하는 별들의 좋은 예시이다.

(E) 태양처럼 종족 I에 속하는 별들은 대부분 수소 가스와 헬륨 가스로 구성되어 있지만, 더 무거운 원소들도 포함하고 있는 상당히 젊은 별들이다.

(F) 우리 은하에서, 종족 II에 속하는 별들이 은하 원반부에서 발견되는 반면, 종족 I에 속하는 별들은 중심부의 불룩한 부분과 그 주변에서 발견된다.

해설 다섯 번째 문단의 내용을 가장 잘 담고 있는 보기는 (A)다. 세 번째 문단의 내용을 보면 종족 II 별들에 대한 설명과, 가용성 물질이 떨어지고 난 뒤 새롭게 형성되는 I 별들의 구성을 담고 있기 때문에 (B)와 (E) 내용의 중심 소재가 잘 포함되어 있음을 알 수 있다.

어휘 exhaust ~을 다 써버리다 cessation 중단, 멈춤

Passage 2

우리 태양계에 속한 행성들

태양은 아홉 개의 행성 및 각 행성의 다양한 달과 위성, 그리고 유성체와 혜성, 소행성 같은 무수한 더 작은 물체들로 구성되어 회전하는 거대한 태양계의 중심을 이루는 천체이다. 우리 태양계 전체 질량의 약 99.85퍼센트가 태양 내에 포함된 반면, 나머지 0.15퍼센트는 집합적으로 행성으로 구성되어 있다. [1(A)]태양으로부터의 거리에 따른 순서대로, 행성들은 다음과 같이 배열되어 있다: 수성, 금성, 지구, 화성, 목성, 토성, 천왕성, 그리고 해왕성. 태양의 중력이 모든 행성들의 움직임에 대한 지배력을 행사하며, [1(C)]이 행성들은 모두 같은 방향으로 이동하고 태양 주위의 타원형 궤도를 유지한다.

우리 태양계 내의 행성들은 지구형 행성 또는 목성형 행성 중의 하나로 분류될 수 있다. 수성과 금성, 지구, 그리고 화성이 지구형 행성, 즉 지구 같은 행성들이며, 목성과 토성, 천왕성, 그리고 해왕성이 목성형 행성, 즉 목성 같은 행성들이다. [1(B)]지구형 행성들과 목성형 행성들 사이에서 가장 분명한 차이점들 중의 하나는 크기이다. 지구가 가장 큰 지구형 행성이기는 하지만, 그 지름은 가장 작은 목성형 행성인 해왕성 지름의 4분의 1 크기에 불과하며, [1(D)]질량은 겨우 17분의 1 정도 밖에 안된다. 따라서, 목성형 행성들은 흔히 거성으로 일컬어진다. 또한, 서로 [2(C)]관련되어 있는 그 행성들의 위치를 바탕으로, 네 개의 지구형 행성들은 내행성이라고 알려져 있고, 네 개의 목성형 행성들은 외행성으로 알려져 있다.

[3(A)]지구형 행성들과 목성형 행성들은 또한 밀도와 구성 요소 측면에 있어서도 상당히 다르다. 지구형 행성들은 평균적으로 물보다 약 5배 더 밀도가 높은 반면, 목성형 행성들은 물보다 약 1.5배 더 밀도가 높은 경향이 있다. [4(A)]실제로, 토성은 물보다 겨우 0.7배 밖에 더 밀도가 높지 않은데, 이는 토성이라는 행성이 이론적으로는 물에 떠 있을 수 있다는 것을 의미한다. 이러한 밀도상의 큰 차이점들은 이 행성들의 구성 요소에 나타나는 차이에 기인한다. ■ 두 범주에 속하는 행성들을 구성하는 물질은 녹는점에 따라 세 가지 그룹(기체와 암석, 그리고 얼음)으로 나뉠 수 있다. ■ [3(A)]지구형 행성들은 주로 밀도 있는 암석과 금속 물질, 그리고 비교적 소량의 기체로 구성된다. ■ 반면에, [4(B)]목성형 행성들은 대체로 수소 가스와 헬륨 가스로 구성되어 있으며, [4(C)]얼어 있는 물과 암모니아, 그리고 메탄의 형태로 된 소량의 얼음도 포함하고 있기는 하지만, [4(D)]암석 물질은 존재하지 않는다. [9(D)]■

목성형 행성들의 대기는 매우 두터우며, 다양한 양의 수소와 헬륨, 메탄, 그리고 암모니아를 포함하고 있다. 지구형 행성들의 대기는 그에 비해 꽤 미약한 수준이다. 행성이 대기를 유지할 수 있는 능력을 좌우하는 핵심 요소는 그것의 온도와 질량이다. 기본적으로 기체 분자들은 탈출 속도라고 일컬어지는 속도에 도달하면 행성의 대기에서 "증발할" 가능성이 있다. 지구의 경우에, 탈출 속도는 초속 11킬로미터이다. [5(B)]목성형 행성들은 더 큰 질량과 더 높은 표면 중력으로 인해 지구형 행성들보다 훨씬 더 높은 대략 초속 21~60킬로미터 사이에 해당되는 탈출 속도를 지니고 있다. 따라서, 기체가 대기에서 우주로 탈출할 수 있게 해줄 필수 속도를 얻게 될 가능성이 훨씬 더 낮다. [6(D)]또한, 기체 분자의 속도는 온도에 크게 영향을 받으며, 목성형 행성들의 낮은 온도는 심지어 가장 가벼운 기체마저도 탈출 속도에 도달하지 못하게 한다. 반면에, [7(A)]지구의 달은 표면 중력이 낮은 비교적 따뜻한 천체로서, 심지어 가장 무거운 기체조차 유지할 수 없어서, 대기가 존재하지 않는다. 더 큰 지구형 행성들인 금성과 지구, 화성은 이산화탄소 같은 일부 무거운 기체를 유지할 수는 있지만, 이 행성들의 대기는 여전히 전체 질량의 극히 일부 비율 밖에 차지하지 않는다.

[8(D)]우리 태양계가 아주 최적의 상태로 조직되어 있기 때문에, 대부분의 천문학자들은 모든 태양계 행성들이 대략적으로 태양과 같은 시기에 그리고 같은 물질로부터 만들어졌을 것이라고 생각하고 있다. 일반적으로 받아들여지는 가설에 따르면, 모든 태양계 행성들은 목성의 구성 요소와 비슷한 구성 요소를 지녔던 원시적인 먼지 및 기체 구름으로부터 응축되었다. 하지만, 목성과 달리, 오늘날의 지구형 행성들은 근본적으로 얼음과 가벼운 기체가 결여되어 있다. 지구형 행성들이 한때 이러한 물질들이 더 풍부하게 존재하면서 훨씬 더 컸지만, 태양과 아주 가까운 위치 및 이 행성들의 비교적 높은 온도로 인해 결국 그 물질들을 잃어버렸다는 점이 한 가지 해석일 수 있다.

[어휘]
1. comprise ~으로 구성되다(= be made up of, be composed of) meteoroid 유성체 comet 혜성 asteroid 소행성 mass 질량 collectively

집합적으로 gravitational force 중력 exert (영향력 등) ~을 행사하다, 발휘하다 elliptical 타원형의 orbit 궤도

2. terrestrial 지구(형)의 Jovian 목성(형)의 be referred to as ~라고 일컬어지다

3. density 밀도 composition 구성 요소 be attributed to ~에 기인하다, 그 원인이다

4. atmosphere 대기 insubstantial 미약한, 실체가 없는 retain ~을 유지하다 molecule 분자 evaporate 증발하다 escape velocity 탈출 속도 (물체가 천체에서 탈출할 수 있는 최소한의 속도) lack ~가 없다, 부족하다

5. optimally 최적의 상태로 astronomer 천문학자 hypothesis 가설 condense 응축되다 primordial 원시의, 태고의 comparable to ~와 비슷한 devoid of ~가 결여된, 없는 proximity to ~와 가까움, 근접함

---

1. 지문에 따르면, 지구형 행성들과 목성형 행성들을 비교하는 다음 내용들 중에서 사실이 아닌 것은 무엇인가?

(A) 지구형 행성들이 목성형 행성들보다 태양과 더 가까이 위치해 있다.

(B) 지구형 행성들의 지름이 목성형 행성들의 지름보다 더 작다.

(C) 지구형 행성들과 목성형 행성들은 다른 방향으로 태양 주위를 이동한다.

(D) 목성형 행성들의 질량이 지구형 행성들의 질량보다 더 크다.

해설 (A)는 첫 번째 문단의 거리 이야기를 통해 확인할 수 있다. (B)는 두 번째 문단의 크기 이야기와 일맥상통한다. (D)는 두 번째 문단의 질량 이야기를 통해 파악할 수 있다. (C)의 경우 '다른 방향'이라는 부분이 잘못된 내용이다.

2. 지문의 표현 "relative to"와 의미가 가장 가까운 것은 무엇인가?

(A) ~와 가까운

(B) ~와 유사한

(C) ~와 관련된

(D) ~에서 멀리 떨어진

해설 relative to(~와 관련된)와 in regard to(~와 관련된)는 동의어로 정답은 (C)이다.

3. 다음 중 지구형 행성들이 밀도가 높은 이유로 세 번째 문단에서 언급하는 것은 무엇인가?

(A) 주로 암석 및 금속 물질들로 구성되어 있다.

(B) 세 가지 그룹의 물질들로 구성되어 있다.

(C) 목성형 행성들보다 더 많은 양의 얼음을 포함하고 있다.

(D) 물을 거의 포함하고 있지 않다.

해설 세 번째 문단의 중간에서 구성 요소의 차이를 이야기하며, 지구형 행성은 소량의 기체와 밀도 있는 암석과 금속 물질이 있다는 점을 토대로 정답이 (A)임을 알 수 있다.

4. 다음 내용들 중 세 번째 문단에서 토성과 관련해 뒷받침하지 않는 것은 무엇인가?

(A) 그 어떤 지구형 행성만큼 밀도가 높지 않다.

(B) 주로 기체로 구성되어 있다.

(C) 냉각 상태의 메탄 같은 얼음을 포함하고 있다.

(D) 소량의 암석 물질을 포함하고 있다.

해설 세 번째 문단의 마지막 문장을 통해 암석 물질이 존재하지 않는다는 점을 알 수 있다. 정답은 (D)이다.

5. 네 번째 문단에 따르면, 다음 내용들 중 어느 것이 목성형 행성과 지구형 행성 모두에 대해 사실인가?

(A) 대기가 더 얇을수록, 행성의 질량이 더 커진다.

(B) 표면 중력이 더 낮을수록, 탈출 속도도 더 낮아진다.

(C) 대기 속에 있는 기체의 숫자가 더 낮을수록, 온도도 더 낮아진다.

(D) 대기가 전체 질량에 기여하는 정도가 더 커질수록, 온도가 더 높아진다.

해설 네 번째 문단의 첫 번째 핵심 내용은 높은 표면 중력으로 인해 기체 탈출 속도가 달라진다는 점인데, 질량이 큰 목성형 행성은 표면 중력이 높기 때문에 요구되는 탈출 속도가 더 높다는 점을 알 수 있다. 이 내용을 토대로 정답이 (B)임을 유추할 수 있다.

어휘 contribute to ~에 기여하다, 도움이 되다

6. 네 번째 문단에 따르면, 목성형 행성들이 지구형 행성들보다 훨씬 더 두터운 대기를 지니고 있는 주된 이유는 무엇인가?

(A) 목성형 행성들은 표면의 중력이 더 낮다.

(B) 목성형 행성들의 기체 분자들은 더 빠른 속도로 이동할 수 있다.

(C) 목성형 행성들은 탈출 속도가 훨씬 더 낮다.

(D) 목성형 행성들은 표면 온도가 더 낮다.

해설 네 번째 문단의 두 번째 핵심 내용은 온도에 따라 기체 탈출 속도가 달라진다는 점인데, 중반부 이하 내용을 보면, 목성형 행성들의 낮은 온도는 기체가 탈출 속도에 도달하지 못한다는 점을 언급하므로 정답은 (D)이다.

7. 네 번째 문단은 행성들의 기체 유지 능력과 관련해 다음 중 어느 내용을 뒷받침하는가?

(A) 행성들은 무거운 기체보다 가벼운 기체를 유지할 가능성이 더 낮다.

(B) 질량이 더 큰 행성들은 상대적으로 질량이 낮은 행성들보다

기체를 유지하기가 더 힘들다.

(C) 목성형 행성들은 가장 가벼운 기체를 유지하는 데 큰 어려움을 겪는다.

(D) 오직 지구형 행성들만 이산화탄소를 유지할 능력이 있다.

해설 네 번째 문단의 마지막 내용을 보면 지구의 달은 무거운 기체조차 유지할 수 없다는 점을 언급하기 때문에, 온도가 낮고 질량을 가지면 무거운 기체는 유지할 수 있다는 점을 유추할 수 있나. 이에 반해 가벼운 기체는 당연히 탈출할 수 있는 필수 속도를 얻을 수 있기 때문에 정답은 (A)이다.

8. 태양과 모든 행성이 응축되기 시작한 기원으로 여겨지고 있는 먼지 및 기체 구름을 "원시적인"이라고 부르는 데 있어, 글쓴이는 그 구름이 어떠했다는 것을 의미하는가?

(A) 다른 어떤 천체보다 더 컸다.

(B) 구조적으로 태양과 유사했다.

(C) 아주 다양한 물질들로 구성되어 있었다.

(D) 우리 태양계가 시작될 때 존재했다.

해설 다섯 번째 문단의 첫 부분에서부터 태양계의 행성들이 태양과 같은 시기에 만들어졌을 것이라고 생각되어지고 있고, 비슷한 구성 요소를 지녔던 원시적인 먼지와 기체 구름으로부터 응축되었다는 점을 통해 우리 태양계가 시작될 때 존재했다는 점을 알 수 있다. 그러므로 정답은 (D)이다.

어휘 inception 시작

9. 다음 문장이 지문에 추가될 수 있는 곳을 나타내는 네 개의 네모 표기 [▇]를 찾아 보시오.

이것이 그들의 비교적 낮은 밀도에 대한 이유이다.

위 문장은 어느 곳에 가장 적합하겠는가? 네모 표기[▇]를 클릭해 지문에 이 문장을 추가하시오.

(A) 1번

(B) 2번

(C) 3번

(D) 4번

해설 해당 문단의 내용 자체가 밀도와 구성 요소를 중심으로 다루고 있으며, 문단의 후반부에 지구형 행성과 목성형 행성 차이를 설명해주고 있다. 이 때 지구형 행성은 밀도 있는 암석과 금속 물질이 있는 반면, 목성형 행성들은 가스로 구성된 점을 언급하기 때문에 마지막 박스에 주어진 문장을 삽입해야 한다. 그러므로 정답은 (D)이다.

어휘 **A account for B** A가 B에 대한 이유이다, A가 B를 설명해주다

10. **설명:** 아래의 답안 선택지 일곱 개 중에서, 지구형 행성의 특징을 바르게 묘사하는 것을 두 개, 그리고 목성형 행성의 특징을

바르게 묘사하는 것을 세 개 선택하시오. 선택하는 각각의 것을 도표의 해당 칸에 끌어서 넣으시오. 남은 두 개는 사용되지 않는다. **이 문제는 3점에 해당된다.**

(A) 상대적으로 높은 탈출 속도를 지니고 있다. (목성형)

(B) 일반적으로 물보다 더 낮은 밀도를 지니고 있다.

(C) 상대적으로 많은 양의 헬륨 가스를 포함하고 있다. (목성형)

(D) 상대적으로 높은 온도로 특징지어진다. (지구형)

(E) 형성될 당시에 기원이 되었던 구름과 비교적 유사한 구성 요소를 지니고 있다. (목성형)

(F) 지구의 달과 같은 범주에 함께 분류된다.

(G) 비교적 작은 크기로 되어 있다. (지구형)

해설 목성형 행성과 같은 경우 높은 질량으로 기체의 높은 탈출 속도를 가지고 있다는 점을 토대로 (A)와 (C)를 답으로 택할 수 있다. 그리고 마지막 문단에서 (E)의 내용이 목성형임을 확인할 수 있다. 이에 반해 지구형 행성과 같은 경우 중심 소재 중 하나인 온도와 크기를 중심으로 내용이 전개된 만큼 (D)와 (G)를 답으로 선택한다.

Passage 3

Answers

1. BC	2. B	3. A	4. D	5. B	6. C	7. D	8. C	9. C	10. BCE

혜성의 구조 및 구성 요소

혜성이 태양에서 멀리 떨어져 있을 때는, 지름이 겨우 몇 킬로미터 밖에 측정되지 않는 비교적 작은 물체이다. 혜성은 깊숙이 박혀 있는 먼지 입자들은 물론, 주로 물 얼음과 메탄 얼음, 그리고 암모니아 얼음으로 구성되어 있으며, 일반적으로 더러운 얼음 공처럼 보인다. [1(B),(C)]혜성이 태양에 더 가깝게 움직일 때마다, 방사선은 그 얼음 물질이 증발되도록 초래하며, 결국에는 포함되어 있는 먼지 대부분을 방출한다. 이는 그 얼음 공을 [2(B)]둘러싸는 거대한 광륜을 만들어낸다. 이 광륜은 코마라고 불리며, 혜성의 얼음 핵으로부터 수만 킬로미터나 멀리 뻗어 나갈 수 있다. 코마는 먼지 입자에 반사되는 태양광으로 인해 지구에 있는 사람들이 흔히 볼 수 있다. 게다가, 증기 분자들은 태양의 자외선에 의해 구성 원소들로 분해되며, 이 성분들은 태양에서 나오는 방사선의 흡수를 통해 여기 상태가 된다. 여기 상태가 된 원자들과 이온들이 에너지가 더 낮은 상태로 돌아갈 때, 빛을 내뿜으면서 코마의 광도에 기여하게 된다.

혜성이 태양과 훨씬 더 가까워지게 되면, 가장 쉽게 알아볼 수 있으면서 주목할 만한 특징(꼬리)이 형성되기 시작한다. 혜성은 엄밀히 따지면 별개의 꼬리 두 개가 있는데, 먼지 꼬리와 이온 꼬리가 그것이다. 먼지 꼬리는 태양광이 코마의 먼지 입자에 반사되면서 나타나는 결과물이다. 광자가 먼지 입자에 반사될 때, 그것은 먼지 입자의 운동량에 약간의 변화를 가하며 코마로부터 먼지 입자를 밀어낸다. 혜성이 궤도 운동을 계속하면서, 활 모양의 먼지 꼬리가 뒤에 남게 된다. 눈으로 볼 수 있는 이 먼지 꼬리는 혜성의 코마로부터 수천만 킬로미터 또는 수억 킬로미터의 길이로 뻗어 나갈 수 있다. [3(A)]대부분의 먼지 꼬리는 완만한 곡선 모양과 희미하게 보이는 황색으로 특징지어진다.

이온 꼬리는 약간 다른 방식으로 형성된다. 혜성이 태양 쪽으로 다가갈 때, 태양풍 속의 자외선이 코마 속의 원자들을 이온화하고 여기 상태로 만든다. 태양풍 속에 들어 있는 높은 속도의 하전 입자들이 코마 속의 전기를 띤 여기 상태의 이온들과 상호 작용하면서, 강제로 이온들을 혜성의 머리 쪽에서 멀리 밀어 보낸다. 이 여기 상태의 이온들이 에너지가 더 낮은 상태로 돌아가면, 광자를 내뿜으면서 혜성에서부터 태양의 반대 방향으로 뻗어 나가는 밝게 빛나는 푸르스름한 색의 꼬리를 만들어낸다. [4(D)]두 종류의 꼬리 모두 태양으로부터 흘러나오는 방사선에 의해 초래되기 때문에, 둘 모두 일반적으로 태양으로부터 멀어지는 방향으로 코마에서 뻗어 나가게 되며, 혜성은 각 종류마다 여러 개의 꼬리를 지닐 수 있다.

혜성이 태양계 내부를 관통해 이동하는 동안, 잔해로 이뤄진 꼬리를 뒤에 남기게 된다. 때때로, 이 물질은 태양 주위의 지구 공전 궤도에 걸쳐 흩뿌려질 수 있다. ■ 지구가 공전 궤도의 이 영역에 도달하는 순간, 먼지 꼬리가 남겨 놓은 잔해를 통과해 이동한다. ■ 이것은 수많은 입자들이 높은 속도로 지구의 대기에 진입하게 되는 결과를 낳을 수 있다. [9(C)]■ [5(B)]그 결과로 나타나는 공기 중의 마찰은 그 입자들이 대기 중에서 타 없어지면서 갑작스럽게 빛 줄기들을 생성할 수 있다. ■

[8(C)]혜성이 태양을 지나쳐 갈 때마다, 더 많은 물질을 잃게 되며, 모든 물질이 고갈되고 나면, 그 혜성은 더 이상 눈으로 볼 수 없는 상태가 된다. 이것이 근본적으로 의미하는 바는 태양과 가까운 곳에서 이동하는 혜성은 한정된 수명을 지니고 있다는 점이다. 혜성의 평균 크기와 혜성이 물질을 잃는 일반적인 속도를 고려해, 천문학자들은 지구에서 보일 정도로 충분히 태양과 가깝게 궤도를 도는 혜성은 우리 태양계의 나이보다 훨씬 더 짧은 수명을 지니고 있다는 결론에 도달하게 되었다. [6(C)]그렇다면, 타버려서 시야에서 사라지는 혜성들을 대신하는 새 혜성은 어디에서 나타나는가?

[6(C)]네덜란드의 천문학자 얀 오르트가 제시한 한 가지 제안은 태양계 형성 후에 남아 있는 물질로 구성된 거대한 구름이 태양을 둘러싸고 있으며 약 50,000AU의 거리에 이른다는 점이다. 이 구름의 범위 내에 존재하는 것은 커다란 물질 덩어리들이며, 그 중 일부는 혜성의 중심핵이다. [7(D)]별이 이 구름을 지나가 갈 때, 그 중력의 영향력이 이 덩어리들 중 하나의 궤도에 영향을 미칠 정도로 커서, 태양계 내부 방향으로 덩어리를 날려보내 태양과 더 가까운 곳으로 이동시킬 수 있다.

[어휘]

1. comet 혜성 be composed of ~로 구성되다 embedded 포함된, 박혀 있는 particle 입자 radiation 방사선 vaporize 증발되다 halo 광륜 reflect off ~에서 반사되다 molecule 분자 break A down into B A를 B로 분해하다 constituent 구성하는 excited 여기 상태의(원자나 분자가 외부에서 방사선 등의 자극을 받아 에너지가 더 커져서 높은 에너지 준위에 있는 것) emit ~을 내뿜다, 방출하다 contribute to ~에 기여하다, 도움이

되다 **luminosity** 광도, 광채

2. **photon** 광자 **exert** (힘 등) ~을 가하다, 행사하다 **momentum** 운동량 **orbit** 궤도 운동을 하다 **arcing** 활 모양의

3. **ultraviolet radiation** 자외선 **charged particle** 하전 입자(전기적으로 양성 또는 음성 전하를 가진 이온 입자) **luminous** 빛을 발하는 **stream out from** ~에서 흘러나오다

4. **debris** 잔해, 쓰레기 **strew** ~을 흩뿌리다 **atmosphere** 대기 **friction** 마찰 **give rise to** ~을 일으키다, 야기하다

5. **deplete** ~을 고갈시키다 **finite** 한정된 **come to the conclusion that** ~라는 결론에 이르다

6. **put forward** ~을 제시하다, 제안하다 **astronomical unit** 천문 단위(= AU, 1AU는 지구와 태양 사이의 평균 거리) **gravitational** 중력의 **proximity** 가까움, 근접

---

1. 첫 번째 문단에서 혜성이 태양 쪽으로 다가갈 때 나타나는 변화를 설명하는 선택지를 두 개 고르시오. 점수를 받으려면, 반드시 선택지를 두 개 골라야 한다.

(A) 혜성의 광륜 크기가 줄어들 것이다.

(B) 혜성의 얼음 물질이 증발하기 시작할 것이다.

(C) 코마가 먼지 입자 및 수증기로부터 형성되기 시작할 것이다.

(D) 중심핵이 물과 메탄, 그리고 암모니아의 응축 과정을 통해 형성된다.

해설 첫 번째 문단의 중간 부분을 보면 혜성이 태양에 더 가깝게 움직임에 따라 얼음 물질이 증발한다는 점을 언급하고 있고 증발과 먼지 방출로 코마라 불리는 광륜이 만들어진다는 점을 토대로 (B)와 (C)가 정답이다.

어휘 condensation 응축, 응결

2. 지문의 단어 "envelops"와 의미가 가장 가까운 것은 무엇인가?

(A) ~을 보내다

(B) ~을 둘러싸다

(C) ~을 흩어지게 만들다

(D) ~을 밀봉하다

해설 envelop(둘러싸다)과 surround(둘러싸다)는 동의어로 정답은 (B)이다.

3. 두 번째 문단과 세 번째 문단에 따르면, 다음 내용들 중 혜성 꼬리와 관련해 사실이 아닌 것은 무엇인가?

(A) 이온 꼬리는 색이 노르스름하며, 곡선 형태를 지니고 있다.

(B) 광자가 이온 꼬리와 먼지 꼬리의 형성에 관여한다.

(C) 먼지 꼬리가 먼 거리에 걸쳐 혜성 뒤쪽으로 뻗어 나간다.

(D) 이온 꼬리의 형성은 자외선을 필요로 한다.

해설 황색 및 곡선 모양은 대부분의 이온 꼬리가 아닌 먼지 꼬리에서 찾아볼 수 있는 특성임을 두 번째 문단 마지막 문장에서 확인할 수 있으므로 정답은 (A)이다.

4. 세 번째 문단에 따르면, 혜성 꼬리는 어떠한가?

(A) 태양 쪽으로 뻗어 나간다.

(B) 혜성이 태양과 더 가까워질수록 더 곡선 모양이 된다.

(C) 강력한 태양풍에 의해 혜성의 핵과 분리될 수 있다.

(D) 꼬리를 만드는 방사선과 동일한 방향으로 움직인다.

해설 세 번째 문단의 내용을 보면 꼬리 모두 태양으로부터 나오는 방사선에 의해 초래되기 때문에 일반적으로 태양으로부터 멀어지는 방향으로 코마에서 뻗어나간다는 점을 확인할 수 있다. 그러므로 정답은 (D)이다.

5. 네 번째 문단에 따르면, 지구가 혜성의 먼지 꼬리를 통과해 이동할 때 무슨 일이 벌어지는가?

(A) 혜성 꼬리가 다른 방향으로 움직인다.

(B) 먼지 입자들이 지구의 대기 속에서 타 없어진다.

(C) 지구의 대기 온도가 증가한다.

(D) 혜성의 궤도 경로가 상당히 바뀐다.

해설 다른 방향, 온도의 증가, 궤도 변경 등에 대한 이야기는 언급되지 않는다. 해당 문단의 마지막 부분에 가면, 먼지 입자들이 대기 중에 타 없어진다는 점을 언급하기 때문에 정답은 (B)이다.

어휘 atmospheric 대기의

6. 글쓴이는 왜 다섯 번째 문단을 질문으로 끝맺는가?

(A) 혜성의 특정 측면들이 논란이 되고 있음을 강조하기 위해

(B) 혜성의 구성 요소들이 더 집중적인 연구를 필요로 한다는 점을 주장하기 위해

(C) 다음 문단에서 상세히 설명하게 될 주제를 도입하기 위해

(D) 지문 내에서 앞서 이야기한 이론들을 거부하기 위해

해설 다음에 이어지는 여섯 번째 문단의 시작을 보면 천문학자가 "제안하는 내용"을 다루고 있기 때문에, 다음 문단에서 디테일하게 설명할 주제를 이어주는 역할을 수행하고 있다고 볼 수 있다. 그러므로 정답은 (C)이다.

어휘 aspect 측면, 양상 elaborate on ~을 상세히 설명하다

7. 여섯 번째 문단에 따르면, 천문학자 얀 오르트는 어떻게 혜성에 대한 우리의 이해에 기여했는가?

(A) 오래된 혜성들이 실제로 사라지는 것이 아니라, 단지 태양계의 경계 너머로 이동한다는 것을 보여주었다.

(B) 다른 별들의 궤도를 도는 혜성들을 우리 태양계 내에서 발견되는 것들과 비교할 수 있는 방법을 제안했다.

(C) 혜성의 수명이 태양계 형성 당시 태양과의 거리에 따라 다르다는 것을 승명했다.

(D) 오래된 잔해 덩어리들이 태양계 외부에서 내부로 밀려 들어올 때 혜성이 만들어진다는 이론을 제시했다.

해설 여섯 번째 문단의 마지막 문장을 보면, 별이 지나치면서 주는 중력의 영향력이 덩어리들 중 하나의 궤도에 영향을 주며 태양과 가까운 곳으로 이동시킬 수 있다는 점을 언급하기 때문에 (D)의 내용이 가장 적합하다.

어휘 dependent on ~에 따라 다른, ~에 달려 있는 theorize that ~라는 이론을 제시하다

8. 다음 문장들 중 어느 것이 지문의 하이라이트 표기된 문장에 담긴 핵심 정보를 가장 잘 표현하는가? 오답 선택지는 중요한 방식으로 의미를 변경하거나 핵심 정보를 배제한다.

혜성이 태양을 지나쳐 갈 때마다, 더 많은 물질을 잃게 되며, 모든 물질이 고갈되고 나면, 그 혜성은 더 이상 눈으로 볼 수 없는 상태가 된다.

(A) 혜성이 태양과 밀접하게 접촉하게 될 때마다, 육안으로 발견하는 것이 점점 더 어려워지게 된다.

(B) 혜성이 태양을 지나쳐 갈 때, 잃게 되는 물질의 양이 혜성과 태양 사이의 거리에 따라 다르다.

(C) 혜성이 태양을 지나갈 때마다 점점 더 많은 물질을 잃게 되어, 결국 모든 물질을 잃어버리고 나면 볼 수 없게 된다.

(D) 혜성은 태양 주위를 도는 궤도 운동 중에 모든 물질이 고갈되고 나면 더 이상 눈으로 볼 수 없게 된다.

해설 여기서 초점을 맞춰야 하는 부분은 "태양을 지나쳐 갈 때"라는 조건, "물질을 더 잃는다"라는 결과, 그리고 "모두 잃으면 혜성을 볼 수 없다"라는 최종 결과이다. (A)는 "물질을 더 잃는다"는 점이 누락되어 있고, (B)는 "거리"라는 불필요한 키워드가 들어가 있다. (D) 역시 "더 많은 물질을 잃는다"라는 내용이 없다. 정답은 (C)이다.

9. 다음 문장이 지문에 추가될 수 있는 곳을 나타내는 네 개의 네모 표기 [■]를 찾아 보시오.

가속하는 이 입자들이 지구 대기 속에 존재하는 다른 입자들과 충돌하게 된다.

위 문장은 어느 곳에 가장 적합하겠는가? 네모 표기[■]를 클릭해 지문에 이 문장을 추가하시오.

(A) 1번
(B) 2번
(C) 3번
(D) 4번

해설 해당 문단의 중간에서, "수많은 입자들이 높은 속도로 지구의 대기에 진입한다"라는 정보를 제공한다. 그렇기에 주어진 문장의 "가속하는 이 입자들이"라는 주어와 흐름이 같아짐을 확인할 수 있다. 주어진 문장을 3번 빅스에 넣을 경우, 그 충돌의 결과로 나타나는 공기 중의 마찰은 입자들이 타 없어지며 빛 줄기를 생성한다는 내용과 잘 맞아 떨어지기에 정답은 (C)이다.

어휘 collide with ~와 충돌하다

10. **설명:** 간략한 지문 요약에 필요한 도입 문장이 아래에 제공되어 있다. 지문에서 가장 중요한 개념들을 나타내는 세 가지 답안 선택지를 골라 요약 내용을 완성하시오. 일부 답안 선택지는 지문에 제시되지 않는 개념을 나타내거나 지문에서 중요하지 않은 개념들이므로 요약 내용에 속하지 않는다. **이 문제는 2점에 해당된다.**

천문학자들은 혜성의 구성 요소 및 태양계를 통과해 이동하면서 변화되는 방식과 관련된 많은 정보를 얻었다.

(A) 혜성은 주된 요소에 따라 여러 가지 종류의 꼬리를 만들 수 있다.

(B) 혜성은 태양을 지나쳐 갈 때마다 물질을 잃게 되어 결국 타 없어진다.

(C) 혜성은 코마라고 알려진 광륜을 만드는 얼음 및 먼지로 구성되어 있다.

(D) 대부분의 혜성에 나타나는 코마는 꼬리보다 상당히 더 크다.

(E) 혜성은 태양과 더 가까워질수록 다수의 꼬리를 비롯해 코마를 형성한다.

(F) 태양계는 먼 옛날에 소멸되었던 오래 전의 혜성들이 남긴 잔해를 포함하고 있다.

해설 네 번째 문단의 내용을 토대로 혜성은 태양을 지나쳐 갈 때마다 점점 물질을 잃게 되어 결국엔 눈으로 볼 수 없다는 정보를 담고 있는 (B)를 답으로 선택할 수 있다. 코마라고 알려진 광륜에 대한 정의는 첫 번째 문단에 아주 상세하게 설명되어 있으므로 (C)를 답으로 채택한다. 첫 번째와 두 번째 문단 내용을 보면, 혜성이 태양 쪽으로 다가갈 때 광륜(코마)과 두 가지 꼬리가 형성된다는 내용과 관련 상세 정보가 나오기에 (E) 역시 정답이다.

어휘 primary 주된 expire 소멸되다

Passage 1

1. A	2. B	3. B	4. C	5. B	6. D	7. C	8. C	9. B	10. BCF

로마 통치 하의 영국 문화

서기 43년에서 87년 사이에 있었던 로마의 영국 침략에는 사회적, 정치적, 그리고 문화적 영향의 물결이 동반되었다. 로마의 상품과 사상이 거리마다 넘쳐났으며, 영국의 정착지들을 점령한 병사들과 행정관들, 그리고 부대들만큼 [1(A)]분명한 것이었다. 이렇게 새로운 문화적 영향들 사이에서 가장 명백하게 드러났던 것은 로마 상품의 유입과 로마 제국 내에서 건너갔던 숙련된 장인들, 그리고 거대한 민간 건축물의 건설 공사였다.

로마인들이 영국으로 들어간 물품들은 결코 예술적 가치를 지니고 있지 않았으며, 실제로, 대단히 실용적인 것뿐이었다. 하지만, 그 물품들이 영국인들에게 미친 영향은 그에 못지않게 중요했다. 수입산 도구들과 조리 기구들, 그리고 의류는 빠르게 영국인들이 애지중지하는 물품이 되었으며, [2(B)]추가적으로 사회적 신분의 표시가 뒤따랐다. 붉은 광택이 도는 로마 제국의 도자기 '테라 시길라타'를 소유한 사람은 설사 그 물품을 장식했던 이야기나 신화에 대해 [3(B)]무지한 상태였다 하더라도 교양 있는 사람이라는 인상을 받았으며, 그리스 로마 문명의 세련된 양식과 예술적 개념을 접할 수 있게 되었다. 대부분의 제품이 대량 생산되고 국내에서 활용되기는 했지만, 작은 조각품 같이 몇몇 더욱 심미적인 제품들도 흔했다. 대부분은 아마 종교 의식에 사용하기 위해 영국에 전해졌거나, 문화적 교류 중에 종교 지도자들에게 선물로 제공되었을 것이다. 외교적, 종교적 가치로 인해 이 작은 조각품들은 사람들이 호감을 갖는 특성을 지니게 되면서 영국 전역에서 그 유행 및 물품 입수가 빠르게 확산되었다.

일부 영국인들은 로마인들의 양식과 문화를 두 팔 벌려 환영하면서 완전히 받아들였다. [4(C)]1세기 후반에 지어진 피시번 저택은 지역의 왕 코기두브누스의 명령에 따라 설계되고 지어지면서 그가 지니고 있던 여러 로마적 성향이 드러났을 가능성이 있다. 이 건물은 당시 로마에서 인기 있었던 수입산 대리석과 화려한 모자이크를 특징으로 함과 동시에, 그리스 로마 조각품들과 기타 예술품이 피시번 저택의 호화로운 홀들을 장식했다. [5(B)]피시번 저택의 디자인이 로마의 미학과 너무 비슷했기 때문에 그곳을 방문한 외교관은 분명 로마가 정복한 일부 지방의 후미진 곳이 아니라 마치 로마 제국의 한복판에 있는 것과 같은 기분이 들었을 것이다. 그 왕에게는 진정한 로마인이라는 사회적 존중이 부족하기는 했지만, 로마 제국의 문화적 상징들과 정체성을 아주 적절히 옹호함으로써 그는 틀림없이 일정 수준의 존경을 받았을 것이다.

이렇게 훌륭한 본보기를 따르면서, 로마의 양식은 번영했고, 유사 디자인에 대한 수요도 증가했다. ■영국 현지인들은 아직 석조 세공처럼 장인이 필요한 작업에 정통하지 못했기 때문에, 본토 출신 공예 작업자들의 유입이 필수적이었다. [9(B)][6(D)]그들이 작업한 초기 결과물이 바스에 있는 장엄한 사원이었으며, 정복 후에 비교적 빠르게 지어졌다. ■ 이 사원은 갈리아 북동부 지역의 디자인과 유사성을 지니고 있었는데, 이는 건축자들이 그 지역 출신이었을 가능성이 있다는 것을 추가로 나타내는 부분이다. ■[6(D)]이러한 시설을 짓기 위해, 로마의 행정관들은 개인 인맥을 활용해 영국의 작업자들을 로마 제국 내에서 온 숙련된 건축가나 석공들과 연결시켜주었다. 결국 그 기술은 현지 출신 작업자들에게 전수되었으며, 이 새로운 장인 기술을 활용한 더욱 독립적인 양식의 출현이 가능하게 되었다. 이는 영국 전역에 걸쳐 모자이크와 장식용 벽화, 도자기, 그리고 금속 세공을 포함한 더욱 폭넓은 예술 작품의 급증을 촉진했고, 그 모두가 결국 독특한 로마 영국 양식의 창조로 이어졌다.

로마의 영향이 모두 영국 문화에 무심코 스며든 것은 아니다. 건축 양식처럼 일부는 정복하는 로마 제국과 함께 의도적으로 유입되었다. 로마 제국 시대 전에는, 영국의 정착지들이 고립되어 있었다. [7(C)]사람들은 좀처럼 이동하지 않았으며, 전쟁 또는 드물게 열리던 종교 축제들을 제외하면, 대규모로 함께 모이지도 않았다. 작은 공동체들이 느슨하게 교류하던 사회였으며, 변변치 못한 오두막과 거주지들이 무리를 이뤄 구성되어 있었다. 대부분의 건물들은 그곳에 살았던 성인들보다 거의 높지 않았으며, 유기재(토탄과 나무)로 지은 건축물과 둥근 형태는 자연 풍경과 어우러졌다. 하지만 로마 건축 양식의 영향은 그 반대였다. [8(D)]거대하고 호화로웠으며, 일체형 구조를 통해 [8(B)]피정복민들이 로마 제국의 힘을 직접 목격하는 과정에서 그들을 두렵게 하려 했다. [8(A)]그 곧은 선과 명확한 각도는 영국의 구조물이 지닌 곡선과 확연하게 대비되었으며, 로마의 공학 기술을 비롯해 원칙 및 권위에 대한 준수를 증명하는 것이었다.

[어휘]

1. accompany ~을 동반하다 invasion 침략 evident 명확한 occupy ~을 점령하다 settlement 정착지 influx 유입 artisan 장인 massive 거대한, 엄청난

2. by no means 결코 ~가 아니다 treasure ~을 애지중지하다, 귀하게 여기다 grant A B A에게 B를 주다 air 인상, 느낌 ware 물품, 용품 introduce A to B A에게 B를 접하게 해주다 rarified 세련된 mass-produce ~을 대량 생산하다 aesthetic 심미적인 statuette 작은 조각품 lend A B A에게 B를 부여하다 quality 속성, 특성

3. adopt ~을 받아들이다, 채택하다 at the behest of ~의 명령에 따라 feature ~을 특징으로 하다 lavish 호화로운 aesthetics 미학 diplomat 외교관 backwater 후미진 곳 esteem 존중, 존경 garner ~을 얻다 aptly 적절히 espouse ~을 옹호하다

4. sterling 훌륭한 live up to ~을 따르다, 충족하다, ~에 부응하다 flourish 번영하다 carving 조각(술) magnificent 장엄한 mason 석공 be passed on to ~에게 전수되다, 물려주다 rise 출현, 발생, 떠오름 artisanal 장인의 upsurge 급증 distinctive 독특한

5. casually 무심코, 우연히, 문득 seep into ~로 스며들다 intently 의도적으로 isolated 고립된 composed of ~로 구성된 cluster 무리 inhabit ~에 살다 merge A with B A를 B와 어우러지게 하다 opulent 호화로운 intimidate ~을 두려워하게 하다, 위협하다 witness ~을 목격하다 monolithic 일체형의 contrast with ~와 대비되다 attest to ~을 증명하다 adherence to ~에 대한 준수, 고수 principle 원칙 authority 권위

---

1. 지문의 단어 "evident"와 의미가 가장 가까운 것은 무엇인가?

(A) 분명한, 눈에 띄는
(B) 강한, 강력한
(C) 필수의, 필요한
(D) 정확한, 옳은

해설 evident(분명한, 눈에 띄는)와 clear(분명한, 보기 쉬운)는 유의어로 정답은 (A)이다.

2. 두 번째 문단에서, 로마에서 제조된 물품을 얻는 것의 가능한 이점은 무엇이었는가?

(A) 품질이 더 뛰어난 결과물
(B) 사회적 지위의 상승
(C) 로마 신화의 소개
(D) 종교 의식 참여

해설 물품이 사회적 신분의 표시가 뒤따랐다는 점과 교양 있는 사람이라는 인상을 받았다는 점에서 사회적 지위의 상승이라는 이점을 누릴 수 있었다는 점을 유추할 수 있으므로 (B)가 정답이다.

3. 지문의 단어 "ignorant"와 의미가 가장 가까운 것은 무엇인가?

(A) 동정하는, 동조하는
(B) 무지한, 알지 못하는
(C) 적대적인
(D) 관련된

해설 ignorant(무지한, 알지 못하는)와 unaware(무지한, 알지 못하는)는 동의어로 정답은 (B)이다.

4. 코기두브누스와 관련해 유추할 수 있는 것은 무엇인가?

(A) 로마의 한 행정관으로 빠르게 대체되었다.

(B) 정복 전에 로마를 방문했다.
(C) 당시 로마 제국의 유행을 잘 알고 있었다.
(D) 정복 중에 로마인들을 도왔다.

해설 세 번째 문단의 초반부에서 코기두브누스는 로마에 대해 호의적인 성향을 가지고 있었으며, 저택의 디자인이 로마의 미학과 비슷했다는 점으로 미뤄보아 정답은 (C)임을 알 수 있다.

5. 다음 문장들 중 어느 것이 지문의 하이라이트 표기된 문장에 담긴 핵심 정보를 가장 잘 표현하는가? 오답 선택지는 중요한 방식으로 의미를 변경하거나 핵심 정보를 배제한다.

피시번 저택의 디자인이 로마의 미학과 너무 비슷했기 때문에 그곳을 방문한 외교관은 분명 로마가 정복한 일부 지방의 후미진 곳이 아니라 마치 로마 제국의 한복판에 있는 것과 같은 기분이 들었을 것이다.

(A) 피시번은 영국 시골 지역에 위치해 있기는 했지만 로마의 저택(빌라)을 면밀하게 본떠 만들어졌다.
(B) 피시번 저택에 간 로마인은 그 저택이 영국의 디자인보다 로마의 디자인과 더 유사하다고 생각했을 것이다.
(C) 길을 잃은 로마인들은 피시번이 로마에 있는 자신들의 집과 닮았기 때문에 결국 그곳에 가 있는 것이 흔했다.
(D) 외교관들은 대부분의 영국 건물들보다 자신들의 필요에 더 적합했기 때문에 흔히 피시번에서 만났다.

해설 (A)의 경우, 유사하다는 생각을 했다 또는 기분이 들었다라는 felt as though절의 의미를 살리지 못하고 있다. (C)의 '그곳에 가 있는 것이 흔했다'는 내용은 하이라이트 문장에는 없는 내용이다. (D)는 비교급 표현이 잘못 사용되었다. 따라서, 로마의 디자인과 더 유사하다고 생각했다는 점을 언급하는 (B)가 정답이다.

어휘 be modeled after ~을 본떠 만들어지다 end up 결국 ~하게 되다 resemble ~을 닮다

6. 네 번째 문단에서, 영국에서 로마 양식으로 된 건축물의 빠른 개발에 도움이 된 가지 요인은 무엇인가?

(A) 국내에서 폭넓게 이용 가능했던 석조 및 대리석
(B) 영국으로 먼저 건너간 로마 제국 출신의 숙련된 작업자들
(C) 영국 현지인들이 지니고 있던 전문적인 석조 세공 기술
(D) 로마 행정관들과 공예가들 사이의 개인적인 친분

해설 해당 문단의 두 번째 문장에서 본토 출신 공예 작업자라는 키워드를 언급하고, 이후 중간 지점을 보면 건축자들이 그 지역 출신이었을 가능성이 있다는 것을 나타낸다는 점이 명확하게 드러난다. 그러므로 그 뒤에 등장하는 개인 인맥을 통해 연결시켜 주었다는 점을 토대로 (D)가 정답이다.

7. 글쓴이는 왜 영국인들이 좀처럼 이동하지 않았다고 언급하는가?

(A) 로마의 정복이 어떻게 교통편 이용 가능성을 제공했는지 알려주기 위해
(B) 영국인들이 다른 문화권과 거의 교류하지 않았음을 나타내기 위해
(C) 영국의 건축물이 왜 크게 지어지지 않았는지 설명하기 위해
(D) 가정 생활이 영국인들에게 우선 순위가 더 높았음을 주장하기 위해

해설 다섯 번째 문단에 좀처럼 이동하지 않고, 대규모로 모이지 않는다는 내용 이후에 작은 공동체들이 느슨하게 교류하던 사회로 구성이 되어 대부분의 건물이 그곳에 살았던 성인보다 높지 않았다는 점을 토대로 정답이 (C)임을 알 수 있다.

어휘 priority 우선 순위

8. 다섯 번째 문단에서, 로마 정복 이전의 건물들이 로마인들에 의해 지어진 것들과 달랐던 측면에 해당되지 않는 것은 무엇인가?

(A) 기하학적 형태
(B) 사람들에게 미친 영향
(C) 무리 내에서의 배치
(D) 규모

해설 문단의 마지막 부분을 보면 곡선, 사람들을 두렵게 함, 그리고 거대하고 호화스러움을 제시하고 있다. 무리 내에서의 배치는 언급되지 않으므로 정답은 (C)이다.

9. 다음 문장이 지문에 추가될 수 있는 곳을 나타내는 네 개의 네모 표기 [■]를 찾아 보시오.

이 장인들은 주로 갈리아와 독일 지역 출신이었다.

위 문장은 어느 곳에 가장 적합하겠는가? 네모 표기[■]를 클릭해 지문에 이 문장을 추가하시오.
(A) 1번

(B) 2번
(C) 3번
(D) 4번

해설 '이 장인들' 및 '갈리아와 독일 지역 출신'의 두 키워드와 관련 있는 부분은, 해당 문단의 두 번째 문장에 제시된 '본토 출신 공예 작업자들의 유입'이다. 그러므로 두 번째 박스에 넣는 것이 가장 적절하다. 정답은 (B)이다.

10. 설명: 간략한 지문 요약에 필요한 도입 문장이 아래에 제공되어 있다. 지문에서 가장 중요한 개념들을 나타내는 세 가지 답안 선택지를 골라 요약 내용을 완성하시오. 일부 답안 선택지는 지문에 제시되지 않는 개념을 나타내거나 지문에서 중요하지 않은 개념들이므로 요약 내용에 속하지 않는다. **이 문제는 2점에 해당된다.**

로마 제국의 영국 정복은 여러 문화적 변화에 영향을 미쳤다.

(A) 영국인들이 선진 무역 기술을 배우기 위해 갈리아로 떠나면서 새로운 교육 기회가 이용 가능했다.
(B) 도자기 같은 일상 용품에서부터 특별 행사에 쓰인 장식용 제품에 이르기까지 다양한 새 물품들이 영국에 전해졌다.
(C) 로마의 건물 및 실내 디자인은 선진 기술을 필요로 했기 때문에, 로마 제국의 여러 다른 지방에서 작업자들이 동원되었다.
(D) 영국의 마을들은 로마 행정관들이 시골 지역으로 이전하면서 고급 저택으로 대체되었다.
(E) 영국인들이 열었던 이교도적 의식은 로마인들이 섬겼던 다양한 신들을 수용하기 위해 변경되었다.
(F) 로마 건축물의 거대한 크기와 곧은 선들로 인해 영국의 별로 크지 않은 건물들이 왜소해 보였다.

해설 두 번째 문단을 보면 일상 용품에서부터 장식용 제품까지 다양한 물품이 전파되었다는 점을 알 수 있다. 그러므로 (B)를 가장 먼저 답안으로 선택한다. 네 번째 문단을 통해 로마 제국의 여러 다른 지방에서 작업자들이 동원되었다는 점을 알 수 있고, 이를 기반으로 (C)를 정답으로 고른다. 다섯 번째 문단을 보면, 로마 건축 양식이라는 키워드와 함께, 로마의 원칙과 권위에 대한 준수를 증명한다는 점을 토대로 (F)를 정답으로 선택한다.

어휘 be replaced by ~로 대체되다 pagan 이교도의 accommodate ~을 수용하다 deity 신 dwarf ~을 왜소해 보이게 만들다

Passage 2

1. B	2. C	3. B	4. C	5. D	6. A	7. A	8. D	9. C	10. ADE

고대 이란의 혁신

이란의 역사는 부분적으로 그 지리적 제약에 의해 정의되어 왔다. ¹⁽ᴮ⁾여러 지역에서 충분히 비가 내리는 비옥한 골짜기와 평원이 가축을 먹여 살릴 수 있었지만, 전체 초목의 양은 충분하지 않았다. 그곳 동물들이 한 장소에서 너무 오래 풀을 뜯는다면, 모든 이용 가능한 먹이를 금방 소비하게 된다. 이러한 환경은 양치기들이 광활하게 펼쳐진 시골 지역에 걸쳐 가축(즉 양과 염소)을 몰고 다니면서 돌보는 전원적인 유목 생활이라는 관습으로 이어졌다. 전원적인 유목 생활은 초기 이란의 경제 및 사회의 여러 다른 측면을 형성하는 데 영향을 미쳤다. 가축 떼들의 움직임은 일반적으로 수직 패턴을 따랐는데, 양치기들이 겨울철에 저지대로 내려갔다가 여름에 다시 고지대로 돌아오는 방식이었다. 유목 가축에 의해 만들어지는 상품은 가치가 높고 다양했다. 여기에는 유제품과 고기뿐만 아니라, 카펫과 의류, 그리고 거처를 만드는 데 들어가는 엄청난 양의 재료도 포함되었다. 유목민들이 여기저기 다니는 가축 떼들을 위해 면적이 아주 넓은 땅을 통제할 수 있는 부족으로 ²⁽ᶜ⁾모여들면서 사회적 정체성을 지닌 집단들이 형성되었다.

전원 생활을 하는 유목민들로 구성된 부족들은 고대에서부터 20세기에 이르기까지 이란 내에서 사회적, 정치적 영향력을 발휘했다. 무엇보다도, ⁴⁽ᴮ⁾그들의 생계에 있어 고유하면서 아주 중요한 기술들, 즉 포식자 사냥, 탁 트인 지역에 대한 탐사, 구성원 기강 확립, 그리고 영토 보호는 군대 목적에 완벽히 부합하는 것이었다. ⁴⁽ᴬ⁾대부분의 통치자들과 병사들은 이 부족들에서 나왔으며, 이 부족들은 국가를 이끌었던 왕조들과 긴밀히 협력하기도 했다. ³⁽ᴮ⁾실제로, 이란의 정치 분야는 이 부족들을 대하는 일과 깊이 연관되어 있었다. 이는 우호적인 부족들에 대해서는 지원과 호의를 제공하는 관계를 구축함과 동시에 그들 중에서 더 적대적인 부족에 대해서는 투쟁이나 위협, 또는 기타 여러 수단을 통해 통치를 시행하거나 완전히 제거하려 했다는 것을 의미했다. ⁴⁽ᴰ⁾심지어 20세기 초 무렵에는, 부족민들이 전체 인구의 최소 4분의 1을 차지하는 상황에서 이란의 부족들이 정치 체계에 대해 여전히 상당한 영향력을 행사하고 있었다. 하지만, 유목 생활 방식은 1930년대에 들어서 기계화된 전쟁의 도래로 인해 정부가 이 부족들의 힘에 맞서 대응하고 정착하도록 강제할 수 있게 되면서 점차 사라지기 시작했다. 이 군사 행동이 성공을 거두면서 이 부족들은 현대 이란의 사회와 경제에서 아주 적은 존재감을 보이고 있으며, 전체 인구의 5퍼센트 미만에 해당되는 사람들만 전통적인 전원 유목 생활 방식을 대표하고 있다.

이란은 물 부족 문제로 인해 추가적인 혁신이 필요했다. ⁵⁽ᴰ⁾고원 지대 전역에 걸친 건조한 환경으로 인해, 이란은 삶을 지탱해주는 강들이 있던 메소포타미아 같은 이웃 국가들에게 충분히 공급되던 물이 없었다. 초기 농부들은 이 문제를 고대의 가장 주목할 만한 농업 혁신들 중 한 가지를 통해 해결했는데, 이는 그 평지 지대에 여기저기 흩어져 있던 부족한 오아시스 너머로 농지를 만드는 일을 가능하게 해주었다. 이 혁신은 바로 카나트, 즉 고원 분지의 자연 경사로를 통해 지하수의 관개를 가능하게 해주었던 대규모 지하 수로의 개발이었다. 이 시스템은 산 속 언덕 지역에 파여 있는 샘에서 시작되었는데, 그곳에 눈이 녹아 발생된 물이 모여 있었다. 거기서부터, 추가 우물과 수직 갱도가 지어져 경작 준비가 되어 있는 다양한 마을의 여러 다른 구역으로 흐르는 지하 수로로 연결되었다. ⁶⁽ᴬ⁾이 자연 경사로가 침식을 촉진했고 우물 및 갱도 내부를 온전한 상태로 유지하기 위해 주기적인 수리 작업이 필요했기 때문에 특별한 주의가 필수적이었다.

카나트는 여러 면에서 경이로운 고대의 창의적 산물이었다. 지상의 시스템들이 증발에 ⁷⁽ᴬ⁾취약했던 반면, 카나트는 지하에 있었기 때문에 그러한 문제를 피했다. 기계적인 시스템도 전혀 필요치 않았는데, 중력이 물의 모든 움직임을 용이하게 해주었기 때문이었다. ⁸⁽ᴰ⁾우물 및 갱도 단위로 수로의 길이를 나눔으로써, 각 구간은 길이가 짧으면서 관리하기 쉽게 유지되었으며, 개별 구역에 대한 수리 작업은 수월하게 처리되었다. ■ 카나트 개발은 여러 세기에 걸쳐 진행되어, 대규모 조직망 구축으로 그 막을 내렸다. ■ 우물과 갱도, 그리고 수로를 포함해 그 시스템 전체는 길이가 30만 킬로미터가 넘는 것으로 추정되어 왔다. ⁹⁽ᶜ⁾■ 하지만, 이러한 지략도 훌륭한 보상으로 이어지지는 않았는데, 이란의 농업은 여전히 전망이 매우 나빴으며, 소작농들은 과세 후에 농산품의 일부만 받았기 때문이다. ■

[어휘]

1. graze 풀을 뜯어 먹다, 방목하다 give rise to (결과로서) ~로 이어지다, ~을 초래하다 pastoral 전원적인 nomadism 유목 생활 tend ~을 돌보다 herd v. (가축 등) ~을 몰다 n. 떼, 무리 facet 측면, 양상 descend to ~로 내려가다, 내려오다 copious 엄청난, 풍부한 pocket 집단, 지역 converge into ~로 모여들다 tract 넓은 지대, 지역 roam 돌아다니다

2. **constitute** ~을 구성하다 **inherent** 고유의, 내재하는 **discipline** ~의 기강을 세우다, ~을 훈육하다 **initiate** n. 구성원, 가입자 **emerge from** ~에서 나오다 **realm** 분야, 영역 **enforce** ~을 시행하다, 강요하다 **intimidation** 위협 **hold sway over** ~에 영향력을 행사하다, ~을 좌지우지하다 **comprise** ~을 구성하다 **diminish** 쇠퇴하다, 약화되다 **push back against** ~에 맞서 대응하다 **campaign** 군사 행동, 작전

3. **scarcity** 부족 **plateau** 고원 지대 **scant** 부족한, 드문 **dot** v. ~에 여기저기 흩어져 있다 **qanat** 카나트(이란에서 지하수를 얻기 위한 지하 수로) **subterranean** 지하의 **canal** 수로, 운하 **irrigation** 관개 **gradient** 경사로(= slope) **basin** 분지 **foothill** 작은 언덕 **accumulate** 모이다, 축적되다 **shaft** 수직 갱도 **erosion** 침식, 부식 **intact** 온전한

4. **ingenuity** 창의성, 독창성 **vulnerable** 취약한 **evaporation** 증발 **facilitate** ~을 용이하게 하다 **culminate in** ~로 끝나다, 결국 ~가 되다 **resourcefulness** 지략, 기지 **dire** 몹시 나쁜, 끔찍한

---

1. 첫 번째 문단에 따르면, 전원 유목민들은 무엇 때문에 한 곳에서 다른 곳으로 가축을 몰고 다녀야 했는가?

(A) 다른 유목민들과의 영토 분쟁
(B) 방목 가능한 초목의 부족 문제
(C) 여러 다른 지역의 계절별 기후 변화
(D) 고도가 높은 지역에서 가축을 기르는 어려움

해설 해당 문단의 두 번째 문장에서 네 번째 문장을 보면 초목 양이 부족해서 금방 먹이를 소비하기에 자연스럽게 전원적인 유목 생활이라는 관습을 택했다는 점을 토대로 (B)가 정답이다.

어휘 dispute 분쟁 altitude 고도

2. 지문의 단어 "converged"와 의미가 가장 가까운 것은 무엇인가?

(A) 경쟁했다
(B) 이주했다
(C) 모였다
(D) 회전했다, 교대로 했다

해설 converged(모였다)와 assembled(모였다)는 동의어로 정답은 (C)이다.

3. 두 번째 문단에서 이란의 통치자들이 유목민 부족들을 활용한 방식과 관련해 무엇을 유추할 수 있는가?

(A) 통치자들이 중대한 행정적 결정을 내리기 전에 부족장들과 상의했다.
(B) 통치자들이 자신들을 지지하지 않는 부족들과 싸우기 위해 우호적인 부족들을 모집했다.
(C) 통치자들이 부족들의 경제 활동에 의해 만들어진 교역에 의존했다.
(D) 통치자들이 부족들의 집단적인 힘을 약화시키기 위해 그들 사이에서 갈등을 조장했다.

해설 두 번째 문단의 첫 번째 문장을 보면, 유목민이 가지는 사회적, 정치적 영향력을 강조하고 있다. 그리고 해당 문단의 중간 지점을 보면, 우호적인 부족에 대해서는 관계를 구축함과 동시에 적대적인 부족에 대해서는 통치 시행 및 제거를 시도했다는 점을 제시한다. 그러므로 통치자들은 우호적인 부족들과 관계를 형

성했다는 정보가 중요하므로 (B)가 정답이다.

어휘 recruit ~을 모집하다 inspire ~을 조장하다, 북돋우다 conflict 갈등 collective 집단의, 공동의

4. 두 번째 문단에 따르면, 전원 생활을 하는 유목민들이 이란의 역사에 있어 중요한 역할을 했던 이유에 해당되지 않는 것은 무엇인가?

(A) 이란의 많은 통치자들이 그 부족 출신이었다.
(B) 그들의 기술이 이란의 통치자들에게 가치 있는 것이었다.
(C) 기계화된 노동 방식을 도입하는 데 도움을 주었다.
(D) 그들이 인구의 많은 부분을 차지했다.

해설 해당 문단에서 20세기 초, 부족민들이 전체 인구의 최소 4분의 1을 차지한다는 점을 언급하므로 (D)를 소거한다. 해당 문단의 두 번째 문장을 보면, 유목민들이 가지는 기술이 중요하다는 점을 언급하므로 (B)를 소거한다. 그 바로 다음 문장에서 대부분의 통치자가 이 부족들로부터 나왔다는 점을 통해 (A)를 소거한다. 따라서 정답은 (C)이다.

5. 세 번째 문단에 따르면, 글쓴이는 왜 이란의 지리적 특징을 메소포타미아의 특징과 비교했는가?

(A) 메소포타미아의 강들이 그 지역 전역에 걸쳐 미친 영향을 입증하기 위해
(B) 인근 지역들이 왜 카나트 시스템을 택하지 않았는지 설명하기 위해
(C) 중동 지역 전체가 어떻게 관개 시스템에 의존했는지 강조하기 위해
(D) 이란의 카나트 개발 이면에 숨어 있는 계기를 알려주기 위해

해설 문단의 시작과 해당 키워드의 앞 문장을 통해 확인할 수 있다. 이란의 물 부족 문제는 고원 지대 전역에 걸친 건조한 환경에서 비롯되었고, 충분한 물이 있던 메소포타미아와 비교되었다. 이로 인해 이란은 농업 혁신을 이뤄냈고 그 중 하나가 바로 카나트 개발임을 알 수 있기에 정답은 (D)이다.

어휘 adopt ~을 채택하다 motivation 계기, 동기 (부여)

6. 다음 문장들 중 어느 것이 지문의 하이라이트 표기된 문장에 담긴 핵심 정보를 가장 잘 표현하는가? 오답 선택지는 중요한 방식으로 의미를 변경하거나 핵심 정보를 배제한다.

이 자연 경사로가 심식을 촉진했고 우물 및 갱도 내부를 온전한 상태로 유지하기 위해 주기적인 수리 작업이 필요했기 때문에 특별한 주의가 필수적이었다.

(A) 카나트는 지속적으로 기능하는 데 별도의 관리가 필요했다.

(B) 침식은 카나트에 여러 구조적 문제를 초래했다.

(C) 경사로에 지어진 것이 카나트 내부의 침식을 방지해주었다.

(D) 카나트를 수리하는 일은 통로의 가파름으로 인해 어려웠다.

해설 ‘특별한 주의가 필수적이었다’는 부분이 반드시 언급되어야 하는데, 이러한 보기는 (A)가 유일하다. 또한 ‘온전한 상태로 유지’라는 키워드가 ‘지속적으로 기능’으로 패러프레이징된 (A)가 정답이다.

7. 지문의 단어 "vulnerable"과 의미가 가장 가까운 것은 무엇인가?

(A) 노출된, 위험에 드러나 있는

(B) 주저하는, 망설이는

(C) 풀어진, 방출된

(D) 손상된, 피해를 입은

해설 vulnerable(취약한)과 exposed(노출된, 위험에 드러나 있는)는 유의어로 정답은 (A)이다.

8. 네 번째 문단에 따르면, 카나트는 왜 다수의 우물 및 갱도와 함께 지어졌는가?

(A) 녹는 눈에서 발생되는 물을 더 많이 모으기 위해

(B) 물의 흐름을 더 빠르게 촉진하기 위해

(C) 다양한 공동체들이 그것들을 통해 물을 얻도록 하기 위해

(D) 분리된 구역들을 더 수월하게 유지 관리하기 위해

해설 해당 문단의 중반부를 보면, 각 구간이 길이가 짧고 관리가 쉽게 유지되었고, 개발 구역에 대한 수리 작업 역시 수월하게 처리되었다는 점을 언급하기 때문에 정답은 (D)이다.

9. 다음 문장이 지문에 추가될 수 있는 곳을 나타내는 네 개의 네모 표기 [■]를 찾아 보시오.

이는 지구와 달 사이의 거리와 동일한 거리이므로, 카나트 건설에 얼마나 많은 시간과 돈이 들어갔는지 쉽게 알 수 있다.

위 문장은 어느 곳에 가장 적합하겠는가? 네모 표기[■]를 클릭해 지문에 이 문장을 추가하시오.

(A) 1번

(B) 2번

(C) 3번

(D) 4번

해설 주어진 문장을 보면 “이는 지구와 달 사이의 거리와 동일”하다는 표현이 들어가 있는 만큼 구체적인 길이가 제시된 문장 이후에 들어갈 것이라고 판단하는 것이 올바르다. 따라서 정답은 (C)이다.

10. 설명: 간략한 지문 요약에 필요한 도입 문장이 아래에 제공되어 있다. 지문에서 가장 중요한 개념들을 나타내는 세 가지 답안 선택지를 골라 요약 내용을 완성하시오. 일부 답안 선택지는 지문에 제시되지 않는 개념을 나타내거나 지문에서 중요하지 않은 개념들이므로 요약 내용에 속하지 않는다. **이 문제는 2점에 해당된다.**

이란의 건조한 기후 및 황량한 풍경은 이란의 사회적, 경제적 발전에 영향을 미쳤다.

(A) 성공적으로 가축을 길러 식량 및 물품을 얻기 위해, 전원 유목민들은 시골 지역에 걸쳐 동물들을 몰고 다녔다.

(B) 이란의 유목민 부족들은 1900년대에 성공적으로 여러 도시 및 마을로 흡수되었다.

(C) 이란의 풍경 속에 나타나는 자연 경사로는 관개용 수로 건설을 가능하게 해주었다.

(D) 유목민 부족 공동체들은 20세기에 이르기까지 수 세기 동안 사회적, 경제적으로 막대한 영향력을 행사했다.

(E) 카나트는 복잡한 관개 시스템을 만들어냈으며, 이란 농업의 확장을 가능하게 해주었다.

(F) 역사적으로, 이란 정부는 유목민 부족들에게 의존해 침략자들을 막아냈다.

해설 첫 번째 문단은 유목민의 발생과 관련된 자세한 설명을 해주기 때문에 (A)를 선택한다. 그리고 두 번째 문단에서부터 유목민 부족 공동체는 강력한 영향력을 가졌다는 점을 알 수 있기 때문에 (D)를 선택한다. 이란이 겪고 있는 물 부족 문제는 단연 이 지문에서 중요한 내용이며, 이를 위한 관개 시스템을 설명해주고 있는 세 번째 문단의 내용을 포함하는 (E)도 선택한다.

어휘 sparse 황량한, 희박한 integrate into ~로 흡수되다, 통합되다 hold influence 영향력을 행사하다, 세력을 떨치다 intricate 복잡한

Passage 3

수메르의 도시 국가들

수메르는 중동의 티그리스 강과 유프라테스 강 사이의 비옥한 지역인 메소포타미아에서 가장 오래된 것으로 알려진 문명이자, 세계 최초의 문명 중 하나이다. 1(A)그것은 메소포타미아 평원의 남쪽 끝자락에서 나타났는데, 그곳은 처음에는 문명을 발전시킬 가능성이 적은 곳이었다. 2(A)그 평원은 목재와 돌, 그리고 금속 같은 천연 자원이 거의 존재하지 않아 대체로 황량한 곳이었다. 2(D)강우량 역시 희박했지만, 2(C)녹은 눈이 평원 전역에서 밀려오면서 연례적인 홍수가 들이닥치곤 했다. 게다가, 약한 자연 경사도로 인해, 평원의 강바닥이 자주 변했다. 하지만, 이러한 어려움들은 문명에 도움이 되는 것으로 드러났는데, 사회 조직 및 협동을 필요로 했던 대규모 작업인 관개 시스템의 개발이 요구되었기 때문이었다. 일단 한 가지 시스템이 도입되어 영양분이 풍부한 토사가 농지 전역에서 넘쳐나게 되면, 농작물은 잘 자랐다. 관개 시스템을 갖춘 토지는 일반 토지보다 거의 다섯 배나 많은 양을 생산했다. 그 결과로 나타난 잉여 농작물은 자원을 관리하고 분배해야 하는 엘리트 계층 및 그 이후에 나타난 사회 계급 질서의 확립으로 이어졌다.

사회 질서가 자리잡기 시작하자, 도시 정착지들이 자연스럽게 그 뒤를 따랐다. 하지만, 최초의 도시 국가 확립으로 이어진 정확한 요인들이 무엇이었는지는 명확하지 않다. 3(C)한 가지 가능성은 종교이다. 기원전 4500년 무렵에 세워진 최초의 도시 국가 '에리두'는 진흙 벽돌로 만들어진 인상적인 한 신전 부근에서 생겨났다. 마찬가지로, 약 1천년 후에 세워진 '우루크'는 도시 중심부에 신전이 하나 자리잡고 있었다. ■ 엘리트 계층은 종교를 활용해 자신들의 권력을 강화하고 신과 관련된 정당화를 통해 권력을 뒷받침했다. ■ 게다가, 도시들마다 수호신이 있었다. ■ 예를 들어, '우루크'에는 하늘의 신이자 판테온(만신전) 최고의 신 '아누'와 사랑과 전쟁의 신 '이난나'라는 두 명의 신이 있었다. 9(D)■ 후대의 종교 문서에 나타나는 것과 동일한 파멸적인 홍수는, 전설 속에서 단지 너무 시끄럽다는 이유만으로 인류를 말살시킨 수메르 신들이 나오는 버전에서 최초로 찾을 수 있다.

신전의 중심적 존재 및 신화의 복잡성은 종교적 인물들이 그 도시들을 이끌었을 가능성이 가장 컸다는 것을 나타낸 부분이다. 4(A)하지만, 현재는 그렇지 않았던 것으로 여겨지고 있으며, 그 도시들은 심지어 초창기부터 세속적인 지도자들이 있었을 가능성이 있었다. 세속적인 지도층 하에서, 다양한 직업이 생겨났고, 도시 생활에 있어 다양성이 창출되었다. 직업 중에는 행정가와 장인들, 그리고 상인들이 포함되었다. 그 지역의 제한적인 천연 자원을 감안하면, 탄탄한 교역 시스템이 발달되었는데, 대부분의 원자재가 수입되어야 했기 때문이었다. 행정 및 교역이 점점 더 고도화됨에 따라 기원전 3300년 무렵에 문자 체계의 발명이라는 결과로 이어졌다. 문자의 최초 버전으로 표어 문자, 즉 단어 전체를 상징하는 기호를 기반으로 했다. 이 표어 문자는 머리 부분이 쐐기 모양인 침을 이용해 점토 판에 5(D)새겨졌다. 나중에 로마인들은 그 침의 모양이 쐐기 같다고 해서 이 문자 체계를 쐐기 문자라고 불렀다.

6(C)가장 오래된 기록을 보면 2,000개가 넘는 표어 문자들이 있는 것으로 설명하고 있지만, 단어 전체가 아닌 음절을 표현하기 위한 기호를 사용하기 시작하면서 그 체계는 간소화되었다. 예를 들어, "주인"을 뜻하는 단어("엔"으로 발음)에 대한 최초의 기호는 왕좌와 닮았지만, 시간이 흐름에 따라 간소화되어, 기호 자체가 음절을 대신 나타내게 되었다. "엔" 발음을 포함하는 모든 단어는 그 기호를 사용했으며, 나머지 음절들은 다른 기호들을 통해 표현되었다. 6(C)처음 생겨난 이후로 약 천년이 지나, 쐐기 문자는 약 600개의 기호로 줄어들었지만, 표현될 수 있는 단어의 종류는 늘어났다. 경제 사안과 관련된 글이 7(C)지배적이기는 했지만, 문학과 신학, 역사, 그리고 법률에 대한 것도 있었으며, 여기에는 길가메시 서사시도 포함된다.

수메르의 도시 국가들은 또한 여러 다른 혁신을 통해서도 혜택을 얻었다. 8(A)기원전 4000년경에 나타났을 가능성이 있는 바퀴는 원래 도예 작업용이었다. 운송 수단에 응용된 바퀴에 대한 첫 기호는 기원전 3000년경에 만든 점토 판에 나타났으며, 바퀴 네 개로 끄는 상자 같은 수레를 묘사했다. 비슷한 시기에 있었던 청동의 발견도 수메르의 주된 발전을 나타내는 것이었다. 수메르인들은 기원전 3500년부터 구리를 사용했지만, 주석과 함께 제련해 훨씬 더 강한 청동을 만들어낸 것은 약 500년 후의 일이었다. 청동이 구리와 석기를 완전히 대체하지는 못했지만, 단조 작업으로 가장자리를 날카롭게 만들면서, 톱과 큰 낫, 그리고 모든 종류의 무기를 만드는 우수한 재료가 될 수 있었다. 청동의 발견으로 인해 청동기 시대가 시작되었으며, 이 시대는 기원전 3000년부터 1000년까지 지속되었다.

[어휘]

1. fertile 비옥한 emerge 나타나다, 생겨나다 foster ~을 발전시키다, 촉진하다 plain 평원 desolate 황량한, 황폐한 sparse 드문, 희박한 descend (불시에) 밀려오다 gradient 경사도 conducive to ~에 도움이 되는 irrigation 관개 undertaking 작업, 일 silt 토사 flourish 잘 자라다, 무성해지다 surplus 잉여, 과잉 subsequent 그 이후의, 나중의

2. in place 자리 잡은, 제 자리에 있는 house v. ~을 포함하다, ~에 공간을 제공하다 consolidate ~을 강화하다, 통합하다 divine 신의, 신성한 justification 정당화 patron god 수호신 deity 신(령) pantheon (모든 신들을 모신) 만신전, 판테온 catastrophic 파멸적인, 대재앙의

3. intricacy 복잡함 secular 세속적인 given ~을 감안하면, 고려하면 robust 탄탄한, 강력한 sophistication 고도화, 세련됨 logogram 표어 문자, 어표(= logograph) incise ~을 새기다 stylus 침, 바늘 cuneiform 쐐기 문자, 설형 문자 cuneus 쐐기

4. resemble ~와 비슷하다, ~을 닮다 throne 왕좌 syllable 음절 predominant 지배적인

5. benefit from ~로부터 혜택을 얻다, 이득을 보다 depict ~을 묘사하다 smelt (광석 등) ~을 제련하다 forge (금속 등)~을 단조하다 initiate ~을 시작하다

1. 지문의 단어 "it"이 가리키는 것은 무엇인가?
(A) 수메르
(B) 문명
(C) 메소포타미아
(D) 중동 지역

해설 it의 앞 문장을 토대로 수메르에 대한 이야기가 이어짐을 알 수 있으므로 (A)가 정답이다.

2. 다음 중 어느 것이 첫 번째 문단에서 메소포타미아 평원의 단점으로 언급되지 않는가?
(A) 나무와 광석 같은 천연 자원이 존재하지 않았다.
(B) 강바닥이 충분한 토사를 포함하고 있지 않았다.
(C) 녹아내리는 눈으로 인해 홍수가 연례적으로 발생했다.
(D) 비가 연중 대부분의 기간에 흔치 않았다.

해설 문단의 초반부에서, 목재와 돌과 같은 천연 자원이 존재하지 않아 황량한 곳이었다는 점을 언급하기에 (A)를 소거한다. 그 바로 뒤의 문장을 보면 강우량이 희박했다는 점을 토대로 (D)를 소거하며, 연례적인 홍수가 들이닥쳤다는 정보를 토대로 (C) 역시 소거할 수 있다. 따라서 정답은 (B)이다.

어휘 ore 광석

3. 두 번째 문단에서, 에리두와 우루크는 모두 어떤 도시 정착지였는가?
(A) 농작물을 얻기 위해 관개에 의존했다.
(B) 수메르의 다른 도시 국가들이 힘겨워했던 것과 달리 번영했다.
(C) 커다란 종교적 건축물을 중심으로 세워졌다.
(D) 엘리트 통치 계급을 지원했다.

해설 두 번째 문단의 세 번째 문장과 이어지는 문장을 보면, 종교에 대한 가능성을 언급한다. 에리두 같은 경우 신전 부근에서 형성되었다는 점, 우루크는 도시 중심부에 신전이 존재했다는 점을 토대로 커다란 종교적 건축물을 중심으로 세워졌다는 점을 알 수 있으므로 (C)가 정답이다.

4. 세 번째 문단에서 도시 국가와 관련해 유추할 수 있는 것은 무엇인가?
(A) 그 기능이 종교보다 경제와 더 크게 관련되어 있었다.
(B) 종교적 관습을 바탕으로 경제를 발전시켰다.
(C) 아주 다양한 교역 기술을 지원하지 않았다.
(D) 문자 체계가 교역 중에 맞닥뜨린 것들을 바탕으로 했다.

해설 해당 문단의 첫 문장을 통해 신전의 중심적 존재를 언급하고, 이후 문장에서 역접과 함께 세속적인 지도자가 있었을 것이라는 점을 강조한다. 그리고 이어지는 문장에서 다양한 직업과 도시 생활의 이야기를 풀어나가는 만큼 도시 국가의 기능이 종교보다 경제와 더 큰 관련이 있었다는 점을 알 수 있다. 정답은 (A)이다.

어휘 based around ~을 바탕으로 practice 관습, 관행 encounter ~을 맞닥뜨리다

5. 지문의 단어 "incised"와 의미가 가장 가까운 것은 무엇인가?
(A) 발견된
(B) 놓인, 위치한
(C) 나타난, 보여진
(D) 새겨진

해설 incised(새겨진)와 engraved(새겨진)는 동의어로 정답은 (D)이다.

6. 네 번째 문단에서, 글쓴이는 왜 쐐기 문자에 사용된 기호의 숫자가 2,000개에서 600개로 줄어들었다고 언급하는가?
(A) 사용 가능한 단어의 범위가 시대에 따라 변동을 거듭했다는 점을 나타내기 위해
(B) 쐐기 문자가 어떻게 더 구체적인 목적으로 사용되기 시작했는지 보여주기 위해
(C) 쐐기 문자가 음절을 표현함으로써 어떻게 더 효율적으로 변했는지 설명하기 위해
(D) 쐐기 문자가 어떻게 사용 빈도가 감소하기 시작했는지에 관한 통계를 제공하기 위해

해설 해당 문단의 첫 문장을 토대로 단어 전체가 아닌 음절을 표현하

기 위한 기호 사용을 기반으로 체계가 간소화되었다는 점을 알 수 있고, 문단의 뒷부분에서 줄어든 기호임에도 표현될 수 있는 단어의 종류는 늘어났기 때문에 효율성이 확보되었다는 점을 유추할 수 있다. 그러므로 정답은 (C)이다.

어휘 fluctuate 변동을 거듭하다 statistics 통계 (자료) decline 감소하다, 줄어들다

7. 지문의 단어 "predominant"와 의미가 가장 가까운 것은 무엇인가?

(A) 복잡한

(B) 아주 긴

(C) 주된

(D) 흔치 않은

해설 predominant(지배적인)와 primary(주된)는 유의어로 정답은 (C)이다.

8. 다섯 번째 문단에 따르면, 수메르인들은 무엇을 하기 위해 처음으로 바퀴를 이용했는가?

(A) 도자기를 만들기 위해

(B) 교역품을 운송하기 위해

(C) 도시들 간의 도로를 개발하기 위해

(D) 상자 같은 카트를 만들기 위해

해설 해당 문단의 두 번째 문장을 토대로 바퀴는 원래 도예 작업용이었다는 점을 알 수 있다. 정답은 (A)이다.

9. 다음 문장이 지문에 추가될 수 있는 곳을 나타내는 네 개의 네모 표기 [■]를 찾아 보시오.

모두 강력했던, 이 신들은 숭배자들의 온순한 삶을 통제했다.

위 문장은 어느 곳에 가장 적합하겠는가? 네모 표기[■]를 클릭해 지문에 이 문장을 추가하시오.

(A) 1번

(B) 2번

(C) 3번

(D) 4번

해설 해당 문단은 도시 국가 확립으로 이어진 가능성을 종교에 대해 이야기를 하고 있다. 그리고 박스 안에 넣어야 하는 문장의 키워드는 "모두 강력했던, 이 신들은"이다. 그렇다면, 주어진 문장의 앞 문장에는 반드시 구체적인 신과 그들이 가진 힘에 대한 설명이 언급되어야 논리적으로 맞고, 이는 4번째 박스 앞 문장이 된다. 따라서 정답은 (D)이다.

어휘 meek 온순한 worshipper 숭배자

10. **설명:** 간략한 지문 요약에 필요한 도입 문장이 아래에 제공되어 있다. 지문에서 가장 중요한 개념들을 나타내는 세 가지 답안 선택지를 골라 요약 내용을 완성하시오. 일부 답안 선택지는 지문에 제시되지 않는 개념을 나타내거나 지문에서 중요하지 않은 개념들이므로 요약 내용에 속하지 않는다. **이 문제는 2점에 해당된다.**

관개의 필요성은 기원전 4500년경 메소포타미아 남부 지역에서 수메르 문명의 발원으로 이어졌다.

(A) 메소포타미아의 엘리트 계층은 평원의 부족한 자원을 모아 최초의 도시 국가들을 만드는 데 활용했다.

(B) 최초의 도시 국가들은 각자의 수호신을 섬겼으며, 커다란 사원 및 예배 장소를 특징으로 했다.

(C) 표어 문자의 형태로 문자가 개발되었지만, 음절을 바탕으로 더 효율적인 체계로 발전했다.

(D) 도시 국가들은 사람들의 경제적, 정치적 활동을 관리 감독했던 사제들에 의해 통치되었다.

(E) 바퀴 및 청동 물품의 제조 같은 기술적 혁신이 도시 국가들이 발전하는 데 도움을 주었다.

(F) 도시 국가 에리두는 관개 농작물에 경제적으로 의존한 반면, 우루크는 도자기 및 금속 세공으로 알려졌다.

해설 네 번째 문단의 핵심 내용을 통해 음절을 바탕으로 문자가 더욱 효율적이었다는 점을 알 수 있으므로 (C)를 선택한다. 바퀴와 혁신은 다섯 번째 문단의 중심부 내용이므로 (E) 역시 선택한다. 그리고 최초의 도시 국가가 가진 종교 및 신전에 대한 이야기는 이 지문 전체의 핵심적인 내용이기에 (B)를 선택해야 한다.

어휘 scarce 부족한 honor ~을 섬기다, 기리다 feature ~을 특징으로 하다 worship 예배, 숭배 evolve into ~로 발전하다, 진화하다 priest 사제

Passage 1

Answers

1. D	2. C	3. A	4. C	5. D	6. A	7. C	8. D	9. A	10. BDE

자전적 기억

^{7(C)}만일 인생에서 갖고 있는 가장 오래된 기억을 이야기해 보도록 요청받는다면, 대략 몇 살에 있었던 일이 될 수 있을까? ^{9(A)}■ 대부분의 사람들은 3세가 되기 전에 있었던 일들에 대한 기억을 떠올리는 것은 불가능하다고 생각하며, 이러한 현상은 영아기 기억 상실이라고 일컬어진다. ■ 심리학자들은 유아 및 어린 아이들이 다른 점에서는 인상적인 기억 능력을 지니고 있음을 보여주는 많은 증거에도 불구하고 왜 영아기 기억 상실이 나타나는지 이해하려 하는 데 수십 년의 시간을 소비해왔다. ■ 일부는 우리가 각자의 삶 속에서 발생된 사건들에 대한 기억을 가리키는 자전적 기억의 일반적인 작용 원리에 관해 더 많이 알게 되면 이러한 현상이 더 잘 이해될 수 있을지도 모른다고 주장해 왔다. ■ ^{1(D)}대부분의 아이들은 3~4세의 나이에 도달하게 되면 과거의 사건들에 대해 상당히 길고 응집력 있게 묘사할 수 있다. 그렇다면, 어떤 요인들이 성장에 있어서 중요한 이 시점에 영향을 미치는 것인가?

^{7(C)}몇몇 가능성 있는 답변들을 스위스의 유명한 심리학자 장 피아제가 제시한 이론들 속에서 찾아볼 수 있다. 예를 들어, 피아제는 2세 미만의 아이들이 더 나이 많은 아이들보다 질적으로 다른 방식으로 사건들을 처리하고 이야기한다고 주장했다. 이는 또한 2살짜리 아이들에게서 나타나는 언어적 능력이 유아의 행동 기반 코딩 방식에 비해 상당히 다른 방식으로 사건에 대한 코딩 및 표현을 가능하게 해준다는 것을 의미할 수도 있다. 실제로, 한 살짜리 아이들의 언어적 능력은 그들이 일 년 후에 사건을 떠올리려 시도할 때의 기억과 연관되어 있다. 연구가들이 한 살짜리 아이들에게 한 가지 연속된 행동을 처음 본지 일년 뒤에 그것을 흉내 내도록 요청했을 때, 그 기억 과제의 성공과 아이가 해당 사건을 처음 봤을 당시의 과거에 지니고 있던 언어적 능력 사이에 상관 관계가 존재했다. ^{2(C)}하지만, 좋지 못한 언어적 능력을 지니고 있는 아이들조차 어느 정도는 해당 사건을 기억할 수 있었으며, 이는 기억이 언어적 능력의 도움을 받을 수는 있지만, 그 능력에 의존하지는 않는다는 점을 나타낸다.

^{7(C)}또 다른 이론은 아이들이 자신의 삶 속에 있었던 과거의 사건들에 관해 이야기할 수 있게 되기 전에 심리적 실체로서 자아에 대한 ^{3(A)}적정한 이해를 지니고 있음이 틀림없다고 본다. 일반적으로, 아이들이 1~2세 사이일 때, 자아에 대한 이해를 발달시키게 되며, 이는 향후 몇 년 동안에 걸쳐 빠른 ^{4(C)}정교화 과정을 거치게 된다. ^{5(D)}이 가설에 따르면, 자전적 기억의 발생은 신체적 자아가 시간 속에서 연속성을 지니고 있다는 자각에 달려 있다.

^{7(C)}세 번째 이론은 아이들이 각자 "삶의 이야기"를 할 수 있을 만한 능력을 갖추기 전에 이야기 구연의 일반적인 구조에 관해 배울 필요가 있다는 것이다. 다시 말해서, 아이들은 이야기 묘사에 관한 필수 지식을 얻기 위해, 사회적 상호 작용, ^{6(B)}특히 부모가 읽어주는 이야기를 듣거나 과거의 사건과 관련해 부모가 해주는 말을 들어보는 행위를 경험해볼 필요가 있다. ^{6(D)}부모가 오늘이나 지난주, 또는 1년 전에 아이들과 함께 했던 것을 이야기할 때, 아이들은 과거의 사건에 관한 이야기를 전달하는 방법을 이해하기 시작한다. ^{6(C)}이는 또한 아이들에게 기억의 기능에 대해 상기시키게 되며, 그러한 기억들은 문화적 경험의 일부로서 가치를 지닌다. 흥미롭게도, 한국의 아이들이 미국의 백인 아이들보다 아주 어릴 적의 기억을 떠올릴 가능성이 더 낮다는 사실을 연구가들이 밝혀냈다. 게다가, 다른 연구가들은 한국의 부모와 아이들이 미국의 백인 부모와 아이들보다 세 배 덜 자주 과거에 있었던 삶의 경험에 관해 이야기한다는 결론을 내렸다. 이는 자전적 기억의 발달이 아이들이 겪는 사회적 경험의 종류에 의해 영향을 받는다는 사실을 나타내는 것이다.

^{7(C)}마지막 한 가지 이론은, 아이들이 각자 과거의 기억을 이야기할 수 있게 되기에 앞서, 반드시 자신을 비롯해 주변 사람들의 생각과 감정, 믿음, 욕망 같은 심리적 상태에 대한 이해를 먼저 발전시켜야 한다는 것이다. 연구에 따르면 기억의 향상은 아이들이 "무언가를 믿는다는 것이 어떤 의미를 지니는가?"나 "무언가를 기억한다는 것이 어떤 의미를 지니는가?"와 같은 질문에 대답할 수 있게 되면 일어나는 것처럼 보인다고 나타났다.

8(D)지금까지 언급한 모든 요인들이 상호 관련되어 있으면서 서로 영향을 미치는 것일 수도 있다. 예를 들어, 부모와 과거의 사건을 이야기하는 것은 자아라는 개념에 대한 이해를 발전시킴과 동시에 아이가 "기억한다는 것"이 무엇을 의미하는지 이해하도록 도움을 줄 수 있다. 어떻든지, 과거에 관해 이야기할 수 있는 능력이 단순히 사람이나 사건을 인식하거나 회상하는 것보다 더 높은 수준의 기억 복잡성을 나타낸다고 확실히 말할 수 있다.

[어휘]

1. autobiographical memory 자전적 기억 (자신이 삶에 있어 역사적 사실과 경험적 사건과 관련해 개인적인 기억) recount ~을 이야기하다, 말하다 recall ~을 떠올리다, 회상하다 phenomenon 현상 be referred to as ~라고 일컬어지다 infantile amnesia 영아기 기어 상실 mechanism 작용 원리 cohesive 응집력 있는, 결합력 있는

2. put forward ~을 제시하다, 제안하다 assert that ~라고 주장하다 qualitatively 질적으로 coding 코딩(정보를 기억하기 편리하도록 부호화하기) verbal 언어의, 말로 하는 imitate ~을 흉내 내다, 모방하다 correlation 상호 관계 be dependent on ~에 의존하다, ~에 달려 있다

3. entity 실체, 존재 elaboration 정밀화, 정교화 hypothesis 가설 continuity 연속성, 지속성

4. be equipped to do ~할 능력을 갖추다 remind ~에게 상기시키다 influence ~에 영향을 미치다

5. state 상태 improvement 향상, 개선

6. interrelated 상호 연관된 foster ~을 발전시키다 simultaneously 동시에 grasp ~을 이해하다 regardless 어떻든지 with assurance 확실히 represent ~을 나타내다 complexity 복잡성

1. 첫 번째 문단에 따르면, 무엇이 아이가 자전적 기억을 발달시켰음을 나타내는가?

(A) 아이가 세 살 전에 있었던 사건을 회상할 수 있다.

(B) 아이가 현재의 사건과 관련된 새로운 기억을 형성할 수 있다.

(C) 아이가 자신이 갖고 있는 일부 생각이 사실 기억에 속한다는 것을 알고 있다.

(D) 아이가 조리 있게 그리고 충분한 길이로 과거의 사건을 설명할 수 있다.

해설 첫 번째 문단의 두 번째 문장을 보면 대부분의 사람들은 3세가 되기 전에 있었던 일들을 기억하지 못하는데, 해당 문단 마지막을 보면, 대부분의 아이들이 3-4세가 되면 과거의 사건을 상당히 길고 응집력 있게 묘사한다는 점을 설명한다. 이를 토대로 정답은 (D)이다.

어휘 coherently 조리 있게 sufficient 충분한

2. 두 번째 문단에서, 글쓴이는 왜 좋지 못한 언어적 능력을 지닌 아이들이 과거의 사건을 기억한 증거를 보여주었다는 정보를 포함했는가?

(A) 한 살짜리 아이들이 충분한 언어적 상호 작용 기회를 제공받아야 한다고 주장하기 위해

(B) 한 살짜리 아이들이 다른 사람들을 인식할 수 없다는 개념에 이의를 제기하기 위해

(C) 기억이 오직 언어적 능력에만 달려 있는 것은 아니라는 증거를 제공하기 위해

(D) 피아제가 말한 기억과 언어적 능력 사이의 상관 관계에 결함이 있었다고 주장하기 위해

해설 두 번째 문단의 마지막 문장을 보면, 좋지 못한 언어적 능력을 지니고 있는 아이들도 어느 정도는 기억을 해냈으며, 언어적 능력의 도움을 받지만 전적으로 의존하지 않는다는 점을 설명한다. 이를 통해 기억이 오직 언어적 능력에만 달려 있는 것이 아니라는 증거를 설명하기 위해 그 정보를 포함했다는 것을 알 수 있다. 정답은 (C)이다.

어휘 ample 충분한 flawed 결함이 있는

3. 지문의 단어 "fair"와 의미가 가장 가까운 것은 무엇인가?

(A) 적당한, 합리적인

(B) 가벼운, 약간의

(C) 외교의

(D) 깊은

해설 fair(적정한)와 reasonable(적당한, 합리적인)은 유의어로 정답은 (A)이다.

4. 지문의 단어 "elaboration"과 의미가 가장 가까운 것은 무엇인가?

(A) 유용, 효용

(B) 유통, 분배

(C) 강화, 향상

(D) 이해(력)

해설 elaboration(정교화, 공들임)과 enhancement(강화, 향상)는 유의어로 정답은 (C)이다.

5. 세 번째 문단에 따르면, 자아에 대한 이해의 발달과 자전적 기억의 발달 사이에 어떤 관계가 있는가?
(A) 아이들이 각자의 삶에서 이전의 사건들을 이야기함으로써 자아에 대한 이해를 빠르게 얻을 수 있다.
(B) 자전적 기억은 아이들이 각자의 장점과 단점을 더 잘 이해하는 데 도움을 준다.
(C) 자전적 기억의 발달은 자아에 대한 이해에 있어 전제 조건이다.
(D) 자아가 시간의 흐름 속에서 변함없는 상태로 유지된다는 점에 대한 이해가 자전적 기억의 발달을 용이하게 한다.

해설 세 번째 문단의 마지막 문장을 보면, 자전적 기억의 발생은 신체적 자아가 시간 속에서 연속성을 지니고 있다는 자각에 달려 있다고 한다. 그러므로 (B)의 장점과 단점이라는 키워드를 소거한다. 이 내용은 하나의 이론이기 때문에 (C) 보기가 언급하는 '전제 조건'이라는 키워드가 문제가 된다. (A)의 경우, 자아에 대한 이해가 결과가 아닌 조건으로 제시되어야 하기 때문에 소거한다. 그러므로 정답은 (D)이다.

어휘 prerequisite 전제 조건 facilitate ~을 용이하게 하다

6. 다음 중 네 번째 문단에서 부모가 아이들에게 이야기 구연의 구조를 이해하도록 도움을 주는 방법으로 언급되지 않은 것은 무엇인가?
(A) 아이들에게 각자의 이야기를 만들어내도록 요구하는 것
(B) 아이들에게 이야기를 읽어주는 것
(C) 기억이 중요하다는 점을 아이들에게 알려주는 것
(D) 아이들과 과거의 사건들을 이야기하는 것

해설 (C)를 쉽게 정답으로 선택할 수 있지만, 해당 문단의 중간 지점을 보면 '기억의 기능에 대해 상기시키게 되며, 그러한 기억들은 문화적 경험의 일부로 가치를 지닌다'라는 내용을 토대로 소거를 할 수 있다. (A)의 경우 명확하게 아이들이 이야기를 만들어내도록 '요구'한다는 점은 언급이 된 적이 없으므로 정답은 (A)이다.

7. 지문의 구성을 가장 잘 설명할 수 있는 것은 무엇인가?
(A) 한 가지 심리적 상태에 대한 정의 및 수년 동안에 걸친 그 상태의 발전
(B) 한 가지 학습 기법에 대한 설명 및 그 기법의 장점과 단점
(C) 한 가지 현상에 대한 설명 및 그 현상의 발달에 관한 여러 이론
(D) 기억 처리에 대한 개요 및 다양한 문화에서 나타나는 기억의 중요성

해설 이 지문의 흐름을 보면 문단별로 이론을 제시하고 가볍게 정의를 내린 후, 구체적인 사례를 들어주는 방식으로 이야기를 전달한다. 그러므로 정답은 (C)이다.

어휘 A followed by B A 뒤에 이어지는 B evolution 발전, 진화 drawback 단점, 결점 outline 개요, 개괄

8. 지문은 자전적 기억의 발달과 관련해 다음 중 어느 내용을 뒷받침하는가?
(A) 무언가를 기억한다는 것이 어떤 의미인지에 대한 이해가 자전적 기억의 발달에 있어 가장 중대한 요인이다.
(B) 장 피아제는 자전적 기억의 발달을 완전히 이해한 첫 번째 심리학자였다.
(C) 자전적 기억의 발달에 대한 연구는 심리학자들이 유아 기억 상실을 막는 데 도움을 줄 수 있다.
(D) 자전적 기억의 발달은 여러 다른 요인들이 결합되어 초래될 가능성이 있다.

해설 이 지문은 이론과 부가 설명으로만 끝나는 것이 아니라, 하나의 가설이 완벽하게 자전적 기억을 설명하지 못한다는 패턴을 가지고 있다. 그리고 마지막 문단의 첫 문장을 보면 '상호 관련되어 있으면서 서로 영향을 미치는 것'이라는 점을 토대로 정답이 (D)라는 것을 알 수 있다.

어휘 comprehend ~을 이해하다

9. 다음 문장이 지문에 추가될 수 있는 곳을 나타내는 네 개의 네모 표기 [■]를 찾아 보시오.

이 기억이 삶의 첫 2년 동안으로부터 비롯될 가능성은 0에 가깝다.

위 문장은 어느 곳에 가장 적합하겠는가? 네모 표기[■]를 클릭해 지문에 이 문장을 추가하시오.

(A) 1번
(B) 2번
(C) 3번
(D) 4번

해설 해당 문단의 첫 번째 문장을 보면 '대략 몇 살에 있었던 일이 될 수 있을까?'라는 질문을 볼 수 있다. 이 질문의 키워드는 몇 살이라는 단어인 만큼 주어진 문장인 '이 기억'이라는 주어와 흐름이 일치하며, 질문의 대답을 하고 있다는 것을 알 수 있다. 주어진 문장이 '첫 2년 동안으로부터 비롯될 가능성이 없다'라는 정보를 제공하기 때문에 1번 박스 이하에서 등장하는 '3세 이전 기억은 불가능'이라는 말과 이어진다. 그러므로 정답은 (A)이다.

10. **설명:** 간략한 지문 요약에 필요한 도입 문장이 아래에 제공되어 있다. 지문에서 가장 중요한 개념들을 나타내는 세 가지 답안 선택지를 골라 요약 내용을 완성하시오. 일부 답안 선택지는 지문에 제시되지 않는 개념을 나타내거나 지문에서 중요하지 않은 개념들이므로 요약 내용에 속하지 않는다. **이 문제는 2점에 해당된다.**

자전적 기억을 만들어낼 수 있는 능력, 즉 과거의 사건들에 관한 조리 있는 이야기는 여러 사회적, 지적 발달에 의해 영향을 받을 수 있다.

(A) 자전적 기억의 발달은 아이들이 각자의 발달을 형성하는 데 도움을 준 의미 있는 순간들을 제대로 인식할 수 있게 해준다.

(B) 언어적 능력 및 이야기 구조에 대한 이해는 자전적 기억의 구성에 있어 중요한 역할을 하는 것으로 여겨진다.

(C) 아이들이 삶의 초기에 단순한 기억 과제를 수행할 수 있기는 하지만, 적어도 3세가 될 때까지는 자전적 기억에 대한 능력을 발달시키지 못한다.

(D) 연구에 따르면 자신의 심리 상태 및 다른 이들의 심리 상태에 대한 이해를 지니고 있는 아이들은 개인적인 기억을 표현하고 이야기하는 일을 더 쉽게 생각하는 것으로 나타난다.

(E) 자아 및 다양한 심리 상태에 대한 개념을 습득한 아이들은 일반적으로 각자의 과거 기억에 관해 이야기할 수 있다.

(F) 아이들의 가장 오래된 자전적 기억은 일반적으로 부모와의 사회적 상호 작용을 중심으로 초점이 맞춰져 있다.

해설 두 번째 문단과 네 번째 문단을 통해 우리는 자전적 기억의 구성에 있어 언어적 능력과 이야기 구조가 가지는 중요한 역할을 이해할 수 있다. 그러므로 (B)를 선택한다. 그리고 다섯 번째 문단을 통해 자신을 비롯한 주변 사람들의 감정 및 심리적 상태에 대한 이해를 발전시켜야 한다는 점을 토대로 (D)를 답안으로 선정해야 한다. 세 번째 문단의 내용을 통해 심리적 실제로 자아에 대한 이해를 지니는 것에 대한 이야기를 다루기 때문에 (E)를 마지막 답안으로 간주한다.

어휘 appreciate ~을 제대로 인식하다 play a vital role in ~에 있어 중요한 역할을 하다 formulate ~을 표현하다

Passage 2

Answers

1. D	2. C	3. A	4. C	5. B	6. A	7. B	8. B	9. B	10. ACF

유아 교육

[1(D)]전 세계적으로, 유아 교육의 목적과 관련해 문화마다 서로 다른 의견을 지니고 있다. 따라서, 일반적으로 5세 이하의 아이들을 대상으로 하는 교육 시설인 유치원도 나라마다 상당히 다양하다. [1(D)]예를 들어, 미국과, 일본, 그리고 중국의 유치원을 비교하면서, 연구가들은 그 국가들 각각의 부모들이 유치원의 기능을 바라보는 방식에 있어 상당한 차이점이 있다는 사실에 주목했다. 일본의 부모들이 유치원을 주로 한 집단의 구성원이 될 기회를 아이들에게 제공해주는 방법으로 바라보는 반면, 중국의 부모들은 유치원을 아이들의 학업 여정에 있어 아주 중대한 첫 걸음으로 여긴다. 한편, 미국에서는, 부모들이 유치원의 주된 목적이 아이들의 독립성과 자립심에 대한 가치를 불어넣기 위한 것이라고 생각하는 경향이 있지만, 아이들에게 집단 경험 및 학업적 배움을 소개하는 것 또한 가치 있게 여겨지는 측면이다.

많은 유치원 프로그램이 주로 사회적, 정서적 요인에 맞춰 준비되기는 하지만, 일부는 인지 발달을 촉진하기 위해, 그리고 유치원생들이 유치원 이후로 계속 경험하게 될 더 공식적인 학습 환경에 더 잘 대비하도록 만들기 위해 고안된다. [2(C)]미국에서는, 미래의 학업적 성공을 촉진하는 것을 목표로 하는 가장 잘 알려진 프로그램들 중의 하나가 헤드 스타트다. 이 프로그램은 미국이 1960년대에 '빈곤과의 전쟁'을 선포하면서 확립되었으며, 지금까지 1,200만명이 넘는 아이들에게 서비스를 제공해왔다. 이 프로그램은 부모들의 참여를 크게 강조하며, "완전한 아이"를 염두에 두고 만들어졌다. 이에 따라, 이 프로그램은 아이들의 사회적, 정서적 발달과 사회적 책임, 신체 건강, 그리고 자신감을 향상시키는 것을 추구한다.

헤드 스타트가 성공적인 프로그램이었는지, 아니면 그렇지 않았는지는 개인적 관점의 문제이다. [3(A)]만약 성공이 장기적으로 증가하는 IQ(지능지수) 점수의 제공이라는 측면에서 평가된다면, 이 프로그램은 실망스러운 존재로 여겨질 수도 있다. 헤드 스타트 프로그램을 졸업하는 학생들이 흔히 즉각적인 IQ 증가를 보이기는 하지만, 이러한 이득은 시간이 흐를수록 차츰 희미해지는 경향이 있다. 반면에, 헤드 스타트는 미취학 아동들이 학교에 입학할 준비를 하게 해준다는 점에서 분명 성공을 거두고 있는 것처럼 보인다. 헤드 스타트 졸업생들은 나중에 평균보다 훨씬 더 높은 학교 성적을 달성하는 경향이 있다. 또한, 연구가들은 설사 성취도 증가 수준이 그다지 크지 않다고 하더라도 헤드 스타트 졸업생들이 결국 고등학교 졸업 시에 더 높은 학업 성적을 보이고 있다는 사실을 밝혀냈다.

마찬가지로, 여러 다른 종류의 취학 전 준비 프로그램을 통해 나타난 결과에 따르면 그 프로그램들을 졸업한 아이들이 수업에서 낙제하거나 점수를 재이수해야 할 필요가 생길 가능성이 더 적으며, 학교를 끝마칠 가능성이 더 높다. 이는 취학 전 준비 프로그램이 장기적으로 좋은 투자임을 나타내는 것이다. 4(C)비용 편익 분석 연구 결과들에 따르면, 취학 전 준비 프로그램 졸업생들이 27세의 나이에 도달할 때쯤, 납세자들은 그 준비 프로그램에 지출한 1달러당 7달러를 절약하게 될 것이다.

최근에, 조기 개입 프로그램에 대한 한 5(B)종합적인 연구에 따르면, 전체적으로, 취학 전 프로그램이 매우 유익할 가능성을 갖고 있으며, 정부들이 잠재적인 향후 비용을 줄이기 위해 그러한 프로그램들에 자금을 보내는 것이 현명할 수 있다고 나타났다. 예를 들어, 조기 개입 프로그램에 등록하지 않았던 아이들에 비해, 이러한 프로그램을 거친 졸업생들은 개선된 건강 관련 행위들, 늘어난 경제적 자급률, 더 나은 교육 성과, 정서적 또는 인지적 발달의 개선, 그리고 범죄 활동 수준의 감소를 보여주었다. 6(A)게다가, 일부 연구가들은 비용이 저렴한 다수의 프로그램들이 헤드 스타트 같이 더 비싼 것들만큼 동일하게 긍정적인 성과를 기록했다는 점도 지적한 바 있다. 전반적으로, 이 연구의 결과물은 조기 개입이 장기적으로 상당한 혜택을 낳을 잠재성을 지니고 있다는 점을 시사하고 있어 대단히 전망이 밝았다.

8(B)하지만, 취학 전의 기간에 학업 능력을 향상시키고자 7(B)시도하는 프로그램에 반대하는 사람들도 일부 존재한다. ▪ 실제로, 유명 발달 심리학자 데이빗 엘킨드는 미국 내의 사회가 어린 학습자들을 너무 가차없이 몰아붙이는 바람에 스트레스와 압박감을 못 이기고 마는 경향이 있다고 주장한다. 9(B)▪ 엘킨드는 학업적 성공이 부모의 통제를 벗어난 요인들, 즉 아이의 성숙 속도와 선천적 능력에 의해 주로 영향을 받는다고 생각한다. ▪ 그래서, 특정 나이의 아이들은 현재의 인지 발달 수준을 고려하지 않고는 학업적 우수성을 달성할 것으로 예상할 수 없다는 결론에 이르게 된다. ▪ 결국, 특정한 한 아이의 고유한 특징 및 대부분 아이들의 일반적인 발달 단계들을 모두 고려하는 적절한 교육을 아이들이 받는 것이 대단히 중요하다.

[어휘]

1. when it comes to ~와 관련해서는 instill (생각 등)을 불어넣다, 심어주다 self-reliance 자립심 aspect 측면, 양상
2. be geared toward ~에 맞춰 준비되다, ~에 맞게 조정되다 cognitive development 인지 발달 place a large focus on ~을 크게 강조하다 with A in mind A를 염두에 두고 Head Start 헤드 스타트(가난한 가정의 아이들을 대상으로 한 미국 공립 유치원 프로그램) enhance ~을 향상시키다, 강화하다 self-assuredness 자신감
3. measure ~을 평가하다, 판단하다 in terms of ~의 측면에서, ~와 관련해서 tend to do ~하는 경향이 있다(= have a tendency to do) fade 희미해지다 modest 보통의, 그다지 크지 않은
4. repeat ~을 재이수하다 cost-benefit analysis 비용 편익 분석 findings 연구 결과들
5. intervention 개입, 중재 channel A into B (자금 등) A를 B로 보내다 enroll in ~에 등록하다 self-sufficiency 자급(률) outcome 성과, 결과 point out that ~임을 지적하다 affordable (가격이) 알맞은 yield (결과, 이익 등) ~을 낳다, 초래하다
6. oppose ~에 반대하다 relentlessly 가차없이 buckle under ~에 무너지다, 굴복하다 maturation 성숙 inherited 선천적인 take A into account A를 고려하다

---

1. 첫 번째 문단에 따르면, 미국과 일본, 그리고 중국의 부모들과 관련해 무엇이 사실인가?
   (A) 유치원이 나중의 교육 프로그램들보다 덜 중요하다고 생각한다.
   (B) 각자의 국가에 존재하는 현 교육 시스템에 불만족하고 있다.
   (C) 여러 다른 국가의 부모들보다 아이들에게 더 높은 기대를 지니고 있다.
   (D) 조기 교육의 목적에 대해 상이한 관점을 지니고 있다.

해설 미국, 일본, 그리고 중국과 같은 예시를 다루는 문장 앞에 있는 큰 개념과 주장을 확인해야 한다. 첫 번째 문단의 첫 문장을 통해 '유아 교육의 목적과 관련해 문화마다 서로 다른 의견을 지니고 있다'는 정보를 알 수 있기에 정답은 (D)이다.

어휘 respective 각자의, 각각의 differing 상이한

2. 두 번째 문단에서 헤드 스타트 프로그램은 어떤 아이들을 돕기 위해 만들어진 것으로 유추할 수 있는가?
   (A) 1950년대에 태어난 아이들
   (B) 일반적인 유치원 학습 내용을 힘겨워 한 아이들
   (C) 경제적으로 어려운 가정 형편의 아이들
   (D) 사회적 능력과 언어적 능력이 부족한 아이들

해설 헤드 스타트 프로그램이라는 개념이 언급된 부분이 해당 문단의 두 번째 문장이며, 이 이후에 프로그램에 대한 설명을 해준다. 세 번째 문장을 보면 '빈곤과의 전쟁'이라는 키워드를 통해 (C)가 정답임을 알 수 있다.

3. 세 번째 문단에서, 글쓴이는 무엇을 하기 위해 "장기적으로 증가하는 IQ"를 언급하는가?
   (A) 헤드 스타트가 인상적이지 못한 성과를 낸 한 가지 요인을 제공하기 위해

(B) 헤드 스타트가 취학 전 준비 프로그램들보다 덜 효과적이라는 주장에 반박하기 위해

(C) 높은 IQ가 대부분의 취학 전 준비 프로그램들에 대해 가장 신뢰할 수 있는 성공의 지표임을 나타내기 위해

(D) 취학 전 준비 프로그램에 참가하는 것의 혜택을 강조하기 위해

해설 세 번째 문단의 첫 두 문장을 보면 답의 근거를 파악할 수 있다. 헤드 스타트가 성공적이었는지를 평가하는 것은 개인의 관점 문제이며, 장기적으로 증가하는 IQ를 평가한다면 실망스러운 존재로 여겨질 수 있다는 점을 토대로 정답이 (A)라는 점을 알 수 있다.

어휘 underwhelmingly 인상적이지 못하게, 전혀 감흥 없이 reliable 신뢰할 수 있는 indicator 지표

4. 네 번째 문단에 따르면, 취학 전 준비 프로그램에 대한 비용 편익 분석으로 드러난 것은 무엇인가?

(A) 취학 전 준비 프로그램들이 미국 내의 납세자들을 대상으로 더 높은 세금을 초래하고 있다는 점

(B) 취학 전 준비 프로그램 참가자들이 27세 무렵에 또래들보다 더 많은 돈을 벌었다는 점

(C) 납세자들이 취학 전 준비 프로그램에 따른 결과로서 장기적으로 돈을 절약하고 있다는 점

(D) 취학 전 준비 프로그램에 할당되는 달러의 액수를 늘려야 한다는 점

해설 해당 문단의 마지막 문장을 보면 '납세자들은 그 준비 프로그램에 지출된 1달러당 7달러를 절약하게 될 것이다'라는 정보를 토대로 (C)를 정답으로 선택한다.

어휘 allocate ~을 할당하다, 배정하다

5. 지문의 단어 "comprehensive"와 의미가 가장 가까운 것은 무엇인가?

(A) 이해할 수 있는

(B) 철저한

(C) 존경할 만한

(D) 아는 것이 많은

해설 comprehensive(종합적인)와 thorough(철저한)는 유의어로 정답은 (B)이다.

6. 다섯 번째 문단에 따르면, 다음 중 어느 것이 조기 개입 프로그램의 혜택과 관련해 사실인가?

(A) 심지어 상대적으로 저렴한 프로그램들도 여러 혜택을 제공해줄 수 있다.

(B) 오직 가장 비싼 프로그램들의 혜택만 투자 가치가 있다.

(C) 해당 프로그램들은 단기적으로 좋은 혜택을 초래하지만, 장기적인 혜택은 거의 없다.

(D) 헤드 스타트 프로그램이 다른 어떤 프로그램보다 더 많은 혜택을 제공한다.

해설 해당 문단의 후반부를 보면 일부 연구가들이 다수의 프로그램들이 더 비싼 것들만큼 동일하게 긍정적인 성과를 기록했다는 점을 지적했다고 언급하기 때문에 정답은 (A)이다.

7. 지문의 단어 "seek"과 의미가 가장 가까운 것은 무엇인가?

(A) ~을 주장하다

(B) ~을 시도하다

(C) ~을 찾다

(D) ~을 끌어들이다, 유혹하다

해설 seek(시도하다, 구하다, 추구하다)와 attempt(시도하다)는 동의어로 정답은 (B)이다.

8. 지문은 무엇을 하기 위해 "발달 심리학자 데이빗 엘킨드"를 언급하는가?

(A) 효과적인 취학 전 프로그램을 시작한 전문가를 예시로 제공하기 위해

(B) 유아 교육 프로그램의 가치에 대해 반대되는 관점을 소개하기 위해

(C) 왜 유아 교육 프로그램이 오직 특정 국가에서만 효과적인지 설명하는 것을 돕기 위해

(D) 학업적 성공이 부모의 통제를 벗어난 요인에 달려 있다는 이론이 틀렸음을 증명하기 위해

해설 문단의 첫 문장에서 '프로그램에 반대하는 사람들도 일부 존재'한다는 정보와 그에 대한 예시를 제공했기에 정답은 (B)이다.

어휘 disprove ~가 틀렸음을 증명하다

9. 다음 문장이 지문에 추가될 수 있는 곳을 나타내는 네 개의 네모 표기 [■]를 찾아 보시오.

엘킨드의 관점으로 볼 때, 이는 정신적 고통으로 이어질 뿐만 아니라, 원하는 인지적 이점을 발전시키지도 못한다.

위 문장은 어느 곳에 가장 적합하겠는가? 네모 표기[■]를 클릭해 지문에 이 문장을 추가하시오.

(A) 1번

(B) 2번

(C) 3번

(D) 4번

해설 문단의 두 번째 문장에서 스트레스와 압박감에 대한 내용을 언급하고 있고, 주어진 문장은 '이는 정신적 고통으로 이어진다'는 점을 명시하므로 정답은 (B)이다.

어휘 distress 고통, 괴로움 foster ~을 발전시키다

10. 설명: 간략한 지문 요약에 필요한 도입 문장이 아래에 제공되어 있다. 지문에서 가장 중요한 개념들을 ㅣ 나타내는 세 가지 답인 선택지를 골라 요약 내용을 완성하시오. 일부 답안 선택지는 지문에 체시되시 않는 개념을 나타내거나 지문에서 중요하지 않은 개념들이므로 요약 내용에 속하지 않는다. **이 문제는 2점에 해당된다.**

취학 전 프로그램은 어린 아이들이 사회적으로, 정서적으로, 그리고 인지적으로 발전할 수 있는 기회를 제공해준다.

(A) 헤드 스타트를 비롯한 기타 취학 전 프로그램은 아이들이 취학할 준비를 하는 데 도움이 되는 것으로 나타났으며, 아이들이 삶과 관련된 다양한 능력을 개발하도록 돕는 데 있어 장기적인 혜택이 될 수 있다.

(B) 학업적인 발전을 강조하는 것뿐만 아니라, 유치원은 재미있는 학습 환경이 되어야 하는데, 아이들은 즐겁다고 생각하는 프로그램을 통해 더 많은 혜택을 보기 때문이다.

(C) 취학 전 프로그램의 주된 목적은 국가마다 다르며, 일부는 집단 경험을 제공하는 데 초점을 맞추는 반면, 다른 곳들은 자립심 및 나중의 교육에 대한 준비를 촉진한다.

(D) 연구에 따르면 취학 전 프로그램이 "완전한 아이"를 위해 도움을 주려 하기보다 오직 한 가지 발달적 요인에 초점을

맞추는 경우에 가장 효과적인 것으로 나타난다.

(E) 데이빗 엘킨드는 부모가 아이들의 정서적 발달에 영향을 미칠 수 없다고 주장하면서 공직 사슴으로 지원받는 취학 전 프로그램에 반대했다.

(F) 취학 전 프로그램을 반대하는 사람들은 그 프로그램이 아이들에게 지나친 압박을 가하는 데다, 아이들이 학업에 대해 발달적으로 준비되어 있지 않은 경우에는 효과적이지 못하다고 주장한다.

해설 이 지문의 가장 중요한 점은 '유아 교육'이라는 키워드며 국가와 문화에 따라 유아 교육에 대한 양상이 다르게 나타난다는 것이다. 그러한 정보를 담고 있는 (C)는 정답이다. 두 번째 문단의 내용을 토대로 헤드 스타트라는 중요 키워드 및 취학 전 프로그램을 소개하는 내용이 핵심적임을 판단할 수 있기에 (A)를 정답으로 선택한다. 여섯 번째 문단에서 제시되는 내용은 교육 프로그램의 단점을 소개하고 있는 중요한 정보인 만큼 (F)를 정답으로 찾는다.

어휘 serve ~을 위해 도움을 주다, ~에 기여하다 put pressure on ~에 압박을 가하다 undue 지나친, 과도한

Passage 3

Answers

1. D	2. B	3. A	4. C	5. B	6. D	7. C	8. A	9. C	10. AEF

교직에서의 성찰

교사는 성찰, 즉 수업을 진행하는 교실 내에서 일어나는 일과 상호 작용에 관해 깊이 있게 생각하고 평가하는 실천으로부터 크게 도움을 받을 수 있다고 많은 사람들이 생각한다. 1987년에, 교육 연구 전문가 T. 와일드먼과 J. 나일즈는 경험 많은 교사들이 성찰 습관을 발전시키는 방법을 간략히 제시했다. ¹⁽ᴰ⁾이들은 성찰하는 습관이 지적 관점에서 볼 때 교직자의 역할에 더욱 몰입된 마음을 갖는 데 도움을 줄 뿐만 아니라, 교직 수련에 있어 과학적 사실의 부족 문제에 대처하도록 도움을 줄 수도 있다고 주장했다.

와일드먼과 나일즈가 특히 관심을 가졌던 것 중에는 성찰이 잘 진행되는 데 있어 잠재적으로 필수적일 수 있는 조건들이 있었다. 이들은 이 주제가 학술적인 문헌에서 충분히 다뤄지지 않았으며 추가적인 연구가 ²⁽ᴮ⁾정당하다고 생각했다. 실험 전략의 일환으로, ³⁽ᴮ⁾그들은 버지니아 지역의 교사 40명이 포함된 집단을 구성해 여러 해 동안에 걸쳐 함께 작업했다. 와일드먼과 나일즈는 많은 참가자들이 이러한 급진적인 교수 개념을 수용하기를 간절히 바라다가 성찰 행위가 교직 같이 복잡한 일에 실제로 적용하기는 어렵다는 사실만 알게 되지 않을까 하는 우려를 품고 있었다. ³⁽ᶜ⁾이에 따라, 이들은 그 교사들에게 하나의 프로그램을 거치도록 안내했고, 그 프로그램에서 교사들은 먼저 가르치는 일과 관련해 이야기하는 법, 그 다음으로 한 집단 내의 특정 문제를 되돌아보는 법, 그리고 마지막으로, ³⁽ᴰ⁾그러한 문제를 혼자 되돌아보는 법을 배웠다.

와일드먼과 나일즈는 교직에 있어 성공적인 성찰은 한 개인이 교실 내의 상호 작용을 ⁴⁽ᶜ⁾객관적으로 평가할 수 있는 뛰어난 능력을 지니고 있

는가에 달려 있다는 결론을 내렸다. 처음에는, 그 프로그램에 참여한 교사들 중 많은 이들이 실리주의자여서 체계적인 성찰을 하지 못할 가능성이 있는 것으로 여겨졌다. 그 이유는 교사들이 공정한 관점에서 각자 자신의 교수 경험, 또는 다른 이들의 교수 경험을 평가할 시간이나 기회를 좀처럼 갖지 못하기 때문이었다. 5(B)와일드먼과 나일즈는 교사들 사이에서 깊이 있고 균형 잡힌 방식으로 잠재적 기여 요인을 평가하는 것이 아니라, 교실 내에서 일어난 일만 고려하는 경향이 있다는 점에 주목했다.

6(D)이 교사 집단에게 교실 내에서의 일과 관련해 생각하는 방식을 바꿔 보도록 권장하는 것이 이 프로그램의 근본적인 목적이 되었다. ■ 이 과정은 아주 많은 인내심뿐만 아니라 대단히 유능한 훈련 진행자들까지 필요로 했기 때문에 상당히 많은 시간이 소모되었다. ■ 이 연구가들에 따르면, 6(L)교실 내에서의 일을 객관적으로 고려하도록 해당 교사들을 훈련시키는 데 30시간이나 걸렸으며, 비슷한 길이의 시간이 성찰 능력을 연습하고 개선하는 데 필요했다.

9(C)■ 연구 중에, 와일드먼과 나일즈는 세 가지 요인이 교직 환경에서의 성찰 습관을 용이하게 한다는 사실을 밝혀냈다. ■ 첫째, 교육 제도 내에서 행정 담당자들의 지원은 교사들이 성찰 습관의 요건과 교직과의 유익한 연관성을 이해하는 것을 가능케 한다. 둘째, 교사는 충분한 시간과 공간을 필요로 한다. 프로그램에 참가한 교사들은 지속적으로 다른 이들의 긴급한 요구 사항을 처리해야 했기 때문에 각자의 성찰 능력을 발전시키는 데 시간을 할애하는 것이 어렵다는 생각이 든다고 불만을 제기했다. 셋째, 협력하는 환경이 만들어지고 다른 교사들의 지지를 받아야 한다. 프로그램에 참여한 교사들은 불만족스러운 직장 생활의 여러 측면에 대처하는 데 지지와 격려가 도움이 되었다고 언급했다. 최종 보고서에서, 와일드먼과 나일즈는 다음과 같은 결론을 내렸다. "아마 우리가 알게 된 가장 중요한 점은 성찰을 실천하는 사람으로서의 교사라는 아이디어가 단순히 좋은 아이디어이거나 심지어 흥미롭기까지 한 아이디어이기 때문에 발생되지는 않을 것이라는 점이다."

와일드먼과 나일즈가 실시한 연구는 교직에서 성찰 습관을 이행하는 일의 어려움을 이해하는 것이 얼마나 중요한지를 강조한다. 다른 연구가들 또한 성찰 습관과 관련해 교사들이 겪는 문화적 억압에 주목했다. 1987년에 작성한 논문에서, 자이크너와 리스턴은 교사들이 두 가지 역할, 즉 학생들을 교육하는 일반적인 교사로서의 역할 한 가지와 성찰하는 결정권자에 더 해당되는 나머지 역할 한 가지를 모두 떠맡으려 할 때 생길 수 있는 문제들을 논했다. 문화적 문제뿐만 아니라, 동기 부여의 문제 또한 존재한다. 7(C)성찰을 실천하는 사람이 되기 위해서는 고된 노력이 필수적이며, 겉으로 보기에 별로 없는 즉각적인 이점 및 명확하게 서술된 목표의 부재로 인해 많은 사람들이 스스로에게 동기를 부여하는 것을 힘들어 한다. 일부 거침없는 비평가들은 교사가 왜 조금이라도 성찰하는 사람이 되고 싶어 할 것 같은 지에 대해 의문을 제기했다. 일부 교사들이 성찰적 실천을 택하기 위해 노력하는 주된 이유는 교사들을 교육하는 전문가들이 그것이 유익하다고 생각하기 때문인 것으로 보인다. 8(A)실제로, 성찰의 동기 부여와 관련해 아직 연구되지 않은 많은 문제들이 존재하는데, 특히 성찰에 대해 외면적으로 동기가 부여되어 있는 사람들을 본능적이고 자연적으로 성찰하는 사람들과 비교하는 경우에 그러하다.

[어휘]

1. reflection 성찰, 반성 practice n. 실천, 습관, 연습 v. ~을 연습하다, 실행하다 outline ~을 간략히 제시하다, ~의 윤곽을 보여주다 reflective 성찰하는, 반성하는 engaged 몰입한, 관여한 scarcity 부족 discipline 수련(법), 훈육

2. flourish 잘 되어가다 warrant 정당하게 만들다 investigation 연구, 조사 strategy 전략 harbor (생각 등) ~을 품다 be keen to do ~하기를 간절히 바라다, 열망하다 embrace ~을 수용하다, 받아들이다 radical 급진적인 reflect on ~에 대해 되돌아보다

3. objectively 객관적으로 utilitarian 실리주의자의, 실용주의자의 assess ~을 평가하다 impartial 공정한 tendency to do ~하는 경향 take place 발생되다, 일어나다 contributing factor 기여 요인

4. fundamental 근본적인 refine ~을 개선하다

5. facilitate ~을 용이하게 하다 comprehend ~을 이해하다 allocate ~을 할당하다 collaborative 협력하는 cope with ~에 대처하다 aspect 측면, 양상 practitioner 실천하는 사람 compelling 흥미로운

6. carry out ~을 실시하다, 수행하다 implement ~을 이행하다, 실행하다 inhibition 억제 arise 발생되다 take on ~을 떠맡다 struggle to do ~하는 것을 힘겨워하다 seemingly 보아하니, 겉보기에 outspoken 거침없이 말하는 at all 조금이라도 adopt ~을 택하다 externally 외면적으로 instinctively 본능적으로

---

1. 첫 번째 문단에 따르면, 성찰 행위가 무엇을 하도록 도움으로써 교사들에게 유익할 수 있는 것으로 여겨졌는가?

(A) 더욱 훈육 지향적인 교수법을 확립하는 일

(B) 교실 기반 학습의 핵심 원리를 이해하는 일

(C) 교수 방법을 개선하기 위해 과학적 사실을 이용하는 일

(D) 교직과의 지적 연관성을 향상시키는 일

해설 첫 번째 문단에 따르면 성찰하는 습관이 교직자의 역할에 더 몰입된 마음을 갖게 할 뿐만 아니라 교직 수련에 있어 부족한 문제에 대처하도록 도움을 줄 수 있다고 주장하므로 정답은 (D)이다. (C)는 '과학적 사실'이라는 키워드가 오답 포인트로 제시되었으며, (B)에서 '교실 기반 학습의 핵심 원리'는 언급된 적이 없다. '훈육 지향적인 교수법'이라는 키워드를 포함하는 (A) 역

시 답이 될 수 없다.

어휘 principle 원리, 원칙 enhance ~을 향상시키다, 강화하다

2. 지문의 단어 "warranted"와 의미가 가장 가까운 것은 무엇인가?

(A) 찬성했다

(B) 정당화했다

(C) 확인했다, 발견했다

(D) 숙고했다

해설 warranted(정당화했다)와 justified(정당화했다)는 동의어로 정답은 (B)이다.

3. 다음 중 두 번째 문단에서 설명하는 실험 전략과 관련해 언급되지 않은 것은 무엇인가?

(A) 가르치는 일과 관련된 성찰 내용을 적어 놓도록 교사들에게 요구했다.

(B) 경험이 있는 교사 집단에 의해 수년 동안 채택되었다.

(C) 교사들에게 각자의 교실에서 발생한 일을 이야기하게 한 것을 포함했다.

(D) 교사들이 궁극적으로 다른 이들의 도움 없이 성찰하는 데 도움을 주도록 고안되었다.

해설 두 번째 문단의 내용을 보면, 교사 40명과 함께 여러 해 동안 걸쳐 작업했다는 점을 토대로 (B)를 소거한다. 그리고 해당 문단의 마지막 문장을 보면, 가르치는 일과 관련해 이야기를 하는 법, 그리고 혼자 되돌아보는 법을 배웠다는 정보를 토대로 (C)와 (D)를 소거한다. 이러한 내용을 "기록"하도록 요구했다는 사실은 언급된 적이 없기에 정답은 (A)이다.

어휘 involve ~을 수반하다, 포함하다 ultimately 궁극적으로, 결국

4. 지문의 단어 "objectively"와 의미가 가장 가까운 것은 무엇인가?

(A) 체계적으로, 조직적으로

(B) 낙관적으로

(C) 편견 없이

(D) 종합적으로

해설 objectively(객관적으로)와 unbiasedly(편견 없이)는 유의어로 정답은 (C)이다.

5. 세 번째 문단에 따르면, 와일드먼 및 나일즈와 함께 작업한 교사들이 성찰하려 시도했을 때 흔히 무엇을 하지 못했는가?

(A) 성찰 행위에 필요한 시간의 양을 정확히 계산하는 일

(B) 각자의 교실에서 일어난 일의 잠재적 원인을 고려하는 일

(C) 여러 일에 대해 성찰하는 데 활용된 다양한 방법을 비교하고 대조하는 일

(D) 성찰을 시작하기에 앞서 달성 가능한 장기적인 목표를 설정하는 일

해설 세 번째 문단의 마지막 문장을 보면, 교사들 사이에서 깊이 있고, 균형 잡힌 방식으로 잠재적 기여 요인을 평가하는 것이 아니라 교실 내에서 일어난 일만 고려하는 경향이 있다는 점을 토대로 '잠재적인 원인'이라는 키워드를 담고 있는 (B)가 정답이다.

어휘 transpire 일어나다, 발생되다 contrast ~을 대조하다 establish ~을 설정하다, 확립하다 engage in ~을 시작하다, ~에 참여하다

6. 네 번째 문단이 지문에 나타난 성찰에 관한 논의의 다른 측면들과 어떻게 관련되어 있는가?

(A) 지문에서 나중에 이야기하는 원리를 정의하는 데 활용된 과정을 설명하고 있다.

(B) 교사들이 각자의 교수 활동을 평가할 시간이 좀처럼 나지 않는다고 앞서 언급한 주장에 이의를 제기하고 있다.

(C) 앞서 언급한 훈련 프로그램을 따랐던 교사들이 얻게 된 이점을 확인해주고 있다.

(D) 지문에서 앞서 설명한 문제를 극복하기 위해 취해진 조치를 간략히 제시하고 있다.

해설 앞서 언급한 문제들을 해결하기 위해 '일과 관련해 생각하는 방식을 바꿔 보도록 권장하는 것' 그리고 마지막 부분을 보면, '능력을 연습하고 개선하기 위해 노력했다'는 내용을 통해 정답은 (D)이다.

어휘 define ~을 정의하다 evaluate ~을 평가하다 follow ~을 따르다, 준수하다 aforementioned 앞서 언급된 overcome ~을 극복하다

7. 여섯 번째 문단에 따르면, 교사들이 성찰을 실행하는 것을 주저할 수 있는 이유는 무엇인가?

(A) 매일 일어나는 일을 기록하는 것이 어렵기 때문에

(B) 일반적으로 교사 교육에 관여하는 사람들에 의해 단념하게 되기 때문에

(C) 성찰에 대한 보상이 즉각적으로 분명히 보이지 않을 수 있기 때문에

(D) 학생들과 함께 보낼 수 있는 소중한 시간을 다 써버리게 된다고 생각하기 때문에

해설 여섯 번째 문단에서 가장 중요한 키워드는 바로 '성찰 습관을 이행하는 일의 어려움'이다. 그리고 그 키워드를 설명하는 내용을 두 가지로 축약하는데 그것이 문화적 억압과 동기 부여이다. 그리고 동기 부여에 대한 정보를 보면, '겉으로 보기에 별로 없는 즉각적인 이점 및 명확하게 서술된 목표의 부재'라는 문제점을 부가 설명으로 제시한다. 그러므로 정답은 (C)이다.

어휘 keep track of ~을 기록하다 discourage ~을 단념하게 하다, 방해하다

8. 다음 문장들 중 어느 것이 지문의 하이라이트 표기된 문장에 담긴 핵심 정보를 가장 잘 표현하는가? 오답 선택지는 중요한 방식으로 의미를 변경하거나 핵심 정보를 배제한다.

실제로, 성찰의 동기 부여와 관련해 아직 연구되지 않은 많은 문제들이 존재하는데, 특히 성찰에 대해 외면적으로 동기가 부여되어 있는 사람들을 본능적이고 자연적으로 성찰하는 사람들과 비교하는 경우에 그러하다.

(A) 무엇이 사람들에게 성찰하도록 동기를 부여하는지에 대해, 특히 성찰하도록 권장 받는 사람들과 자연스럽게 그렇게 하는 사람들 사이의 차이점에 대해 더 많은 연구가 분명히 실시되어야 한다.

(B) 대부분의 교사들은 다른 이들의 지원을 필요로 하기보다 독립적으로 성찰하는 데 도움이 되는 여러 다른 전략을 탐구해야 한다.

(C) 성찰하는 습관과 관련해 알려지지 않은 요인들 중 많은 것들이 외적 동기 부여 없이 성찰하는 사람들을 연구함으로써 더 잘 이해될 가능성이 있다.

(D) 우리가 교사들에게 그들의 표준 교수법에 성찰 내용을 포함하도록 동기 부여할 수 있는 방법과 관련해 실시된 연구가 거의 존재하지 않는다.

해설 주어진 문장을 보면, '아직 연구되지 않은 많은 문제들'이라는 키워드와 함께 외적으로 동기 부여가 된 사람(those who are externally motivated)과 자연적으로 성찰하는 사람(those who reflect instinctively and naturally)의 비교가 들어가는 것이 중요하다. (A)의 경우, '더 많은 연구가 분명히 실시되어야 한다'라는 점과 함께 'differences between people(encouraged & naturally)'을 명확하게 다루고 있다.

어휘 carry out ~을 실시하다, 수행하다(= conduct) external 외적인, 외부의 incorporate A into B A를 B에 포함하다, 통합하다

9. 다음 문장이 지문에 추가될 수 있는 곳을 나타내는 네 개의 네모 표기 [■]를 찾아 보시오.

하지만, 성찰에 대한 교사들의 태도를 바꾸는 일은 교직 환경에서 성찰에 대한 지지가 존재하지 않는 한 성공적이지 못할 것이다.

위 문장은 어느 곳에 가장 적합하겠는가? 네모 표기[■]를 클릭해 지문에 이 문장을 추가하시오.

(A) 1번
(B) 2번
(C) 3번
(D) 4번

해설 우선 1번과 2번 박스의 경우 흐름상 문제가 전혀 없다. 주어진 문장을 보면 '교직 환경에서 성찰에 대한 지지가 존재'해야 한다는 의미이다. 따라서, 이를 가능하게 하는 세 가지 요인이 뒤에

등장해야 하기 때문에 정답은 (C)이다.

어휘 attitude 태도

10. **설명:** 간략한 지문 요약에 필요한 도입 문장이 아래에 제공되어 있다. 지문에서 가장 중요한 개념들을 나타내는 세 가지 답안 선택지를 골라 요약 내용을 완성하시오. 일부 답안 선택지는 지문에 제시되지 않는 개념을 나타내거나 지문에서 중요하지 않은 개념들이므로 요약 내용에 속하지 않는다. **이 문제는 2점에 해당된다.**

와일드먼과 나일즈는 교직에서의 성찰에 대해 광범위한 연구 조사를 실시했다.

(A) 와일드먼과 나일즈는 교사들이 충분한 자원을 비롯해 다른 이들의 협조 및 격려가 있다면 성공적으로 성찰을 실행할 수 있다는 결론을 내렸다.

(B) 버지니아의 교사들과 협업함으로써, 와일드먼과 나일즈는 성찰이 다양한 면으로 교사와 학생 모두에게 유익하다는 점을 결정적으로 입증할 수 있었다.

(C) 와일드먼과 나일즈는 교사들이 성찰의 결과로 발생되는 문제들을 처리하는 데 도움을 받기 위해 활용할 수 있는 세 가지 전략을 설명했다.

(D) 교사가 성찰과 관련된 어려움을 극복할 수 있는 능력은 성찰을 시작하는 초기의 동기 부여에 달려 있다.

(E) 연구에 따르면 학교에서 성찰을 실행하는 데에는 여러 장애물이 있을 뿐만 아니라 왜 교사들이 성찰하고 싶을지에 대한 이해가 불충분한 것으로 나타나 있다.

(F) 와일드먼과 나일즈는 교실 내의 일들을 이해하고 성찰에 필요한 능력을 발전시키는 데 상당한 훈련과 연습이 필요하다는 것을 알게 되었다.

해설 네 번째 문단에서, 성찰에 필요한 능력을 발전시키는 데 상당한 훈련과 연습이 필요하다는 중요 포인트를 언급하기에 (F)를 정답으로 선택해야 한다. 이 지문의 중요 키워드는 '동기 부여'와 '서포트'이며 이를 다루고 있는 (A)를 정답으로 선정한다. 그리고 마지막으로, 교직에서의 성찰은 실행에 많은 어려움이 있고, 성찰해야 하는 이유에 대한 이해가 더욱 필요하다는 점이 등장해야 하기에 (E)를 고른다.

어휘 sufficient 충분한(↔ insufficient) conclusively 결정적으로 overcome ~을 극복하다 involved in ~와 관련된 depend on ~에 달려 있다 obstacle 장애(물) implement ~을 실행하다, 시행하다

Passage 1

Answers

1. C	2. A	3. D	4. A	5. B	6. C	7. C	8. A	9. D	10. BCE

목재의 상업화

1800년대 미국에서는, 건축되는 거의 모든 것이 나무로 제작되었다. 건축용으로 가장 가치 있는 나무 종류 중의 하나가 소나무였다. 소나무는 단순한 수공구를 이용해 쉽게 만들 수 있을 정도로 충분히 부드러우면서도 비교적 내구성이 좋고 튼튼하다. 또한 물에서도 잘 떠다니기 때문에, 전국 곳곳에 멀리 있는 시장으로 운송하는 것이 수월하다. 5대호 주변에 자리잡고 있는 미시간과 위스콘신, 그리고 미네소타 같은 주는 모두 광활한 소나무 숲과 큰 강을 자랑했기 때문에, 5대호와 나아가 국제적인 해상 운송의 중심지들을 향한 통나무 수송을 용이하게 해주었다.

19세기 중반 무렵, 동부 지역의 목재용 수목 부족 문제 및 미국 서부 지역 정착이 모두 5대호 주변의 소나무 숲에 영향을 미쳤다. 이후의 30년 동안에 걸쳐, 목재 산업은 미시간과 위스콘신, 그리고 미네소타에서 호황을 누렸다. 새롭게 설립된 벌목 회사들이 엄청난 지역에 걸친 소나무 지대를 매입해 빠른 속도로 나무를 베기 시작했다. 목재용 수목이 식민지 개척자들과 나중에 등장하는 실업가들 모두에 의해 가치 있는 상품으로 여겨졌지만, 후자의 경우가 나무를 잘라내는 데 있어 훨씬 더 포괄적이고 공격적인 접근 방식을 취했다. 그 결과, 1860년에서 1890년 사이의 기간은 과거에 목재가 거래되었던 방식에 있어 급격한 변화를 보였다. ^{1(C)}돈을 벌 수 있는 별도의 방법을 찾던 농부들은 더 이상 장작 또는 기타 나무 제품들에 대한 주요 공급원이 아니었다. 일찍이 1870년대부터, 농부들과 도시 사람들 모두 직접 나무를 베어내거나 지역 공급원을 통해 목재를 사들이는 대신 5대호 주변의 여러 주를 기반으로 하는 대형 제조업체들을 통해 목재 제품을 구입하기 시작했다.

^{2(A)}기술의 발전은 목재의 상업화에 있어 큰 역할을 했다. 기존에 사용되었던 두꺼운 톱날은 너무 비효율적이어서, 각 통나무에 대해 3분의 1에 달하는 많은 부분을 낭비하게 되어, 톱밥이나 폐품으로 남겨지곤 했다. ^{2(A)}하지만, 1870년대에, 영국에서 발명된 띠톱은 더 얇은 날을 지니고 있어, 곧 5대호 주변의 여러 주 곳곳에 자리잡은 목재 공장에서 선호하는 절단용 도구가 되었다. 비슷한 시기에, 증기로 가동되는 제재소의 출현이 더욱 지속적이고 효율적인 통나무 절단 작업을 ^{3(D)}가능하게 함으로써 목재 생산을 용이하게 해주었다. 실제로, 증기 동력은 아주 다양한 작업에 자동화를 가져왔는데, 이들 중 하나가 폐기물의 수송이었다. 증기로 가동되는 제재소는 또한 통나무 연못에 열기를 제공해, 목재 생산이 지연되지 않고 지속될 수 있도록 일 년 내내 얼지 않은 상태로 유지해 주기도 했다.

목재 회사들은 산업용 목재 생산이 성공을 거둘 수 있도록 계절의 영향력을 무력화시킬 방법을 강구해야 했다. 목재 절단 작업은 일반적으로 겨울 중에 진행되었는데, 통나무들을 썰매에 실어 눈과 얼음을 가로질러 강둑으로 쉽게 끌고 갈 수 있었기 때문이었다. 강과 호수들이 녹는 대로, 작업자들이 통나무들을 뗏목에 싣고 제재소로 옮겼으며, 그곳에서 여름 중에 잘라 목재로 만들었다. ■ ^{5(B)}만일 계절에 맞지 않게 겨울이 따뜻하거나 봄철 해빙 기간이 지연되는 것처럼 계절이 예기치 못한 반응을 보이는 경우, 목재 생산은 악영향을 받았다. 벌목 작업자들은 기후 조건이 이상적이지 않을 때 숲에서 통나무를 수송할 수 있는 여러 기술을 고안해 냈다. ■ 1870년대에, 5대호 주변의 여러 주에 속한 벌목 작업팀들은 수송을 ^{4(A)}용이하게 하기 위해 썰매 이동로에 물을 뿌려 인공 얼음 층의 형성을 촉진시키기 시작했다. ■ 이 얼음에 의해 감소된 마찰은 작업자들이 더 많고 더 무거운 양을 수송할 수 있게 해주었다. ^{9(D)} ■

하지만, 평소답지 않게 썰매 이동로가 빠르게 진흙탕으로 변하는 따뜻한 겨울철에 따른 더 큰 문제에 아주 빠르게 대응할 해결책은 존재하지 않았다. ^{7(C)}연속적으로 눈이 내리지 않은 일련의 겨울을 보낸 끝에, 목재 회사들은 대자연 및 계절에 대한 의존도를 줄일 수 있는 방법에 초점을 맞추기 시작했다. 이들이 생각해 낸 첫 번째는 철도의 확장이었다. 처음에는, 소나무 숲의 ^{6(C)}고립으로 인해 철도 운수회사들이 제안된 철도를 놓기를 꺼려 했지만, 1870년 말의 목재 가격 상승 및 간간이 나타나는 따뜻하고 건조한 겨울로 인해 벌목 작업자들이 철로로 눈을 돌릴 수밖에 없게 만들었다. 1887년경에, 미시간은 89개의 벌목용 철도망을 갖춘 본거지가 되었으며, 벌목 작업은 단순히 겨울에만 한정되는 것이 아닌 일 년 내내 이어지는 활동으로 탈바꿈했다.

심지어 통나무들이 강가에 도착한 후에도, 하류를 따라 제재소로 향하는 이동 과정의 나머지 구간이 흔히 어려운 부분이었다. 15킬로미터에 이를 정도로 길게 이어질 수도 있었던 통나무 정체(통나무들이 모이게 되면서 강을 따라 떠다니지 못하게 된 것)가 나타나는 것은 흔한 일이었으며, 이러한 문제는 미국 중서부 지역의 북쪽 소나무 지대에 가해진 압박이 늘어남에 따라 가중되었다. [8(A)]통나무들이 꾸준히 움직이도록 유지하고 이것들의 방향을 통제하는 데 도움을 주기 위해 방재라고 부르는 통나무 및 쇠줄로 된 방벽이 만들어져야 했다.

[어휘]

1. commercialization 상업화 fashion ~을 만들다 durable 내구성이 좋은 Great Lakes 5대호(북아메리카 대륙의 동부에 있는 다섯 개의 큰 호수) boast ~을 자랑하다 facilitate ~을 용이하게 하다 timber 목재용 수목, 가공 전 베어진 수목 log (운반을 위해 자른) 통나무 lumber 목재, 가공이 끝난 수목

2. boom 호황을 누리다 tract 지역, 지대 commodity 상품 colonist 식민지 개척자 industrialist 실업가, 기업가 comprehensive 포괄적인, 종합적인 aggressive 공격적인

3. play a large role in ~에 있어 큰 역할을 하다 be left behind as ~로 남겨지다 scrap 폐품 advent 출현, 도래 mill 제재소 allow for ~을 가능하게 하다

4. neutralize ~을 무력화시키다 take place 발생되다, 일어나다 thaw 녹다, (추운 날 등이) 풀리다 behave 반응을 보이다 unpredictably 예기치 못하게 unseasonably 계절에 맞지 않게 adversely 부정적으로 affect ~에 영향을 미치다 devise ~을 고안하다 sprinkle ~을 뿌리다 artificial 인공적인 friction 마찰(력)

5. fix 해결책 uncharacteristically 평소답지 않게 consecutive 연속적인 dependence on ~에 대한 의존(도) Mother Nature 대자연 common carrier (철도, 항공 등의) 일반 운수업체 be reluctant to do ~하기를 꺼려 하다, 망설이다 remoteness 고립, 원격성 intermittent 간간이 나타나는, 간헐적인 leave A little choice but to do A에게 ~할 수 밖에 없게 만들다

6. leg (전 과정 중의) 한 구간 downstream 하류를 따라, 하류의 accumulation 모임, 쌓임, 축적 stretch (길 등이) 이어지다, 뻗어 있다 exacerbate ~을 가중시키다, 악화시키다 boom 방재

---

1. 두 번째 문단에서 1860년 이전의 미국에서 목재와 관련해 유추할 수 있는 것은 무엇인가?
(A) 목재가 1860년 이전에는 덜 손쉽게 이용할 수 있었기 때문에 더 비쌌다.
(B) 목재가 동부 지역을 기반으로 하는 대형 회사들에 의해 주로 생산되었다.
(C) 소득에 보탬이 되기를 바랐던 농부들이 주된 목재 공급원이었다.
(D) 미국 서부 지역의 농부들이 새롭게 찾아오는 정착민들에게 목재를 판매해 부자가 되었다.

해설 해당 문단의 하단에 '돈을 벌 수 있는 별도의 방법을 찾던 농부들은 더 이상 장작 또는 기타 나무 제품들에 대한 주요 공급원이 아니었다'라는 점을 토대로, 이들이 소득을 위해 목재 공급을 해왔었다는 점을 유추할 수 있으므로 정답은 (C)이다.

어휘 supplement ~을 보충하다

2. 글쓴이는 왜 "영국에서 발명된 띠톱"을 언급하는가?
(A) 새로운 기술이 목재 산업에 미친 영향의 예를 들기 위해
(B) 증기 동력이 어떻게 여러 기술적 발전이라는 결과를 낳았는지 설명하기 위해
(C) 더 두꺼운 톱날이 어떻게 통나무에서 나오는 폐기물을 줄이는 데 도움이 되었는지 설명하기 위해
(D) 미국의 목재 회사들이 어떻게 영국의 목재 회사들과 긴밀히 협력했는지 보여주기 위해

해설 해당 문단의 첫 번째 문장을 토대로 왜 예시가 등장했는지 알 수 있다. 기술의 발전은 목재의 상업화에 큰 기여를 했다는 점을 토대로 정답이 (A)임을 알 수 있다.

어휘 exemplify ~을 예로 들다

3. 지문의 표현 "allowing for"와 의미가 가장 가까운 것은 무엇인가?
(A) 승인함
(B) 장려함
(C) 준비함
(D) 가능하게 함

해설 allowing for(가능하게 함)와 enabling(가능하게 함)은 동의어로 정답은 (D)이다.

4. 지문의 단어 "facilitate"과 의미가 가장 가까운 것은 무엇인가?
(A) ~을 용이하게 하다
(B) ~을 생산하다
(C) ~을 평가하다
(D) ~을 단축시키다

해설 facilitate(용이하게 하다)와 ease(용이하게 하다)는 동의어로 정답은 (A)이다.

5. 네 번째 문단에 따르면, 따뜻한 겨울이 어떻게 목재 생산에 부적적으로 영향을 미칠 수 있었는가?

(A) 강물이 목재 제재소에 동력을 제공할 정도로 충분히 빠르게 흐르지 않았다.

(B) 강과 호수로 통나무를 옮기는 일이 너무 어려워졌다.

(C) 일부 나무 종은 만족스럽지 못한 품질의 목재를 생산해냈다.

(D) 통나무들이 수상 운송 경로에서 정체될 가능성이 더 컸다.

해설 해당 문단의 첫 문장부터 '계절의 영향력을 무력화시킬 방법'이라는 키워드에 초점을 맞추고 글을 읽는 것이 중요하다. 이어지는 문장을 보면, 통나무들을 썰매에 실어 강둑으로 쉽게 이동시키고, 뗏목을 통해 제재소로 옮겼다는 정보를 확인해볼 수 있다. 이후 계절이 따뜻해지는 경우, 수송할 수 있는 여러 기술을 고안해냈다는 점을 토대로 (B)를 정답으로 유추할 수 있다.

어휘 species (동식물의) 종 yield (제품, 결과물 등) ~을 내다, 산출하다, 생산하다

6. 지문의 단어 "remoteness"와 의미가 가장 가까운 것은 무엇인가?

(A) 밀도, 농도

(B) 불경기, 정체

(C) 고립, 격리

(D) 부족, 품귀

해설 remoteness(고립, 격리)와 isolation(고립, 격리)은 동의어로 정답은 (C)이다.

7. 다섯 번째 문단에서, 글쓴이는 왜 "미시간은 89개의 벌목용 철도망을 갖춘 본거지가 되었다"라는 정보를 포함하는가?

(A) 극한의 기후 조건이 철로 설치 작업을 막았다는 주장에 반박하기 위해

(B) 미시간이 목재 산업보다 철도 산업을 우선시하기 시작했다는 점을 보여주기 위해

(C) 목재 산업에 있어 철도 교통의 중요성 증가에 대한 증거를 제공하기 위해

(D) 미시간의 숲이 최상의 품질을 지닌 목재를 생산했다는 견해를 뒷받침하기 위해

해설 썰매 이동로가 작업자들에게 있어서 너무나 중요한 개념이었고, 계절에 대한 의존도를 줄일 수 있는 방법으로 고안해낸 것이 바로 철도의 확장이라는 점을 토대로, 목재 산업의 운송에 철도 교통 수단은 매우 중요했다는 점을 알 수 있다. 그러므로 정답은 (C)이다.

어휘 refute ~에 반박하다 prioritize ~을 우선시하다

8. 어섯 번째 문단에 따르면, 방재의 설치가 벌목 업계에 어떻게 유익했는가?

(A) 통나무가 하류를 따라 더욱 신속하고 쉽게 이동하도록 도움으로써

(B) 5대호 주변에 있는 여러 주의 벌목 작업 지출 비용을 감소시킴으로써

(C) 벌목 장소에서 제재소로 이어지는 하류의 이동 시간을 단축시킴으로써

(D) 호수에 보관할 수 있는 통나무의 숫자를 증가시킴으로써

해설 해당 문단의 마지막 문장을 보면, 꾸준히 움직이고, 방향을 통제하는 데 방재를 이용했다는 점을 알 수 있으므로 정답은 (A)이다.

9. 다음 문장이 지문에 추가될 수 있는 곳을 나타내는 네 개의 네모 표기 [■]를 찾아 보시오.

실제로, 몇몇 썰매는 무게가 100톤을 초과하는 많은 양의 목재를 옮길 수 있었다.

위 문장은 어느 곳에 가장 적합하겠는가? 네모 표기[■]를 클릭해 지문에 이 문장을 추가하시오.

(A) 1번

(B) 2번

(C) 3번

(D) 4번

해설 해당 문장에서 주목해야할 점은 '실제로'라는 표현과 '100톤을 초과하는 많은 양의 목재'이다. 따라서, 마지막 문장인 '더 많고 무거운 양을 수송할 수 있게 해주었다' 뒤에 예시로 제시되어야 알맞으므로 (D)가 정답이다.

어휘 exceed ~을 초과하다, 넘어서다

10. **설명:** 간략한 지문 요약에 필요한 도입 문장이 아래에 제공되어 있다. 지문에서 가장 중요한 개념들을 나타내는 세 가지 답안 선택지를 골라 요약 내용을 완성하시오. 일부 답안 선택지는 지문에 제시되지 않는 개념을 나타내거나 지문에서 중요하지 않은 개념들이므로 요약 내용에 속하지 않는다. **이 문제는 2점에 해당된다.**

19세기 미국에서 목재에 대한 수요 증가가 5대호 지역의 벌목업을 탈바꿈시켰다.

(A) 띠톱 같은 새로운 기술에 대한 혁신을 통해, 미국의 목재 회사들이 영국 및 기타 국가들을 대상으로 벌목용 장비를 수출함으로써 수익을 얻었다.

(B) 증기 동력의 개발 및 기타 기술적인 발전이 목재 산업의 생산성 및 효율성, 그리고 상업화의 증가로 이어졌다.

(C) 1800년대에, 벌목업은 지역 농부들에 의해 만들어진 지역 기업 대신 제조 회사들을 포함한 하나의 대규모 산업

이 되었다.

(D) 1860년 이후에, 농부들이 효율적으로 통나무를 수송하고 나무 제품으로 제조하기 위해 목재 회사들과 협업하기 시작했다.

(E) 통나무를 제재소로 옮기는 새로운 기술이 도입되었으며, 이것이 벌목 작업을 계절적인 활동에서 연중 지속되는 활동으로 탈바꿈시키는 데 도움을 주었다.

(F) 5대호 주변의 여러 주에 나타나는 예측 불가능한 계절별 날씨로 인해 벌목용 철도 교통을 위한 철로를 설치하는 것이 사실상 불가능했다.

해설   세 번째 문단과 다섯 번째 문단의 내용을 보면, 목재 산업의 생산성 및 상업화의 증가로 이어진 부분은 기술의 발전과 증기 동력의 사용이었다는 점을 중심적으로 다루고 있기에 (B)는 맞다. 첫 번째와 두 번째 문단을 보면 1800년대 벌목업이 어떻게 본격적으로 커질 수 있었는지를 확인할 수 있기에 (C)를 답으로 선정한다. 마지막으로 지문의 후반부는 '어떻게 계절에 구애받지 않고 목재를 이동시킬 것인가'라는 점에 초점을 두고 있기에 (E)를 선택한다.

어휘   innovate ~을 혁신하다 profit 수익을 얻다 efficiency 효율성 large-scale 대규모의 involve ~을 포함하다 enterprise 기업 collaborate with ~와 협업하다, 공동 작업하다 unpredictable 예측 불가능한 virtually 사실상, 거의

Passage 2

Answers

1. B	2. D	3. B	4. D	5. C	6. A	7. C	8. D	9. B	10. ACF

저가 인쇄의 혁명

인쇄물의 경제적 환경에 있어 상당한 변화가 19세기 전반기에 미국과 유럽에서 모두 나타나기는 했지만, 그 변화는 일반적으로 미국에서 더 빨리 시작되어 더 폭넓은 영향을 미쳤다. 1830년대와 1840년대에, 저가 인쇄 시대의 [1(B)]도래는 미국 내 도서 및 신문에 대한 급격한 가격 인하를 통해 예고되었다. 일간지의 가격이 보통 한 부에 6센트였던 반면, 어떤 것은 겨우 1~2센트의 가격에 팔리기 시작했다. 마찬가지로, 한때 가격이 2달러였던 도서들도 25센트에 팔리기 시작하기는 했지만, 동일한 도서가 영국에서는 7달러에 상당하는 가격이었다. 인쇄 비용의 하락은 너무 급격했고 너무 빠른 속도로 나타난 나머지 정보 가격의 혁명으로 묘사되었다. 급격한 가격 하락의 여러 유사한 사례들이 당시와 현대 사이에 꾸준히 나타나면서, 우리의 문화 및 정보 확산에 깊이 영향을 미쳤다.

19세기 중반에, 미국에서 인쇄물과 관련해 나타난 두 차례의 문화적 혁신이 그 저렴한 가격을 인지할 수 있도록 명명되었다. "다임 나블(10센트짜리 소설)"과 "페니 프레스(1센트짜리 신문)"는 두 가지 의미로서 저렴한 것으로 여겨졌는데, 가격이 기분 좋을 정도로 저렴한 것이었을 수도 있지만, 그 세련됨의 저조한 수준으로 인해 비난받기도 했다. [2(D)]하지만, 저렴한 가격이 항상 저렴한 취향을 의미한 것은 아니었으며, 출판사들은 가능한 한 많은 고객에게 다가가기 위해 높이 평가받는 작품을 저렴한 방식으로 점점 더 많이 출간했다. 정보 가격의 혁명은 또한 종교와 정치에도 깊은 영향을 미쳤는데, 두 분야에 속한 단체들이 모두 역사상 처음으로 인쇄물의 출간이 가장 효과적인 대중 설득의 수단이라는 점을 이해했기 때문이었다.

저가 인쇄물의 이용 가능성이 완전히 [3(B)]전례 없던 일은 아니었다. 1600년대와 1700년대의 잉글랜드와 프랑스에서는, 더 낮은 계층의 사람들 사이에서 소설과 발라드, 그리고 희곡의 저렴한 소장본을 돌려보는 것이 꽤 흔한 일이었다. 대다수의 가난한 사람들은 글을 읽을 줄 몰랐기 때문에, 읽을 줄 아는 사람이 많은 사람들이 모인 앞에서 큰 소리로 작품을 읽어주곤 했다. 이렇게, 저가 인쇄물은 읽는 사람들보다 듣는 사람들의 마음을 훨씬 더 많이 사로잡았다. 1800년대 미국과 유럽에서 출현한 저가 인쇄는 훨씬 더 큰 규모로 발생되었으며, 읽고 쓰는 능력의 상당한 증가와 동시에 일어나면서 일종의 문화적 분수령이 만들어졌다. ■ [4(D)]역사적으로, 심지어 글을 읽고 쓸 아는 사람들의 집에서도, 책을 비롯한 기타 출판물은 상당히 흔치 않은 특별한 물품이었으며, 흔히 반복적으로 읽었던 종교 서적으로만 구성되어 있었다. [9(B)]■ [4(C)]하지만 저가 인쇄의 급증으로 인해, 글을 읽는 습관이 더욱 다채로워졌으며, 사람들은 신문과 잡지, 그리고 저가 도서를 읽고 나서 [4(B)]다른 이들과 공유하는 것을 즐기기 시작했다. ■ 사람들이 여전히 집중적인 종교 서적 독서에 빠져 있기는 했지만, [4(A)]빠르게 읽는 것 또한 즐겁고 느긋하게 해주는 여가 활동의 형태로서 인기를 얻게 되었다. ■

저가 인쇄의 출현에 대한 설명을 제공하기 위해 시도할 때, 대부분의 자료들이 기술 발전의 중요성을 강조하는 경향이 있다. 의심의 여지없이, 기술의 변화는 저가 인쇄의 발전에 있어 중요한 부분이었다. 하지만, 미국에서는 기술 발전이 일어나기 저부터 이미 인쇄 기격이 하락하기 시작했다. 다시 말해서, 가격 인하가 이미 진행 중인 상황에서 새로운 기술이 나타났기 때문에, 그것이 그러한 추세를 가속화하는 데 도움이 되긴 했지만, 속발시키진 않았다. [5(C)]실제로, 새로운 기술에 혁신을 일으킨 원동력을 촉발시킨 것은 인쇄술의 지속적인 확대였다. 기술을 저가 인쇄의 주요 원인으로 여기는 것은 다소 무지한 일일 수 있는데, 정치와 문화, 그리고 시장이 인쇄 목적의 새 기술에 투자하는 일을 실현 가능하게 만든 조건을 형성하는 데 있어 아주 중요한 역할을 했기 때문이다.

유럽의 각국 정부가 신문 같은 인쇄 출판물에 대해 세금을 부과한 반면, 미국은 그렇게 하지 않았으며, 심지어 우편 제도를 통해 보조금을 지급하기까지 했다. [6(A)]미국 내 저가 인쇄물의 인기 상승은 또한 19세기 미국 소비자 시장의 명확한 추세를 집중 조명해 주기도 했다. 경제 역사학자 네이선 로젠버그는 식사용 도구, 총, 부츠, 의류의 경우들을 언급하면서 "미국인들은 저가 대량 생산 방식을 위해 의도적으로 고안된 제품들을 선뜻 받아들였습니다."라고 말했지만, [8(D)]영국 같은 나라에서는 소비자들 사이에서 독특하면서 맞춤 생산되는 제품에 대한 수요가 [7(C)]지속되었다. 따라서, 도서가 이러한 패턴을 따른 것은 놀라운 일이 아니다. 더욱이, 도서의 대량 생산을 용이하게 하기 위해 도입된 새로운 제조 기술의 많은 부분이 미국의 독창성에서 나온 산물이 아니었다. 실제로, 1850년 이전에 인쇄 분야에서 나타난 대부분의 주요 발전상은 대서양을 가로질러 동쪽의 영국으로 건너간 것이 아니라, 그 반대였다. 하지만 도서의 대량 생산은 시장이 영국보다 훨씬 더 컸고 품질보다 가격을 더 우려했던 미국에서 더 빠르게 발전했는데, 아마 그 이유는 도서 구매자들 중에서 상대적으로 교양 있는 독자의 비율이 낮았기 때문이었을 것이다.

[어휘]

1. revolution 혁명, 변혁 have a wide impact 폭넓은 영향을 미치다 advent 도래, 출현 herald ~을 예고하다 drastic 급격한(= steep, sharp) equivalent 상당하는 것 profoundly 깊이 있게

2. acknowledge ~을 인지하다, 인정하다 criticize ~을 비난하다, 비판하다 sophistication 세련됨 highly regarded 높이 평가 받는 sphere 분야, 영역 mass persuasion 대중 설득

3. unprecedented 전례 없는 circulate ~을 돌려보다, 유포하다 captivate ~의 마음을 사로잡다 take place (일 등이) 발생되다, 일어나다 on a much greater scale 훨씬 더 큰 규모로 coincide with ~와 동시에 일어나다 literacy 글을 읽고 쓸 줄 아는 능력 watershed 분수령 consist of ~로 구성되다 indulge in ~에 빠져들다, ~을 탐닉하다

4. tend to do ~하는 경향이 있다 emphasize ~을 강조하다 instrumental 중요한 underway 진행 중인 accelerate ~을 가속화하다 trigger ~을 촉발시키다 drive 원동력 ignorant 무지한 play a critical role in ~에 있어 아주 중요한 역할을 하다 feasible 실현 가능한

5. subsidize ~에게 보조금을 주다 deliberately 의도적으로, 고의로 bespoke 맞춤 제작되는 persist 지속되다 facilitate ~을 용이하게 하다 ingenuity 독창성 sophisticated 지적 수준이 높은, 교양 있는

1. 지문의 단어 "advent"와 의미가 가장 가까운 것은 무엇인가?
(A) 이상(적인 것)
(B) 시작
(C) 원인
(D) 기간

해설 advent(도래, 출현)와 onset(시작)은 유의어로 정답은 (B)이다.

2. 두 번째 문단에 언급된 저가 출판과 관련해 다음 중 어느 주장이 제시되었는가?
(A) 도서 출판업체들이 잘 알려진 문학 작품 출판을 중단하고 값싼 이야기에 초점을 맞췄다.
(B) 소비자들이 다임 나블에 담긴 글의 높은 수준에 깊은 인상을 받았다.
(C) 비싸지 않은 소설이 상류층에서 대체로 인기를 얻게 되었다.
(D) 모든 저렴한 소설이 세련되지 못하다는 비판이 항상 정확한 것은 아니다.

해설 해당 문단의 내용을 보면 However 이하 내용에서 '항상 저렴한 취향을 의미한 것은 아니었으며'라는 내용을 토대로 글쓴이의 의도가 반영이 되어 있다. 그리고 이를 통해 가능한 한 많은 고객에게 다가가기 위해 높이 평가받는 작품을 저렴하게 더 출간했다는 점을 기반으로 정답이 (D)임을 알 수 있다.

3. 지문의 단어 "unprecedented"와 의미가 가장 가까운 것은 무엇인가?
(A) 한결같은
(B) 전례 없는, 이례적인
(C) 받아들일 수 있는
(D) 문서로 기록된

해설 unprecedented(전례 없는, 이례적인)와 exceptional(이례적인)은 동의어로 정답은 (B)이다.

4. 세 번째 문단에 따르면, 다음 중 저가 인쇄의 출현 이후에 나타난 독서 방식의 변화가 아닌 것은 무엇인가?

(A) 즐거움을 위한 독서가 더 흔한 일이 되었다.

(B) 독자들이 지인들과 책을 공유하기 시작했다.

(C) 사람들이 더욱 다양한 출판물을 읽기 시작했다.

(D) 사람들이 더 집중적으로 종교 서적을 공부하기 시작했다.

해설 이 문단의 내용을 보면, '역사적으로, 심지어 글을 읽고 쓸 아는 사람들의 집에서도, 책을 비롯한 기타 출판물은 상당히 흔치 않은 특별한 물품이었으며, 흔히 반복적으로 읽혔던 종교 서적으로만 구성되어 있었다'라는 문장을 토대로 사람들이 더 집중적으로 종교 서적을 공부했다기보다 저가 인쇄 이전에 흔했던 현상이라는 점을 알 수 있기 때문에 정답은 (D)이다. 공유를 즐기고, 다양한 글을 읽으며, 즐거움을 주는 여가 형태의 활동이었다는 점 역시 해당 문단의 하단부에서 확인할 수 있다.

5. 네 번째 문단에서, 글쓴이는 기술과 저가 인쇄의 발전 사이의 관계에 대해 다음 중 어떤 관점을 나타내는가?

(A) 신기술의 도입이 저가 인쇄의 초기 발전을 가능하게 해주었다.

(B) 상당한 기술 발전이 아니었다면 인쇄 혁명이 일어날 수 없었을 것이다.

(C) 저가 인쇄의 성장이 신기술을 발전시키기 시작하는 자극제가 되었다.

(D) 문화 및 정치 단체들이 저가 인쇄물을 생산하기 위해 신기술을 활용하는 것에 반대했다.

해설 '실제로'(In fact)라는 시그널을 토대로 문장의 내용에 집중할 필요가 있다. 새로운 기술에 혁신을 일으킨 원동력을 촉발시킨 것이 바로 인쇄술의 지속적인 확대라는 내용을 기반으로 저가 인쇄의 성장이 신기술로 이어지는 자극제 역할을 했다는 점을 알 수 있다. 따라서 정답은 (C)이다.

어휘 incentive 자극(제), 동기 opposed 반대하는

6. 글쓴이는 왜 "식사용 도구, 총, 부츠, 의류의 경우들"에 대한 네이션 로젠버그의 발언을 언급하는가?

(A) 도서들이 19세기 미국 소비자 시장에서 관찰되던 경향과 어울린다는 생각을 뒷받침하기 위해

(B) 도서를 만드는 데 쓰인 제조 기술이 어떻게 다른 상품을 생산하는 데에도 활용되었는지 강조하기 위해

(C) 영국과 미국 내의 소비자 경향 사이에 존재하는 유사성을 보여주기 위해

(D) 맞춤 제작된 제품이 왜 다른 나라보다 미국에서 덜 인기 있었는지 설명하기 위해

해설 글쓴이의 의도를 파악하는 경우, 주어진 키워드의 앞을 보는 것이 중요하며, 해당 문단의 상단을 보면, 미국 내 저가 인쇄물의 인기 상승은 19세기 미국 소비자 시장의 명확한 추세를 집중 조명해 주었다는 점을 토대로, 그 당시 관찰되던 경향과 흐름을

같이 했다는 점을 알 수 있으므로 정답은 (A)이다. 해당 문장 뒤를 보더라도 미국인들이 대량으로 생산된 제품을 받아들였다는 점을 보아 이러한 부분 자체가 트렌드였다는 점을 알 수 있다. (C)의 경우 유럽은 미국과 대비되는 개념이기에 오답으로 빠르게 소거한다.

어휘 fit ~에 어울리다, 적합하다 similarity 유사성

7. 지문의 단어 "persisted"와 의미가 가장 가까운 것은 무엇인가?

(A) 언쟁했다, ~라고 주장했다

(B) ~을 높였다, 들어올렸다

(C) 계속되었다

(D) ~을 보존했다

해설 persisted(지속되었다)와 continued(계속되었다)는 유의어로 정답은 (C)이다.

8. 다음 중 어느 것이 다섯 번째 문단에서 영국의 도서와 관련해 언급된 내용인가?

(A) 영국은 1850년 이전에 도서 인쇄를 위한 가장 혁신적인 기술을 개발했다.

(B) 정부 보조금으로 인해 유럽의 출판업체들이 더 많은 책을 생산할 수 있었다.

(C) 영국과 미국의 도서 시장이 19세기에 직접적인 경쟁 관계에 있었다.

(D) 대량 생산된 도서가 미국보다 영국에서 덜 인기 있었다.

해설 이미 해당 문단 중반부에서 미국인들은 저가 대량 생산 방식을 위해 고안된 제품을 선뜻 받아들였다는 점을 시사했다. 그리고 이러한 개념은 도서에도 동일하게 적용이 되었다. 그러나 이후 내용에서 영국은 독특하고 맞춤 생산되는 제품에 대한 수요가 지속되었고, 도서 생산 시장이 영국보다 미국이 훨씬 컸다는 점을 토대로 정답이 (D)임을 알 수 있다.

9. 다음 문장이 지문에 추가될 수 있는 곳을 나타내는 네 개의 네모 표기 [■]를 찾아 보시오.

비록 사람들이 아주 다양한 것들을 읽은 것은 아니지만, 제한적인 수량의 도서를 마음껏 집중적으로 그리고 주기적으로 읽는 경향이 있었다.

위 문장은 어느 곳에 가장 적합하겠는가? 네모 표기[■]를 클릭해 지문에 이 문장을 추가하시오.

(A) 1번

(B) 2번

(C) 3번

(D) 4번

해설 주어진 문장은 '사람들이 아주 다양한 것을 읽은 것이 아니다'라는 중요 정보를 내포하고 있으며, 이 문장 뒤에 역접을 나타

내는 'But'을 토대로 사람들이 다채로운 독서 습관을 가질 수 있었다는 점이 이어서야 가장 이상적이라는 것을 알 수 있다. 따라서, 2번째 박스가 정답이다.

어휘 at one's disposal 원하는 대로, 마음대로 intensively 집중적으로 on a regular basis 주기적으로

10. **설명:** 간략한 지문 요약에 필요한 도입 문장이 아래에 제공되어 있다. 지문에서 가장 중요한 개념들을 나타내는 세 가지 답안 선택지를 골라 요약 내용을 완성하시오. 일부 답안 선택지는 지문에 제시되지 않는 개념을 나타내거나 지문에서 중요하지 않은 개념들이므로 요약 내용에 속하지 않는다. **이 문제는 2점에 해당된다.**

저가 인쇄는 미국에서 초기 성공을 경험했다.

(A) 일찍이 1830년대에, 미국은 영국보다 훨씬 더 저렴하게 출판물이 팔리는 현상이 나타난 정보 가격의 혁명을 경험하기 시작했다.

(B) 17세기와 18세기의 잉글랜드와 프랑스에서는 종교적이지 않은 인쇄물을 읽는 데 관심 있는 독자가 거의 없다시피 했다.

(C) 아주 다양한 제품에 해당되었던 경우와 마찬가지로, 미국의 소비자들은 유럽의 소비자들보다 더 기꺼이 대량 생산

된 도서를 수용했다.

(D) 저가 인쇄는 종교 서적이 사라지고 세련되지 못한 인쇄물로 대체될까 우려했던 몇몇 정부의 반대에 부딪혔다.

(E) 대부분의 인쇄 기술 발전은 유럽에서 비롯되었으며, 미국의 출판업체들은 이 새로운 접근 방식을 수용하기를 꺼려 했다.

(F) 저가 인쇄의 급부상은 미국의 독자들에게 여러 다른 종류의 출판물을 더 많이 이용할 수 있게 해주었고, 이는 사람들이 책을 읽는 방식 및 독서하는 주된 이유를 변화시켰다.

해설 다섯 번째 문단을 보면, 미국의 소비자들은 대량 생산된 도서와 같은 제품을 받아들였다는 점을 기반으로 영국과의 비교가 이뤄진다. 그러므로 (C)를 답으로 선택해야 한다. 세 번째 문단을 보면, 일정하고 다양하지 못했던 사람들의 독서에 변화를 주고 사람들이 독서라는 행위를 즐길 수 있게 만들어 주었다는 내용을 확인할 수 있다. 그러므로 (F)를 답으로 선택한다. 그리고 첫 번째 문단에서 유럽과의 가격 비교 및 정보 가격의 혁명과 같은 키워드가 등장하므로 (A)를 답으로 선정한다.

어휘 be willing to do 기꺼이 ~하다, ~할 의향이 있다 embrace ~을 수용하다, 포용하다 be replaced by ~로 대체되다 originate 비롯되다, 유래하다 be reluctant to do ~하기를 꺼려 하다, 망설이다 access 이용, 접근

Passage 3

Answers

1. D	2. B	3. D	4. B	5. C	6. D	7. C	8. C	9. C	10. BCE

17세기 유럽의 경제 성장

[1(D)]16세기 말과 17세기 초에, 유럽에서 경제 성장이 지속되면서 대부분의 유럽 국가들이 덜 번영하던 중세 시대를 지나 상당한 경제적 이득을 누릴 수 있게 되었다. 여러 요인이 이러한 성장에 있어 아주 중요한 역할을 했으며, 여기에는 교역망의 확대 및 농업 생산성의 증대도 포함되었다.

농촌 경제가 모든 사람을 충분히 먹일 정도로 여분의 식량을 생산해 낼 수 없다면 인구가 증가하는 것은 사실상 불가능하다. [2(B)]16세기에는, 농부들이 방대한 지역의 숲과 저지대 습지를 농작물 경작에 적합한 땅으로 변모시켰다. 이에 대한 한 가지 주목할 만한 예시가 16세기와 17세기에 네덜란드에서 있었던 간척 사업이다. 이 광범위한 농지 확장 사업으로 인해 네덜란드에서 1590년과 1615년 사이에 36,000에이커가 넘는 간척지를 만드는 결과를 낳았다.

[4(B)]작고 평범한 마을의 형태로 보일 수도 있었던 것이 사실 유럽 경제 발전에서 상당한 역할을 했다. 시골의 이 정착지들은 일반적으로 농업 생산이 비교적 발전되어 있던 지역에 자리잡고 있었으며, 이는 마을 거주민들의 생계뿐만 아니라 판매 및 거래용 잉여 농산물도 보장해주었다. 더욱이,

이 작은 마을들에 살았던 농부들은 상당히 수월하게 도시의 상인과 시장, 그리고 거래 경로를 접할 수 있었다. 농산물이 시골 지역에서 증가하면서, 회사들이 시골 지역에 산업 시설을 세우기 시작했고, 이는 산업의 확장에 있어 중추적인 역할을 했다. 특히, 직물 제조업체들은 값싸고 풍부한 시골 인력을 이용했고 수많은 소작농을 고용해 마을의 개인 집에서 상품을 생산했다. ^{4(B)}독일 전역에 걸쳐, <mark>30년 전쟁</mark>(1618-1648)에 의해 초래된 파괴로 인해 직물 생산 작업이 시골 지역으로 훨씬 더 깊숙이 파고 들었다. 가난한 마을 사람들의 가족 전체가 일에 비해 형편없이 임금을 지급받았음에도 불구하고 일반적으로 ^{3(D)}<mark>변변치 않은</mark> 가족 수입에 보탬이 되기 위한 노력으로 자신들의 초라한 판잣집에서 실을 잣거나 엮어서 천과 리넨 제품을 만들었다.

교역망의 확대 또한 이 기간 중에 유럽 경제를 끌어올리는 데 도움을 주었다. 영국과 네덜란드에서 선박이 출항해 발트해 국가들에게서 호밀을 받아간 다음, 돌아가는 여행 중에 다양한 상품을 거래하기 위해 스페인과 포르투갈에 잠시 머물렀다. 잉글랜드와 벨기에, 북부 이탈리아, ^{5(C)}그리고 스페인의 여러 지역 같은 장소에서 나타난 인구 증가 및 그로 인한 인력 증가는 그 지역들 내의 소규모 직물 제조 및 금속 생산의 확대로 이어졌다. 당시에, 제조 산업은 자본금은 거의 필요로 하지 않으면서 빠르게 이익을 냈다. 초기의 상당한 재정적 투자를 필요로 했던 유일한 모험적 사업은 광산업과 제철업이었다.

교역의 확대는 은행 산업 및 금융 서비스의 발전으로부터 도움을 받았다. 16세기 중반 무렵, 대금업자들과 상인들이 금 또는 은의 사용을 고집하는 대신 환어음을 받아들이기 시작했다. ■ 환어음이 처음 사용된 곳은 중세 이탈리아였다. 이는 개인이 특정 날짜까지 명시된 금액을 지불한다는 서면 보증이었기 때문에, 오늘날의 사회에서 신용을 제공하는 방식과 유사했다. ■ 같은 세기 중반 즈음에, 앤트워프의 한 자본가는 "물 없이 항해하지 못하듯이 환어음 없이는 교역할 수 없다"라는 대담한 주장을 펼쳤다. ^{6(D)}환어음의 사용은 상인들이 더 이상 길고 위험한 이동 중에 사람들이 탐내는 금과 은을 갖고 다니는 위험을 감수하지 않아도 된다는 것을 의미했다. ^{9(C)}■ 마드리드의 한 상인에게서 올리브를 구입하고 싶어한 한 런던 상인은 환전상에게 가서 영국 통화인 파운드로 동일 금액을 지불할 수 있었다. ■ 그런 다음, 그 환전상은 마드리드에 있는 동료에게 환어음을 보내, 런던 상인에게 상품이 건네지면 그 마드리드 상인에게 당시 스페인의 통화였던 레알로 지불하도록 승인해주는 것이었다.

스페인 선박들이 아메리카 대륙에서 캐낸 금과 은을 싣고 유럽으로 돌아가자, 이 자본의 투입이 국제 교역의 확대에 더욱 ^{8(C)}<mark>박차를 가했다</mark>. 자본의 증가는 상품의 생산을 촉진했고, 유럽 대륙 전역에서 교역뿐만 아니라 심지어 신용 거래의 증가로 이어지기도 했다. 더욱이, 은행가들과 부유한 상인들이 여러 국가에 투자금과 대출금을 제공하면서 신용 공급이 늘어났으며, ^{7(A)}주식 합자 제휴 관계라고 부르는 영국의 혁신적인 방법이 더욱 흔한 일이 되었다. ^{7(C)}주식 합자 회사는 투자자와 업체 사이의 전형적인 단기 금융 협정과 달랐는데, ^{7(D)}부유한 상인 및 다른 투자자들에게 주식을 매각하고 ^{7(B)}주식을 통해 만들어진 돈을 회사를 강화하는 데 활용함으로써 장기간의 영구적인 자본금을 제공하는 것이었기 때문이다.

[어휘]

1. economic gains 경제적 이득 prosperous 번영하는, 번창하는 medieval 중세의 play a crucial[considerable, pivotal] role in ~에 있어 아주 중요한[상당한, 중추적인] 역할을 하다
2. virtually 사실상, 거의 rural 농업의, 시골의 tract 지역, 지대 low-lying 저지대의 land reclamation 토지 간척, 토지 개간 result in A -ing A가 ~하는 결과를 낳다 reclaim ~을 개간하다, 간척지를 만들다
3. unremarkable 평범한, 특징 없는 surplus 잉여, 과잉, 흑자 take advantage of ~을 활용하다, 이용하다 peasant 소작농 bring about ~을 초래하다, 야기하다 spin (실 등)을 잣다, 방적하다 weave (직물 등)을 엮다, 짜다 supplement ~을 보충하다 meager 변변치 않은
4. boost ~을 촉진하다, 증대하다 subsequently 그 후에, 나중에 capital 자본(금) turn a profit 수익을 내다 business venture 모험적 사업 smelting 제철업
5. bills of exchange 환어음 insist upon ~을 고집하다 specified 명시된 risk -ing ~하는 위험을 감수하다 equivalent 동등한, 상당하는 hand A over to B A를 B에게 건네다, 넘겨주다
6. infusion 투입 spur ~에 박차를 가하다 affluent 부유한 state 국가 joint-stock partnership 주식 합자 제휴 관계 bolster ~을 강화하다, 개선하다

1. 첫 번째 문단에 따르면, 중세 시대 유럽과 관련해 사실인 것은 무엇인가?
(A) 농업 생산성의 감소가 발생했다.
(B) 국제 교역이 경제를 튼튼하게 만들기 시작했다.
(C) 대부분의 상인들이 더 부유해졌다.
(D) 경제 성장이 비교적 느렸다.

해설 가장 첫 번째 문장을 보면, 유럽에서 경제 성장이 지속되면서 대부분의 유럽 국가들이 덜 번영하던 중세 시대를 지났다는 정

보를 확인할 수 있다. 정답은 (D)이다.

2. 두 번째 문단에 따르면, 식량 생산을 늘리기 위한 열망에 따른 한 가지 영향은 무엇이었는가?
(A) 생물 다양성이 습지 내에서 감소했다.
(B) 숲이 농지로 전환되었다.
(C) 농촌 경제가 번영하기 힘겨웠다.

(D) 농부들 사이에서 경쟁이 늘어났다.

해설 식량은 인구의 증가와 상관관계가 있다는 첫 번째 문장에 이어, 농부들이 방대한 지역의 숲과 저지대 습지를 경작을 위한 땅으로 변화시켰냐는 점을 기반으로 정답이 (B)임을 알 수 있다.

어휘 biodiversity 생물 다양성 struggle to do ~하기 힘겨워 하다, ~하기 위해 발버둥치다

3. 지문의 단어 "meager"와 의미가 가장 가까운 것은 무엇인가?
(A) 점차적인
(B) 간헐적인
(C) 보통의, 평범한
(D) 불충분한

해설 meager(변변치 않은)와 inadequate(불충분한)은 유의어로 정답은 (D)이다.

4. 글쓴이는 왜 세 번째 문단에서 "30년 전쟁"을 언급하는가?
(A) 좋지 못한 교역 관계의 부정적인 결과를 보여주기 위해
(B) 시골의 산업 증대로 이어진 여러 요인들 중 하나를 설명하기 위해
(C) 유럽에서 있었던 두 가지 갈등 사이의 차이점을 대조하기 위해
(D) 국제 교역이 그 전쟁 전에 더 튼튼했다고 주장하기 위해

해설 작고 평범한 마을의 형태가 유럽 경제 발전에서 큰 영향을 미친 주역이라는 점을 첫 번째 문장에서 언급하고 있다. 그리고 이후 독일 전역에서 일어난 파괴가 시골 인력의 활용으로 이어졌다는 점을 설명하고 있기 때문에 정답은 (B)임을 알 수 있다.

5. 네 번째 문단에서, 글쓴이는 직물 산업이 무엇에 따른 결과로 성장했다고 주장하는가?
(A) 시골 정착지의 개선된 상태
(B) 업계에서 쓰일 새로운 종류의 원자재 발견
(C) 일할 수 있는 근로자 수의 증가
(D) 광산업과 제철업을 통해 축적된 수익

해설 해당 문단에서 교역망의 확대가 유럽 경제를 끌어올리는 데 도움을 주었다는 점을 설명한다. 그리고 중반부를 보면, 이러한 것들로부터 파생된 인구 증가 및 인력 증가는 그 지역 내 소규모 직물 제조 및 금속 생산의 확대로 이어졌다고 한다. 따라서 정답은 (C)이다.

6. 다섯 번째 문단에서 유럽 내에서 출장에 임하는 상인들과 관련해 유추할 수 있는 것은 무엇인가?
(A) 일반적으로 그룹을 이뤄 출장을 떠나기로 결정했다.
(B) 좀처럼 환어음을 받아들이지 않았다.
(C) 중립 지역에서 구매자와 만나는 것을 선호했다.

(D) 귀중품을 강탈당하는 위험을 감수했다.

해설 다섯 번째 문단의 핵심 키워드는 은행 산업과 금융 서비스의 발전이고 그 예시 중 하나가 바로 환어음의 등장이다. 해당 문단 중반부를 보면, 환어음의 사용은 사람들이 위험한 이동 중에 금과 은을 가지고 다니는 위험을 감수하지 않아도 된다는 정보를 제공하는데, 이는 기존의 위험한 항해에서 귀중품을 강탈당할 위험을 감수하고 교역을 진행했다는 점을 의미한다. 따라서 정답은 (D)이다.

어휘 undertake ~에 임하다, 착수하다 neutral 중립적인 be robbed of ~을 강탈당하다 valuables 귀중품

7. 여섯 번째 문단에서, 다음 중 주식 합자 회사와 관련해 언급되지 않은 것은 무엇인가?
(A) 처음에 영국에서 착안되었다.
(B) 업체들을 대상으로 재정적 지원을 제공했다.
(C) 일반적으로 단기 금융 협정을 체결했다.
(D) 업체 주식 매각과 관련되어 있었다.

해설 해당 문단에서는 자본의 투입을 통해 상품 생산 증대와 신용 거래의 증가로 이어졌다는 내용을 중심으로 다루고 있다. 주식 합자 회사는 투자자와 업체 사이의 전형적인 단기 금융 협정과 달랐다고 명확하게 언급하고 있기 때문에 정답은 (C)이다. 이 문단에서 영국의 혁신적인 방법이 흔해졌으며, 투자금과 대출금을 제공하며 신용 공급이 증대하고, 주식을 매각하고 주식을 통해 만들어진 돈을 기반으로 회사를 강화하는데 활용했다는 정보를 제시하고 있기에 나머지 보기는 언급되어 있다.

어휘 conceive (생각, 계획 등) ~을 착안하다, 생각해 내다 enter into (협약, 관계 등) ~을 체결하다, 시작하다

8. 지문의 단어 "spurred"와 의미가 가장 가까운 것은 무엇인가?
(A) ~을 저해했다
(B) ~을 간략히 설명했다
(C) ~을 촉진했다
(D) 협업했다

해설 spurred(박차를 가했다)와 promoted(촉진했다)는 유의어로 정답은 (C)이다.

9. 다음 문장이 지문에 추가될 수 있는 곳을 나타내는 네 개의 네모 표기 [■]를 찾아 보시오.

그들은 또한 각 교역 목적지에서 쓰이는 다양한 통화의 가치를 확인하고 평가해야 하는 일을 피할 수도 있었다.

위 문장은 어느 곳에 가장 적합하겠는가? 네모 표기[■]를 클릭해 지문에 이 문장을 추가하시오.

(A) 1번
(B) 2번

(C) 3번

(D) 4번

해설 주어진 문장에서 중요한 힌트 중 하나는 '또한'(also) 이라는 표현이다. 이를 보면, 해당 방식이 도입되기 이전에 있었던 번거로움이나 문제점이 앞선 문장에서 등장해야 함을 의미하고 이는 '금과 은을 갖고 다니는 위험을 감수하지 않아도 된다는 것을 의미했다'라는 정보이다. 따라서, 3번째 박스에 삽입하면 논리적으로 글을 이어나갈 수 있다.

어휘 identify ~을 확인하다, 식별하다 assess ~을 평가하다

10. **설명:** 간략한 지문 요약에 필요한 도입 문장이 아래에 제공되어 있다. 지문에서 가장 중요한 개념들을 나타내는 세 가지 답안 선택지를 골라 요약 내용을 완성하시오. 일부 답안 선택지는 지문에 제시되지 않는 개념을 나타내거나 지문에서 중요하지 않은 개념들이므로 요약 내용에 속하지 않는다. **이 문제는 2점에 해당된다.**

16세기 말과 17세기 초의 유럽에서는, 농업 생산량 증가와 교역의 확대가 경제 성장을 촉진하는 데 도움을 주었다.

(A) 대부분의 시골 지역 정착지들은 도시의 시장들과 협정을 맺어 직접 생산한 모든 수공예품을 판매할 수 있었다.

(B) 교역의 확대는 금융 서비스의 개선 및 아메리카 대륙에서 들여온 금과 은으로 인한 엄청난 양의 자본 유입으로 인해 용이하게 되었다.

(C) 시골 산업의 출현 및 그곳의 많은 인력이 직물 제조업의 호황이라는 결과를 낳았으며, 그 대부분이 마을 주민들의 집 안에서 이뤄졌다.

(D) 자본의 증가가 유럽의 소비자들이 점점 더 많이 호감을 갖게 된 더 정교한 제품의 생산에 필수적이었다.

(E) 토지를 농지로 전환하면서 농부들이 시골 경제를 개선하기 위해 더 많은 식량을 생산하고 교역에 필요한 여분의 제품을 축적할 수 있게 되었다.

(F) 은행들이 상인들에게 대출금을 제공하기 시작하자 한어음은 점차 국제 무역상들의 눈 밖에 났다.

해설 토지를 농지로 전환하며 시골 경제가 개선되기 시작했다는 정보를 두 번째 문단에서 확인할 수 있으며, 이 정보는 전체 글의 흐름에서 매우 중요한 역할을 한다. 그러므로 (E)를 먼저 선택할 수 있다. 이후 세 번째 문단에서 시골 산업이 등장하며, 각기 집에서 작게 직물 제조에 기여를 했다는 내용이 유럽 경제에 기여했다는 글의 흐름상 중요하기에 (C)를 고른다. 마지막으로 교역 확대 및 금융 서비스는 후반부 내용 흐름의 중심이 되기 때문에 (B)를 선택한다.

어휘 facilitate ~을 용이하게 하다 influx 유입 take place (일 등이) 발생되다, 일어나다 fall out of favor with ~의 눈 밖에 나다, ~가 선호하지 않게 되다

Actual Test 1

1. D	2. B	3. C	4. B	5. A	6. B	7. C	8. D	9. C	10. BCF
11. A	12. D	13. C	14. D	15. B	16. B	17. D	18. A	19. A	20. BCD

Questions 1-10

종의 지리적 고립

종의 정의를 제공하도록 요청받았을 때, 에른스트 마이어라는 이름의 생물학자는 종을 "실제로 또는 잠재적으로 이종 교배하는 개체군으로서, 그와 같은 다른 개체군과 이종 교배할 기회가 있을 때 그렇게 하지 않는 개체군"이라고 설명했다. 많은 종의 유래는 한 개체군, 그리고 그 전체 유전자 풀이 동일 종의 다른 개체군들과 분리되어, 개체군들 사이의 이종 교배를 불가능하게 만드는 중요한 사건에 의해 영향을 받는다. 분리되어 고립된 유전자 풀을 갖게 되는 개체군은 그 후 자체적으로 뚜렷이 다른 진화 경로를 따르게 된다. [1(D)]새로운 종이 만들어지는 많은 경우에 있어, 지리적 장벽은 개체군의 고립에 대한 첫 번째 이유이며, 이렇게 새로운 종의 진화가 나타나는 방식을 이소적 종분화라고 일컫는다.

[2(B)]개체군의 지리적 고립은 다양한 요인에 의해 촉발될 수 있다. 예를 들어, 산맥이 서서히 출현하면서 호수 및 하천 연결망을 갈라놓을 때 저지대 호수에 서식하는 특정 물고기 개체군이 분리될 수 있다. 마찬가지로, 서서히 나아가는 빙하가 결국 한 개체군을 분리시킬 수도 있고, 파나마 지협처럼 다리 역할을 하는 육로가 나타나 해양의 개체군들이 육지 양측으로 분리되는 결과를 낳기도 한다.

[3(C)]지리적 장벽이 개체군을 분리된 상태로 유지하려면 얼마나 실질적이고 거대해야 하는가? 이는 특정 종이 그러한 장벽을 넘나들 수 있는 능력에 달려 있다. 산과 강은 조류에게, 또는 심지어 코요테처럼 적응력이 좋은 포유류에게도 아무런 장애물이 되지 못한다. 식물의 경우에, 바람에 날리는 꽃가루 또한 그러한 장벽에 의해 방해받지 않으며, 식물의 씨앗도 여전히 곤충 및 다른 동물들을 통해 이리저리 옮겨질 수 있다. [4(B)]반면, 작은 설치류는 넓은 강이나 깊은 협곡을 지나다닐 방법을 찾지 못할 것이다. 이에 대한 한 가지 좋은 예시가 미국 남서부의 그랜드 캐니언에 의한 흰꼬리 영양 다람쥐 및 그와 밀접하게 관련된 해리스 영양 다람쥐의 분리이다. 해리스 영양 다람쥐는 그랜드 캐니언 남쪽 사막의 제한적인 범위에 살고 있는 반면, 더 작은 흰꼬리 영양 다람쥐는 그 협곡 북쪽의 사막과 콜로라도 강 서쪽의 캘리포니아 남부에 서식하고 있다.

[5(A)]지리적 고립이 새로운 종이 발생될 기회를 야기하기는 하지만, 이소적 종분화는 유전자 풀이 모체가 되는 개체군과 고립되는 개체군 사이에서 충분히 생식 장벽을 확립할 정도로 상당히 변화되는 경우에만 발생될 수 있다. 이소적 종분화의 발생 가능성은 한 개체군이 작으면서 고립되어 있는 경우에 모두 해당될 때 높아지는데, 그 유전자 풀이 상당히 변화될 가능성이 더 높아지기 때문이다. 예를 들어, 2백만년도 되지 않는 기간에, 남아메리카 본토에서 유래한 외래 동식물 종의 작은 개체군들이 갈라파고스 제도에서 군락을 이뤄 [6(B)]냈으며, 이로 인해 현재 그 제도에 살고 있는 모든 고유 종이 만들어졌다.

[7(C)]이따금씩 개체군 이동이 발생되도록 할 수 있을 정도로 충분히 가까우면서도, 대부분의 개체군이 고립된 상태로 진화하도록 보장할 정도로 충분히 멀리 떨어져 있는 해양 섬들은 진화의 과정이 한 눈에 보이는 소중한 야외 실험실의 역할을 한다. 이러한 경우가 갈라파고스 제도보다 더 명확히 나타나는 곳은 존재하지 않는다. 이 제도는 수중 화산 분출에 따른 결과로 생겨났으며, 흔히 바람과 해류에 의해 멀리 떨어진 대륙과 섬으로부터 옮겨지면서 서식지에서 벗어난 생물체들이 점차 정착하게 되었다. 또한, 일부 종은 바다 새의 깃털에 엉긴 씨앗처럼 다른 생물체에 의해 옮겨져 그 열도에 도달했을 가능성도 크다.

오늘날 갈라파고스에 사는 대부분의 종은 다른 어디에서도 발견되지 않고 있으며, 남아메리카 본토에서 바다를 건너 날려 왔거나 떠내려 온 생물체들의 후손이다. 예를 들어, 이 열도는 밀접하게 관련된 13가지 조류 종이 속한 갈라파고스 핀치의 서식지이다. 이 새들이 많은 유사성을 공유하고 있기는 하지만, 부리 형태가 다르듯이, 먹이 섭취 습성도 서로 다른데, 부리 형태가 각자의 먹이 섭취 습성에 더 적합하도록 특별히 적응되어 있기 때문이다. [8(D)]이 13가지 핀치 종이 모두 그 섬들 중 한 곳에 군락을 이뤘던 단 하나의 작은 조류 개체군의 후손임을 보여주는 증거가 많이 수집되었다. 시조에 해당되는 개체군이 본토로부터 이동해온 후 그 섬에 고립된 상태가 되자, 근본적으로 새로운 종을 만들어내며 그 유전자 풀이 상당한 변화를 거친 것이 틀림없다. ■ 나중에, 이 새로운 종에 속하는 몇몇 생물체가 아마 폭풍에 의해 인근 섬으로 옮겨졌을 것이다. ■

이 두 번째 시조에 해당되는 개체군은 당시 그 섬에 고립된 채로 그 후에 두 번째 새로운 종으로 진화했을 것이며, 최초의 개체군이 다른 곳으로 이주한 그 섬에서 나중에 다시 군락을 이룰 수 있었을 것이다. ^{9(C)}■ 최근의 연구에 따르면 갈라파고스의 각 섬에는 현재 다수의 핀치 종이 있으며, 몇몇 섬에는 10가지나 되는 뚜렷이 다른 많은 종이 있는 것으로 나타나 있다. ■

[어휘]
1. species (동식물의) 종 isolation 고립, 분리 interbreed 이종 교배하다 population 개체군 gene pool 유전자 풀(한 집단에 속하는 모든 개체가 지닌 유전자 집합) evolutionary 진화의 allopatric speciation 이소적 종분화(한 개체군이 지리적으로 분리되어 상이한 종들이 새롭게 생겨나는 것)
2. trigger ~을 촉발시키다 inhabit ~에 서식하다 split apart ~을 갈라놓다 advance 나아가다, 전진하다 glacier 빙하 Isthmus of Panama 파나마 지협(지협: 큰 육지 사이를 잇는 극단적으로 좁아진 지형)
3. substantial 실질적인, 상당한 traverse ~을 가로질러 건너다 mammals 포유류 unhindered 방해 받지 않는 rodents 설치류
4. give rise to ~을 야기하다, 유발하다 reproductive 생식의, 번식의 substantially 상당히, 많이 colonize ~에서 군락을 이루다
5. evolve 진화하다, 발전하다 on full view 한 눈에 보이는 emerge 나타나다, 드러나다 volcanic eruption 화산 분출 populate ~에 살다, 거주하다 stray from ~에서 벗어나다
6. descendant 후손, 자손 finch 핀치, 되새류(부리가 짧은 작은 새) adapted 적응된, 알맞은 descend from ~의 후손이다, ~로부터 전해지다 emigrate 이주하다

1. 첫 번째 문단에 따르면, 이소적 종분화는 어떤 경우에 가능한가?
  (A) 한 가지 종의 개체군 하나가 다른 종과 이종 교배하는 경우에
  (B) 한 가지 종이 성공적으로 지리적 장벽을 극복하는 경우에
  (C) 같은 서식지를 공유하는 개체군들 속에서 유전적 돌연변이가 발생하는 경우에
  (D) 지리적 장벽으로 인해 한 개체군이 고립되는 결과를 낳는 경우에

해설 해당 문단의 마지막 내용을 보면, 지리적 장벽은 개체군 고립의 첫 번째 이유이며, 이종 교배가 불가능해지며 새로운 종의 진화가 나타나는 것을 이소적 종분화라고 설명하기 때문에 정답은 (D)이다.

어휘 overcome ~을 극복하다 genetic mutation 유전적 돌연변이

2. 두 번째 문단은 첫 번째 문단과 어떻게 관련되어 있는가?
  (A) 두 번째 문단은 첫 번째 문단에서 지리적 고립이 많은 종의 감소로 이어졌다고 제시한 결론을 더욱 상세히 설명한다.
  (B) 두 번째 문단은 첫 번째 문단에서 개괄적으로 서술한 지리적 고립 현상이 발생될 수 있는 여러 가지 방법을 설명한다.
  (C) 두 번째 문단은 첫 번째 문단에서 한 개체군이 고립되고 나면 유전적으로 덜 다양해진다고 말한 이론을 증명하는 증거를 제공한다.
  (D) 두 번째 문단은 왜 "이소적"이라는 용어가 첫 번째 문단에서 상세히 언급한 종분화 방법을 말하는 데 사용되는지 설명한다.

해설 첫 번째 문단에서 지리적 장벽이라는 키워드로 마무리를 짓고 있고, 두 번째 문단에서는 지리적 고립의 다양한 요인이 키워드로 등장한다. 따라서 정답은 (B)이다.

어휘 elaborate on ~을 상세히 설명하다 phenomenon 현상 take place (일 등이) 발생되다, 일어나다 detail ~을 상세히 말하다

3. 세 번째 문단에서, 다음 중 어느 요점을 설명하기 위해 다양한 생물체를 활용한 예시를 제공하는가?
  (A) 식물 개체군이 동물 개체군보다 지리적 장벽에 의해 분리될 가능성이 더 낮다.
  (B) 대형 생물체 개체군이 소형 생물체 개체군보다 지리적 장벽에 의해 고립된 상태로 유지될 가능성이 더 크다.
  (C) 생물체가 지니고 있는 지리적 장벽을 가로질러 이동하는 능력이 해당 장벽의 유효성과 직접적으로 관련되어 있다.
  (D) 한 가지 종에서 오직 진화적 적응 과정을 거친 구성원만 지리적 장벽을 가로질러 건널 수 있다.

해설 해당 문단의 첫 번째와 두 번째 문장을 보면, 장벽을 넘나들 수 있는 능력에 따라 다르다는 주장을 하고, 이후 다양한 예시를 들어주고 있다. 따라서 정답은 (C)이다.

어휘 relate to ~와 관련되다 undergo ~을 거치다, 겪다 evolutionary adaptation 진화적 적응

4. 세 번째 문단에 따르면, 흰꼬리 영양 다람쥐와 해리스 영양 다람쥐는 다음 중 어떤 공통점이 있는가?
  (A) 캘리포니아 토종인 두 가지 가장 작은 설치류이다.
  (B) 그랜드 캐니언을 가로질러 건널 수 없다.
  (C) 미국 대륙 전역에 걸쳐 발견된다.
  (D) 사막 환경에서 생존하기 힘겨워한다.

해설 해리스 영양 다람쥐가 등장하기 전 문장을 통해 핵심 정보를 파악할 수 있는데, '작은 설치류는 넓은 강이나 깊은 협곡을 지나

다닐 방법을 찾지 못할 것이다'라는 점을 확인할 수 있다. 그러므로 정답은 (B)이다.

5. 다음 문장들 중 어느 것이 지문의 하이라이트 표기된 문장에 담긴 핵심 정보를 가장 잘 표현하는가? 오답 선택지는 중요한 방식으로 의미를 변경하거나 핵심 정보를 배제한다.

지리적 고립이 새로운 종이 발생될 기회를 야기하기는 하지만, 이소적 종분화는 유전자 풀이 모체가 되는 개체군과 고립되는 개체군 사이에서 충분히 생식 장벽을 확립할 정도로 상당히 변화되는 경우에만 발생될 수 있다.

(A) 지리적 고립은 고립된 개체군의 유전자 풀이 모체가 되는 개체군과의 번식을 막을 정도로 바뀐 경우에만 새로운 종의 발생이라는 결과를 낳을 수 있다.
(B) 지리적으로 고립된 개체군 내의 유전적 변화는 흔히 생물체의 번식 행위를 변화시키며, 이는 한 종의 유전자 풀이 줄어드는 결과를 낳을 수 있다.
(C) 지리적 고립은 분리된 개체군이 각자 독립적으로 진화할 수 있게 해 원거리의 서식지에 서식하는 개체군과 번식할 수 있게 해준다.
(D) 지리적 고립은 흔히 모체가 되는 개체군과 그 후손에 해당되는 개체군 사이에 생식 장벽의 형성으로 이어진다.

해설 '~에도 불구하고'(Although)라는 정보를 담기 위해서는, 지리적 고립이 가지는 긍정적인 면을 담고 있어야 한다. 그 내용은 종이 발생될 기회라는 부분이며, 'new species to develop'(새로운 종이 발생될)을 담고 있는 표현은 'the development of new species'(새로운 종의 발생)이기 때문에 이 부분에서 이미 (A)가 답으로 결정된다. 그 이후 내용에서 'only'(~에만)라는 조건을 거는 부분 역시 포함하고 있는 것이 중요하다. '유전자 풀이 모체가 되는 개체군과 고립되는 개체군 사이에서 충분히 생식 장벽을 확립할 정도'라는 조건을 담아야 하는데, 그 내용은 (A)의 'the gene pool of the isolated population was altered to the such an extent that it prevents reproduction with the parent population'(유전자 풀이 모체가 되는 개체군과의 번식을 막을 정도로 바뀐 경우에만)이라는 표현에서 잘 담고 있다. 그러므로 정답은 (A)이다.

어휘 alter ~을 바꾸다, 변경하다 to such an extent that ~하는 정도로 shrink 줄어들다

6. 지문의 단어 "managed"와 의미가 가장 가까운 것은 무엇인가?
(A) 조절되었다
(B) **할 수 있었다**
(C) 했을 가능성이 있었다
(D) 이용 가능했다

해설 managed(어떻게든 해냈다)와 were able(할 수 있었다)은

유의어로 정답은 (B)이다.

7. 다섯 번째 문단은 갈라파고스 제도가 주로 무엇 때문에 지구상에서 "소중한 야외 실험실" 중의 하나에 대한 좋은 예시라는 뜻을 나타내는가?
(A) 그 제도를 주로 구성하는 풍부한 화산토
(B) 생물체가 그 제도에 군락을 이루는 데 걸렸던 오랜 기간
(C) **개별 섬들 사이의 거리 및 본토와의 거리**
(D) 여러 가지 종이 번성하는 데 필수적인 최적의 기후

해설 '소중한 야외 실험실'이라는 키워드 앞 문장을 보면 답의 근거를 찾을 수 있는데, 그 내용이 '이따금씩 개체군 이동이 발생되도록 할 수 있을 정도로 충분히 가까우면서도, 대부분의 개체군이 고립된 상태로 진화하도록 보장할 정도로 충분히 멀리 떨어져 있는 해양 섬들'이라는 내용을 담고 있으므로 정답은 '거리'라는 키워드를 제공하는 (C)이다.

어휘 volcanic soil 화산토 be composed of ~로 구성되다 optimal 최적의 flourish 번성하다

8. 여섯 번째 문단에 따르면, 13가지 갈라파고스 핀치 종과 관련해 사실인 것은 무엇인가?
(A) 13가지 종 모두 현재 갈라파고스 제도의 섬 대부분에 존재한다.
(B) 13가지 종 모두 존재하는 숫자가 적으며, 멸종 위기에 처해 있다.
(C) 13가지 종 모두 본토에서 진화한 후에 그 제도로 이동했다.
(D) **13가지 종 모두 동일한 새들이 조상인 개체군의 후손이다.**

해설 해당 문단의 중간 부분을 보면 '이 13가지 핀치 종이 모두 그 섬들 중 한 곳에 군락을 이뤘던 단 하나의 작은 조류 개체군의 후손임을 보여주는 증거가 많이 수집되었다'라는 내용이 있다. 그리고 이를 기반으로 '섬이 고립된 상태가 되며 새로운 종이 만들어지고 유전자 풀이 상당한 변화를 거쳤을 것이다'라고 한다. 따라서 정답은 (D)이다.

어휘 extinction 멸종 ancestral 조상의

9. 다음 문장이 지문에 추가될 수 있는 곳을 나타내는 네 개의 네모 표기 [■]를 찾아 보시오.

이러한 종분화 및 군락 형성 과정은 세 번째와 네 번째 종 그리고 그 이후에도 지속되면서, 서서히 그 제도의 모든 섬 전역에 걸쳐 확산되었을 것이다.

위 문장은 어느 곳에 가장 적합하겠는가? 네모 표기[■]를 클릭해 지문에 이 문장을 추가하시오.
(A) 1번
(B) 2번
(C) 3번

(D) 4번

해설 주어진 문장에서 'This process'와 'would have continued'를 통해, 앞 문장은 종분화의 과정 설명이 있고, 뒤에는 구체적인 종분화 과정의 결과가 등장할 것임을 예상할 수 있다. 이러한 점을 고려할 때, 정답은 (C)이다.

어휘 disperse 확산되다, 흩어지다

10. 설명: 간략한 지문 요약에 필요한 도입 문장이 아래에 제공되어 있다. 지문에서 가장 중요한 개념들을 나타내는 세 가지 답안 선택지를 골라 요약 내용을 완성하시오. 일부 답안 선택지는 지문에 제시되지 않는 개념을 나타내거나 지문에서 중요하지 않은 개념들이므로 요약 내용에 속하지 않는다. **이 문제는 2점에 해당된다.**

한 개체군의 지리적 고립은 새로운 종의 출현이라는 결과를 낳을 수 있다.

(A) 연구에 따르면 갈라파고스 제도에서 군락을 형성한 첫 생물체는 13가지 뚜렷이 다른 종으로 점차 진화한 핀치였던 것으로 나타나 있다.

(B) 종분화는 고립된 개체군의 규모가 작을 때 발생될 가능성이 더 큰데, 규모가 큰 개체군보다 작은 개체군에서 상당

한 유전적 변화가 더 흔하기 때문이다.

(C) 고립은 지리적 장벽이 개체군을 분리하는 경우에, 또는 일부 생물체가 무심코 바람이나 바다를 통해 지리적 장벽을 가로질러 이동해 새로운 개체군을 만드는 경우에 발생될 수 있다.

(D) 갈라파고스 제도의 지리적 고립으로 인해, 그곳에 서식하는 많은 종이 많은 진화적 변화를 거치지 못했다.

(E) 조류 개체군은 날 수 있는 능력으로 인해 어류 및 포유류 개체군보다 지리적 장벽에 의해 덜 쉽게 고립된다.

(F) 갈라파고스 제도는 종분화에 이상적인 곳인데, 개체군을 고립시킴과 동시에 섬들 사이에서 이따금씩 나타나는 생물체 확산을 가능하게 하기 때문이다.

해설 이 지문의 키워드인 '갈라파고스 제도'를 명시하면서, 개체군을 고립시킴과 동시에 생물체 확산이 일어난다는 점을 네 번째와 다섯 번째 문단에서 찾을 수 있는 (F)를 가장 먼저 고를 수 있다. 네 번째 문단을 보면, 이소적 종분화의 가능성이 한 개체군이 작으면서 고립되어 있는 경우에 해당할 경우 높아진다고 이야기하며, 이는 유전자 풀이 상당히 변화될 가능성을 높인다는 점을 토대로 (B) 역시 정답이다. (C)의 경우, 첫 번째와 두 번째 문단을 통해 지리적인 장벽과 이러한 변화에 의해서 진화가 이뤄지는 점을 찾을 수 있기에 정답이다.

어휘 inadvertently 무심코 dispersion 확산, 분산

공생 관계

두 가지 이상의 종 사이에서 한 가지 종이 나머지 종의 내부 또는 외부에 살며 상호 작용이 존재하는 경우, 이는 공생 관계의 예시에 해당한다. [11(A)]공생적 상호 작용은 기생과 편리 공생, 그리고 상리 공생으로 크게 분류될 수 있다. 생물 군집, 즉 모든 생물체 개체군이 주어진 생태계 내에서 서로 상호 작용하는 구조에서, 기생과 상리 공생은 특히 중요한 공생 관계 유형이다.

일반적으로 말해서, 기생은 한 생물체, 즉 숙주가 특정한 희생을 통해 공생 파트너인 기생 생물에게 먹이 또는 자원을 제공하는 포식자와 먹이의 관계로 설명된다. 대부분의 경우에, 기생 생물체는 숙주 생물체보다 더 작다. 기생 생물의 한 가지 흔한 예가 촌충인데, 더 큰 생물체의 내장 속에 살면서 숙주로부터 영양분을 빨아먹는다. 숙주를 찾아내고 그것을 통해 먹을 것을 얻는 데 잘 적응되어 있는 기생 생물은 자연 선택에 의해 [12(D)]선호되며, 이는 숙주의 방어 능력도 마찬가지이다. 예를 들어, 일부 식물은 곰팡이류 및 박테리아 기생 생물에게 유독한 화학 물질을 생성하며, 다른 것들은 포식 동물에게 유독한 화학 물질을 생성한다. 그리고, 대부분의 척추 동물에게 있어, 신체의 면역 체계가 내부의 기생 생물을 대상으로 하는 다양한 방어 수단을 제공한다.

때때로 우리는 숙주와 기생 생물의 관계에서 자연 선택의 영향을 관찰할 수 있다. 예를 들어, 1940년대 호주에서는, 수억 마리의 유럽 토끼가 시골 지역마다 들끓었다. ■ [19(A)]이 토끼들은 호주 농지의 많은 구획을 망쳐 놓았으며, 양과 소를 이용한 축산업에 심각한 위험 요소가 되었다. ■ [13(C)]1950년에, 호주 정부는 이 토끼 개체군을 급격히 줄이기 위한 노력의 일환으로 토끼에게 치명적인 기생 생물인 점액종 바이러스를 의도적으로 도입했다. ■ 이 바이러스는 모기를 통해 빠르게 확산되어, 토끼 개체군을 몰살시켰다. ■ [14(B)]하지만, 이 바이러스는 생존한 토끼의 새끼를 죽이는 데에는 덜 효과적이었으며, 해가 거듭될수록 점점 덜 유용한 것으로 드러났다. [14(C)]기생 생물에 저항력이 있는 유전자형, 즉 생물체의 유전적 구성이 토끼 개체군 내에서 유리하게 작용하고 있었다는 점이 분명해졌다. [14(A)]따라서, 이 바이러스의 가장 치명적인 균주가 숙주 토끼들과 함께 소멸되었는데, 자연 선택이 숙주를 감염시킬 수는 있지만 죽이지는 않는 균주의 편을 들어주었기 때문이다. 이에 따라, 이 숙주와 기생 생물의 관계는 자연 선택을 통해 안정화되었다.

편리 공생은 그 관계의 한쪽이 영향을 받지 않으면서 다른 한쪽이 이득을 얻는다는 점에서 기생과 다르다. 절대적인 편리 공생은 자연에서 비교적 드물게 나타나는데, 이득을 보지 않는 쪽이 전적으로 영향을 받지 않게 될 가능성이 별로 없기 때문이다. 편리 공생적 상호 작용은 흔히 한 가

지 종이 다른 종에 의해 ^{15(B)}무심코 노출된 먹이를 얻는 일과 관련된다. 예를 들어, 풀을 뜯는 소들이 풀 속의 곤충들을 노출시키면 많은 조류 종이 위에서 덮쳐 먹게 된다. 이런 상황이 어떻게 소들에게 해로운 영향을 미칠 수 있을지 상상하기란 어렵지만, 아직 밝혀지지 않은 어떤 측면에서 그 관계가 소들에게 도움이 되거나 방해가 될 수 있을 가능성은 남아 있다.

마지막으로, 상리 공생이라고 부르는 공생 유형이 있는데, 이는 해당 관계 속의 양측 모두에게 이득을 제공해준다. 이 상부상조적 유대 관계는 꽃식물과 꽃가루 매개자 사이의 상호 작용에서, ^{16(B)}그리고 콩과 식물과 그 식물의 질소 고정 세균 사이에서 전형적으로 나타난다. ^{17(D)}첫 번째 경우에, 새와 곤충 같은 꽃가루 매개자는 꽃식물이 바람에만 의존하는 것보다 훨씬 더 효율적으로 꽃가루와 씨앗을 퍼트리도록 돕는 과정에서 그 식물로부터 먹이를 얻는다. ^{16(B)}두 번째 경우에, 박테리아가 식물로부터 탄수화물과 기타 유기 화합물을 공급받는 한편, 식물은 박테리아가 서서히 흙 속에 추가해주는 질소를 이용한다. 상리 공생은 중앙 아메리카 및 남아메리카 전역에 걸쳐 발견되는 황소뿔 아카시아 나무의 경우에서도 분명히 나타난다. 수도머멕스 속에 해당되는 개미들은 흔히 이 나무를 보금자리 장소로 이용한다. ^{18(B)}이들은 이 나무의 크고 텅 빈 가시에 서식하면서 나무가 분비하는 당분을 먹고 산다. 이 나무는 또한 작은 잎 끝부분이 황색 구조로 되어 있는데, 단백질이 풍부한 이 특징은 개미들을 끌어들이는 것 말고는 아무런 쓸모도 없어 보인다. ^{18(C)}숙주인 이 나무는 개미들이 나무에 가까이 접근하는 거의 모든 다른 종을 공격한다는 점에서 이득을 얻는다. 다른 곤충과 대형 초식 동물은 개미에게 쏘일 위험을 감수해야 하기 때문에, 이 나무를 그냥 놔두는 경향이 있다. 심지어 나무가 자랄 공간을 더 많이 제공하기 위해 이 개미들이 주변의 초목을 깎는 모습이 관찰되기도 했다. ^{18(D)}이 개미들이 없어지면, 이 나무는 보통 죽게 되는데, 더 이상 초식 동물로부터 보호되지 못할 뿐만 아니라 공간 및 자원을 두고 주변 식물들과 어쩔 수 없이 경쟁해야 할 것이기 때문이다.

[어휘]
1. symbiotic relationship 공생 관계 parasitism 기생 commensalism 편리 공생 mutualism 상리 공생 population 개체군 organism 생물체 ecosystem 생태계
2. host 숙주 parasite 기생 생물 tapeworm 촌충 intestine 내장 leech ~을 빨아먹다 natural selection 자연 선택(환경에 적응한 것이 생존 경쟁에서 살아남는 것) fungal 곰팡이류의 vertebrates 척추 동물 immune system 면역 체계
3. overrun ~에 들끓다, ~에 급속히 퍼지다 swath(e) (띠 모양의) 긴 구획 myxoma virus 점액성 바이러스 decimate ~을 몰살시키다 offspring 새끼, 자식 genotype 유전자형(생물체가 갖고 있는 특정 유전자의 조합) composition 구성 strain 균주 stabilize ~을 안정시키다
4. inadvertently 무심코 graze 풀을 뜯다 swoop down (새, 비행기 등이) 위에서 덮치다 detrimental 해로운 hinder ~을 방해하다, 저해하다 have yet to do 아직 ~하지 않았다
5. confer ~을 주다 be exemplified in ~에 전형적으로 나타나다 pollinator 꽃가루 매개자 legume plant 콩과 식물 nitrogen-fixing bacteria 질소 고정 세균(공기 중에 존재하는 질소를 고정하는 미생물) disperse ~을 퍼트리다, 분산시키다 carbohydrates 탄수화물 organic compounds 유기 화합물 take advantage of ~을 이용하다 genus (생물 분류 단위) 속 Pseudomyrmex 수도머멕스(개미의 한 종류) secrete ~을 분비하다 herbivore 초식 동물 risk -ing ~하는 위험을 감수하다 tend to do ~하는 경향이 있다 clip ~을 깎다, 잘라내다 perish 죽다, 소멸되다

11. 다음 중 첫 번째 문단에서 편리 공생과 관련해 유추할 수 있는 내용은 어느 것인가?
(A) 생물 군집이라는 조직 속에서 비교적 작은 역할을 한다.
(B) 생물 군집이 번성하는 능력에 있어 필수적이다.
(C) 일반적으로 두 가지가 넘는 종 사이의 상호 작용을 배제한다.
(D) 생물 개체군의 구조에 심각하게 지장을 줄 수 있는 잠재성이 있다.
해설 기생과 상리공생이 특히 중요한 공생 관계 유형이라는 점을 토대로 편리 공생은 비교적 중요도가 떨어진다는 점을 유추할 수 있기에 정답은 (A)이다.
어휘 play a minor role in ~에 있어 작은 역할을 하다 integral 필수적인 flourish 번성하다 exclude ~을 배제하다, 제외하다 disrupt ~에 지장을 주다, 방해가 되다

12. 지문의 단어 "favored"와 의미가 가장 가까운 것은 무엇인가?
(A) 연결된

(B) 감당할 수 있는
(C) 꺼리는, 마지못해하는
(D) 선호되는
해설 favored(선호되는)와 preferred(선호되는)는 동의어로 정답은 (D)이다.

13. 다음 중 어느 것이 세 번째 문단에서 호주의 토끼 개체군에 관한 이야기에서 내릴 수 있는 결론인가?
(A) 숙주와 기생 생물의 관계에 대한 인간의 간섭이 환경에 부정적으로 영향을 미칠 수 있다.
(B) 생물 군집에 외래 종을 유입시키는 것의 이점이 위험 요소보다 훨씬 더 크다.
(C) 인간의 개입이 숙주와 기생 생물, 그리고 그들의 관계에 변화가 나타나도록 초래할 수 있다.
(D) 기생 생물의 공격에서 살아남는 종이 기록적인 숫자로 번식할 가능성이 있다.
해설 인간이 바이러스를 의도적으로 도입하고, 개체 수에 영향을 미

첬다가, 자연 선택에 의해 감염은 가능하되 죽이지 않는 균주의 등장을 만들었기 때문에 여러가지 변화가 일어났다는 내용이 포함된 (C)가 정답이다.

어휘 interference 간섭, 개입(= intervention) outweigh (중요성 등이) ~보다 더 크다 reproduce 번식하다

14. 세 번째 문단에 따르면, 「다음 중 자연 선택이 호주의 토끼 개체군을 안정화한 방식의 특징이 아닌 것은 무엇인가?
   (A) 가장 치명적인 바이러스 균주가 숙주와 함께 사라졌다.
   (B) 살아남은 토끼들이 해당 바이러스에 대한 면역력 증가를 나타냈다.
   (C) 특정 유전자형을 지닌 토끼들이 해당 바이러스를 견뎌냈을 가능성이 더 컸다.
   (D) 모기 개체군의 감소가 해당 바이러스의 유효성을 떨어뜨렸다.

해설 바이러스가 모기를 통해 확산되어 토끼 개체군을 몰살시켰다는 문장 이후에 생존한 토끼의 새끼를 죽이지 못했으며 점점 더 영향력이 줄어들었다는 점을 확인할 수 있다. 이후 기생 생물에 저항력이 있는 유전자 형이 유리하게 작용했다는 점을 보면 (A), (B), 그리고 (C)의 내용을 확인할 수 있다. 그러나 모기 개체군의 감소와 바이러스의 유효성 사이의 상관관계를 나타내는 내용은 지문에 등장하지 않으므로 정답은 (D)이다.

어휘 immunity 면역력 resist ~을 견디다, ~에 저항하다

15. 지문의 단어 "inadvertently"와 의미가 가장 가까운 것은 무엇인가?
   (A) 거꾸로, 반대로
   (B) 무심결에, 고의가 아닌
   (C) 상당히, 중요하게
   (D) 간헐적으로

해설 inadvertently(무심코)와 unintentionally(무심결에)는 동의어로 정답은 (B)이다.

16. 다섯 번째 문단에 따르면, 콩과 식물과 박테리아 사이의 관계가 어떻게 토양에 유익한가?
   (A) 토양으로부터 탄수화물을 흡수함으로써
   (B) 질소로 토양을 비옥하게 만듦으로써
   (C) 대기 중에서 독소를 없앰으로써
   (D) 유기물의 분해를 가속화함으로써

해설 해당 문단의 초반부 내용을 보면 콩과 식물과 그 식물의 질소 고정 세균 사이에서 전형적으로 나타난다는 점을 설명하고 있다. 그리고 이후 문장에서 두 번째의 경우 박테리아가 식물로부터 탄수화물과 기타 유기 화합물을 공급받는 한편, 식물은 박테리아가 서서히 흙 속에 추가해주는 질소를 이용한다는 점을 설명해주고 있다. 이를 통해 식물이 질소를 유용하게 활용하고 있

다는 점을 알 수 있기에 정답은 (B)이다.

어휘 enrich ~을 비옥하게 하다, 풍요롭게 하다 accelerate ~을 가속화하다 decomposition 분해, 부패

17. 다음 문장들 중 어느 것이 지문의 하이라이트 표기된 문장에 담긴 핵심 정보를 가장 잘 표현하는가? 오답 선택지는 중요한 방식으로 의미를 변경하거나 핵심 정보를 배제한다.

   첫 번째 경우에, 새와 곤충 같은 꽃가루 매개자는 꽃식물이 바람에만 의존하는 것보다 훨씬 더 효율적으로 꽃가루와 씨앗을 퍼트리도록 돕는 과정에서 그 식물로부터 먹이를 얻는다.
   (A) 동물과 곤충은 각자 매일의 식사에서 많은 부분을 차지하는 먹이를 발견하기 위한 노력의 일환으로 꽃식물을 찾아낸다.
   (B) 일부 경우에 있어, 조류와 곤충은 바람에 의해 옮겨지는 꽃가루와 씨앗을 쫓아다님으로써 꽃식물에 이끌린다.
   (C) 바람은 꽃식물들이 자신의 씨앗과 꽃가루를 먹는 조류와 곤충들 사이에 그것들을 퍼뜨릴 수 있게 해준다.
   (D) 조류와 곤충은 꽃식물로부터 먹이를 얻으면서 바람보다 더 나은 꽃가루 및 씨앗 확산 수단도 제공한다.

해설 주어진 문장은 'while'이라는 키워드를 중심으로 두 가지 핵심을 분석할 필요가 있다. 가장 우선적으로는 현재 시제를 통해 매개자는 꽃식물로부터 먹이를 얻는다는 정보를 통해 (B)와 (C)를 소거할 수 있다. 그리고 while 이후 내용을 통해 바람에만 의존하는 것보다 더 효율적으로 씨앗을 퍼뜨린다는 내용을 확인할 수 있기에 정답은 (D)이다.

어휘 comprise ~을 차지하다, 구성하다 A enable B to do A가 B에게 ~할 수 있게 해주다 distribute ~을 퍼뜨리다 consume ~을 먹다, 소비하다 means 수단 dispersal 확산, 분산

18. 다섯 번째 문단에 따르면, 다음 중 어느 것이 황소뿔 아카시아 나무와 수도머멕스 개미 사이의 관계에 대해 사실이 아닌가?
   (A) 수도머멕스 개미가 황소뿔 아카시아 나무에게 자체 화학적 방어 체계를 만드는 데 도움을 준다.
   (B) 황소뿔 아카시아 나무가 수도머멕스 개미에게 있어 소중한 영양분 공급원의 역할을 한다.
   (C) 수도머멕스 개미가 숙주인 황소뿔 아카시아 나무를 잠재적 포식자들로부터 방어해준다.
   (D) 수도머멕스 개미가 주변 초목과의 경쟁을 감소시킴으로써 황소뿔 아카시아 나무를 돕는다.

해설 숙주인 이 나무는 개미들이 나무에 가까이 접근하는 거의 모든 다른 종을 공격한다는 점에서 이득을 얻는다는 정보를 통해, 나무에게 자체적인 화학적 방어 체계를 만들 수 있도록 도움을 준다는 내용은 사실이 아님을 알 수 있다. 따라서 정답은 (A)이다.

어휘   serve as ~의 역할을 하다   defend A against B A를 B
로부터 방어하다   potential 잠재적인   predator 포식자
competition 경쟁   vegetation 초목

19. 다음 문장이 지문에 추가될 수 있는 곳을 나타내는 네 개의 네
모 표기 [■]를 찾아 보시오.

이 엄청난 숫자는 한 세기 전에 들여와 빠른 속도로 번식한 불
과 12쌍 밖에 되지 않았던 외래 토끼들에서 비롯되었다.

위 문장은 어느 곳에 가장 적합하겠는가? 네모 표기 [■]를 클
릭해 지문에 이 문장을 추가하시오.

(A) 1번
(B) 2번
(C) 3번
(D) 4번

해설   '이 엄청난 숫자는'이라는 주어를 통해 앞 문장에서 이미 구체적
인 숫자가 제시된다는 것을 알 수 있으므로 첫 번째 박스가 정
답이라는 점을 확인할 수 있다. 그리고 외래 토끼라는 키워드를
통해 첫 번째 박스 이후 내용에서 '이 토끼들은'이라는 주어로
지칭함을 확인할 수 있다.

어휘   originate from ~에서 비롯되다   reproduce 번식하다

20. **설명:** 간략한 지문 요약에 필요한 도입 문장이 아래에 제공되어
있다. 지문에서 가장 중요한 개념들을 나타내는 세 가지 답안
선택지를 골라 요약 내용을 완성하시오. 일부 답안 선택지는 지
문에 제시되지 않는 개념을 나타내거나 지문에서 중요하지 않
은 개념들이므로 요약 내용에 속하지 않는다. **이 문제는 2점에
해당된다.**

공생 관계는 두 가지 이상의 생물체 사이에서 나타나는 상호

작용 및 관련된 한 가지 또는 두 생물체 모두에게 유익한 결과
를 수반한다.

(A) 생물 군집의 구조는 해당 군집 내의 종들 사이에 존재하는
관계의 유형에 따라 다르다.
(B) 편리 공생 관계는 통상적으로 해당 관계를 구성하는 한
생물이 다른 생물에 대한 어떠한 인지된 대가 없이 이득을
얻을 수 있게 해준다.
(C) 상리 공생은 해당 관계에 관련된 두 생물 모두에게 이득
을 준다는 점에서 공생 관계들 중에서 특별하다.
(D) 기생 관계는 일반적으로 기생 생물과 숙주를 포함하며,
기생 생물이 숙주의 희생으로 이득을 얻는 결과를 낳는
다.
(E) 기생 생물의 도입이 숙주와 기생 생물 사이의 관계가 자연
선택을 통해 안정화될 때까지 처음에 호주의 토끼 개체수
를 통제하는 데 도움을 주었다.
(F) 상리 공생은 서로 다른 종의 두 생물보다 같은 종의 두 생물
사이에서 더 흔히 발생한다.

해설   이 지문의 경우 첫 문단에서 제공하는 공생적 상호 작용은 기생
과 편리 공생, 그리고 상리 공생으로 크게 분류될 수 있다는 정
보를 토대로 세 가지 개념과 이를 뒷받침하는 내용을 선택한다.
두 번째와 세 번째 문단에서 중심적으로 다루고 있는 기생 관계
를 설명하는 (D)를 먼저 고를 수 있다. 편리 공생의 경우 네 번
째 문단에서 다루고 있으며 한 생물이 다른 생물에 대해 대가
없이 이득을 제공한다는 정보를 담은 (B)를 선택한다. 상리 공
생의 경우 다섯 번째 문단의 핵심 내용이고, 두 생물 모두에게
이점을 준다는 경우를 설명하고 있기 때문에 (C)가 정답이다.

어휘   beneficial 유익한, 이득이 되는   outcome 결과   be
dependent on ~에 따라 다르다, ~에 달려 있다   ordinarily
통상적으로, 보통   perceived 인지된   confer ~을 주다, 수여
하다   result in A -ing A가 ~하는 결과를 낳다   at the
expense of ~의 희생으로   stabilize ~을 안정화시키다

Actual Test 2

Questions 1-10

금성과 지구의 표면 유체

일반적으로 액체 또는 기체 상태인 물질이 서로 지나쳐 움직일 수 있는 입자들로 구성될 때, 우리는 그것을 유체라고 일컫는다. 유체가 어떤 유형의 용기 안에 담겨 있든, 그 유체는 해당 용기의 형태에 맞추게 된다. 유체가 행성의 표면에 걸쳐 이동할 때, 발생되는 지질학적 과정이 그 행성의 표면을 상당히 변화시킬 수 있다. [1(D)]이러한 과정의 대부분은 태양열과 해당 행성 자체의 중력에 의해 촉진된다. 유체가 표면에 걸쳐 흐르는 동안, 입자들이 이리저리 이동하게 되고, 해당 유체는 입자들을 변경하거나 새로운 물질을 만들어낼 수 있는 화학 반응을 유발한다. 일반적으로, 행성 질량의 아주 적은 양만이 수권 및 대기권이 있는 고체 행성에서 표면 유체로서 흐른다. 하지만, 이러한 유체의 움직임은 여전히 행성을 [2(C)]급격히 변모시킬 수 있다.

대기를 지니고 있는 두 곳의 지구형 행성인 금성과 지구를 한번 생각해보자. 금성과 지구가 흔히 쌍둥이 행성으로 일컬어지고 있기는 하지만, 이 둘은 전혀 똑같지 않다. 탄생 당시, 두 행성은 비슷한 수준의 이산화탄소와 산소를 갖고 있었을 가능성이 있으며, 둘은 대략 같은 크기이고 유사한 물질들로 구성되어 있다. 하지만, 태양으로부터 서로 다른 거리에 위치해 있는 관계로, 이 쌍둥이 행성은 진화하면서 서로 상당히 다른 차이점을 갖게 되었다. 금성은 내부에 엄청난 양의 열기를 품고 있어서, 화산과 단층 작용, 그리고 습곡 형성으로 인해 지질학적으로 대단히 활동적이다. ■[4(A)]하지만, 어떤 종류의 물 순환 체계(물의 순환 및 분배)에 대한 증거도 없기 때문에, 어떤 빙하나 강, 또는 수역도 전혀 존재하지 않는다. [9(B)]■ 우주로 보내진 탐사선에 따르면 금성은 한때 지구만큼 물을 많이 가지고 있었을 지도 모르는 것으로 나타나지만, 그 물은 액체의 형태로 지속되지 못했을 것이다. ■[5(C)]금성이 태양으로부터 받는 열의 양이 증가되어 내부에서 방출되는 그 물이 증발해 상층부의 대기권으로 올라가면서, [5(D)]그 분자들이 태양의 자외선에 의해 분해되는 결과를 초래했다. ■[5(A)]방출된 수소 대부분이 우주로 떠나려 나가면서, 금성을 지구와 아주 다르게 대기권에 이산화탄소가 많고 물이 존재하지 않는 상태로 만들었다. 대기 속의 이산화탄소는 극심한 온실 효과를 만들어, 지표면의 온도를 아주 극도로 높은 수준으로 치솟게 해서 납을 녹이고 탄산염 광물 생성을 [3(D)]막을 수 있다. 셀 수 없이 오랜 세월에 걸쳐, 화산들이 지속적으로 분출되어 오면서 대기를 점점 더 많은 이산화탄소로 가득 채웠다. 지구에서는, 이산화탄소가 액체 상태의 물에 의해 대기 중에서 제거된 다음, 암석 풍화 작용에 의해 생겨나는 칼슘과 결합하면서, 결국 탄산염 퇴적암을 형성하게 된다. 이러한 액체 상태의 물이 없는 금성은 대기 중에서 탄소를 없앨 수 없기 때문에, 대기 중의 이산화탄소 수준이 계속 대단히 높게 유지되고 있다.

지구는 중력장이 대기를 유지하고 지질학적으로 활동적일 정도로 충분히 거대하다는 점에서 금성과 유사하다. [6(A)]하지만, 태양과의 이상적인 거리로 인해 물이 액체와 고체, 그리고 기체로 존재할 수 있게 해주는 바람직한 온도가 만들어진다는 점에서 금성과 상당히 다르다. 이는 물의 이동성을 높여주면서 지속적인 물 순환 체계에 따라 지구 곳곳을 자유롭게 옮겨 다닐 수 있게 해준다. 바닷물은 태양에 의해 가열되어 대기 중으로 진입하며, 그곳에서 비를 형성해 떨어지면서 대륙마다 교차하는 하천 체계를 만들었다가 결국 다시 지구의 거대한 바다로 모이게 된다. [7(A)]이러한 지속적인 체계에 따른 결과로, 지표면에 수많은 변화들이 생겨났고, 강 계곡들로 이뤄진 복잡한 연결망 구조로 침식된 지구의 표면은 충돌 분화구들이 특징인 다른 행성의 표면들보다 더 두드러져 보이게 되었다.

[8(B)]지구의 거의 모든 부분이 물의 흐름에 의해 형성되어 왔다. 유사한 방식으로, 바람도 천년 동안에 걸쳐 암석들을 침식시켜 고운 입자를 먼 거리에 걸쳐 날려보내면서, 모래 언덕들이 주를 이루는 광활한 모래 바다나 뢰스라고 부르는 미세 입자 토양 퇴적물 층을 형성해왔다. 이러한 유체 이동은 대체로 중력과 태양열에 의해 촉진된다. 지질학적 변화는 또한 지구 표면의 암석들이 물 또는 대기 중의 기체와 반응하면서 독특한 성질을 지닌 새로운 화합물이 생길 때도 발생된다. 이 과정의 한 가지 주목할 만한 예시는 대기 속에서 지구의 이산화탄소 대부분이 제거되는 것에 따른 결과로 나타나는 탄산염 암석의 형성이었다. 하지만, 만일 지구가 태양에서 더 멀리 자리잡고 있다면, 바다는 완전히 얼어붙을 것이며, 태양

과 조금이라도 더 가까이 있다면, 모든 물이 증발해버릴 것이다. 액체 상태로 존재하는 물 덕분에, 지구는 자동 재생되는 탄소와 수소, 그리고 산소 분자들을 이용해 생명체를 발전시키고 지탱할 수 있었으며, 그 결과 무성한 초목들로 덮여 있는 모습으로 변형된 대륙들이 생겨났다. 따라서, 산소와 질소가 풍부한 대기 및 온화한 온도를 지닌 지구는 모든 방식의 생물체들이 자라고 번성할 수 있는 이상적인 행성이다.

[어휘]

1. fluid 유체 consist of ~로 구성되다 particle 입자 refer to A as B A를 B라고 일컫다 conform to ~에 맞추다, ~을 따르다 gravitational force 중력 mass 질량 hydrosphere 수권(지구 표면과 대기 중의 물이 있는 곳)

2. terrestrial planet 지구형 행성 comparable 비슷한, 비교할 만한 be composed of ~로 구성되다 harbor ~을 품고 있다 rifting 단층 작용 folding 습곡 형성 probe 탐사선 sustain ~을 지속하다, 지탱하다 evaporate 증발하다 molecule 분자 soar 치솟다 erupt 분출하다 weathering 풍화 작용 sedimentary rocks 퇴적암

3. gravitational field 중력장 mobility 이동성 crisscross ~을 교차하다 erode ~을 침식시키다 impact crater 충돌 분화구

4. dune 모래 언덕, 사구 fine-grained 미세 입자의 loess 뢰스, 황토(바람에 날려온 퇴적토) give rise to ~이 생기게 하다, ~을 일으키다 self-replicating 자동 재생되는, 자가 복제하는

1. 첫 번째 문단에 따르면, 무엇이 지구와 금성의 지질학적 과정에 영향을 미치는가?
(A) 수위 및 폐하 지수
(B) 계절별 기후 및 강우량
(C) 공전 속도 및 지름
(D) 중력 및 태양
해설 첫 번째 문단의 중간을 보면, 지질학적 과정의 대부분은 태양열과 해당 행성 자체의 중력에 의해 촉진된다는 점을 알 수 있다. 그러므로 정답은 (D)이다.

2. 지문의 단어 "drastically"와 의미가 가장 가까운 것은 무엇인가?
(A) 처참하게
(B) 영구적으로
(C) 상당히
(D) 지속적으로
해설 drastically(급격히)와 significantly(상당히)는 유의어로 정답은 (C)이다.

3. 지문의 단어 "prohibit"과 의미가 가장 가까운 것은 무엇인가?
(A) ~을 촉진하다
(B) ~을 감소시키다
(C) ~을 근절하다
(D) ~을 막다
해설 prohibit(막다)과 prevent(막다)는 동의어로 정답은 (D)이다.

4. 두 번째 문단에 따르면, 지구와 금성이 다른 한 가지 방식은 무엇인가?
(A) 오직 지구에만 물 순환 체계가 있다.
(B) 지구의 대기에 금성보다 물이 더 적게 있다.
(C) 금성이 지구보다 지질학적으로 덜 활동적이다.
(D) 지구에 금성보다 이산화탄소가 더 많이 있다.
해설 해당 문단의 중반부를 보면 금성에는 어떤 종류의 물 순환 체계(물의 순환 및 분배)에 대한 증거도 없기 때문에, 어떤 빙하나 강, 또는 수역도 전혀 존재하지 않는다는 정보를 확인할 수 있다. 그러므로 정답은 (A)이다.

5. 두 번째 문단에 따르면, 다음 중 금성의 대기 중에 이산화탄소 수준을 높게 유지하는 데 있어 한 가지 역할을 하지 않는 것은 무엇인가?
(A) 우주로 빠져나가는 수소
(B) 탄산염 물질의 생성
(C) 그 행성으로부터 방출되는 물의 증발
(D) 태양광에 의한 물 분자의 분리
해설 해당 문단의 중반부를 보면 태양으로부터 받은 열 때문에 금성엔 물이 증발하고, 그 분자들이 분해되며, 수소가 우주로 빠져나간다는 점을 알 수 있다. 따라서 금성이 이산화탄소 수준을 높게 유지하는 데 관련이 없는 것은 (B)이다.

6. 세 번째 문단에 따르면, 물이 왜 지구에서 그렇게 자유롭게 옮겨 다닐 수 있는가?
(A) 지구의 온도로 인해 물이 고체와 액체, 그리고 기체 형태로 존재할 수 있다.
(B) 지구의 중력장이 바다의 조수에 영향을 미칠 만큼 충분히 강력하다.
(C) 지구의 산악 지역들이 강물의 흐름을 가속화한다.
(D) 지구에 여러 바다에서 해류를 만드는 활동적인 바람이 있다.
해설 지구와 태양의 이상적인 거리가 바람직한 온도를 만들어 주고 이는 물의 이동성을 높여주면서 지속적인 물 순환 체계에 따라 지구 곳곳을 자유롭게 옮겨 다닐 수 있게 해준다는 정보를 통해

(A)가 정답이다.

어휘   tide 조수, 밀물과 썰물   accelerate ~을 가속화하다
             current 해류, 기류

7. 세 번째 문단에 따르면, 지구의 지표면은 다음 중 어떤 방식으로 다른 많은 행성들의 표면과 다른가?

    (A) 물의 흐름에 의해 침식되었다.
    (B) 충돌 분화구가 특징이다.
    (C) 더 두터운 암석 층을 포함한다.
    (D) 더 빈번한 온도 변화를 겪는다.

해설   지구의 특성을 설명하는 세 번째 문단의 내용을 보면 태양과의 거리 덕분에 바람직한 온도가 만들어진다는 정보를 시작으로 비의 형성 이야기까지 확인을 할 수 있다. 이때 지속적인 물의 순환으로 지표면에 많은 변화가 생겨났고, 강 계곡들로 이뤄진 복잡한 연결망 구조로 침식된 지구의 표면은 충돌 분화구들이 특징인 다른 행성의 표면들보다 더 두드러져 보이게 되었다는 정보를 기반으로 정답이 (A)임을 알 수 있다.

8. 글쓴이는 왜 "지구 표면의 암석들이 물 또는 대기 중의 기체와 반응하면서 독특한 성질을 지닌 새로운 화합물이 생길 때"를 지적하는가?

    (A) 지구의 특정 지역이 왜 흐르는 물에 의해 훼손되지 않은 상태로 유지되어 왔는지 설명하기 위해
    (B) 행성의 표면이 변화되는 다양한 방식들 중의 하나에 대한 예시를 제공하기 위해
    (C) 화합물이 어떻게 물의 흐름을 용이하게 하는 데 있어 중대한 역할을 하는지 설명하기 위해
    (D) 지구가 금성보다 더 폭넓은 지질학적 변화를 거쳐왔다는 증거를 제공하기 위해

해설   해당 문단의 첫 문장을 보면 지구의 대부분이 물의 흐름에 의해 형성되어왔다는 내용을 전제로 시작한다. 다시 말해 이 문단은 지구의 모래 언덕이나 퇴적층 등 표면 형성에 대한 이야기를 전개하고 있는데, 주어진 문장 역시 결국은 행성의 표면이 변화하는 방식들 중 하나의 예시를 제공하는 역할을 하기 때문에 정답은 (B)이다.

어휘   play a crucial role in ~하는 데 있어 중대한 역할을 하다
       facilitate ~을 용이하게 하다

9. 다음 문장이 지문에 추가될 수 있는 곳을 나타내는 네 개의 네모 표기 [■]를 찾아 보시오.

금성은 사실 과거에는 상당히 달랐을지도 모른다.

위 문장은 어느 곳에 가장 적합하겠는가? 네모 표기[[■]]를 클릭해 지문에 이 문장을 추가하시오.

    (A) 1번
    (B) 2번
    (C) 3번
    (D) 4번

해설   주어진 문장은 '과거에는 상당히 달랐을지도 모른다'라는 내용이기에 해당 문단에서 금성의 과거 모습을 묘사하는 내용이 등장할 수 있음을 유추할 수 있다. 이러한 내용의 문장, '우주로 보내진 탐사선에 따르면 금성은 한때 지구만큼 물을 많이 가지고 있었을지도 모르는 것으로 나타나지만, 그 물은 액체의 형태로 지속되지 못했을 것이다'라는 문장 앞의 박스인 두 번째 박스에 해당 문장을 삽입하면 자연스럽게 이야기가 전개된다.

10. 설명: 간략한 지문 요약에 필요한 도입 문장이 아래에 제공되어 있다. 지문에서 가장 중요한 개념들을 나타내는 세 가지 답안 선택지를 골라 요약 내용을 완성하시오. 일부 답안 선택지는 지문에 제시되지 않는 개념을 나타내거나 지문에서 중요하지 않은 개념들이므로 요약 내용에 속하지 않는다. **이 문제는 2점에 해당된다.**

시간이 흐르면서, 표면 유체의 움직임이 금성과 지구를 크게 변화시켜왔다.

    (A) 지구와 금성이 크기가 비슷하기는 하지만, 금성의 더 많은 화산 활동이 그곳 대기의 이산화탄소 수준을 상당히 증가시켜왔다.
    (B) 지구의 대기에 금성의 대기보다 훨씬 더 높은 수준의 산소 및 질소가 있다.
    (C) 유체를 수반하는 화학 반응이 탄산염 암석을 생성함으로써 지구의 대기에서 이산화탄소를 제거하는 반면, 바람은 한 곳에서 다른 곳으로 미세 입자를 운반한다.
    (D) 금성에서 모든 물이 증발되었기 때문에, 이산화탄소가 많은 대기로 인해 그 행성의 온도가 상승하는 결과가 초래되었다.
    (E) 지구에서는, 거듭되는 물 순환 체계가 대기 중의 탄소를 조절하며, 강 계곡들이 특징인 지표면 풍경을 만들었다.
    (F) 지구의 지표면에서 발생되는 액체 상태 물의 증발이 대부분의 대륙에 존재하는 광범위한 초목 범위로 인해 차단되고 있다.

해설   지구의 물 순환 체계는 가장 중요한 내용 중 하나로 두 번째 문단의 중심 내용이기도 하다. 따라서 (E)는 정답이다. 그리고 같은 문단에서 금성은 물의 증발과 이산화탄소가 많은 대기로 인해 온도가 상승하였다는 차이점을 설명하기에 (D) 역시 정답이다. 탄산염 암석의 생성이 이산화탄소를 제거한다는 내용과 바람의 퇴적물 층 형성 등의 내용은 네 번째 문단에서 다루고 있는 지구 구성의 핵심 내용이므로 (C)도 정답이다.

어휘   continual 거듭되는, 끊임없는 coverage 범위

유아기의 청각적 지각

유아들이 ^{11(C)}상당히 좋은 청각적 지각을 지니고 태어나는 이유는 출생 전에 놀라울 정도로 많은 청력 훈련을 받기 때문이다. ^{12(B)}실제로, 태어나서 첫 2년 동안, 유아는 성인보다 특정한 아주 높고 낮은 주파수에 더 민감하다. ^{12(C)}반대로, 유아는 처음에는 성인에 비해 중간 범위의 주파수에 덜 민감하다. ^{12(A)}하지만, 시간이 흐를수록, 중간 범위에 대한 청각적 지각이 훨씬 더 민감해진다.

^{13(C)}유아의 소리 민감성 향상에 대한 결정적인 설명이 존재하지는 않지만, 많은 연구가들은 그것이 신경계의 성숙과 연관되어 있다고 생각한다. 왜 유아기 이후에 아주 높고 낮은 주파수를 듣는 아이의 능력이 점차적으로 약화되는지에 대한 설명과 관련해서는 의견 일치가 훨씬 덜 이뤄져 있다. 한 가지 이론은 큰 소음에 대한 노출 증가가 이러한 극도의 주파수에 해당되는 소리를 감지하는 아이의 능력을 낮출 수 있다는 점이다.

효과적으로 듣기 위해, 유아는 소리를 감지하는 능력뿐만 아니라 여러 가지 다른 능력들도 필요로 한다. 예를 들어, 소리 위치 인식을 통해 유아는 소리가 나오는 방향을 정확히 알아낼 수 있다. 유아는 이러한 능력과 관련해서 성인에 비해 불리한 입장에 있는데, 효과적인 소리 위치 인식은 두 개의 귀가 개별적으로 소리를 듣는 시간의 근소한 차이에 의존하기 때문이다. 유아의 양쪽 귀 사이의 거리가 성인보다 더 짧기 때문에, 성인의 경우에 나타나는 것보다 소리가 양쪽 귀에 더 빨리 도달한다. 하지만, 심지어 이러한 잠재적 제약이 있다 하더라도, 유아의 소리 위치 인식 능력은 심지어 출생 당시에도 상대적으로 뛰어나며, ^{14(D)}일반적으로 유아가 한 살이 될 때쯤이면 성인 수준의 효율성에 도달한다. 그 능력의 향상이 직선적이지 않다는 점에 주목해보는 것은 흥미로운 일이다. ^{14(D)}소리 위치 인식 능력은 실제로 출생 후의 첫 두 달 동안에 걸쳐 약화되었다가 향상되기 시작하며, 왜 이러한 일이 나타나는지에 대한 명확한 설명은 존재하지 않는다.

^{15(C)}영유아들은 또한 다양한 소리들 사이에 존재하는 미묘한 차이를 인식할 수 있으며, 이는 향후의 언어 이해력에 있어 중대한 부분이다. 예를 들어, 한 가지 잘 알려진 연구에서, 4주에서 4개월 사이의 유아로 구성된 그룹이 빨기 시작할 때마다 성인이 "바"라고 말하는 녹음 소리가 나오는 젖꼭지를 빨았다. 처음에는, 이 유아들이 녹음된 목소리에 대한 강한 흥미로 인해 힘차게 빨기 시작했다. 하지만, 얼마 후에는, 그 소리에 대한 흥미를 잃어지면서 젖꼭지를 빠는 것이 덜 열정적으로 변했다. 실험 진행자들은 그 후에 소리를 "파"로 변경했는데, 그 유아들의 열의가 즉시 새로워지면서 한 번 더 더욱 힘차게 빨게 되었다. ^{15(C)}이 실험 결과는 4주 밖에 되지 않은 어린 유아들이 두 가지 유사한 소리들 사이의 차이를 구별할 수 있다는 사실을 분명히 보여주었다.

^{17(D)}유아의 청각적 지각에 있어 또 다른 흥미로운 측면은 다양한 음성 언어 사이에서 차이를 구분 짓는 특정한 특징들을 식별하는 능력이다. 연구에 따르면 심지어 태어난 지 이틀 밖에 되지 않은 아기도 익숙하지 않은 언어보다 주위에 있는 사람들이 말하는 언어를 더 좋아하는 것으로 나타났다. 언어 사이의 차이를 구별하는 능력은 출생 후 첫 몇 달 동안에 걸쳐 빠르게 발전한다. 5개월쯤 되면, 심지어 말하는 사람이 동일한 언어 구사 속도와 억양, 그리고 음절 수를 ^{16(B)}활용하는 경우에도 영어와 스페인어의 음성 구절들 사이의 차이를 인식할 수 있다.

유아들이 두 자음 사이의 차이점 같이 말 속에 담긴 아주 경미한 차이를 식별할 수 있다는 사실을 안다면, 이들이 목소리를 바탕으로 서로 다른 사람들도 알아볼 수 있다는 점이 놀랍지만은 않다. 나이가 어릴 때, 유아는 특정 목소리에 대한 명확한 선호도를 보인다. ^{18(B)}이는 신생아들이 이야기를 읽어주는 성인 목소리가 담긴 녹음 내용을 작동시키는 젖꼭지를 빨도록 허용된 한 실험에서 그 결과가 크게 나타났다. 그 목소리가 낯선 사람의 것일 경우에, 그 녹음이 엄마의 목소리일 경우보다 유아들이 훨씬 덜 열정적으로, 그리고 더 짧은 시간 동안 젖꼭지를 빨았다.

연구가들은 오랫동안 어떻게 이러한 선호도가 발생될 수 있을지에 대해 궁금해했다. ^{19(A)} ■ 이 이론의 지지자들은 흔히 신생아들이 다른 남성의 목소리에 비해 아빠의 목소리에 대한 선호도를 보이지 않는다는 점을 보여주는 입증 자료를 제시한다. ■ 더욱이, 신생아들은 출생 후에만 불러주는 노래들보다 자궁 속에 있는 동안 불러주었던 노래들을 듣는 것을 선호한다. ■ 따라서, 유아의 듣기 선호도는 액체로 된 자궁 속 환경으로 인해 소리가 약화된다 하더라도 엄마 목소리에 대한 출생 전의 노출에 의해 영향받는 것이 분명하다. ■

[어휘]
1. auditory 청각의 perception 지각, 인식 infancy 유아기 infant 유아 frequency 주파수
2. definitive 결정적인, 확정적인 maturation 성숙 consensus 의견 일치, 합의 when it comes to ~와 관련해서, ~의 측면에 있어 diminish 약화되다, 감소하다
3. detect ~을 감지하다, 발견하다 localization 위치 인식 at a disadvantage 불리한 입장에 있는 discrepancy 차이 linear 직선적인, 선형의 worsen 약화되다
4. subtle 미묘한 distinction 차이, 구별 vigorously 힘차게 renew ~을 새롭게 하다, 갱신하다
5. aspect 측면, 양상 employ ~을 활용하다 intonation 억양 syllable 음절
6. discriminate ~을 식별하다, 구별하다 consonant 자음
7. proponent 지지자 womb 자궁 muffle (소리 등) ~을 약화시키다, 죽이다

11. 지문의 단어 "fairly"와 의미가 가장 가까운 것은 무엇인가?
(A) 동등하게, 똑같이
(B) 명확히, 분명히
(C) 꽤, 상당히
(D) 때때로

해설 fairly(꽤, 상당히)와 reasonably(꽤, 상당히)는 동의어로 정답은 (C)이다.

12. 첫 번째 문단에 따르면, 유아의 청각적 능력과 관련해 다음 설명 중 어느 것이 정확하지 않은가?
(A) 중간 범위의 주파수에 대한 유아의 민감성이 아이가 나이를 먹으면서 더 향상된다.
(B) 최대 두 살까지의 유아는 성인보다 극도의 주파수를 더 잘 들을 수 있다.
(C) 유아는 중간 범위의 주파수에 대한 것보다 높고 낮은 주파수에 대해 더 민감하다.
(D) 유아는 출생 전에는 어떠한 종류의 청각적 자극에 대해서도 익숙하지 않다.

해설 해당 문단의 두 번째 문장은 (B)의 정보를 담고 있다. 세 번째 문장에서 (C)의 정보를 담고 있으며, 마지막 문장에서 (A)를 담고 있다. 출생 전이라는 키워드는 '청각 훈련' 외에 연결되는 지점이 없으므로 정답은 (D)이다.

13. 다음 중 어느 것이 두 번째 문단의 구성을 가장 잘 설명하는가?
(A) 청각적 지각에 관한 두 가지 이론 뒤에 이어지는 그 이론들을 증명한 실험에 대한 설명
(B) 청각적 지각 연구의 역사 뒤에 이어지는 해당 주제에 관한 두 가지 최근의 연구들에 대한 비교
(C) 청각적 지각의 두 가지 발달 과정에 대한 간략한 논의와 함께 그에 관한 잠재적 설명
(D) 두 살 이하의 아이들이 지닌 청각적 지각 능력을 테스트하는 데 활용된 두 가지 방법

해설 해당 문단의 첫 번째 문장과 두 번째 문장을 통해 청각적 지각의 과정에 대한 논의를 하고 있다는 점을 알 수 있다. 세 번째 문장에서 하나의 이론을 제시하는 것을 통해 잠재적 설명을 이어간다는 점을 토대로 정답은 (C)이다.

14. 세 번째 문단에 따르면, 다음 설명들 중 어느 것이 유아의 소리 위치 인식 능력을 정확히 특징 짓지 못하는가?
(A) 한 살이 될 때쯤, 유아의 소리 위치 인식 능력이 기본적으로 성인과 똑같아진다.
(B) 유아의 소리 위치 인식 능력이 꾸준히 향상되지 않는 이유는 알려져 있지 않다.
(C) 유아의 소리 위치 인식 능력이 상대적으로 짧은 양쪽 귀 사이의 거리로 인해 성인보다 잠재적으로 덜 정확하다.
(D) 소리의 위치를 정확히 인식하는 능력이 출생 두 달 후에

꾸준히 약화되지만, 그 후 한 살이 지나면 증가된다.

해설 해당 문단의 마지막 문장을 보면 소리 위치 인식 능력은 실제로 출생 후의 첫 두 달 동안에 걸쳐 약화되었다가 향상되기 시작한다고 쓰여 있고, 앞선 문장에 한 살 때쯤이면 성인과 같은 수준에 도달한다고 언급되어 있으므로 (D)가 정답이다.

15. 다음 설명들 중 어느 것이 네 번째 문단에서 이야기하는 유아의 청각적 지각에 관한 잘 알려진 연구의 결과를 말하는가?
(A) 유아는 계속 들어오던 소리가 바뀔 때 흥미를 잃는 경향이 있다.
(B) 일부 자음의 소리는 유아가 다른 것들보다 더 쉽게 인식한다.
(C) 심지어 아주 어린 유아도 소리의 작은 차이를 감지할 수 있다.
(D) 유아는 물체에서 나는 소리보다 말 소리에 더 큰 흥미를 보인다.

해설 영유아들이 다양한 소리들 사이에 존재하는 미묘한 차이를 인식할 수 있으며 실험을 통해 4주 밖에 되지 않은 어린 유아들도 소리의 차이를 구별할 수 있다는 사실을 보여주었다는 점을 토대로 (C)가 정답이다.

어휘 tend to do ~하는 경향이 있다

16. 지문의 단어 "employ"와 의미가 가장 가까운 것은 무엇인가?
(A) ~을 모집하다
(B) ~을 활용하다
(C) 애쓰다
(D) ~을 배우다, 알다

해설 employ(~을 활용하다)와 utilize(~을 활용하다)는 동의어로 정답은 (B)이다.

17. 다섯 번째 문단의 요점은 무엇인가?
(A) 아이들은 다양한 언어에서 오직 소리가 유사한 단어들만 쉽게 인식할 수 있다.
(B) 억양과 말하는 속도가 아이들이 어느 언어를 듣고 있는지 알아내는 데 활용하는 두 가지 특징이다.
(C) 많은 아이들이 아주 어린 나이에 영어와 스페인어를 모두 배울 수 있다.
(D) 심지어 출생 후 몇 달밖에 되지 않은 경우에도, 유아는 서로 다른 언어의 소리를 구별할 수 있다.

해설 해당 문단의 첫 번째와 두 번째 문장은 명확하게 다섯 번째 문단의 요점을 정리해주고 있으며 유아는 서로 다른 언어의 소리를 구별할 수 있다는 내용을 전달하고 있다. 그러므로 정답은 (D)이다.

18. 여섯 번째 문단은 다음 중 유아의 청각 능력과 관련된 어떤 질문에 대한 답변에 해당되는가?

(A) 신생아는 엄마가 읽어주는 여러 이야기의 차이를 인식할 수 있는가?

(B) 유아는 녹음된 이야기를 읽어주는 사람이 바뀔 때 그 차이를 구별할 수 있는가?

(C) 신생아는 익숙하지 않은 사람이 말하는 이야기를 듣는 것으로부터 더 많은 이득을 얻는가?

(D) 어떤 종류의 목소리가 어린 아이에게 가장 잘 진정시키는 효과를 내는가?

해설 언어의 차이에서 목소리를 바탕으로 인지를 한다는 내용으로 넘어가는 구간이 바로 여섯 번째 문단이다. 그리고 실험 결과를 통해 낯선 사람의 목소리와 엄마의 목소리에서 젖꼭지를 빠는 시간이나 강도 등의 차이를 알 수 있었기 때문에, 녹음된 이야기를 읽어주는 사람이 바뀔 때 구별을 할 수 있는가라는 질문을 던지는 (B)가 정답이다.

어휘 soothing 진정시키는, 달래는

19. 다음 문장이 지문에 추가될 수 있는 곳을 나타내는 네 개의 네모 표기 [■]를 찾아 보시오.

한 가지 이론은 가장 중대한 요인이 엄마의 목소리에 대한 출생 전의 노출이라는 점이다.

위 문장은 어느 곳에 가장 적합하겠는가? 네모 표기[■]를 클릭해 지문에 이 문장을 추가하시오.

(A) 1번
(B) 2번
(C) 3번
(D) 4번

해설 첫 번째 박스 뒤 문장의 this theory는 주어진 문장의 One theory를 지칭하는 것이므로 정답은 (A)이다.

어휘 prenatal 출생 전의

20. **설명:** 간략한 지문 요약에 필요한 도입 문장이 아래에 제공되어 있다. 지문에서 가장 중요한 개념들을 나타내는 세 가지 답안 선택지를 골라 요약 내용을 완성하시오. 일부 답안 선택지는 지문에 제시되지 않는 개념을 나타내거나 지문에서 중요하지 않은 개념들이므로 요약 내용에 속하지 않는다. **이 문제는 2점에 해당된다.**

연구에 따르면 유아의 청각적 지각이 상당히 수준 높은 것으로 나타났다.

(A) 엄마의 목소리 및 임신 기간 중에 들었던 노래에 대한 신생아의 선호도는 소리에 대한 출생 전의 노출이 자궁 속에 있을 때 청각적 발달에 영향을 미친다는 것을 나타낸다.

(B) 한 가지 잘 알려진 연구에서, 유아는 "바"라고 말하는 사람의 녹음 소리를 듣자마자 열심히 젖꼭지를 빨았지만, 그 소리가 "파"라고 바뀌었을 때 덜 활기 있게 변했다.

(C) 액체 상태인 자궁 속 환경이 아빠의 목소리에 대한 노출을 제한하기 때문에, 신생아는 일반적으로 엄마의 목소리에 대한 선호도를 나타낸다.

(D) 출생 후 첫 2년 동안, 유아는 극도의 주파수에 해당되는 소리보다 중간 범위의 주파수에 해당되는 소리에 더 정확하게 반응한다.

(E) 아주 높고 낮은 주파수를 듣는 유아의 능력은 심지어 어른을 능가하며, 소리의 진원을 알아내는 능력도 엄청날 정도로 좋다.

(F) 나이가 어릴 때부터, 유아는 청각적 지각으로 인해 두 가지 유사한 소리뿐만 아니라 서로 다른 언어 및 목소리 사이에 존재하는 청각적 차이도 구별할 수 있다.

해설 해당 지문의 첫 문단부터 세 번째 문단까지 유아는 높고 낮은 주파수를 듣는 능력이 뛰어나고, 소리 위치 인식 능력 역시 뛰어나다는 점을 설명하기 때문에 (E)를 가장 먼저 답안으로 선택한다. 이후 네 번째부터 여섯 번째 문단까지의 내용을 토대로 유아는 청각적 지각으로 인해 소리 사이의 미묘한 차이, 언어적 차이, 그리고 목소리의 차이까지 구별할 수 있다는 점을 알 수 있으므로 (F)를 선택한다. 엄마의 목소리에 대한 신생아의 선호도가 청각적 발달에 영향을 미친다는 내용은 일곱 번째 문단의 중심 내용이기에 (A)를 정답으로 선택한다.

어휘 sophisticated 수준 높은, 세련된, 정교한 surpass ~을 능가하다, 뛰어넘다 extraordinarily 엄청날 정도로, 특별히, 이례적으로

시원스쿨 LAB

시원스쿨 LAB